hints and
help from

Heloise

hints and
help from

Two Volumes in One

Bonanza Books
New York

To my Mother,
who put homemakers on the pedestal they deserve...
and to homemakers 'round the world, who responded
with their love and affection.

Copyright © 1980, 1981 by King Features Syndicate, Inc.

This 1986 edition is published by Bonanza Books,
distributed by Crown Publishers, Inc., 225 Park Avenue
South, New York, New York 10003, by arrangement
with Arbor House.

Printed and Bound in the United States of America

Library of Congress Cataloging-in-Publication Data
Heloise.
    Hints and help from Heloise.

    Includes index.
    1. Home economics   I. Title.
TX158.H444   1986   640   85-30896
ISBN 0-517-60524-4

r   q   p   o   n

Acknowledgments

Like my syndicated column, this book was written not just *for* but *by* homemakers. Believe me, friends, if I listed every last one of you who took the time to send me a super shortcut, a thrifty hint, share a great idea or a giggle, there'd be more names here than you could find in the telephone directories of New York, London and Tokyo combined. So, bless each and every one whose sharing and caring contributed. I couldn't have done it without you—or without the encouragement and support of the men in my life, dad and David, who cheered me on and helped choose the hints they thought men would like most. Thanks also to the homemakers who help me hunt, find, test and research the best hints and the right answers, with special hugs and kisses to

Hazel Bolton, Anne Mundy and Pinky Cad because they're the greatest.

This book just grew as a result of the suggestions and input of many people, and especially Joan O'Sullivan, King Features senior editor. Thanks also to Joan Marlow, managing editor of Arbor House, and Judith Riven, Avon Books senior editor, who lent their expertise, encouragement, and enthusiasm throughout.

—Hugs, Heloise

Contents

hints from

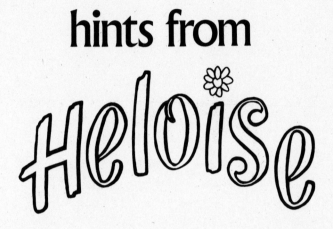

General Introduction

Hi!

Since the first "Hints from Heloise" column appeared in a newspaper and got itself syndicated around the world, lots has happened . . .

F'rinstance:

"Housewives" have become "homemakers" and, believe your friend Heloise, there's a dadgum good reason why . . .

Lots of us are men!

More bachelors than ever are pushing carts around supermarkets and joining the Mop and Broom Brigade.

Not to mention the "house husbands" who've changed things around. While their wives work, a lot of them are discovering what many of us gals instinctively knew—there's something very satisfying about raising kids, keeping a home, cooking, cleaning and nipping about in search of a bargain (these days, it's a triumph for sure when you find one!).

These are just some of the changes.

The things we're doing! Running locomotives, working oil rigs, digging coal, tip-tapping our high heels right into those posh executive suites.

Not that it means we're excused from KP.

Mostly we're not because, come to think of it, in some way or other almost everyone is a homemaker, contributing a little, a lot, or maybe the whole works to running a household.

And there's something else new too—lots more "single" households, and that means lots more men and women finding their way around a kitchen for the first time.

Well, I guess you know what I'm saying. It's that whatever you do and whoever you are, your home's very important.

It can be a lot of work if you do things the hard way. But who says you have to? Not Heloise! That's why I'm here . . . to lend a hand and share some of the best housekeeping hints you'll ever find.

Seem like I'm blowing my horn? Then let me explain . . .

First, I grew up in a home that had more than a "test kitchen." So help me, Hercules, it was a whole "test house."

Looking back, seems the first thing I can remember is mother and I "testing" some hint or other, trying to find a way to make gravy lumpless . . . or an easier way to take up a hem, make a mend, paint, wallpaper, you just name it.

Well, nothing's changed. I'm still at it, testing and besting, trying to get a handle on the quickest, easiest, most economical ways to get things done.

Second, I've had lots of help rounding up the shortcuts, the savers, the quick and easies in this book—and not just from the homemakers on my testing panel who keep their dust clothes at the ready to take a quick swipe at each new hint that comes down the pike. No sirreee!

They're great . . . but the homemakers who've sent me their own special tips, why they're the greatest!

So this book is by your friend Heloise and a cast of thousands, all the homemakers—the marrieds and singles, the males and females —who've contributed to it.

Bless 'em all, and bless you too.—Hugs and kisses, Heloise.

Cooking Up a Storm

INTRODUCTION

HI!

Did you ever stop to think how important food is—and not just because it provides the energy we need to get up and go?

Think about it, friends, and you'll see my point. Food is love. It's our way of showing family and friends we care.

It's what makes any occasion—from an everyday dinner to a birthday party—extra special.

It's recipes we make for ourselves 'cause we need a lift, or prepare for a friend because that friend's sick and needs cheering up.

Life revolves around food . . . and families and friendships revolve around meals shared.

Take it from me, the secret ingredient in every good recipe is love!

Some folks get their kicks doing the darndest things. But for most of us nothing can compare to the satisfaction that comes from making and baking something really great, from cooking up a storm.

The very best cooks of all are you . . . everyone who cooks for self or someone else. And the real test kitchens are in apartments and houses all over the U.S. because the best time- and money-saving tips are the ones that carry your own personal HSA, "Homemaker's Seal of Approval."

The truth is, friends, that necessity's the mother of invention—especially in the kitchen. You not only learn by doing, you discover —new ways, easier ways, tastier ways.

So, sit a spell, pour yourself a cup of coffee, and work up an appetite. You're bound to when you read all the fantabulous cooking hints and recipe tips I've collected from good cooks clear across the good old U.S.A. Better keep a marker in hand, too, because some of the budget-wise ideas are just what you need to s-t-r-e-t-c-h that food dollar as far as it'll go.

Love to you all from the bottom of my heart.—Hugs, Heloise.

P.S. When you get to the goodies—and there are lots of 'em—do me a favor. Forget about your diet—at least till tomorrow. Give yourself a treat from your friend, me.—Heloise

Soup

INTRODUCTION

Land sakes, ever notice the way they're always putting up monuments to people, some of whom you never heard of, or can't remember who they are? The wonder is that someone hasn't erected a statue to honor that unsung homemaker who invented soup. Bless his/her ingenuity.

Soup stands right next to bread, the staff of life, in my cookbook. It's feed-your-family food that makes you feel warm inside and out on a cold day.

It's the just-before-payday meal that sneaks you through deliciously when the old food budget's battered.

5

It's the kind of make-do emergency ration that got the pioneers over the mountains and through the deserts, and that soldiers in all the wars of history have cooked up over campfires with whatever vittles they had.

But the greatest thing about soup is that it's just plumb good, hits the spot, fills you up, makes you feel satisfied.

Soup can be a mini-course or the main course. That's up to you. Just don't forget it's a great catch-all for a little of this, a little of that, and whatever you've got on hand.

Of course you can cook soup from scratch—nothing wrong with that—but you don't have to. If you're in a hurry, you can start with canned soup or with packaged soup mix, then doctor it up with a few additions until it tastes downright homemade. And don't tell a soul—a cook's secrets are his and her own!—Hugs, Heloise

Bean Soup

From New York: "My Greek sister-in-law makes a fabulous bean soup. She cooks a pound of navy beans. When they're soft, she adds finely chopped celery, onion and carrots, a can of tomato paste and a little olive oil and cooks until the vegetables are tender, adding water as needed. The soup can be as thick or as thin as you prefer. Sometimes she puts it in a blender and pureés it."

Bisque (see Shrimp Bisque, p. 10)

Bouillon

From Iowa: "Bouillon is the base for 'Leftover Soup' in my house. I add slivers of sliced meat and any vegetables I have on hand. Sometimes I throw in sliced cold cuts or a package of frozen vegetables too. No work at all!"

Mix beef bouillon and tomato juice to make a delicious instant soup. Season with pepper, bay leaf and celery salt.

From Colorado: "I always keep bouillon cubes on hand—and not just for soup. They're great flavor-making additions to rice, main dishes, casseroles. I often make gravy from a base of chicken bouillon, then spark it up with seasonings."

From Nebraska: "You can doctor up chicken bouillon in many ways to make soup. I like to throw in a cup of fresh chopped parsley and a head of chopped romaine lettuce and some diced potatoes. I simmer this for an hour or so, then put it in the food processor and give it a whirl. Serve in mugs with a spoon of hot melted butter. Delicious!"

To make bouillon more interesting, spark a cup by floating a lemon slice on top. It looks great!

You can make a fabulous soup by adding a mashed avocado to three cups of chicken bouillon. Season with salt and pepper, then heat. When piping hot, remove from burner and stir in a cup of milk or cream. Heat again (don't boil), and serve.

Cabbage Soup

From Pennsylvania: "My family loves cabbage soup and it's easy to make. I shred a 1½-to two-pound head of cabbage and sauté it in a stick of butter for twenty minutes; tossing in a tablespoon of sugar to speed browning. Then all I do is add six cups of beef bouillon (made from cubes) and simmer for another half hour. I season it with salt and pepper and serve."

Chicken Soup

From Illinois: "Try flavoring canned cream of chicken soup with a dash of curry."

Consommé

From Vermont: "Chicken consommé has saved the day many a time for me. I add frozen vegetables to it, sometimes beat an egg and swirl it into the soup (Oriental style). It makes an instant course that supplements meager fare or creates a nice soup-and-sandwich entrée."

Cream Soup

When serving cream soup, beat for a few seconds with your egg beater before heating and you'll have soup that's ever so wonderfully smooth.

Fish Soup

From New Jersey: "I make the best for-free soup—that's because our local fishery doesn't charge for fish heads, bones or tails.

"I simmer them in a pot to make a fabulous stock, then strain it. You can poach fish in this (wrap it in cheesecloth). Sometimes I just add vegetables, such as leeks, carrots, potatoes, onions and celery, after sautéing them for fifteen minutes in olive oil. A family favorite."

Garnishes (see Soup Garnishes, p. 11)

Meatball Soup

From Ohio: "My Greek sister-in-law makes a fabulous meatball soup. She mixes chopped beef with rice, salt, pepper and parsley, then rolls it into tiny balls with floured hands. These she simmers in a mixture of stewed tomatoes and chicken bouillon. A fabulous party dish—and economical too."

Milk Soup

From Minnesota: "My grandmother makes a delicious milk-buttermilk soup, using a quart of each. She thickens one cup of milk by stirring in 2½ tablespoons of flour. She heats the rest of the milk and adds the flour mixture, stirring constantly while it heats and thickens. Next, the buttermilk is stirred in. After the soup boils, she slowly pours it over two beaten egg yolks in the bottom of a big soup-server bowl, stirring all the time. This is great served with a little brown sugar sprinkled on the top."

Onion Soup

From New Jersey: "While boarding at school, I discovered a delicious onion soup made from the few items I had on hand. Dissolve beef bouillon in boiling water. Add a small handful each of rice and dehydrated onion flakes and a dash pepper. Cook until rice is soft. Served with a sprinkling of Parmesan cheese, it sure beat cafeteria soup!"

Pea Soup

From Idaho: "I like to make chilled pea soup in summer. I mix the soup with a small can of tomato sauce and stir in a can of minced clams with their juice. I thin this out with 1½ cups of milk and let it stay in the refrigerator until it's icy cold."

After cooking split-pea soup remove the ham bone and bay leaf and put the soup through the blender, a little at a time. Then warm it up and serve it. Ohhh, so smooth!

From Iowa: "Pea soup mix is marvelous when you add sliced frankfurters or slivers of ham. I serve it as a main course, and the family loves it."

Potato Soup

From California: "Did you know that instant potato flakes can make fabulous potato soup?

"I stumbled onto the idea when I was making instant mashed potatoes one night and tipped the milk bottle too far. My family cracked up when I served mashed potatoes in a bowl, but they were great!

"Just make mashed potatoes with the recipe on the box. Then keep adding milk to the desired consistency. When you're through, add extra salt and pepper to taste. Yummy!"

This can be served cold, too.—Heloise

Shrimp Bisque

From Washington, D.C.: "The hit of my last dinner party was Shrimp Bisque—made with frozen shrimp, simmered with diced green pepper in butter, then heated in canned tomato soup thickened with cream.

"How's that for quick and easy?"

Soup, cooling

If you eat soup with a plastic spoon, it'll cool faster. Metal spoons retain the heat.

Soup, removing fat

It's best to make meat soups a day ahead, so they can be stored in the refrigerator. This allows fat to solidify on top and makes it easy to remove.

If you can't do this, here's a trick that works like a charm: Put ice cubes on top of the soup! Fat will harden up around the cubes in about ten minutes and can be lifted right off!

Soup, serving

From Iowa: "We serve soup in mugs placed on a plate with crackers and spoon. We use the spoon for the vegetables in the soup and drink from the mug. This system simply evolved when mugs came into use because we didn't like the dip-and-drip routine."

Soup, thickening

To thicken soup, add instant rice or mashed potatoes.

Soup Garnishes

Dress up soup with top-offs, such as: thin slices of lemon, chopped parsley or chives, sliced mushrooms, olive rings, toasted croutons, bacon bits, a dollop of unsweetened whipped cream or sour cream.

Soup Helper

You've heard about hamburger and tuna helpers, now hear about Heloise's soup helper.

I cook one cup of macaroni or noodles in plain water, adding no salt, but often some chopped onion or chopped celery, depending on my mood.

After I drain off the water, I add two cans of vegetable or other soup to the macaroni plus the amount of water called for. Sometimes I substitute tomato juice.

This will make enough soup for at least four or five.

For a little extra nutrition, I always dissolve an envelope of unflavored gelatin in hot canned soups.

Soup Stock

To save broth or stock of soup, strain while hot then put in a bowl. Don't skim off the fat. It will solidify and seal the stock pretty much like paraffin seals jelly in a glass.

The stock will keep quite a while if it is left undisturbed in the refrigerator.

But if you use some of the stock, bring the leftover stock to a full boil, cool and put it back in the refrigerator, again leaving the fat on it.

When making stock with bones, wrap them in cheesecloth. This keeps bits of gristle from mixing into the soup.

Don't throw out vegetable cooking water or bones from a roast. Freeze 'em away and you've got the beginning of soup stock.

Tomato Soup

From Louisiana: "My family loves tomato soup egg-drop style. All I do is drizzle a well-beaten egg into canned tomato soup while it's boiling. It's important to keep stirring as you slowly add the egg."

Try seasoning canned tomato soup with dill. Just love it.

From Idaho: "I always have a lot of tomatoes from our garden in the summer. One of the things I do with them is make soup. I simmer eight or ten peeled tomatoes in six cups of chicken bouillon for an hour or so, then mush them up with a fork (try a potato masher—Heloise). Really good! Sometimes I add a drop or two of food coloring to 'pink' up the soup's color. I season this with salt and pepper and put in a pinch of sugar to cut the acid."

From New Mexico: "For a quick supper, I poach eggs in tomato soup. Really gives them flavor! The soup serves as a sauce which I spoon over the eggs and melted cheese on toast."

Vegetable Soup

A sweet doll wrote:
"Heloise says don't throw it out if you can use it some way . . .
"Well, my seven-year-old son likes vegetable soup but only the store-bought kind. I make it with one can of vegetable and one can

of vegetable-beef combined. When his lunch is over I usually have a lot of broth left.

"I like my own soup more homemade-like, so I then add a can of mixed vegetables to the broth and I have soup that tastes almost as if I made it from scratch."

2

Main Dishes

INTRODUCTION

Anyone who creates a painting or sculpture, designs a dress or writes a novel is creative.

Good cooks are creative too!

Innovating and experimenting are what cooking's about. And that's creative, for darn sure it is, and yet some homemakers do it every day of their lives . . . and sometimes two or three times a day.

Wow! Doesn't it wipe you out to think of all that creativity in homes and apartments north, south, east and west? It bowls me over and makes me wish I could have a taste or a sample of all the good things that are sizzling and simmering on front or back burners and in ovens coast to coast.

You'll find some of them in this chapter because it's about main dishes. Mainly, that's things like meat, fish, poultry and pasta, plus other menu-makers.

These hints are the greatest, so thanks to each of you who shared your creativity and clever cooking cues. 'Twas right neighborly. Wish I could lean over my back fence and say "thanks" in person because you're special.

Lots of creative people don't share—but good cooks do! That's a very nice thing about them. When they hit on a super recipe or a great idea, they just can't wait to tell someone . . . and sometimes the someone they tell is me!

So in this chapter I'm sharing what was shared, because it's only fair and square. Enjoy every morsel.—Hugs, Heloise

Bacon

If you have a family to feed and you're worried about the price of bacon but like the taste, try this:

Purchase a three-pound package of bacon ends and pieces. Chill thoroughly.

Using an electric slicing knife, or just an ordinary sharp carving knife, cut the bacon into one-half inch cubes, first slicing lengthwise, then crosswise.

Place the pieces in a large kettle and render slowly over your kitchen burner until cooked but not crisp. Drain off the bacon fat. Cover and referigerate the fat to use instead of oil, butter or margarine for gravy or flavoring.

Refrigerate the cooked bacon. Use two tablespoonfuls with two scrambled eggs in sandwich fillings, or to flavor salads, sauces or vegetables. This'll satisfy you until better days . . .

Here's another good way to stretch that expensive bacon:

Let the bacon come to room temperature. Slice the long pieces in halves or thirds. Before frying, dip the bacon in flour. This not only makes bulk but gives you something to chew on. Makes bacon go twice as far.

As for drippings, they sure do make good gravy if you're cooking biscuits.

One sweet man wrote that he uses a mixture of flour and sugar for dipping, and it sure does give the bacon an entirely different taste. I tried it and it tastes like sugar-cured. Great!

With meat prices out of sight, let your family have a little taste of bacon without having to use a lot by making "bacon pancakes." Fry the bacon 'til partially crisp, break it up and arrange the pieces in circles, each the size of the anticipated pancake. (An alternate method is to cut the bacon into small pieces first and then fry.)

Pour the batter over each circle, being sure all the bacon is covered with the batter. And, of course, serve with butter and heated syrup.

Scrumptious!

No time to defrost that package of bacon you bought on sale and put in your freezer? Those slices seem welded together?

Just pick up the whole frozen pound and start rolling it up as you would a magazine. (It will roll because the fat keeps it a little flexible.) Do it two or three times.

Now you can peel off those slices, easy as pie!

I positively do not like to fry bacon!

I buy two or three pounds at a time and fry it all at once. Doesn't make any more mess than a few pieces do . . . just takes a little more time, which I save later on.

When the fried bacon has been well drained on paper towels, I spread it out on cookie sheets and freeze so the pieces do not stick together. After freezing, the strips can be put in plastic bags or a freezer container.

A few pieces of frozen bacon can be heated quickly in the oven or on a back burner while the eggs are cooking or while preparing a lettuce and tomato sandwich with bacon. Also great for crumbling on a salad or into soup!

Bologna

I always divide packages of bologna into slices and store them, three pieces per pack, in individual plastic sandwich bags, then freeze 'em. They thaw faster that way.

But sometimes I get in a hurry long about noon . . .

So I remove the three slices from the package, lay them in a small skillet and pour boiling water from my teakettle over 'em.

In less than a minute they're all thawed. But the best part of it is this: That old skin peels off smoothly and instantly with absolutely no waste whatsoever of the meaty part.

Place "thawed" slices on a paper towel. Zingo!—all the water's blotted up and the bologna is edible quick as lightning.

The bologna can be eaten cold or put back in the same emptied skillet and heated.

Use that same paper napkin to wipe the skillet out (it's not dirty) and put the skillet away.

Glory be to bologna!

Chicken

When you are frying chicken, did you know that if you add a few drops of yellow food coloring to the oil (before it's heated, or it will pop) your chicken will absorb it and become a beautiful golden brown?

Looks like it's been fried in pure butter, honest, friends!

If you like a good crust on chicken but don't like the bother and mess of battering, try this:

Mix flour and seasonings in a large plastic bag. Add the chicken pieces, a couple at a time, close tightly and shake.

Leave the chicken in the bag for at least half an hour (you can leave it all day).

It gets nice and gooey and fries to a perfect golden crust.

You know how, after you've browned the chicken and are ready to add a bit of water for steaming, you're liable to have your hands sprayed with hot fat?

Try an ice cube instead. By the time it melts, the lid is safely on the pan, your hands are in no danger of spatters, and you're smiling smugly for being so smart.

Make stewed chicken and dumplings often?

If you do, I have a suggestion for you. Did you know that you can put poultry seasoning in your dumpling dough?

All you have to do is make up the batter, using two cups of any prepared biscuit mix. Add one teaspoon of poultry seasoning to the flour mixture before you add the liquid and you have an entirely new recipe that's absolutely delish!

From South Carolina: "With today's prices what they are, this is a reminder to use all those extra chicken parts that get thrown away. Freeze parts until you collect enough to make something.

"Freeze livers separately and when you have enough, sauté them with eggs for brunch or combine with bacon, mushrooms, etc. for a mixed grill supper. You also can use them to make pâté.

"When gizzards are boiled until tender they really are very good. Save up a few and try them!

"You may think that back piece that comes in a package of cut-up broiler isn't worth frying, but collect a few and make yourself a delicious chicken soup. Put bits of meat from the bone in the soup or enjoy it as broth and save the meat to make yourself a chicken salad sandwich.

"You also can use both the stock and bits of meat to make ready-to-eat and frozen foods taste homemade. For example, stuff the meat into chicken pot pies, mix into chicken chow mein or chicken à la king; use the broth to flavor gravy."

Chicken, crumb-coated

From Oklahoma: "I make my own crumb mixture for coating chicken, cutlets or pork chops by putting a package of dry mix dressing and stale bread into my blender and turning it on for a few seconds.

"I end up with the best coating for my meat that ever was. The dressing has its own delicious seasonings, but for extra zest I added paprika and garlic salt. Try rosemary or oregano for pork chops."

Corned Beef

From Montana: "I always used to break the key off the corned beef can before I got halfway around when opening it. I find now that I have no trouble if I wind the can instead of the key."

From Pennsylvania: "Here's how to get even slices of corned beef hash. Open each end of the can with an electric can opener.

"Remove one of the round lids, and with the other end gently push the corned beef hash out a little at a time, just enough each time for the width of the patty. With a sharp knife, cut along the edge of the can until it is sliced.

"Continue pushing and cutting until the canned hash is sliced to perfection.

"Put the slices on a cookie sheet in the freezer; when frozen, store in a plastic sherbet container, which is just the right size.

"They never stick together. You can reach in and take out just as many as you need. After flouring, they fry perfectly—nice and smooth and brown.

Dressing (See Stuffing, p. 42)

Flounder

From Connecticut: "I've found the most fabulous way to fix flounder. Put it on foil on a cookie sheet; make slits crosswise from head to tail and then make slits lengthwise from head to tail. This makes a checkered design and allows your favorite sauce (oil and lemon's great) to seep down into the fish.

"Put under the broiler at medium temperature and broil until tender and brown. Instead of turning the fish over to get the underside brown, put it in the oven at medium temperature and bake it until the bottom is done.

"When the fish is ready, trace the outline of the fish with a knife, cutting through the foil. Use a spatula to lift the fish (with the foil still on the bottom) and place it on the plate. The fish looks like a magazine picture."

Frozen Dinners

To avoid burned fingers and spills, use a cake rack when removing frozen dinners from the oven, especially the larger ones with gravy.

Just hook two of the feet of the cake rack over the first bar on the oven rack. Hold the rack with one hand and ease the foil pan onto the cake rack. Place rack and pan on the counter to cool.

Have you seen the frozen chicken à la king and creamed chipped beef dinners which come already cooked and packaged in a plastic cooking bag? You just drop the bags in boiling water and heat for about twenty minutes, then pour the contents over toast.

I keep my freezer stocked with these dinners. Bought on sale, they are inexpensive meals, so I watch for the specials . . .

The only thing I have against them is that sometimes one portion isn't enough if you are very hungry.

So, here's what I do:

I boil an egg in the same pan of water the chicken or beef

heats in. Yep, it's great! You get two-in-one service from that one pan.

I pour the water off, peel the egg and dice it saving the yolk. Cut open one end of the plastic bag, drop in the diced egg and stir.

All that's left to do then is pour it over some toast.

If you have company, just multiply the eggs by the bags and use a bigger pan. Dice only the egg whites. Open all the bags and dump contents in a bowl and stir. Pour over canned biscuits or toast.

Grate or run the yellows of the eggs through nylon net. (See Nylon Net, p. 217). Sprinkle on top of your main dish, adding a dash of paprika for color and you've got a dish to set before any king . . .

So cheap, so quick, so easy—that's the kind of dish I like!—Heloise

Giblets

From Colorado: "To cook giblets, put them in a covered casserole dish, barely cover them with water and place the dish in the oven alongside the turkey. Cooks the giblets 'free' without using a surface burner."

Gravy

If the gravy gives out before the roast does, don't use those expensive gravy mixes in packets. Instead, use instant beef or chicken bouillon to stretch beef, chicken and turkey gravy.

Add a teaspoon or two of the bouillon to a tumbler of water; add flour or cornstarch, then mix with a fork and add to what's left of the gravy. You can stretch it for days this way. Careful with the salt as bouillon is salty. Add the bouillon to taste and thicken it as you like.

I guarantee you won't have lumps if you stir it in the tumbler with the fork. I stir almost everything with a fork and believe me, it works! But if you do have lumpy gravy or sauce, pour it in the blender and buzz a bit to turn a disaster into a triumph.

If gravy is too thin, add some instant potatoes until it is the thickness that you want. It is so easy and it gives the nicest texture.

When no gravy mix is available to color gravy, try this: put some flour in a custard cup or a foil pie pan when you roast meat in the oven. The flour browns slowly as the roast cooks. If it is put in the oven at the same time as the roast, it will brown evenly and be ready to make a rich brown gravy when the meat is done.

From Georgia: "When you have made thickening for your gravy and there is a little left over, pour it in a small jar with a tight lid and put it in the refrigerator. Sometime you might need a little extra thickening, and there it is all ready for you."

From Minnesota: "I have found the perfect gravy thickener . . . no lumps. It's pie crust sticks. Just cut off about a half-inch and drop in the pan drippings. Let melt, then add water as needed.

"French chefs use a combination of flour and butter to thicken gravy and these pastry sticks are made of vegetable shortening and flour."

Ground Beef, substitutes for

From Connecticut: "In recipes that call for cooked ground beef, substitute the less desirable parts of a beef roast or the edges of a chuck steak or roast. Trim the meat, brown these pieces, then simmer them in a little water for about an hour. Cut them into slivers, then use instead of ground beef in such dishes as chili con carne, enchiladas, etc.

"This meat lacks the grainy quality that you so often find when hamburger is fried and then crumbled. Also, the fat can be sliced off before you prepare the meat, something you can't do with ground meat.

"If you have venison in your freezer, it is out of this world when used in dishes that call for cooked ground meat."

Ham

When slicing a warm baked ham, place several thicknesses of paper towels under the cutting board. This catches the juices. When finished, you can just roll up the towels and toss in the trash.

Hamburger (also see Meatballs, p. 27, Meat Loaf, p. 27, Pasta, p. 30, Ground Beef, substitutes for, p. 22 and Lids, plastic, p. 256)

Hamburger's not as cheap as it used to be, so when it's on sale, lay in a good supply, then freeze it. But, here's the trick:

You'll use less energy (yours and the metered kind) if the hamburger is prepared for meatballs, meat loaves, hamburger patties or spaghetti sauce before you freeze it.

When I buy six pounds on sale, I press some of it into patties with or without onions. Place pieces of waxed paper between each patty. Put these inside a plastic bag and freeze. All I have to do when I'm ready to cook is hit the package on the side of the drain board and the patties fall apart.

Put the remaining hamburger in a mixing bowl. I grate one big onion into it and add one egg for each pound of hamburger, mixing it well with the meat. Use salt, pepper and any other seasonings that you like.

Shape some of this into meat loaves. (If you like bread crumbs in your meat loaf, add it now.) You should make one big meat loaf and a few small ones. Use the small ones when you're pressed for time. They cook quickly. Use the big one when you have plenty of time to thaw it.

What is left of the meat can be made into meat balls for spaghetti

sauce. These are always good. Roll into balls, place on cookie sheets and freeze. Remove and place in a plastic bag and you can remove as many as you need at one time!

And . . . do you know that you can separate, prepare and freeze all these recipes in less than thirty minutes? But, best of all, it eliminates that last-minute worrying over "What's for supper?"

I always had to thaw frozen hamburger patties before cooking so that the centers would get done. Now I make a hole about the size of a nickel in the center before I freeze 'em. The hole disappears as the patty cooks and no more raw centers. No more thawing before cooking either, and that preserves the meat juices.

When you make hamburgers to take on a picnic, cook the patties at home and wrap them individually in foil.

When you get to the picnic site and it comes time to eat, put the whole package in the coals.

The burgers will be steaming hot and juicy in a jiffy, and you'll never have burned or dried-out hamburgers. Chop onions and put them on top of the meat before closing the foil.

From Kentucky: "Spooning or pouring off grease from browned hamburgers was always a problem until I discovered that a syringe turkey baster is a perfect 'grease remover.' It gets out almost all of the grease and you won't lose any ground beef trying to pour the grease into a can."

I'm thinking about those of us who really like lots of meat in our hamburgers and like it cooked quickly or with lots of smoke over a grill:

Make the burgers thinner and use two slim patties for each burger. I tried this, putting mustard and chopped onions between the thin patties after charcoal broiling them over the grill. Twice as much charcoal taste, too.

Here's the way I prepare thin hamburger patties with a press—but I'm also going to tell how to make them if you don't have a press, so hang on a minute.

If you have a hamburger press, put a piece of waxed paper in the press first, then a ball of hamburger, mashing it a bit with fingers until it has spread perfectly. Place another piece of waxed paper on top, smooth out with the back of a spoon, then top with another ball of hamburger and a third piece of waxed paper, then press. Result? Two thin patties with one push of the press.

If you don't have a press, roll your hamburger meat in a ball and put it between two pieces of waxed paper. You can kinda mash it a bit. Next, take a small salad plate that has a rim around the bottom and put the plate on top of the ball of meat and mash it down on a chopping board.

This will make your patty exactly the size of the rim on the bottom of the plate and will make a very thin patty.

A great cook fried frozen hamburger patties (because she wanted them in a hurry) and do you know how she did it?

She took a heavy skillet and put the frozen patties in it, then she poured some water out of her tea kettle into the skillet full of patties before they even got hot.

Quickly she put on the heavy lid, then cooked away.

The steaming made 'em tender. No grease spatters. Very juicy. No crust. And, best of all, they didn't shrink.

From Wisconsin: "Wear hand-saving rubber gloves (kept especially for this purpose) the next time you shape hamburger patties. You will get neat, smooth burgers with no shaggy edges to break off during cooking. Not one smidgen sticks to the gloves and they rinse clean of grease under hot water."

Hot Dogs

From Missouri: "My kids love soup and hot dogs for lunch so, to cut preparation time in half, I put the hot dogs (cut in bite-sized pieces) right in the soup pot to cook. Serving the soup and the hot dog in one dish tastes just as yummy.

"The big plus: there's only one pot and dish to clean!"

Liver

From Tennessee: "Instead of slicing liver, I partially freeze it until the food membrane (or skin) around it peels off easier. After that it's a cinch to slice any thickness you prefer."

From Arizona: "Has anyone tried cutting liver into strips, as for French fries?

"Coat the liver strips in a bag of seasoned cornmeal and fine cracker crumbs (a blender does a great job making crumbs), then fry it in deep fat. It fries in minutes and is very tender. This is the only way my family eats liver anymore.

"The kitchen shears are just great for clipping the liver into strips."

Macaroni (see Pasta, p. 30)

Meat, cold, garnish for (See Beets, garnish for cold meat, p. 96)

Meat, defrosting

I learned something a long time ago that I should have told you about then. Why I haven't, I don't know. Lazy, maybe?

It's about defrosting meat, whether it's a package of frozen hamburger or what.

We usually just pull it out of the freezer and put it on the drain board to defrost and wonder why it takes so long. Because we just put it on the drain, that's why.

For years I have always put a spoon under the package to let the air get under it so it would thaw faster. Now I've got a better idea: I pick up a grill from one of the burners on my stove, put it on a newspaper on the drainboard, put the frozen package of meat on the grill and let it thaw away. Much better.

I suggest that you don't put your meat on the stove itself because some meats bleed and drain while thawing. Might save you a clean-up mess on your stove later, honeypots.

So remember this trick next time you thaw a roast.

Meat, leftover (see Leftovers, Meat, p. 148)

Meatballs

If you want really great meatballs, put them in the refrigerator for twenty minutes before frying and they won't fall apart so easily. It's that simple!

Use a release ice cream scoop to mold meatballs. If you want to make little hamburgers, drop on wax paper and flatten with a pancake turner.
If the scoop gets sticky, just run it under hot water.

From New Jersey: "Have you ever tried Norwegian meatballs?
"Make small meatballs seasoned with ginger and nutmeg. Brown well in butter or margarine and then make a flour gravy from the drippings. Return meatballs to gravy and simmer 'til done. Serve with mashed or boiled potatoes. They're also delicious with a bit of sour cream added to the gravy at the very last minute."

Meat Loaf

Never make one meat loaf. Save time and energy and make two. You can freeze the extra one cooked or uncooked.
All I do when I'm ready to cook a frozen meat loaf is pour on a little ketchup, chili sauce or canned tomatoes and place in the oven!
Meat loaf is great when served hot the first night with baked potatoes (and always throw a few extra spuds in the oven because they can be pan-fried or used for making potato salad the next day). As long as the oven is going, utilize that heat.
The next night you can slice your loaf in thick pieces and broil under your broiler. Delicious when spread with margarine, barbecue sauce or chili sauce. And what a change it makes for that old taster of yours, as it disguises that hamburger in a big way.
It can always be pan-fried quickly for either open-faced or regular sandwiches. Or dice it and, when slightly browned, scramble with eggs for a quick hot meal.
Here's another timesaver when you are baking meat loaf. Al-

ways place baking potatoes in the oven at the same time and utilize this heat. Open a can of biscuits, pop in the oven, and dinner is ready.

And did you know that individual meat loaves can be made in muffin tins? They cook in less than half the time a large loaf will take. Even if you are not pressed for time, try this method once, as it's a change.

When freezing these little loaves, I place cupcake liners in each muffin tin, pat the meat loaf to shape, freeze it and then . . . remove liner and all from the muffin tins and pack in plastic bags. This leaves me with a muffin pan that's clean and ready to use for other things. When ready to cook the mini-loaves, remove the paper, place loaves in the muffin tin and cook as usual.

You also can hurry it up if, after plopping your meat loaf in an iron skillet, you heat it on one of the burners a wee bit before putting it in that oven . . . I leave the skillet (or baking pan) on top of the burner until it barely starts to "bubble," then pop it in my oven.

To vary meat loaf, you can always add a package of onion soup mix. Try grated carrots, too—they're fantastic, give color, are cheap and make the meat go further.

As far as stretchers go, add seasoned bread crumbs, farina, crushed corn flakes, pre-cooked or raw oatmeal. I always add a bouillon cube that has been liquefied with a tablespoon of hot water. Great! This can be varied by using hot sauce, Worcestershire or a dash of chili powder.

When mixing all the goop together, try putting ingredients in a heavy plastic bag and blend by squeezing the bag. Saves greasy hands and extra bowls to wash. Lots of folks use their potato mashers to mix with, too.

For those who are on low-fat diets and want to get rid of the fat that drips out of a meat loaf, try putting the loaf on a small cake rack, then placing it in the pan. The meat will brown on all sides and the fat will drop in the pan.

And don't ever forget, as long as you're mixing the goop, anyway, why not make up an extra amount and divide some of it into thick patties and freeze 'em in plastic bags. I add dehydrated onions with these separate portions—and make what they call "Salisbury Steaks." Whoever gave that fancy name to a hamburger patty had lights turned on in the gray matter in his cranium, eh?

Before baking meat loaf, pre-slice it by running a knife through it to suggest the desired slices. When serving after the meat loaf is cooked, slice it through the previously made marks. It seems to come out so much nicer looking this way.

Some people love meat loaf but hate to find a piece of onion in it.

No problem! Pop the onion in the blender with an egg, carrot and sometimes the heel of the bread and no one will notice there's onion in the meat loaf!

From Colorado: "As I have arthritis in my hands, I try to do things the easy way, and I think my method of making meat loaf is the greatest!

"I take ground meat just as it comes from the package, place it on foil, put one package of onion soup mix on top, then close the foil and put in a pan just in case of leaks and bake slowly—at least an hour, at 350° F, depending on the amount of meat used.

"Slices beautifully! No mixing, no fuss and just delicious."

Make your favorite biscuit recipe, then make your old standby meat loaf recipe but, instead of putting the meat loaf in a pan, roll it into small balls. Flatten out biscuit dough, put a meat loaf ball in the center, and completely cover with the biscuit dough. Bake them all on a cookie sheet at 350° F until done (about thirty-five minutes).

These little meat pies are a perfect meal served with a salad, vegetable and dessert.

You can make them the day before and put in the refrigerator overnight. Or they may be frozen for later use.

From Idaho: "Want a different tasting meat loaf? Try pouring peach or apricot juice over the loaf just before it is done.

"Really spruces up the old standby!"

Meat, lunch box

Perhaps some of the other "brown-baggers" of the working world can use my lunch ideas.

As I don't care much for sandwiches, I had to devise something else for standard fare, so here's what I do:

I make a batch of "basic" meat dishes, such as stewed chicken, beef stew, meat sauce, etc. When finished, I package individual servings in containers, properly labeled, and freeze them.

While I'm getting breakfast, I take out a container of one of these "basics" and put it in a pan, along with a handful of noodles, a shake of rice, or a serving of frozen vegetables . . . plus seasoning variations.

While I'm eating breakfast, "basic" has become a uniquely seasoned and complete main-course meal. It goes into a wide-mouth vacuum bottle and, presto!, lunch.

Cooking the big batch can be done whenever I've the time or inclination; fixing a lunch-size serving is unbelievably speedy.

I have a refrigerator at the office, so I round off the menu with a salad of some sort and a "tasty" for dessert.

For cold lunches, in addition to that old standby fried chicken, I make individual meat loaves in foil pans and keep them frozen and handy for lunch.

Noodles (see Pasta, below)

Pasta (also see Spaghetti sauce, p. 39)

With the price of food reaching up to the moon, looks like we are going to have to get back to eating pasta more. Since everyone loves pasta, what could be nicer?

Well, one of my dearest readers has sent me a hint that I have tested many times. Every time, I find it not only perfect but the easiest yet. (And don't you take any bets, 'cause you're gonna lose.)

I have never had a failure, and it's really a fuelsaver and timesaver since there is absolutely no pot-watching. I love it because I have overcooked, underboiled and burned many a pot of pasta. No more!

Here's the way:

Put three quarts of water in a four-quart pot that has a tight-fitting lid; bring to a full rolling boil. (Rolling boil means the bubbles come to the top and burst quickly.) Then add a tablespoon of salt.

After the water is again bubbling fast and furiously, put in eight ounces of spaghetti, adding it slowly so the water continues to boil. Then give it a good stir or two. Immediately put the lid on the pot and twist it (that makes a vacuum) and turn off the heat.

Remove from the burner—and that frees the burner for cooking something else—and let the pot sit for exactly twenty minutes. Don't remove the lid during this time. That's the secret. Then drain quickly because it's done, folks.

Another thing I have found since using this method:

When you cook elbow macaroni in the morning (I usually do this for casseroles) but don't finish your recipe till that afternoon, it's important to drain the hot water immediately once the macaroni's cooked and then cover the macaroni with cold water. This prevents overcooking, which is what causes sogginess.

Here's something else that I learned from restaurant chefs:

They cook spaghetti, macaroni, and other pasta ahead of time to use in salads next day. They keep it refrigerated—under water—in stainless steel or glass jars for as long as two or three days.

And we often wonder how we can go into a restaurant and get good spaghetti in seven minutes? They just drop it in boiling water for a minute to heat, then drain it.

And, folks, try something I discovered which costs you practically nil and makes any pasta look scrumptillious:

Add yellow food coloring to the water in which you boil the pasta. You'll get the happiest shock of your life at the difference. Looks like you've used a pound of butter, makes it into a rich new dish entirely. Not just plain old pasta.

I finally got the recipe for shell macaroni and cheese from my favorite restaurant.

Use the cheapest cheese you can buy. Cube the cheese (cut in squares) and add undiluted canned evaporated milk and a dash of Worcestershire sauce. (A dash means a couple of blops; in other words, let the bottle go gurgle, gurgle and you have it—perfecto!)

Then melt this, stirring constantly, over a low burner. Make sure you stir in a figure-eight motion and use a wooden spoon.

The secret is in pouring the cooked, drained macaroni into the same pot in which you melted the cheese.

You can serve this immediately or bake it in the oven (350° F) for twenty minutes or so.

When I tested this gem, I added pimiento for color and cubed leftover ham 'cause it's good. Now that really gives you something to chomp your teeth into! All you need to complete the meal is a salad.

So easy and so magnifique!

When I bought a box of macaroni and cheese dinner, they were out of the brand I've used for years. So, I decided to try the cheapest brand, one I'd never bought before. It was great! I did improvise to make it out of the ordinary—but I usually do that anyway.

Here's what I did:

I cooked and drained the macaroni. Then to the sauce mix, I added a blub-blub of hot sauce, some fancy pepper (ordinarily used for steaks), a tablespoon of Worcestershire sauce, and a sprinkling of grated onion. I poured this into a buttered casserole dish on top of the macaroni.

Now, as Cheddar cheese isn't cheap-o, I used my potato peeler to slice some for topping. Talk about s-t-r-e-t-c-h-i-n-g cheese! Then I sprinkled on paprika and put the casserole in the oven until the cheese got yummy melted.

It sure was good! The hot sauce and Worcestershire changed the flavor of plain old "mac-and-chee"!

Do you know that this can be varied umpteen ways? For example: add bits of leftover meats. Add Vienna sausage cut in skinny rounds. Top with a medley of different cheeses (a super way to use odds and ends of 'em).

From Missouri:

"When I boil water for macaroni or spaghetti I put a little cooking oil in the water.

This keeps the pasta from sticking together or to the pot without constant stirring. It also keeps the pasta from boiling over."

Need a pick-up for noodles? Boil as many as you need for your family. Open a can of cream of chicken soup, pour on as much as needed to generously coat the noodles, heat a little more.

Salt and pepper to taste. Quick and delicious!

Here's a simple way to get ravioli out of the can without breaking them by digging into the can with a spoon:

Simply open the can and place it, open end down, in a pan; puncture the other end with a can opener and lift. The ravioli oozes right out.

From Indiana: "Instead of cooking spaghetti or noodles in a pot of boiling water the regular way, I cook them in a deep fryer basket. No sticking to the bottom because they are in the basket.

"All one has to do is lift the basket out, and quick as a wink, it's drained!"

I dearly love spaghetti and am always looking for new ways to cook it.

The other night when I was making salad while I waited for the spaghetti water to boil, I happened to spy a beautiful bunch of celery. Know what I did?

I chopped up three stalks about one-quarter inch thick.

I dumped this into my boiling water and waited for it to come to boil again before putting in the spaghetti.

You talk about a knockout? Those crunchy bits of celery really gave that old spaghetti zing. The celery doesn't turn out soft like the spaghetti, but adds a little crunchy bite to it.

Sure makes it different.

If you cook spaghetti in one of those big oval roaster pans on top of the stove, the spaghetti strands won't get tangled.

From Hawaii: "When I serve pasta, half of us want macaroni instead of spaghetti. So, here is my solution!

"I take a large pot about twice the size I'd normally use for cooking macaroni, and begin cooking the macaroni according to package instructions.

"After it's cooked five minutes, I lower my French fry basket (or large strainer) with the spaghetti into the pot. (Make sure the water covers the spaghetti.) Lift the basket and shake or stir from time to time. Stir the macaroni, too.

"They both will be ready at the same time—and only one pot to wash!

"This tip is handy too if you run short of spaghetti or macaroni 'cause you can supplement one with the other."

Pork Chops (also see Chicken, crumb-coated, p. 19)

Here's a tip from a Wyoming widower who had to start cooking for himself after losing a companion of forty-four years:

"I love breaded pork chops and finally figured out a way to have both sides nice and crisp—and practically greaseless.

"I place the breading mixture on a sheet of wax paper, then press the chops into it firmly until no more will adhere. Do both sides this way.

"Now, place on a wire cake rack in a baking pan and bake away. The grease will be in the bottom of the pan, and both sides of the chops will be delightfully brown and crisp.

"To facilitate cleaning of the pan, place a piece of aluminum foil in the bottom before you start cooking."

I have a little cooking hint that is going to make your supper great tonight:

After you fry pork chops in a heavy iron skillet, try this:

Pour a cup or two of water in the skillet and let it bubble for a little while with some pepper and salt. Then, in another pan, have some egg noodles boiling. Now drain them in a colander.

Take the drained egg noodles from the colander and put them in that good boiled-down gravy (fat skimmed off) in your skillet.

Pork chops with browned egg noodles are out of this world—

about on cloud nine. Guess that's floating way up in the heavens somewhere.

These noodles can be put in a large casserole and the browned pork chops laid on top and sprinkled with a dash of paprika, then put back in the oven. (Really no need to do this unless dinner is delayed.)

Thickening may or may not be added to the gravy; suit your own taste. I personally think the starch from the noodles is enough.

Salmon

Pink canned salmon is cheaper than red and tastes just as good. If you want, tint it a tiny bit with red food coloring—not too red, just pinker—and the family will never know the diff!

Looking to save your food dollar by substituting fish for meat? Well, here's a dandy and inexpensive dish I discovered quite by accident while trying to salvage a can of salmon after testing another recipe. And believe me, it's delicious! Here's all it takes:

One 15-oz. can pink salmon; one whole egg, one heaping teaspoon baking powder, one-half cup flour,

Plus only about five minutes of your time from start to finish. (And what else can you cook that fast that's really good—and inexpensive, too?)

Now . . . here's how:

Open the can of salmon. Pour the juice into a measuring cup and set aside. Dump the drained salmon in a mixing bowl. Drop in one whole egg.

Use a fork to break up the salmon and mix in the egg real good. When it's gummy, add the sifted flour. Stir in flour thoroughly with a fork again. This mixture will be real thick. Don't worry . . . it's supposed to be that way!

Don't add any salt. Pepper is OK.

Take one-fourth cup of the salmon juice (pour out any excess—brands of salmon differ in liquid content) and add the baking powder to the juice; beat with a fork. It's going to foam. Good . . . it's supposed to. Your measuring cup should be three-quarters full of foam! This is what makes the difference in your recipe! If it doesn't foam, your baking powder may be old.

After the foaming process has worked, pour this into your salmon mixture. Mix again with that fork. It's going to be really thin this time. That's the secret of it all . . .

Pick up two iced teaspoons and use 'em to scoop out a ball of the salmon, then drop it into a deep fryer half-full of hot oil.

And the scoops of batter don't have to be perfect. The "crookeder" they are, the better.

These tidbits don't have to be turned. They will float on top of the hot oil! They turn themselves as they cook and are completely done in just a few seconds.

Your luscious brown tidbits will look as if you have dipped them into a secret, time-consuming, lacy batter and the crust browns beautifully. Another funny thing, they aren't greasy.

All I can figure out is that the bubbles which I got from the mixture of salmon juice and baking powder seem to be what makes them light, lacy and crunchy.

This batter cannot be made ahead of time and saved. It must be cooked within fifteen minutes after mixing in the foamy baking powder and juice.

This recipe can be varied by adding grated onions, garlic salt, etc. Wonderful for parties when served on a toothpick and served with or without a dip. Or pile 'em up on a plate for supper and serve with a hot sauce over them.

And you know what else? They're even great cold the next day.

A friend tried this recipe but was out of flour. She substituted cornmeal and said it was superb.

From Illinois: "While making salmon patties, I discovered I was out of onions so I substituted two tablespoons of packaged onion soup mix.

"You'll never believe how delicious those patties were! The best ever. Try it and see."

I did and I agree. Delish!—Heloise

From Nebraska: "When frying salmon patties, flour the side which you are going to put in the shortening and the patties won't fall apart as easily when you turn them over."

Sauces

From a Pennsylvania bachelor who knows his way around the kitchen:

"If I say so myself, I'm not a bad cook . . . but I do take shortcuts.

"My secret when fixing a cheese sauce mix is to whirl it up in the blender.

"I also do this with instant gravy."

From Vermont: "Anybody need an idea for pepping up everyday vegetables? If so, try my Chinese sauce.

"Just thicken chicken broth with cornstarch, add a little sugar or molasses, a teaspoonful of soy sauce and some onion salt or chopped green onions.

"This may be used on any vegetable . . . and you can also add a can of bean sprouts and/or sliced water chestnuts. Just use your imagination."

From Wisconsin: "To thicken creamed or buttered vegetables, here is a slick trick:

"Take one stick of softened butter or margarine and one-half cup of flour . . . mix well and put in a covered bowl and keep in the refrigerator.

"When you want to thicken vegetables, just add some of this mixture to the vegetables. It will melt all through and will thicken without lumps."

Sauce, lump-free

From Oregon: "Most of us housewives have a set of matching kitchen utensils, including a potato masher we hardly ever use.

"When cooking white sauce, I use my potato masher to stir with. It fits flat on the bottom of the pan and makes a perfect stirrer that eliminates lumps in the sauce.

"When you stir with its flat surface, you keep the bottom of the pan clean and no scorching. I just love the idea!"

Sausage

From North Dakota: "If you put sausage in the freezer just long enough for it to chill, you can slice it as thin as you wish.

"I slice the whole package, then store it in the refrigerator. Next time I'm ready to cook sausage, it's sliced and ready."

From Oregon: "If you like sausage patties, you may want to make a doughnut hole in the center of each before cooking.

"This way, they never have a partly done center."

From Minnesota: "I buy pork sausage in one- or-two pound rolls. Since sausage spoils quickly, here's what I do:

"I cut the whole roll, paper and all, into slices. Then I wrap the sliced roll in foil and put it in the freezer. "When I get ready to cook sausage, I take the edge of a knife and break off as many slices as needed, rewrap the roll and return to the freezer. No need to thaw the frozen slices before cooking, either."

From Kentucky: "Did you know that if you link two or three sausages together with a couple of toothpicks, it keeps them from curling when you fry them?"

From Maryland: "If you wet your hands with cold water before shaping sausage patties, the grease won't stick to your fingers."

Sausage, Vienna

From Idaho: "I cut Vienna sausages in half, then cut canned biscuits in half and roll 'em around the sausage to fry in deep fat.

"When golden brown, I drain on paper towels and dip in ketchup or mustard.

"They're mmm-good!"

To remove Vienna sausages from the can without mutilating them, take the center one out first. If that doesn't work, look on the bright side: at least you'll have only one mutilated sausage.

Shrimp

For best results with canned shrimp, pre-chill 'em and they'll hold their shape and texture better when added to hot mixtures and be at their best for cocktails or salad. Pre-chilling in the can firms the meat, helps shrimp stay curled, plump, pink, and unbroken until ready for us. P.S. Always rinse well in ice cold water before using.

Want to substitute canned shrimp for fresh in a recipe? Then hear this: One 4½-ounce can equals about one cup shrimp. Now figure that out!—Heloise

When using frozen shrimp, soak in ice-cold salted water for ten minutes. The shrimp will taste darn close to fresh . . . could really fool you!

Spaghetti (see Pasta, p. 30)

Spaghetti Sauce

For dieters who miss eating spaghetti:
Make spaghetti sauce . . . but pour it over lean hamburger.
It may not come up to the real McCoy, but for the time being it does satisfy that yearning.

Another low-cal treat for pasta lovers is zucchini lasagne. Just cut the zucchini into broad strips, parboil and layer in a casserole dish as you would lasagne noodles, with sauce and cheese between the layers. Mmm:good!

From Arkansas: "When making spaghetti sauce, rub cold butter or oil all around the inside of the pot, from the top right down to where the sauce is. Do this and you'll never have sauce spatter on your stove. It will simmer just to the butter line and no further. Sure helps keep the stove clean."

From New York: "I usually make spaghetti sauce from scratch, doubling ingredients, including the chopped meat. After it has cooked awhile, I add a pre-browned pot roast to the sauce and finish cooking both.

"When the roast is done, I remove it, wrap it in aluminum foil and freeze.

"Then, I remove a portion of the sauce and add to it a can of red kidney beans and some chili powder. I freeze this in a plastic container for chili con carne.

"Next, I remove another portion of sauce and freeze it for sloppy joes.

"For a fourth meal we have sauce with spaghetti that evening.

"There you go! Four meals in one pot."

From Georgia: "Do you use your gravy boat only for gravy? I discovered it is great for serving spaghetti sauce. Everyone loves pouring their own and children can do this with a minimum of dripping."

Steak

A neighbor of mine had some friends over for steak, baked potatoes and a lovely salad. She had a fantabulous idea I've just got to share with you all:

Instead of having just one kind of steak, she had a potluck of different steaks. There were T-bones, rib eyes, sirloins, and even a couple of porterhouse steaks.

After they came off the grill, she cut each steak in half—some in quarters.

I had three of those "quarter" steaks and I gnawed on three different kinds of bones—all at one meal. Imagine! A few bites of T-bone, rib eye and sirloin—now that's living!

Try it and if your guests don't eat it all, wrap the leftovers in foil as soon as folks leave and refreeze so you won't have to light that old grill again when you want steaks with great flavor. These steaks can be reheated in the oven any time.

From Ohio: "If you will brush the oven broiler rack lightly with oil and put a cup of water in the drip pan before broiling, cleaning up after you broil a steak is a cinch."

From Kentucky: "When pounding flour into meat for Swiss steak, wash the bottom of an unopened can of soup and use it as a pounder. The can fits the hand, has weight and an edge at the right angle to score the meat without cutting it."

From Hawaii: "Here's a tip for those who like their steaks rare inside but browned on the outside: Wrap the steaks in aluminum foil and place in the freezing compartment of your refrigerator until time to cook.

"Do not thaw before cooking and the center will remain rare while the outside gets browned to your liking."

Stew Meat

Subject? Stew meat, those little chunks we buy to slow cook with vegetables, etc.

Natcherlee, you should always buy the ones with the least bit of fat on 'em. Why pay for fat at the price of beef today?

But with today's cost of living and every dadgum penny adding up and counting, let me tell you what I did with some stew meat this week . . .

You won't believe it, but it does work and is scrumptiously scrumptious stuff. (Just don't you tell anyone it's stew meat.)

First thing you gotta have is a meat pounder. Cut your stew meat crosswise into bite-size pieces. Crosswise is against the grain. Then pound it with the meat pounder.

Next, sprinkle water on the meat and shake tenderizer on each chunk of meat you've hammered flat. You can cook immediately or stack each piece, one on top of the other, and put in a plastic bag and refrigerate overnight.

When ready to cook, dip in flour and fry in oil or bacon grease. Wow!

You will never know you're eating stew meat. Tastes like tips of steak and so tender that you won't even have to use a knife to cut it.

Make milk gravy with the pan drippings.

Now, how is that for saving money!

Your meat goes twice as far, and you've got twice as much of that beautiful crust on the outside because the meat's been pounded flat. Far better than any chicken-fried steak I ever shook a shaking stick at.

Whew! A new dish with stew meat! Can you beat that?

And remember that smiles are the same in any language. So give a smile to someone today.

Bet you a nickel with a buffalo on it that you will get one back. Give yourself another smile—this one in the mirror—and see how much prettier you look.

Stuffing

From Texas: "While puttering around the kitchen one day I discovered a trick that really helps me.

"I sometimes like to make stuffing for dinner, but never think about it 'til noon. Not usually having day-old bread on hand, I use bread from the freezer. Cuts much better."

From California: "Dressing made with crusts and heels of bread or stale bread stretches any kind of meat, so think about dressing with beef, lamb and other main dishes—not just with turkey."

From New Hampshire: "To make delicious dressing for roast chicken, use white raisin bread in your regular recipe.

" 'Swunderful!"

From Texas: "I used a seasoned Mexican corn bread mix to make stuffing, only adding a little sage. The seasoned corn mix did the rest. Just delicious!"

Stuffing, for turkey

Making do sure is an art . . . one a New Jersey bride has already mastered. She didn't have a bowl big enough to mix stuffing for a twenty-five pound turkey so . . .

"I used a plastic bag (the size for lining small kitchen garbage pails). First I tossed in the chopped and diced vegetables, then the chopped gizzards and water chestnuts, then the bread crumbs—mixing and tossing vigorously as each was added.

"The last thing I poured in was the liquid.

"I was so amazed—no vegetables or other stuff to wipe off the work counter and, needless to say, none on the floor either."

Sometimes we sure get in a rut when it comes to using kitchen aids. F'rinstance, a Minnesota housewife only used her electric knife to cut roast beef until one day when inspiration hit her while making turkey stuffing:

"I used my electric knife to cube the bread and dice the celery and onion.

"I left the celery in a bunch and, starting at the top, sliced down. The whole bunch was cut in seconds!"

A working wife in New York came up with this quick and easy "substitute" for stuffing:

"Just lay a few slices of bread on a plate, sprinkle with your favorite herbs or seasonings, chop a couple of bits of onion on top, then fold each slice in half, and insert it in the cavity of the bird."

We all love turkey with stuffing. But what a job to scoop it out of that old bird!

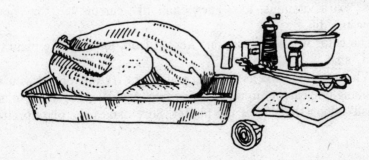

So let's hear a cock-a-doodle-doo for a homemaker in Missouri who has licked that problem:

"I make a cheesecloth bag about the size of a five-pound flour package and put it in the cavity of the cleaned turkey.

"After stuffing is made, I pack it lightly in the bag. When the turkey is finished, I pull out the stuffing bag and turn it inside out into a hot dish. Presto, I'm ready to serve!"

Does the family snack up on turkey and the trimmings when you're cooking up a feast? Do you shoo 'em away, fearing there won't be a morsel left to put on the table?

Here's a solution from an Ohio mother who knows her stuff, and stuffing:

"I started making twice as much stuffing as needed to fill the bird.

"The first thing I do is fill as many buttered muffin pans as I can with it. I bake them while the family's eating breakfast.

"If baked in a very hot oven, they come out crunchy on the outside and moist and tender on the inside.

"Then, when folks come into the kitchen for a taste of the feast, there's a platter of stuffing muffins waiting for them."

Now, that's a thoughtful mom!—Heloise

Tuna Fish

I was visiting a friend recently who had only one can of tuna for sandwiches. She just didn't see how she was going to stretch it for all her kids. So she put in lots and lots of chopped celery, which gave it quite a bit of crunch.

I took a carrot and grated it on the smallest part of her grater and added it to the mixture. Heaven help a duck, not only did it help stretch the tuna and make it tastier, but the kiddos got those extra vitamins, too. They don't like carrots but they never knew the diff.

The color was appealing and kept it from looking like plain old tuna salad.

When serving tuna as a salad, you might try (as long as you are grabbing one carrot anyway) taking two. Make carrot sticks to add "dash" along the side of the platter. Sure makes the plate pretty!

One thing my friend taught me is to add a bit of mustard to the mayonnaise. Wow, does that give tuna salad a lift!

I never buy solid pack tuna any more. I buy flaked or chunk. Why pay extra for solid pack and then waste time crumbling it up with a fork? Makes no sense whatsoever, does it?

Tuna packed in water is great, and less fattening. If you wanna make it taste like chicken salad, get out that old grater and grate an apple in it. Bet you'll think, "What is this? Chicken?"

In case you don't know the difference in the varieties of tuna, in reality there is none, as I learned when I went through a tuna packing plant. It all comes off the same fish. They take the big pieces and put 'em in one can and call it solid pack, which means it's all one big piece.

The chunk types are the ones that fall off around the big pieces. They cut the chunks to fit that round can.

The flaked types are the smaller pieces that are left on the cutting board after they have picked up the chunks.

The price difference in the types can sure make a difference in your budget, folks.

From Maryland: "I've found a unique way of draining the oil from a can of tuna.

"Here's what you do: after you open the can, take a round potato masher and, bracing the can on the side of the sink, push that potato masher into the can. Works like a gem!"

Turkey (also see Stuffing, for turkey, p. 43)

Remember when you only got the big bird on Thanksgiving?

Times sure have changed. Now turkey's likely to turn up on the menu any old time because it's a good buy . . . one of the best!

Don't take my word for it . . . check out the price per pound . . . lots cheaper than red meat!

And you don't have to buy the whole bird either. You can buy turkey parts—drumsticks, breasts, turkey patties and the like. Those patties are great dipped in egg, breaded and fried. Yummy.

If turkey's on sale, go whole hog and get a big bird. Have your butcher whack it in half. Serve one half, freeze the other.

And never ever worry about turkey leftovers. Sure as snow needs shoveling, you can do lots of delicious things with 'em.

Second time around, I always serve them "as is" with reheated stuffing and gravy.

For their next return engagement, I might make Turkey Divan (that's a fancy way of saying turkey with broccoli in cream sauce) or Turkey Tetrazzini (that's with spaghetti and cream sauce). I like both with lots of Parmesan cheese.

Don't go 'way because I haven't even warmed up on turkey leftovers yet.

They can be stir-fried with vegetables in peanut oil for chow mein.

You can bake 'em with cooked vegetables and sauce for a two-crust pie.

Or sauce them up and use as filling for crepes.

Or make a chef's salad . . . or stuffed tomatoes.

Not to mention heating 'em in curry sauce and serving over rice; dicing into hash, or chopping for croquettes.

And when you get right down to that old carcass, don't toss it out. Instead toss it into a Dutch oven with the turkey neck and make what I call "For Free Soup."

Talk about good to the last drop . . .

Turkey, steak

Did you know about turkey steak?

I always buy a big turkey and, after it's completely thawed, slit the skin on one side of the breast and remove the meat carefully to make turkey steak. I replace the skin over the turkey and bake the rest of it as usual.

I then cut the raw breast crosswise (across grain) and freeze it.

Turkey steak may be broiled, fried, or barbecued. Delicious, inexpensive, and different.

3

Dairy Foods

INTRODUCTION

Can you imagine breakfast without milk, cream and butter?
Dessert menus without ice cream?

Or life without cheese? Not if you're a born mouse like me, you can't.

If a cow hadn't clambered aboard Noah's Ark, cooking would've come to a standstill. And so would my waistline! But I wouldn't give up milk, cream, butter or cheese—not even to make Scarlett O'Hara pea-green with envy!

And there's something else in the dairy department that'd sure be hard to replace. It's a marvel of perfection and gift-wrapped to boot, because the hen delivers it packaged. It's the egg!

Eggs are a favorite breakfast food for many people and they're used as a main ingredient in lots of other dishes, like soufflés and quiche—not to mention cakes, cookies and bread!

So a cockle-doodle-doo for the hen! And an eighteen-moo salute for the cow! Most of all, a round of applause for the good foods they contribute to your table and mine.—Hugs, Heloise

Butter (see Margarine, p. 60)

Butter, herbed

Herbed butters are fantabulous with corn and other foods and it's cinchy to make 'em. There are so many combinations. For starters, try one of my eight favorites or dream up your own buttery concoction.

1. Cream one-third cup butter with one-eighth teaspoon ground black pepper, one-half teaspoon parsley flakes, one-quarter teaspoon onion powder, one-sixteenth teaspoon garlic powder and two teaspoons lemon juice.

2. Mix one-half cup softened butter, one-half teaspoon ground oregano and one-eighth teaspoon ground black pepper; blend well.

3. Combine one-half cup softened butter, two tablespoons wheat germ, one-quarter teaspoon garlic powder and one-eighth teaspoon salt.

4. Combine one-half cup softened butter, one teaspoon grated lemon peel and one-sixteenth teaspoon ground white pepper.

5. In small saucepan melt one-half cup butter or margarine. Stir in one-half teaspoon crushed dried dill weed, one-quarter teaspoon salt, one-sixteenth teaspoon ground black pepper and two teaspoons lemon juice. Simmer, uncovered, for two minutes.

Cheese (see specific cheese listings; also see Fondue, p. 58 and Leftovers, Cheese, p. 147)

Cheese, moldy

From Iowa: "Instead of throwing moldy cheese away, I take a knife or a cheese slicer, dip it in vinegar and slice the mold off.

"Dip the knife in vinegar after each slice of your knife.

"The vinegar kills the mold and keeps it from coming back."

Cheese, slicing and grating (also see Leftovers, Cheese, p. 147)

Don't have a cheese slicer? Use extra strength thread—it works better than a knife. Holding both ends, pull the thread tight and slice down through the cheese with it.

Keep grated cheese handy in the refrigerator for sprinkling on everything from soups to salad.

A neat way to grate cheese is to stretch a plastic sandwich bag over the end of a four-sided grater. Insert a wedge of cheese, grasp it through the plastic, then grate your cheese and it's in the bag. No mess!

Cheddar cheese grates better if placed in the freezer for ten to fifteen minutes before grating.

If you dip a knife into hot water before cutting processed cheese, you can slice it as thin as you wish and it won't curl.

Of course, you have to dip the knife into the hot water before cutting each and every single slice.

From South Carolina: "I was too lazy to grate cheese, so I used that good old stand-by—the potato peeler. It worked like a charm!"

From Missouri: "After grating cheese, clean the grater by grating a slice of bread. The cheese residue comes off easily and the resulting crumbs may be added to the grated cheese or refrigerated for later use as a casserole topping."

The quick way to grate or shred cheese is in a blender or food processor.

Cut the cheese in small cubes and drop them in.

The cheese will be shredded in nothing flat. If the cheese sticks together in globs, either as it is shredded or in the storage pack, sprinkle a tablespoon of flour over it. It'll coat the cheese bits enough so you can shake the cheese on pizzas or casseroles easily.

Cheese, storing

I must be part rat . . . the way I eat cheese . . .

I love all kinds and am always trying a new flavor.

I can't resist trying something new when I go shopping. I think I must be addicted, the way I seem to be drawn toward the cheese displays.

If they would let me sample-taste cheese the way they do ice cream, I would probably spend all my time at the cheese counter and cry like a baby when they said, "No more."

It never fails that I don't buy a little piece of some new, exotic cheese.

My big problem is storing. Now, I can eat a lot of cheese but there is a limit—even for me.

Cheese used to dry up before I could get to it, no matter how well I wrapped it. But I've got the problem solved:

I put the cheese back in its original wrapper and drop it in a big quart jar, then twist the lid on tight.

It stays fresh for what seems like ages.

From North Carolina: "The cut edge of boxed cheese won't dry out if you rub a bit of butter or margarine over it before rewrapping."

If you wrap cheese in a cloth dampened with vinegar and put it in an air-tight container, it'll stay fresh and moist.

Ever buy cheese in a two-pound cardboard box? The loaf keeps getting smaller as it is used, but the box still takes up the same amount of space in the fridge.

Cut the box in half. Keep sliding the two halves of the box within one another like a telescope as the cheese is used up.

If you are real industrious, you can keep trimming the cut ends of the box to make it custom-fit the block of cheese you have left!

From Minnesota: "I buy cheese in the two-pound carton. With only two of us in the family, it doesn't get used up very fast.

"I find that if I slip a plastic sandwich bag over the end of the cheese before returning it to the carton, it stays moist instead of becoming hard and dry."

From Vermont: "Know what I do with odds and ends of different kinds of hard cheese? Grate 'em, store them together in a jar, then use them for a 'cheese medley' topping for spaghetti or casseroles."

Cheese, cottage

From Washington, D.C.: "Here's an idea for a quick snack: mix cottage cheese, lemon pepper, salt, regular pepper and a small amount of pimiento. Stir together and spread on crackers. Sure is delicious!"

This is the greatest for drop-in guests.—Heloise

Cheese, ricotta

For a yum-yum low-calorie dessert, treat yourself to a scoop of ricotta cheese. Then spark it with a dash of vanilla, almond extract or rum flavoring. So delish, it positively tastes fattening, but there are only seventy calories per ounce.

Top melon or sliced fresh fruit with a scoop of ricotta. For the absolute greatest, mash some strawberries into the ricotta, then use it as topping. Fabulous!

Cream

Say cream, and I start thinking yummy thoughts like strawberry shortcake or peaches and cream.

Cream's the greatest, but would you believe that nobody used it until the ninth century? That's when a Roman chef had a brainstorm and started skimming the cream off the top of the milk so he could use it separately. What a genius!

It took a Viennese cook—and that was only 300 years ago—to come up with the idea of whipping it! He probably was concocting a topping for Viennese pastry!

Chill cream first and you'll find it whips a lot more easily.

Chill the bowl and beaters too. In fact, pop 'em in the freezer for a bit. The colder they are, the quicker the cream whips.

It's better to whip one-half pint of cream at a time rather than the full pint. Makes it fluffier.

Whip cream only until soft or stiff peaks form. Don't overwhip.

If you're putting whipped cream through a pastry tube, it should be stiffer than whipped cream you're going to fold into other ingredients. When folded in, cream has to be stiff enough to give firmness, but soft enough to blend in smoothly.

Wait until after the cream's whipped to sweeten it. Then fold two to three tablespoons of sifted confectioners' or granulated sugar into two cups of whipped cream. Adjust the sugar measurement if you have less cream.

Store cream in the coldest part of the refrigerator. Remember, it's perishable.

Once whipped, cream can be frozen in dabs or dollops. Don't freeze unwhipped cream!

Cream, powdered (see Coffee, powdered cream for, p. 124)

Cream, whipped, substitute for

From Utah: "My mother uses bananas as a substitute for whipped cream.

"She adds a sliced banana to the white of an egg and beats it with an electric beater until it's stiff. The banana is absorbed, leaving a very tasty substitute for whipped cream."

Lots less calories, too, friends!—Heloise

Eggs (also see specific egg listings and Leftovers, Omelets, p. 145)

What comes gift-wrapped by Mother Nature in its own fragile white package?

Why the egg, of course, one of the wonders of the world. Versatile? You betcha! It can be served in so many super ways.

If you're wondering what's the best way to separate an egg, it's to crack it and drop the whole egg in your cupped hand. Let the white slip through your fingers into a cup and only the yoke will remain in your hand.

As for a super way to beat an egg, try a jar! Just break the egg in the jar, cover and shake! Doesn't that beat everything? And, oh yes, don't forget to put a "for sale" sign on your eggbeater.

White eggs? Brown eggs? Which should you buy? The cheapest! The color of the shell doesn't have anything at all to do with how good those eggs taste . . . or with their food value or quality, either.

From New Jersey: "Here's a small tip: When you are taking eggs from a carton, dampen your fingertips and the eggs will be easier to pick up."

Eggs, baked

If there's anything I love, it's scrumptious baked eggs with different trimmings. Must be good 'cause I never get tired of them. I've found a new way to fix 'em that's real easy.

First, I set my little electric broiler-oven to 350° F, then I put the coffee pot or a kettle of water on—most days I use instant coffee so it's the kettle . . .

Next, I drag out my nonstick six-muffin pan and butter a piece of bread (for toast), cutting it in fourths and placing them in two separate muffin cups.

I put a small, thin patty of sausage in a third and bite-size bacon strips in a fourth.

In the fifth and sixth, I put one pat of margarine, one teaspoon of instant rice and one full teaspoon of boiling water (that's for the rice). Then I stir in salt and pepper and break an egg over the rice.

That's all there is to it. I put the pan on the middle shelf of the oven, and set my timer for fifteen minutes.

This idea gives you bachelors time to shower, shave and shine, or you career gals to bathe and buff it.

From the time you walk into your kitchen until you pop breakfast in the oven, it's only two minutes of fixing and, later on, only one pan to rinse.

The eggs will rise like muffins. The toast is melba-type and crisp on both sides. You'll absolutely love it.

I have varied these eggs in many ways. I've broken the yellows and slightly stirred the eggs into the rice and water before cooking. This is good!

One morning I put leftover cooked bacon chips in and stirred slightly. That was good, too, real good. I cooked two more of those . . .

Another morning I had some company and was short on eggs, so I used four tablespoons of boiling water and four tablespoons of instant rice. Mixed good, then dumped in four eggs and beat well by hand. I poured this into six margarined muffin tins, and if I didn't come up with six beauteous eggs!

This is the grandest way I know to stretch eggs.

Now, if we could stretch our dollars and our strength that much, it would be wonderful.

Eggs, boiled

Ever wonder why some hard-boiled eggs don't peel easily? The fresher they are, the harder to peel, say egg experts.

Let me tell you something about hard-boiled eggs.

Peel them immediately while they are hot—under cold water—either running from the faucet or in a pan. Crack the egg and roll it so the shell's all broken up first, and the skin just pops right off with no raggedy edges whatsoever.

If you are like me and always boil an extra egg or two for salads or egg sandwiches for the next day, go ahead and peel the extra eggs then.

Put it (or them) in a glass jar filled with cold water in the fridge so the egg will sink below the level of the water. Eggs keep beautifully this way for about three days and don't shrink at all.

It's always nice to have hard-boiled eggs on hand for stuffed eggs, to add to casseroles, or slice in salads or sandwiches.

Use a potato masher—the kind that is flat on the bottom with little round holes in it—to dice hard-boiled eggs.

It's much faster than any other method.

If you want to chop a hard-boiled egg, put it in a slicer. Slice all the way through. Then pick up carefully so that the slices stay together. Now reslice the egg in the opposite direction by placing it crosswise in the slicer!

From Alaska: "To keep egg shells from cracking when they are boiled, wrap each in aluminum foil, then put them in the pan to boil. Nary a one will crack! It has never failed me."

Eggs, deviled

Don't you just love yummy deviled eggs?

Don't you just dread the thought of making them?

I do both, and that's why I want to tell you what I did the other day when I was packing food to go on a hike.

I stood there looking at the box of hard-boiled eggs and, being honest with myself, I knew that I did not want to go through the mess and hassle of deviling them.

So, I decided not to!

Being a basically lazy person . . . now, I could have said I just do things with the least amount of effort and time, and that I am not lazy . . . but, like I said, I'm lazy.

I found the quickest and easiest way. I just peeled all of the eggs, plopped them into a jar and covered 'em with water.

That's pretty basic, huh?

The next step was the mixture for the yolks.

I keep a small jar of this deviled egg "goop" mixed up in the fridge. This is merely mayonnaise, mustard, a dab of vinegar, chopped pickle, plus seasonings.

It already was taken care of, so all I did was put both jars in a plastic bag with a knife and fork.

When it was time to eat, I did get some strange looks when I pulled out the jar of eggs.

I explained that it would have been difficult to carry the eggs already deviled, so instead everyone could make his own. (Good excuse, huh?)

I fished out a whole egg, sliced it and, being lazy, spread some "goop" on it.

It was good . . . to my surprise!

One of the fellows sliced his egg, plopped out the yolk on a plastic lid, and mashed it together with the deviled egg stuff and made his own.

You are probably saying to yourself, "How lazy can that girl be —or how smart!"

I think a little bit of both, but who cares? It was easy for me and everyone else liked the idea.

I wouldn't do this for a party or dinner, but I think it is a darn good way to travel with deviled eggs.

I plan to do this from now on. One added attraction: if someone doesn't like deviled eggs, they can have plain hard-boiled ones.

From Oregon: "Those little spoons that babies receive for presents are absolutely perfect for filling deviled eggs. They're just the right size and make the job so much easier."

Eggs, poached

I think the easiest way to poach eggs—it saves lots of time cleaning the poacher—is to first put water under the poacher trays, then lightly grease the little egg compartments with corn oil.

Put a paper baking cup in each egg compartment and then break the eggs into 'em. Put the lid on the pan.

For soft-poached, serve in the paper baking cup; for hard-poached turn upside down for a beautiful fluted egg.

From New Jersey: "Don't have an egg poacher—and don't need one. All I do is give a small saucepan a squirt of vegetable spray, then add a few drops of vinegar and a little water. Bring the water to a boil; break in an egg; cover and turn heat to low for a few minutes —until the egg's set."

From Ohio: "Use herb-seasoned stuffing under poached eggs. It soaks up the juices and stays crisp."

Eggs, scrambled

To make scrambled eggs go farther, add a little water and a dash of baking powder. The eggs come out nice and fluffy!

Eggs, storage

From Virginia: "My refrigerator has no egg compartment on the door but does have shelves. By cutting the top from an egg carton and fitting the carton on the shelf, I have an egg compartment. The shelf holds two cartons so I have storage for two dozen eggs."

The best way to store egg whites is in a tightly covered container in the refrigerator. They'll keep seven to ten days.

Egg yolks should be covered with water and stashed away in a covered container in the fridge. But use 'em within two to three days.

Eggs, substitute

Here is an idea I use for a change from fresh eggs. I buy the frozen egg substitute popular with those who are watching cholesterol. It includes only the white of the egg, but with seasonings to make it taste good, extra vitamins too.

It's advertised for scrambled eggs, but I like to pour it out from the package in dollar-size "pancakes" and cover with good maple syrup. Makes the easiest pancakes you'll ever find, and they're tasty and good for you.

Fondue

From Iowa: "We are fond of giving fondue parties but our fondues always were stringy and never completely blended. My error was in preparing the cheeses. I had always grated them, then stirred 'em in a circular motion with a metal spoon.

"I was lucky enough to ask a Swiss chef about fondues. He told me, 'Never stir with a circular motion because the cheeses won't blend. Never, never use a metal spoon.' I also discovered that my cheeses were not aged and I was keeping the flame too high.

"So, for a perfect Swiss fondue, cube your cheeses unless the recipe specifically calls for grated cheese. Stir with a wooden spoon in a figure eight motion. Keep the fondue heated on a low flame.

"Bon appetit for your pièce de résistance."

Ice Cream (also see Baked Alaska, p. 107)

Ice cream is an instant dessert you can fancy up in countless ways. F'rinstance:

Spoon crème de menthe, apricot or chocolate sauce over it.

Top with sliced peaches, strawberries, blueberries or other fruit.

Use flaked coconut or chopped nuts as a topping.

Swirl hot fudge or butterscotch sauce through it.

Crush peppermint candy, sweet chocolate or peanut brittle and sprinkle on vanilla ice cream.

Cut fruit gelatin into cube shapes and serve with ice cream.

Serve ice cream on pancakes, waffles, sliced pound or angel food cake or on pie to make it à la mode.

Just recently I discovered that by adding a small amount of un-sweetened, flavored powdered drink mix to vanilla ice cream, and mixing well, you can make different flavored ice cream that's delicious.

The amount of powder you add depends on the amount of ice cream you want to flavor. One-half teaspoon to an average dish of ice cream would be about right. Use the unsweetened mix so the ice cream doesn't become overly sweet.

It's fun to have different flavors without having to have a freezer full of umpteen different ice cream containers.

From Vermont: "My favorite dessert: chocolate ice cream mixed with Maraschino cherries. It's a new flavor!"

From Texas: "For instant dessert, spoon canned crushed pineapple on ice cream and top with melted marshmallows."

From Utah: "Maple syrup's not only good on pancakes. Heat it and try it on ice cream."

From Pennsylvania: "Instead of mince pie, I serve mincemeat topped with vanilla ice cream for Thanksgiving dessert. Oh, so good! Another good Thanksgiving combo—cranberries and ice cream!"

Ice Cream, storage

From Illinois: "Put aluminum foil over ice cream in refrigerator trays to keep beads of moisture from forming ice crystals that spoil the texture of your dessert."

Ice Cream Parfaits

From Indiana: "I use my crystal water glasses to serve my jellied ice cream dessert. I spoon two kinds of jelly between layers of ice cream."

From Massachusetts: "I make parfait by alternating layers of ice cream and sherbet or whipped cream."

Ice Cream Sandwiches

Like ice cream sandwiches? Try making your own with bulk ice cream and cinnamon-sugared graham crackers.

When you put a thin slice of ice cream between two crackers, spread it on the sugared sides. The sugar won't wear off on little hands, clothing—or the floor.

Isn't that a fresh, crisp treat? And a bit more economical than buying the commercial product, too!

Margarine

Do you want to be real fancy, not only for dinner guests, but for your family too? Let me tell you what to do with your butter and margarine:

First, slice the butter for individual servings and lay the slices out on wax paper. Next, take a raw potato, cut the end of it off and carve an initial or design on the cut end.

Then press the design in the slightly softened butter pats. Those butter pats will be just adorable!

Place the wax paper in your refrigerator or freezer until you are ready to use the butter pats . . . and while you're makin' the pats don't make just a few. Make lots and lots. They keep a long time when frozen.

I found something I surely enjoy using, squeeze-bottle margarine. When I use it all up, I melt the amount of margarine I need and pour it back in the bottle to use on baked potatoes, waffles, pancakes, etc. Don't put the bottle in the fridge, though, or you'll never get the margarine out!

From Illinois: "I thought other mothers might like my way of softening butter to make it go further.

"I mix a pound of butter with a pound of soft margarine, and a small amount of milk.

"Let it stand until quite soft, then whip it well, and pack it in empty margarine containers.

"The result is delicious 'butter' that's always soft enough to spread, and already in serving dishes."

Milk

This may surprise you but . . . while you can't freeze cream, it's perfectly safe to freeze milk . . . and it will retain all its nutritional value in the freezer.

To defrost frozen milk, put it in the refrigerator or set the carton in ice water.

Never defrost frozen milk at room temperature.

Here's a Letter of Laughter from a seasoned homemaking hand in Idaho:

"Gave a recipe to a new bride that called for a tablespoon of milk. Guess what the sweet young thing asked? 'Level or heaping?' "

Yogurt

Put some small containers of yogurt in the freezer for a healthful frozen dessert.

You can even pour a diet drink over a large spoonful of this frozen yogurt to make a "float," then luxuriate in its wickedly good taste.

At last I have solved the delicious problem of how to take my favorite flavor yogurt to work for lunch. I put the yogurt in the freezer the night before, and have an icy cold dessert defrosted by lunch time.

Bread, Potatoes, Cereal and Rice

INTRODUCTION

Sorry about this, calorie counters, but I've got to confess:

This is one of the most fattening chapters in my book . . . but it's also one of the most delicious!

We can't watch our weight all the time, can we? Got to live a little now and again. So sneak a peek, because lots of good things follow.

In the bread department, you'll find biscuits (don't you love 'em hot and buttered?), dumplings, French toast, pancakes, rolls, sandwiches . . . and that's just mentioning a few of the goodies.

And then come potatoes—all kinds, including baked potatoes, which I love topped with sour cream or melted butter.

I know a potato's not fattening without sour cream or butter
. . . but it's not as good, either. So, once in awhile, forget dieting. I
do. Sometimes I'm sorry . . . and sometimes I'm not!

You'll flip for the cereal tips. If you serve yours plain with milk,
you're missing some good bets, like serving cereal with chocolate
milk or topping it with ice cream, or with raisins, dates and nuts!

Aren't they the greatest ideas? Sure are—and there's lots more.

I haven't even warmed up to rice, one of my favorite foods because
it's so versatile. Land sakes, the things you can do with rice! Every
time you serve it, it can seem like a brand new dish!

So read on. One thing's for sure, you won't gain an ounce—at least
not while you're turning pages. After that, you're on your
own!—Hugs, Heloise

PART I: BREAD

Biscuit Mix (also see Applesauce Dessert, p. 106)

Here's my very own recipe for biscuit mix:

Mix together thoroughly eight cups flour, one-third cup baking
powder, two teaspoons salt and eight teaspoons sugar (optional).
With a pastry blender, cut in a cup shortening to a very fine consistency.

This mixture keeps well in your cabinet, but I keep mine in the
refrigerator as I don't use it very often. It stays fresh for months.

When I want to make biscuits, I use one cup mix to one-third cup
milk. Many times I don't even roll them out as the mix makes
excellent drop biscuits, but if you want to go to a little more trouble,
do this:

After adding the milk to the mix, stir it well, then turn it onto a
floured surface. Knead gently for a few seconds, then roll out to
approximately one-half inch thickness and cut with a biscuit cutter
or small juice glass.

Place in a greased pan and bake at 425° F until lightly browned.

Gee whiz! Just noticed my mouth is watering so, I can't type!

If yours is, let's go make up a batch of these biscuits and have a
feast! I'll even put the coffee on!

Biscuits (also see Leftovers, Biscuits, p. 146)

I have one of those handy little toaster-broiler ovens just the right size to hold a TV dinner. The catch is I also like biscuits with my TV dinner.

My solution? I put the TV dinner in the oven. About ten minutes before it's ready, I wipe the foil cover with a piece of paper towel dipped in shortening, lay on three or four refrigerator biscuits and pop the TV dinner back in the oven.

Result—biscuits and dinner ready at the same time. No need to heat up a big oven for two small items . . . and only silverware to wash.

From Alabama: "Who said biscuits have to be round? Instead of the usual round shapes, I use cookie cutters and make hearts, diamonds, clubs, stars, squares, crescents and bells! My family was positively stunned first time I did this."

From Maine: "My husband loves the ready-mix biscuits I make. The instructions tell you to just spoon-drop them, but that way they never turned out really great like his mother's.

"All my mother-in-law does is lightly roll out the dough. Then, she dips the rim of a glass in flour and uses it to cut out the biscuits! This trick makes all the difference in the world."

From New Mexico: "Like the difference it makes in a packaged cake mix when you improvise and add other ingredients, canned biscuits can be improved on, too.

"Preheat the pan with a little margarine in it. Then dip the biscuits in the melted margarine as you place them in the pan. Let them sit for a few minutes before baking in a slower than recommended oven —twenty-five to fifty degrees cooler.

"Remove when brown and enjoy light-as-a-feather biscuits without having to make them from scratch. They're much more flavorful, too!"

From Massachusetts: "I am one of those men who loves to cook, therefore I'm always looking for unusual foods to prepare and different ways to prepare them.

"The other day I stumbled onto a goody:

"Open a can of biscuits, separate and grease them as usual, and then pop them into your waffle iron. Set the iron on 300°F.

"If you like thin, crisp biscuits you are really in for a treat. Be sure to keep a close watch on them because they cook quickly."

From South Dakota: "Have you ever tasted fried biscuits? A couple of years ago when it was too hot to fire up the oven, I fried biscuits over a very low fire, almost as low as I could get it.

"Then when they were brown, which only takes a few minutes, I browned them on the other side, and they were better than when baked in the oven.

"I use canned biscuits and they taste very much like the shortbread my mother used to make. We like them better than the baked ones. Be sure to cover the pan so the heat will bake the sides.

"Some biscuits separate and, if they do, fry them very thin and crisp.

"Really delicious!"

Bread (see specific bread listings; also see Rolls, p. 72)

Bread, frozen

Here is a helpful hint for those who enjoy making fresh baked bread with those popular frozen loaves.

After the bread is baked, lay it on its side on a cooling rack. You will find the wires from the rack leave a slight impression on the bread at just the right places for slicing.

Bread, home-baked

Because of the mess of floured pastry boards or cloths that are difficult to clean up, I nearly gave up breadmaking. Thank heavens I thought of my nonstick-coated cookie sheet.

It's perfect for kneading and shaping! The dough never sticks and you can keep on kneading 'til every speck of flour is well absorbed into the dough.

Best of all, when I bake round loaves, I can cook the bread in the same pan!

Do you bake nice hot bread and dinner rolls, then put them on the napkin in your straw breadbasket, only to find they get cold before dinner's over?

Well, here is a way to prevent this problem.

When you put your rolls in the oven to bake them, put a ceramic tile in, too. When the rolls are done, this tile is hot. Place it in the basket and put your rolls on top.

The tile sure keeps 'em warm.

From Maryland: "I use two-pound coffee tins for baking bread instead of the conventional bread tins.

"These make high, pillar-type bread that is just as good as the conventional loaves."

From Utah: "Here is a wonderful treat for homemade bread lovers: Just shape the dough into a roll, then slice it with a knife. Dip each piece in melted butter and then in a cinnamon and sugar mixture.

"Stand these slices straight in a loaf pan and let rise, then bake.

"You end up with a very delicious and different loaf."

From Alaska: "As you know, caraway seeds are used to flavor rye bread. However, I do not like to bite into the seeds, so I grind them in my peppermill. I have two mills, one for pepper and one for caraway seeds."

Bread, stale (also see French Toast, p. 69 and Leftovers, Pizza, p. 149)

From Ohio: "My daughter always cuts slightly stale bread into shapes with her cookie cutter and freezes them. When unexpected company arrives, she takes the bread out of the freezer, pops it under the broiler and spreads it with a cheese spread.

"Instant snacks for her friends with no trouble at all."

Bread, store bought (also see Rolls, p. 72)

From Montana: "I dislike those bread twistems that come on the bread bag, but didn't know how else to keep the bread fresh. Then came a brainstorm . . .

"I took a child's plastic barrette, the kind that has straight bars without the metal pieces, gathered the top of the bread bag and clipped the barrette across it. Just a snap seals the bag—and it opens just as easily."

From Idaho: "A friend showed me how to keep bread wrappers secure without bothering with twistems or those little plastic tabs: Take the open end of the wrapper, twist it a few times to get out the air, then pull the ends of the wrapper back over the bread. As the slices of bread are used, the remaining part of the loaf gets a double wrap, which gives extra protection and keeps the loaf fresher."

Bread Crumbs (see Chicken, crumb-coated, p. 19 and Pork Chops, p. 34; also see Leftovers, Breading, p. 147 and Leftovers, Bread Crumbs, p. 146)

Cornmeal (also see Leftovers, Breading, p. 146)

From New Jersey: "To keep cornmeal from getting weevils, I store it in the freezer. The cornmeal doesn't freeze solid . . . and it doesn't get bugs."

Croutons

If you love croutons in salad, make your own. I do—because it's cheaper.

I take a whole loaf of bread, buttering each slice, then stacking four to six slices at a time. With my electric knife I slice the stack of bread in four sections, then into smaller sections. The little crouton squares may be made large or small, whichever suits your fancy.

I put all the little bread squares on a cookie sheet, sprinkle them with garlic salt and put them in the oven at 250° F for about an hour, turning once.

These homemade croutons are far better than the commercial product.

Crust (see Pie Crust, p. 120)

Dressing (see Stuffing, p. 42)

Dumplings

Here's a trick for all you darlings who dote on dumplings:

Dip the spoon in the hot gravy each time before filling the spoon with the batter and the batter will drop readily from the spoon into the gravy.

Take my word for this one: For delicious dumplings, add about a quarter-cup of crisply crumbled bacon to the batter. The taste is delightful.

Flour (also see Leftovers, Breading, p. 147)

Store two paper plates with your flour sifter; sift from one to the other.

Paper plates bend easily for pouring flour back into the sifter, or for returning excess flour to its container.

French Toast

From Utah: "I make a variation of French toast I call "Pineapple French Toast." It's delicious.

"First I cut slices of bread in half, then into the bowl go the eggs, sugar, and cinnamon. (Very often I substitute honey for the sugar, using one tablespoon for each egg.)

"I beat all this until it's fluffy. You can add just a little milk if desired, but I usually don't find this necessary.

"Set this aside and put on a skillet with a lot of butter and about a quarter of a cup of crushed pineapple. Let this get real hot. Now you are ready to dip your bread into the egg mixture and fry quickly in the butter and pineapple.

"The bits of pineapple will stick to the bread. Fantastic!"

This Indiana bachelor can cook! Here's his own recipe for "Fraffles:"

"Batter up French toast as usual but cook in a waffle iron. Makes a great brunch!

Pancakes and Waffles (also see Bacon, p. 15 and Potato Pancakes, p. 76)

Did you know that when you cook waffles and pancakes they are twice as good if served on a warm plate?

I know you're going to think it's too much trouble—nobody warms plates. Well, let me tell you something: Set your plates under the hot water faucet and turn the hot water on.

Just when you turn over the pancake or when the waffle is almost done, pick up a plate and towel-dry it. Then throw (I love that word, 'cause some mornings that's exactly how I feel!) that nice hot pancake or waffle on it. The butter melts and it tastes ever so much better.

So warm your plates tomorrow morning. (The china ones that is . . . not your dentures!)

Let me tell you how to make better waffles to put on those nice warm plates.

Did you know that if you substitute club soda for milk, you will have lighter, crisper waffles?

I use two cups of a good biscuit mix, one egg, one-half cup of oil, and one and one-third cups of club soda.

Try this recipe and you'll think those waffles fell from heaven! Let me tell you that these are the most scrumptious waffles I have ever eaten.

I also tried this idea with a box of pancake mix and just substituted the club soda for the milk. It too is delightful. So light and fluffy! Nothing like ordinary pancakes.

From New Hampshire: "After pouring batter into your waffle iron, let it cook for awhile before closing the lid. This assures a fluffier waffle. Mainly, it will keep batter from running down the sides and creating a mess to clean."

From Nevada: "Have you ever tried adding buttermilk to buttermilk pancake mix? My husband says, 'Now I know what they mean when they say, melts in your mouth.' "

From South Carolina: "An easy way to warm plates for waffles or pancakes is to put them on the rack in the oven with the pilot light on while you're cooking. By the time you are ready for pancakes, the dishes are toasty warm."

Many people skip pancakes because, for health reasons, they must restrict their intake of sugar.

If this is the case, just sweeten the pancake batter with artificial sweetener. After cooking, add butter and you have a very tasty pancake with no need for syrup.

From Vermont: "I use a pizza cutter to cut pancakes into bite-size squares for my three children. I butter, cut, then pour on the syrup. It's really a great timesaver."

From Texas: "I have discovered a simple and delicious method of reheating waffles because each time I make 'em, I make plenty so I'll have leftovers to freeze.

"To reheat: add butter and syrup and place under the broiler (use ovenproof plates) until butter melts, syrup sizzles and the waffles are warm and tasty.

"I have found this method a great improvement over using the toaster which often burns the edges of the waffles.

"The broiler method melts the butter and heats the syrup and the waffles all in one operation. It's positively Heloisian!"

Pancakes, cake-mix recipe for

I was in a rip-roaring hurry to get dessert ready recently, so I turned my oven to preheat, and started making a chocolate cake.

I'd just gotten my batter mixed when, wouldn't you know it, I noticed a cloud of smoke coming from the oven. I'd forgotten that the night before a blueberry pie had overflowed while baking.

There was nothing to do but turn off the oven. There I was with a batch of cake batter that I wasn't about to waste . . .

So I turned on my electric grill to 400° F and poured the batter out on it as if I was making pancakes. And I was—lovely chocolate ones about 4½ inches in diameter.

I repeated this until I had used all the batter. Then I whipped up some packaged dessert topping mix (which I always keep on hand) and blended some chocolate shavings and finely chopped nuts into it.

Then I stacked the pancakes, four to a stack, alternating with the topping mixture. I topped it off with a large dollop of cream and a few additional chocolate shavings.

It was beautiful!

I popped it back in the refrigerator until ready to serve and then cut it into quarters. It was very rich and a quarter serving was plenty.

Fortunately, I had used a small package of cake mix, but still had enough for four stacks. The first couple of pancakes I made didn't look so good because I hadn't learned the knack of turning them.

I'd suggest you use a large pancake turner as these little cakes are very soft. It seems to me this would be a good idea for campers who don't have an oven.

There are variations you can try. Afterwards, I thought I could have added chopped, drained maraschino cherries.

You also could use white or yellow cake mix, or mix the cream with strawberries, or make spice cake pancakes with canned apple pie filling for topping.

I made cake pancakes again in a nonstick skillet and had no trouble whatsoever turning them. Also I made some the size of cookies and stacked them in fours. The smaller pancakes make perfect individual servings.

You know what sold me completely? The dessert was all ready to put in the refrigerator and chill in only fifteen minutes.

How about that for a dessert you'd write home to mom about?

I think it's great. When the rest of you cooks try it, I know you will echo my sentiments exactly.

Pizza (see Leftovers, Pizza, p. 149)

Rolls

Here's a hint I think will help save a little on fuel bills.

To heat rolls, don't turn on the oven. Instead invert the lid of the pot in which you're cooking vegetables—or use a pie tin. Put the rolls in it; sprinkle a very small amount of water over them, and cover with a larger lid or pie tin.

The rolls will heat while you're cooking your vegetables.

To freshen rolls that have gotten hard, turn on the kitchen faucet gently, wet the rolls quickly, shake, then pop into the oven with the roast to heat. This is a "Heloise quickie" and it works!

Sandwiches (also see Leftovers, Sandwich Fillings, p. 145)

From Vermont: "If I don't have time to hard-boil eggs for egg salad sandwiches, I scramble them very dry and add the usual seasonings."

From Massachusetts: "My quick way to make a BLT (bacon, lettuce & tomato) sandwich is to use imitation bacon bits.

"Try it for a quickie—no work, no bother and no mess. Three cheers for bacon bits!"

Here is a helpful hint for mothers who are called on to make jelly sandwiches:

Instead of spreading the bread with butter, take the jelly and butter and mash them together with a fork, then put the mixture on the bread and your bread slices won't slide when they're sandwiched.

Also, the jelly can be mixed this way with peanut butter and you have a firm sandwich that can be cut in shapes without slipping.

From Missouri: "When the church guild prepared the food for a wedding reception, I noticed they placed all the fancy sandwiches on regular cafeteria trays.

"The food was covered in the usual way to prevent drying out, then the trays were stacked. They used four empty wooden thread spools as 'legs' between them—one spool at each corner of the tray.

"The trays were stacked as high as space in the refrigerator permitted and none of the carefully prepared sandwiches were squashed or packed down while stored."

From Ohio: "By accident I discovered it's much easier to make sandwiches using frozen bread. The butter's a cinch to spread."

From Maine: "I love bacon, lettuce and tomato sandwiches, but when lettuce is expensive, I use tender, chopped leaves of celery instead.

"Delicious!"

Here's a recipe for my favorite olive nut sandwich:

Let six ounces of cream cheese stand at room temperature until soft. Mash with a fork and add one-half cup mayonnaise.

Chop pecans until you have one-half cup full. Chop olives until you have one cup. Put in your bowl with the cream cheese and add two tablespoons of the olive juice with a dash of pepper. No salt.

Stir well. This will be mushy. It's supposed to be that way.

Put in a pint fruit jar and refrigerate for at least twenty-four to forty-eight hours. It will then become thick. You won't believe it but it will.

You will have nearly a pint of delicious, deluptious, delicate spread such as you never have put on your poor palate in the past!

This should be served on very thin toast. Fresh, thinly sliced bread will do, too.

I always serve mine topped with shredded lettuce. Be sure to cut the sandwiches into tiny fingertip sizes. Then you will really feel as if you are going first-class.

A jet-set traveler whose home base is California returned from Europe with these yummy sandwich suggestions:

"Try soft cream cheese with cucumber or watercress or tomatoes.

"I went bananas over European sandwiches. In fact, cream cheese and bananas is 'jolly' good."

And how about cream cheese with olives; peas or avocado on toast or rye bread?—Heloise

When packing a lunch, here's a different way to make a sandwich:

Slice the meat thin enough so two or three slices can be put on the sandwich. Put condiments or pickles between the slices of meat instead of next to the bread.

That keeps the bread or bun from becoming soggy before it's time for lunch!

Sandwiches, substitutes for (see Meat, lunch box p. 29)

Stuffing (see Main Dishes, p. 14)

Toast (also see French Toast, p. 68)

From Montana: "When making toast with small bread slices, put a toothpick through the top edge of the bread so that the toothpick will lie across the top of the toaster.

"This keeps the bread from falling to the bottom of the toaster, and makes it easier to remove."

Here's a make-do idea from a smarty in Georgia:

"I don't have a toaster so I grill toast in a cast-iron skillet.

"I butter the bread on both sides and brown to my liking. Works great!"

From Illinois: "To keep toast hot, wrap in aluminum foil after buttering it."

Toast, cinnamon

From West Virginia: "Here's my easy way to fix cinnamon toast:

"I mix the sugar and cinnamon with the margarine in a large bowl, then spoon into a margarine tub.

"It's always ready to spread when someone wants a toast treat."

I tried this but used diet margarine and sugar substitute. Scrumptious!—Heloise

Toast, French (see French Toast, p. 69)

Waffles (see Pancakes, p. 69)

PART II: POTATOES

Potato Chips

You know what the big problem is with potato chips, friends? They get soggy. What to do about it?

Many people store them in a gas oven. The pilot light keeps them crisp. (You can keep cereal there, too.) The proper way is to keep them in the freezer.

Once the bag has been opened, remove as many as you want. Re-twist, seal the bag, and pop in the freezer.

Once potato chips have become soggy, spread on a cookie tray and heat in your oven at a low temperature for a few minutes.

I love potato chips done this way, whether they are soggy or not.

Potato Pancakes

From Ohio: "On hunting trips, I make potato cakes with pancake mix. Here's how: First, I add two parts of pancake mix to one part instant potatoes, then add the other ingredients listed in the directions on the pancake mix package.

"Works very well and they really are delicious."

Potato Salad

Use a wire cheese slicer to make paper-thin slices of cold cooked potatoes for potato salad.

Potatoes, baked

Here's to you and you . . . and had we not met it might never have been.

But now that we have met, I want to tell you how I bake potatoes.

After washing 'em, take a paring knife and jab each potato full of holes—I put about fifteen or sixteen in each big spud. Then bake 'em in the oven.

I lay the potatoes on the top shelf and really don't worry much about the temperature setting of the oven. I'm usually cooking something else at the same time and have never really noticed that it makes a big difference when baking potatoes whether the oven is set at 350° F or 450° F.

I do not wrap potatoes in foil because a connoisseur of baked potatoes told me that potatoes were 87 percent moisture and foil wrapping makes them soggy. After I tested baking potatoes with and without foil, I found there was all the difference in the world between the two. Without foil's much better.

When I think they are done, I stick an ice pick through them to see if they are completely baked (not steamed!). Then I tear off foil in squares. Beginning at one corner of the square, I start wrapping each potato.

Don't serve or cut yet, please.

We now have them wrapped in foil, diaper-fashion.

All we do now is cut a big X across the foil and pinch each potato with two hot pads until it blossoms out over the top. The pinching breaks up the spud and makes it flaky as snow.

You are going to bake potatoes anyway, so try it—you don't have to buy it.

One thing more: If you grease the potatoes after stabbing them with holes, it will make the skins crispy. Do try this. You won't be sorry at all.

From Kentucky: "My husband loves baked potatoes, but not the skins. So he suggested I peel them before cooking, place them in a piece of foil, add a little butter, seal and cook as usual.

"They taste just as good and are a lot easier—no burned fingers trying to remove hot peelings, either."

I recently discovered an easy way to reheat baked potatoes.

I cut the medium-sized potatoes in half and place them, peel-side down, in the cups of my egg poacher (no need to oil the cups), then add water to the bottom of the poacher. Just put the lid on and place over the burner. In minutes—hot potatoes.

For those who can't have fried foods, this hint is a quickie.

From Florida: "Scrub potatoes with nylon net (see Nylon Net, p. 217) and then place them whole in the roaster pan right along with the roast to bake for two to three hours at 325° F. Makes the easiest ever baked potatoes."

From Louisiana: "Use those rough, yellow, square pot scrapers to scrub potatoes for baking. Better than a brush."

Potatoes, boiled

When you buy potatoes, boil them with the jackets on to retain vitamins, then peel, cut them up in bite-sized pieces and refrigerate.

Now, when you come home from work, you have five ways to fix them.

1. Just fry as many as you need.

2. Make potato salad. The potatoes are ready, just add vegetables, etc.

3. Company coming? Make a quick cheese sauce, adding a sliced onion, and pop in the oven while you prepare the meat

and salad. Presto! Potatoes Au Gratin.

4. You can also boil a few of these potatoes for about ten minutes and add an onion, then mash them down a bit, add milk and butter, and season to taste for potato soup.

5. Creamed potatoes can be made by adding white sauce and a little butter. Season to taste and heat.

When boiling potatoes for dinner, wait until the water starts to bubble, then drop in a plastic cooking bag of frozen vegetables, too. When the potatoes are cooked the vegetables are hot.

This saves space on the stove (especially when cooking large holiday meals), electricity or gas, and wear and tear on the dishwasher because there's one less pot to wash.

From Wisconsin: "Did it ever occur to you to use your dish drainer to drain boiled potatoes in their jackets, hard-boiled eggs or even artichokes?

"I think it's a whiz-bang idea and, when tried and tested, I think you'll agree."

From Kentucky: "I love small new Irish potatoes, but hate to scrape them, so I fill the pot with hot water from the tap, put in my potatoes, place on the stove over high heat and bring to a boil. I remove immediately; drain off the hot water and run cold water over them. The skins come off easily, eyes and all."

Potatoes, canned

Buy canned potatoes when they are on sale. They are great for many things.

Heat them in the gravy and serve with your pot roast. Keep them in the refrigerator so they will be cold for a quick potato salad. They are great sliced and fried for breakfast, especially when camping.

Potatoes, diced

From Delaware: "If you have a lot of potatoes to dice, first put them through a French-fry cutter, then cut across to dice them. Saves a lot of time."

Potatoes, French-fried

I always keep a couple of pounds of French-fried potatoes in the freezer for emergencies.

In a buttered casserole, put a layer of frozen French fries, freshly sliced onions, salt and pepper. Build up the casserole, layer by layer, then pour a thick cream sauce over it.

Plunk in the oven for forty-five minutes, or until your dinner is completely cooked, then serve.

It's such an easy dish to prepare and so delicious to eat.

Potatoes, fried

Ever try running an unpeeled potato through the grater before frying it for hash browns?

It sure tastes good and different. Saves potatoes and uses the skin, too!

Did you know if you sprinkled a little flour on potatoes before frying them, it helps make 'em very crisp?

Potatoes, mashed

From Arizona: "Did you ever oven-cook potatoes for mashing?

"I do this when I know I am going to be gone for awhile and would like to have my potatoes done when I return.

"I put peeled potatoes in a stainless steel bowl, cover with water and then cover the bowl with foil. (Punch a hole in the foil with a fork to allow the steam to escape.)

"Put this in your oven at 200° F and cook until you return home. The potatoes are ready to mash! No waiting."

From Missouri: "To make mashed potatoes taste richer and creamier without adding calories, add some non-dairy coffee creamer to them. The more you add, the creamier they taste."

Potatoes, storing

Don't you just hate those pithy potatoes that grow eyes? They seem to stare you in the face, saying, "Go buy some new ones."

When you see white buds growing on potatoes, take your fingernail or a knife, and pop them off and your potatoes won't shrink and shrivel . . . and they will keep longer.

Try it. It works.

Test it this way yourself:

Save two potatoes from the same batch. Let one grow eyes but keep the eyes scratched off the other.

Leave them in your potato bin for a month or so . . . and see if I'm not right. I am.

From Michigan: "I'm fond of potatoes but I live alone and if I buy them in bags (which is cheaper) they begin to get old and sprout before I can use them.

"To avoid waste, I buy the five-pound bag, pare and cook them, then freeze them in small quantities.

"I can then drop the potatoes in boiling water and they are soon ready to mash. I also can slice them for frying."

From Louisiana: "To keep peeled potatoes from turning dark, cover them with water and place in a sealed jar or container. Air's what causes the color to change."

Potatoes, sweet

Cut oranges in half and ream them out on the juicer.

Now fill the hull with homemade mashed sweet potatoes. Top each little filled goody with miniature marshmallows and bake until they are slightly brown and melted.

You can buy canned mashed sweet potatoes, add a dab of brown sugar and mix, then fill the orange hull and top with the marshmallows. Plop them in the oven at the last minute, just before dinner's done.

From Pennsylvania: "When boiling sweet potatoes, rub the inside of your pot with cooking oil or margarine before adding the water and potatoes. When washing the pan, you'll find it's much easier to clean."

PART III: CEREAL

Cold Cereal

From New Hampshire: "It is most annoying to me to take a box of cereal from the shelf and find the top torn and the wax inner lining in shreds. I solved this by doing the following:

"Before putting a new box in the cupboard, I open the top gently (no hungry child in a hurry has the patience), unfold the lining and cut it off to the exact height of the box.

"There is always plenty of lining left to fold over when the contents have settled. Now I have a neat looking box, and the cereal pours out smoothly without scattering all over the table."

From Minnesota: "If your diet forbids milk, how do you eat dry cereal? Soaked in warm or cold coffee! I love it."

From Minnesota: "Would you believe I let my children eat the cereal bowl?

"I do—because the 'bowl' is half a cantaloupe filled with dry cereal and milk."

From California: "My family loves cereal flakes for breakfast, but sometimes I use it as topping only. For example, for special occasions I serve cantaloupe filled with cottage cheese. I use granola, grape nuts, rice krispies or frosted flakes as topping and add a dollop of jelly. Yummy!"

From Maine: "The favorite breakfast dish in our house is 'Medleys.'

"I put five or six different kinds of breakfast flakes, puffs and krispies on the table and the kids make their own combinations."

Did you know that whole grain cereals should be refrigerated because of their fat content? Well, they should . . . and this is true even if the package is unopened. Keep 'em tightly covered and they'll stay fresh up to five or six months.

Hot Cereal

I just had to tell you fellow homemakers how I have been making hot cereal for years and years . . .

I always add a tablespoon of sugar to each cup of water I put in the pan.

Then I cook the cereal as usual—but you can't convince me that it doesn't taste better cooked this way.

Sometimes I use brown sugar instead of the granulated—this makes a nice change.

From Washington, D.C.: "Stir chopped nuts, dates and/or raisins into hot cereal for a breakfast treat."

From Utah: "My ten-year-old daughter came up with this recipe:
"She stirs semi-sweet chocolate morsels into her cereal.
"It's ever so good!"

From Oregon: "Try crumbling crisp bacon on top of hot cereal. Serve with lots of butter—but no sugar."

From Illinois: "No cereal problems in my house because I cook hot cereal in cocoa instead of water and the kids love it."

From New York: "My daughter wouldn't eat hot cereal until I had a brainstorm:
"Instead of serving it with milk or cream, I top her cereal with a scoop of ice cream."

From Idaho: "Hot breakfast cereal becomes an adventure when you fold honey, apple butter or your favorite jam or jelly into it."

For lump-free hot cereal, make sure the water's boiling before you add the cereal. And don't add it in one fell swoop, friends. Instead, sprinkle it slowly into the water, stirring all the time. Keep stirring until the cereal thickens.

Oatmeal

Packets of instant chocolate-flavored oatmeal are quite expensive, so create your own.

Add cocoa mix to regular quick-cook oatmeal or add brown sugar and cinnamon.

Delicious and it costs much less!

From Montana: "When cooking quick oats, I add a cup of fresh or drained canned fruit. I have to cook it about five minutes longer than package instructions, but it's really delicious."

PART IV: RICE

Rice, boiled

There's nothing easier to cook than rice, so if yours comes out gluey and phooey, you're doing something wrong.

I hope you're not washing that rice before cooking or rinsing it afterwards. Both are no-nos.

If your rice is soggy, you're using too much water. If it's dry, you're using too little.

Or maybe you're peeking while the rice cooks. Don't—it lets out steam and lowers the temperature.

Do you stir rice after it comes to a boil? This mashes grains and makes the rice gummy.

Know the best way to cook rice? Follow package directions to the letter!

Rice, doneness (see Rice, test for doneness, p. 85)

Rice, freezing (see Rice, storing and reheating, p. 85; also see Leftovers, Rice, p. 149

Rice, liquid for cooking

Know what's so wunderbar about rice? It's a go-with that goes with everything. Don't just cook it in plain old water. Instead, substitute chicken broth, beef broth, consommé, or tomato juice. With a curried dish, try orange juice. Tomato soup's good, too.

Rice, oven-baked

From Utah: "To conserve energy, I cook my rice in the oven when I'm baking a roast. I use 2½ cups of water to one cup of rice. I put this in a covered casserole and bake at 375° F until tender. "My rice always turns out light and fluffy cooked this way."

Rice, special recipes with

To make rice pilaf from scratch, use your food processor to chop celery, onions and carrots fine. Sauté them in olive oil, then add to the water for rice along with a couple of chicken bouillon cubes. Superb!

Children love spaghetti and meat balls but find those long strands messy to cope with, so try substituting rice for spaghetti, using the sauce and meatballs as usual.

Good to eat and neat to eat.

From Ohio: "As a change, my family loves hot cooked rice for breakfast with butter, cream and sugar. For an added touch of flavor, sprinkle on a small amount of cinnamon or top the rice with fresh or frozen fruit."

To make rice nice and white and give it extra flavor, add some lemon or lime juice. Just a dash to the water when cooking. Great!

For a special effect, tint rice with food coloring. Try pink for Valentine's Day or green for St. Patrick's.

Rice, storing and reheating (also see Leftovers, Rice, p. 149)

Keep cooked rice in the refrigerator about one week in a tightly covered container.

To reheat, place enough liquid in the pan to cover the bottom and keep the rice from scorching. Heat to boiling and add rice. Cover tightly, turn heat to simmer and heat until warm.

Cooked rice freezes nicely. You can store it up to eight months. To serve, thaw and reheat by cooking with a few tablespoons of water in a covered saucepan.

You can rustle up regular rice in a few minutes as my friend does, if you do this:

Cook lots of rice (not the instant kind) at one time and then, after it's cooked and drained, bag the leftovers and freeze.

In this way, anytime you want quick "real" rice, all you have to do is take a package out of the freezer, put it in a colander and let the hot water run over it until it is completely thawed, then heat and serve immediately.

Imagine that! And just think of all the quickie dinners you can use that rice for.

Rice, sweeping up

If you serve rice to the kids, some of it is bound to land on the floor. Leave it there while you do something else for awhile, because fresh it'll only gum up your broom. Later, when it has dried, it will sweep up easily. No one's going to scold you . . . it's your house and your energy.

Rice, test for doneness

To test rice for doneness, press a kernel with a spoon. When ready for serving, it should be soft throughout.

5

Fruit and Vegetables

INTRODUCTION

I owe you calorie counters one—and here it is, a chapter on fruit and vegetables that's right down your weight-watching alley.

When you get to thinking that everything you really like to eat is fattening, start thinking about fruit. It's the greatest! You just can't beat a ripe peach or a juicy orange for naturally sweet goodness! Sure hits the spot when you need a food fix that'll make those yearning-for-something-yummy tastebuds sit up and take notice.

One of the things I've discovered about fruit is that it's addictive. Once you get a yen for it, fattening goodies taste blah! They lack that naturally good taste.

Of course, sometimes I have to convince myself of this when I'm eyeball to eyeball with a chocolate mousse—but you know what I mean. And sometimes—not always—I take a nibble of that mousse and it doesn't live up to expectation because fruit leaves a fresher taste. It's better—better for you, better for your waistline.

There are calorie bargains to be had in the vegetable department, too. Lots of them. You can fill up on lettuce, string beans, broccoli, cucumbers, escarole and all the leafy greens and, if the needle on that bathroom scale moves at all, it'll move down.

Of course, some fruit and vegetables are more thinning than others. But all fruit and vegetables are a treat Mother Nature whipped up to give us variety and vitamins.

Most of us tend to play favorites when we shop for produce. That's not playing fair, because it means you're missing some good bets. Live a little and buy something exotic next time you shop . . . or check out a new way to serve an old favorite.

F'rinstance:

Bet you mostly serve lettuce in salads or sandwiches. Ever think about cooking it? Oh so good when steamed for ten minutes, then seasoned with salt, pepper, nutmeg and a splash of lemon juice.

Ditto for celery: It loses some of its crunch when you cook it—but that celery flavor intensifies! Think what celery does for soups and stews and you'll get the picture of how tasty a vegetable bowl full of it is.

Except when pie-making, lots of people eat fruit raw! Nothing wrong with that, but it's not the only way. Cooked fruit's fantabulous!

Try baking pears, peaches or plums as well as apples. Put a little water in the baking pan, then sweeten it with sugar. Throw in some spices or a dash of vanilla flavor or fruit juice. Baste occasionally.

Fit for a king, queen and the whole royal family!

Or simmer dried apricots, prunes and raisins with sugar to taste in water until they're tender. (Soak the apricots and prunes for a few hours first to plump them out).

You can make a low-calorie crust-less pie with strawberries, blueberries or sliced peaches . . . or a combination of all three. Just put them in an unbuttered pie plate then sprinkle on a crumb topping made by mixing flour, sugar, butter, cinnamon and/or nutmeg. Bake at 350° F until the topping browns. Sheer heaven!

Nature's bountiful . . . so take full advantage. You won't be sorry you did.—Hugs, Heloise

PART I: FRUIT

Apples, baking

When you bake, use your potato peeler and remove just a tiny slice of peel all the way around the middle of the apple.
This will prevent the apple from shrinking while baking.

Apples, cutting

If you have a child who always wants his apple cored and cut and you just hate digging for that old core, try this: Slice the apple off on both sides of the core. Voilà, what's left at center? The core! Don't throw it away. You can nibble on it.

Apples, snack

Here's a snack idea from a mom in Wisconsin: "Spread peanut butter on a halved apple. Children just love it! Grownups, too!"

Cantaloupe (see Melon, p. 91)

Bananas

Bananas are most digestible when the brown spots appear.

Citrus Fruit, rinds

From West Virginia: "Do not discard rinds of grapefruit, lemons or oranges. Grate them and place in a tightly covered glass jar and store in the refrigerator.

"Makes excellent flavoring for cakes, frosting and such. Also you can sprinkle the orange rind over chicken and the grated lemon rind over fish. Magnifico!"

Fruit, lunch box

When packing cut-up pieces of honeydew, watermelon or cantaloupe for picnic or school lunches, use discarded margarine containers and lids. Pack a toothpick right in the container.

The margarine containers seal in the flavor for quite some time, and the toothpicks help do away with toting extra spoons or forks.

Isn't this a neat-o way to have fresh fruit for lunch without getting juice all over?

Fruit Salad

From Kentucky: "When you use fruit cocktail to make salad, save the cherries and use them to doll up the top of the salad."

From Maine: "Apple salad is a favorite at my house, so I make it in large quantities. It distressed me that the first of the apples turned dark before I had the last ones diced. But not any more . . . now I start by putting several tablespoons of mayonnaise and a large wooden spoon in my mixing bowl. I dice awhile, then stir. Result, no discoloring."

Grapefruit (see Citrus Fruit, rinds, p. 88)

Grapes

From Washington: "When preparing grapes with seeds for a salad, slice them slightly off center.

"This way the seeds are all on one side and a flick of the knife point removes them."

From Kentucky: "Wash seedless grapes, put them in a plastic bowl and freeze. They are truly delicious when frozen and a good substitute for calorie-laden junk food snacks."

Honeydew (see Melon, p. 91)

Lemon (also see Citrus Fruit, rinds, p. 88)

Instead of high-calorie butter, substitute a squeeze of fresh lemon juice on baked potatoes. For extra flavor, add a little freshly grated lemon peel. Yummy on squash, broccoli, asparagus, too.

Diet tip: Squeeze two or three lemon wedges on tossed green salads in place of salad dressings. There are only seven calories in a table-spoon of fresh lemon juice.

Squeeze a wedge of lemon into diet colas to cut the sweet taste.

Lemon, substitute for

When you don't have fresh lemon or lime to use in ice tea, try using a tablespoon of lemon or lime gelatin.
It's really great.

From Pennsylvania: "Did you ever make lemon pie, and discover you didn't have any lemon flavoring for the meringue?

"I did! But lemon-flavored powdered drink came to my aid. I sprinkled about one-half teaspoon in the meringue."

Lemon Juice, containers for

Know those plastic containers shaped like lemons which contain reconstituted lemon juice? Doesn't it get you mad how quickly that juice is used up?

So, know what I did? I bought a 32-ounce bottle of the reconstituted juice (it also comes in smaller-sized bottles) and found there was no trouble at all in taking off the top of the plastic container and filling it with juice from the bottle.

Smart idea, what!

From Indiana: "Recipes that specify sprinkle with lemon juice were a bit of a problem until I found that a small, glass salt shaker provides an excellent way to sprinkle small quantities of lemon juice."

Maraschino Cherries

Maraschino cherries are rather expensive if you are on a tight budget. After they are eaten . . . what to do with the juice? I put it in whipped cream topping. Talk about something tasty! Real yummy!

Melon

After watching some ladies at the supermarket trying to pick out a good melon, I suspect many didn't really know what to look for. Methinks some enlightenment on the subject is in order.

Here, according to an old produce man, is how to tell when a melon is ripe, and good:

1. Cantaloupe: skin should be tan, not green. Ends should be soft with plenty of aroma, which is easier to detect if the melon is not so cold.

2. Watermelon: select three or more. Thump vigorously with your knuckle. The one that gives the most hollow sound is the ripest.

3. Honeydew: hold to your ear and shake. If you can hear the seeds and juice sloshing around inside, it's ripe.

4. Papaya: squeeze gently. If it feels "rubbery," it's probably ripe.

But if it isn't when you open it, close it and leave it out of the refrigerator for a day or two.

To make serving cantaloupe or honeydew melons easier, eliminate their tendency to slide on the plate. Here's how:
After slicing the melon in half, turn the halves over, rind side up. In the middle of each piece, slice a thin layer of rind off. This will give the melon halves a level base.

From Pennsylvania: "If you'll put cantaloupe in a bread wrapper and tie the end in a knot or secure tightly with a twistem, you will not be bothered by its odor in your refrigerator."

Orange Juice (also see Citrus Fruit, rinds, p. 88)

Mix a 12-ounce can of frozen orange juice in a three-quart pitcher; add one cup of powdered orange drink mix. Fill the pitcher to the brim with cold water, and stir until dissolved.
The powder gives the drink sweetness and the frozen juice gives it body. Delicious—I think it tastes better than freshly squeezed oranges and it's much easier to make.

Buy a 32-ounce glass bottle of citrus juice . . . not a can. Keep that wonderful wide-mouthed bottle when it's empty and put a small can of frozen orange juice in it. Measure the water and, with fingernail polish or tape, mark a line on the bottle. Cap and shake.
Next time no measuring . . . just fill with water to the mark.

From Montana: "To dissolve frozen orange juice concentrate, mix with a potato masher instead of a spoon."

Papaya (see Melon, p. 91)

Peaches

Most people will dip whole peaches in boiling water to remove the skins. I find it's much easier to halve the peaches first, then remove the pits.

Tie the halves in nylon net (see Nylon Net, p. 217) and put in very hot water: very ripe peaches, thirty seconds; ripe peaches, sixty seconds; not-so-ripe peaches, ninety seconds. Lift the net out and, voilà! the skins slip off easily. This isn't as messy as trying to remove the pits from whole peaches after they've been dipped.

Pineapple (also see French Toast, p. 69)

From Rhode Island: "To core fresh, sliced pineapple, use a doughnut cutter. Press its center ring on a pineapple slice and it will core it beautifully."

Prunes

From Indiana: "There's no need to cook prunes for hours. Place them in cold water, put on the fire with a couple of lemon slices and let come to a mad boil. Turn off the heat and let them stand all night. They will be nice and plump and taste great in the A.M.

"Soon as I turn off the heat, I put in a few spoonfuls of honey and a pinch of powdered cloves. Yum!"

From Oregon: "When making prune butter, cut fresh plums in half, discard pits and freeze. When frozen, they're a cinch to put through the food chopper—no juice running all over the place."

Watermelon (see Melon, p. 91)

PART II: VEGETABLES

Beans, baked

From New York: "Have you ever cooked dried beans that were hard as rocks? And you had to keep cooking them until the skin came off to get them tender?

"I happen to be a cook in one of New York's biggest hotels and, as I was trained in Boston where they are famous for beans, I know my beans, you bet.

"We chefs never ever put salt pork or strong salt-seasoned meat in beans until after they are completely tender.

"We boil this seasoned meat in water (that means juice and seasonings in liquid form). Then we add it to the beans twenty minutes before they are ready to serve."

Beans, green and wax

If you dieters who eat lots of low-calorie string beans get a little tired of them, try something new:

Add beef bouillon when you cook 'em and they really taste different and good!

If you want to zip up canned green beans, try topping with a dash of horseradish and those beans will taste as good as any you pick right out of your own garden.

Bean Salad (see Salad, bean, p. 100)

Beets

For years I have been making Chinese pickled beets and never thought to share the recipe my mother learned in China when she lived there after World War II.

This lush dish is great any way you swallow it . . . good served as a hot vegetable for dinner . . . fantabulous when served over hot steaming rice . . . the way the Chinese eat it . . . and, you won't believe it, but super, hot or cold, spooned over cottage cheese! Dig that?

It's the most beauteous dark cherry-red color you ever shook a stick at, and really makes a dinner party. Above all, it's inexpensive, which is what we are looking for. Right?

Here 'tis:

 3 (one-pound) cans of beets
 1 cup sugar (or an equivalent amount of artificial sweetener)
 2 level tablespoonfuls cornstarch
 1 cup vinegar
 24 whole cloves
 3 tablespoons ketchup
 3 tablespoons cooking oil
  Dash of salt
 1 teaspoon vanilla
 1½ cups beet juice
 5 minutes of your time!

If you want to make less, then just divide everything by three, but I always whip up three cans of beets at a time. Why waste five minutes more making it again the next day? It keeps in the refrigerator.

1. Using a large shallow pan, I dump in the sugar and cornstarch and stir, mixing well. Add vinegar, cloves, ketchup, oil, salt and vanilla. Stir again well.

2. Open the cans of beets and add 1½ cups of the juice. Discard the rest.

3. Cut all the beets into bite size and dump in the pan.

4. Cook over medium heat three minutes, stirring all the time until thick and that's all there is to it.

Another thrilling thing about this, besides its being cheap (I love that word), is that it looks beautiful when used to top that routine salad which we all get so tired of. Makes it taste sorta sweet and sour.

Put any leftovers in an empty glass jar and keep in the refrigerator. It will congeal a bit when chilled. This is the reason we must slightly warm it when used for salads, etc.

Though they cost a few more cents a can, it sure pays to buy tiny whole beets and cut them in fourths, especially when you have company.

Happy eating!

Beets, garnish for cold meat

From California: "Here is a delicious garnish to use with cold meat or fowl: add some chopped cooked beets to a thin layer of lemon gelatin that has been slightly chilled. This can be cut into different shapes and served right along with the meat."

Broccoli

From Oregon: "My family loves fresh broccoli prepared in my own special way. I wash the broccoli, cut into clusters, then boil in salt water until tender.

"Meanwhile, I sauté one or two finely chopped garlic cloves until well browned. Then, I add enough butter or margarine for the broccoli, adding the garlic. Strain this mixture to remove the garlic particles and pour over the broccoli.

"Broccoli prepared this way may be used as a vegetable, in salads, or on a canapé tray, and it is delicious."

From Pennsylvania: "What can you do with the stem part of broccoli? Don't throw it away. Instead, peel off the thick skin, then, when making your next tossed green salad, cut the stems in thin slices (crosswise, like a cucumber) into it. Broccoli stems have a good and different taste, and not many people will recognize what it is!"

Cabbage

When I chop cabbage in the blender for slaw, I line the sieve with about three layers of net (see Nylon Net, p. 217)—cut much larger than the sieve—and dump the chopped cabbage in to drain.

If you're in a hurry, gather the top of the net together and squeeze all the water out.

Quick and easy!

Carrots

From Utah: "Everyone praises the carrot sticks I serve at parties and they always want to know how I make them.

"Well, after peeling the carrots, I lay 'em on my wooden chopping board and slice each one down the middle the long way. Then I turn each half flatside down on the board and push my knife through lengthwise from the top down, making the strips as thin as desired.

"This way I get more uniform sticks and it's much, much faster."

Celery

I can't use a whole bunch of celery before it spoils, so I clean it and chop it up in small pieces.

Now here's the trick. As you know, celery can be kept in the freezer until needed (for cooking only), so I freeze mine in one-serving pouches. I put a one-serving pouch in the bottom of a large plastic bag and put a rubber band around the outside. Then I put the next serving pouch in on top of the first bunch and so on until the bag is full.

When I need a small quantity of celery for cooking, I merely remove one rubber band and take out just the amount I need. The rest is left in the freezer until next time.

From Georgia: "If celery goes limp, don't discard it. Try cleaning it real well, then put in a container. Pour enough ice water over the celery to cover it and put in the refrigerator. Within the hour it will be crisp and ready for use again."

From Texas: "For working wives and mothers who pack husband's and children's lunches the night before: "Use chopped celery instead of lettuce. It won't wilt like lettuce and is good on cheese spread or ham salad sandwiches."

Corn

Here is a hint for spreading butter on a hot, boiled ear of corn on the cob.

Spread quite a bit of butter on one side of a slice of bread, lay the ear of corn on the bread, and roll. Even children love doing this.

You kill two birds with one stone, so to speak. Buttered bread and buttered corn. Easy—yummy, too.

This hint is especially nice for those who wear dentures.

To enjoy eating corn on the cob, take a sharp paring knife and shave off each row of kernels, then butter up and start eating.

The juicy goodness slips out and is yummy . . .

From Massachusetts! "Have you ever used nylon net (see Nylon Net, p. 217) for removing silks from ears of corn? It's great and I'm not being corny."

Eggplant

From Idaho: "Peel and thin-slice an eggplant, then shake the slices in a plastic bag with flavored crumbs until well coated. Drop in hot fat and fry. Crisp, crunchy and easy fixing."

Onions

Did you know that you could take an old pithy cooking onion that is sprouting "greenery" and plant it in a pot in soil? Then set it in your kitchen window (or outside) and it will continue to grow the most beautiful tops that you have ever seen.

Just snip off these tops for salads, soups and Oriental dishes. Great in spaghetti.

It's a knockout.

The old pithy onion will take root in the soil and grow away in a few weeks.

Try one for yourself.

From New Mexico: "Since some members of our family do not like chopped or grated onion in anything, I make onion juice.

"Do not remove the onion skin. Cut the onion in half, then use the squeezer and squeeze the onion just as you would an orange or a lemon!

"Onion juice can be used in anything you are cooking."

Never throw away the juice from a bottle of olives. Save it and make something that is real, real good: olive-pickled onions!

Cut onions in one-fourth-inch thick slices. Put them in the olive juice, cap the bottle and put it back in your refrigerator for a couple of weeks.

Great in salads.—Heloise

From Kansas: "I like to use the new spray-on vegetable coating for pans. Last week I decided to spray it on my hands before cutting raw onions. I was delighted to find the odor washed off my hands completely and didn't linger on . . . and on . . . and on."

From Rhode Island: "Here's an easy way to clean white onions: put one pound of onions and four cups of water in a saucepan; let boil two minutes. Dip onions in cold water and the skins will slip right off."

Use an extra small jar of mayonnaise and add a measure (to each his own, when it comes to the amount) of dehydrated or fresh chopped onions to it. Let this stand until the onions are soft.

This mixture can be quickly used in recipes that combine onions and mayonnaise—sandwich spreads, salad dressings, whatever.

It's "ready-and-onioned" for just about anything. And it keeps beautifully in the refrigerator.

From West Virginia: "Would you like to always have fresh green onion tops on hand when you need them?

"Chop the tops finely, put them in ice cube trays half filled with water; freeze. When frozen, pop out the cubes and keep frozen in a tightly closed plastic bag.

"When you need some onion tops, just remove a cube or two. Let thaw and there you are."

Onions, cocktail

I am always trying to think of something new and different. Once in a while that ol' gray matter in my belfry jiggles a little . . .

I was looking at a bottle of sour cocktail onions a while back and thought to myself, "Why are they white? Wouldn't they be much more appetizing if they were colored? White seems so dull."

So I bought a couple of bottles and put some green food coloring in one of them. I used about fifteen drops to a two-ounce bottle, but you could let your eyes be your guide in creating any shade you like.

The onions won't look good at first, and you are going to think Heloise has lost her marbles when the onions don't absorb the color right away.

Put them in the refrigerator and forget all about 'em, as I did. A month later I was cleaning out the fridge and, what do you know, they were the most beautiful green you ever saw. Each little tidbit had absorbed all the color!

These look great when used to top salads . . . especially potato or egg. Or for their intended purpose . . .

So why don't you buy a bottle? After all, we need to splurge and spend a quarter once in a while. Eh?

Ratatouille (see Leftovers, Medleys, p. 145)

Salad, bean

For an easy way to marinate kidney, garbanzo and string beans for that delicious three-bean salad, put all the ingredients in a plastic container with a lid that locks in place and store in the refrigerator. There is no need to stir! Each time you open the fridge, just flip the container over. Works like a charm . . .

Salad, leftovers in (see Leftovers, Salads, p. 145)

Salad, mixing

A chemist explained to me that a salad should never be mixed ahead of time in wooden bowls. He said the acids from tomatoes and oil-vinegar dressings are the major cause of that stickiness.

If you still want to get everything done ahead of time, including the salad, do what I do:

Place a piece of wax paper in the bowl before you put the salad in. Put the dressing in a small jar and set the whole kit and caboodle in the fridge.

Then, when it is time for dinner, slip out the piece of waxed paper, pour the dressing on the salad and give it a real good toss.

Salad, tossed

From Arizona: "I've found a new way to put a little zest into a tossed lettuce and tomato salad.

"When I buy celery, I chop the small upper ends of each stalk very fine and put these pieces in a jar. Cover the celery bits with half vinegar and half water, then add a teaspoon of sugar. Shake well and refrigerate. This mixture will keep for days.

"After this has marinated, it gives the celery tidbits a sweet-sour tang. When I make a tossed salad I add a few teaspoonfuls of this delicious concoction. Sure gives it extra zing and is quite unusual."

From South Carolina: "To give a new twist to a tossed salad, add crumbled taco or corn chips. Crunchy, zesty, and a nice change."

From New Mexico: "To put attractive scalloped edges on thin cucumber slices for salad, run the tines of a fork lengthwise over the peeled cucumber. Slice as usual."

From Montana: "After cutting greens for a salad, I put them in a metal bowl and place them in the freezer for just a few minutes— I set my timer so I won't forget them.

"Try this just before serving dinner and your salad will be crisp and tasty."

This is a super trick—Heloise.

And here's a Letter of Laughter from a salad-tosser in Utah:

"One evening as I was preparing a salad for supper, I broke the lettuce head in two with my hands. (I had read once you should do this.)

"Well, my husband was standing right nearby, talking to me. When he saw me do that he started backing away and saying, "Yes, dear, yes dear, yes dear.""

Salad, Dressing (also see Vinegar, p. 140 and Oil, p. 139)

When they mix oil and vinegar salad dressing in Europe, they add water to it.

"Everyone knows that," you're saying . . .

Well, I didn't, and I have been making my own dressing for years. I have always put in vinegar and herbs mixed, then added the oil, mixed some more and that was that.

For those who don't like to use too much oil because of calories or who don't like the vinegar to taste too strong, the European idea of adding water is great.

Now you are saying, "But how much of each?" I have to leave that up to you. I'm not one to measure things, but I have been trying, and for me it comes out to about twice as much vinegar as oil because I am watching calories (as always). Then I add a few tablespoons of water, plus all the herbs or spices I want.

Good idea? You bet. Lower in calories and stretches your salad dressing too.

Also, the secret of a good salad is to toss and toss until each leaf is covered—and you don't need a lot of dressing to do this. You will use much less dressing if you mix your salad right.

From Ohio: "If you use dehydrated salad dressing mix, adding oil and vinegar according to the package directions, you'll find it has better texture, taste and appearance if you mix it in the blender. It doesn't seem to separate so readily either."

Sauce, vegetable (see Sauces, p. 37)

Tomatoes, peeling

From Iowa: "Take a dull table knife and rub over a tomato as though you were peeling it. Set it aside and do a second tomato the same way.

"Then go back to the first tomato—you will find the skin peels off as though it had been scalded."

From North Dakota: "Here's a little touch of glamour that utilizes tomato peels.

"Take a nice, red ripe tomato and, with a potato peeler or knife, take off the peel in a continuous strip, then wind it into a handsome tomato rose.

"Delightful for garnishing salads, cold cuts, etc."

Tomatoes, ripening

Wrap green tomatoes in newspaper and store in a cool, dark place and they ripen nicely.

Vegetables, boiling (also see listings for individual vegetables and Leftovers, Vegetables, p. 150)

At some time or other, nearly everyone has a pot boil over while cooking vegetables.

If a toothpick is inserted between the lid and pot, just enough steam escapes to prevent boil-overs.

Did you know that? Betcha didn't!

See, it's the little things that make life easier.

From Idaho: "I was very pleased to find I could use the bottom half of a little two-cup drip coffee pot to boil one vegetable; the top, right in place above it, to steam another.

"And it only takes one burner!"

Vegetables, freezing

I thought those who freeze vegetables might like to try my method of blanching them, using nylon net (see Nylon Net, p. 217).

I always keep eight or more thirty-inch squares of nylon net ready. After using, they can be rinsed, stored, and used over and over.

Place no more than a quart of prepared vegetables in each square. Gather up the corners and as much of the sides as is needed to keep the vegetables from spilling out. Fasten with a wire twistem, as close to the top of the net as possible. This allows the vegetables to float around inside the bag in the boiling water.

Drop one "net" bag of vegetables at a time into your pot of boiling water for required blanching time. Then simply lift the bag out, shake it, drop it into a pan of cold water for a minute or two, then into a pan of ice water.

Pick the bag of vegetables out of the ice water, give it a good shake, open it and package your product. No colanders, no fishing for elusive vegetables.

From beginning to finish, it's "in the bag."

Desserts And Beverages

INTRODUCTION

Remember when you were a kid and the one thing you looked forward to at meals was dessert?

It's what got you through spinach and things you didn't like because you knew mom had a grand finale up her sleeve.

If you're like me, you probably haven't changed. I still look forward to dessert . . . it's the happy ending, because a meal is something like a play. It moves along from Act I. What it needs is something smashing for the last act curtain. That's dessert, and you'll find a lot of goodies in this chapter to choose from, plus some super shortcuts to use when you're baking or making 'em.

Beverages are included because it's never just dessert . . . it's dessert and coffee or tea. And you know how your friend Heloise likes coffee.

I love tea, too, and I've got some super tea-making tricks for you to try that spice it up and make it special. Just the thing to warm the cockles of your heart on a cold evening and wind up a meal with style.—Hugs, Heloise

PART I:

DESSERTS

Applesauce Dessert

Anytime you're looking for a really great dessert that doesn't take a lot of effort to make, think biscuit mix and applesauce. Flatten out the biscuit dough and bake on a cookie sheet. Then, spoon on applesauce and top with cottage cheese for what I call "Snow on the Mountain."

Not counting calories? Add a scoop of ice cream instead and it's "Glacier on the Mountain."

Some like sweetened milk poured around a "mountain" and sometimes I substitute other puréed fruits for the applesauce. For extra flavor, cooks, butter those hot biscuits.

Bake Sale

Here is a suggestion for you folks who make those very special cakes, pies or cookies for bake sales.

You'll find that if you write or type out the recipe on an index card and tape it to the plate or box, your goodies will sell quick as a wink. This way, when buyers find your goody to their liking, they can whip it up themselves.

Baked Alaska

From Alaska: "For a darling difference when making baked Alaska, try putting the ice cream into individual shortcakes. The packaged cakes bought at the grocery store for making mini-strawberry shortcakes are ideal for this. Cover them with the beaten egg whites and bake. They are absolutely terrific and no mess when serving."

Baking

Here's one of those handy dandy little tips that make baking a breeze:

When mixing anything using eggs and shortening, try dropping an egg in the measuring cup before measuring the shortening. Stir the egg a little to make sure the white has touched all sides of the measuring cup.

Empty the egg into the bowl with the sugar. Then measure your shortening and see how nicely it leaves the measuring cup!

From Texas: "When baking, measure all the dry ingredients the day before and it makes baking almost as easy as using a mix."

Batter, mixing

From Oregon: "When using a blender to grate, you must add liquid—but who wants to use water and then have to drain it—whatta mess!

"I make carrot cake and zucchini bread often. Both recipes call for oil.

"So, I put the oil in the blender and add the carrots, zucchini or whatever, and turn on the blender. Works great and certainly saves a few skinned knuckles as well as time.

"Also works for a cranberry salad I have which calls for ground cranberries as well as pineapple juice. I use the juice for the liquid in the blender."

Cake (see specific cake listings)

Cake, angel food

A wonderful idea for making all kinds of angel food cakes is to use the regular recipe for angel food but substitute one-third cup flavored gelatin in place of the same amount of sugar.

You can make practically any kind of angel food cake you want to—raspberry, strawberry, cherry, orange, lemon or what have you. Try it—you'll like it!

Before frosting an angel food cake, chill the cake in the refrigerator. The frosting is easier to put on and no mess.

Cake, cooling

From Maine: "To cool a cake layer, turn your colander upside down and put the cake pan on it."

From Indiana: "When I bake a cake or cupcakes, I place the pan on a damp towel for a few minutes after taking it out of the oven. This helps cool the cake and keeps it from sticking to the pan."

Aren't these tips great, folks! Others have written me about this same damp towel idea for cooling cakes. Honest, I think you are all about the brainiest because you come up with such super solutions to the little problems that give all us cooks kitchen conniptions.

Cake, cutting

To cut a 9 × 13-inch cake into fifteen equal parts rather than the usual twelve, do this: Slip four rubber bands across the thirteen inch area at equal distances and cut along the side of each. The two cuts across the nine-inch side are simple to eye up.

Cake, heart-shaped

Here's an idea for those who want to make a heart-shaped "love cake" but do not have any of those heart-shaped cake pans.

Simply pour cake batter into one round and one square cake pan of about the same size (eight or nine inches). When putting the batter in the pans, try to have it the same depth in each so the cakes will be the same thickness when they're baked.

When the baked cakes are removed from the pans, cut the round one in half. Place the cut edges against two adjoining sides of the square cake and, faster than you can say, "I love you," you've got a heart shape.

Conceal your cake pieces under a coating of pretty pink icing— and no one but you will know the difference, luvs.

Cake, layers

If your layers stick to the bottom of the pans, return them to a warm oven briefly. The layers will come out intact in just a short time.

From Illinois: "Rather than separating a cake at the batter stage into two or three different cake pans to make layers, I find it's much easier to use all the batter to bake one layer. When I remove it from the pan after it has cooled, I wrap it in clinging plastic wrap and freeze it.

"When the cake is frozen, it is very easy to handle. I slice it with my long, fine bread knife into as many layers as I want. The layers are flat, fit perfectly on top of each other and, being cold, are easier to frost."

Cake, mixes

In using cake mixes, if you put the water in the bowl before putting in the dry mix, you won't have any dry pockets of powder on the bottom of the bowl after you've mixed the cake. The powdered ingredients float on top of the water and mix evenly.

Cake, mixing

When I have any mixing to do, such as cake batter or cookies, I put the bowl in my sink on a damp cloth.

It can't slide all around, and spilling and splashing accidents are kept in the sink so there is no mess to clean up.

Best of all, if you are short, there is no ache in your arms or back as the sink is lower than the counter!

Cake, quick

From Omaha: "If you are pressed for time and want to bake a cake, try my speedy method:

"Make your favorite white or spice cake recipe and put in a long loaf pan. Mix together three-fourths package of brown sugar and one-half cup of chopped nuts. Put on top of the the unbaked cake.

"Then bake the cake as usual and it will come out of the oven already frosted and delicious."

Cake, sponge

This hint is right down my alley. It seems I never have time to do all the little things, like making yummy desserts, that I would like to. Every little timesaver helps, like this one:

From Vermont: "I love to cook, but have always met my Waterloo trying to make sponge cakes! Since I love to serve Italian rum cake for special occasions, this presented a problem until I hit on the idea of using ladyfingers!

"They are packaged six in a row—you'll need about six packages. Separate the tops and bottoms. Line up enough bottom sections, overlapping slightly, to make the size cake you want, then sprinkle rum over this layer. Spoon pudding on, then top with another layer of ladyfingers. Keep alternating this way to make at least two or three layers of pudding. (You can use chocolate and vanilla, the prepared kind sold in dairy cases.)

"When you finish your cake, the top layer should be ladyfingers. Cover very, very tightly with plastic wrap and refrigerate overnight. Before serving, ice with whipped cream. When you cut into the cake all the separate ladyfingers will have blended into what appears to be one cake. It is delicious and saves hours and hours of hard work."

Cake, storing

Here's one I'd like to share with all you homemakers who find your families growing smaller.

Instead of cutting your favorite cake in half, which often does not give the desired results, go ahead and bake the same size cake you always have, then frost when cool.

Next, cut the cake into servings and place them in the freezer at once, without wrapping.

The next morning, cut enough pieces of foil to wrap each section individually. With a wide spatula, lift the frozen pieces out and wrap them. Once frozen they can be stacked, so they take up less room in the freezer.

Before mealtime, or for company, remove the number of servings you need from the freezer. (Unwrap at once, so the icing doesn't stick to the foil.) This eliminates stale or wasted baked goods, friends, and saves you time, effort and energy (the oven kind). How's that for using the old noodle?

Cake, tube

From Louisiana: "Before placing a tube cake in a cake server, put a glass or a plastic bottle filled with water in the center of the cake. This will keep the cake extra moist for a week or longer."

Cake Pan, greasing

From Tennessee: "I have a wonderful cake-pan coating that takes the place of 'greasing and flouring' and I'm so-o-o-o happy to share it with you!

1. Mix until creamy (do not heat or cook):
   1¼   cups of shortening
   ¼   cup salad oil
   ¼   cup flour
2. Use pastry brush or fingers and coat cake pans before using them.
3. Put this mixture in an air-tight container and keep it in your fridge. Keeps excellently."

When you're finished greasing a cake pan with your hand inside a small plastic sandwich bag, grasp the two inside corners of the bag and pull your hand out. This turns the bag inside out so you won't get any of the leftover margarine or butter on anything when discarding the bag. Clever, what!

Candy

From Wisconsin: "When sending homemade candy, particularly fudge, to the kids away at college or in the service, try pouring it into plastic dishes, the kind margarine and some other foods come in.

"Butter the dish, pour in the candy, and, after the candy is set, pop it out, put in a liner of plastic wrap, return the fudge to the dish, then pop on the lid.

"Sometimes if the container is not quite full, I put in miniature marshmallows before lidding it. Makes the candy ship very nicely."

Cookie cutter

Here's a hint for those who do a lot of baking.

Keep a bowl of water next to your dough and, instead of dipping your cookie cutter in flour, dip it in water. Your dough will drop right off the cutter with no flour mess.

It works every time, friends, honest.

Next time you're rolling in dough, cooks, here's a trick that will make cookie dough the same thickness:

I broke a yardstick in half (you could devise something of your own), laid one half on each edge of the pastry cloth, put the ball of dough in between and rolled away until the dough was as thick as the yardstick halves.

All of my cookies are the same thickness and therefore bake evenly too.

Cookies

The fragrance of cookies baking has never been bottled or packaged! Remember opening the front door after a hard day at school and being greeted by the most wonderful, glorious aroma in the whole wide world? It didn't take two guesses to know what mom had been doing.

A plate of freshly baked cookies and a cold glass of milk . . . complete ecstasy!

When a cookie recipe directs you to "drop from a spoon," try a knife instead.

Just swipe it through the cookie dough, scoop it up and roll it off with your finger. It works much easier and isn't as messy.

When making icebox cookies, mold the dough and place in oiled empty twelve-ounce frozen juice cans. Give each can a good whack

on the kitchen counter to settle the dough, then place in the freezer
or the fridge.

To remove for easy slices use the zip-off lid of the can, then remove
the other end and push the cookie dough through, slicing as you push
for even slices.

When removing cookies from the cooling rack, place it over the
sink and all the crumbs will drop through, avoiding a crumby mess
elsewhere.

Has anyone ever tried sprinkling a presweetened drink mix on
cookies!

When I was baking some sugar cookies, I used this mixture on top
of the cookies instead of sugar. Not only pretty, but dee-licious.

From New Mexico: "If you run out of cookies but have some
graham crackers on hand, try spreading them with a mixture of
brown sugar and a dab of butter. Then top with a pecan and toast.
This is a surprise for adults as well as children . . . No matter what
age, they all say, 'yum!' "

From Kansas: "Baking a batch of cookies has been a three-fold
bonus:

"First of all, it is an excellent tranquilizer; second, it saves lunch-
fixing money; third, it's the best air-freshener found anywhere."

From Michigan: "When cutting candy orange slices for cookies,
etc., I drop each bit in part of the sugar called for by the recipe. This
way the pieces will not stick together."

From Iowa: "When baking cookies in large amounts, cut two
sheets of aluminum foil the size of your cookie sheet. Place the
unbaked cookies on each piece of foil. Place one piece of foil and
cookies on cookie sheet and bake as usual.

"When they are finished, slide the foil off and slide the next sheet
of foil on, again placing in the oven. The cookie sheet is already hot,
so you may have to cut down on the baking time by two or three
minutes.

"While these are baking, you can remove the baked cookies from the foil and put more cookies on it and have them ready to slip onto the cookie sheet as soon as the other batch is done."

From Oregon: "In addition to making cookies with cake mix I have just made the most delicious coconut macaroons with a package of angel food cake mix, one egg, two tablespoons butter, a fourth cup water, two cups of coconut. Drop by teaspoonfuls and bake at 375° F for eight to ten minutes. This makes you about forty-eight macaroons."

From South Carolina: "Though my baking pan was well-greased and floured, my oatmeal cookies were difficult to loosen, and so I placed the sheet of cooled cookies over a pan of boiling water, letting the steam loosen them easily."

From Maryland: "If you have trouble with drop cookies spreading, try this trick:

"After spooning the chilled dough onto a cookie sheet, I placed the sheet in the refrigerator for an additional ten to fifteen minutes before baking. This allowed the first of the spooned cookies, which were warm and slightly softened. to rechill. Worked like a charm!"

From Alabama: "When cookies get hard, put half a raw apple in the jar. In a day or so the cookies are like fresh baked and even have a little apple fragrance."

Cookies, lunch box

When opening a new package of cookies for lunches, why not pack a week's worth in plastic bags? Then, when needed for the lunch box, the cookies will be ready.

These bags can be reused when a new package of cookies is opened. Bonus: the cookies stay fresher when repacked in these bags, and the whole process saves the one thing we never have enough of—time!

Cookies, storing

If you don't have a cookie jar, stash those crisp goodies in an ice bucket. Keeps 'em fresh and yummy.

Cupcakes

From Texas "I finally figured out a neat way to pour batter into cupcake tins. Pour the batter from the mixing bowl into a clean one-half gallon milk carton. Let the top partially close and start pouring from the spout portion of the carton into cupcake papers or, if you prefer, right into the greased tins. No spills, no waste! Why didn't I think of this before!"

Dough

From Mississippi: "When rolling out dough on wax paper, aluminum foil or plastic wrap, wet the surface of the counter before smoothing the paper down and the water will keep the paper in place."

Frosting (see Icing, p. 118)

Gelatin Desserts

From Florida: "When making gelatin dessert, add a thin slice of lemon while the gelatin is hot."

From Illinois: "One day I baked too many cream puff shells and didn't have enough filling for them. Know what I filled the remaining ones with? Gelatin. They were delicious!"

From Iowa: "I'm always on a diet so when I make gelatin dessert, I usually pour it in the little individual custard cups. In this way, I am not tempted to eat as much as I would if I were taking my serving out of a large bowl.

"This, however, did pose a problem. I was forever spilling it while putting the little cups in the refrigerator, or someone was forever knocking one over in the refrigerator before it was set.

"Now I make my gelatin, put it in little custard cups which I place in a small pan large enough to hold them all. I find it's so much easier to get the gelatin to the fridge, without spilling. If I do, it doesn't matter, it's in the pan."

From Kansas: "For years I hated to make a gelatin salad with cream cheese as I spent so much time trying to get the cheese into the hot gelatin without lumps.

"Then a friend told me to mix the softened cream cheese with the dry gelatin before adding the liquid.

"It was so easy I couldn't believe how much time I saved."

From Georgia: "Directions on packages of fruit gelatin tell how to use ice cubes for a fast set, but if ice cubes are different sizes, or smaller than usual, as they are from an ice maker, results may be disappointing.

"I solve this by putting the contents of a three-ounce package of gelatin and one cup of boiling water into a quart measuring cup. Then I note where the liquid level is and add ice cubes until the liquid reaches one cup higher.

"I have always had success with this method."

Gingerbread

From North Dakota: "I am very fond of gingerbread and often make it from scratch. One day I started to make gingerbread and found I was out of molasses. But I had some dark brown corn syrup on hand so I substituted it. The result was wonderful. The gingerbread had a finer texture, was much moister, and the ginger flavor was much more predominant, as well as that of the other spices."

Glazing (See Icing, p. 118)

Ice Cream (See Ice Cream, p. 58)

Icing (also see Leftovers, Icing, p. 148)

When getting ready to put icing on a cake, cut a piece of wax paper into quarters and place them on the plate before putting the bottom layer of cake on the paper.

After the icing job is completed, gently pull the wax paper out from under the cake. This makes for a neat icing edge and a clean cake plate!

From Vermont: "When I decorate a cake with white frosting, I sometimes shave colored gum drops very thin and put them on the cake. They curl like little roses and make a beautiful topping."

From Utah: "Here's a great way to make icing for a cake.

"Take one package of whipped topping and beat according to directions. Now, add powdered sugar until it is the desired consistency for spreading. (Usually takes about one-half to three-fourths pound of sugar.) Blend well.

"Presto! The best seven-minute icing you ever tasted."

From Oregon: "Icing a lot of cookies at one time is a breeze when you 'paint' them with a baster brush. Quick as a wink the cookies are iced."

Marshmallow

Here's a goody from a clever kiddo in Michigan who's found a great way to get around some sticky business:

"If you keep marshmallow packages in the freezer, they won't dry out and when you cut them to add to desserts, your kitchen shears won't get stuck."

From Nevada: "If the mixture sticks to the spoon when you're making marshmallow treats using cereal, try buttering the spoon and the mixture will slide off nicely."

Meringue, topping (also see Lemon, substitute for, p. 90)

From Idaho: "If you like to use meringue on pies made with instant pudding, prepare the meringue as usual, then arrange the meringue only on a greased pie tin and pop it into the oven. When done, place it on the pudding pie."

Nuts

Use a plastic bag when cracking quantities of thin shelled nuts.

Lay the bag flat on a breadboard and put in one layer of nuts. Then hold the bag shut with one hand and use a hammer to crack all the nuts. Pour them in a pan and pick out the goodies.

Big plus: no bruised fingers or flying nut shells.

Pie (also see Lemon, substitute for, p. 90)

Lovers of apple pie that's served topped with a slice of cheese, try this:

Just grate Cheddar cheese over the filling, then plop on the top crust and bake. What a treat is in store for you!

From Alaska: "I usually bake two pies with four flavors. I do this by building up the bottom crust across the middle, making a ridge.

"Sometimes I bake half chocolate and half lemon for one pie, half apple and half peach for the other.

"Of course, you can vary this according to your family's taste. Only be sure that the two fillings in the same crust have the same baking time."

From New Hampshire: "Put a layer of marshmallows in the bottom of a pumpkin pie, then add the filling. When it's cooked, you will have a nice topping, as the marshmallow will rise to the top. Try it and see!"

From Indiana: "When making pies, I add one-quarter teaspoon of baking powder to the meringue. This makes it stand up better and look lovely."

Pie Crust (also see Leftovers, Pie Crust, p. 149)

Does the crust get soggy when you bake pumpkin pie? Try this: Bake the pie crust until it's just lightly tan—about ten minutes. Remove from oven. Add the filling and return to the oven to bake while you relax and enjoy the aroma . . . Mmmmm, Mmmmm!

From Oklahoma: "I was rolling out pie dough and it cracked all around the edge. What to do? I turned up the cracked edges and pressed them down, then turned the dough over and rolled it out again. Not one crack in the edge."

From Washington, D.C.: "Save those plastic bags that bread comes in. They're handy for so many things. For example, when I make graham cracker crumbs for pie crust, I use two of these bags. I put one bag into another and then put the crackers in and roll away on any hard surface with a rolling pin. This makes very fine crumbs that I easily can pour into the pie plate without any mess or trouble."

The directions on frozen pies say to cut slits in the top crust but you don't have to run for an axe, chisel or hammer to penetrate that cement-hard dough. After the pie has been in the hot oven for a few minutes, it will be soft enough to open up at the drop of a knife point.

From New Jersey: "To save time in preparing pie crust, try my shortcut. Instead of mixing the dough for one crust at a time, mix enough for at least four. Bake all at the same time. Cool. Stack one on top of the other in the pans they were cooked in. Put in a plastic bag and tie securely. Place on the pantry shelf. (These keep real crisp for several weeks.)

"It's so easy to take one or two off the shelf, fill with your favorite filling (already cooked, that is!) and top with a boxed topping, whipped cream or even ice cream.

"This gives you a lush dessert at a moment's notice without much effort at all."

From North Dakota: "When making pie crust, add a few drops of food coloring to the water you mix it with, and you'll have a tinted pie crust that's especially nice for the holidays."

Pies, no-bake

From Utah: "Make chocolate, lemon or pumpkin pie filling; keep in a covered jar in the refrigerator.

"When ready for pie, crumble up one or two honey graham or other kind of crackers in an individual dish, cover the crumbs with the desired amount of cold pudding. It's instant pie!"

From Iowa: "A pie only serves about six people—but make mini-pies in baking cups and you can serve ten to twelve.

"The recipe I use is for no-bake cream pie. I spoon my cookie crumbs in the cups, add filling and chill to set, then top with my favorite fruit.

"These little pies have to be eaten with a spoon or fork. They are ever so tasty."

Pudding

From Mississippi: "Here's a quick way to make cooked pudding.

"Instead of standing at the stove, stirring and stirring while waiting for it to boil, put most of the milk into a pan and heat it almost to boil.

"In another pan, have a small amount of milk mixed with the other ingredients. Add the hot milk to the mixture, stirring constantly, then pour back into the hot pan, and you will only have to stir for a short time before the pudding thickens.

"Turns out perfect. Add vanilla after the pudding has cooled."

Use a spatual to stir, too! Makes it much easier.—Heloise

From Ohio: "If you don't like standing over a hot stove waiting for pudding to come to a boil, mix it in a ten-inch skillet over a large burner, and you'll find it comes to a full boil in just a few minute's time."

PART II: BEVERAGES

Coffee, drip and percolator

I would love to have a cup of coffee with you. I like mine hot, especially on cold winter mornings.

So the first thing I do when I go into the kitchen is to pour real hot water into my mug. By the time I have prepared my breakfast, the cup is hot.

Then I pour out the water and put in the fresh coffee . . . it seems to stay hot much longer.

I find if I give the basket of my coffee pot a few taps and shake it over the sink after I have put the coffee in, most of the fine particles that normally end up in the bottom of my cup are eliminated.

Be sure to do this before you put the basket in the percolator!

You will be surprised how good and clear the coffee will be down to the last half-cup . . . and the very last drop.

Bad coffee bother you?

Fill a pitcher with water and leave it on the drainboard or stove. When you make coffee, use this water.

When water sits, the gasses escape. Keep adding water to the pitcher every time you take some out of it.

For a good cup of coffee, remove the basket or coffee container as soon as the coffee has perked or dripped through.

This prevents coffee oils from getting into the brew, and causing an "off" taste. Try it!

If you use a percolator, you probably spill coffee in the stem. Next time you're making coffee, hold your finger over the stem while filling the basket, and you won't have grounds in your cup. Simple but super!

Rinse the basket of your percolator with water before making coffee and grounds won't go through it. Instead, they'll stick together, making 'em too large to fall through. No more trouble with grounds in your coffee.

Coffee, filters for

From Arizona: "My dripolator has four-inch filters that I haven't been able to purchase. This morning I took a heavy quality white paper towel and cut out a filter. It did the trick! Costs less than the regular filters too."

Coffee, instant

Do you have instant coffee you don't drink very often, so it's caked in the jar?

Did you know that you could just pour hot water in the jar and dissolve it?

Well, you can! When it's dissolved, place the jar in your refrigerator. To use, pour a small amount of this liquid in your cup and add boiling water.

I've been doing this for a number of years now and find it absolutely great!

I have used this method with onion and garlic salt, instant tea too. Try it. Don't waste a thing, friends!

Save dollars by making your own spiced coffee. Here's how:

1. Mix one cup instant coffee powder, four teaspoons dehydrated lemon peel, four teaspoons ground cinnamon and one teaspoon ground cloves.

2. Store in a tightly covered container.

3. For each serving, spoon a rounded teaspoon of the aromatic mixture into a coffee cup; stir in six ounces of boiling water.

4. Sweeten to taste and enjoy. You can make iced coffee with this, too.

5. For added flavor, sprinkle with grated nutmeg.

Coffee, powdered cream for (also see Milk, p. 61)

The instant powdered cream for coffee is supposed to be sprinkled on top of the hot coffee after the coffee has been poured in the cup.

You would be surprised at the number of people who put instant coffee and powdered cream in the cup together then pour boiling water over 'em or pour hot coffee from the pot over the cream powder. It just doesn't work as well. For some reason when that powdered cream's sprinkled on top, it blends right in beautifully.

You know I'll have to "fess" up! I was a doubting Thomas. Just couldn't believe it would make a difference. But, I tried it once, thought my old eyes were deceiving me, tried it again (could be just a coincidence) and, the third time I mixed up the brew, I was convinced.

I just gotta admit it makes all the difference in the world, and, while I'm fessin' up, might as well make the slate clean: I was one of the worst offenders, but live and learn.

Drinks (see Iced Drinks, p. 125)

Eggnog (see leftovers, Eggnog, p. 147)

Iced Drinks (also see Tea, iced, p. 126)

From Hawaii: "To keep iced drink glasses from sweating wrap a colorful paper napkin around the glass, then insert into a plastic sandwich bag that's a protective, disposable jacket. Different colored napkins may be used to identify glasses so you don't goof when it's time for refills."

When you make cool drinks on a hot day with a flavored mix that calls for added sugar, dissolve the sugar in a small amount of very hot water before adding it. Works like a charm—and you will use far less sugar this way. Add lots of ice.

Tea

You know those special spiced-up teas you buy in gourmet shops? Delicious, yes? But expensive, right?

Well, why not save those shrinking dollars and make your own. For example, I love to mix up spiced tea. Here's how:

1. Wrap six (two-inch long) cinnamon sticks, one teaspoon whole cloves and a whole nutmeg in a double thickness of cheesecloth; crush with a mallet.

2. Combine the spices with two cups tea leaves, two tablespoons grated orange peel and two tablespoons grated lemon peel. Mix well.

3. Store in an airtight container or pack into jars with tight fitting lids for gifts.

This little recipe makes about 2¼ cups of spiced tea.

When I want a cup of this spicy treat, I heat my teapot by rinsing it with boiling water. Then I spoon in a teaspoon of the mixture for each teacup of boiling water. I let the tea stand for two to five minutes, then strain it into teacups.

What aroma! What bouquet! What a fantabulous treat!

Another great mixture is anise and lemon tea. Here's how I make it:

1. Crush three tablespoons anise seed and add to two cups tea leaves and one-half cup grated lemon peel.

2. Store in an airtight container.

This makes a 2½ cup mixture.

Tea, brewing

From Hawaii: "Put loose tea leaves in the filter of a drip coffee maker and follow the same procedure as if making coffee.

"Makes good, strong tea in a short time. Normally, you don't have to use as much tea as when making it in a teapot. Your own taste will determine how much."

Tea, iced (also see Lemon, substitute for, p. 90)

From Vermont: "When making instant tea, fill the pitcher or glass with water first, then add the tea and stir, instead of vice versa, and it won't be foamy."

Tea, instant mix

Budgeteers, it costs less to make your own sweetened iced tea mix than to buy it.

Get a jar of unsweetened instant tea. Pour into two jars. Now divide a package of sweetened lemonade mix between them. That's it.

Now, get out your piggy bank and sock away those pennies saved in it. The day is coming when they will come in mighty handy.

P.S. For dieters, use artificially sweetened lemon mix.

Tea, leftover (see Leftovers, Tea, p. 150)

When a large jar of instant tea mix hardens because of dampness, know what I do?

I put the uncapped jar in a pot of water and let the water heat, warming up that jar so it doesn't crack when I get to step number two.

Know what that is? It's covering the hardened tea in the jar with boiling water.

Result: instant tea syrup.

It mixes with hot or cold water and is easier to use than crystals. I keep it in the refrigerator.

This same trick also works with hardened instant coffee.

Tea Bags

From Illinois: "The paper tag on a tea bag won't get in your brewed tea if you remember to tuck it through the handle of the cup so it stays put."

From Kentucky: "If the little tag comes off the string on a tea bag, dip the string into the hot water before you put the bag into it. The string will then cling to the outside of the cup or pot . . . and you won't have to fish for it."

Seasonings, Condiments and Preserves

INTRODUCTION

It's the little things that count when you're cooking up a storm—
little things like seasonings and condiments, which add flavor to
savor and make a recipe not just great but the greatest!

Call 'em sugar and spice and everything nice, 'cause that's what
they are!

Condiments like ketchup, mayonnaise and pickles—which add zip
and zing—count, too.

It's primarily spices that make a magical difference in the taste of
things. Don't they ever! But you've got to know or be able to guess
what goes with what—that's what this chapter's all about.

My trick is to sniff and season. If a spice smells right for what I'm making, I add a dash, put it to the taste test, then maybe add more.

But before you read further, do me a favor. Put down this book and check out your spice shelf. Count up those jars. Now count how many you really use.

What's the answer?

I'm willing to wager a fortune cookie that there are jars on that shelf that have never been opened. They came with the spice set and, from force of habit, you automatically ignore 'em and reach for your old favorites.

For shame! Where's your spirit of adventure?

In 1492, Columbus sailed the ocean blue in search of spices—that's how highly prized they were and are. He discovered a New World—and you will, too, if you learn how to spice up meals with a dash of this or that. Nobody will enjoy the good results more than you.

There's a bonus to using spices: they not only make recipes taste extra good but also add an aroma that whets the appetite and gets you in a just-right mood to enjoy.—Hugs, Heloise.

P.S. Just in case you jam and jelly lovers and makers think that I've forgotten your specialty, of course I haven't. Right at the end of this chapter are some great how-to hints especially for you. Sweets to the sweet—enjoy!

PART I: SEASONINGS

Allspice

For yum-yum results, add a sprinkling of this baking spice to squash, turnips, beets or baked beans. Dee-lish!

Apple Pie Spice

You can substitute apple pie spice in any dish in which cinnamon or nutmeg are called for.

Basil

Add a few basil leaves to tossed salads or a pinch to creamy scrambled eggs.

Bay Leaves

Some people say that putting a bay leaf in the flour cannister will keep those nasty weevils away!

Brown Sugar (see Sugar, brown, p. 137)

Caraway Seed

Always add caraway seeds when you cook sauerkraut. They're good with pork and add tang to cheese dips. I sometimes toss in a few when steaming cabbage

Cardamom Seed

Ground cardamom's great with nutmeg and cinnamon to flavor pumpkin pie. Also try adding one whole seed to demitasse coffee.

Chervil Leaves

Instead of parsley, add chervil leaves to salads, stuffings, sauces, omelets and seafood. Also great with peas.

Chili Powder

Chili powder, that hot, heavenly, spicy mixture, really zips up Mexican dishes, eggs and stews. Try a dash in meat loaf.

Chives

There's nothing like chives to spark vegetables and salad dressings. Sprinkle some on cream soups to add color, taste and texture.

Cinnamon

Stir hot apple cider with a cinnamon stick. Or use one to stir mulled wine.

After you've cooked cabbage, fish or anything else that will smell up the house, place a teaspoon or two of ground cinnamon in a small pan with some water on the stove and very slowly let it heat.
This produces a wonderful aroma throughout the house.

Shake a little powdered cinnamon over your coffee some time. Mmmm-good.

Cloves

You can stud a pork butt with this spicy-sweet flavoring. Cloves also go great with yellow squash.

Coriander Seed

This lemony spice adds oomph to cookies, cakes, biscuits and gingerbread. Try it with a mixed green salad, too.

Cumin Seed

Use cumin when you make deviled eggs or sauerkraut to add zest.

Curry

Curry's not one spice, but a mixture of sixteen to twenty spices (ginger, turmeric, fenugreek seed, cloves, cinnamon, red pepper, cumin seed and others.) Add curry to seafood to really pep it up. Fantabulous!

Dill Seed

Crushed dill seeds give homemade potato salad an out-of-this-world flavor. I also like dill in sour cream and mayonnaise sauces.

Fennel Seed

Fennel is a little like licorice and mighty good in chicken dishes, seafood sauces, bread or coffee cake recipes.

Garlic

For some folks, garlic goes with everything—and it practically does . . . if you're discreet. It can spark meat, chicken, seafood, soup or salad. Don't you just love it with butter spread on hot French bread?

For the barest aroma of garlic, use about one-eighth to one-sixteenth teaspoon of garlic powder or minced garlic for six servings of meat or vegetables. But use lots more if you're a garlic freak.

This is for those of you who like to cook with garlic but hate to use a big chunk of it.

Remove both ends and the outside skin of any dry garlic bud and cut it in very tiny pieces.

I usually do this in a small wooden or crockery bowl that I save just for this.

Sprinkle lots of salt in the bowl with the garlic.

Now—this is where the magic starts—using the end of anything wooden, like a spatula, start smashing and stirring.

The garlic bud dissolves and it's now ready to use in sauce, salad dressing, etc.

Want to get the garlic odor off your hands? Wash them with baking soda and water.

From Illinois: "Here's a great idea for crushing whole garlic cloves:

"Peel the garlic and put it in a plastic sandwich bag, but do not tie it closed.

"Crush the garlic with a hammer, etc., then invert the bag over your hand and rub the salad bowl.

"Holding onto the bag with your fingers, turn the bag right side out, and discard.

"Your hands stay free of the smell and mess."

A thoughtful hostess in Utah came up with this goody: "I don't want anyone to bite into a garlic clove so . . . When I stuff garlic into the sides of a roast, it's skewered on toothpicks so I can pull it out before serving the meat."

Now hear this, garlic lovers:

People aren't the only ones who love a whiff of this highly distinctive spice. Man's best friend likes a little in his doggie dinners—especially if he's a doggie who's sure he's a people. Some makers of dog food know this and add dehydrated garlic to the packaged food!

Garlic, storing

Know the best way to solve the pungent problem of storing garlic?

First, peel the garlic and break the buds apart. Take a jar with a tight-fitting lid and, after putting the garlic into it, cover it completely with cooking oil. It will keep indefinitely and always be ready to use.

The oil will become very "garlicky" in just a few days, and this can be used in various recipes, but very sparingly (just a few drops, and I mean a few). As the oil is used, add more from time to time.

Happy eating, all you garlic lovers.

Garlic, too much

From Indiana: "Whenever you goof and put too much garlic in something you're cooking, place parsley flakes in a tea ball and dunk it in or sprinkle on directly. This will eliminate the 'too-much-garlic' taste."

And chewing a few fresh parsley leaves after a garlicky meal will take the garlic odor right off your breath.—Heloise

Ginger

Of course, you need ginger in gingerbread and spice cookies but try a smidgen in beef casseroles and use it to flavor mayonnaise for fruit salad topping. A dash in hot coffee makes a delicious after-dinner drink.

Lemon (see Lemon, p. 90; also see Citrus Fruit, rinds, p. 88)

Mace

You know what makes cherry pie the most delicious? A dash of mace. It's fabulous for pound cake and fruit cake, and works wonders for whipped cream topping.

Marjoram

Try a little marjoram in corn bread or when making croutons.

Mint

Fabulous in tea, mint flavor adds a special touch to carrots. The Greeks use it to flavor lamb dishes.

Nutmeg

When you bake, nutmeg's the spice to use for cakes, cookies and other desserts. Try a pinch with spinach or corn, too.

Onion Salt

Add a little onion salt to the crust of your meat pies . . . Delicious!

Some of the world's greatest recipes begin by sautéing onion in butter. Onion salt or onion flakes can be substituted for fresh onions.

Poultry Seasoning

Great in stuffing, this ground blend of sage, thyme, marjoram and savory can make flavor magic for hamburgers and meatloaf, scrambled eggs and omlets, too.

Pumpkin Pie Spice

Not just for pie, this ground blend of cinnamon, nutmeg, ginger and cloves is a pick-me-up for fruit desserts and sweet yellow vegetables.

Rosemary

Rosemary is good in salads and with vegetables like green beans, squash and mushrooms. Try it in soups and dumpling dough, or with chicken.

Saffron

Saffron is an expensive spice that works magic with rice, chicken and seafood.

Salt, shakers

When filling shakers from the bottom, I always ended up with a lot of salt on the counter top. Today I found a solution to this pesky job!

First, I put in enough rice to completely cover the shaker holes in the top cover, then I poured in the salt and it didn't sift through the holes. Besides, as so many of you know, rice absorbs moisture and keeps salt from caking or lumping when it's humid.

Salt, too much

From Illinois: "If you use too much salt in soup, correct it by adding a raw potato (or piece of one). Cook only five minutes, remove it and you'll find the potato has absorbed the extra salt."

Spices, freshness

It's a good idea to check your spice supply twice a year. Remember that spices lose their pungency with age.

Put each spice to a "sniff" test. If the delicate, distinctive aroma doesn't rush out to greet you when you open the container, chances are you need a replacement. Herbs and bright-colored spices like paprika betray their age by fading or darkening in color.

Spices, sampling

A great way to discover what a new spice flavor's like is to mix a little of the spice with two or three tablespoons of butter, cream cheese or cottage cheese. Let the mixture sit for an hour or so to give the flavor a chance to develop. Then, spread it on crackers and enjoy a tasting.

Spices, storing

Spices should be stored in a cool, dark place. Keep them away from the range and radiator. During hot, humid weather you might even move paprika, chili powder and cayenne into the refrigerator for better keeping.

Be sure you cover all containers immediately after using, and keep them tightly sealed so flavor and aroma won't escape.

Spices, using

If in doubt about how much spice to use, remember Grandmother's rule and "season to taste."

Sugar

From Vermont: "It's easy to make granulated sugar into powdered sugar if you have a blender.

"Just pour a little of the 'sweet stuff' into the blender and push the button.

"A half cup of granulated sugar makes about a cup of powdered sugar, so measure accordingly."

Sugar, brown

Here's a way to soften hardened brown sugar: put it in a pan, add a little water and bring it to a boil. It makes the most wonderful syrup, but the secret is always to add a dash of vanilla or imitation maple flavoring. Sure makes good homemade syrup to use on waffles and hotcakes.

A marvelous mom from Washington keeps brown sugar from hardening by putting a small piece of bread in the sugar box. The bread gets hard instead of the sugar.

From Virginia: "If you store brown sugar tightly closed in its original box in your refrigerator, it will not get hard.

"I have an opened box in my refrigerator that has been there eight months, and it's still soft."

Sugar, brown, substitute for

When a New Hampshire smartie ran out of brown sugar, it didn't stump her for a minute. Here's what she did:

"I took a half cup of white granulated sugar, one-half teaspoon imitation maple flavoring and one-half teaspoon molasses.

"This may not be the perfect solution but it is darn close to the real thing!"

Tarragon

Salad dressings and meat sauces need a dash of tarragon. Be sure to add some to tartar sauce and chicken salad.

Turmeric

Turmeric adds saffronlike coloring to rice, chicken, seafood and eggs.

Vanilla

A natural sweetener, vanilla's the answer to a dieter's prayers. Add a drop of vanilla to coffee and you'll never miss sugar.

PART II: CONDIMENTS

Catsup (see Ketchup, below)

Ketchup, bottle

Do you know how to open a ketchup bottle so the ketchup flows right out without your having to shake the bottle to death?

Before you take the cap off, simply hold the bottle neck down and give it a good shake.

Now open the bottle and the ketchup is right there and ready to flow.

Caution! Be sure the cap is on real tight before doing this. Do I have to explain why?

Ketchup, container for

From Alabama: "To make fixing six school lunches every day easier, I put ketchup and mayonnaise in empty mustard squeeze bottles that have shut-down tops. I soaked off the labels and, with a felt-tipped pen, marked the contents. These are a real convenience and so easy to refill."

My little useful "thing" for working people:
Use empty pill containers to tote ketchup, mustard or mayonnaise in your lunch box.
They're just the right size.

Mayonnaise (also see Ketchup, container for, above)

From Ohio: "A really neat way to make homemade mayonnaise is to use a syringe-type baster rather than a tablespoon to add the oil, drop by drop. It is a perfect way to control the flow of oil and eliminates the mess of going back and forth with a spoon."

Oil (also see Salad Dressing, p. 102)

All vegetable oil bottles drip and drup. They make our shelves messy, and we don't like that, do we?
We've all heard about wrapping a paper towel around the oil bottle, anchoring it with a rubber band. This works, I'll admit, but that oil seeps through the paper towel and gives with the glop in a few days.
My solution: Try stretch socks! Use only the part from the ankle to the sock top. It won't ravel; just take your scissors and whack away. That's about all there is to it.
If you want the label on the bottle to show, cut the sock shorter or roll it down as if you were a flapper rolling her stockings in the roaring twenties. The little roll at the top absorbs the glop.

Isn't that nice?

These "bottle-girdles" can be thrown in your washing machine and need no care whatsoever. Best of all, they cost you absolutely nothing and give you something useful to do with unmated socks.

Olive Oil

Olive oil will keep indefinitely at room temperature in the kitchen cabinet—but not a cabinet over the stove. It need not be refrigerated. Keep the container tightly capped and the oil will keep its flavor and purity.

From Mississippi: "To keep salad oil from running down the side of the bottle and onto the cabinet shelf, I cut off the bottom of a box of salt and just set the bottle in it.

"No oil on anything and so easy to replace when worn out."

Pickles

From Minnesota: "If you like those yummy sweet dill pickles that are expensive, try this recipe:

"Buy a quart jar of whole dill pickles—not kosher (because they contain garlic). You will also need three-fourths cup of sugar and a teaspoon of celery seed.

"Slice the pickles thin, round-wise. Now use a wide-mouthed jar or any bowl that has a lid. Put in a layer of pickles, some celery seed and sugar. Repeat this process 'til all ingredients are in the jar.

"Leave on the counter a couple of days, then refrigerate.

"If you like them not quite as sweet, and with more dill flavor, add three tablespoons of the dill pickle juice when making the pickles. So easy and so good!"

Vinegar (also see Salad Dressing, p. 102)

Vinegar is so versatile, folks, so don't use it for salad dressing only. It's got many more cooking uses than that.

From Nebraska: "To give pie crust sheen, take the pie out of the oven when it is almost baked and brush the top with white or cider vinegar, then pop it back in the oven for a few minutes."

No, folks, it won't taste like vinegar pie . . . and it does the trick.—Heloise

From Wisconsin: "I use vinegar to tenderize tough meats by making a marinade (one-half cup of white, cider or wine vinegar to a cup of liquid bouillon)."

From Iowa: "My meringues come out really fluffy because I add one-fourth teaspoon of white vinegar to three egg whites to make them."

From California: "We all have our hang-ups. What I hate most: dingy, gray potatoes. I find if I add a teaspoon of white or cider vinegar to the water in which I boil potatoes, they stay nice and white."

From Kentucky: "To sour milk for soda bread, add one tablespoon of white vinegar to a cup of milk; let stand five minutes to thicken."

Vinegar, storing

So you won't pour vinegar with too heavy a hand, store it in an empty liquid sweetener bottle that has a plastic pointed top—be sure

to wash the bottle thoroughly first. Voilà! The vinegar will shake out by the drop instead of pouring in torrents.

PART III: PRESERVES

Jam and Jelly

Here's how I solved the problem of sticky jam jars . . .

I put my jam in a plastic squirt bottle, the kind used for mustard, and it works great! The jam flows right onto the bread or toast and doesn't get on the container.

From South Dakota: "I always stir with a stainless steel potato masher when making jelly. Works wonders."

From Idaho: "When I make jelly, I add butter or margarine to the hot juice to prevent the foam that rises on the top. This foam has to be skimmed off before pouring into the jars.

"To four or five cups of juice I add a tablespoon of margarine and, presto, no foam!"

From Maryland: "When melting paraffin to seal jelly, line a small pan with foil and use that for the job.

"If there is leftover paraffin, cool it and fold the foil around it so it's ready to unfold and use again.

"If all the paraffin is used, the liner is simply thrown away and the pan is clean—what a bonus! I hate to scrape that stuff out of the pan!"

Preserves, canning

From Wyoming: "Wear a tight pair of lined rubber gloves when trying to get jar ring bands on canning jars really tight. The jars are hot from the scalding procedure and always seem to be hotter when filled.

"The gloves serve a dual purpose. They protect the hands from burning and prevent a possible accident because the jars are more likely to slip out of your hands if you use a towel instead of wearing gloves."

Preserves, wrapping

From Oregon: "To wrap a jar of preserves to give as a gift, use one of the plastic mesh bags that fruit comes in. Put the jar in the bag and tie it together at the top with leftover yarn and make a bow or a puff ball, or attach a plastic flower."

Leftovers

INTRODUCTION

Leftovers could be the subject for a great big cookbook. I know for sure Heloise readers could write it because they believe in "waste not, want not." I do too!

The teeniest tiniest bite shouldn't be thrown out. It doesn't make sense—especially not when food costs so much you have to float a bank loan to feed a family.

But some people just aren't savvy when it comes to recycling food. Actually, it's a cinch. Here are some ideas for using them as:

Sandwich Fillings: They're a great way to get rid of leftover fish, meat or vegetables. Use mayonnaise, mustard or ketchup to bind them together.

Salads: A medley of this, that and the other makes a super salad. Toss together leftover vegetables, meat, fish, odd bits of cheese, cubed stale bread.

Soups: Boy, oh girl, if you know your stuff, soup is for free (cross my heart it is!).

F'rinstance . . .

Every time you buy a broiler, fryer or a family pack of chicken, save necks, wings, gizzards and hearts in one bag in the freezer. In another, stash salad "throwaways," like the tops of scallions; the outer leaves of lettuce and cabbage; the top leaves and skinny stalks of celery; the cores of cabbage, lettuce and endive; the stems of spinach.

What do these all add up to—the chicken parts and the greens? Soup for free! Delicious.

Omelets: There's just no end to the things you can toss into an omelet —leftover meat and vegetables of all kinds. Be creative! Use those odds and ends.

Medleys: A Minnesota mother says she feeds her family a pick of "medleys" once a week. Medleys are a round-up of leftover main dishes—each wrapped and reheated in foil. Everyone in the family can choose his or her favorite.

When it comes to food recycling, for thrift's sake, don't forget your blender or food processor.

I'm always processing vegetables for soup . . . stale bread for bread crumbs . . . odd bits of cheese into grated.

Sometimes you've just got a single helping of main dish left over. Know what to do with it? Freeze it until you have two, three, four or more (whatever you need to feed your family).

And don't forget that stale bread is the basis for all those yummy bread puddings you can spark with fruits in season.

If you give food a good think, you shouldn't have to waste a morsel.

Honest, I've scored lots more than Brownie points by heating assorted leftover vegetables together, sprinkling 'em with grated cheese and browning the resulting casserole in the oven. The French call this "Ratatouille." I call it "Make-do."

—Hugs 'n' Kisses, Heloise.

P.S. Don't stop here. More variations on the "make-do" theme follow. They should get you thinking thrifty.

PART I USING LEFTOVERS

Biscuits

Even if there's only one left, leftover biscuits, rolls, muffins, etc., can be put in a large plastic bag and frozen.

Not too many days later, treat your family to a meal accompanied by a crazy variety of breads. They will love it, and it's great for the cook—quick, easy and no extra work.

From New Jersey: "When you take biscuits from the oven, put them in a glass oven-proof dish with an oven-proof lid and they'll stay hot. If there are any left over, keep them in the same dish and reheat them for the next meal. They'll be good and fresh!"

Bread Crumbs

From Idaho: "When we have leftover bread crumbs and eggs after breading something, we make use of them. Here's how:

"Pour the egg into the bread crumbs and shape into little balls. Fry in oil until brown.

"No more waste and our kids love these fried goodies."

From Montana: "I save stale bread, biscuits and rolls for bread pudding.

"If necessary I freeze them until I have a sufficient amount to make a large mixing bowl full of crumbled bread.

"Check out a bread pudding recipe in your favorite cookbook. Then vary it by adding fresh fruits (apples, peaches, berries) in season."

Breading

From Florida: "When I prepare too much meal for the food I want to bread, I keep it in an empty garlic salt jar (any such container with a shaker top will do). I just shake the meal onto whatever I need to bread. This way, I'm sure to use the right amount and I never have leftover meal to be tossed away."

Just seal and store for the next use.—Heloise

Cheese

What to do with odd bits and pieces of cheese?

Grate them all, then mix together with some spices added and make a cheese ball or use to top off spaghetti or lasagna.

From Washington, D.C.: "Grate leftover cheese on top of a tossed salad. Delicious!"

Eggnog

From Maine: "For an after-the-holiday hint, how about using leftover eggnog to make tasty rice pudding. If you happen to have leftover rice too, you're in business.

"Pour them together, bake as usual, and delicious rice pudding is the end result!"

From New Mexico: "I use up leftover holiday eggnog by serving it over hot or cold cereal."

From Washington: "Leftover eggnog is a great topping for vanilla ice cream."

Icing

How many times have you thrown out leftover icing because there never seemed to be anything to put just a dab on? I save it in little jars in the freezer. When I have a selection of colors, I whip up a dozen or so cupcakes, adding a few drops of warm water to the icing after it has thawed.

From Minnesota: "I save odds and ends of colored icing until I have enough to cover a cake with a rainbow of colors or a patchwork, depending on the design I choose when applying the icing."

Mothers always keep crackers on hand, don't they?
How about using leftover cake frosting as a filler between crackers? This makes a delicious and quick snack for children.

Meat

Cut leftover hot dogs and sausages in half-inch slices and put them in the freezer in a plastic bag. Let them accumulate for a party. Warm in a flat pan, stick a toothpick in each one, serve with a sauce, and take credit for being the clever homemaker you are.

Chop leftover beef or ham with boiled potatoes and onions for hash, then top with poached eggs. Sure is good for a change.

Onion Soup Dip

From Kansas: "I used leftover onion soup dip as a topping for baked potatoes. Delicious!"

Pie Crust

From Mississippi: "If you've ever wondered what to do with left-over pie crust trimmings, I have a good solution.

"I put all the trimmings together in a ball and knead it a little to blend into smooth dough.

"I then roll it out as if making another crust. Spread butter lightly over the dough and sprinkle a little sugar and cinnamon on it.

"I roll this into a 'jelly roll' and slice. Place the slices on a cookie sheet and bake along with the pie until golden brown.

"Delicious! And the kiddies just love their 'own' surprise."

This is a nifty idea, friends, but you can go another route:

Sprinkle the dough with cheese and make hot hors d'oeuvre.
—Heloise

Pizza

From Louisiana: "I make great pizzas with leftover French bread.

"I slice it in half horizontally, then spoon readymade spaghetti sauce over the halves, sprinkle on Italian seasonings and Parmesan cheese, and top the halves with shredded mozzarella. (Any semi-soft cheese could be used as a substitute.)

"I put the bread in the oven and bake the pizzas at 425° F for about ten to fifteen minutes or until the cheese bubbles and begins to brown slightly."

Rice

From New Jersey: "I reheat leftover rice by adding about one-half cup to a can of vegetable soup.

"It's a nutritious and filling lunch."

From Montana: "Store leftover rice in a plastic cooking bag, closing the end tight. Keep in the refrigerator. When needed, just set it in hot water and heat."

Tea

From Delaware: "Pour leftover tea into ice trays and freeze it, then use the cubes in tea the next day."

There also are things you can do with leftovers besides eat them. F'rinstance:

Put eggshells or leftover tea leaves in water, let stand overnight, then use to water your plants. And you can do ditto with the tea or coffee itself. One of my plants is absolutely flourishing on the coffee or tea left in my pot each day. No sugar or cream, natch.

Used teabags also can be used to reduce under-eye puffiness. Store them in the refrigerator and dampen with ice water before applying.

Vegetables

From New Jersey: "After making crisp vegetable sticks or salads, I carefully wash cabbage cores, celery leaves and ends, even potato peelings. I then put them in my blender, puree, add spices, nonfat dry milk and water and make a low-calorie cream soup.

"The soup can be dressed up for family or company with cheese

cubes or croutons. For pennies I have a first course or sometimes, if I add a sandwich, a whole meal for my family."

From Mississippi: "My refrigerator has two vegetable crispers. I labeled one of them 'Snacks and Leftovers.'

"Now, my family knows that anything in this section can be eaten between meals.

"This keeps whatever I'm planning for dinner safe from nibblers."

PART II: STORING LEFTOVERS

So leftovers won't be forgotten in the refrigerator, try this:
When opening a can or package of vegetables, save the label, especially the picture part. Tape it to the appropriate leftover container. You'll be able to see at a glance what's in the container without having to open it.

From Virginia: "When I cover a bowl of leftovers with aluminum foil, I write the contents on the foil with a felt-tipped pen."

To use up all leftovers, I sometimes pretend I'm making a mini-smorgasbord and put each leftover in a small ovenproof container, then line 'em all up on one flat cookie sheet. I need only turn on the oven and sit back waiting for dinner to be served. When I've enjoyed it, whoopee!

From New Mexico: "I keep a rather large container in my freezer, labeled 'Soup Seed', adding to it any leftovers that are suitable for soup. When I have enough, I add whatever is missing and have an instant pot of soup."

From Texas: "I shape foil into bowls just big enough to hold whatever I have left over from meals (or I use foil pie tins). I simply place the foil bowls in the electric skillet, set it at 200° F and heat all the leftovers at the same time. Then I set the skillet in the middle of the table and serve from it. Saves on dishwashing too."

SECTION TWO

All Through the House

INTRODUCTION

DEAR Fellow Homemakers: Bless you all, because this is your book, crammed full of the wonderful hints and super shortcuts you've discovered. And, believe me, your discoveries are important, so thanks for sharing them.

Whether you're a he or a she, young, old, or in between, if you keep house you know for sure it's a never-ending job because there's always something you should do, ought to do, need to do. So now and again, if you let things slide for a spell, don't feel guilty—everyone deserves a vacation, and especially you.

And don't you worry about any mistakes you make, hear! Everyone goofs occasionally. It's a good way to learn, and it's how some of the best tips in this book were discovered—by trial and error.

Homework won't go away, but cheer up, friends, it's not so difficult when you know the shortcuts. So pour yourself another cup of coffee and settle down with me for a tour all through the house.

Just so it will be easy for you to find the hint you need when you need it, here's what I did:

First, I gathered all the hints that work all through the house—hints for everything from air-conditioners to woodwork—and turned them into the first chapter of this section. Got that? Good!

Next, I put on my glasses and did a room-by-room tour, asking myself what special tips you'd want to know for every nook and cranny.

So, friends, in this section there are chapters that tell you what you need to know about each room and area—hints on caring for furnishings and tips about things that are stored or used in each room, too.

To give you an example:

In the bathroom chapter you'll find all the how-to's for cleaning that you need to know . . . plus first-aid instructions. Of course, I know that lots of accidents—burns and cuts, especially—happen in the kitchen—but the bathroom is where you store that first-aid stuff, right?

So give a flip through the chapters in this section and get your bearings. Find out where every tip is, then you'll know just where to look for what.

One last thing: Bet your coffee's cooled down, so heat it up and let's go over all these great time- and money-saving tips together.

What to do with all that time and money you're gonna save? Why, luvs, enjoy it with your family, your friends and yourself—because that's what makes life worthwhile.

—Hugs, Heloise

1

A Houseful of Hints

PART I: GENERAL HOUSEHOLD HINTS

Air-conditioning

From Louisiana: "Home air-conditioning and heater vents seem to be high up on the wall (especially for shorties) and hard to reach.

"Well, I cut off a three-foot length of an old broom handle and screwed a cup hook into the cut end. It's just right to push the lever up or pull it down.

"Really makes adjusting that old vent a snap."

Batteries

Money is thrown away needlessly because people think batteries are completely shot and throw them out. Using sandpaper, a nail file or an emery board to scrape both ends of a battery often will prolong its life and give it another shot when it seems useless!

Remember that, honeychile, when your flash doesn't operate or your transistor radio or tape recorder slows down . . . and always keep an extra set of batteries around for those toys that need 'em. Sure saves tears when a favorite toy won't perform because the batteries are kaput!

Bird Cage

Here's a nifty hint from a bird lover in Utah:

"The bottom tray in my canary's cage kept getting rusty from spilled water. I got the bright idea of cutting a vinyl tile to fit the tray. Then I bored a hole in it and strung a piece of cord through it.

"All I do now when I have to clean the cage is grab hold of the string and pull the piece of tile out."

Bookcase

I have a little decorating tip for you that I snitched from a friend.

It particularly applies to college students and newlyweds who are starting out with their first apartment and limited funds for furniture.

We have all seen bookcases made out of cinder blocks and boards.

My friend, John McDonald took this idea a step further and covered the blocks and the boards with burlap.

It makes all the difference in the world!

You don't just have yucky old cinder blocks, but a custom-made bookcase that looks smashing! Even better than smashing—classy!

The way he did it was to cut pieces of cardboard the height of each stack of blocks and wide enough to wrap around all sides, and tuck in back.

Next, he measured and cut the burlap, allowing an inch or so of extra material in order to wrap it across the cardboard and glue the edges to the underside of the cardboard. This assures a nice finished edge.

Before he glued the burlap to the cardboard with white liquid glue, he smoothed out all the wrinkles.

If you do this and there are any lumps or bumps after the glue dries, you can touch them up with a warm iron.

Got the picture?

Fold the covered cardboard around the cinder blocks so it overlaps slightly at back; staple together.

The shelves were next, each covered with burlap the same as the cinder block stacks were. The fabric ends were tucked and folded like wrapping a package, then secured with staples.

Try this and for a couple of bucks and a little effort, you will have something you can really be proud of.

My thanks to John McDonald for letting me spill his secret.

Get a gleam in your eye and go to it. It will look great when you're finished.

Smile, you know what you're doing . . . don't you?—Love, Heloise

Candles, wax stains

If you get candle wax on a painted or wallpapered wall because you didn't hold your hand right behind the flame when you blew the candle out, here's what to do:

Wait until the wax gets cold and congeals. When it does, pick it off with your fingernail, or scrape off as much as you can with a blunt knife or a plastic credit card. Then grab about six facial tissues—paper towels, I find, do not work as well here—and turn your iron to a low setting. Hold the facial tissues against the wall, and put the hot iron on the tissues.

As soon as you see wax coming through, remove the tissues and replace with clean ones. Continue until no more wax irons off.

Not to worry about scorching your wall because if your iron is hot enough, and it will be, it will scorch the facial tissues first. Note: thermostats on irons are not the same, so be mindful of that fact, and take care.

Sometimes a good cleaning fluid will remove the rest of the wax, especially if the wall is painted. However, I have never found cleaning fluid necessary after the iron-and-tissue treatment.

P.S. Incidentally, friends, use this same technique to remove wax from a carpet but set your iron for "synthetic" or very low heat.

Carpet (see specific carpet listings; also see Rug, p. 180)

Here, thanks to my friend Rose, is a super sensational way to keep kiddos from tracking mud, snow or what-have-you over a pale carpet.

She lined up six carpet samples on her carpet right inside the front door. If they get soiled—and 'deed they do—she cleans them instead of her wall-to-wall stuff.

From Montana: "Know how to raise the pile on a shag carpet that's flattened out? My daughter used her new, light bamboo yard rake. Worked great!"

Carpet, faded

From Illinois: "My red carpet's old and faded in spots, so I took a chance, bought some red dye, diluted it with water, as per package instructions, and sponged it over the faded spots. What a face-lift! Honest, it's a big improvement. I'm glad I took the chance."

And, believe me, it is a chance, one that's worth taking only as a last resort.—Heloise

Carpet, casters

From Vermont: "The beige casters on the legs of my sofa seemed so noticeable and ugly against my dark green carpet. Know what I did? Painted 'em green to match the carpet and now they blend right in."

Carpet, repairs

From Tennessee: "I discovered a great way to repair a cigarette burn in a wall-to-wall carpet.

"With curved nail scissors, I cut out the blackened fibers, leaving a little pit. Into it, I squeezed some liquid glue and into the glue I placed some fuzzy fiber cut from a remnant of the carpet.

"I stood up to see how it looked and couldn't find the spot! It has withstood wear and vacuuming for a couple of years now and I still can't locate the spot."

Carpet, stains on (also see Spot Check chart, p. 377)

My neighbor spilled shellac on her carpet, and tried to remove it with rubbing alcohol. It was no go, so I checked this out with a rug cleaning expert and this was his answer:

"The stain is reappearing simply because the rubbing alcohol has been softening the shellac, but not really removing it.

"Alcohol is an excellent solvent for shellac, but you have to be sure that you blot the area with clean white tissues or toweling; and that you repeat the application of alcohol and continue blotting until the tissue or towel no longer blots a yellowish residue. Always work from the outside in towards the spot.

"Be careful that the alcohol doesn't make your carpet bleed (it is if your tissues are blotting up the same color as your carpet!).

"Allow the carpet to dry completely and then examine the area. It should have a softer feel, but if not, repeat the process, being careful not to apply too much of the alcohol. You should have good results if you are careful."

And be sure to spot test first to see how alcohol affects your carpet.

Here's what an expert advises to remove bloodstains from a carpet:

Try to get to the stains while fresh, blotting up as much blood as you can with paper towels. Then flush the stain with cold water. Never use hot—it sets bloodstains. If necessary, apply a light application of household ammonia to any remaining stain.

Don't use peroxide unless you test an inconspicuous corner first. Remember peroxide's a bleach and could remove not only the stain but your carpet's color.

Ceiling

Here's a "Letter of Laughter" from a Minnesota mother who has the right idea: "Dear Heloise: Know the best time to clean ceilings? It's when the kids have the house turned upside down!"

Clock

From Indiana: "Ever heard the old tale that when an electric clock quits running, you should turn it upside down for three days and it will start running again?

"Know why this works? Because the oil in the mechanism of the clock drips upside down and gets itself redistributed in the works!"

Cracks, filling (see Energy Savers, window, p. 166 and Plaster, p. 177)

Curtains, beaded

Try this method of cleaning beaded curtains:

Take a bucket of suds and soak one or two strands of beads while scrubbing 'em with a good-sized soft brush.

Double or triple the strand of beads in your hand so that you are scrubbing several rows at once.

To avoid tangles, handle each strand separately. Rinse thoroughly. Drain in the sink. Then hang to dry.

Curtains, hanging

Ever get home and have to press new curtains to get the creases out before hanging them?

If they're the drip-dry kind or 100 percent cotton, water in a spray bottle does the trick.

Just spray on a fine mist after hanging the new curtains. When they're dry, the creases should be gone, so no ironing is needed.

When hanging sheer curtains on a rod, cut a finger from an old glove, slip the finger over the rod end, then push the rod through the curtain channel and it'll keep the rod from ripping the sheer fabric.

Curtains (see specific curtain listings; also see Draperies, p. 165)

Curtains, tiebacks

Can't match tiebacks to your curtains? Here's what two clever homemakers did.

One used tasseled shade pulls; the other used metallic chain from the hardware store.

Aren't these ideas inventive? Shows that where there's a will, there's always a way.

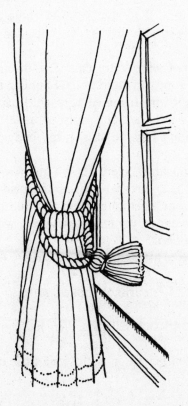

From Wisconsin: "Recently, tiebacks were needed for some curtains so I bought six fancy chain belts. I now have the best-looking tiebacks ever!"

Door, repair

From Wyoming: "I was sanding the edges of a new bedroom door my husband had hung but it kept sticking along the top and side.

"Suddenly I got the idea of using carbon paper to find the places where it was rubbing. I placed the paper against the facing, carbon-side out, pushed the door shut, then opened and sanded where the black marks were instead of doing it by guess work.

"Made this job almost painless."

Doorknob

From Connecticut: "I've always loved china doorknobs, but my budget just doesn't stretch that far. So I decided to do the next best thing.

"I bought a can of refrigerator enamel and some decals and made real beauties out of my old doorknobs. I applied the enamel, let dry, stuck on the decals, and trimmed with gold paint.

"I'm proud as a peacock and satisfied at last. I have attractive doorknobs and didn't have to stretch my budget either."

From New Hampshire: "Here's how I got new doorknobs for free:

"I just took all the knobs that were on the inside of closets or other doors where they didn't get much wear and put them on the outside. The outside ones went on the inside. After all, who sees an old knob on the inside of a door?

"All it took was a little time and my trusty old screwdriver!"

From Florida: "My doorknob looked worn so I painted it. Here's how:

"I cut an 8 × 10-inch cardboard in half, giving me two 4 × 10-inch cards.

"Then I cut a semi-circle in each one a little larger than half the doorknob stem.

"I put one of the cards above the doorknob and the other one below and overlapped them and taped them in place. Only the knob was exposed. I gave the old knob two or three coats of bright gold spray paint and discarded the cardboard.

"Looks good as new and I didn't even have to remove the knob to do it."

From New Jersey: "I had a doorknob that banged against the wall whenever it was opened. So I took a cotton-filled powder puff, ripped one side open, put it over the knob and sewed it closed. It did the trick."

Door, louvered (see Louvers, cleaning, p. 171)

Door, sliding glass (see Sliding Glass Door, p. 180)

Draperies (also see Curtains, p. 163)

With the high cost of draperies, here are some buying tips.
Select fabrics to fit individual needs.
For sunny locations, choose fibers that have resistance to sunlight. Synthetics are more resistant than cellulose; silk is least resistant.
Line all draperies as an added precaution against fading or rotting.
Select colorfast fabrics that resist fading.
Atmospheric conditions will change draperies constructed from cotton or rayon.
To prevent rotting, yellowing and mildew, clean draperies at least once per year. Remember, synthetic fibers collect dry soil due to static; cotton and rayon tend to yellow with age.
If you will abide by these rules your drapes will last longer.

Draperies, cordless

From Indiana: "We don't have draw drapery rods, so opening and closing the drapes was a hassle until my genius husband got a brainstorm. Now, instead of standing on a chair, I open and close the draperies using a yardstick."

Draperies, cords

From North Dakota: "Everytime I wanted to open or close my drapes, I invariably pulled the wrong cord. So I used fingernail polish and painted the cord pull used to open the drapes. What a nice solution!"

From Florida: "To give drapery cords additional life, I rub soap or wax on them when I take down the drapes. Then, when I adjust the drapes to an open or closed position, the cords move against each other with very little friction.

"By thus preventing extra wear and tear, the nasty job of replacing the cords is postponed.

"This tip works well on Venetian blind cords, too."

Energy Saving, lights

One love from Maine wrote:

"I found I had plenty of company in my mistaken notion that it took a lot of electricity to turn a light on or off. Not so! The cost is virtually nil.

"What a difference this knowledge has made because I thought that when I went from one room to another I shouldn't waste electricity by turning the light off if I was coming right back. Then something would come up and it would be hours before I got back to that room and the light would still be on.

"Since I've turned onto the trick and turned off lights, my electric bills are cheaper."

From Georgia: "Save electricity by using night lights in hallways, kitchen and bath. Plug one in any place you would keep a light burning after dark so folks who wake up during the night won't stumble."

Energy Saving, windows

If you close your drapes and pull down your window shades during the day, you can save on heat in winter, air-conditioning in summer and energy all year around.

This is great in rooms you do not use daily.

If you need a little insulation to block that crack between the bottom of the window and the sill, here's just the thing:

Use strips cut from plastic foam meat trays.

From Nevada: "Everybody's trying everything to keep a little warmer in winter without going bankrupt to pay the fuel bills.

"I hung a large sheet of plastic like a curtain at my picture window between the blind and the nylon curtain. I bought plastic that's as clear as glass, pinning it to the top edge of the curtain. It sure keeps cold air from flowing across the room."

Extension Cord

From New Mexico: "To coil electric extension cords without kinking, hold one end in your hand and wind around your elbow, crossing your forearm in a figure-eight motion.

"Take a few turns around the coil with the end of the cord and tuck it into a loop.

"Works best if you start at the socket end and finish with the plug."

Fireplace

From Arizona: "So I know whether the fireplace flue is an open or shut case, here's what I do:

"When I close the flue, I use a paper napkin to hold the black sooty handle.

"After it is closed, I insert the napkin through the ring on the flue handle. The napkin is easily seen days later when I look into the fireplace, not remembering the position of the flue."

From Michigan: "To avoid getting ashes on hands and arms when I clean the fireplace, I wear long plastic bread bags, secured with loose rubber bands, as gloves."

Fish Tank

From Vermont: "Try adding a few drops of food color to your goldfish bowl.

"We love ours blue, green or aqua.

"It's fun and harmless to the fish."

Floors

From Indiana: "For best results when shining hardwood floors, wax them on a warm, sunshiny day. It's much better than doing it when it's damp or cold, as the wax job lasts much longer."

From Kentucky: "You'll find wax won't streak if, when using your electric floor polisher, you make long sideways strokes to buff floors. Do this until the shine shows through, then you can revert to the usual up-and-down strokes."

Foot Locker

From Illinois: "Turn an old foot locker into an extra seat by topping it with a slipcovered foam pillow. It makes a super storage seat for a kid's room . . . great for stashing skates, shoes, whatever."

Frames (see Picture Frames, p. 176)

Furniture (see specific furniture listings, also see specific furniture listings and room-by-room listings for Chair, Table, etc.)

Furniture, polishing

No matter how careful we are with furniture, accidents will happen.

One woman came home from work to find her feline friend had knocked over a vase filled with water on her coffee table.

Another complains that her ebony piano is covered with greasy fingerprints that no amount of polishing removes.

Let's just admit it—spray polishes are convenient to use for a quick shine—but week after week and month after month is too much, so let's get down to basics.

Fine furniture needs to be waxed only once or twice a year. Overwaxing should be avoided.

A reputable furniture refinisher told me that the finest furniture could be washed with a soft cloth dipped in a mixture of mild soap or liquid detergent and water, then wrung out. The point: the cloth should be damp, not sopping wet. After washing, rinse with a clean damp cloth, then dry thoroughly and apply polish.

There again, only once or twice a year is all that's necessary.

Furniture, staining (also see Woodwork, scratched, p. 185)

From Arkansas: "It seems like every furniture project requires a different size paint brush . . . and that gets expensive . . .

"So one day I cut a kitchen sponge into the size I needed and used it to apply the stain for my current furniture project. Worked great!

"A sponge can be cut to the exact size needed for a job and, best of all, it leaves no brush marks when used to apply varnish."

Furniture, water rings

If you remove water rings while they're fresh, a little elbow grease and a soft cloth should do it. If they've been there awhile, try an oil-based furniture polish and a lot of elbow grease.

Homemaker

An overworked homemaker from Arizona wrote that she needed help. "As I go from room to room I find myself thinking, 'Now what did I come upstairs for?' " she said. "I talk to myself. I have four children, but when one interrupts me, I forget what I was talking about. Am I going crazy?"

You know what I told her?

Aw, come on now . . . you just have too much on your mind, honeychile. And if it will make you feel any better at all, lots of women say the same thing. It's just because homemakers and moms have too much to do and there never seems to be an end to the work.

The job of homemaker is never-ending!

You make the beds every day and yet they are unmade the next morning and have to be re-made again.

You wash the dishes after every meal, but the next meal you have to wash the same dishes over again and this happens every time you eat.

It takes you hours to prepare a meal and it's eaten in fifteen minutes. Then, dirty dishes again . . .

You wash clothes each week but the following week you wash the same clothes over again. It's never-ending, isn't it?

If you are ever lucky enough to hit the bottom of your ironing basket, give yourself a big smile.

Talk to yourself? I do! Half the time it's the only way I can remember to do something when I walk from one room to the other. So, absent-minded homemakers, join the crowd of those who talk to themselves and be one of us.

Housekeeping Routine

From Delaware: "As a full-time professional woman with a large home to care for, I found myself dreading weekends because of the tasks awaiting me—oven to clean, floors to scrub, clothing to mend, etc. Then I hit on the idea of using my stereo to help me get through tedious jobs. I estimate the time it will take, then put on one, two or more records.

"If the record is still playing when the job is finished, I have 'won' the game.

"Now the kitchen floor is a two-record job, the ironing is a three, and so on. This makes chores more enjoyable because the rhythm gets me cleaning with a beat."

Humidifier

From Kansas: "If you find that your humidifier begins to smell musty four or five days after it has been cleaned, add a tablespoon of bleach to the water.

"This will make it smell fresh again."

Lamp Shade

From Alabama: "Don't be tempted to use the cellophane strips wrapped around a new lamp shade as a 'dust cover'. They may keep off dust but the sun will cause them to darken the rim of the shade and cause streaking and shrinkage.

From Kentucky: "An easy way to dust accordion-pleated lampshades is with a soft paintbrush kept just for this purpose."

Light Bulb

From Hawaii: "To store loose light bulbs that you sometimes buy unpackaged . . .
"Set them in drinking glasses—large bulbs (100-watt or more) in big glasses, smaller ones (40s for example) in smaller glasses.
"The glasses will keep your light bulbs from rolling around or getting broken. And nearly all of us have extra glasses on hand that are seldom used."

Know what to do with three-way lamp bulbs when the top two wattages (100 and 150) wear out? Put 'em in a hall socket and use until the lowest wattage (50) wears out.

Lights (see Energy Saving, lights, p. 166 and Lamp Shade, above)

Louvers, cleaning

From Florida: "To clean louvered doors, remove them, take outdoors, then use a two-inch paintbrush to 'paint' each louver with a mild household cleaner. Rinse, then repeat the process on the other side. I think 'painting' should work like a charm for heating vents, too."

Mirror (also see Ammonia, p. 192)

From Minnesota: "We salvaged the oval-shaped mirror from an old bureau. My husband removed it, base and all, and had it resilvered. Then he refinished the base and attached a brass chain to the bottom side. Now it hangs (upside down) in our living room where everyone admires it."

What to do about black spots on mirrors?

Aside from having them resilvered (which is expensive but rewarding), you might try taping a small piece of aluminum foil behind the bad spot to make it less noticeable.

Moving

Here are a few timely hints on the fine art of picking up lock, stock and barrel and moving to a new address:

To begin with, when packing clothes, pack only enough in each carton to fit snugly without wrinkling. Cram things in and you'll have to press them on arrival.

Pack books on edge in the carton. Pack records with paper between them.

Protect framed pictures by applying crisscross strips of masking tape to reinforce the glass.

Wrap medicine, perfumes and lotion bottles individually in paper before stashing them in a carton.

To correctly pack stemware, each piece should be placed upright for greater protection.

Special crating should be provided for fragile odd-size pieces, such as folding screens, framed tapestries, etc.

Before you pack your mattresses, place a clean bottom sheet on each. Then put a top sheet and a blanket in the box with the mattress.

Upon arrival at your new home, all you need to do is set up the beds, put on the top covers, and "fall" in!

Happy moving day!

Odors, musty

From Maine: "Here's a way to keep musty, damp odors out of a house you're closing for the winter.

"Fill shallow boxes with cat-box filler. Place one in each room before closing up.

"Sure soaks up any lingering odors or mustiness."

Paint

I'm bursting to tell you all about those walls in my kitchen which were painted only last year with the water-base paint so many of us use.

Soon as you finish reading this, go look at yours and see if you find what I did—bare spots around light switches, behind the wastebasket, the kitchen table and chairs—all caused by too much scrubbing with harsh cleansers which removed the paint.

Well, here's what I did. I "patch-painted" every one of these spots.

First, I scrubbed like mad, getting off what soil I could.

Next, I got a new sponge, wet it thoroughly with water, wrung it out good, and dipped it in some of the leftover paint which I save after a paint job.

Then I pretended I was washing the wall again. I started in the middle of each soiled spot with lots of paint and, using a circular motion, spread it out. This is called "feathering." But I call it patch-painting.

You can't do this with a dry sponge. Or an old one that has been used in your kitchen and has grease and soap film on it.

When the paint dried, I couldn't even tell the diff.

My kitchen looks clean and bright as a new penny . . . and for just the price of a new sponge.

But please wear gloves on this job. Do what I say this time, and not as I did . . .

From Idaho: "Ever try to paint the baseboard molding in a room with wall-to-wall carpeting?

"Nothing to it if you tear newspaper into twelve-inch strips and

lay on the rug an inch or two from the wall.

"Using masking tape, fasten down the paper, tucking the tape down over the edge of the rug. Paint to your heart's content.

"Let paint dry completely, then pull up the paper and tape. You'll have no paint on the rug. An added bonus: the tape will pick up a lot of the dust the vacuum cleaner missed."

From Oregon: "When you paint the inside of your kitchen cupboards, use the electric trouble light that you keep in your car. It has a little shield that keeps the light out of your eyes but directs it so you can see what you're painting."

From South Dakota: "Instead of removing hardware from cabinets and doors when I paint, I just coat them with petroleum jelly and I can easily wipe off any paint that gets on them."

From Texas: "Can't stand that just-painted smell? Then prevent it by adding a little vanilla to the paint."

From Montana: "I just got a wonderful hint from the painter who varnished my doors this morning:

"To keep the doors from being accidentally closed and messing up the paint job, he used a spring clothespin under each door as a door stop.

"Just slip the clip end under the door and it will work like a charm."

From Iowa: "When we painted the window sills of our house, we had to force the windows open.

"After three days of stuck windows I hit upon an idea:

"I sprayed the sill and around the bottom of the windows with furniture wax and now the windows are non-stick."

From New Mexico: "When painting a room, isn't it a mess when you get to the ceiling?

"Let me tell you what to do:

"Put on a rubber glove and turn the cuff back a few inches. As you hold your hand up, the paint may drip . . . but right into your cuff!

"When the cuff gets full of paint, turn your hand over and the paint will run back into the can or pail!"

From Utah: "When I repainted my room, it looked nice except for the wires of the electric wall clock and lamp . . . so I painted them the same color as the walls.
"It makes a big difference."

From Ohio: "I painted over a darker paint with white only to find that every time my sweeper got too close to the quarter rounds at the baseboard, the white paint chipped off and the dark paint showed through.
"Instead of constantly touching up the white, I covered the quarter rounds with strips of white plastic tape.
"Some of it has been on for a year now and is still doing the job."

From Florida: "When painting a room, write down the amount of paint that it took and the color name or number on the back of a picture frame in that room.
"When it's time to repaint, turn over the picture and there is the information you need."

Paint, removal

From Tennessee: "To remove fresh paint from your face or hands, use shaving cream or shampoo.
"Sure feels a lot better than the regular paint remover."

From Washington, D.C.: "I could go on and on with uses for nylon net (see Nylon Net, p. 217). I especially like to use it to clean paint from my hands as I am always painting something.
"It does a wonderful job, and doesn't scratch or irritate the skin. I use it with a little detergent."

Painting, velvet

From Washington: "I have a painting on velvet that was dusty. I wanted to clean it but didn't know what to use.

"Nylon net (see Nylon Net, p. 217) to the rescue! I just brushed it lightly and the velvet looks as bright and pretty as new!"

Paneling

From Maryland: "It was easy to fill in the nail holes in our paneling with a matching shade of plaster, but to get off the excess plaster was a tough job until . . .

"I thought of your nifty nylon net (see Nylon Net, p. 217). It scrubbed that excess plaster off in a wink."

From Alabama: "Erase pencil marks from wall paneling with a soft rubber eraser.

"After erasing, vacuum up the eraser shavings and go over the wall with a light detergent and water. When dry, apply polish."

Picture Frame

Here's a moneysaver: use shoe polish to finish wood picture frames. It works amazingly well.

Go over the frame thoroughly with chalk to fill up the pores.

Next, take a powder puff and dip it into a can of paste-type shoe polish. Smear the polish over the frame. Be sure to get it very thick in the corners.

Place a piece of paper toweling or tissue on the soiled side of the puff. Use this to buff the frame thoroughly. You will get a sheen on that frame that is amazing.

The chalk, which has gotten into the pores of the wood, will provide that antique look.

I want you to know that after I finished a frame, I compared it with one finished professionally. There wasn't much difference at all . . . and mine cost pennies at the most!

Picture Hanging

From Texas: "To hammer a small nail into the wall without hitting your fingers, try this:

"Stick the nail through a strip of thin cardboard, hold the cardboard and start hammering the nail.

"When the nail takes hold, tear away the cardboard."

From New York: "If you're hanging a lightweight object, you can hang it on straight pins instead of a nail. Bonus: a pin won't leave a big hole in the wall."

Plaster

From California: "To patch plaster on a painted wall, my clever husband mixed spackling compound with leftover paint (same color as the wall) instead of water.

"It was a perfect match . . . and all in one simple operation."

From Hawaii: "In an emergency, you can use toothpaste instead of spackling to fill in small holes in plaster . . . but let it dry well before you paint over it."

Roaches

Instead of fighting roaches and never getting rid of 'em, why don't you find out where they lay their eggs?

Take your flashlight and peek in any place you think they might be hiding.

You probably will find scads of eggs around the motor of your refrigerator. Look in the tray under the motor too.

Remove the drawers from kitchen cabinets and take a long peek underneath with your flashlight. Look at the pipes under the sink in both kitchen and bathroom.

Also check out the bottoms of chairs where the corners are glued with a triangle of wood for reinforcement. These little devils absolutely love glue!

If you pull up the eggs with your vacuum cleaner, be sure to empty your cleaner after using it. It will be dark and warm in there and they will multiply faster. So, empty it immediately.

If you want to apply bug juice, the time to do it is when you are cleaning these spots. Paint it on while the drawers are opened. (This paint-on type stays on for months.)

Check your closet hot water heater and any places that are warm and dark. That's the kind of climate roaches love.

Your washing machine is not only warm and dark, but damp too, and so's the dryer. The tops of these two appliances usually pull open (or the back does). Get your husband to open it up and take a look.

Awful thought: Eggs hatch oodles of roaches—so destroy them before it's too late.

Also, look back of bookshelves! Remove all the books. Remove the dust with your vacuum attachment and apply bug killer. Roaches like the glue in book bindings.

A radio is another likely spot. Also your stereo set, or pianos and organs, as well as TVs.

Remember: darkness, heat and moisture are potential breeding places for these pests.

In a friend's house, these places had all been cleaned. There still were roaches. Guess where I found loads of them. Not in the kitchen cabinet, but in the folds and headings of all the draperies! Ugh!

Draperies (especially if they are heavy draw drapes) are seldom cleaned. The pleats at the top can be home for roaches! Then the little devils even get into the curtain rods!

Don't waste time putting bug juice around unless you put it on the right places. Let's kill 'em the easy way.

And one last thing:

Roaches are often in the cardboard cartons in which we bring home our groceries from the store. They love the glue in that corrugated stuff. They also sneak under the gummed labels on canned goods, hide out in paper-wrapped goods and nest in egg cartons. So keep eyes alert when you're putting groceries away.

Maybe you can avoid roaches and other pests. The trick is: don't hang out a welcome sign.

For example: spilled foods, crumbs, open packages or open garbage containers are an invitation to dinner.

Use a soapy sponge and clean all surfaces where food is spilled or prepared.

Sweep and mop floors regularly or, if you are lucky enough to have a carpeted kitchen, vacuum it after each meal, or at least once a day.

Since the kitchen or dining room may not be the only place where food is served, food wipe-ups may also involve a family room or even a bedroom.

Wash dishes, pots and pans, etc. after each meal. Dispose of the garbage each day and make sure the containers are clean and odor free.

Of course your kitchen isn't the only place where pests love to hide out (sometimes they don't hide—they come out at the wrong time —when one of your eagle-eyed friends is there).

Clean your mattress and springs regularly as well as all upholstered furniture.

As you can see, I've only hit the high points but every little bit helps.

Hang in there—with lots of effort and very little spare time left, you'll make it!

Bless the heart of the helpful homemaker in Wisconsin who sent me a get-rid-of-roaches recipe that dates way back to the 1800s.

Yup, I said "1800." Does that knock you out? Well, hang on, because roaches have been around lots longer than that . . . like for thousands of years.

This is a real goody, using boric acid, but—and this is important —before you do anything drastic, here's a word of caution.

WARNING: The Poison Control Center says boric acid can be harmful to small children and pets if taken in large quantities. So, precautions, please.

And now for the hint:

"Sprinkle powdered boric acid mixed with a little sugar (the little devils will go for it even quicker this way) under the refrigerator and stove, in cupboards, around the drain, in cracks and crevices. You can use a baster to blow it into corners that are hard to reach. Or put it in lids or beverage bottle tops—the roaches will then take the poison back to their nest.

"Leave it around for about ten days.

"Take it from me, it works like a charm."

Rug (also see Carpet, p. 160)

From Illinois: "Rugs used as wall coverings are quite attractive. Here's one novel idea:

"We had a flush door that was in bad shape, with several large dents and kick marks at the bottom.

"To remedy this, we bought carpet squares with adhesive backing in colors that match the decor of the room and applied them to the door. Now we have a very good-looking door that is both unusual and inexpensive!"

Here's a foolproof way to keep throw rugs from skidding:
Cut a piece of one-half-inch thick foam rubber the shape of the rug and place it under the rug. This foam rubber can be found in department and dime stores.

From Alaska: "When fringe on a rug gets worn, trim it the first time, then take your scissors and just 'whack' it off that old rug. But don't cut it too short.

"You'll find a small piece of cloth underneath that fringe that looks like a selvage. Turn this under, fold your rug back a little and apply iron-on tape, ironing it to the back of the rug. This will do away with that fringe and make your rug look like new again."

Sliding Glass Doors (also see Doors, p. 164)

A safety precaution for those of you who have sliding glass doors and worry about burglars:
Take a wooden rod about an inch thick and cut it to fit the track. I used an old broom and made it about an inch shorter than the width of the door.
Drop the rod in the track and the door can't be opened.

Television

Many the time I have jumped up from a comfortable chair to adjust the color dial on my TV set, only to have to readjust it again when daylight dawned in the TV scene I was watching. Thanks to an expert from Delaware, I know why.

He says, "Please tell those who have color TVs and who try to adjust them whenever the faces turn greenish to wait until the scene changes before trying to adjust.

"While there could be trouble with the set, the green color might be due to the fact that the scene was filmed at night.

"If viewers will wait until a daytime scene appears, the greenish glow usually disappears.

"You can test by flipping channels and comparing faces before calling your repairman."

From Oregon: "When the tiny bulb that shows the channel numbers on my TV burned out, I cut a circle from a gummed label and pasted it on the glass in front of the burned-out bulb.

"When the TV was turned on, I turned the dial to a program I knew was on a certain station and marked the channel number on the label in big red numbers.

"Continuing on around the dial, I marked all other channels. Saved myself the expense of a repairman . . . until something really big goes wrong. Then I'll have him replace that little light, too.

Upholstery

Ever notice how inflation brings out the ingenuity in people? Here's a marvelous make-do tip from a super smarty in New Jersey:

"When our cat clawed the arms of the sofa, we couldn't afford re-upholstering so we cut fabric from the back of the sofa and redid the arms, sewing with transparent nylon fishing line.

"The sofa looks brand new. As for the back of the sofa, who's going to pull it away from the wall anyway?"

Vacuum Cleaner

From New Hampshire: "It's very important to keep the roller brush on your vacuum or sweeper clean. This will assure you of the best possible results from your appliance.

"I use my seam ripper to clean the brush, running it along the roller to catch hair and string caught in the brush.

"Try it—you'll see!"

From California: "Recently I ran out of disposable bags for my vacuum.

"I cut off about a half inch at the top of the bag and emptied the dirt out through that end. Then, when the bag was empty, I simply folded the top part of the bag down about a half-inch and stapled and taped the top shut.

"The used bag is slightly smaller but gets the job done. This should be done only in a pinch."

When you are using your vacuum cleaner, here is a hint to keep in mind:

Vacuum your way into a room instead of going into the room first with the vacuum and all that cord.

Venetian Blinds

From Montana: "Here's an easy way to wash Venetian blinds:

"Soak them in the tub. Then wear a pair of garden gloves and wipe each slat clean. No cut hands!"

From Iowa: "I didn't want to buy new blinds when the tape got worn spots, so I repaired it.

"I cut a piece of white iron-on tape the length and width I needed and ironed it over the worn tape.

"It has lasted two years and is still in good shape."

Walls, cleaning (also see Plaster, p. 177, Ammonia, p. 192, Salad Bowls, wooden, p. 231 and Spot check chart, p. 377)

From Indiana: "I put a dash of fabric softener in my bucket of sudsy water for washing up wall smudges. It gives walls a lovely clean smell, plus it's so gentle on my hands."

From Kentucky: "To keep the sofa from marking the walls, I attached a couple of screw-in doorstops to the bottom back of the couch. Now the sofa can't bang into the wall."

From Maryland: "Use a sponge mop to clean the upper parts of walls and you won't need to stand on a ladder."

Here's a super household hint from a school custodian in Florida: "Use a sponge mop to wash walls, then throw a dry towel over it to dry them quickly!"

Windows (see specific window listings and Energy Saving, windows, p. 166)

Windows, burglar-proofing

Friends, if you have a broken lock on your window and want to feel a little better about spending the night alone . . . leave the window closed and slip a knife in, between the frame and the window.

It will give you an extra sense of security . . . and I guarantee that from the outside no one will be able to get that window open without breaking it.

Window, decorating

A dear friend, Mary McBeth, has the cutest idea she said I could share with you.

She framed a window instead of making a valance.

Her husband took molding that was about three inches wide by one-half-inch thick and cut it to fit the length and width of the window.

She covered the board in the same fabric she used for curtains, tacking it on the back—you could put padding under the fabric first to make it look smoother.

The real clincher is that the material she used was a sheet that she had bought on sale! Permanent press, too!

Windows, dust-proofing

From Idaho: "Save the ends of used white candles and rub them on the corners of wood next to the windowpane.

"The wax keeps the corners free of dust and moisture."

Windows, screens

Nylon net scrubbies (see Nylon Net, p. 217) are great for cleaning window screens. Run dry net over the screen section of the window and all that dirt that has been gathering on the screens just flies out beautifully.

Windows, shades

From Washington: "My neighbors and I have worked out a 'Do Not Disturb' system:

"We pull down a particular shade whenever we don't want to be disturbed. As soon as we are ready for visitors, the shade is raised.

"As dear as friends are to me, there are moments when unexpected company is a terrible intrusion, no matter who comes calling."

Windows, washing (also see Gas Lights, p. 433)

From Iowa: "I'm elderly and washing windows is a challenge but I have found a way:

"I use a child's toy cotton mop to wash the window over my sink. Then I take an old towel, put it on the mop and dry the window.

"Doing outside windows, I use a regular mop, the hose, and dry them in the same way, using a towel wrapped around the mop head."

When your windows are so dirty even twenty-twenty vision doesn't help, use pure vinegar to clean them.

Did you know that if you pour this used vinegar in a tall, narrow container, the dirt will settle at the bottom?

Then you can pour off the clean vinegar and use it again for window washing.

From New York: "The sap from our maple trees seems to gravitate to my windows, and ammonia cleaners can't remove it.

"I apply baking soda on a paper towel, scour away and it works!

"It is not as abrasive as scouring cleanser and, as the baking soda dries, I rub and the windows are brilliant.

From Georgia: "I've discovered another use for that ever versatile nylon net (see Nylon Net, p. 217).

"We live close to salt water and have a great deal of trouble with the salt sticking to our windows.

"To get the windows really clean, we use nylon net to scrub them when washing. It takes a lot less effort and they get sparkling clean."

From Wisconsin: "If you hate to wash the outside of windows . . .

"Put a long-handled carwash brush on the hose. Dip the brush in a pail of soapy water and wash away. Then turn the hose on to rinse the windows."

Woodwork, scratched (also see Furniture, staining, p. 169 and Salad Bowls, wooden, p. 231)

From Iowa: "When my antique table was moved, one leaf was slightly marred.

"I had no commercial product on hand and so I mixed a level teaspoon of instant coffee and two teaspoons of water. I went over the surface with the mixture, using a small wad of cotton. All the scratches disappeared.

"Some months later, soapy water was splashed near a modern walnut chest of drawers. Some drops left slightly noticeable marks. Again I restored it with the coffee mixture.

"All splash marks are gone and the wood has a soft sheen as if furniture polish had been used."

Note from Heloise: this works like magic!

We managed to uncover a place on one of the desks in our office and tried the coffee treatment on a badly scratched area.

The coffee covered the scratches and put a sheen on the desk that has lasted over a week.

Now I guess we will have to do the rest of the desk . . .

From South Carolina: "All my woodwork is stained walnut. With our children around, scratches appear quite often. So I made myself a quickie first-aid scratch-remover kit.

"I filled an empty shoe polish bottle with walnut stain and linseed oil, and threw in a few bee-bee pellets so they'd stir it up when I shake the bottle. Now, whenever I see a scratch, I just daub my stain over it and wipe off with a cloth . . .

"Presto . . . no scratch!"

Know what I do to cover the nicks and scratches that seem to crop up from time to time on my furniture?

I use a paste shoe polish in a color to match the furniture, rubbing in lightly over the scratch.

Scratches seem to disappear like magic and the furniture buffs up to a beautiful shine.

SECOND TIME AROUND: HOUSEHOLD RECYCLE

INTRODUCTION

Know how you get when it's spring-cleaning time? Well, I know how I get—hopping around like a jumping bean, not just cleaning, but cleaning out.

Have you ever noticed that when you decide to get rid of something, instantly isn't a moment too soon? I mean you want it out pronto.

That used to be me to a T. Not any more!

I've discovered if I sorta let discards sit for a bit, then give 'em another look-see, I can spot possibilities.

That's how a friend of mine turned an old-fashioned typewriter into a home-office lamp that's a real conversation piece.

And how another friend got the idea of removing the center shelf of an old-fashioned vanity table and using the three-drawer units on either side as free-standing night tables.

But it's also true you can think, and think, then think some more about some things, and not get inspired.

Still, why throw 'em out? Save up—discarded furniture, drapes, curtains, picture frames and all kinds of furnishings. Then have a yard sale!

You won't make a fortune but it's found money, and it's fun.

One tip: price everything in advance (but make prices negotiable —remember you want to unload that stuff, not store it forever!).

Get the word around—an ad in your local newspaper, a note on the bulletin board at the market. Tell friends and neighbors. Don't keep it a secret if you want a success.

Before you do anything, run through the make-over tips that follow. Could be they'll come in handy.—Hugs, Heloise

Carpet

Recently I was in a shop where I saw a carpet made by putting odd pieces of carpeting together. The owner told me how she did it.

Glue the carpet samples to a rug pad. This way the glue won't hurt the floor. When or if the carpet wears thin, there's no problem removing it.

From Idaho: "When the rubber backing wears off a cotton shag rug, you can use the rug to make scrubbers to wash down painted walls and woodwork.

"Cut the rug in 8 × 8 inch squares, then stitch around the outer edges with the sewing machine so they won't ravel.

"This takes only a few minutes but prolongs the life of the scrubber."

A reminder for anyone who has had shag carpeting installed:

Those little pieces of leftover carpeting make wonderful shoe polishers!

Newspaper

From South Carolina: "Get rid of cobwebs that appear overnight with a disposable duster made from a section of newspaper.

"Roll the paper tightly, securing it with a rubber band at midsection. Fringe the other end with a few snips of your scissors and gather the cobwebs with the fringed end.

"Then toss the duster away! It's quick, easy and a good use for yesterday's paper."

Paint

Here's a hint from a painter in Vermont who knows how to get his money's worth:

"Here's a way to save money after painting ceilings with white water-base paint. I had a roller, roller pan and paintbrush plus the empty paint can to clean—all heavily coated with paint.

"First, I added a little water to the bucket and cleaned the paint from the sides and bottom.

"I put a little water into the roller pan and cleaned the roller, brush and pan. I then added this water-paint mixture to the paint can.

"What resulted was a clean brush and roller—and about a gallon of 'whitewash' which I used in the garage and basement to paint the concrete blocks."

Window Shade

From Washington: "Window shade rollers can be used to hang curtains.

"I hem the new ones with a casing wide enough to fit the larger rod."

2

Kitchen Capers

INTRODUCTION

Right here, while we're in the kitchen where lots of chores get done, put down your eggbeater and lend an ear.

Let's talk housework in general. Sure isn't a giggle, is it?

You new homemakers, guys and gals, sometimes don't know where to start when it comes to cleaning. Should you shine up pots, chase dust balls, do dishes first? Or what?

Bet it makes you realize how hard mom worked to keep things shipshape, right?

Well, don't you worry. Let's sit down together and find easy ways to banish the can't-cope blues.

First of all, don't feel guilty about not getting everything done every day! Housework is one thing you can put off 'til tomorrow.

Do what you can today and just don't worry about the rest. Life's too short to waste trying to keep a spotless house.

Know what I always say? Dust never killed anyone, not ever!

Some things have to be done (dishes, mopping, laundry). But who looks under beds or rubs a finger across our blinds every day? Do these kinds of jobs when time and energy permit.

The main thing you need to remember: always put things back in place.

Before going to bed at night, check around:

Newspapers picked up? Snack dishes washed?

In the morning, before leaving for work, go back over things again, putting away makeup, shaving cream, etc. See that dishes are washed or, if you're rushed, stacked in the sink. Make the beds. Be consistent.

Now, when you come home in the evening, things should be pretty well in order (on the surface). But what about the cleaning you know needs doing? Will anyone notice if it's not?

Here's where a schedule comes in handy.

Make a list of chores for each room—from dusting to cleaning blinds and straightening out the closet. Or from polishing silver and washing crystal to cleaning out cabinets.

Got the idea?

Tack up the list some place in a closet. Each evening, as time permits, choose one job that needs to be done in addition to regularly scheduled daily chores. And do it! You'll be surprised how much you get done when you have a checklist.

Be sure to mix up jobs. Do a difficult hate-to-tackle-it task with a couple of easy ones.

If you don't complete a project one day, carry it over to the next. Eventually it'll get done.

Now for the regularly scheduled jobs—the ones which have to be done on a regular basis—choose one for each day of the week. Make your own list but . . .

For example: washing on Mondays, floor vacuuming or mopping on Tuesdays, mending and dusting on Wednesdays, bathroom scrubbing on Thursdays, changing sheets on Fridays.

You can adjust this schedule to your own preference, but you get the idea.

Try to save weekends for shopping and outings.

After a week of all work, you need to play . . . or be dull guys and dolls.

Nobody likes a clean house better than your friend Heloise but . . . you've got to take shore leave once in a while.

Just listen to what a Maryland mother wrote me:

"I think your best hint ever was, 'Every once in a while, just let the house go. The dirt will still be there tomorrow. Get out and enjoy a day with your loved ones'.

"Heloise, can you see a twenty-five-year-old woman out in a tent in the yard with three boys (ages seven, five and two)? We played cowboys, ate peanut butter and jelly sandwiches, and had a ball!

"The kids couldn't have been happier if I'd taken them to the circus! Thank you!"

You know what I said to this marvelous mom: "Atta girl—you're on the right track."

What I really believe in more than anything is freedom from drudgery. That means doing things quickly, easily and economically so there's time—and money—to spend on the good things in life.

Starting right here in the kitchen, that's what my book is all about.

—Hugs 'n' Kisses, Heloise

PART 1: KITCHEN HINTS

Adhesive-Backed Paper

Adhesive-backed shelving paper sure is an improvement over the old tacked-down kind.

However, I went crazy trying to get it smooth in the closed-in end of my kitchen cabinets. You should have seen the contortions I went through attempting to get the job done!

Even getting it down right on an open shelf took a bit of doing.

So, I finally just removed a wide border of the backing on all four sides of the paper, leaving the center with its backing intact.

It took me just half the time to cover the shelf! All the edges were firmly in place and the center so taut and smooth, you'd never guess it wasn't stuck in place!

From West Virginia: "It can be pretty frustrating when you get a bubble in adhesive-backed paper you're applying to a shelf. I've found that if I cut a small 'X' into the bubble with a single-edged razor blade, and re-lay the four parts formed by the 'X' cut, the problem is solved."

From Vermont: "There's one place in my house that has never been pretty: That's under the kitchen sink where I keep soap, cleanser, waxes, etc.

"To brighten up that ugly cabinet, I lined the sides and bottom with flowered adhesive-backed paper . . . Now it looks great!"

From North Carolina: "Don't throw away the backing of adhesive-backed paper. It makes excellent lining for kitchen drawers.

"So easy to clean with a damp cloth, too, because of its wax coating."

Aluminum, cleaning (see Pots and Pans, cast aluminum, p. 224)

Ammonia

Want to make fingerprints on those walls, tiles or mirrors do a disappearing act? A mixture of equal parts of plain old nonsudsing household ammonia and water (I mix mine in a spray bottle) gets fingerprints off like magic. This is really great for cleaning the shower and plumbing fixtures, too.

Appliances, oiling

To make appliances with moving parts, such as can openers, run smoother, wash and dry thoroughly, then spray the moving part with nonstick vegetable spray.

Baking Soda (also see Refrigerator Odors, p. 230)

From Idaho: "I am a nut about baking soda. I use it for scrubbing anything that I do not want to mar: porcelain, enamel, chrome, glassware, etc. Well, thanks to a lovely accidental discovery, I have the sweetest smelling kitchen cleanser ever . . .

"If I poured baking soda from the box, it came out in a big sploof! What to do?

"I pried the top off an empty plastic talcum powder shaker and filled it with baking soda and a couple of glass marbles to keep the soda from caking, then I replaced the snap-on sprinkle-type top.

"When I give the container a shake or a squeeze, it works like a dream and there's a bonus! It is the most deliciously talcum powder-scented cleaning powder you can imagine! Now I feel feminine every time I scrub a pot."

From Maine: "For years, I've kept a box of baking soda near the stove in case I needed it to extinguish a small grease fire. But I didn't mark this box 'For Fires' and when I really needed it, guess what? Smoke was pouring from the house before I found it. Now it not only says, 'For fires', but has a red 'slipcover' so I can't miss it in an emergency."

Blender, cleaning

From California: "The easy way to clean a blender: pour water in up to the halfway mark, add a drop or two of detergent; put the lid on tight and 'buzz' the blender, blades, *et al.*, clean."
And rinse well, well, well!—Heloise

Bottle Washer

If your bottle washer brush doesn't do the job, try this: wrap a few folds of nylon net (see Nylon Net, p. 217) around the bristles, fastening with a rubberband. Then scrub away. Works super!

Broiler (also see Steak, p. 40)

Hesitant to use the broiler in your electric oven because you dread cleaning up? Nothing to it! Fill the broiler pan with at least one inch of water and place meat on a rack under the broiler unit and over the broiler pan. Result: No messy oven and just a greasy water-filled broiler pan to wash.

Broom (also see Mop, p. 216)

Here's a handy hint to save pain and strain on your back! Why struggle to sweep dust up from the floor with a long-handled broom in one hand, the dustpan in the other? There's no need.

Since you have to stoop anyway to pick up the dust pan, why not use your whisk broom? Soooo wonderfully simple!

And another thing . . . don't hang up that whisk broom separately, hang it and the pan together so you'll be ready for next time. I put a cup hook on top of my whisk broom's handle so I can hang it on a nail.

A great guy in Alaska told me how to recycle a broom with lopsided bristles. First, he soaked the broom in hot water. When they were soft, he pulled them straight and gave the longest straws a trim. The broom's just like new—and it's gonna stay that way cause he drilled a hole in the handle to hang it—and that keeps the bristles from getting lopsided.

Bulletin Board

From Kentucky: "There's a lot of unused bulletin board space on the inside doors of kitchen cabinets. It's especially handy if you happen to have a phone in your kitchen.

"On the inside of my cabinet doors, I tape our monthly church events calendar and a regular calendar. Under each month I list the birthdays and anniversaries of our children, relatives and friends I want to remember with a card or gift.

"I have also marked on the calendar under the appropriate month those things which I might slip up on, such as license renewal, taxes, etc.

"A large envelope, which is cut lower on one side, is taped to the door. This is a handy catchall for all sorts of odd clippings and perhaps a recipe which I intend to try.

"I've used this door space to tape up Heloise hints and various bits of information. It takes up no extra room and sure is handy."

Any of you who have a tiny kitchen will appreciate this hint. Sure saves lots of things from getting buried—and forgotten.—Heloise

Cabinets, organizing (see Storage Space, organizing, p. 237 and Pantry, organizing, p. 222)

Cake Carrier (also see Boxes, cake, p. 251)

From Nevada: "I have a cake carrier that is rather large and takes up quite a bit of storage space. I finally found a use for it while it's in storage: I stash my supply of paper plates in the cake carrier and they are kept clean and out of the way."

Calendar (see Bulletin Board, p. 194)

Can Opener (also see corned Beef, p. 19)

A punch-type can opener (the kind that makes a triangular hole in a beverage can) makes a very good shrimp cleaner and deveiner.

Hang a punch-type can opener on the inside of the pantry door so it will be handy for getting the lids off cocoa, baking powder and spice containers, as well as jars of home-canned goods.

From New Mexico: "If the can opener just won't fit the top of a can, try turning the can upside down and opening the bottom instead of the top."

From Virginia: "To clean my nonelectric wall can opener, all I do is boil a kettle full of water, remove the opener from its hook, place it in the sink and pour the boiling water over it.

"I clean any spots left with a toothbrush. Then I dry it well, oil the necessary parts with spray-on or vegetable oil and it works like new.

Cart

Know those three-tiered metal kitchen carts which most of us have? I'll bet yours is pushed in a corner and the top shelf holds a small electric oven, steamer cooker, electric skillet or toaster.

Anyhow, the top shelf usually is reserved for whatever your household uses most frequently. Second shelf, whatever won't fit on the top one; third shelf, whatever you use a little less often.

Well, heaven-help-a-duck, when I've been visiting lately I've noticed that the top shelf always is in pitiful condition. People either paint it, put plastic over it or a towel to hide the rust, etc.

I looked at my cart recently . . . no better than anyone else's. So I thought to myself, "Why don't you take that thing apart (only has a few screws in it) and put the worn-out scratched shelf on the bottom and the practically new bottom shelf on the top? Nobody sees that bottom shelf anyway."

I did just that.

When that new shelf (the old bottom one) gets a few scratches I'll swap it with the "new" middle shelf.

You all don't have to spend a penny for this and what's a few minutes of your time working a screwdriver?

You are just gonna love me for pouring this hint in your coffee cup, eh what?

Casseroles

From Idaho: "When making a crusty casserole, I like to line the baking dish with foil. I first mold the foil over the bottom of the dish, then it custom-fits the inside. No more tears in the foil to let juices leak through and bake onto the dish."

Ceramic, cooking surface

From Maine: "I have a stove with a smooth ceramic cooking surface. The burner areas had turned a dirty brown color. All attempts to clean 'em failed until I tried white vinegar.

"I poured a small amount on the discolored area and let it stand for five minutes then wiped it up with a paper towel. Amazing!"

Compass

From Iowa: "I am an ex-schoolteacher and always keep a drawing compass in my kitchen drawer. It's so handy for many things: I use it to punch holes in a shoe strap or belt, to make a hole in woodwork before screwing in a cup hook, or to make a circle for pastry, and on and on.

"It also comes in handy to poke out the holes in the salt and pepper shakers when they get clogged."

Great idea!—Heloise

Cookbook

From Kentucky: "When a thick cookbook won't stay open to the page you're using, set a clear glass pie plate over the page. It will hold the book open, keep the page clean, and you can read the recipe right through it!"

Counter, cleaning

From Illinois: "Got a dried spot, such as cooked oatmeal, that has splattered on the counter?

"Don't waste time scrubbing. Wet that sponge in warm soapy

water, leaving it a little soapy and plop it down on the spot. Then
go have a cup of coffee or dust the living room.

"When you come back that dried spot will be soft and whoosh
. . . off it comes!"

Cruet, cleaning

From Washington, D.C.: "When I clean cruets, I use a plastic
drinking straw to clean the corners and curves.

"It is flexible enough to bend into any angle, yet strong enough to
do the job."

Cutting Board

From Iowa: "Storing my cutting board was a problem until I
decided to hang it.

"I centered a cup hook on one end of the board and now it can
be hung on the wall or in the bottom cabinet where it is always handy
when needed."

And here's a thrifty-nifty from a clever husband in Vermont: "My
wife doesn't like wooden cutting boards because she doesn't think
they're sanitary, so I made her three from a scrap strip of plexiglass.
And all three cost less than a dollar."

Ohhh . . . don't you just love it!—Heloise

Dishcloth

From New Hampshire: "I like a large, soft dishcloth and they are
hard to find in the stores. So I bought a package of disposable
dishcloths, sat down at the sewing maching and stitched two together all the way around. Then I had a nice, big, soft cloth that
lasted for quite a while."

Sew a pompom of nylon net (see Nylon Net, p. 217) in a corner
and you have a scrubber-dubber for dried-on foods.—Heloise

Dishwasher

I have a great hint that I got from Bill Emick, a bachelor friend.

Like most people who live alone, he finds it usually takes a day or two to fill up the dishwasher so there are enough dishes and glasses in it to make it worthwhile to run.

His trick is that when he washes, he fills only one cup with detergent and runs the washer for one wash and rinse cycle.

I have been trying this at home because it really would save a lot of money over a period of time.

I also rinse my dishes well before putting them in the dishwasher so they are basically almost clean to start with. If you put greasy plates directly in the dishwasher, you're going to have to run them through twice.

There are so many different types of dishwashers, you will have to check yours out and see if you can run it for one cycle only.

Since doing this, I am using only half as much detergent as before so a box really lasts a long time now. That's what I call a real savings!

Give it a try and see for yourself.

From Oregon: "Here's a hint for the lady of the house: Use your dishwasher as a facial steam bath.

"Just when the dishwasher finishes the rinse cycle, and before it starts drying, I turn it off and open the door a few inches. This lets the first blast of really hot steam escape.

"Then I quickly throw a beach towel over the opening, trapping the steam. With my hair covered with another towel, I stick my head under the beach towel for a few minutes or so. It is so relaxing!"

From Wisconsin: "To keep small, thin objects like chopsticks or fondue forks from falling through the silverware basket in your dishwasher, try this:

"Place a plastic scrubber in the bottom of the basket and poke the thin objects into it.

"They will stay put and your scrubber will come out clean and fresh, too."

Dishwashing

From Utah: "When I wash my good china and crystal, I line the sink with a terry cloth towel. The soft fabric acts as a cushion and guards against chips and scratches."

From Alabama: "Whether you have a dishwasher or not, here is an idea for draining those extra dishes, especially pots and pans.

"Lay a clean shelf from your oven on the drainboard. Holds much more than a drainer.

"If you put a newspaper under it, the water won't run like a creek emptying into the ocean and swamp everything."

From Florida: "To avoid finding a sink full of dirty dishes each day when I return from work, I have a stand in my kitchen on which I leave paper plates, paper napkins and paper cups for the kids.

"Whenever my daughters and their friends want a snack, they use the paper articles, thus eliminating dirty dishes and glassware."

From Illinois: "I love to bake—but hate to clean up. The thought of a counter full of dirty dishes has often kept me from even starting.

"But no more!

"I've found it works wonders if I fill the sink with hot sudsy water before I start. As I empty each utensil, I slip it into the water to soak.

"When my goodies are done, my dishes are clean. A quick swipe with a dishrag, a rinse, a wipe and I'm finished."

From Ohio: "A cup hook mounted next to the sink is ever so handy for holding rings, bracelets and watches while you're doing dishes."

And you'll always know where they are if you get in the habit of putting them there.—Heloise

From Kansas: "Before doing dishes, I remove my rings and put them on the little spout on my hand lotion bottle which I keep by the sink.

"It's a perfect place for rings because when I finish with the dishes, I always put on hand lotion, and never forget my rings."

Dishwashing Detergent

From Maine: "In order to economize, I buy a cheaper brand dishwashing detergent and add a half bottle of it to a half bottle of a name brand detergent.

"The name brand detergent is always strong, so when it's used half and half, it goes a long way."

Double Boiler, cleaning (see Pots and Pans, mineral deposit, p. 227)

Drain

From Minnesota: "My plumber told me to pour one cup of baking soda in my sink drain followed by one cup of cider vinegar. As this foams up, I flush the drain with at least a pint of boiling water. I do this procedure once every week and have never had a clogged sink."

Drainboard

From Illinois: "My rubber dish drainer was coated with a lime deposit from hard water.

"I used scouring powder, bleach, you name it, I tried it.

"Now, I use vinegar! I use it all the time to clean the alkali from my tea kettle, so I said to myself, 'Why not on the drainboard?'

"It came clean as a whistle. No fuss! No muss!

"I pour the vinegar on the crusted area, let it sit a few minutes, and then scrub it off."

Drawers, organizing (also see Storage Space, organizing, p. 238)

Let's talk about the kitchen drawer where you keep your favorite knives, spoons, gadgets and no telling what else.

While you are reading this, think to yourself, "Now what is in that drawer?" (Bet you can't make a complete list before you look!)

How much of it is really necessary? What do you actually need? Can you find your favorite knife or bottle opener immediately?

When you clean the drawer, do you just remove all the "stuff," get the crumbs out, line it with paper, replace everything and let it go? Don't!

You will be right back where you started—still having to knock everything aside to find that favorite spoon or knife.

Put some newspaper down on the drainboard and literally pour out everything in the drawer onto the paper.

Just look at all the excess junk and clutter! Whatever do you need all this mess for? There are umpteen spoons, three peelers, two bottle openers, etc.

Wipe out the drawer and line it with adhesive-backed paper, foil, whatever.

Now don't throw all that stuff back in the drawer! Stop, look and think, "What do I really use every day?"

Pick out your favorite butcher knife, paring knife, spatula, egg turner, can opener and enough silver for the family. Put these back in your drawer.

Put the bag of excess items in the garage or a closet. If you don't go into that kitchen grab bag within a week, then it's a fact that you can do without those extra gadgets. If you decide you need a certain item, it's there.

How many bottle openers do you have? Three? Six? You can open only one bottle at a time. You keep the extras because you think someday one might not work. You still can only open one bottle at a time, so pick out the best two and put them back in the drawer.

Go through all your equipment this way.

What you can do without, you don't need. Get rid of it so you can find what you do need quickly. Saves your time and nerves. Eliminates excess cleaning, clutter, etc.

Don't faint when you see how little will be in this favorite drawer after it's organized. It pays off! You will have a glorious feeling tomorrow when you open the drawer and immediately find what you are looking for.

Simplicity is the solution to a lot of problems.

From Arizona: "Put a couple of magnets on the inside of your kitchen junk drawer . . . great for holding paper clips that would otherwise be all over the bottom of the drawer.

"You can put the magnets anywhere on a metal drawer."

Egg Poacher

Use an egg poacher for warming a baby's or toddler's meal. After the water boils, turn the burner off and insert the cups of food. Then let the pot sit with the lid on for five to ten minutes.

The steam alone does the job. You can even heat a wiener in the water below.

The baby's vegetables won't get cold and you won't have three pans to wash. Hooray!

Electric Frying Pan

From Florida: "Found an easy way to clean my electric frying pan:

"I covered the bottom with an ammonia-soaked cloth, slipped the skillet into a plastic bag, tied it shut and let it stand overnight.

"Grease and stains came off like magic."

Faucet, dripping

Ever bothered by a drip in your sink?

Cut a piece of string about two feet long and tie it around the nozzle of the faucet, then put the rest of the string down the drain as far as it will go.

The dripping water will hit the string; then run down it and into the drain.

Eureka! You can get a good night's sleep!
This is a great stop-gap measure but get that faucet repaired!

Feather Duster

From Utah: "I've found a feather duster will last considerably longer if a rubber band is placed a little below the base of the duster, but not on the handle. This keeps the feathers together. The end feathers are soft and fluffy, but they're less apt to break off."

Floors, cleaning

And here's a great hint from a kitcheneer in Montana: "If you have a wax build-up (which usually turns yellow) in the corners of your kitchen floor and under the cabinet overhang, here's a suggestion:

"Scrub the areas that get the most wear and dirt, then thoroughly wash your mop (to keep from spreading the soil under the cabinets and to the corners) and wash these areas with cool, clear water only.

"I never use hot suds around the baseboards or in the corners, nor do I wax these areas. I only rewax the area that gets the wear and tear. This avoids getting coats and coats of wax in out-of-the-way places that will only become yellow and dirty looking."

From Iowa: "For the woman who does her kitchen floors on her hands and knees, a sponge car mitt is mighty handy.

"Use this between regular scrubbings for a quick going over."

Food Grinder (see Grinder, p. 209)

Freezer

From Maryland: "At one time or another, we've probably all had electricity problems or failures that caused food spoilage in freezers and refrigerators. And what an awful odor that makes!

"My freezer is located in an area away from everyday traffic so we didn't notice that it wasn't operating until I opened the door and the odor almost knocked me over.

"I went to the supermarket and bought a bag of cat box filler, emptied out the freezer, washed it all down (sides and shelves) and dried it thoroughly. Then, I poured the filler in a flat box, placed it on the middle shelf and shut the door.

"Five days later, absolutely no odor of any kind. It worked like a miracle!"

From Louisiana: "This is how I organized my upright freezer:

"I bought wire bicycle baskets, 12 × 18 × 6 inches. They keep packages from falling out of the freezer, and can be removed to make it easier to find the food I'm looking for."

Freezer Containers

From New Jersey: "I have quite a collection of freezer containers in all sizes and shapes but could never find the right lids for them. One day I hit on a bright idea: I coded them, marking each container and its cover with a matching symbol—squares, circles, crosses, etc. I used indelible marking ink.

"Now, when I pull out a square container marked with two stars, I know exactly which lid fits it, no searching party needed."

A clever Montana husband had this idea: "My wife was canning for the freezer and was having trouble filling the plastic bags because she could not hold them open and fill at the same time.

"I found a plastic margarine tub that fit the opening of the bag and cut out its bottom. Then I placed the tub in the opening of the bag to use as a funnel.

"The filling was a cinch."

Freezer Wrap

From Michigan: "Freezer wrap has lots more uses than the one for which it was intended . . .

"The piece you just took your frozen meat out of makes a great little chopping board (wax side up). Just throw it away when you're done.

"When rolling out pie crusts, roll them out between freezer wrap (wax side next to dough). Won't slide around like wax paper usually does.

"Use it to line your cupboard shelves (wax side up). It's sturdier and dishes and pans slide out easier.

"Use it to cover the children's school books (wax side out). Very cheap and good protection from the weather.

"When shaped as a cone (wax side in), it makes great funnels, even for icing cakes. Then just throw away.

"It's great to wrap packages you send through the mail, (dull side out). Very sturdy."

Garbage (also see Trash Bag, p. 243)

I was tired of using the wastebasket clear across my kitchen—and isn't that usually the only space there is for it?—until I realized I could eliminate this situation for less than a dollar. Here's what I did:

I screwed two cup hooks about twelve inches apart on the inside top of the door under the sink. (Of course, your doors must be wooden!)

With pliers, I bent the hooks out a little to form two "L" shapes sticking straight up.

Next, with an ice pick I punched two holes on the side and near the top of a rectangular plastic wastebasket, spacing them to fit over the hooks on the door.

I hung my basket on the inside of the door. It's the greatest because, if you analyze how you spend your kitchen time, you will find that most of it is spent right at the kitchen sink!

Why walk across the kitchen when all you have to do is open that cabinet door and drop in a peeling, a paper or whatever.

This idea doesn't cost you anything except two cup hooks and an inexpensive wastebasket. You can't lose because the basket can always be used somewhere else if you don't like my system.

This will reduce "basketball" practice in your family and save you time—and the kitchen wall!

A clever air force bachelor from Connecticut wrote that when lining a garbage can, he uses several layers of plastic bags so he can fill and lift out one at a time.

Isn't that a super idea? And if you already do this, then shame on you for not letting me know before this!

From Rhode Island: "We have a plastic trash basket in our kitchen. We line the basket with a paper bag to keep it clean and also clip a plastic bag to the edge of the basket so that it falls down into the paper bag.

"Dry trash goes into the paper bag; wet trash, such as coffee grounds, peelings and sink scraps, into the plastic one.

"This prevents wet trash from soaking through the paper bag and keeps the basket clean."

Garbage Disposal

From Connecticut: "When a bottle cap, or some other small, hard object gets into the garbage disposal and is clattering around, I have a way of getting it out without having to put my hand down into it (always a scary feeling, even with the motor off).

"After turning the disposal off, I put a small lump of floral clay (available at any florist shop) on the end of a wooden spoon handle, push it down on the object and, presto, up it comes!"

Glassware

From Nevada: "So that I don't have to wash all my glasses for a big party, I devised a system to keep them constantly sparkling and ready.

"Each day I use a different glass for myself, taking them in order from the cabinet. I do the same with special dishes, using them at least once a week on my rotation system.

"Now I never have to spend time washing stacks of dishes or glassware because they don't have time to collect dust."

From Georgia: "If you want to stack glasses for storage, place a small square of tissue paper between the glasses. It will prevent them from sticking."

You know how terrible you feel when you get a nick in the rim of a good crystal glass? You're afraid to throw it out—and you're afraid if you use it you'll cut yourself! Know what to do? Take a diamond-tip fingernail file or emery board and gently file the rough edge smooth. This'll minimize the nick and make the glass safer to drink from!

Grater

From Kentucky: "To clean the grater after using it, how about a toothbrush?

"I keep one handy in a kitchen drawer for this and many other uses.

"It really gets in those little holes in the grater and gets out most of the lemon rind, etc."

From Idaho: "When I have two or more things to grate for one dish, I always grate the softest one first. Then as I grate the firmer food, it 'cleans' the openings in the grater."

Grease

From Illinois: "I take a plastic lid from a shortening can, cut the inside out, leaving the heavy outside rim.

"Then I cut a circle of clean muslin 1½ inches larger than the outside of the lid.

"I place this on top of the empty shortening can, place the plastic rim on top of the muslin and strain used grease.

"I label the can and keep it in the refrigerator tightly sealed with a plastic lid, saving the cut-out rim for re-use.

"I keep separate cans for different kinds of grease.

"Bacon grease is especially good in green beans."

From South Carolina: "I borrowed this idea from my mother and really can't understand why I never thought of it before.

"She stores grease in a small two-cup coffee pot on the stove.

"The basket that was used for the coffee can serve as a strainer for the grease.

"The best thing of all is that you can pour it out with less chance of spilling the grease on the stove or having messy drips on the side of the container."

Grease Fire

From Iowa: "I was broiling a steak when the grease caught on fire and flames started shooting out of my broiler-oven. I was stunned for a second, but then I took a box of baking soda, opened the oven door and sprinkled it over the broiler pan. The fire was put out and no damage done. I even saved the steaks."

Remember, friends, never, ever, put water on a grease fire—Heloise

Grinder

Having difficulty in finding a place to clamp your old-fashioned food grinder?

Attach it to the top of a wooden stepstool.

There is plenty of room on top of the stool for the food grinder and for a good-sized dish to catch the food, too.

Grocery Shopping

All right now . . . pull up your rocking chair because I am going to give you your money's worth of free advice—right now!

I just went price-and-ad checking and came home mad! Here's why:

One local store had canned biscuits on sale at a give-away price. When I got there, women were complaining that some of the cans leaked.

Lo and behold, all I did was pick up a can and check the date stamped on it. All those cans were outdated.

None of those complaining shoppers knew the cans were dated. Did you? Don't ever fail to check for the date when you buy canned biscuits.

Whenever you pick up a can, especially one that's on sale, check the date before (not after!) you put it in your cart. Compare it to the other brands next to it. And compare the prices, too.

Now most stores do not sell outdated merchandise, but sometimes it happens so do watch for it, please.

Why should you get home and cook a beautiful dinner and put those biscuits in your oven and have them come out like lead bullets?

At the same store one day, they had salad dressing on sale. Your pal Heloise carries her magnifying glasses with her. Right next to the sale-priced quart jars were pints. Two pints (which weren't advertised) were cheaper than one quart!

I watched for fifteen minutes and not one poor soul who bought

the sale quart bothered to compare prices with other brands or check the pints . . .

What price hurry?

From Kentucky: "To keep grocery bags and cartons of soft drinks from falling over and tumbling about in the back of my station wagon, I keep two cardboard boxes side by side near the back door of my car.

"I load grocery bags right into them and have no more spills."

From New Hampshire: "When shopping for meat, dairy products or frozen foods on a hot day, put some ice in an ice chest, set it on the back seat of the car and put those perishables in it."

Grocery Shopping, spices

Did you know that most stores have spices displayed in alphabetical order on the shelves?

Sure saves time if a person knows about it!

Ice, storing

Don't know if you've tried this, but it's a real honey of an idea.

When you need to store ice for a party, pack it in plastic bags and use your washing machine instead of an ice chest. Either front or top loading machines will work.

After the party, when the leftover ice melts, just spin out the water.

Caution: Be sure to unplug the washer so some "wise" guest doesn't start the machine . . . Otherwise, this tip is the greatest party helper!

Ice Cubes

You know why it's hard to get ice cubes out of the trays? Because some of you people fill your ice trays with hot water and place them in your freezer chest to defrost the freezer more quickly. Do not do this.

Most refrigerator companies "coat" these trays. When you put hot, hot water in them, it melts and removes this coating. Nothing should be placed in these trays except cool water.

Also, these trays should never be put in dishwashers or extremely hot, soapy dishwater. This removes the coating and causes cubes to stick when you try to get them out.

The only thing I have found to remedy this is:

Wash and dry the tray thoroughly and then coat it with spray used for fry pans and casserole dishes to prevent sticking.

I am well aware that this spray is not sold for this purpose, nor do directions mention using it for this purpose, but it works!

From Florida: "When we are having a lot of company and need lots of ice, I use plastic egg cartons as ice trays.

"The ice cubes are nice and round. Needless to say, I always have plenty of ice for those get-togethers—and very inexpensively!"

Ice Tray

From New York: "I got so sick and tired of ice trays sticking to the bottom of the freezing unit that I finally put two rubber fruit jar rings under each tray.

"Do you know that they never stick anymore?"

Instruction Books

From Missouri: "Here's a hint for keeping track of a kitchen full of appliance instruction books.

"I took an old loose-leaf binder, then punched holes in construction paper.

"I pasted the back cover of each booklet to a page. Now I have a handy file when I need a hint for my stove, blender, frying pan, etc.

"No more rummaging through drawers for hours and hours to find just the one book I want to use."

Jars

Here is a hint for opening jars:

Don't sprain your wrist . . . instead, take an ice pick and punch a little hole in the lid.

As the vacuum seal is broken, the lid will come off that jar like magic.

Store almost empty jars of jam, mayonnaise, mustard, relish, etc., on their sides.

Makes it so much easier tc scrape out that last little bit without wasting any!

From Missouri: "After washing and drying jars, always place part of a crumpled paper towel in the container, then replace the lid.

"In the event that moisture remains, the towel will absorb it and the jar will smell fresher the next time you use it.

"This also will prevent rust in a metal container or lid."

Labels

This is a gem of a trick that saves the mess and fuss of scraping labels from bottles when I want a special label for some coupon offer.

Put the bottle or jar in a container that's deep enough for the water to cover the label. Extra hot water (that's the secret) is then poured in to cover the label, and the bottle is left to soak until the label comes loose.

When you take the label out of the water, lay it on a paper towel to absorb the moisture. Be sure to have the glue side up or the label will end up being stuck to the towel!

From Texas: "Believe it or not, hair spray will remove the stubborn sticky 'goop' remaining after a label has been soaked or peeled off.

"Aim directly at the offensive glue with the hair spray and limit wiping strokes (don't smear the glue around).

"Repeat if necessary, then wash in sudsy water."

Lime Deposits

Here's how to remove lime from a teakettle:

Pour half water and half white vinegar into the kettle, place on the stove and let boil for about ten minutes to loosen most of the sediment.

Now shake the kettle and pour off the solution; rinse well.

If the lime has really built up, you may have to scrape the bottom with a wooden spoon to remove all of the remaining residue. Repeat the vinegar treatment if necessary.

Linoleum

From Texas: "Our kitchen linoleum was curled at the edges. Instead of buying new linoleum, we cut nine inches off all around the old linoleum. Then we installed nine-inch tiles as a border. Looks great . . . and isn't it a great money-saving idea!"

Magnifying Glass

"Why, oh why, do most manufacturers who put ingredients and instructions on bottles, packages and boxes use such tiny, tiny print?

"Most of them can't be read with a naked eye. So I keep a magnifying glass in the kitchen at all times for this purpose."

Measuring

I do believe I have lost my last marble . . .

And if I haven't, please tell me why a jar that says "contents one quart," won't measure out to be four cups! All my cookbooks say a quart equals four cups. But it doesn't always . . .

When I measure water into jars that say "one quart"—and with two different kinds of measuring cups—I come up with 4½ cups.

I have tried this with three different kinds of fruit jars.

I caught this mistake when trying to make a batch of fillings for six pies. Instead of measuring out twelve cups of milk, I just grabbed a one-quart fruit jar and filled it three times. I knew immediately that the recipe wasn't right . . . way too watery and thin. Then I measured with a cup and, sure enough, I had 1½ cups of extra liquid.

Now, you all remember this when you do your canning.

Always use standard measuring cups, not commercial containers when following a recipe because, as I've explained, sometimes a quart bottle holds more than a quart.

And you should have seen my pickles last year! And chowchow! They were so sour, people's lips puckered when they ate 'em.

Know why? A darn quart bottle of vinegar isn't always a quart!

For that matter, it isn't always even thirty-two fluid ounces as it says. Sometimes it's thirty-six ounces!

My recipe called for two quarts of vinegar and, being a brainless wonder, I poured in two one-quart bottles of the sour stuff which was exactly one whole cup too much. How does that grab you? It sure didn't me.

For family gatherings and guild suppers, I am always asked to bring my famous potato salad. The quart bottle of mayonnaise isn't a quart (or four cups). It's 4½ cups, my loves. Measure it and see for yourselves.

Now let's get down to pints. Same thing. When a recipe calls for one pint of mayonnaise don't grab a new jar and dump it all in. A "jar" pint is sometimes two cups plus some!

Measuring Cups and Spoons

Do you ever have trouble reading the markings on measuring cups and spoons?

Paint red nail polish over those markings. Then, take a knife and carefully scrape the polish off the markings. The markings will stand out against the polish around them and be so much easier to read.

Memos (also see Bulletin Board, p. 194)

From Florida: "Messages always seem to get lost at our house or else just aren't seen. Well, I discovered a way to keep that from happening:

"Write them on your fridge! A regular crayon or grease pencil is perfect and it rubs right off with a dry towel.

"Just write lightly with either one and make sure there is no residue on them that might scratch."

From Louisiana: "I've found a wonderful place to post important notices and memos.

"It's the inside of a cupboard door.

"The nicest feature of this idea is that it keeps everything out of sight. No messy bulletin board clutters my kitchen!

"I use masking tape to attach clippings or notices so I can easily remove them when I want to, yet when I need the information, I open the cupboard door and there it is."

Mirror (also see Ammonia, p. 192)

From Iowa: "If your kitchen lacks a window, add one.

"Hang a mirror on the wall above the kitchen sink and frame it with pretty kitchen curtains. I find this 'window' even gives me more light from reflections, thus making my kitchen brighter. The curtains dress up the mirror, too."

Mixer

From Iowa: "Here is the brainstorm of a seventy-two-year-old that may make life a little less sticky for some:

"Ever get yourself, the sink and what have you all splattered up using an electric mixer?

"If so, just cut the bottom out of a large paper shopping bag and slip it over your bowl, mixer and all.

"High speed, low speed . . . all that fly-away mess will be on the inside of the little old brown bag—not on you, or the surrounding area."

Mop (also see Broom, p. 194)

Mops and brooms must be washed from time to time. For those of you who have drain hoses on your washing machines that empty into the laundry basin . . . think about this:

All that good water goes down the drain. Why not use it a second time? I put my broom and mop in that basin right under the drain and leave them there until all the suds have gone through. You can use a bucket, but it's really not necessary.

We all know that dirty mops make dirty floors, but that old broom: when was the last time it was washed?

If you don't have the kind of washer I have, take a bucket and fill it with hot water, add a little ammonia and suds. Soak your broom and mop while you are having that second cup of coffee. Then rinse well.

Perhaps your floor coverings won't become soiled so quickly.

Instead of buying a new mop when the ends got hard and stiff, I decided to give my mop a haircut.

I took my scissors and trimmed off all the stiff ends.

Now the mop is like new again and the ends are soft.

It can have three or four more "haircuts" before I have to buy a new mop.

Know something? I just thought maybe this will work on my broom, too . . . tried it and it does!

Muffin Pan

Can't find the aid you need in your kitchen? Then be innovative like this Iowa homemaker:

"A muffin pan can be used as a tray for cold drinks. It can carry six at a time without worrying that they'll slide off as they might on a regular tray."

Nylon Net

As you go through my book, here, there and everywhere you're going to find hints that mention "nylon net."

Know what it is? The greatest discovery since the wheel—well, almost.

I get carried away when I think about how cheap it is (a few cents a yard), how useful (I'll get to that later), and how attractive (all those great colors).

But first things first: What is it and where can you get it?

Think bridal veils, crinoline, and tulle . . . then think of a coarser kind of net.

You'll find it sold by the yard at fabric counters. The best kind to buy is the nylon net with the smallest holes.

Now for its uses—and my name's not Heloise if they aren't nigh on endless . . .

F'rinstance:

It makes the greatest mops, dish rags, pot-and-pan scrubbers . . . and lots more as you'll discover throughout my book.

But, remember, not any old nylon net will do. So shop carefully.

Pick up a piece of net and test it yourself (I can't buy it for you . . . wish I could!). Put one piece of net against the other or on top of the other. Compare the holes in each bolt of net (yes, even if it is on the same table and the same price). Buy the net with the smallest holes! The smaller the holes, the better the bargain. This is the easiest way I know of to test net yourself.

Don't waste your valuable time making curtains, scouring pads, floor mops, or dish cloths out of inferior net.

Your time and energy are valuable.

Only you, my dear homemakers, can search, shop and demand to get your money's worth.

Learn to compare for yourself.

When you find the right net and choose your favorite color from the rainbow assortment, know what's the first thing you'll want to do? Make a nylon net pompom (see next hint) to scrub-a-dub-dub pots, pans and dishes . . . not to mention walls, cabinets, bathroom fixtures and linoleum.

Make an extra one for your grooming kit . . . great for giving heels and elbows the old one-two.

And another for his closet—a super aid for giving his hats and suits the brush-off.

Better make a lot because you'll find a zillion uses for 'em.

Best of all, you don't have to be arts and craftsy or super at sewing to make a nylon net pompom. It couldn't be easier.

Nylon Net Pompom

Buy a half-yard of seventy-two-inch wide nylon net. Cut three six-inch strips across the eighteen-inch side. Stack them one on top of the other.

Thread a big needle with nylon yarn and, with one-inch basting stitches, stitch down the middle of the 72 inches of stacked net.

Pull the thread as you'd do if making a ruffle. Make it as tight as you can, then tie the ends of the yarn together. Be sure it's tight.

Wrap yarn around the middle of the pompom again, tie tightly on the other side, cutting excess yarn off at the knot.

Take each layer of net, one at a time and yank so it separates. It must stand apart.

When you've done this, you have a big pompom to scrub pots and pans and dishes.

These pompoms also are wonderful for all kinds of scrubbing—but find out for yourself. You'll be glad you did.

Organizing (see Storage Space, Organizing, p. 237; also see Drawers, organizing, p. 202, Pantry, organizing, p. 222 and Time, organizing, p. 242)

nylon
net
pompom

Oven, cleaning

A dirty oven's the absolute pits, a job we'd all like to avoid but . . .

To begin with, clean the inside of a glass oven door with baking soda on a damp cloth. It won't scratch the glass.

Recently, I was visiting with a neighbor and, after eating our get-together meal, we all helped clean up the kitchen.

She had a cookie sheet lined with foil in the bottom shelf of her oven on which something had overflowed from the shelf above. Ugh!

I was doing the oven. I looked at the soiled piece of foil and decided to save it.

I couldn't take the foil off the cookie sheet so I turned on the hot water and let it run over the foil without removing it. Then I picked up a soapy dish rag, ran it across the foil and, believe it or not, all the wrinkles came out of that foil and it molded to the cookie sheet.

All that was left to do was give it a quick rinse under the faucet, shake the water off and return the sheet, still foil-covered, to the oven.

To save yourself work, use a foil-covered cookie sheet on the lower rack in your oven. Sure saves cleaning the oven's bottom. Which, may I say (outside of defrosting a freezer), is about the most hateful job I know of when it comes to housekeeping . . .

If you're using a strong oven cleaner and don't have plastic gloves, improvise! Wear long plastic bread bags. Fasten 'em with a rubber band or a piece of tape. You can then use your cleaner or whatever without getting the gunk from the oven all over your arm.

When all through, roll the bag, scrubbing pad and all, down and off your hand and throw the whole thing in the garbage can.

Who says men aren't savvy about housework? You can't beat this tip from a New York bachelor:

"Instead of using cleaning rags to remove oven cleaner, I use crumpled-up newspaper. No need to rinse it out—just toss it out and reach for a new wad of crumpled paper when the old one gets messy."

Oven Racks, cleaning

Here's an easy way to do oven racks.

Put an old towel in your bathtub to protect the tub from scratches, and then lay the oven racks on it.

Cover the racks with very hot water, then sprinkle about one-half cup of automatic dishwasher detergent (not your liquid dishwashing detergent) over the racks.

Let them soak for awhile and the burned-on goop should wipe off easily. Try it, you'll like it.

From Idaho: "When cleaning oven racks, I place one on top of the other and by pushing one a little forward and to one side, I'm able to scrub both at the same time.

"I turn them over and do the undersides the same way."

This timesaver came from a Minnesota bride who credits her mother-in-law for it: "Cleaning oven racks is easy her way. First, place a bunch of sheets of newspaper down on the table or countertop to protect it. Then, put both oven racks on top of one another on the paper and spray your oven cleaner on the racks. Cover with some more sheets of paper.

"Now, clean the rest of your oven or have a cup of coffee. When you get around to cleaning the racks, they practically rinse clean by themselves."

From Nebraska: "My 'continuous-cleaning' oven works great except for the racks, and you know how dirty they can get.

"After years of broken fingernails, scratched fingers, and not really getting the racks clean, I learned to put them in a garbage bag, pour in a cup or two of ammonia, tie the bag securely and forget them overnight.

"When I take the racks out, I lay them in the bathtub on an old plastic tablecloth, run water over them and brush. Presto! Everything comes right off and they look like new."

A good idea but be sure little ones and pets can't get at them. —Heloise

Pans (see Pots and Pans, p. 224)

Paper Bags

A disco fan in New Mexico knows just what to do with an old spring-type record holder: "Place it under the sink and use it to store paper bags.

"Really keeps the bags neat and orderly."

From Vermont: "If you use grocery paper bags to line wastebaskets and find they collapse when you toss something in, try this:

"Just dampen a few inches of the top of the bag, then carefully fold over the top edge as many times as needed to fit the basket. This will make it stick to the side of the container and eliminates torn bags or messy misses."

Pantry, organizing (also see Storage Space, organizing, p. 237)

Everyone has his or her own methods and ideas on keeping house, most handed down from generation to generation—"the way momma did it is the way I do it."

So, consequently, I've followed in my mother's footsteps in storing canned goods. She found the best way to do it—by color.

Place all your canned green foods in one section and mark the edge of the shelf "green." Anything green which comes in a can should be located in this space: peas, green beans, asparagus, pickles . . . yes, even pickles. Here's why:

Let's pretend you're making a sandwich and you need pickles. Why move ketchup bottles, mayonnaise jars and such to find them?

No need to. Pickles are green, so look on the "green" shelf.

Same goes for the rest:

RED SHELF: beets, tomato sauce, cranberries, pimientos, cherries, and the like.

ORANGE SHELF: canned yams, carrots, peaches.

YELLOW SHELF: corn, pineapple.

WHITE SHELF: apples, applesauce, kraut, onions, pears, potatoes, mayonnaise.

Reserve one section for all canned meats. Another space for dried and boxed goods, such as biscuit mix, custard, rice, macaroni, etc.

Another point to remember: place items most often used at eye level or waist level for easier access.

Perhaps you will want to reserve a special place for spreads, which include anything that goes on a piece of bread, such as honey, jellies or jams.

We all have different amounts of cabinet space, but no matter how much we have, it's never enough, right?

So hopefully this will get you started on thinking and planning what will best serve your particular need.

I do believe you will find that a well-planned kitchen can save you many extra steps and minutes and, believe me, those minutes begin to add up especially on a day when you can't seem to spare a one.
—Heloise

Pastry Blender

I've discovered my pastry blender has many uses. It is great for cutting shortening into flour, but it can't be beat for mashing avocados, bananas, or any slightly soft food.

I use it for dips or anything that is too stiff for the blender, such as liver pâté, cream cheese, etc.

It is a good substitute wire whisk for beating eggs. Once you start using this handy little gadget, you will think up more and more uses for it.

My only regret is that it runs on elbow grease.

Pilot Light

From Louisiana: "To make a kitchen match long enough to light or relight a pilot light, twist a pipe cleaner around the end of the match.

"If the end of the pipe cleaner chars, no harm is done."

Plastic Wrap

From Vermont: "Plastic wrap that becomes frustrating when un-rolled, because it is so unruly, has always been one of my pet peeves.

"I've found that this helps:

"Try keeping it in the refrigerator, box and all, and the problem's solved. And it even adheres to the bowls, etc. a lot better."

Pots and Pans, cast-aluminum

So many people have problems with cast-aluminum pans that I have secured some good hints from a company that makes them.

So, just put the coffee pot on and sit down and let's learn something. OK?

Discoloration on the inside of any aluminum utensil is merely a coating or deposit of minerals on the surface of the metal and is absolutely harmless! Isn't that nice to know? It's comparable to tarnish on silver.

If you clean the pot with soap-filled pads each time you use it, you won't have this trouble.

However, if pans do discolor, add two tablespoons of cream of tartar to each quart of water and boil in the pan twenty minutes or more. Let stand until the water's cold. Then pour out and rub the pan with soap-filled steel wool pads and rinse well. That's all there is to it!

Don't store these pans with the lids on. This seals the moisture in and may cause white spots.

Never "boil out" any aluminum pot with soda, water softeners or cleansers containing alkali. These types of cleansers cause discoloration and, in time, pitting.

Don't let any aluminum utensil soak or remain in soapy water for long periods of time. This causes discoloration.

Don't immerse a very hot utensil in cold water. This can cause warping.

For grease burned on hammered surfaces, use a fine wire brush like the kind used for suede shoes. Mix pumice (bought at drug or paint store) with powdered soap and sprinkle it on the brush to make the job easier. (Never use the above mixture on nonstick or porcelain.)

Pots and Pans, cast-iron

Most of the cast-iron pots sold nowadays have already been pre-seasoned so they should not require first aid if you give 'em care.

For most cooking purposes, no further seasoning is necessary. All that is needed is to wash thoroughly, dry, and always lightly grease before storing.

But I'll bet a lot of you guys and gals have old utensils that have been handed down from your mothers and grandmothers and need re-seasoning.

Cast iron should never be scoured with powders. To scour them is to remove that very necessary seasoning.

Rust, discolored food or food that has a metallic taste are indications that the seasoning has been removed from the pores of the metal. You've got to re-season. Here's how:

First, clean all that old rust off, using a scouring pad only if necessary, then wash and dry. Next, coat the inside of the pan with a heavy film of unsalted grease (preferably suet) and don't forget to coat the lid, too.

Place the pan in the oven and leave it there for about two hours at the lowest possible temperature. It's a good idea to wipe more grease on the sides again after about an hour. Wash in good soapy suds and it should now be ready for use.

After each use, wash in warm, soapy water. Wipe thoroughly, dry, then coat the inside of the utensil with oil or shortening. Crumple up newspaper and put in the pan to absorb moisture. Turn the lid upside down on the pot to store.

When ready to use next time, wipe well with a paper towel. Grease again and cook food as usual.

Follow the plan of coating the utensil before and after using the first few times. Many successful cooks always coat the inside of a cast-iron utensil with grease before putting foods in to cook to help control the rust problem.

Be sure to keep in a dry place after use. Those of you who cook with gas will find that the heat of the oven pilot light makes the oven an ideal storage place.

With plenty of tender loving care your cast ironware should give you years of service.

Pots and Pans, cleaning (also see Aluminum Foil, p. 246)

Made a bet I could get all the burned-on gook off a friend's aluminum pan, cause I knew I'd win.

Here's what I did: I turned that old pot bottom-side-up, put an old terry washcloth over it and poured a half cup of ammonia on it.

Then I placed the whole thing in a large plastic bag and secured it tightly with a wire twistie so I wouldn't get "gassed." (Those fumes are murder!)

The next morning, I used a soap-filled pad and you should have seen that pan shine! My friend was simply delighted!

Even if you don't own a dishwasher, you should keep dishwasher detergent on hand because that stuff is dynamite. F'rinstance . . .

The next time you have a pan that needs soaking to loosen food, boil some water in the pan and add dishwasher detergent.

Saves time and fingernails! Never fails!

Pots and Pans, copper-bottom

For those of you who have copper-bottom pans, here's a cleaning quickie I use: Sprinkle table salt on the copper bottom and pour a little vinegar over it, then rub slightly.

Quick as a flash, it's gleaming again.

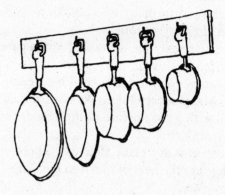

Pots and Pans, grease build-up

Don't let jobs pile up, especially not dirty pots and pans, friends, 'cause mark my words, you'll regret it! For example:

Grease goes on one coat at a time. Two coats take nearly twice as long to remove as one! Getting my message? If your pans have a build-up of black grease, try to estimate how many coats are built up. Then you can just about guess how long it's going to take you to clean it—a long, long time!

When you don't get off that grease the first time, it cooks and cooks and cooks and gets all the harder to remove.

So, clean those pots and pans after each and every use.

And put a little zip into that elbow grease, you sweet chickens. There's nothing like a nice clean pot, unless it's a clean home . . .

Pots and Pans, mineral deposit

Do you spend extra time cleaning the mineral deposit left by hard water on the bottom part of your glass double-boiler?

Add a little vinegar to the water in the bottom part of the boiler next time you're using it; sure enough, it will wash clean as a dish with no strain on your part.

Pots and Pans, nonstick finish

One of the problems with pots and pans that have a nonstick finish is that they discolor and turn dark. I checked this out and discovered why. Using them at high temperatures causes this problem. They shouldn't be used at temperatures over 450° F—so watch out, especially when using baking pans with a nonstick finish.

Greasy film also mars the way a non-stick finish looks. I think some folks are afraid to use soap and water on these pans! It won't hurt. What you've got to watch out for: steel wool and scouring powder. They head the no-no list.

For a stubborn spot or a bit of stuck-on food, detergent suds and my nylon net pompom (see p. 217) work like a charm.

To clean away burned-on food, soak the pan in water or boil some water in it to soften the burned-on stuff, then go over the pan with the nylon-net pompom or a rubber scraper until the burned-on gook comes loose.

To remove stains from a nonstick finish, try this formula: Mix two tablespoons of baking powder with one-half cup of chlorine bleach and a cup of water. Put this in the stained pot (double the formula for big pots) and boil for about ten minutes. This should remove stains nicely. Don't let the bleach mixture boil over, or it could spot the outside finish of the pot.

Wash the pan thoroughly with soap and water, then dry it. Before cooking with it, pour a little vegetable oil on a paper towel and wipe it over the non-stick finish.

Pots and pans, storing (see Meat Trays, plastic foam, p. 257)

Recipes

From Wisconsin: "I've collected so many yummy recipes through the years that I needed a larger file box. The lunch box my daughter had outgrown proved perfect . . . holds a lot of cards, too."

Here's a nifty tip from a Utah mother who gets her best recipes from the backs of food packages, bottles and cans:

"If I was paid for the compliments I've received on my pumpkin pie, I'd be rich. I got the recipe from the back of a can.

"When the manufacturer gives a recipe for a product, you can bet it's good."

And you can bet this cook's a smartie. Read those labels, guys and gals, and you'll come up with the greatest recipes ever.—Heloise

Refrigerator, cleaning

When you call a repairman to fix an appliance, for goodness sakes, watch and see what he does because you could learn a thing or two.

My fridge was making noise like the whirrr and tap, tap, tap of a woodpecker, and was frosting up badly.

Lo and behold, when the repairman took off the front plate, if there wasn't enough dust in it to stuff a pillow!

The dust build-up, which I should have removed at least every two or three months, caused it to heat up and I had to have a whole new part.

So that this doesn't happen to you, friends, here's what to do:

Just remove the bottom panel, called the kick plate. (I found it easier to remove and replace with the fridge door open.)

The condenser is housed in back of the plate. Just clean it with the suction wand of your vacuum, then replace the kick plate.

If this little cleaning job is done properly, according to the instructions, it will keep the motor in good condition.

Your fridge may not be the same type as mine and you may never have this trouble, but do get your instruction manual out and check this out. Quicker yet, look on top of your kick plate! The repairman pointed to a big label that warns about this very thing!

Where there's a will, there's an easy way to do that job you dislike. Like how about this nifty idea from a grandmother in Nebraska:

"After growing tired of dusting the top of my refrigerator because it is hard to reach, I got a brainstorm. I covered it with a towel.

"Now I never have to dust the top of the refrigerator. I just change the towel as needed."

A husband in Maryland had this neat notion: "Take your snow brush out of the car and use it for cleaning under the refrigerator.

"The long handle and narrow brush are great for getting into those hard-to-reach spots."

From New York: "I tried to figure out how to clean the coils on the back of my refrigerator since I can't move it.

"Then I got an idea. I used a long-handled car brush (the kind you use to wash the car) to clean the inside and outside of the coils.

"I even sprayed a little dust remover on the brush before using it. I cleaned the wires and tubes near the coils also."

Refrigerator, defrosting

A helpful husband in Texas had this idea: "Use a trigger spray bottle filled with hot water to aid in the final defrosting of your refrigerator.

"It sure cuts the ice near the upper coils, reducing the time needed for the job."

You'll cut defrosting time way down if you put a pan of hot water either inside your freezer box (but not on the coils or plastic parts!) or the top shelf of the fridge (if it's near enough to the bottom of the freezer box to do the trick). Or use a hand-hold dryer and it works like a charm.

Refrigerator, odors

Get rid of refrigerator odors by sponging off shelves bins and walls with baking soda on a damp sponge.

Roaches (see Roaches, p. 177)

Rolling Pin

From Rhode Island: "Hollow, plastic rolling pins, designed to be filled with cold water, make ideal beverage containers that fit easily into a golf bag.

"Simply fill (leaving a little room for expansion) with your favorite non-carbonated beverage the night before.

"Place in the freezer and you will have an ice-cold drink ready when you really need one on the course.

"On especially hot days wrap the pin in a terry towel to keep the contents from thawing too fast."

To keep your rolling pin clean, store it in a plastic bag.

Put one handle through a small hole you've made in the unopened end and fasten the other end of the wrapper around the handle with one of those wire twisters.

Rubber Gloves

From Ohio: "Here is a little hint to help prolong the life of your rubber gloves:

"Because rubber gloves are more apt to tear at the fingertips, I turn them inside out and attach a piece of adhesive tape on finger areas that receive the most wear. Then I turn the gloves right side out again and they're ready to wear."

From Kentucky: "It sometimes is hard to remove rubber gloves. I found that if I run cold water over my gloves I can peel them off quick as a flash."

Salad Bowls, wooden

Here is what I have learned about getting rid of the gummy stickiness on the inside of wooden salad bowls:

Use raw walnuts or pecans as cleaners. First, crack the nut and remove the meat. Break the meat in half and use the broken side to rub away on those icky, sticky bowls.

I have learned, too, that those of you who have beautiful wood-paneled walls with scratches on them can use this same idea. Just wipe with a soft cloth after rubbing with the nut meat, and that's all there is to it.

Here's another little trick for protecting wooden salad bowls. After washing quickly in lukewarm water, dry thoroughly, then rub the entire bowl briskly inside and out with wax paper. This keeps the surface of the wooden bowl sealed.

Remember, always wash a wooden salad bowl *immediately* after using it. Never set it aside on the drainboard with all the other dishes you intend to do in the morning. Absolutely ruins 'em . . .

And don't, repeat luvs, don't fill that messy salad bowl with water and leave it in the sink. Talk about warped wood . . .

Silverware, cleaning

No need to rush out and buy silver polish because your sterling's tarnished . . . there's a budget way to take care of the problem. In fact, there are two budget ways . . .

One: fill an aluminum pan with water, then stir in a teaspoon of baking soda. Lay your silver flat in the pan, then place the pan on the stove and heat it for a few minutes. Don't boil, just heat.

When you take the silver out of the pan, the tarnish will have transferred itself to the pan—and a pan is a lot easier to clean, right? Your silver will be tarnish-free but a bit on the dull side. Not to worry. Buff it with a soft cloth and you'll get instant shine.

Two: make your own silver polish. My chemistry teacher friend, Tony Wedig, gave me the formula:

Just mix powdered white chalk and enough ammonia to make a paste . . . then apply just as you would regular silver polish.

And guess what Tony says? This is the formula they use to clean the Queen of England's silver. Doesn't it beat everything?

Know what I say? What's good enough for Buckingham Palace is good enough for thee and me.

For ever-ready, on-the-spot cleaning of silverware, fill a small decorative cosmetic jar (empty, of course) with a little silver polish, and leave it on your counter.

With a nylon net (see Nylon Net, p. 217), my favorite scrubber-dubber, it's easy to attack those stains as they occur. Just plunge the

wet fork, or whatever, into the silver polish and rub with the nylon net. Rinse and dry.

You'll never have an "all-at-once" big silverware-cleaning chore to do, if you clean as you go along.

From Nevada: "I always help clean the silverware at home but have trouble with tarnished forks.

"I found if I wrap a cloth with silver polish on it around a knife and use it to get between the tines, this job's a snap."

From Mississippi: "For years, whenever silver polish became hard and dry, I just threw it away. What a waste!

"Now I add warm water and stir it until it's nice and creamy again. Works like new."

From South Dakota: "When I empty my dishwasher I don't put the silverware basket back in the washer.

"I leave it out on the drainboard and, as the silver is used, I put each piece into the basket right then. (If you have a family, teach them to do the same.)

"This way, all one has to do is rinse basket and silver under the faucet and place in the washer in one fell swoop."

Here's a real nifty idea I came across in a roadside café recently, and I am sure it could be used in every household.

Wrap your silverware—a knife, fork, and spoon—together in a paper napkin and store them that way. Then they can either be slapped on a table quickly or picked up by anyone in a hurry. I watched a waitress do this. Clever, huh?

But that isn't all! Do you know what else she did? (She was a real smart one, what.) She wet her fingertips in a bowl of water before picking up the paper napkin to wrap the silverware. The moisture on her fingers made it easy to grasp.

Why can't we homebodies do this, too, before we store our silver back in the drawer? Then, instead of doing four jobs (picking up knife, fork, spoon and napkin out of the drawer and putting them back later) we'd get it down to one!

Here's a sterling idea from an Iowa mother who knows there is more than one way to skin a cat: "Had an old sterling silver ice bucket, and since the kids hate putting the silverware in the drawer when they take it out of the dishwasher, I let them put it in the bucket instead.

"Saves time and drawer space and the bucket can just be carried to the table when setting it."

Sink

Here's an idea improvised by a clever husband in Delaware:
"The kitchen sink is set for my wife's height and is too low for me.
"So I have an old discarded plastic dishpan that I put in the sink, upside down, and set the real dishpan on it—which makes it just right to avoid a cramped back from bending over."

From Mississippi: "My stainless steel sink is blooming like a flower garden and is the talk of the neighborhood!
"I decorated it with those little floral decals that are used in the bottom of bathtubs to avoid slipping. You just can't imagine what a bright, blooming, colorful sink I have!"

From New Mexico: "I found myself constantly turning on the hot water in my kitchen sink to rinse things during the day when cold water would have done as well.
"To solve this, I put a piece of red tape on the cold water faucet. This attracts my attention to it when reaching to turn the water on.
"Saves a lot of hot water and electric bills."

Sink, stainless steel

In normal use, the secret of keeping a stainless steel sink clean and new-looking is to wipe it out with a damp cloth, then dry it with a soft cloth.

If it needs a more thorough cleaning, use a solution of ammonia and water or dishwashing detergent and water.

If it's stained, use rubbing alcohol or baking soda, then wash the sink thoroughly with detergent and hot water.

Dry thoroughly to avoid spots, especially if the water is hard.

Never use a gritty abrasive cleaner on a stainless steel sink as it will mar the finish and make cleaning even more difficult.

If water spots or hard water build-up have dulled your sink, wipe it out with vinegar, then flush well with water. Buff with a dry cloth until it shines.

Once the surface of the sink is clean, try polishing it with mineral oil on a soft cloth, again buffing with a dry cloth afterward.

As I said in the beginning, the main thing is to wipe the sink out after each use. Keep a dry cloth handy and remind everyone to use it, even though only clean water has been run in the sink, because when the water evaporates, mineral deposits are left. They mean spots and eventually a dull finish.

Sink Mat

From Texas: "I have made a discovery . . .

"After trying unsuccessfully to clean the rubber mat used in my kitchen sink. I tried soaking it overnight in one-fourth cup of household bleach and water to cover.

"Worked great!"

Skewers

From Kentucky: "A clear, large-size empty bottle that contained effervescent medicinal tablets makes a wonderful container for the short skewers you use to hold a fowl closed when roasting.

"You can easily see them and they don't get lost."

From Louisiana: "When you empty your next spice jar (with a plastic shaker top), wash it, dry it, and replace the top.

"Drop your trussing skewers through the holes. They won't go all the way through.

"Place the jar on the spice rack next to the poultry seasoning. No more rummaging through the drawer with greasy fingers looking for those skewers next time you're stuffing the bird."

Spatula, rubber

When your rubber spatula gets battered edges, trim them off and it will be good for many more cooking sessions.

After several trimmings, when it's down to the lean and narrow, it still can be used to scrape out the contents of small narrow-necked bottles.

Spices (see Grocery Shopping, spices, p. 211)

Sponges

From Kentucky: "Put that much used—and abused—kitchen sponge into the dishwasher (on the top shelf) once a week to keep it smelling sweet. Or toss your sponges into the washing machine— but not the dryer."

I have a neighbor who keeps not one, but two sponges on his kitchen sink. One is used for rinsing, the other for washing. He keeps a few drops of liquid detergent on the washing sponge. Now I'm doing the same.

It's great when the dishwasher is full of dishes and there is no room for the pots and pans. I just take my soapy sponge, which I covered with nylon net (see Nylon Net, p. 217), and scrub out the scrambled egg skillet, mashed potato pot, etc., then rinse with the other one.

You are going to be mighty surprised at how long the soap in that extra scrub sponge will last.

Helps keep the kitchen clean, too, and reduces the clutter, because you'll find you wash each pan immediately after using it and put it away right then.

And so it goes . . .

From Idaho: "Want to keep the sponge dry between usings?

"Take a heavy darning needle and thread it with heavy string or cord and poke the needle through the dry sponge. Then push the needle back through about an inch from where it went in and tie the ends of the cord together. Gives you a nice loop to hang the sponge up with.

"I have two cup-screws on the inside of the cupboard door and hang my sponges on them—one color for the dish sponge, the other for the mop sponge."

Spray Bottle

When the suction tube of a spray bottle isn't reaching the liquid, drop a handful of glass marbles in the bottle. This raises the level of liquid and you're in business again.

Keeps the marbles off the floors, too!

Squeegee

From Nevada: "The small rubber squeegee that I use on my windows is excellent for scraping the crumbs off my tablecloth."

Stainless Steel, cleaning (see Sink, stainless steel, p. 234)

Stapler

From Minnesota: "I keep a small stapler in my kitchen to staple shut the tops of potato chip and cookie bags."

Steel Wool Pads

From Georgia: "To keep soap-filled steel wool pads from rusting, I wrap them in plastic wrap and place in the freezer.

"This way I can use them over and over many times."

Storage Space, organizing (also see Drawers, organizing, p. 202 and Pantry, organizing, p. 222)

Have you ever taken a look at the shelves in your kitchen cabinets? A mess, eh?

Well, let's take a few minutes and see what's wrong with those low-down shelves.

Take everything out of all those bottom cabinets and spread it all out on your kitchen floor.

Then, stand back and look at all that stuff!

You will die laughing . . .

Here's a pan that you never use, but just hate to part with because you've had it so long. Why keep it? It just clutters up your cabinet and makes it harder to find the things you do use.

You don't need fifteen pans, anyway (and this is average!). You don't have fifteen burners in your home to cook on! Ever stop to think of that?

Here's the secret:

If you are one who can't bear to throw things away . . . at least divide 'em up. Put things you haven't used in a year in one pile and set this aside to store in less easily-reached cabinets or, better yet, to discard. Don't put these things back in your convenient cabinet.

I like to line my cabinet shelves with foil. It reflects light and wipes clean easily with a sponge.

Now, take some antiseptic and make a solution with water (read the directions on the bottle), and wash the inside of all your cabinets thoroughly. It's supposed to be a fact that roaches are anti-antiseptic and won't walk across it.

If you do have roaches, now is the time to spray some bug stuff in the cabinets. It's easy. They are empty and you can do it twice as fast. Besides, no use to do one cabinet at a time. When a roach finds one cabinet fumigated, it just runs across to the next one.

The shelves (especially if they're wood) should first be lined with wax paper. This keeps the foil or shelf paper from sticking to the paint. Then put your foil over this.

I line shelves with triple layers of paper or foil, one on top of the other. This way, when the top paper gets soiled, all I have to do is roll it up and remove it, revealing a clean layer of foil underneath. To do this, remove a few articles from the cabinet and pull up the end of the top layer of foil. Continue across the shelf, rolling back the paper a little at a time (and replacing the articles) until the entire soiled top paper has been removed.

By using this method, you will save yourself many hours next time you have to clean your shelves.

I also find when lining shelves (especially those which contain canned goods or pots and pans), that if you will put a newspaper under the foil it cushions it and makes the foil last longer.

Some women use linoleum, oilcloth, or adhesive-backed paper to line shelves. All good ideas!

Now, let's start to replace our pans.

First, use the "hidden" space in the back of the cabinets for those odd pans seldom used.

In front of them, put the pans you use more frequently.

Then, pick up the ones you use all the time. Your favorite skillet, a big saucepan, and two small ones—and place 'em where you can reach 'em pronto.

Put one inside the other and put them in the most convenient place in your cabinet. This will be at the front of the cabinet nearest the stove.

It takes two, three, but never more than four pans to cook a meal (remember, you don't have more than four burners and can't possibly use more), so keep this stack light.

Try to adapt yourself to new ideas. If we didn't, we would still be boiling our clothes over a wood fire!

From Washington, D.C.: "My daughter stores all of her spray bottles, polishes and cleaning gear in two shoe bags which she hangs on each side of the stairway going to the basement. This is so handy, yet out of the way."

From Texas: "Here are a few ideas about how to make better use of the space underneath your sink:

"Take one of those plastic vegetable bins that has one side lower than the other sides and, by maneuvering it, place it underneath the garbage disposal or those pesky drain pipes that take up so much room.

"You can use this as a catch-all for sponges, pads, rubber gloves —whatever.

"Next, take two spring-type, expandable curtain rods with rubber tips.

"Place one in front and one behind the pipes or disposal, high enough to be above bottles, etc.

"The front rod can hold the roll of paper towels or even that oversized roll of tin foil.

"With some drapery hooks, you can hang brushes or even awkward-sized utensils.

"You will probably even have room to store those seldom-used appliances or large vases. I keep my cutting board propped up against the wall.

"You really can use that space efficiently if you put your mind to it."

Stove, cleaning (also see Ammonia, p. 192)

Here's an idea that will save you hours of scrubbing:

At least once a day (whenever you are doing your main meal dishes), you should pick up two of the grates on your stove and the drip pans underneath them, and plop 'em in the dishwasher before you start it. If you have no dishwasher, then wash two of 'em along with your dishes each night.

Amazingly, these parts come clean in a jiffy, because spills haven't "cooked" into them.

But, the best part is: you still have two burners in workable condition on the stove, and no one in the family will complain, because they can use those two.

Try to remember not to wash all of the top stove parts in any one day because then it becomes a big chore.

No more dishpan hands roughed up by steel wool pads and, instead of taking hours to get the grates clean, they are done in seconds.

I asked a chemist friend of mine why it sometimes takes us so long to clean a stove. his answer was that carbon, grease spots and spills go on one coat at a time and, if you let them add up, must be taken off that way. He's right

From Maine: "Save squeezed lemons and grapefruit shells, put in a jar and close. Store in the fridge.

"When you get grease splatters on your stove, take one of the shells out of its jar, run hot water over it and scrub the spot with the inside part. Grease Comes off and—a bonus—leaves a nice clean smell."

Stove, safety

From Illinois: "Children sometimes are severely burned when they turn on the stove and their clothes catch on fire.

"Well, I solved that problem when my child was two. He began to get up in the morning and go downstairs while I was still asleep.

"I always worried that he'd turn the stove on, so before I went to bed at night, I took off the knobs and put them in the cupboard. The next morning, I put them back on."

Table, kitchen

If you are using your kitchen table and need extra eating space for the children's snack, pull out a lower cupboard drawer, place a cookie sheet on the top and close the drawer until the cookie sheet fits tightly and you have an "instant table."

Cookie sheets with edges or rims work best.

From Montana: "When we needed to put the leaf in our kitchen table, we found the underneath rail had rusted from spills and stuck.

"After getting the table open we applied a thin coat of petroleum jelly to the rail. It did the trick."

Tea Kettle, cleaning (see Lime Deposits, p. 214)

Telephone

Know what you can't have too much of? Telephone cord. The longer, the better, I say, 'cause it lets you move around.

I've given the dishes a dunking, hustled up a meal, and even taken a swipe at cleaning the refrigerator . . . all the while talking on the kitchen extension.

Couldn't do this if I had a short cord that kept me glued to one spot, now could I?

Thermos Bottle (see Vacuum Bottle, p. 243)

Time, organizing

From Louisiana: "To organize my time more efficiently, I have 'in' days and 'out' days.

"I reserve my 'in' days for housework, extra baking, painting, etc.

"On an 'out' day I try to do all my errands. If a doctor's appointment has to be made, I choose an 'out' day for it.

"It doesn't always work, but aiming for it helps keep me more organized and I seem to avoid that panicky 'no time' feeling."

Tobacco

From Florida: "Your suggestion to keep tobacco in a plastic bag, twisted shut, and replaced in the original can was very good for keeping the tobacco fresh.

"My husband, a chemist, always insists that I keep our can of freshly ground coffee in the refrigerator to keep the flavor at its peak. It worked so well that I suggested we do the same with his tobacco. It was a 'real cool' idea."

Towels

The best place I know to hang a hand towel in the kitchen is on the refrigerator door handle where it's handy as can be.

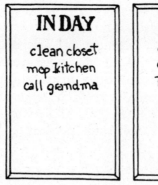

Transparent Wrap (see Plastic Wrap, p. 224)

Trash Bag (also see Garbage, p. 206)

From Oregon: "After helping my sister-in-law empty trash into one of those large plastic trash bags and hearing her tell about spilling it when she does this chore herself, I showed her how I got an 'extra hand' for this chore:

"I open a drawer or cupboard door, put the edge of the bag in it, close it, and have a 'third' hand to help one of mine hold the sack open while I use the other one to empty the trash.

"It's a lot easier than cleaning up spills."

Vacuum Bottle

From Vermont: "My husband has a stainless steel vacuum bottle which was stained with coffee.

"Nothing I did would remove this stain until I tried soaking it with hot water and two tablespoons of automatic dishwasher detergent for about a half hour.

"A few swishes with a bottle brush and it was spotless."

Vase, cleaning

Place a little automatic dishwasher detergent in a dirty bud vase. Then fill the vase with water and leave overnight. Wunderbar!

Next morning, all you have to do is rinse for a sparkling-clean vase. Even gets out the dregs at the bottom!

To remove a stain in the bottom of a cut glass vase or vinegar cruet, put some water in the cruet, drop in one denture cleanser tablet and watch it clean beautifully.

Vinegar Cruet, cleaning (see Cruets, p. 198 and Vase, cleaning, Walls, cleaning (see Walls, cleaning, p. 183 and Ammonia, p. 192; also see Spotcheck Chart, p. 377)

Water

From Minnesota: "I have a pet peeve that just bugs me silly. It concerns keeping a water jug in the fridge. It's bad enough in the winter, but in the summer that door opening and closing all the time drives me bonkers.

"First, the door is opened to get the jug out, the glass of ice cold water's poured and the door is opened again to put the jug back in. Kids don't seem to like to open and close the door, so they open it and leave it open while they pour their drink.

"And to top the whole thing off, the once in a great while that I want a cold drink, the last person who took one didn't take time to refill the jug!

"Well, this problem irritated me to the point where I just had to find the answer. And you know, the answer was so close, it almost bit me!

"I got into the habit of saving empty baby-food jars—saving them for what I didn't know, I just thought sure they would come in handy for something, and come in handy they did!

"I ran all the jars I had through the dishwasher and after they had cooled, I filled each one with water and put the lid on. (This keeps out any refrigerator odors.) Then I placed all the jars on a low shelf so they could be reached by every member of the family, including youngsters.

"All my kids have to do is open the refrigerator door, remove a jar, close the door, drink and put the jar on the counter to be put through the dishwasher.

"I have found this to be not only sanitary, but less work for me. I don't have to stop what I'm doing to get a drink for the littlest child who can't handle the large jug. I am defrosting less often and when I want a cool drink, there is always one available.

"I often surprise the clan and instead of water in all the jars, I put fruit juice in some of them.

"My individual water jars have worked wonders and so far the only problem I have had was when I first started this and my nine-year-old brought all the neighborhood kids in to have a cold drink."

If that little one really wants a drink of water in the middle of the night and not just reassurances from mom and dad, here's a terrific idea:

Save all those plastic containers you get at your favorite drive-in —the kind that sodas, milkshakes, etc., come in with the plastic top and straw that fits through the lid.

Take them home—wash well and store. They are just the thing for a drink of water you can put on his bedside table to solve that midnight thirst problem.

The water is covered, so there is no danger of spills in the middle of the night.

PART II: SECOND TIME AROUND: KITCHEN RECYCLE

INTRODUCTION

Sometimes packaging gets me all riled up. It's such a waste.

Ever buy some iddy biddy thing that was factory-packaged in a box four or five times bigger than it needed to be?

What a waste . . .

. . . of materials,

. . . of shelf space,

. . . and of money!

That's your money I'm talking about 'cause you're paying for the whole kit and caboodle.

Not to mention all the paper and cardboard packaging that you toss out in the trash . . . or the trees that got chopped down to produce that packaging!

Doesn't it make you furious?

Know what I do when I find packaging that's wasteful? I sit down and write the manufacturer a letter and give him a piece of my mind, and some chapters and verse on conservation.

Bet if everyone did the same, things would change because manufacturers want to please the public. And know who the public is? That's you and me.

But it's not just manufacturers who are wasteful. Almost everyone is a little . . . or maybe even a lot.

Land sakes, the useful things that get the old heave-ho. But, know something? Before they throw something out, people are beginning to take a second look, maybe even a third, and they're asking themselves an important question: "Couldn't I use this for something?" Nine times out of ten the answer is "Yes."

Not only folks on tight budgets are doing this . . . everyone is.

I was reading a story on thrift tips in the newspaper. And guess who the reporter was interviewing? Society women.

One of them, the wife of a chairman of the board, said she reused plastic vegetable bags . . . even as you and I do, friends. Another woman, president of her own company, allowed that she washed out aluminum foil, sometimes using the same piece two or three times.

Sure makes you think. If women who can afford not to, practice thrift, why, Heloise help us, we all should, because if you save pennies, the nickels, dimes and dollars take care of themselves.

A good place to start saving pennies is in the kitchen. It's a gold mine of things you can use, re-use and use some more.

Bet a penny you've thought of some of the ideas that follow . . . but I'll bet lots more that many of these nifty thrifties are brand new to you.—Hugs 'n' kisses, Heloise

Aluminum Foil

From Idaho: "Instead of throwing away used aluminum foil, I use it as a pot and pan scrubber.

"I was out of the soap-filled pads one day and found I could do a great job scrubbing away burned-on pudding by sprinkling a little cleanser on the wet pan, loosely crumbling a small square of the foil into a ball, and using it as I would a soap pad.

"It sure comes in handy between shopping days. The foil can be thrown away afterward, or rinsed and re-used."

Bags, mesh

From New Jersey: "The mesh bags onions come in can be used for gift bags.

"Cut both ends straight, fasten one end with an elastic band, tie with a ribbon and fill with small things such as cookies, candy, toilet articles, playing cards or fruit. Fasten the top with another elastic band and ribbon."

From Indiana: "I found the handiest kitchen helper and it didn't cost me a cent! I used to use a brush to scrub fruits and vegetables. When it wore out, I got the bright idea of using the mesh bag onions come in.

"I just slip it over my hand like a glove. Found if you wear one on each hand the work goes much faster."

Bags, plastic

The plastic bags with holes that vegetables come in are wonderful for the beach.

Simply put a string through the top and make a draw-string bag. When the toys are covered with sand, put them in the bag and swish it through water. All clean in a jiffy! Then the bag with toys can be hung to dry outdoors on a convenient nail or hook.

Baskets, bushel

From Maryland: "A bushel basket makes a great basketball hoop.

"Cut out the bottom and nail the basket up someplace, and you'll have a very good substitute for a regular hoop and net."

Baskets, plastic

You know those plastic baskets that strawberries and tomatoes come in?

When you have outdoor barbecues, use the baskets to serve potato chips, corn chips, etc.

Bottles, bleach

If there was no such thing as a plastic bleach bottle, somebody'd have to invent one. So help me, Heloise, they would! Once empty, the things folks use 'em for. Just blows my mind, it does.

First, they soap-and-water wash them out ("thoroughly" is the key word). Then—why you won't believe the uses they put them to. And it's all for free . . . That's the best part.

To give just a sampling of their multi-uses:

F'rinstance, they are teachers' pets:

A gym instructor on the New Jersey shore has her students fill small empty bleach bottles with sand to make dumbbells.

A Kansas basketball coach has his cheerleaders cut them in half and use the tops as megaphones.

A Pennsylvania kindergarten teacher got her tots to bring 'em in, cut off the tops, and use the bottoms as crayon caddies.

This same crafty gal had another idea: at Christmas, her kindergarteners cut the sides of these versatile bottles into stars, Santas, and wreaths. Zingo! A present mom and dad can hang on the tree.

They are great outdoors, sure as shooting they are.

Don't you just love this idea from a freshman who earned his college spending money berry-picking all summer?

"I cut the top off a plastic bleach bottle, leaving the handle intact. Then I tapered the front of the bottle down to about the halfway mark. I ran my belt through the handle of the jug (now a berry container) and had both hands free for nonstop berry-picking."

A green-thumbed Vermont gardener cuts them up to make shields

for small plants. She also cuts some in one-inch strips to make plant markers.

If you do this, use a waterproof pen to write the name of the seedlings.

And in a New York apartment, a bachelor who says water that seeped through clay saucers made his metal windowsill rust, has found a solution: "I've got everyone in our laundry room saving me those big bleach jugs . . . I cut 'em off and make leak-proof saucers for my plants."

The big scoop on bleach jugs is in the kitchen. Can't tell you how many homemakers here, there and everywhere cut them into scoops for flour, sugar and rice. And a clever mom in Montana turned two into scoops for her children's sandbox.

A mother in Oregon saves 'em up and, instead of wasting money on "loot bags" when her daughter has a birthday party, she gives each homebound guest a "bleach bottle basket" filled with goodies.

"Part of the pre-party fun is stapling handles in place and decorating each basket with the guest's name and whatever design strikes my seven-year-old's fancy," she says.

Talk about kitchen capers, a thrifty bride in Missouri cut a big circle out of the side of a giant bleach bottle and now it's a vegetable bin for onions—easy to grab too because it has a handle!

This same penny-saver made a set of nesting bowls out of large, medium-size and small bleach bottles. Now I ask you, is that smart or isn't it? Sure takes the cake.

And here's another zinger, one I love because I've sure wasted lots of soap powder because it spilled out when a box tipped over.

"I pour soap powder out of its box and into a bleach bottle (you need to use a funnel). It makes a detergent container I can cap so it positively won't spill."

A Hawaiian handyman uses the bottom of one of these jugs as a caddy for tools; a Tennessee teen as a catch-all for rollers. A Georgia fisherman says they make great floats and, when filled with cement, super anchors.

A hot rodder in Pennsylvania cuts a hole in the side of an empty bleach bottle and uses it when changing oil to catch the dirty stuff. "And in the summer," he says. "I always keep a water-filled bleach bottle in the car in case my radiator needs a drink."

Sure beats everything, doesn't it? But my very favorite tip of all —it's such a super problem solver—is this one from a home handyman in Maine:

"During cold spells I let the faucet drip so the pipes wouldn't freeze . . . but then the sink got rusty. Not any more.

"I took a bleach bottle (any plastic bottle would do), cut the bottom out and made a giant funnel. I placed the cap end of the bottle (cap removed) in the sink drain.

"Got the picture? The water drips into the funnel and right down the drain. No more rust spots."

Now does that rate an "I" for Ingenious or doesn't it? In my book, it sure does!

Bottles, glass

From Utah: "I created interesting additions to my collection of "window bottles," as you call them, by using leftover antiquing paint on nicely shaped liquor and juice bottles.

"I followed the instructions for antiquing furniture and had wonderful results.

"I used gold paint on raised areas, tops and corks. The antiquing gives the bottles a lovely wood grain effect."

Bottles, milk, plastic (also see Bottles, bleach p. 248)

From Iowa: "We had a covered-dish luncheon at a family gathering. For an easy way to carry the dish she prepared, my niece cut off the top half of a clean plastic milk bottle. She covered the lower part with foil and brought up the edges of the foil around the sides of the "bowl" and neatly tucked them inside at the top of the bowl.

"I had to look real hard to see that it wasn't a silver dish, and the best part was that she didn't have to take it home again."

Bottles, mustard

From Texas: "Recently, before going on a picnic, an idea struck me . . . I use the mustard bottle with a pump, and had saved some empty ones. I decided to use one for mayonnaise, one for jelly and another for ketchup.

"They were handy and everyone liked the idea."

Bottles, squeeze

Keep cooking oil in a clean squeeze bottle, the kind liquid margarine comes in.

It's much easier than trying to twist off an oil bottle cap with messy hands. A plus: the squeeze bottle takes less shelf space than most oil bottles do.

A plastic squeeze bottle with the tip on top makes a terrific baster! (Be sure to wash and rinse it well first.) All you do is squeeze and draw in the juice and squirt away.

Be sure the top is on tight so it won't leak.

Bottles, tops

From Mississippi: "Save the dispenser top of a liquid dish detergent bottle and replace the regular shampoo bottle top with this cap. Then it will be a simple matter to shake out an application without spilling it.

From Maine: "If your teenagers are like mine and never put the tops back on shampoo bottles, toothpaste, etc., do what I do:

"I save tops in a bag—all kinds, all sizes, all shapes. I can always find one to fit a capless bottle or tube. How's that for one-upmanship?"

Boxes, cake

From Washington, D.C.: "I live in a small apartment and do not have room for a lot of extras.

"One of the things that I do without is a cake holder. Instead, I recycle a cardboard bakery cake box!

"I just turn the box upside down and set the cake down on the inside of the cover.

"The box then becomes a lid, and covers the cake completely. When I want to cut a piece, all I have to do is lift up the lid and I don't have to take the cake out of the box."

Boxes, cereal

From Vermont: "I cut an empty cereal box in half, covered it with flowered paper and used the bottom as a holder for 45 rpm records."

Burner Covers, foil

From Kansas: "When you buy foil covers to keep your stove burners clean, don't keep throwing them away and buying new ones. Just re-cover them with clean aluminum foil and they are good as new again."

Cans, potato chip

If you think a tube-shaped potato chip can is only a potato chip can, you're right off your ever lovin' rocker. Once the chips are down—and eaten—the empty can has lots of possibilities.

Who knows better than your friend Heloise? I've got stacks of letters to prove it. Know what I think? Some people buy chips just for the can!

F'rinstance:

A craftsman in North Carolina uses chip cans to package the ceramic vases he ships to customers.

A Wisconsin family finds them the moisture-proof, space-saving, unbreakable answer for storing staples in their camper. They label them so they'll know the contents.

A Florida grandma says they get her home-baked cookies off to her granddaughter at college with nary a break or a crumb.

In Mississippi, a thrifty mom says she uses one as a lunchbox for her daughter: "I drop her milk money in the bottom, followed by a small apple, a sandwich cut in rectangles (packed one atop the other), a few wrapped cookies and a napkin."

And, guess what? On the way home from school, her daughter rolls test papers and pops them in her "lunch box."

In New Mexico, a new mom finds a tube-type chip can will hold exactly three jars of baby food and "the paper padding keeps them from breaking." She pops them in her diaper bag, then refrigerates them when she gets to grandma's. If that's not using the old noodle, what is?

All over the USA folks are using them as canisters for such things as bread crumbs, flour, biscuits, sugar. The trick is to cover them with adhesive-backed paper so they've got eye appeal, then tack on a label of contents.

A kindergarten teacher collects them to make individual crayon kits for her moppets.

And there are lots and lots and lots of other uses, I'm sure you've just thought of one, two or more.

Bet you didn't realize how "canny" people were. I'm the same way myself. There's something about a nicely sized can, jar or package that starts those wheels turning. If I think hard enough, I usually think up a good use for it. You can too. Remember, waste not, want not.

Cans, tabs from

From Massachusetts: "With the help of our friends we saved dozens of soft-drink-can tabs and strung them together forming chains of different lengths. Then the fun began in our playroom.

"We hung the longer chains vertically in the doorway and used the shorter ones to curtain a window. Gives us plenty of light and privacy as well.

"Sweeping through the chains makes you feel like you are entering a really festive spot! They add so much pattern and interest to the room that we're tickled pink with our idea."

Cartons, milk

From New Hampshire: "When you know you're going to move, start saving milk cartons. When empty, rinse, dry thoroughly and store away. Pack odd shaped dishes, vases, knicknacks, jars, small statues, even silverware in them when ready to move.

"I've even put plants in the half-gallon containers. You can use the quart size to pack glasses, using tissue, newspaper or paper towels to cushion them."

From Alaska: "When I have a lunch box to fill, I cut a milk carton down to the size I need and use it to pack salads, desserts, etc., by folding the top down over the food.

"These containers can be washed and reused any number of times, and best of all, they're free."

Cartons, soda pop

From Oregon: "I took a couple of cardboard cartons that soda pop comes in and made handy carriers for backyard picnics.

"I reinforced all four corners of each carton so they would be strong, spray-painted the insides and covered with adhesive-backed paper.

"In one carton, I put the ketchup, mustard, salt and pepper, instant coffee and cream. I used the other carton for plastic spoons, knives and forks, napkins, paper cups or plastic glasses.

"All I have to do is pick up the cartons, head for the backyard and my job is half done! When we're through eating, it's just as simple to bring everything back in."

From Minnesota: "My husband found a good use for those cartons that bottled drinks come in.

"He put them in the cabinet under my sink to hold cleaning items, such as furniture polish, sink cleanser, brushes, etc.

"You can tote your little carton with you to do your cleaning and it saves you a few steps back and forth to the kitchen (it also organizes the bottom of your cabinet)."

And saving your energy is what it's all about.—Heloise

Coffee, measures

Don't throw away the plastic measurer that comes with coffee. Have you ever thought of keeping one in your flour canister?

It is perfect for scooping out flour for your pastry board or adding it to your plastic bag of chicken-coating mix.

The bonus is that it's a two-tablespoon measure—just right for most gravy and sauce recipes!

Coffee Cans (see Lids, plastic, p. 256)

Containers, lemon-shaped

From Delaware: "I save lemon-shaped plastic bottles, remove the inner plug, wash, fill with white glue, replace plug and glue away.

"This enables me to buy the large bottles of glue (less expensive)."

Leave it to a fisherman to fish around and hook this good idea:
From Minnesota: "A while back when fishing, I got snagged and lost my hooks and last bobber.

"In my picnic basket was an almost-empty lemon-shaped juice container. I emptied it, twisted my line around the threads on the neck and screwed the top back on tight.

"It turned out be one of the best bobbers I ever had."

Containers, margarine (also see Lids, plastic, p. 256)

From New Hampshire: "Instead of washing out the aluminum containers with plastic tops in which whipped margarine is sold, do this:

"Store leftover mashed potatoes, green peas, etc., in the empty container. Then, when you are ready to reheat leftovers, the extra margarine is already there."

Egg Cartons

From Kentucky: "Turn the bottom half of an egg carton upside down. Cut a hole in each little hill, being careful not to cut it too large.

"Makes a great holder for lipstick, mascara, eyebrow pencil, makeup brush, etc.

"You can spray paint it a color to match your room."

From Michigan: "I organized my silverware drawer with the tops of egg cartons—one for knives, one for forks, etc.

"This saves the painted metal, and my silver caddies are easily and often replaced."

Egg cartons also are great for organizing and storing sequins, buttons, beads, etc.—Heloise

Electric Knife

From Indiana: "My electric knife quit on me so my husband carefully removed the blades.

"After shaping two blocks of wood to fit each blade, and smoothing off the corners, he attached a blade to each new handle.

"I now have two of the sharpest nonelectric butcher knives a person could want."

Foil Burner Covers (see Burner Covers, foil, p. 252)

Frozen Dinner Trays

From Wisconsin: "I save the divided aluminum plates that frozen TV dinners are packaged in.

"They're great for camping since they're sturdy and seem to keep the food warmer than regular paper plates. They're also super for packaging leftover meals when my children come to visit and I give them 'care' packages to take home."

Lids, plastic

The lids of margarine tubs must have been designed for reasons like the following:

Press hamburger meat between two lids, then stack and store in a plastic bag in the freezer. Result? Separate, stickless uniform patties of just the right size!

Occasionally, one patty will stick to a lid instead of peeling right off. Prevention: a little margarine on the lid. Cure: a dash of hot water.

To keep half a grapefruit juicy, store it, cut side down, on the plastic lid of a coffee can or other container.

From Oklahoma: "Here is a use I found for plastic lids. I snip out the centers of the lids, cutting close to the first inside ridge, to make plastic rings.

"Then I use the rings as ties for my curtains. Just run the curtains (I have white plastic ones) through the ring, bringing it up as far as necessary.

"Keeps curtains from blowing against the window screen when windows are open."

From Hawaii: "I use plastic lids of different sizes several ways. They save a few cents and also time.

"A two-pound coffee can lid makes a very handy small cutting board for a little job and can serve as a spoon or fork saucer near the stove.

"I use different sizes of lids as flowerpot saucers and as covers over small bits of leftovers."

From Indiana: "To remove the lettering on margarine lids, I use nail polish remover. Then, when I use the containers to store various things, I write the contents on the lid.

"Real neat!"

Margarine Containers (see Containers, margarine, p. 255)

Meat Trays, plastic foam

From Minnesota: "I've found another use for plastic foam meat and vegetable trays. I needed to stack two dishes of gelatin salad in my refrigerator because of lack of room, but was afraid they'd slip and one would fall into the other.

"So I placed one of those little trays on top of the bottom dish and set the other dish on top of that.

"It worked beautifully and sure saved space!"

From Minnesota: "To keep pans with nonstick finishes from being scratched when stacked, I cut a circle from a plastic meat tray and put it in the bottom of each pan.

"These trays also make good spoon rests (but don't get them close to a burner on the stove). In fact, there are so many uses for them I find myself saving each one I get.

"I use a tray to gather sewing aids—thread, scissors, etc., and I can stick needles and pins in edges so they won't fall on the floor.

"They're also great under flower pots and they make great throw-away picnic plates, too."

From Michigan: "I save plastic meat and vegetable trays to slip under the tomatoes, squash or cucumbers that might be touching the ground in my garden.

"This keeps them from rotting on the bottom."

From Connecticut: "Another use for plastic foam meat and vegetable trays: dry and use them for paint palettes for arts and craft classes."

Mesh Bags (see Bags, mesh, p. 247)

Mops

From Washington, D.C.: "The best wax mop I have is one I made from my old string mop.

"I cut off the strings of the mop down to six inches in length. It has a long, strong handle and is easy to wash. It's absolutely the best for waxing floors."

Plastic Bags (see Bags, plastic, p. 247)

Silverware Tray

From Kentucky: "I made a useful sewing box and pin cushion using a discarded silverware tray. I cut plastic foam to fit the compartments.

"I use one compartment as a pin cushion the others to hold sewing machine bobbins, thread, tape measure, binding, etc."

Spice Jars

From Oklahoma: "When empty, the shaker bottles that dried parsley and onion flakes come in are great for filling with flour and seasonings for those small flouring jobs. Use them when sprinkling flour on Swiss steak, veal, stew meat, etc."

Spice Rack

From New York: "Don't throw out an old spice rack. Give it a coat of paint and hang it as a caddy for nail polish, perfume, etc."

Tablecloth, plastic

From Kansas: "When a plastic tablecloth starts looking the worse for wear, I use the sections that aren't worn to:

"Line kitchen shelves.

"Make place mats.

"Re-cover the seat of a kitchen stool.
"Make 'painting aprons' for toddlers."

Trays (see Meat Trays, plastic foam, p. 257 and Frozen Dinner Trays, p. 256)

3

Your Bathroom

INTRODUCTION

Whoever said, "The secret of a happy marriage is two bathrooms," sure knew his stuff.

Bet parents of teenagers won't argue that . . . 'cause there's nothing like kids to give the order of the bath a double whammy.

Not to mention what some teens do to the hot water bill—for heaven's sakes, they'll wash that hair right off of their heads 'cause they over-shampoo.

It's sure the truth: no bathroom's big enough for two, not to mention three, four or more. Not when every last one has his or her own supplies—medicinals, makeup, shaving stuff, rollers, and ad infinitum.

It's not just his, her and their paraphernalia, it's the temperaments, too.

He can't stand her drip-dry wash . . .

She wishes he'd file his laundry in the hamper and not on the floor . . .

And they (the kids) never put tops back on toothpaste or caps on shampoo.

And the tempers that flare in the A.M. rush hour because she's blow-drying her hair when he wants to shave.

And how about the numbers of towels and facecloths involved?

Lord love a duck, it's one crisis after another.

Wouldn't you wonder why bathrooms weren't designed big as barns? Sure would make sense and solve lots of problems. But it didn't happen, so we've got to make do.

One thing that helps is the extra towel racks and rings and the shelf units you can buy to provide more hang-up and shelve-it space.

I mean, every inch counts.

You could even install a second medicine chest. Come to think of it, I could use one, too—and I live alone.

But the really important thing about baths is to keep 'em looking spotless, so shiny bright they make you squint.

Know something? Even though the bath's the smallest room in the house, it's not the easiest one to clean. There's so much to remember.

Like sponging off behind the toilet paper holder . . . coping with mildew on a shower curtain . . . avoiding goop in the soap dish . . . and a zillion etceteras.

Well, as the old saying goes, it's easy when you have the know-how, and that's just what you'll have when you finish this chapter.

—Hugs 'n' kisses, Heloise

PART I: BATHROOM HINTS

Appliqués

From New Mexico: "If you have trouble removing appliqués from your tub when they start to peel and you want to replace them, I have the answer. Most appliqués are made in three layers. Be careful not to remove the top layer first! If you do, the thin film left may be very tough to get off.

"Try to lift a corner or edge of the film. Use any rigid, sharp-edged plastic or wooden scraper (like a cuticle stick) to get it started. Then pull up and peel back the film from all corners, working towards the center.

"If this does not work for you, the next step is to try to lift an edge of each appliqué and apply a generous amount of a pre-wash spray evenly over the bottom of the tub. Allow the solution to soak the film for about two hours, then try lifting the appliqué.

"Usually you can roll bits of adhesive off with your thumb after you've peeled off the appliqué.

"Be sure to wash the tub thoroughly and air-dry before installing new appliqués.

"Pre-wash spray will not harm tub surfaces whether porcelain, fiberglass or steel."

Back Scrubber

Here's a hint for those of you who have a hard time scrubbing your backs while bathing.

Take an old nylon stocking and tie a knot near the center of it. Drop in a bar of soap and tie another knot on the other side of the soap.

Now, just take hold of both ends of the stocking and kind of seesaw it across your back.

Does it ever feel good! But for those who like a little more "scratch" to your scrubber, take a strip of nylon net (see Nylon Net, p. 217) and tie a bar of soap in the middle of it, by simply folding the strip of net over the soap a couple of times and tying a knot at each side of the soap.

Nice, huh?

Bath

Take a bath the easy, fast and thorough way.

Use a pair of jersey cotton gloves in place of a washcloth. Put them on and start scrubbing yourself.

They don't roll up like a washcloth and you can use both hands. Try it, 'cause this works just great!

Bath Mat

From Minnesota: "We often had a soggy rubber mat in the bathtub so my husband got the idea of sticking it on the tile wall at the end of the tub.

"With its suction cups, it sticks great and is fresh and ready to take down for the next bath."

From Wisconsin: "To remove sticky marks from a bathtub after removing a nonskid mat, try fingernail polish remover. Works like a charm!"

Bath Pillow

I'd like to pass this hint along to those who like to soak in the tub and don't have a bath pillow.

Try filling a hot water bottle with warm water (not hot). Use as you would a pillow. This is the greatest for relaxing your neck.

Bathroom Scales (see Scales, bathroom, p. 272)

Bath Toys (also see Hamper, p. 269)

If you share a bathtub with a toddler and his bath toys:
Store them in a nylon mesh bag with a zipper top that can be hung with a plastic clothespin hanger. Then the toys will be out from under foot when you shower, will drip-dry into the tub and the shower curtain will hide them.

Bathtub, cleaning (also see Appliqués, p. 263, Porcelain, Enamel, cleaning, p. 270 and Toilet Bowl Cleanser, p. 278)

From New Mexico: "Here's how to use soap slivers to clean the bathtub:
"Cut a square of nylon net (see Nylon Net p. 217) and fold four thicknesses around several bits of soap. Secure the net with a rubber band and use this to go around the tub a few times just after you pull the plug."

Bathtub, drain

A savvy teenager in Montana is saving her parents plumbing bills with this idea: "When I shampoo my hair, I place a piece of nylon net (see Nylon Net, p. 336) inside the drain. It is a real surprise to find out how much hair this net traps and, of course, it saves the drain from getting clogged.

"As soon as the nylon net is dry—which is just a matter of minutes —the hair is easily removed.

"Then I fold the net, put it between my shampoo and my bottle of rinse and fasten them together with a rubber band. Everything is ready for the next shampoo.

"My friend's parents just paid an expensive plumbing bill, mostly because of hair trapped in the drain. So I guess this idea is really a money-saving tip."

Bathtub, getting out of (also see Shower, slip-proofing, p. 273)

From Illinois: "To help you get out of the bathtub, wring out your washcloth and lay it on the edge of the tub. It will not move, and you can use it to help yourself out of the tub."

Carpeting (also see Rugs, p. 180)

If you haven't been able to figure out how to measure around the sink and toilet when you want to put down snip-and-cut carpeting in your bathroom, here's a wing-ding of an idea from a bride in Texas:

"All you have to do is lay the carpet against the surface and put straight pins on the right side, sticking them through the crease you

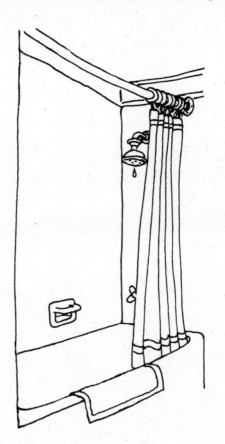

make in the carpet, folding it back where you want it cut. Then pull it back and cut along the line of pins.

Zip, a perfect cut and very easy."

A bachelor in Arizona solved the problem of cutting a big shag bathroom carpet to fit.

Instead of putting it down in one piece, he cut the carpet in half. (The big plus: now he can get it in the washing machine without having to resort to taking it to the washateria.) Also, it was easier to cut around the sink, etc., when he had two small pieces instead of one big one to work with.

When re-laying, he overlaps the seam and it doesn't show one iota. Besides, if only one half gets soiled before the other, he doesn't have to wash the whole carpet. Bachelors are great, don't you think?

So you've finally found the new carpeting with foam rubber backing you want for the bathroom.

It is too wide and too long and already your hand is aching as you remember the last time you "cut a rug" (no pun intended). Well, cheer up, help is on the way!

Use the electric carving knife. (Remember? That's the gadget you used on roast beef when you could afford it?) But, watch out! It cuts fast and you can get off the line in a hurry, so take your time and easy does it.

Just had a ball cleaning the rubber-backed shag carpeting in my bathroom! It's an orlon and nylon blend.

I hung it over my strong clothesline. Then I took the four-gallon glass sprayette that I use for my garden, put a half cup of dish detergent in the bottle part and filled to the top with water. I attached this to a hose and sprayed away.

It took a bit of rubbing with my free hand, here and there, to get the stubborn spots off. I got soaked, but it was worth it!

I took the bottle attachment off the hose when empty and rinsed with the hose quite a few times. Had to get all the soap out.

Since I did this "fun" thing on a sunny, windy day, it didn't take long to dry the carpeting and it went right back into the bathroom.

I was so proud of myself. If you like, you can brush the carpeting with a wire doggy brush when dry.

Ceramic Tile

If you've wondered whether you could give your bathroom a new color scheme by painting ceramic tile, here's the answer from a handy husband in Alabama:

"My wife has been after me (nagging, really) for months to do something about our bathroom.

"So the other day I decided to put my talents to work! (Mostly to keep peace in the family.)

"I took vinegar and washed all the ceramic tile and woodwork, including the tile around the tub. Then I took some good oil-based, high-gloss enamel and painted the tile lime green.

"After I finished the decorating, I waxed all the tile with a good quality self-polishing wax.

"This is to keep the tile from having water spots on it. All I have to do is just wipe it dry—it takes only a minute."

From Maine: "For years I've battled soapy scum build-up on the ceramic tile in the shower.

"Tried all sorts of things: soap-filled pads, scouring powder, bathroom cleaner sprays, etc.

"I now have the problem solved. Spray the tile liberally with any pre-wash spray. Wait a couple of minutes and rub the scum away with a damp sponge."

Clock

Nothing's more frustrating to a clock-watcher than not having a clock to watch. It sometimes happens . . . like when a man's shaving or his mate's putting on makeup.

That's because most people don't think to hang a clock in the bathroom. It's a good idea. Or, if not a clock, at least a clock radio.

Cup

From Oklahoma: "When I discovered I was spending $15 a year on disposable bathroom cups for the family, I bought a very attractive mug tree.

"Now each of us has an individual cup which is both economical and hygienic.

"And to make it easy on me, it's each family member's responsibility to keep his or her cup clean."

Fashion Accessories

Hey, friends, here's an idea. I get dressed in the bathroom . . . do you? If so, it just makes sense to stash fashion accessories there—so they're handy.

I've hung up belts, scarves, ties, and pin-on flowers. Bonus: they provide a real pretty touch of color. You guys could have a tie rack.

This is the greatest because when you need an accessory, it's right where it ought to be—within reach so you can see how it looks with your dress or suit.

Simple but super.

Hamper

From Vermont: "Improvise a hamper for a bathroom with limited space by using a molded plastic tote, a good-looking shopping bag, or a zippered, plastic pillow cover suspended from hooks on the back of the door."

From Kansas: "Clothes hampers can be used for a lot of things besides storing soiled laundry. For example:

"Storing towels and washcloths, extra bed linens, socks and underwear, toys, things that need mending or ironing.

"They come in so many different sizes and colors that you can find one to match most any room in the house."

Hot Water Bottle

Before you screw the top into an empty hot water bottle or ice pack to store it away, blow into the bottle and then replace the top immediately. This keeps the sides from sticking together. . . . Makes the bottle last much longer.

Medicine Cabinet (see First Aid, p. 293)

Mirror

From New Jersey: "My children are too short to see themselves in the bathroom mirror, so I put three mirror tiles on the wall between the bottom of the medicine chest and the sink. They look as if they were made for this spot.

"Now the kids can see their faces and keep them clean."

From Idaho: "We use the bathroom mirror for messages. A bar of soap is our 'pencil.'

"This system is especially useful when family schedules don't mesh. The message is never missed and removing the lettering gives us the bonus of a clean mirror."

Porcelain Enamel, cleaning (also see Bathtub, cleaning, p. 265 Sink, cleaning, p. 276 and Toilet Bowl Cleanser, p. 278)

This cleaning lesson could save you big bucks, friends, so read this as though you were back in school and had to take a test on it. It's about how to properly clean and care for porcelain enamel surfaces such as your bathtub and sink.

New porcelain enamel surfaces should not be cleaned with abrasive cleansers of any kind. If you use them, you are likely to shorten the life of your tub or sink by ten to fifteen years!

An abrasive cleanser will dull and scratch the glossy surface. After this surface has been scratched, stains get down into those scratches and become really hard to remove.

This means no abrasive cleansers for your sink or bathtub, not if you want them to serve you well in the years to come.

Ah, you say, what about the new creamy liquid cleaners that manufacturers claim are only mildly abrasive?

Honeychile, you listen and listen well. They are abrasive, too. No, not as harsh as the old standbys we are used to, but, even so, they can scratch porcelain enamel surfaces and the painted enamel surfaces of appliances.

If you continue to use these on certain surfaces, they will eventually remove the protective glaze and even, in time, wear away a painted surface.

What, you ask, am I supposed to use? All of us, including me, have been brought up believing there's nothing like a good scouring to get that tub clean. Well, if you want your tub or sink to last and last and stay in good condition you are going to have to change your ways.

You can and should use a spray-on, foamy-type bathroom and kitchen cleanser. It will not harm the finish. Yes, you may have to scrub a bit more but it is worth it to save the finish on your tub.

There are one or two types of powder on the market that can be used that have less abrasiveness than the others. One is the all-purpose powdered cleanser we usually use for walls and floors. It has been around for ages, and I bet you never thought to use it on your tub.

You can also use dishwasher detergent. I called the Porcelain Enamel Institute and they tested this and said it would work fine. Just be sure to wear gloves 'cause it's very hard on hands.

So, if you want that sink or tub to last, take care of it.

Rugs (also see Carpeting, p. 266)

If you have several limp bathroom rugs that are so worn out they skid and wrinkle, try using two—one on top of the other. They sure do stay put better when you double up.

When the top one becomes soiled, just switch 'em. Put the soiled one on the bottom.

After using this method for six months, I came up with a better idea!

I turn the rugs back to back and, using the largest stitch on my sewing machine, sew around the edge. (Or, I fold one over to make a two-sided mat that's half the size. That's called a "Heloise Mat.")

A two-sided rug can be turned over in a jiffy when one side gets wet. Moreover, because a rug side is always on the bottom, it can be used to scoot across the floor for those dribbles of water, etc. Great in the kitchen in front of your sink or refrigerator, too.

Saves the energy of pushing a handle around when you can just pull or push it with your footsies.

I had a nylon bath rug that looked like fur when it was new. After a few washings, it was so matted I was going to throw it away—you know how awful it must have looked for me to do that!

But I decided to wash it once more. Then, while it was still damp, I took a wire doggie brush and sat down with the rug over my knee and brushed away.

I couldn't believe my eyes! All those tangles brushed out and it really did look like fur again.

The next time I washed it, I added one-half cup of vinegar to the rinse water and the tangles seemed to brush out easier.

Fabric softener will work, too. Use it instead of vinegar in the rinse water, but not both at the same time.

Rust

Here's an idea from a clever kiddo in Vermont: "My dad had a good idea to stop bathroom rust stains made by metal cans. When the can is open, switch the plastic cover to the bottom of the can.

"The fact is that plastic and water don't rust, while metal and water do! So check those cans!"

Scales, bathroom

From Oklahoma: "I re-covered my bathroom scale when the linoleum-like covering started curling up around the edges.

"I used a twelve-inch square of stick-on tile, trimming away the edges to conform to the curve of the scale, and cutting out a space for the numbered dial.

"With that done, it was simple to pull off the adhesive backing and press the tile in place.

"Now, after cleaning up the scale's chrome trim, I have a smart 'almost new' bathroom scale for less than fifty cents."

From Indiana: "I wanted to change the color of my round bathroom scale but couldn't figure out how to do it.

"While shopping for a new bathroom rug, I noticed the matching toilet lid cover. It fit the scale perfectly and all I had to do was cut out an area for the dial."

Shower, slip-proofing (also see Bathtub, getting out of, p. 266)

I get so many letters from people who have broken a hip or an ankle or some other bone, either while taking or stepping out of a shower.

For years, I doubted this because I didn't see how anyone could be so careless.

Well, yours truly just about broke her fool neck . . . the same way! Instead of my neck, it was my ankle. It was badly sprained and it hurt, believe me!

I was so mad at me that I just sat down and cried . . . and more tears when I couldn't do such simple things as run the vacuum, lift the laundry, etc.

I immediately yelled at myself, "Whatcha gonna do to prevent it next time?"

So, I bought some nonskid decals which are meant for the bottom of the tub. Believe me, because it's the truth, I put the whole package on the shower floor! I was taking no chances!

Play it safe and buy some of these decals if you use a shower stall. Much, much cheaper than a doctor bill and crutches, not to mention the pain involved.

Be sure and scrub the shower floor first. It has a buildup of soap film in it, which is why I slipped.

"And never leave a bar of soap that you have dropped (while showering) where it landed. I'm not going to tell you where I landed but it wasn't funny!

When a hotel or motel shower or tub lacks a mat to keep it from being slippery, do this:

Wet a terry hand towel or washcloth and spread smoothly in the tub or shower. It makes a more slip-proof standing surface.

P.S. Be sure to put the side with the label on the bottom, friends, so you won't catch your toe in it!

Shower Cap (also see Shower Cap, p. 285)

As everyone knows, the plastic in a shower cap lasts forever . . . but the elastic doesn't last five days, it seems.

So this is my idea and, believe me, it works. All I do after the original elastic wears out is to make a narrow hem around the edge of the cap and run new elastic out through a small opening on the outside surface of the cap so I can tighten it as I use it. Simple, what! But sensationally effective.

Shower Curtain

Know what to do when shower curtains get grimy looking, develop a film and mildew spots? Toss 'em in the washing machine with some terry towels.

They help buff your curtains while they're coming clean.

Just fill your machine with warm water, add your detergent and about half a cup of bleach. Let the machine run a few seconds, then put in the shower curtains and three or four white bath towels.

The grimy build-up and mold will be gone by the time the wash cycle is finished.

From Tennessee: "After washing and drying plastic shower curtains, rub cream wax over them.

"This coating prevents their soiling so quickly, and the folds of the curtain do not stick together.

From Montana: "I purchased some of those new wild print towels but couldn't find a shower curtain to do them justice.

"So I bought a single flat sheet in the matching print. It was too long, so I cut off part of it, and hemmed the raw edge. Then I made buttonholes across this hemmed portion with my machine attachment and hung the curtain with a clear plastic liner on the tub side.

"The bathroom looks terrific and, best of all, the sheet doesn't require ironing.

"Isn't that great?"

From Iowa: "I'm so excited about the inexpensive shower curtain that I made for our bathroom that I just have to share it!

"I bought a plain white shower curtain liner, complete with magnets. Then I bought a package of plastic daisy appliqués. These flowers are waterproof and come in assorted sizes and colors.

"I peeled the backing off and put them all over the shower curtain liner.

"Sure brightens up the bathroom and costs so little!"

Shower Curtain, mending

From Indiana: "For years I have tried to salvage shower curtains that are in good condition but have torn ring holes.

"I've finally found something that works! Strapping tape! (Not masking tape.) It can be found at hardware and stationery stores, etc., and is primarily used for wrapping packages for mailing. It wraps them so securely you practically have to dynamite to get it off.

"Just press the tape over the damaged hem area, press tightly, then punch an opening in the tape (over the covered hole) for the curtain ring.

"This tape holds for a long time and no one can see the mended spots. Better then pins or sewing!"

Know what works too? Waterproof plastic tape. It comes in lots of colors and holds up pretty well—but if there's lots of steam you may need to patch it.—Heloise

Shower Doors

Sliding glass shower doors are exasperating! The dirt that collects in the door runners and the splashes that get on the door take time and effort to clean.

To eliminate this extra work, I installed a curtain rod—the kind held in place with suction cups—inside the shower door. Then I hung a shower curtain on the new rod and now my sliding shower door is a delight. It is most attractive with my pink curtain showing through the glass.

Lo and behold, the water hits the curtain and not one smidgen on my door or runners.

Don't know why I didn't do this years ago.

Shower Head

This little hint concerns keeping the shower head from getting clogged with mineral deposits.

Twice a year I remove the shower head, take out the rubber washer, and soak the head in a pan containing about one cup vinegar and one cup water. I bring this to a boil, then continue to simmer for a few minutes.

I replace the rubber washer, install the shower head and once again I have nice hot showers with well-distributed water instead of dribbles in one place and needles in another.

Try it!

Sink, cleaning (also see Porcelain Enamel, cleaning, p. 270 and Toilet Bowl Cleanser, p. 278)

From Maine: "To clean my bathroom sink drain, I use an old percolator brush. I call it my little plumber brush because it cleans the drain with no trouble."

Soap

I have discovered something wonderful to do with leftover smidgens of soap. Put them in your blender, add some water, set your blender for "grate."

You'll get the creamiest liquid soap. Then pour this liquid into plastic squeeze bottles and set a bottle at each sink.

You'll not only use up leftover soap, but you'll eliminate dirty, goopy soap dishes.

A squeeze bottle is so much quicker and easier to use, too!

When a bar of soap gets too small to use, many people save soap slivers in an old nylon stocking. But, I wonder if they have ever thought to hang one of these stockings on an outdoor faucet?

It gives a quick cleanup before you come in after gardening and, better still, children seem to like the idea of washing their hands this way. Sure cuts down on dirty little fingerprints on the woodwork.

From Montana: "My aunt places a small sponge in each soap dish to absorb moisture and melted soap. It sure makes soap dishes easier to clean."

From Kansas: "Here's something you might have fun with if you enjoy experimenting:

"I was saving soap chips in a bowl to make soap on a rope. I put in just enough water to cover them and let them stand for a few days 'til they melted down. Then I took my electric beater and whipped the mixture up till it was creamy and smooth.

"The mixture was too mushy for soap on a rope, so I had to improvise. First, I tinted portions of the mixture different shades with food coloring. Then, I got out my cake decorating bag and tips and made designs like rosettes and seashells.

"I set it aside for a few days and found the designs had shrunk some but the little soaps were still cute.

"I used one to wash my hands and it sort of just melted like cotton candy but it gave a lot of suds.

"I had so much fun with this that I can't wait until I get another bowl full of chips. I'm using my little designs as guest soap in my bathroom."

From Kentucky: "All you have to do to dissolve a sink full of soap suds is sprinkle salt on them."

Here's a thrifty-nifty a Nevada homemaker learned from her mother-in-law: "Soap was literally melting away in our tub soap dish because water collected in it . . . until my mother-in-law got a brainstorm. She took one of those square latticed baskets (the kind fresh strawberries come in) and hooked it over two stick-on hooks above the shower line, but within easy reach.

"Drains instantly."

A bachelor in New Mexico came up with this money-saver:

"When a bar of soap is getting too small, open a new one and do this:

"Before you go to bed, wet the old sliver and the new bar and, using a toothbrush, scrub up some lather on the smooth side of the new bar and the softest side of the old one.

"Place both surfaces together and squeeze firmly for 20 seconds or so. Carefully place the double bar in the soap dish with the small one underneath.

"When you awaken, you will find that the two bars are 'welded' together, and the only way they will come apart is if they are dropped onto the floor or left in water.

"When using, always rub from the small side, and always replace with the small side down. Soon the small bar will disappear and you will never again be bothered with slivers of soap in your soap dish."

Tape Recorder

A clever businesswoman I know doesn't waste a minute:

"Sometimes when I'm putting on makeup, I get a great idea," she says, "but I don't want to rush out to my desk to jot it down . . . so I keep a tape recorder in the bathroom. Just a flick of the switch and the idea's noted for future use."

Isn't that a goody? But I've got a different system. I tape memo sheets on the inside of the medicine chest door. When inspiration strikes, I reach into my makeup bag for a pen and write myself a note. —Heloise

Toilet Bowl Cleanser

Honeychile, if you don't know of the danger of mixing chlorine bleach with other household cleaners, I'm sure there must be thousands of other people who are also uninformed. And take it from me, this can be hazardous to your health.

Two housewives in separate cases. Both were using an ordinary toilet bowl cleaner. Not satisfied with the way it was removing stain, each one added some household bleach and stirred with a brush. One died quickly, the other spent a long time in the hospital.

A medical newsletter told about twenty people being overcome by gas or gases released from a cleaning mixture. Investigation revealed the mixture included a well-known liquid household cleaner, chlorine bleach, and ammonia.

What happened in the above cases was that a poisonous gas was liberated when the users decided to use a mixture of two or more common household cleaning agents.

When the widely used household chlorine bleach (a sodium hypochlorite solution) is combined with an acid or acid producing substance, such as a toilet bowl cleanser or vinegar, there is a sudden release of a quantity of chlorine gas.

Likewise, when a chlorine bleach is mixed with ammonia, lye or other alkaline substance, the action will liberate a highly irritating gas.

If the gas is inhaled, in either case, it can cause serious injury and possibly death. Accidents of this type have occurred not only in the kitchen and bathroom, but also in the cleaning and treating of the water in swimming pools.

Don't make the mistake of thinking that because certain household products are good and useful, the combination of two or more of them will do a better job than one alone. Very often mixing them is useless and unnecessary; combining them may be disastrous.

Follow the safe rule—use chemical cleaners as the manufacturers direct on the labels, and keep in mind some scouring powders now contain chlorine bleach.

It is best, anyway, not to use a hypochlorite (chlorine) bleach in toilet bowls, sinks, or bathtubs, or on electrical appliances, as it can, in time, injure, dull or roughen a fine, smooth porcelain surface.

In short, don't mix chlorine with any other cleaning agent.

Please heed this advice. This is a lesson I want to teach you before you learn it the hard way:

DON'T—I repeat, DON'T use toilet bowl cleansers in your bathroom basin or tub because such cleaners are meant for toilet bowls only.

Nine times out of ten, the toilet bowl is made of vitreous china.

Tubs and basins are made of cast iron (or steel) with a bonded porcelain finish, or glass fiber or plastic.

If your basin or tub is rough and you can't get it clean, the reason may be that you have been using toilet bowl cleansers on it and have ruined the finish. Lots of people try squirting some on because it's easy. Thousands of bathtubs are ruined this way!

Toilet Brush Holder

From Iowa: "I keep a sponge in the bottom of the holder for the mop that I use to clean the toilet. It soaks up any moisture that drips from the brush and keeps the holder cleaner."

Toothbrush

Sometimes kiddos have the best ideas . . . like this one from a ten-year-old "hostess" in Wisconsin:

"When I have friends spending the night with me, they sometimes forget to bring their toothbrushes.

"So I bought three brushes when they were on sale and took a piece of masking tape and wrapped it around the handles of each.

"I wrote the names of my friends on them and that way, when they forget to bring their toothbrushes, they have one to use."

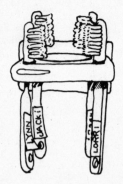

Towels, buying

I don't think all of you know how to buy bath towels and wash-cloth sets when you stock up.

Never buy "just a set" and walk out.

Here's why:

Have you ever noticed that the washcloth is worn out completely and the hand towel is rather worn, while the bath towel is like new?

Well, sweethearts, it's because you use that washcloth umpteen times more, and for lots harder work, than you do that hand towel. Sometimes you even pick it up and wash out the wash basin or bathtub. That's a no-no!

Even if you don't use cleanser for this chore, the rubbing helps wear the cloth out. Then, too, while it's in your hands, you might wipe the vanity top and the edge of the basin.

This is a habit you should break.

Next on the agenda, hand towels:

Rinse your ten little fingers, wash your face or neck and you dry away with that hand towel. It gets lots of use.

Then when company is coming, you look for a decent set of matching towels, you "no-can-find." Everything is shoddy except those beautiful bath towels. Know why? Because you don't rub-a-dub with them; you use 'em to blot yourself dry.

So there you are, you need a new washcloth and a new hand towel. You know how hard it is to find some new pieces to match? Things are changed and a new pattern is out. You can't match yours! You're sorry you didn't listen to Heloise.

So listen now, sugar pies. Next time you buy a set of towels, buy two bath towels, four hand towels and four washcloths. (I personally buy six—yes, you read correctly—six washcloths. I find it evens out.)

Know what? I have never been without matching sets.

Now, if you are a smarty and have a good matching set that is fairly new, run, don't walk, to the nearest store and buy those extra washcloths and hand towels.

The reason I wrote about this little idea is that many of you are complaining to me that today's towels are OK but manufacturers aren't making hand towels and washcloths good enough.

It isn't their fault, friends. It's ours because we give hand towels and washcloths a lot more wear!

It happens all the time . . . mothers of teenagers complaining about the hair shampooing and the towels, towels, towels!

These towels are used to dry clean hair. They are not dirty, just wet! Throw them over the shower rod or any place to dry. Use them again the next day.

They are drying clean hair! They are not dirty!

Invest in color-coded towels and personal towel hangers for each teen. Let them use their towels an extra day or two. Less laundry—less energy for mom!

Tub, appliqués (see Appliqués, p. 263)

Water Conservation

Which is the most economical in using less water—a shower or a bath?

According to a spokesperson for the government's Consumer Information Center, it depends . . .

"Showers use from five to fifteen gallons of water per minute. Baths use from thirty to fifty gallons," they say.

"If you have a shower with a flow control device to cut the amount of water the shower uses, or if you just turn the water on a little, you can take up to a six minute shower and still save water.

"But, if you have the shower on as hard as it will go and stand under it for thirty minutes, you will indeed use a great deal more water than a tub bath."

Now, the only question is how to convince those teenagers to get out of the shower after only a few minutes.

"And on that score," said the spokesperson, "the U.S. government has no advice whatsoever." (Think he or she might also have teenagers at home? Sure sounds like it.)

Here's a hint on saving hot water and energy (and that means saving your money, too):

When taking a bath, if the water runs too cool, turn down the cold —not up the hot!

PART II: SECOND TIME AROUND: BATHROOM RECYCLE

Some folks never throw anything out and that's a mistake that results in clutter. My motto is: never throw anything out until you're rootin' tootin' sure you can't find a really good use for it . . . like maybe give it a brand new purpose and use. F'rinstance:

Carpet

From Iowa: "My bathroom carpet was limp and ready to be discarded. I had an idea—maybe I could use it as shelf paper for the bathroom and kitchen cabinets.

"Great—and when it becomes soiled, I just toss it in the washing machine."

From Kentucky: "I had one of those contour shag bathroom carpets that fit around the bottom of the basin. Well, it shrank when washed. What to do?

"I cut the two 'ears' off evenly across the top of the rug, whip-stitched them together around the curved edges with heavy button-hole thread and, presto! A super-duper car-washing mit for my husband!

"The rest of the rug, now with a straight edge at the top, fits nicely in front of the basin.

"How's that for killing two birds with one stone?"

Pill Bottles

From Maryland: "The other day I needed a cover for my tooth-brush, so I could take it traveling. So I used a clear plastic pill bottle.

"I cut a hole in the plastic top for the handle to go through, put the bottle over the brush, then snapped the top back on."

From Massachusetts: "Plastic-topped pill bottles make great sewing kits for the traveler. Fill with a needle and thread (wrapped around a little piece of cardboard)."

From Indiana: "Empty pill containers are great for toting ketchup, mustard or mayonnaise if you carry your lunch to work."

A lady from Georgia who has saving ways came up with this dandy:

"I drop empty prescription bottles in a storage bag. They are handy for 1,001 storage uses—from holding thumbtacks to buttons.

"They are great for fish hooks in hubby's tackle box. I use 'em to hold razor blades I'm throwing out, etc., etc., etc.

"They also make great 'blocks' for visiting kiddos."

Here's a dandy from a trailer park resident in Florida: "I keep spices in plastic screw top pill bottles. Not only keeps bugs out but, should I drop one, it doesn't break."

From Connecticut: "Plastic prescription bottles make excellent storage containers for spools of thread. If you use clear bottles, you can see the color of the thread.

"My sewing basket used to have ravelled threads all over it, knotted together. Oh, such a horrible mess! No more!"

This idea from a ten-year-old in Kentucky is clever as clever can be: "For a present for mom or dad, all you need is a bottle! Remove the plastic snap-on top; punch two little holes in the lid and insert a key chain through the holes. Then put the following poem inside the bottle with the typed side out so it can be seen:

'Keep me full of nickles,
'And never you'll be stuck.
'How to feed the meter,
'With only half a buck!'

"Snap on the plastic lid and you've got a gift key carrier with space for those parking meter dimes and nickels."

Roaches (see Roaches, p. 177)

Shower Cap (also see Shower Cap, p. 274)

From Maryland: "I buy shower caps that have terry lining.

"When the elastic gets all stretched out and I cannot use the cap anymore, I cut the lining out and use it for cleaning rags."

Shower Curtain

Shower curtains usually don't wear out all over . . . just in places. Or sometimes you dispose of 'em 'cause you're sick of the pattern. Whichever, don't throw your old shower curtain out. It has uses . . .

A New Jersey mother made covers for a picnic table and two benches with a shower curtain. She sewed elastic at each corner to anchor 'em.

A handyman in Texas says an old shower curtain makes a super drop cloth for painting jobs.

A lady who's handy with a needle recycled a shower curtain into a whole mess of aprons.

You see—everything has a use, so find it before you toss something useful away. And here are other ideas . . .

From North Carolina: "I made the cutest rain outfit for my daughter from an old shower curtain.

"The bottom was covered with mildew, so I cut off that portion and the rest was fine for a poncho and matching hat.

"It was easy to sew the plastic, too."

From Illinois: "When plastic shower curtains fade or I get tired of them, I save them to use as runners on the carpet to protect it when it rains or snows."

From Alaska: "I made curtains for my basement windows with an old shower curtain.

"When I wash the windows I take down the curtains, put them in warm sudsy water, and rinse. By the time the windows are clean, the curtains are too, and ready to hang."

From California: "A has-been shower curtain can be cut to fit and used as an extra layer of protection under a mattress pad."

From New Hampshire: "I converted an old shower curtain into a couple of laundry bags. I used the upper half of the curtain so I could insert a cord drawstring through the holes where the shower hooks attached and close the bags."

Shower Curtain Rings

From North Carolina: "Don't toss out old metal self-closing shower rings. They make great key chains."

A keen teen who uses the same idea says she clips her shower curtain key ring to a loop on her jeans or to her belt. That way she never has a "what-did-I-do-with-my-keys" crisis.—Heloise

From New York: "I've found a good use for old shower curtain rings: they can be hung on towel racks to hold your washcloths by the tags on the corners. More room for hand towels and bath towels.

"They also could be used on your shower rod, behind the curtain, to hang hand-washed items to dry. This way you can close your shower curtain and no one is the wiser."

I love it!—Heloise

Toilet Paper, cardboard rolls

From Kansas: "The cardboard rolls that toilet paper comes on make jumbo rollers for long hair. I hold 'em in place with clips."

You can cut 'em up, cover them with fabric or patterned paper and make the dandiest napkin holders too!—Heloise

Toilet Seat Covers, fabric

From Mississippi: "Run a cord or elastic through the casing of an old fabric toilet seat cover and pull it so it fits over your dust mop. Does a good job of picking up the dust and is easy to launder."

Toothbrushes

From Ohio: "You can use old toothbrushes for many cleaning jobs:

"They're great for cleaning ridges and grooves on clocks, stoves, can openers, tables, vegetable bins and refrigerators. I could go on and on."

And they're super for cleaning jewelry . . . and for grooming eyebrows!—Heloise

From Connecticut: "My kitchen windows have fifteen panes—I really mean 'pains'. Those corners are murder to try to get a cloth into.

"I spray the corners with a cleaner then do a scrub-up with a toothbrush. You wouldn't believe how great it works!"

Towels

Some of you just throw things away without thinking about how they can be mended or repaired . . . it's a waste. Sometimes, with the

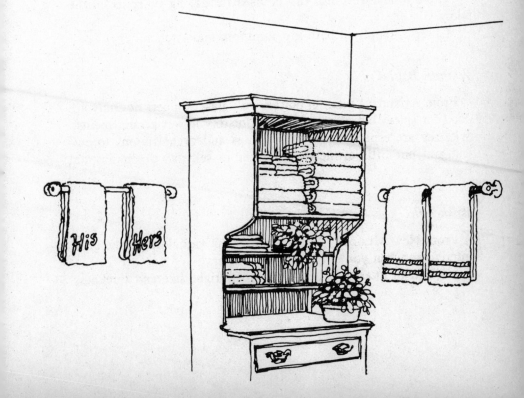

kind of ingenuity a college girl in Florida has, you can make something worn as good as new. Here's what she did: "I have a large bath towel with a beach scene on one end, which became slightly worn in the mid-section. I cut a large orange-colored washcloth into a circle to represent either a sun or a beach ball and appliquéd it into the worn spot. Good as new and also a changed scene!"

From Michigan: "Our puppy chewed holes in several towels. I patched the holes with fabric scraps and since my shower curtain was faded, I carried out the patchwork theme, making a new curtain.

"I used six-inch squares of fabric, and lined the curtain with a plastic liner left over from another curtain.

"To carry the patchwork theme even further, I made a cover of patchwork squares for a wastebasket.

"This all costs nothing if you sew and have scraps around.

"Another advantage: when I buy new towels or rugs, I can buy whatever color is on sale because it will go with my patchwork."

From South Dakota: "I save old worn-out bath towels and, when I mop my floor, I put each foot on one and walk around the room, rubbing and drying the floor.

"These foot towels also can be used for drying up spills on the floors.

"I keep a supply in both my bathroom and kitchen."

Vitamin Bottles

From Arizona: "Vitamin bottles with glass stoppers not only are good for spices but also make vases for tiny flower arrangements.

"They are especially nice for groups and organizations to collect and put little artificial flowers in to sell or put on hospital trays."

Washcloths

From New Mexico: "Worn-out, beat-up washcloths make great interfacing when you're making pot holders.

"Folded in quarters, they are just the right size and thickness.

However, three or four cloths may be stacked together and trimmed to the desired size.

"For the outside cover, I use fabric scraps left over from sewing projects, put the covers and insides together and machine-stitch a few lines (or designs) over the top to hold them securely. Then I bind the edges with matching bias tape.

"Not only are they very attractive, but very inexpensive as well."

First Aid: In Case of Emergency

PART I: MEDICAL SUPPLIES

The things that wind up in medicine chests . . . deodorant, aftershave, blemish coverup, skin cream, facial masks, cologne, nail polish, etc., etc., etc.

And it's not just your medicine chest, friends; it's mine, it's every-one's.

That may be life . . . but what do you do in a real emergency—especially if your bandage box is empty and you can't remember the last time you saw the adhesive tape?

The truth is that no one likes to anticipate trouble but, anticipated or not, it sure crops up.

Maybe you don't want to think about it but you'd better, and right now while all is quiet on the home front.

What I did when I suddenly came down with a case of the suppose-there's-an-emergency jitters was this:

I nipped around and found a small cardboard box and stocked it with things I might need . . . just in case. (A good list follows.)

Then I went a step further and bought extras for day-to-day, can-happen-any-time mishaps (stick-on bandages, adhesive tape and that kind of stuff). These things I put in the medicine chest . . . just so it could live up to its name.

But, so help me, Hannah, I had to move out a mess of stuff to do it. Know something? I should have chucked those things sooner—stuff like dried-up mascara wands, lipsticks worn down to the nub, foundation caked in bottles, and so on.

Getting rid of that stuff sure made me feel better . . . and made the medicine chest look darned near empty!

But to get down to serious stuff like a first-aid box. You should have a well-equipped one you can call on in an emergency. Why a box? Why not a shelf of supplies?

Because a box can be toted along if you go on a camping trip or trek off on vacation, or even rush from top floor bathroom to basement.

What to put in that box? Here's a list of supplies, alphabetically arranged, that cover most emergencies:

Adhesive Tape: If you're trying to secure a dressing or hold bandages in place, you certainly need this. I buy the wide kind, then if I need just a narrow strip, I slit the tape with scissors or a razor blade and pull off a strip of the width I need.

Bath Towels and Sheets: Remember *Gone With the Wind*—Miss Melanie and other hoop-skirted belles rolling bandages?

Time marches on but some things don't change! Clean white bath towels and sheets (the older and softer, the better) still make great bandages and dressings.

Sheets should be cut in strips and rolled (just like in GWTW).

The thing is to wash and iron them and wrap 'em in heavy brown paper to keep out dust. And, this is important, throw them into the wash every three months!

Eye Dropper: You could need one to rinse out eyes.

Roller Bandages: If you injure a finger or a toe, you might need to wrap it up. A roll of one-inch wide gauze bandages will do the job.

While you're at it, get a roll of two-inch wide gauze bandages, too. It'll come in handy to hold a dressing in place.

Safety Pins: If you have some in the first aid box, at least you'll know where they are when a slip strap breaks or a case of "gaposis" hits at the waist.

Scissors: You honest to goodness need a pair exclusively for your first-aid box. Why? Because if you need scissors to cut bandages or tape, you'll know where to find them in an emergency. Can you ever find your pair of desk scissors? Probably not. That's why you should stash away a medical pair (blunt-ended) for emergency use only. And pack a bottle of rubbing or grain alcohol too for sterilizing them.

Soap: When you run out of first aid spray, know what to replace it with? Plain old soap! Honest injun! Would Heloise fool you?

I checked this out with my own M.D. and he says: "If you clean a wound, scratch or cut thoroughly with soap, you don't need to use an antiseptic."

How about that for a moneysaver!

Sterile Bandages: These are what you need to cover open wounds or dry dressings for burns. You can use 'em as a compress to stop bleeding, too. They come all sealed up in sterile packets (twelve to a box). You should buy a box of the 4 × 4-inch size. This is one first aid item you can't make yourself because sterile is sterile—and if you cut bandages they're not!

Triangular Bandages: That's the biggie 37-inch square that you fold in half (on the diagonal) if you need to put an arm in a sling.

Tweezers: What I said about finding scissors goes ditto for tweezers. Keep a pair in the first-aid box in case you have to remove a stinger or a splinter. Dip 'em in the alcohol first.

If your first-aid box is going traveling, also pack things like: any medication you regularly take, paper cups, a flashlight, splints. And don't forget aspirin and other remedies for common ills.

PART II: FIRST-AID MEASURES

INTRODUCTION

The medical dramas on TV make emergency measures seem easy, but those guys and gals are medics, so don't fool yourself.

In an emergency, know what you could do? Panic!

It happens! It's like trying to remember whether to feed a fever or starve a cold (or is it starve a fever and feed a cold?).

See what I mean?

Maybe you've taken a first aid course (and if you haven't, you should—it could save a life). Even so, in a split second of crisis, your mind could go blank. That's why this first aid section is in my book —so you can find it when you need it, when you're responding to an SOS.

To be on the safe side, know what you should do? Make copies of this mini-manual. I've got copies of it everywhere. Paste 'em in the first-aid box, on the kitchen bulletin board, in the basement, garage and laundry, on the inside of the medicine chest door, in your car's glove compartment, too . . . which reminds me.

Keep a first-aid kit in the car at all times . . . even if you never drive further than 'round the block. You never know . . .

Here's hoping an emergency never crops up. Know who's keeping her fingers crossed on your behalf? Me!—Your friend, Heloise.

FIRST AID FOR THE FAMILY

Everyone should obtain training in standard first aid procedures and in cardiopulmonary resuscitation (CPR). Call your local Red Cross for information about classes in your community. The directions here will serve as brief reminders. Review them *before* you need them.

Asphyxiation: (breathing stopped) Get victim to fresh air. Start ABC of life support. (See end of chart.) Send for help.

Bites, Animal: Wash wounds with soap under running water. Have animal caught alive so that it can be tested for rabies. Take patient to physician.

Bleeding: Press hard with clean compress directly over wound until bleeding stops. If bleeding is severe, continue pressure and send for help. For minor cuts, wash with soap under warm running water and apply clean compress. For nosebleed, keep patient quiet and seated with head tilted forward. Pinch nose while patient breathes through mouth, or pack bleeding nostril with gauze and pinch. If bleeding does not stop, call physician.

Burns: For mild to moderate burns (skin or blisters unbroken), immerse area in cold water or apply cold, wet towels. Do not apply butter, grease, ointment. For severe burns (loss of skin), cover area with clean cloth. Keep victim warm to prevent shock and get him to the hospital. Never break blisters, clean burns or remove charred clothing. For chemical burns, flood area with water for five minutes, apply clean dressing and call physician.

Choking: (foreign body in throat or windpipe) Do nothing momentarily. Give cough reflex a chance to expel the object. If choking continues, give four sharp blows between the shoulder blades. If ineffective, get behind victim, place the thumb side of your fist just below the victim's rib cage, grasp your fist with other hand and press into the victim's abdomen with a quick upward thrust. Repeat. If choking persists and victim becomes unconscious, pull his tongue and jaw forward and dislodge any visible foreign matter with your hooked index finger. Perform mouth-to-mouth resuscitation or cardiopulminory resuscitation, as necessary, until help arrives.

Convulsions: See that patient is where he cannot hurt himself. Push away nearby hard objects. Do not restrain victim; do not put spoon or other hard object between his teeth. When convulsions stop, turn victim's head to side. If breathing stops, begin ABC of life support.

Electric Shock: Turn off electric power if possible. Do not touch victim until contact is broken. Pull him from contact using dry rope, wooden pole, or loop of cloth. If breathing has stopped, start mouth-to-mouth or cardiopulminary resuscitation. Send for help.

Eye, Chemicals in: Have victim turn head so injured side is down. Flood inner corner of eye with water for five minutes. Cover both eyes with clean compresses. Call physician.

Eye, Foreign Bodies in: If object can be seen, touch it lightly with moistened corner of handkerchief. If object does not come out or if it cannot be seen, cover both eyes with clean compresses and take patient to physician. Never rub the eye; this may force the foreign body in deeper.

Fainting: If a person feels faint, have him lie down or sit down and lower his head between his knees. If a person has already fainted, lay him flat on his back. Anyone who has merely fainted will regain consciousness almost immediately. Keep victim lying down and quiet until recovery is complete—about ten minutes. If victim does *not* regain consciousness almost immediately, send for help. If victim stops breathing, begin mouth-to-mouth or cardiopulminary resuscitation.

Falls: Stop any bleeding and cover wounds with clean dressings. Keep victim comfortably warm to prevent shock. If fracture is suspected, do not move patient unless absolutely necessary (as in case of fire). Call physician.

Poisoning: If poison is unknown, immediately give milk or water to dilute it. Call Poison Control Center. If poison is known, induce vomiting *unless* the poison is a petroleum product (gasoline, kerosene, lighter fluid, furniture polish); a strong acid (bleach, toilet-bowl cleaner), or a strong alkali (lye, drain cleaner). Get victim to a hospital. Take along poison container or sample of vomited material. Do not give fluids or induce vomiting if victim is unconscious or having convulsions.

Stings, Insect: Remove "stinger" if possible. Apply solution of ammonia and water, or paste of baking soda. In case of unusual swelling, call physician. Allergic persons should receive desensitization treatment from physician to prevent severe reactions.

Unconsciousness: (victim cannot be aroused) Make certain that victim's airway is open. If victim is not breathing, begin mouth-to-mouth resuscitation. Have bystander call ambulance. To prevent shock, keep victim comfortably warm. Never try to give an unconscious person food or liquid.

Emergency Telephone Numbers

Rescue Squad (Ambulance):

Poison Control Center:

Fire:

Police:

Physician:

PART III: FIRST PERSON HINTS: ACCIDENTS AND ILLNESS

Medical books don't tell it all . . . not by a longshot, friends. Why, when it comes to tricks that ease ills or accidents, who knows better than the patients themselves?

So here are just a few tips from folks who have been there . . . They're hints that helped them and could help you.—Hugs, Heloise

Ankle, sprained

From Nevada: "I sprained my ankle and had to wear a heavy taping for some time. Of course, that made one foot larger than the other.

"The best answer was to buy two pairs of inexpensive house shoes —one pair in my regular size, the other a size larger.

"When my ankle was well, I wore the smaller pair and gave the larger pair away."

Arm, broken

Hate the way a sling looks on your arm? Give it a fashion touch and use a colorful silk scarf instead of a bandage for the sling.

Bandaging

From Utah: "I need to have a fresh tension bandage put on each day, but just couldn't figure out how to manage it by myself.

"Then my son suggested that I just unroll the bandage, close one end of it in the door (at the latch) and, starting at the other end, turn my body, guiding the bandage, until I reach the door.

"Doing this, I can control the tension to perfection."

Cast, arm

From a caring, careful mom in Maine:

"When my baby was two weeks old, I had to have my arm put in a cast. I worried that it might scratch the baby and be hard on her neck while handling her.

"So I took a tube-type work sock and cut the toe off. I pulled it up over my cast and then cut a place for my thumb. Not only was it easier on my little one, but it protected my clothes from snags."

Cast, leg

From Indiana: "My daughter's broken leg required a cast from toes to thigh during the summer months. I found a neat trick for cooling her leg and adding 'itch-relieving' powder under the cast.

"I fastened the hose of my vacuum cleaner to the blow outlet of the tank. By cupping my hands around her toes and the hose end, the air circulated upward to her knee.

"I sprinkled baby powder generously on her toes and blew it into the cast.

"I repeated the same process at the top of the cast for the upper part of her leg. She said it felt great, and it certainly stopped the itching . . . for a little while.

"Also, as an added benefit, it cut down the odor inside the cast."

Finger, soaking

From Montana: "I soaked a sore finger in a wide-mouthed thermos filled with hot water.

"The thermos kept the water hot for a long time.

"When you are as clumsy as I am and always hurting yourself, you have to think up ways that are easy and convenient for taking care of sore spots."

Ice Pack

From Massachusetts: "I injured my hand and the doctor told me to use an ice pack but I had a problem getting ice out of the trays and making the pack.

"Then I noticed a can of frozen juice in the freezer.

"It fit right into the palm of my hand. No melting either. When I was finished, I just returned it to the freezer for the next treatment."

Keep folded squares of blanket-type material dampened and cased in sandwich bags on the freezer shelf. These "icebags" stay cold long enough for the hurt to go away and they sure help reduce swelling. They're also great packs for pouchy under-eyes.

From Alaska: "A wet but squeezed dry quilted oven mitt filled with ice cubes makes an efficient icebag."

Medication, taking

I don't know how you are when it comes to taking medication. But I know how I am—forgetful. That's why this Vermont husband gets a hip-hip-hooray for his simple—but simply great—memory prodder:

"Recently I was ill and had to take medication four times a day for twelve days.

"What a feat for an absent-minded professor like me . . .

"My husband came up with a clever idea.

"Since I was taking four capsules a day, each morning he'd place four capsules in an empty bottle.

"I could tell at a glance whether or not I had taken the right amount for that day."

Important: remember there are certain medicines that must be in amber bottles. This is required by law and is for your safety. —Heloise

Splinters

From Ohio: "I always use a threaded sterilized needle when getting out a splinter or thorn because then, if I drop the needle, it is easier to find."

5

Your Bedroom

INTRODUCTION

I don't know about your bedroom but mine is a very private room, someplace special that's just for me.

If you're married, then a bedroom is a retreat for two—the place where you talk over problems, make plans and dream those dreams. Just two, just you.

Everyone's taste is different so I bet you can't guess the one thing I've got to have in a bedroom? Red carpeting! When I look at its rich, radiant color first thing at dawning, I think happy thoughts. You can't look at red and feel blue, now can you?

Another thing I like is white walls. They're what I see as I open my eyes. It's like looking at clouds . . . nothing to distract or seem busy or bold when my eyes aren't wide open or even awake.

Most folks buy bedroom furniture in sets, and that's all right, but it's not my way.

I like a bedroom uncluttered—it's a lot more restful looking that way.

So guess what I did? Built a closet clear across one wall!

That's where I stashed my bureau. I knew if I left it out, I'd be dumping odds and ends on it. Instant clutter!

Now if the top's cluttered, and sometimes it is, it's behind closed closet doors.

I thought about night tables, but tossed that thought out. Instead, I found a one-of-a-kind carved round coffee table. It's bigger than the biggest night table I ever saw so there's lots of room for things like . . . a tall reading lamp, a radio alarm, my telephone, books or magazines I'm reading and a pad and pencil in case inspiration strikes in the night.

I don't own a bedspread . . . bet that surprises you. It shouldn't! Remember me, Heloise, the gal who likes doing things quick and easy? That's why no bedspread.

I hate making beds, tucking in, straightening out, fussing around. So instead I've got a pretty quilt that I just pull straight up over the blankets, sheets and pillows. In five seconds—maybe less—my bed is made because it's an on-the-floor type in a beautiful oriental-style frame. The quilt just tops it off and doesn't have to be tucked in.

The great thing about quilts: they're bumpy and lumpy by nature so if everything underneath isn't quite flat, why who's gonna know?

Know what else is in my bedroom? A giant stuffed bear I've had since college. Maybe it's an odd thing for a woman to cherish but it's special to me . . . and special things belong in your own special room.

My bedroom suits me fine . . . just as yours should suit nobody else but Y-O-U.

So forget decorating trends and "in" colors when you furnish your bedroom. Only put in it things you truly like whether they're all the rage or not.

Remember your bedroom's your very own room . . . and that "your" is meant singular for singles and plural for doubles.

—Hugs 'n' kisses, Heloise

PART I: BEDROOM HINTS

Bed (see specific bed listings; also see Box Spring, p. 305, Dust Ruffle, p. 306, Headboard, p. 307, Mattress, p. 308, Mattress Pad, p. 309)

Bed, getting out of

A hint to help arthritics or older people who have difficulty getting out of bed:

When you are lying flat in bed, raise one knee and hook your hand behind it. Straighten out the leg and lower it to the bed while still holding it.

This will automatically raise you to a sitting position with no effort.

Slide your legs off the bed and you're ready to stand up.

From Kentucky: "In winter, anyone without an electric blanket who must get out of bed during the night should keep this in mind:

"When you get out of the bed, don't just throw the covers back. Instead, pull those covers right up to the pillow—just as if you were going to make the bed.

"With the covers pulled up, you can be gone several minutes and your bed will retain some of your body warmth. It's a lot better than going back to an icy bed. Yuck!

"The moral is, don't waste heat, even when it's your own!"

Bedspread

From Illinois: "When I buy a new bedspread, I buy a larger size than I need.

"I cut off the excess and use it to make a matching headboard."

I'd like to pass along an easy method of putting the spread on a king-size bed.

When removing the spread at night, fold down the top to where the pillows start and then fold again to the middle of the bed.

Fold up the bottom to the edge and fold in half from side to side to the size you wish.

In the morning, put the spread on the bottom end of the bed, unfold one, two, three, and you've made it.

Sure beats running around a bed.

Bedspring

Why spend hours cleaning and dusting a coil spring when it can be done in minutes?

Take your bedsprings out to the yard and put the garden hose on it and you'll have the cleanest spring in town.

When it's warm weather, it will dry in a few minutes—in cool weather about a half hour.

Bed Table

Here's how to make an ideal bed table for anyone confined to bed:

Place an adjustable ironing board parallel to the bed, slide the legs under, adjust the height and you'll have a large surface for books, papers, magazines.

Some adjustable ironing boards have wheels and can be rolled away when no longer needed.

Some have an outlet to plug in a radio or other appliances that might be needed.

You can serve the patient's meal on the ironing board table. Just cover with a plastic cloth to protect it from spills.

Blanket

There's a solution to every homemaking problem, including differences of opinion between husbands and wives. Here's how an ingenious Washington, D.C., wife kept the peace:

"My husband wants sheet blankets on our double bed in cold

weather, while I prefer regular sheets all year round.

"To keep peace and happiness, I sorted out my two oldest sheets and sheet blankets, split them down the middle and sewed half a sheet to half a blanket, selvage edges together, and hemmed the outside.

"Now he has sheet blankets on his side and I have sheets on mine. We're both happy!"

For owners of electric blankets who dislike getting out of bed on chilly mornings, try this . . .

At night, spread your bathrobe on top of the bed, over the electric blanket. I find I can face the world a lot better when I slip into a nice warm robe.

From Texas: "When putting blankets on my bed, I put the first blanket on the bed lengthwise (as usual) so that I will have plenty to tuck in real good at the foot of the bed.

"When I put on the second blanket, I put it on crosswise so that I'll have plenty of blanket to tuck in at both sides.

"Honest to goodness—you'll be as snug as a bug in a rug if you make your bed the way I make mine."

From Oklahoma: "If you own a blanket or quilt that is too small to give you adequate overhang on a large bed, try this:

"Machine-stitch an extension (such as a two-foot wide strip of old sheeting) along one long side of the quilt.

"This extension gets tucked under the foot of the mattress when making the bed. What used to be the length of the quilt now goes crosswise on the bed and hangs over adequately; what used to be the width of the quilt now runs lengthwise on the bed. And because the quilt itself is not used for tuck-in at the foot, it should reach up to your chin nicely."

From New Hampshire: "Electric-blanket users who cannot see the numbers on the controls in the dark can put a piece of adhesive tape over the most often used number on the control."

Box Spring

If you have a new mattress and box spring set and want to keep it looking new, don't forget to cover the box spring, too. Most of us protect our mattresses but leave the box springs uncovered.

I slipped an old white fitted sheet over the spring, and launder it as necessary.

The box spring is three years old and still looks new.

The cover also keeps out a lot of the dust that normally would sift down through the mattress to the spring.

Bureau

"My son's bureau kept hitting the wall and marking it. I finally found that empty thread spools, placed between the base of the bureau and the wall, work great because they keep the dresser in one spot."

From Idaho: "Cleaning under dressers and chests is a very easy task, but it took me two years to figure that out.

"Don't try to move the entire piece of furniture. Take out the bottom drawer, vacuum and then replace the drawer.

"So easy with a little know-how. Right?"

Carpet (also see Carpets, p. 160 and Rugs, p. 180)

From Ohio: "My bedroom has shag carpeting, so I put a piece of plastic runner under the bed near the headboard where most of the dust seems to accumulate.

"Now all I have to do is mop it with a child's small dust mop. Up comes the bulk of the dust!"

Comforter

Do you have one of those satiny down comforters that keeps slipping off the bed, and you've chased it for years?

Well, here's the answer:

Just sew a piece of muslin, about as wide as the comforter itself, across the edge of the bottom of the cover. This is about mattress width.

Then just tuck the muslin extension under the mattress along with the sheet.

Result: no more chasing in the night.

From Minnesota: "Comforters usually begin to show wear on the muslin or plain side . . .

"By stitching a flat bed sheet over that side, they will be much warmer and may last for a few more winters."

Desk

From Georgia: "When we decorated our daughter's bedroom, we took a leftover scrap of carpeting and tacked it around the foot rest on her desk.

"This protects the wood finish from scratches left by her shoes. Also looks nice because it matches her carpeting."

Dust Ruffle

From Alabama: "I have a dust ruffle around my box spring. It has elastic around it and never stays in place and always looks messy.

"So I sewed the dust ruffle around a fitted sheet and placed the sheet on the box spring, not on the mattress.

"Now it stays in place and looks much neater."

From Vermont: "I made a dust ruffle for my bed and thought of an easy way to remove it for laundering.

"I took an old sheet, measured the width and length of the bed and marked it. Then I measured the length of the skirt and I sewed snap-on tape to the top of the skirt and around the sheet.

"I placed the sheet between the mattress and springs and snapped on the skirt.

"When the skirt is soiled, it pulls off; when it's washed, it snaps back on."

Electric Blanket (see Blanket, p. 303)

Guest Room

I realize that many people buy several bars of soap at a time, especially when it's on sale. Then they remove the wrappers and tuck it in the linen closet, in stored luggage, etc. But I wonder if anyone ever thought of my idea?

I always save one bar of soap for the guest room. I put the unwrapped bar between the pillows on the bed so there is always a refreshing smell.

I never have to worry about a musty odor in the guest bed, and my guests love it.

From Kansas: "Do you have a guest bedroom that's used only now and then?

"I like to keep mine made up neatly. Over my nice bedspread, I keep a plastic drop cloth that I can whisk off quickly when I need to.

"It keeps the dust off the spread and doesn't spoil the looks."

Headboard (also see Bedspread, p. 302)

From Hawaii: "When I got tired of the dingy-looking vinyl headboard on my bed, I tacked a fluffy rug over it. It's a whole new look —and it wasn't expensive."

Jewelry Boxes

You know the jewelry boxes with separate little compartments for earrings, rings, pins and necklaces? Everyone knows they are hard to clean unless you remove the contents. But you don't have to!

Lay a strip of nylon net (see Nylon Net, p. 217) across the top, securing tightly, then vacuum the box out with the wand of your vacuum. All the dust comes through the net . . . but not the jewelry!

Linen Closet

From Arkansas: "In my linen closet I keep sheets of cardboard (cut to the proper size) and slide them between each sheet, tablecloth, place mat, etc.

"In this way, if I want to use the one on the bottom of the pile, it is easy to lift up the whole pile and slide out the one I want."

From South Dakota: "I never have enough room in my linen closet to store extra blankets for guests. So I made some decorative pillow cases from old drapery material with a zipper at one end of them.

"Then I stuffed them with blankets not in use. They make fine throw pillows on sofas and beds, and I now have lots of room in my linen closet."

Mattress

Boy, oh, boy! The price of a mattress set is enough to make you want to sleep on the floor.

When I decided on the one for me, I got some good advice from the salesman which I want to pass along to you.

He suggested that I turn my new mattress once a month for the first few months. When the mattress has deep padding on it, that padding gets packed down very easily.

If you are like me, even though I have a queen-size bed, I always

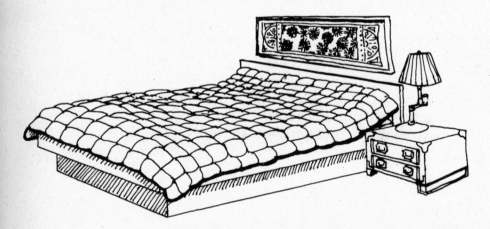

end up on one side right next to the edge. Night after night I sleep in the same place and the mattress gets all the wear on that side. So turn your mattress as often as you can. Once every month isn't too often either.

From Tennessee: "Here's an easy way to turn a mattress:
"Put plastic trash bags between the mattress and the box spring. You'd be surprised how easily your mattress slides around with the help of those little ol' plastic bags."

Does hubby need a nudge to help with a job like mattress turning? Here's what a wife in the state of Washington did:
"I made up the bed at the wrong end and that night when he pulled down the bedspread, he found that the mattress had to be rotated if he wanted to sleep with his head against the headboard. He laughed, but he did switch the mattress around."

From Nevada: "We have no guest room, nor space to store a rollaway bed. But we do have a spare twin mattress just in case.
"Guess where we keep it? Under our queen-size bed!"

Mattress Pad

From Wisconsin: "I used iron-on tape to cover a stain on my mattress pad that wouldn't come out."

From Florida: "When bleach wouldn't remove a stain on a mattress pad, I appliquéd a patch cut from a white sheet over it."

From California: "When the elastic corner anchor bands on mattress pads stretch out, I buy the same kind of anchor hooks that are used underneath the ironing board to keep that cover snug and tight. They usually come five on a cardboard with the hooks and springs.
"I use the hooks with inch-wide elastic pulled tight—two lengthwise and three across—to keep mattress pads flat and smooth."

Pillow

From Georgia: "Here's a handy hint when overnight guests are coming and you don't have enough pillows.

"Put two throw pillows in a pillowcase and slip a second pillow-case over the loose end of the first."

Pillowcase, satin

From South Dakota: "I needed a satin pillowcase to protect my hairdo, but didn't want to go to the expense of purchasing one.

"I slipped a satin half slip over my pillow, case and all, and had a temporary 'coiffure-saver'."

Radio

There are many of us who can't sleep at night for one reason or another . . .

Well, if you have a little transistor radio and your husband (or wife) can't stand the thought of music or noise at night, did you know that you can put it *under* your pillow and hear it perfectly?

Not only this, but it takes out some of the static and noises that you get from certain programs! And even dims some of that snoring!

Sometimes this soft music is exactly what we need to put us to sleep, and one thing about it . . . it won't disturb anyone at all, will it?

Sheets

A hint for couples who still sleep in a regular-size double bed.

Buy queen-size top sheets and a queen-size blanket to avoid fighting for the covers at night.

In the morning, a regular-size spread covers all!

Here is my money-saving hint for the owners of king-size beds: Buy queen-size top sheets!

They work just as well with less (but enough) overhang and they are usually several dollars less expensive than king-size.

From New Mexico: "I had an idea several years ago that solved the problem of all my sheets wearing out at the same time.

"Each year during the white sales, I buy one set of sheets (top and bottom) whether I need them or not.

"Then by the time the others start to wear out, I have a good backlog and don't have to completely restock my linen closet all at one time—which really puts a strain on the old budget.

"I practice rotation in using my sheets and in this way each set gets the same amount of wear."

From Massachusetts: "I had several sets of old white sheets, that were not as white as I'd like, so rather than weaken the cloth by bleaching, I decided to tie-dye them.

"I grabbed the sheet in the center, tied a strip of old material from the rag bag around the center and kept wrapping it around and around till I got to the outside edges, then fastened it tight.

"One set I dyed tangerine, another set olive green. I dried them in the dryer, still tied, then wet them again, untied them and dried again. They're rejuvenated and beautiful!"

From Mississippi: "I do not use a pillow when I sleep, but I do use a night cream.

"So, I always put a small hand towel under my head at night. This really saves the sheets.

From West Virginia: "I have devised a space-saver system for storing my linens.

"In the room that has twin beds, I store the sheets for those beds on the closet shelf. Regular-size sheets are on the shelf in the room with a double bed, etc.

"This helps keep the sheets straight and leaves more space in the linen closet for towels and wash cloths and other necessary linens."

From Louisiana: "Put a dot of nail polish on the inside of the hems of your double sheets, at the middle fold. The middle is always visible so, at a glance you can tell the doubles from the singles."

From Illinois: "One twin flat permanent-press sheet makes a lovely dress."

From Ohio: "I have two complete sets of king-size sheets and pillow cases, one blue and one pink. I wash the blue set, put it on the bed fresh off the clothes line. The pink set on the bed is retired to the dirty clothes bin to stay until next bedding change day.

"When that day comes, I wash the pink set, stuffing the soiled blue set I have just taken off the bed into the rear of the hamper until the next change.

"I never have to fold big awkward sheets; my linen shelf space is not used up on them; and we always have sweet-smelling (just washed) sheets on the bed."

Storage (also see Linen Closet, p. 310)

Here's a great stash-away suggestion from an eleven-year-old in Colorado:

"Have you ever had trouble finding places to put your special little items? Here's what to do:

"Cut some cloth the size of your bedroom door and sew different size pockets on it. Mount it on the back of the door.

"It's attractive besides being useful. You could even sew on extra big pockets and store your small phono records in them."

Wallpaper

From Michigan: "Many paint and wallpaper stores are willing to give away wallpaper sample books. I have used these sample pages for lining drawers and shelves and they work great. Plus, they're free and you can't beat that!"

Window Shades

From Wyoming: "When we covered our daughter's bedroom with wallpaper which had figures of little girls all over it, we had some scraps left over.

"I cut out the individual characters, spaced them on the window shades, and glued them down.

"Now when she pulls the shades at night, instead of an all-white shade she has one that matches her walls."

PART II: CLOSET TALK

INTRODUCTION

I had a funny thought the other day:

What did folks do before someone came up with the idea of closets?

A friend of mine had the answer:

"It's not what they did—it's what they didn't . . . they didn't worry about what their closets looked like."

Isn't it the truth!

Sometimes it seems as if closet is just another way of saying "clutter."

It gets discouraging. It gets so you don't even want to open that closet door . . . at least not when anyone's looking.

I was talking about this everyone's-got-it problem with a decorator who had some really good ideas. So tune in, friends, because organizing's not as difficult as you might think. There's hope for that cluttered closet if it's yours alone . . . and even if you share it with him or her.

First off, just empty everything out onto the bed. Yup—everything. But please don't tackle this job unless you've got a couple of hours to see it through. I never said it would be a cinch-o. But I promise you'll like the results so much, you'll be showing off that closet to total strangers.

Next—and this is the only hard part—give the old heave-ho to everything you haven't worn for a year or two.

You've got to be ruthless. That means, out with clothes that don't fit . . . clothes that are out of style . . . shopping mistakes. (If you're like me you have a few "bargains" hanging there that are hopeless.)

Now, what's left? The clothes you really wear.

I'll bet you're surprised at the size of the discard heap. You'll be even more surprised when you see how much space there's gonna be in that closet.

Next, sort those separates by color, so you can see what goes with what. Think how the separates displays look in a department store and you've got the idea.

Now just leave those sorted clothes and walk right up to that empty closet and give it the X-ray eye.

Wouldn't it help if you put shelves at one side? Super for shoe boxes, etc., right?

How about the shelves over the hanging rod? Betcha they can be improved on because usually there's too much space between them. So add a third shelf and make every inch of closet space work for you.

Another thing: Sometimes closet shelves are too shallow. You can extend them out—right to the door frame—and gain more S-P-A-C-E.

Take care of these little notions, honeybuns, and then start hanging your clothes back up—but not any old way. You're getting organized, remember? So here's what you do:

Hang all the short things—blouses, jackets, shirts—together. Hey, look what's under them—more found space. You can fill it in with a small chest of drawers for accessories and odds and ends. Or, if you're organizing a his-her closet, you can install a second clothes rod and hang his jackets above her blouses.

Finally, hang your long clothes—coats, robes, etc.

Doesn't everything look neat and nifty. Isn't that closet lots bigger than you thought?

Right now, while you're feeling someone should strike a medal in your honor, pour yourself a cup of coffee and read on . . . 'cause there are more closet capers to come.

They're from experts too . . . because in my book an expert is someone like y-o-u whose reaction to a problem is a super solution.
—Hugs, Heloise

Clothes, off-season (see Off-Season Storage, p. 319)

Clothes Rod

From Alabama: "Take a few extra seconds to rub a bit of wax on the clothes rod and you'll find hangers can be pushed back and forth along it lots easier."

From Nebraska: "For a more durable and easier sliding clothes rod try using the translucent tubes that golfers use. I slit mine open and snapped it on over the rod."

Garment Bag

From New Jersey: "When my plastic garment bag began to tear I bought some remnants and, using the metal frame, made another cover for it. I kept the quilted pieces of the plastic which ran down the center on each side of the zipper and sewed these pieces on under the new covering."

Handbags

From Illinois: "I drove four small-headed nails in my closet wall and placed an empty thread spool over each.

"I then painted the spools to match the wall and hung my purses over the spools. This saves storage space and also looks very neat."

Hangers

Do you wish you could afford padded clothes hangers for knitted pantsuits, dresses and sweaters? You can!

If you're anything like me, you probably have discarded pantyhose. It is simple to pad the hangers with them instead of throwing them away.

Poke the hanger hook through the crotch of the panty and wrap each leg loosely around the hanger. Pull the panty over all this. The elastic in the waistband will hold the legs in place.

These padded hangers may not be the most elegant in the world, but they are inexpensive and work great.

From a new husband in Arizona:
"Like most folks who have a closet space problem with half of the space devoted to pants, I was wrestling with the problem today and found an unused skirt rack.

"By simply pushing the clips to the end of the hangers I could lay my pants across the wires."

Here is a tip from a retired Iowa air force sergeant and a charter member of the M.I.M.A.S. (May I Make A Suggestion) Club:

"To eliminate the problem of tangled clothes hangers, remove the wooden closet rod from the closet and notch it at half-inch to one-inch intervals, depending on the bulk of your clothes.

"Make the notches the same depth as the hook on the hanger.

"Replace the rod in the closet with notched side up. As you replace hangers, face the hooks open side toward the back of the closet.

"No more hangers slipping and a neat uniform-looking closet."

From Kentucky: "When you remove a garment from a hanger in your closet move that empty hanger to the end of the rod.

"Then when you wish to rehang the garment, there is no mad scramble to find an empty hanger."

Can you encourage your family to hang up their clothes? One wife and mom in Indiana had this idea:

"I went to the dime store and bought four of the cheapest towel racks I could find.

"I screwed two on the inside of each closet door about three feet apart. One is at head level, the other is just above the doorknob.

"Then I gave my family orders . . . 'When you take off your pants or skirts, open the closet door and drape them over the towel rack from now on.'

"I gave them the excuse that the towel rack would keep their clothes from wrinkling. By golly, it really does."

Hooks

From North Dakota: "Using white household glue, I glued clip-type clothespins across the slanted ceiling of an attic closet.

"Now we clip gloves, scarves, caps, little sweaters, etc. Each item has its own clothespin. Result: a neat closet, added space, easy to find items."

This is from a lazy man in California: "I have some clothes hooks on which I hang my everyday jacket.

"I don't like to bother putting a coat on a clothes hanger every time and having to hang it up. Nor do I like to damage a good coat with the sharp end of a clothes hook.

"So . . . I got a rubber ball about the size of a golf ball and cut a hole in it and stuck it on the end of the hook. It doesn't damage the coat . . . and it saves me from fooling around with a coat hanger.

"Now, if someone can just tell me what to do with the time I save."

From Louisiana: "I screwed a cup hook to the edge of my closet shelf so I can hang garments (on their hangers) on it to button them before placing them back on the clothes rod.

"Simple but great."

Light Pull

From Ohio: "When I was hanging up ironed clothes in my daughter's closet the other day, I noticed she had attached an empty plastic lemon juice container (the kind that looks like a lemon) to the light cord pull.

"This makes the pull easy to spot and it's heavy enough so it doesn't get caught up in her clothes."

Luggage Rack

From Indiana: "We always leave a couple of folding camp stools stashed away in the closet in the guest room. These stools make great luggage racks."

Odor

This is not the "sweetest" subject to bring up but I would like to answer a question that you frequently ask . . . and that's "Why do my closets smell?"

Well, if a garment is clean enough to wear again, don't immediately hang it in the closet after you take it off.

Put the garment on a hanger and hang it on a curtain rod or over a door. Leave it at least overnight to allow it to air.

If you take off a damp garment and put it right back in your closet and squash it between other clothes, the odors cannot possibly escape. Nor can the moisture it picked up from the air . . . or from you. This is what causes closets to smell!

If you perspire a lot, turn the garment wrong side out and then hang it up to air. (Remember, you did not perspire on the outside of the garment.)

Some people say horses sweat, men perspire, and ladies "glow" but, doing housework, we work like horses . . . so give your clothes the air!

Off-Season Storage

If you're short of storage space for off-season clothes, store them folded up in large, heavy plastic garbage bags.

Put a bar or two of unwrapped soap in among the clothes—they'll smell great when you get them out. Tie the tops of the bags closed to keep out winged creatures.

Overshoes

From Maryland: "With four boys sharing one big bedroom there's always a slew of overshoes on the closet floor.

"My solution: a plastic shoe bag hung on nails at a low level behind the door of their room.

"Now the children can put their own wet, grubby overshoes away by themselves. The bag is easy to brush out or wash, and it keeps soil from collecting on the floor."

Padded Hangers (see "Hangers", p. 315)

Shelves

Not every handyman uses a hammer. For example, how about this easy do-it-yourself idea from a bachelor in Ohio:

"Here's an easy way to gain a second shelf above the usual one in closets where about thirty inches of hard-to-organize space exists from shelf to ceiling.

"Place a wastebasket at each end of the existing shelf and rest a board across them. You also could use bricks or concrete blocks.

"I've done this 'carpentry' in several closets recently and gained lots of storage space.

"I use matching slender metal or plastic wastebaskets twelve or thirteen inches tall, and cheap pine boards from a discount store.

"The inside of the baskets can even be used for long-term storage."

From Virginia: "I hated the sight of all the things I had stored on my closet shelves so I bought a spring-tension rod to fit the width of the closet. I placed the rod a few inches above the top of the door (on the inside of the closet), and made short curtains that hang from the rod and extend down to the bottom of the shelves, hiding the clutter."

Shoe Boxes

From Alabama: "I always wondered what to do with shoe boxes. I like to keep my shoes in them and stack them one on top of the other in my closet.

"This was very awkward, especially when I wanted to get to a certain pair of shoes that happened to be in the box at the bottom of the stack.

"So, I cut out one of the ends (not the sides) of each box and then put the tops back on. I stacked them one on top of the other and now I can get to any pair of shoes I want without juggling the boxes."

PART III SECOND TIME AROUND: BEDROOM RECYCLE

INTRODUCTION

Before you rip up a sheet to make dust cloths or cleaning rags . . . before you throw out a mattress pad that's worn thin in the middle . . . before you relegate an old bedspread or blanket to the discard heap . . . take a look at the hints that follow.

Sure hope they get those rusty wheels turning because if there's one thing your friend Heloise can't stand, it's w-a-s-t-e. That's a five-letter word nobody, nohow, can afford to have in his or her vocabulary.

Sometimes I get to thinking how spoiled we are. Why, back in grandma's day, know what they used old sheets for? They washed them up, ripped them into neat squares, and used them to remove makeup . . . that's before facial tissues were invented, maybe even facecloths.

And they rolled 'em into bandages too.

And they used them as dust covers to keep sun from fading the good parlor furniture.

And back even earlier than that, ladies would dye them, cut 'em up and make patchwork quilts.

Nothing went to waste . . . not a thing.

Know what I think? It's time to adopt some old-fashioned ways, 'cause every little bit saved adds up.—Hugs 'n' Kisses, Heloise

Bedspread

From New York: "I cut several small pieces from a chenille bedspread I was ready to discard, hemmed them and made the most wonderful dishcloths. The chenille knots are the greatest for removing hard-to-clean food from dishes and pans."

From Pennsylvania: "I was going to throw out two quilted bedspreads, then I took a second look and turned them into Chinese jackets for my twins."

From Illinois: "Next time you need drapes consider making them from bedspreads.

"Bedspreads already have three sides finished so all you have to do is make a heading at the top!

"Bedspread-drapes can be pleated or made with a double heading at the deepest hem to slip a rod through.

"If you buy queen- or king-size spreads, split them down the middle and hem the torn edges, then make your casing or pleats."

Blanket

From Oregon: "My eighty-nine-year-old mother has a great idea.

"When our sheet blankets grow worn and thin in spots, she makes pillowcases out of the good parts.

"Lots snugglier to lay your head on soft flannel in winter than on percale."

From New York: "Worn lightweight blankets make the greatest polishing cloths for shoes."

Mattress Pad

From Arkansas: "To my surprise, I didn't think of the great money-saving idea this time. My husband did!

"When I was trying to think of a filling for a baby quilt I was making, he suggested that I use an old quilted mattress pad. I had thrown it away twice but he kept fishing it out of the discards, insisting we could do something with it."

From Idaho: "Here's how I recycle unworn areas of quilted mattress pads:

"I make place mats, using an oval plastic mat for a pattern. I cover the pad with machine washable and dryer-safe fabric in a weight suitable for matching napkins, then zigzag the three layers together and cover the raw edges with bias trim."

From Florida: "I was going to discard a worn-in-the-middle mattress pad, then inspiration took over . . . I used it to make the filling for pot holders that I made as hostess gifts."

From Nevada: "Ever notice how mattress pads wear out in the middle?

"I cut off the good portions and save them for patching and reinforcing when other pads start getting worn."

From Nebraska: "As a confirmed recycler (they used to call us pack rats), I'm always finding new ways to use the unworn areas of quilted mattress pads.

"My list includes: Oven mitts, wet pads for baby cribs, knee pads for gardening, quilted linings for booty-type slippers and silverware drawer linings."

From Kentucky: "When quilted mattress pads wear out I put the ends and sides to good use.

"With pinking shears I cut pieces the size of platters and they have good protection between them when they're stacked."

From Georgia: "Here are two ways you can put an old mattress pad to very good use:

"After laundering, use the good parts as padding for homemade scuffs or slippers. Or, using an old oven mitt as a pattern, cut out padding and cover it with a piece of colorful print."

Sheets

From Alabama: "When a contour sheet wears out, put it on the bed and pin a flat mattress pad to it.

"Sew (I make a double row of stitching along the edge of the pad), then trim the worn sheet away close to the line of stitching.

"You've saved money by making yourself a fitted mattress pad."

Desk Work

INTRODUCTION

Everyone doesn't have a desk but, sure as there are little green apples in the summertime, everyone's got "desk work."

And it sure adds up!

There are bills to pay, calls to make, letters to write, gifts to wrap and send.

Land of Goshen, I bet you busy guys and gals could use a P.S. (Personal Secretary).

So this chapter's all about that mountain of paper work that no one can escape . . . and all the supplies needed to make it go easier.

If you're like me, I'll bet you bless the genius who invented transparent tape. But if he was such a genius, how come he didn't invent a way for you to find that useful old tape when you need it? Huh?

Not to fret, friends, because if you look up "Transparent Tape" in this chapter, you'll find a tip that'll help you find that tape every time.

Honest, I never ever stop marveling at how folks find solutions to the stickiest problems . . . and tape is one of 'em.—Hugs, Heloise.

Bills (see Budget, below and Computers, p. 327)

(see Budget, below and Computers, p. 327)

Book, repair

From Iowa: "If you spill water on a book, place paper towels on each side of the wet pages to absorb the moisture and prevent wrinkling of the pages. Or use facial tissues and a moderately warm iron to dry out the moisture."

Bookmarks

From Iowa: "To make a pretty bookmark, take two playing cards from an incomplete deck and glue them together with the numbers on the inside."

Budget

From South Dakota: "To keep track of how you spend your money, rule off a page in a spiral notebook into four columns: Necessities, Comforts, Luxuries, Vices.

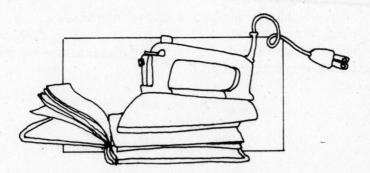

"It doesn't take long to do this and it really helps a person become aware of what is really important in his or her spending habits."

You may be shocked!—Heloise

Calendar (also see Date Book, p. 329)

From Wisconsin: "I have a suggestion for those who are a little forgetful. Make a list of birthdays and anniversaries which you want to remember and color that particular date on the calendar with a crayon.

"I use orange for anniversaries and blue for birthdays and write the name of the person on the date.

"By just glancing at the calendar on the first of each month, I know what cards to buy."

Camera

From New Jersey: "When you have to remove the flash cube from your camera and have one or two unused flashes, place a small piece of masking tape on the used sides.

"You can tell at a glance which flashes are left. No more fumbling or ruined pictures!"

Cellophane Tape (see Transparent Tape, p. 338)

Chair

From Pennsylvania: "I wanted to put some type of protectors on the bottom of my desk chair because it was scratching my hardwood floor something terrible.

"While searching for the felt and glue, my retired husband handed me a pack of bunion pads.

"Since they are made of a felt-like material and the glue is already there, they are perfect for this."

Checkbook

From Mississippi: "When refilling your checkbook, tear out the last two blank checks of the new set and slip 'em into your billfold. Then when you think you've run out, you'll have two more to tide you over!"

From Hawaii: "I have one of those new type of wallets that have the checkbook and balance book in it. I would get so frustrated trying to find the balance sheet to enter the amount, and I thought there must be an easier way. There was—a paper clip! I just clip the used pages back, so I'm always able to find my place in that little book.

"An end to another one of life's small frustrations!"

Clippings (also see Newspaper Clippings, p. 333)

From Tennessee: "Clip the 'up-lift' sayings from advertisements, magazines, or from needlework catalogs and paste them on your bulletin board.

"They are a gentle reminder to think of brighter things."

Computers

Folks who have felt as frustrated as I have may like my solution to mix-ups in our computerized world.

When an incorrect computer statement arrives with all those little holes punched through it, I don't fool around, I wrinkle the card and return it with a note of correction.

It is the only way that I can get attention from the people who run the computers. Before this discovery, I kept receiving repeated mistaken statements. Nothing had been done.

Computer people have to look at a wrinkled card!

This is for people who love to play Scrabble.

In keeping score, I find it easier to use a little shopping calculator than to bother with paper and pencil.

It's a whiz!!!

Correspondence (also see Greeting Card, p. 331, Labels, p. 332, Mail, p. 332, and Stamps, p. 336)

From Alaska: "I have a large family with many letters to write and I used to make carbons of my letters to send out, since I usually said about the same thing to everyone, anyway.

"But then I began to wonder if those who got the carbons felt that the letter was a little impersonal, even though I added a few personal lines at the end.

"So I came up with this idea . . .

"We have four children all scattered in various states. They have small children and time is precious, but we like to hear from each other.

"As everyone got busier and busier, letters were becoming fewer and fewer. So I started what we called a 'round robin' letter.

"I write a letter and mail to our oldest daughter. She in turn adds her letter and mails it to the next in line and so on. When it comes back to me I take my original letter out, add a new one, and start the letter on its rounds again.

"This really cuts down on the time involved in letter writing and, also, we are sure to hear from everyone once in a while. And you have no idea the pleasure we get when all those letters arrive—it's almost like having everyone here for a visit at the same time."

From Connecticut: "Use a black felt-tipped pen and white paper when writing to older people. The contrast between the white paper and black ink will make the letter easier to read.

"Do not cramp your letters or use fancy script. Write plainly in a large script.

"If you do this, you'll have the pleasure of hearing an older person say, 'I enjoy your letters so much because I can read them myself.' "

From Hawaii: "My parents live out of the state so we see them only once a year. My mother kept asking me to tell her more about the children but when I sat down once a week my mind went blank.

"So I came up with the idea of a week-long letter, recounting the news of each day as it happens.

"Mom said, "You'll never know how much cheer your nice long

letters bring. They really provide dad and me with chuckles and cheer.' "

Credit cards

From California: "Next time you pass a copying machine, stop!

"Take your credit cards, social security card, bank cards, and other important papers and line them up in the machine.

"Then you'll have a record in case you lose them or they are stolen. If the name and address of the company is printed on the back of the card, turn it over and print the other side.

"Put the copies in a safe place for future reference."

Date Book (also see Calendar, p. 326)

From Montana: "For her birthday, her grandchildren gave Nana a date book for her desk. In it, each of us filled the date when we wanted to take her out to dinner or shopping or have her for a visit. It gave her something to look forward to and will help keep her active all year round."

Desk Chair (see Chair, p. 326)

Embosser

Buy one of those little gadgets that embosses your name and address on envelopes or stationery and you'll not only save the cost of engraving, but the effort of writing the return address yourself.

You'll bless this idea, especially when writing Christmas cards.

Gift Wrap (also see Mail, p. 332)

From Wyoming: "Here is a suggestion for wrapping a gift when you find you don't have a proper box to place it in.

"I always save the plastic foam cartons that meats are packaged in. By using two of these in the size I need and taping the sides together, I create a gift box.

"These trays are especially nice when mailing pictures or anything you want to protect."

And from a creative guy in New Mexico, here's a money-saving idea for creating your own original gift wrap paper . . . we all know when you buy it, it sometimes costs more than what's wrapped in it:

"You will need large sheets of white or solid-color paper and real bright fingerpaints. Place the paper on the floor and put your finger-paints in an aluminum pie plate next to the paper.

"Put your hand flat (palm down and fingers spread) in the paint. After you get the paint on your hand, take your hand out of the pan and lay it, palm down, on the paper (still with your fingers spread apart). Now gently bring your hand up from the paper without moving your fingers around.

"You can put prints all over the paper or just a few here and there. Be sure to let the paint dry thoroughly before you use the paper."

Wouldn't grandparents just love this?—Heloise

A thrifty gal in Mississippi came up with this winner:

"Here is my idea for using the small or odd-size pieces that are always left after wrapping gifts.

"I cut the paper into equal sheets, the larger ones for letters and the smaller ones for short notes.

"This paper also can be cut round or oblong or any shape your little heart desires.

"The heavier paper works best but either way your stationery will be original."

From Rhode Island: "Here's an idea for decorating a gift:

"I save chicken wish bones, spray them gold and tie them on the package with a bow."

From Colorado: "The other day, while wrapping a very large gift, I discovered that crepe paper streamers make a very nice and novel bow for big packages.

"It requires a little extra care when trying to tie the streamers, but you can do almost anything with crepe paper that you can with ribbon."

. . . And it costs less!!—Heloise

From Arkansas: "When I have a large package (such as an ironing board) to give as a gift, I take flat wall paint and a roller and paint the box to cover all printing and pictures. Then I add ribbons.

"It is so much easier and less expensive than trying to wrap a biggie!"

Glue

From Tennessee: "Glue can be a sticky mess when used from a large economy-size bottle, so I filled an empty nail polish bottle with glue. The brush makes it easy to apply.

"No mess, no waste and the glue doesn't dry out."

From South Carolina: "I have many kinds of glues, cements, etc., on hand. Since only a small quantity of cement or glue is required for each job, I find that the rest of the tube is usually too dry when the next project comes along.

"So, for the past few years I have been keeping all these tubes in tightly closed glass jars and they seem to last indefinitely."

Greeting Cards

From Missouri: "Here's an idea on reprocessing the special greeting cards you save:

"Cut the cards in various sizes and shapes to include the signatures and verses.

"Glue the cards and verses to an old chest, bookcase or screen, following the proper procedure for découpaging.

"Those precious cards will then continue to spread their love and cheer through each day of the year."

"I make place mats with greeting cards. Here's how:

"Take a sturdy piece of poster paper and, using pinking shears, cut it to place mat size. Cut the front off the card and glue onto the paper. After they are all in place, cover front and back of the place mat with clear adhesive-backed paper so it can be sponged clean."

Hole Puncher

From Tennessee: "Know how to clean up the little circles of paper that litter the floor when you use a hole puncher? Wrap masking tape around your hand, sticky side out, then pat over the circles. The tape attracts 'em like a magnet."

Ink Stains (see Spot Check Chart, p. 377)

Labels

From Kansas: "Before I go on vacation I take adhesive-backed mailing labels and write down the names and addresses of the people I want to send postcards to while I'm away.

"This way I'm sure not to forget anyone, and it certainly saves time when I can just stick on the label, stamp the card and drop it in the mail.

"I buy stamps beforehand, too, because they are not always readily available everywhere."

Letter Writing (see Correspondence, p. 328)

Loose-Leaf Covers

From South Carolina: "The plastic covers used for loose-leaf papers are also great for old sheet music. I have saved several old, old songs. By taping them in these covers, they are preserved."

Mail

From Ohio: "When you send a card to someone in the hospital, use the patient's home address as the return address on your envelope. It will insure delivery of the card even if the patient has been discharged."

From Alabama: "When mailing paper items you don't want folded or bent, here's what to do:

"Wrap the paper to be mailed around an empty cardboard tube from a box of foil. Then wrap a piece of foil around it—one long enough to overlap a bit, and fold it into the ends of the tube.

"Return this to the foil box. Wrap with wrapping paper and address.

"It is ready for safe mailing and it's waterproof, too."

From Rhode Island: "It makes your job much easier when wrapping a package to be mailed if you put a large rubber band around the package. Then you can easily tie the cord around it without a third hand."

Mail Order

You know how you write a check and send it away to buy something through the mail? Then weeks pass and no goods are delivered.

True, you will have the canceled check to show the amount you sent but to what address did you send it?

The recording method I use is to write the name, address and what I ordered on the back of the check stub.

No problem for me to check up on the item if it isn't received within a reasonable period of time.

From Wisconsin: "I have film developed by a mail-order house. Once the envelope came open in shipment, but my film was saved because I always put a small address sticker on each cartridge."

This is a good habit to get into.—Heloise

Markers (see Pens and Pencils, p. 335)

Newspaper Clippings

I want to pass along a fantabulous hint for those of you who have old, yellowed newspaper clippings in scrapbooks, etc.

I have been knee-deep in the restoration of some of mine and have learned that those old clippings can be bleached so they look almost new by soaking them in a weak solution of household bleach and water.

This soaking also removes all of the old paste and scrapbook paper that adheres to the back of the clippings when they're removed from the pages of a scrapbook.

When testing this hint, I tore a number of clippings in half and bleached only one part of each. The bleached clippings came out white as snow, and the print did not smear!

The amount of bleach used is optional. On very yellow papers, I used one cup of bleach to three cups of water; for others, about one cup of bleach to a gallon of water was about right. It depends on the age and the yellowness of the paper.

Soak for ten to fifteen minutes, checking often. And be sure to test a small piece before you do the whole clipping.

Now for those who want to try this, let me give you a few tips:

First, do not put more than one clipping at a time in the bleach water. I tried three at once and it doesn't work. The clippings stick together and will not turn white where they touch each other.

The next secret is this: as soon as you take your old clipping out of the bleach-water solution, rinse it under the water faucet. Or, dip it in pan of plain water. Next, slap it on the door of your stove or refrigerator, and smooth it out.

When it dries, it will fall off. Absolutely beautiful! It's so nice to have those old wedding clippings and birth announcements white again.

The very best gadget for snipping gems of wisdom from a newspaper is a seam ripper.

It's unobtrusive, has a safety cap, and can be kept right on the coffee table with your reading glasses.

For handicapped people and those with bursitis and arthritis in their shoulders who are unable to raise their arms very high, here's my idea:

Just open up your newspaper to the middle, lay it all out on a table, and cut it down the center fold. Half sheets can be easily held and also are much easier to clip if there's a story they want to keep.

Pens and Pencils

From Connecticut: "When I carry a pencil in my purse I usually end up with a broken pencil point.

"Now I just put one of those plastic tubes from a flash bulb box on the point of the pencil. Saves many a broken point.

"These tubes also can be used to cover ballpoint pens to keep the ink from getting all over everything."

From Texas: "When the felt tip markers in our office got stiff and we couldn't use them, I took a sharp razor blade and cut a slice off at the same angle of the original tip.

"Gee, they're great!

"Also . . . when using felt-tipped pens, never store them tip up.

"Put the cap on and stand them tip down, and you'll find they are always ready to use. Otherwise, the ink flows back into the pen and it's difficult to get it flowing again."

From New Mexico: "I do a lot of painting with ball point markers. They have to be stored with the point down so I keep them in a canister, but it's a nuisance to have to hunt around in the can every time I need to change color.

"I took an egg carton, turned it upside down, and cut a round circle in each little cup, large enough to insert a marker.

"It organized them just right."

Record Keeping

From Maine: "When making entries in your family bookkeeping journal or listing telephone numbers, alternate blue ink and black ink. It will be easier for your eyes to follow the correct line across to the number."

Rubber Bands

From Rhode Island: "If you have trouble keeping rubber bands together when you store them, try this: hang them on an old shower curtain hook. In turn, this can be hung where it's convenient. In a desk drawer, you also can use a safety pin to gether 'em together."

Scotch Tape (see Transparent Tape, p. 338)

Stamps

From Kentucky: "If a stamp won't stick, apply clear fingernail polish to the back, then press the stamp on the envelope.

"Just be sure to let it dry before mailing.

"I discovered this one time when I was out of glue."

Tape (see Transparent Tape, p. 338)

Telephone (see specific Telephone listings)

Telephone, cleaning

From Illinois: "Here's how I clean my telephone:

"I twist cotton around toothpicks, dip them into rubbing alcohol and go to work getting into the crevices and inside the dial.

"Then I take a piece of cotton, wet it with the alcohol and rub over the rest of the phone and the cord.

"Our phone really shines."

Telephone, long-distance calls

From North Dakota: "To save money on long distance calls to close friends, I have their names at the top of a wax pencil memo board next to my phone.

"When I think of things I want to tell or ask them, I jot them down so I'll have it in front of me when we talk.

"It saves a lot of 'uhs' and regrets that I forgot to mention something of interest or importance."

Telephone, ring

From Michigan: "My mother is hard of hearing.

"While waiting for the telephone company to install a louder bell, she placed the phone on a ceramic tile. That sure amplified the sound!"

Telephone Numbers (also see Telephone, long-distance calls, p. 336)

Is it seek and search for your address book every time you call a friend? Here's how an Ohio woman licked that problem:

"I typed frequently used telephone numbers plus numbers for police, fire, doctors, etc., on a sheet of paper and put it in a picture frame that hangs near my wall phone.

"It's always there when needed."

From New York: "I had to have our phone number changed and unlisted.

"My husband, who can never remember numbers, thought of writing our new phone number with a marking pen on the inside of his belts.

"When he has to call home, he has the number handy.

"Eventually, he may remember it, but I doubt it very much. It has helped him out many times already."

Telephone Numbers, emergency

From Massachusetts: "The best place for emergency phone numbers is on the underside of the phone receiver.

"Cover the strip of paper they are written on with clear plastic tape. They can't get lost, and won't show unless you are looking for them."

A mother in Nebraska sure is well prepared for emergencies ... and you should be, too: "I've put one of my own gummed address labels right at the top of the list of emergency numbers for fire, police, doctor, etc.

"That's so a baby sitter, who mightn't be able to remember our address straight off in a crisis, has it right at hand.

Transparent Tape

Here's a gem from a man in Kentucky who's starting his own lost-and-found department:

"Everyone has one item which disappears whenever he needs it most.

"Sticky tape's the elusive item 'round here. Oh, the things it has caused me to do. Like trying to wrap a package with string, or a gift with white household glue.

"I've found a solution that's sure to work. Just look at the logic behind it: I'm going to tape my sticky tape to the top of my desk! That is, when and if I ever find it."

Now isn't this a honeybunch of a clever idea, folks!

I did find my tape—now if I can just find the top of my desk . . .
—Heloise

What do you do when transparent tape breaks off and sticks to itself so you can't find the end?

Whoa! Before you round up a searching party, listen to your friend Heloise:

First of all, don't use a knife to try and get it started. You end up cutting through several layers, ruining that much more of the tape.

Just drop the roll in a small container of hot water, after removing it from the dispenser.

Leave it in the water only a *few* seconds and you will marvel at the results.

Typewriter

From Florida: "Tired of expensive, ineffectual typewriter cleaners? Try plain old rubbing alcohol on a soft, lint-free cloth.

"It also cleans the hands afterwards!"

Warranty

From Maryland: "When buying a gift that carries a warranty, please remember to include the necessary information needed to complete the guarantee.

"Most ask for the place and date of purchase—which is impossible for the recipient of a gift to know.

"Only the purchaser can supply that information and without it the warranty may be worthless!

"So, please, open the package if you must, but fill out that form!"

7

Your Dining Room

INTRODUCTION

A dining room is a dining room is a dining room but, listen to
Heloise, maybe it's a card table or a fold-up shelf in the kitchen, too.
It's where you eat and that's what makes it your dining room.

Even if you're not the greatest cook in the world, remember that
it's not just food that makes a meal festive—it's the atmosphere. And
atmosphere is nothing more than lots of little things that mean a lot.

Like a pretty tablecloth or place mat, candles for special occasions,
a centerpiece.

Honest, luvs, these things are important . . . even if you bachelor
guys and gals are dining in solitary splendor.

Okay, you're saying, "Heloise has lost her marbles because who has time for that kind of stuff?"

You do! Because it's important. It makes a difference.

F'rinstance . . .

Why is your favorite restaurant your favorite restaurant?

The food? The decor? The candles on the table? Think about it, dearies, and you'll discover it's not only the food but the atmosphere.

So even if you dine alone, dine in style. Treat yourself as you'd treat a guest . . . and we all know that's good—in fact, the absolute best!

A bachelor in Missouri says he always uses the "good china" his mom gave him as an apartment-warming present even though he has a kitchen set. He swears that on china a hamburger tastes like prime ribs.

Another New Jerseyite, who is counting pennies, said he just couldn't live with that heavy-duty cheap-o pottery or glass stuff. So know what he did? He picked up two good china plates and two crystal goblets at a thrift shop. And I hate to even mention what he paid for them—only pennies.

A New York working gal on a tight budget wrote me that she always has a "centerpiece" on her table—even if it's a single flower or a bouquet of weeds plucked from the vacant lot next door—because "flowers are good for the soul."

Sure, I know everything is expensive these days but . . .

A centerpiece can be a bowl of fruit or vegetables. They're natural beauties.

Once a friend of mine made a centerpiece by filling a bowl with eggs and lemons. It knocked me over, it looked so beautiful with yellow place mats and white napkins. Just the greatest.

A centerpiece can be just anything that gladdens your eye.

And who says you have to have a double damask tablecloth? Why folks have been sending me all kinds of sensational ideas for making tablecloths for pennies with fabric remnants, like wonderfully washable and colorful terrycloth or upholstery plastic. Fantabulous!

One thrifty working gal in Mississippi said she made an elegant tablecloth with lace curtains she bought for a dollar at a yard sale. Another one in New Jersey used a patterned drip-dry sheet.

How's that for clever!

If you really look around—even at today's prices—you sure can find a bargain. Garage sales. Auctions. The "china rooms" in department stores where they keep odd lots and discontinued patterns and sell 'em for a song.

An artist in Missouri got all his candle holders for free—by asking his favorite restaurant to save him a couple of empty wine bottles.

Food is one of the good things in life, luvs, so add to its enjoyment by creating a little atmosphere. Take it from me, Heloise, it counts.

For more hints on that room where you do your dining, read on. And next time you light the candles in the jelly glass jars on your dining room table, think of me.—xxxx's, Heloise

Candle Wax (also see Candles, wax stains, p. 159 and Spot Check Chart, p. 377)

To get candle wax off the dining room table, wait until it hardens, then gently remove as much as you can with the edge of a plastic (*not* metal) credit card. Don't use a knife! Next, turn your hair dryer on warm and direct the air on the waxy residue to soften it. Blot off with a facial tissue.

Candles (also see Centerpieces, p. 343)

From Montana: "After our daughter's wedding I took the candles from the candelabra at the reception and melted them into one large candle, using a potato chip can as a mold.

"This makes a lovely large candle centerpiece for the newlyweds to burn on their anniversaries."

From Vermont: "I love to use candles on the table when having guests for dinner but used to forget to light them before everyone was seated.

"Now, early in the day, as I decide what dishes or serving bowls I will be using, I place a book of matches in one of the bowls I will be filling just before dinner is served.

"As soon as I start to use this particular bowl, I am reminded to go in and light the candles before doing anything else."

From Minnesota: "I save the cardboard tubes from wrapping paper or paper towels, cut them to the right length and use 'em to store candles.

"To be sure they don't break, I wrap each candle in tissue before inserting it in the tube."

Centerpieces

From Rhode Island: "I melt odds and ends of candles in an empty coffee can to make a decorative centerpiece for the dinner table.

"You can create your own colors by cutting up bits of colored crayons and adding the pieces to the melted candles.

"Pour the melted wax into aluminum gelatin molds. Add wicks to the centers. When the wax gets hard, remove the candles from the molds.

"You will have beautiful flower-like candles which, when floated in a flat dish of water, give the appearance of lighted water flowers."

From Georgia: "Instead of sticking a corsage in the refrigerator after wearing it and then disposing of it when its beauty is gone, put it in a low dish with a small amount of water and use it as a centerpiece on your dinner table."

China

Watch how you stack your china in the china cabinet. To protect plates, separate them with circles of felt or with foam. You can make plate separators from foam meat trays or from that bumpy plastic that stores use to protect fragile items they're shipping by mail or UPS.

For longtime storage of good china, put it in china bags available from department stores or wrap it in transparent wrap or in plastic bags. Keeps it dust-free and ready to use.

Don't stack china cups. They'll be less likely to break if hung on hooks screwed into the underside of a shelf.

China Closet

From Pennsylvania: "When I cleaned out my china closet, I discovered I had no lacy paper doilies to replace the old ones.

"I did have some gay flowered paper place mats. I traced around a small plate and cut several doilies out of each mat.

"They are colorful and very pretty."

From Delaware: "I lined the back wall and the shelves of my china closet with metallic adhesive-backed paper. It really catches the light and makes my crystal sparkle plenty."

Crystal

When you buy a china closet, check to see that it has adjustable shelves so you can arrange them at the right height for cocktail glasses, old-fashioned glasses, etc.

Store odd-shaped glassware so that every other glass is upside down. This will help you make the absolute most of every inch of storage space.

Don't crowd crystal on a shelf or you'll wind up with chipped glasses and goblets.

Get good use from water goblets by using them for other things. They can double as champagne glasses (only half-fill them) and are great for serving ice cream, pudding and gelatin.

If you don't have a china cabinet, show off your sparkling crystal on open shelves.

Decanter

From North Carolina: "When the stopper gets stuck in a cut-glass bottle or decanter, pour a few drops of glycerine around the neck of the bottle.

"The glycerine will work down and the stopper can be removed after awhile."

Flower Arrangements (also see Flower Arrangements, p. 443)

Wow! Bet you thought artificial flowers would last forever. Nope! The sun fades them too and then they look wishywashy.

When that happens, get some color back in those blooms.

Use any kind of all-purpose dye. Mix it up rather strong in very hot tap water, and dip your buds in this. I tie a bunch with some string and let them soak in the dye bath for thirty minutes to two hours according to how dark I want them.

I hang them on the clothesline to dry with the buds hanging down. I sure saved some pretty flowers this way.

Sometimes I use strong food coloring. This takes a little longer. You can leave them in for three or four days until they get the color you want them.

I took a faded pink rose and dipped it in strong yellow food coloring mixture and it turned out perfectly exquisite.

From Georgia: "When I want my plastic flower centerpiece to sparkle, I spray it with air freshener. Not only makes the posies shine, but makes them smell like the real thing."

Here's an idea from a flower fancier in Mississippi that rates a blue ribbon:

"Did you know that a dish drainer over a sink full of water makes a fine flower holder when you are making an arrangement and want the blossoms to stand apart?"

Meal Serving

From New York: "Having a large group for a sit-down dinner?

"Instead of passing bowls of hot food or casseroles right out of the oven, place all the food on a server and let guests help themselves, buffet-style, before sitting down at the table."

From Maryland: "I keep a lazy Susan on the dining room table to hold sugar, cream, salt and pepper. A spare one is great in my bedroom for a selection of grooming aids and perfumes."

Place Mats (also see China Closet, p. 344)

Come listen, honeypots . . .

I'm gonna tell you something I think is terrific, cheap, and so darn simple that you might fall out of your chair...

It's cute and it's different . . . and I learned this trick from a neighbor.

At any dime store you can buy a cowboy bandana, one of those little printed eighteen-inch squares that's navy blue or red.

And, oh, what you can do with 'em, you wouldn't believe! My neighbor sure did and how!

You can fold them triangle like a diaper and use as place mats, letting the point hang off the table.

If you want to fold them exactly in half for a rectangular place mat, you still have plenty of room for silver, etc. Great again!

But the most fantabulous part of it: use a matching bandana for a napkin! I'll swear this is the greatest because on red or navy, barbecue sauce doesn't show.

And you know something else? They're drip dry! It's an added bonus.

From Kansas: "Instead of stashing place mats in drawers or the linen closet, I keep them piled on top of each other on the center of the dining room table with a pretty potted plant or a bowl of fruit centered on them.

"Since they're so handy, the kids remember to use them when they are eating alone or having a snack."

Silverware

Don't save your good sterling silver for special occasions only. It should be used frequently. Use gives it a mellow finish and improves its appearance.

If you wash silver after each use and dry it pronto with a soft cloth, you won't have to polish it so often.

Never ever use rubberbands to secure paper you're wrapping silver in. They can corrode silver even through paper or cloth.

Watch what you serve in silverplated bowls. Salt can leave marks on silver. Eggs and olives are to be avoided as well. Also watch out for salad dressing, fruit juices and vinegar. Never use a perfume spray near silver as perfume can mark it.

Silver should be kept in a special silver drawer or box designed to retard tarnishing. If you don't have a silver drawer, wrap silver in plastic bags. It's gases in the air that cause tarnish.

Table (see specific Table listings)

Table, extending size

From Illinois: "Here's a solution to the problem of more people for dinner than can be seated comfortably at the dining room table:

"Enlarge the table by topping it with a piece of plywood that's four feet by eight feet. To protect the table top, I cover it with a thin piece of foam rubber or table pads. I find the foam rubber provides enough adhesion between the plywood and the table so that the plywood stays in place.

"After covering the plywood with two overlapping tablecloths, the 'table' is ready to be set for dinner.

"Everyone is together and plenty of room for food and place settings!"

Table, improvised

From Iowa: "If we don't have enough room at the table for everyone when company comes, I put my adjustable ironing board in front of the sofa as a table for the children.

"Of course, I protect it with a plastic cloth.

"The kids love the idea of having their own party."

Table, leaves

From Iowa: "When I wanted to put the extra leaves in my dining room table I had a tough time pulling the table apart in order to insert them.

"I finally got smart and used spray wax on the runners and the little wooden pegs that hold the two halves of the table together. Now I can pull it apart without struggling."

Can't figure out where to store the leaves of your dining room table? Install felt-covered runners in a closet on the underside of a shelf and "run" your leaves into them. Be sure they're covered (slip into a plastic bag), so they won't get scratched.

Table, setting

From Vermont: "When I'm going to have company I set the table a day ahead, when I'm not rushed and can take my time.

"I then take a large sheet of clear plastic and completely cover the entire table and the buffet on which the serving dishes are laid out.

"This saves a lot of time and confusion at the last minute. Minutes before guests arrive, I remove the plastic sheet and everything is clean and in place."

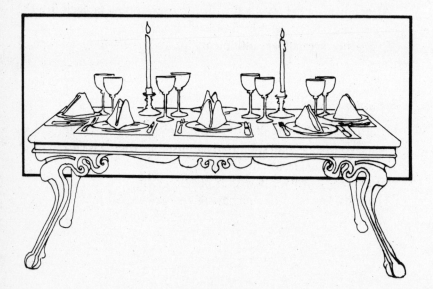

To help remind children where the silverware goes when they set a table, let them think of the number of letters involved in each word.

Both "fork" and "left" have four letters. While "knife," "spoon" and "right" have five!

Tablecloth

From New Mexico: "For a fancy tablecloth, put a 72-inch wide length of nylon net (see Nylon Net, p. 217) over a white or colored sheet. Looks great and launders like a breeze."

From Georgia: "No matter how carefully I used to iron table-cloths before storing them in a drawer, most had to be touched up before I could use them.

"Here's how I got around that: Now, after ironing them, I fold them carefully, hang them over a padded pants hanger and cover them with a plastic bag to keep them dust-free.

"Amen! And they're not wrinkled when I want to use them!"

From Indiana: "I make tablecloths with sixty-inch wide polyester-blend knitted lace that costs one-fifth of what ready-made cloths cost. Want to try? Here's how:

"First, measure your table. If it is thirty-six inches across, you will have an overhang of twelve inches on each side.

"Then, measure the length. Add twenty-four inches in order to have a twelve-inch overhang on each end plus the amount of fabric needed for hems.

"These cloths launder great, dry quickly and need no ironing."

From New York: "Years ago when I was assistant manager of a hotel dining room I learned an easy way to fold a tablecloth.

"Fold it in the middle with the right side out. Then fold each side back slightly beyond the center. When the tablecloth is opened, the side creases will be alike and if the tablecloth is stored for a while you won't have a streak down the middle from dust."

Tablecloths, ironing (see Tablecloths, p. 388)

Table Pads

There are several things you can use to make a table pad.

When cut to fit your table, quilted mattress pads work fine. Foam carpet padding also can be made into table pads. If you don't happen to have any on hand, scraps can sometimes be bought inexpensively at carpet stores. Some have a plastic film on top which keeps spills from going through.

One reader used an old cardboard cutting board (a sewing notion found in fabric shops) though she had to use a thin sheet of foam underneath to keep it from slipping.

Another suggestion is to use an old quilt or quilted bedspread. These would need to be bound with wide bias tape after they were trimmed to fit your table top.

Indoor-outdoor carpeting scraps make an adequate pad, too.

So you see, luvs, there are many budgetwise possibilities to consider. The main thing is to protect a wooden table top from spills and hot dishes.

A pad alone often is not thick enough to do this, so always use trivets of some kind.

Your Laundry

PART I: THIS IS THE WAY WE WASH OUR CLOTHES

INTRODUCTION

Whoever said "Monday's washday" must have been a hermit or a hobo because every day's a washday . . . whether you do a little or a lot.

Why, if you let everything pile up and accumulate you'll be swamped with wash by week's end.

Just think of big families and a mountain of wash that'd make Mt. Everest look like a mole hill.

My best advice about laundry is: make a daily dent in it.

When you take those drip-dries off, soak 'em in the sink and by the time you're ready to brush your teeth goodnight those clothes'll be clean and ready to rinse and hang up.

No pain, no strain, and a minimum of effort . . . that's the way we like to get our chores done, right?

Then, when it's time for your weekly rendezvous with the washer, half your work's done.

Okay, I know this isn't as easy as it sounds, especially if you've got kiddos. But they can learn, too.

A mom in Montana says she keeps a plastic pail filled with soapy water in the bathroom: "I've trained the little ones to drop their drip-dries in it when they change into their 'jamas."

A mother in New York who has two teenage girls says she licked the laundry problem this way:

"I make each do her own wash and, since both hate going to the laundromat, something super happened.

"They stopped using ten towels each per week.

"They also stopped stuffing clean clothes in the hamper every time I told 'em to clean up their room.

"They started rinsing out undies, blouses and nighties by hand.

"I've saved myself a fortune—plus lots of aggravation."

So there are lots of ways to skin that old laundry cat.

Washdays used to mean lots of problems but there are many super aids around—from heavy duty detergents to pre-wash sprays—that make 'em cinchier, not that this always means new ways are always the best ways.

For example, an absolutely fantabulous cleaner-upper for ring-around-the-collar, spots and stains is plain old-fashioned brown laundry soap. Works like a charm every time but maybe takes a little extra rub-a-dub-dubbing.

Grandma used brown soap on everything from collars to white kid gloves and she sure knew her way around a washtub.

And aren't we lucky too, now that "care" labels are stitched right into clothes. Wow! They're the greatest . . . sure keep us from going wrong.

But—and here's something I found out from a designer—"care" labels are sometimes extra cautious.

F'rinstance have you ever wondered why the label in a 100 percent cotton dress says "dry clean" when cotton is washable? I have.

Well, this designer says sometimes manufacturers play it safe because someone might wash cotton in super-hot water and shrink it, then holler and complain like all get out.

So . . . if you know a fabric is washable, you could take a chance but be careful, please, and only try it if you know what you're doing.

Use cold water, gentle suds and avoid wringing out. Press out the excess water. Then blot up more by gently rolling the garment in a towel. Finally, hang it up or stretch it out flat to dry completely.

And, for goodness sakes, don't take chances with a dress or shirt you really love. You could be sorry. I only get daring with the older numbers in my wardrobe.

There's an old saying, "Everything comes out in the wash." Everything includes the great tips that follow from some super smarties in the laundry department.

Sometimes I get to thinking you guys and gals are the greatest because when it comes to saving time, money and effort, nobody but nobody knows more than you do.—Hugs, Heloise

Apron Strings

From Mississippi: "Have you ever had apron strings tangle into a real puzzle in the wash?

"Before I load the clothes, I tie a large bow in each apron. The strings are then short and don't twist up."

Basket (see Laundry Bag, p. 362)

Bathtub Mat (see Tub Mat, p. 368)

Clothesline (see Wash, hanging up, p. 369)

Clothesline Post

From Illinois: "The posts supporting my clotheslines are steel and the bars at the ends of the posts are hollow. All sorts of things—from birds to wasps—were taking up residence in them.

"I closed the Clothesline-Post Hotel by covering the ends of the hollow steel bars with aluminum foil."

Clothespin Bag

Save one of those mesh bags that onions and potatoes come in for clothespins. It can be hung with a heavy cord.

If you leave the pins outside, the rain will never collect in the bottom of the bag and rot the pins. Bonus: after their rainy washing, the pins will dry out much faster.

From Oklahoma: "Throw away that clothespin bag that hangs on the line and make a handier, dandier one.

Get a half yard of strong cotton, double it and make yourself a shoulder strap clothespin bag about 9 × 12 inches.

Put a single strap where it is comfortable for you, then load it up with clothespins and hang away. A shoulder bag even makes taking down the wash easier."

Collars

For those of you gals—and guys, too—who have real nice drip-dries and get back-of-the-neck collar lines and perspiration marks . . . here's my solution:

I take a piece of folded nylon net (see Nylon Net, p. 217), fill a tub with lukewarm sudsy water, and dip my pretty new dress or blouse in it. Then I scrub the collar with nylon net instead of a scrub brush or my hands.

The marks go away like magic.

One thing good about this is that because I use warm water I have no pressing to do!

If you have a double sink, put the soiled spots and dirty collar lines on the block between the two sinks and gently scrub away. I find the nylon net does not wear out the material or leave wrinkle marks, and it does remove soil immediately.

I have tried scrub brushes and even scouring powders but they just seem to ruin the material. The nylon net works like a whiz and doesn't harm the fabric at all.

Be sure when you rinse the garment thoroughly, that you take it up while it's still full of water, put it on a hanger and then hang it up to drip-dry in the shower!

From Minnesota: "I find it very easy to eliminate 'ring-around-the-collar' with nylon net (see Nylon Net, p. 217), cold water and pieces and ends of bar soap, even in hard water areas.

"When I have accumulated enough small odds and ends of soap to make a golf-ball-size cake, I wrap them in nylon net and secure with a rubber band so I can add more soap pieces later.

"Rubbing this across dampened soiled collars (or any particularly dirty spots) before I put clothes in the washer really works."

Colored Clothes (also see Wash, sorting, p. 372)

A college quiz kid in Kansas had this useful suggestion:

"When I went away to the university, I chose bath towels and wash cloths in gay, bright colors.

"I soon regretted this, as I discovered almost all my laundry (blouses, tennis shorts, socks and lingerie) was white.

"While there was room to include my supply of towels in my first wash load, I couldn't do it, lest their color wash out on my whites.

"So I had to use a second machine and run it half empty. My penchant for colored towels doubled my laundry expenses."

If you've already got yourself into this situation, you might knock on your dormmates' doors and see if you can team up with someone who has the same problem, sharing the machines to do "light" and "colored" washes separately. Good way to meet your classmates, too!—Heloise

Curtains

From Nebraska: "Doing up twenty-two pairs of straight sheer curtains in the fall and ruffled sheers in the spring was a killer until I got the Heloise smarts.

"I purchased a long, thin curtain rod and attached brackets to my attic wall. After ironing, I hung all of them on the rod and then covered them with a plastic drop cloth. This way they stay wrinkle-free and are ready to hang when I need them for the next season."

From Ohio: "To give limp glass fiber curtains a new look, rinse by hand in a solution of one cup Epsom salts to one gallon lukewarm water. Even ruffled ones won't need ironing.

"This solution will do long curtains for four big windows.

"Experiment and you'll soon discover how much salt is needed for different curtain fabrics.

"I don't even use curtain stretchers—just hang 'em on the clothesline."

From Tennessee: "When washing matching curtain panels that are different lengths, put a small safety pin in the shorter ones. No more measuring when you hang them."

Detergent

From Arkansas: "When I buy a box of laundry detergent, I measure a cup each into plastic sandwich bags and twist-tie them. I store these until wash day. Then I grab as many bags of detergent as I have loads of laundry and stuff them into my laundry bag."

From Vermont: "When I use a liquid heavy-duty laundry detergent on the collars and cuffs of shirts, I always feel I'm wasting a lot when I pour it on, so . . .

"I took a skewer and heated it by passing it over the burner of my stove. With the heated end I melted a hole through the top of the plastic bottle cap so I can drip it out instead of pouring.

"Once you fix a cap in this manner, you can switch it from an empty bottle to a full one."

Dryer

Have you ever had only one load of wash and were in a hurry and couldn't wait around to dry "like" materials or "like" garments on three different time settings? Here's what to do:

Put all the clothes in the dryer at one time and set your timer for ten minutes.

When the signal goes off, take out the quick-drying shirts. Then set the timer for ten more minutes and take out things that require a little more drying; set the timer again for twenty minutes and finish drying the larger, heavier pieces.

Use a kitchen timer if your dryer does not come equipped with one.

More dryer advice: overdrying takes out natural moisture and can result in wrinkles or shrinkage. Articles containing rubber or plastic (shower curtains, for example) should be dried only on an "air" setting. Never put anything in the dryer that has dry cleaning solvent on it—not even if the solvent's dry.

Did you know that if your dryer stops and cools off before you take out the clothes (and this is what causes wrinkles) you can wet a towel, wring it out real good and then throw it in the dryer with your clothes and let 'em tumble through again to remove those creases?

Works every time.

From South Dakota: "Here is an energy-saving tip;

"When drying the laundry in the dryer, save small lightweight pieces until last.

"Many times the heat left over from a load of clothes will dry these items without your having to turn on the machine."

From Georgia: "I've discovered that a short time in the dryer will dry some things totally and will fluff towels, etc.

"Then, if they are hung on the line to get the last bit of dampness out, they will finish drying, stay fluffy and smell better."

From Mississippi: "Here is a hint my dryer repairman gave me: He said to remove the lint after doing each load as the lint retards the flow of air into the dryer and thus clothes take longer to dry and use more energy, hitting us where it hurts: in the pocketbook."

From Ohio: "I reset my washing machine after the cycle is finished to give the clothes an extra spin-dry treatment.

"You would be surprised how much water still comes out.

"With the clothes nearly dry to start, less time is needed in the dryer.

"Less energy is used to spin washers than heat dryers."

Dryer, lint hose (also see Lint, p. 363)

Necessity sure is the mother of invention as this tip from a super smartie in Nebraska proves:

"There was no place to put an outlet for the lint hose on my dryer, so I made a large sack out of doubled nylon net (see Nylon Net, p. 217) with a casing in the open end. I ran elastic through it and pulled it tight enough to fit the hose on the exhaust.

"It catches the lint and, when it's full, I just take it off and remove the lint. Keeps it from flying all over my laundry room."

Drying, mittens

From California: "I've found metal shoe racks are just great for drying wet mittens.

"They allow the air to circulate through them so they dry faster, especially if you leave the rack on the floor near a warm air register."

Drying, pillows

From Omaha: "After checking the ticking to make sure it doesn't need repair, I wash feather pillows in the washing machine and put them in the dryer instead of hanging them on the line.

"To get the nice fresh smell that comes from line-drying, I spray a washcloth with my favorite room deodorizer and put it in the dryer with the pillows.

"They come out fresh and sweet smelling."

Dye

From Kentucky: "My sister and I are teenagers who like tie-dyed clothing so we tie-dyed Dad's discarded white shirts and T-shirts in different colors. We did sets of matching T-shirts and men's shirts.

"We wear the shirts as jackets over the matching T-shirts. The outfits are really nifty and cost only the price of a package of dye."

Fabric Softener

I've collected some do's and don'ts about the proper use of fabric softeners from experts.

Everyone is aware that fabric softeners give softness and fluffiness to washable fabrics. And the nicest thing is that they reduce or eliminate the static cling that often makes it necessary to peel synthetic and permanent-press items away from each other when folding laundry. This static cling seems to be a problem for everyone.

With the use of softeners, some fabrics no longer need ironing. Those that do, dry with fewer deep-set wrinkles.

There are several types of fabric softener.

You probably are most familiar with the one used in the rinse cycle. Either dilute it with water first and then add it to the rinse water or, if your machine has one, pour it into the washer's fabric softener dispenser.

It is important not to add other agents—bluing, water conditioner, etc.—when you use a rinse-cycle fabric softener. Although fabric softener is effective in both hard and soft water, it should not be used in rinse water containing packaged water conditioner.

Another type of fabric softener can be used in either the wash or rinse cycle. Because it is compatible with other wash cycle compounds, such as detergents, you add it to the wash water before putting in detergent and laundry. Then proceed as usual.

Experts say you should not pour a wash-cycle fabric softener into a fabric softener dispenser unless you want it used in the rinse cycle because that's when the dispenser is triggered to release it.

Never add any kind of fabric softener to a bleach dispenser or a detergent dispenser. They are not equipped to handle softeners.

Something else to remember: don't pour softeners directly on fabrics because they may cause staining. If this accidentally happens, immediately hold the stained area under cool, running water and rub with a bar of soap.

Another category of fabric softeners can be used in dryers. One kind comes in sheets—you use one sheet per load.

There also is a semi-permanent softener pocket that you can attach to the fin of the dryer drum. This means it's there so you don't have to worry about softener every time you dry a load because that attached pocket's going to do a softening job for you.

In some places, you can buy a pump spray that dispenses softener around the dryer drum.

There are a lot of choices when it comes to softeners, but one word of advice:

You may not need to use softener every time you wash items, such as towels or diapers that you like fluffy but that also should absorb moisture. Occasionally, if towels or diapers don't lap up moisture in a thirsty way, as they should, then skip softener for a wash or two. You're the best judge of when you need to do this.

Whichever type softener you use, know what the best tip of all is? Why, it's read the instructions carefully, then follow them to the letter.

When using a fabric softener that needs mixing with water, avoid trips to the faucet: have a batch mixed up and ready to use right beside your machine.

Graying

Ever wonder what makes a wash gray instead of whiter than white? There are lots of factors. F'rinstance:

The water may be muddy and cloudy and have sediment in it. That sometimes happens temporarily. If it does, why not postpone washing until the water runs clear again?

Or maybe the water's hard. If so, a softener will help.

Also, it could be you're not using enough detergent. If clothes are heavily soiled, pour in a little more to be sure they'll come out of the wash white, whiter, whitest.

Hamper

From Delaware: "Looking for a bargain buy in a clothes hamper that's big enough to hold a week's wash for a family? Do what we did:

"We purchased a wire trash burner with a hinged lid and covered it with decorator burlap. Around the lid I attached ball fringe in coordinating color."

Hand Wash (also see Wool Knits, p. 374)

From Colorado: "Whenever I put a load of clothes in my washer, I immediately do my hand-washables separately.

"They then are ready to be put in the machine on its last spin (with the other clothes) for some drying out."

Jeans

If faded jeans aren't your cup of tea, heed a hint from a honey-bunch of a homemaker in Kentucky:

"Before you put your jeans in the wash, turn them inside out. Also, dry and iron them that way and they'll keep their dark-blue color."

From Wisconsin: "Here's a way to make jeans soft with the very first washing:

"Fill the washer with cold water and add about two cups of fabric softener. Wash new jeans in the water along with old ones in order to save on the softener.

"Run through three wash cycles by setting the timer back and using the same water, then spin out and dry in the dryer for fifteen to twenty minutes.

"This also gets all the excess blue dye out so that next time they need a washing, new jeans can be washed with other dark clothes without running on them."

If you wear jeans—and doesn't everyone—have you ever noticed how dirt collects around the cuffs? Know how to beat it?

Go out and splurge and buy starch! This will "seal" the fibers and keep the dirt out. I don't care what kind of starch it is. The cheapest (cooked starch) will do just as well as the most expensive.

Here's why starch helps:

When you put the pants in your washing machine, the gentle warm water and suds loosens the starch and all of the soil that has clung to the outside of the starch.

I've also learned—for those who wear wash-and-wear trousers and carry keys on the belt or back pocket—that after ironing, if you give that area a light spurt of spray starch, it will prevent the silver marks that ruin pants.

Lace Tablecloth

From Maine: "To keep lace tablecloths in shape and to prevent shrinkage in a hot dryer, remove your cloth from the washer, fold it in half and place it over a clean shower curtain rod. Then pull and straighten lengthwise and crosswise to the desired shape and let it dry.

"Only takes a touch of the steam iron to smooth the edges but, better yet, this method will give you a perfectly straight cloth every time!"

Laundry Bag

From Indiana: "I was carrying the laundry basket down to the basement, missed a step and landed in the hospital. I wouldn't have if I'd done what a friend does:

"She puts her clothes in a plastic bag and throws them down the steps!"

Laundry Room

From Indiana: "My washer and dryer are in the garage. The floor is not always spotless, so I put down an old plastic tablecloth in front of the machines when doing my laundry.

"This catches all the clean (and usually wet) clothes that get dropped during the process. It's a real tempersaver.' "

Lint (also see Dryer, lint hose, p. 373)

By Zeus, if there is one thing calculated to drive a person right off the edge, it's lint on dark clothing. So avoid it by heeding these hints:

First, don't wash your dark things after you have done the rest of the laundry. Do them first. Lint from bath towels and cottons can cling to your washer and dryer walls after the cycle has completed.

If you do your laundry at a commercial laundromat, carry some paper towels along. Dampen them and thoroughly wipe out the inside of the washer and dryer before you put in dark garments. Who knows, perhaps the person ahead of you washed and dried a shag rug!

Another way to eliminate unsightly lint is to turn dark garments wrong side out before they go in the wash. They will get just as clean. Besides, most of our body oils and perspiration accumulate on the inside of our clothes, right?

Bonus: garments that are turned inside out for washing and drying will keep looking good longer because the good side doesn't take such a beating.

How I love that fantabulous nylon net (see Nylon Net, p. 217) because it has so many super uses, including this notion from a smartie in Colorado:

"Did you know that if you throw a yard or so of nylon net into your dryer when you put your wet clothes in, there won't be any lint on anything?"

From Montana: "The drain hose from my washer empties into a sink in the washroom which was forever getting stopped up with lint.

"But, thanks to our plumber, I now have the problem solved.

"I cut off panty hose at the knee and slipped the leg over the drain hose and secured it with a rubber band.

"Never a clogged drain. And I only change it about once a month."

Mildew, on washables

Mildew is a fungus; therefore, it grows, so you can't just brush it off and let it go at that because you won't get rid of it that way.

Treat mildew as soon as you discover it.

Brush off what you can and then, depending on the fabric, launder the article with chlorine bleach, hydrogen peroxide or sodium perborate bleach.

If the article is permanent press or double knit, soak it in lemon juice, then rub salt into it, letting it stand overnight or placing it in the sun.

Odor

To remove odor from clothing, add one-half cup of white vinegar (or one-half cup of household ammonia) to the rinse cycle in your machine.

Do not rinse again. All traces of vinegar or ammonia will be gone when the garment is completely dry.

Pants

Where the cuffs of wash-and-wear slacks and work pants are tacked, sew on medium-size snaps. This way you can unsnap them easily for laundering and wash out accumulated dirt and lint.

Pillow Cases

From Utah: "My mother always turns her permanent press pillow cases wrong side out before laundering.

"When she is ready to put them back on the pillows, she puts both hands into the case, catches both corners of the pillow and turns the case right side out onto the pillow. Neat-o, what!"

Pre-Wash Spray

From Ohio: "This is my own recipe for pre-wash spray.

"Combine one-third cup each of water, liquid detergent and ammonia. Mix, then store in a spray bottle.

"This is excellent to spray on collars, spots and resistant stains. It's also safe for delicate fabrics."

I might add, guys and gals, that you wash the garment immediately after spraying just in case some fabrics are sensitive to the ammonia.

Sneakers

From Indiana: "After purchasing a new pair of white or colored sneakers, give them a blast of spray starch before wearing.

"The starch keeps soil from grinding in when the sneaker gets dirty."

"Just wash the sneakers in the machine and the dirt's gone."

From New Jersey: "While washing colored sneakers in the machine, put the laces in a small jar and pour in bleach, water and soap. Then, while the sneakers process, the laces are soaking clean as can be."

From Louisiana: "I wash the boys' sneakers once a week. Before they go in the machine, I remove the laces so I can clean the inner soles.

"I hold the sneakers under the hot water faucet, work in a bit of detergent and scrub the inner soles with a brush.

"Then I dump them in the machine and run through the entire cycle. I hang them on the line by the tongue of each shoe to dry."

From Idaho: "When drying sneakers, I take a drapery hook and hook it through the top eyelet of the shoe, then over the clothesline. Simple but super effective!"

Socks

A traveling salesman whose home state is Missouri came up with this winner:

"When traveling I had difficulty laundering handknit woolen socks, since at home my wife blocks them on wire sock forms.

"Necessity led me to an even better drying device.

"I bought one yard of nylon net, the coarse type (see Nylon Net, p. 217) and cut the net in half.

"When the socks are wet, I crush the net inside them and form it evenly.

"The socks dry in less than half the time needed on the sock stretcher, and the net can be folded and carried on the trip with no trouble at all."

Stains (also see Spot Check, p. 373 and Spot Check Chart, p. 377)

What I always say about some spots and stains in washable fabrics is this:

If detergent and bleach won't take 'em out, the chances are good that hot sun and lemon juice will.

Don't hang 'em on the line. Instead spread them out on an old sheet on the grass, on a picnic table or a plastic cloth. The idea is to get 'em flat so the sun's rays will focus on them full strength and work their magic bleaching process. Leave them out all day.

If the stains are still not out, re-wet the stains with lemon juice and turn the garment over on the other side. I tried this on some stained sheets and pillowcases. I left them out overnight and let the dew drip down on them. I found this was even a more terrific peach of a bleach.

As a last resort, here's a tip from a resourceful homemaker in Kansas:

"If you can't remove a stain on a blouse or jeans, sometimes— depending on its location—you can conceal it by appliquéing a flower or patch over it.

"No one will ever detect the reason for the appliqué, and the outfit will be even prettier for it."

From North Dakota: "Many times I have 'set' stains in a piece of clothing unaware that it needed pre-treating before washing. Finally, I found a solution!

"Each family member ties an article of stained clothing in a loose knot before putting it in the hamper, indicating that it needs special attention. Soon as I see the knot, it takes no time to find the spot. I treat it then and there."

Suede, simulated

Do you remember when man-made simulated suede came out and everyone flipped because it was an honest-to-goodness looks-like-suede you could throw in the washing machine?

So what happened? It was expensive and people who bought it were afraid to wash it.

Phooey on that!

Washable simulated suede—unless it has a non-washable lining, which just doesn't make sense—is, as it promises, washable. Just follow those "care" instructions and you won't go wrong.

Fact is, according to a designer I know, this mock suede improves with washing. It's sorta stiff to start out with but wash it a few times and it gets soft, supple, and suede-ier.

The trick, says this designer, is to throw a couple of towels in the washing machine with your looks-like-suede outfit and let them buff it to perfection in the washing process.

T-Shirts

There's a "right" technique for everything, chums—even washing T-shirts:

From Montana: "My son has the nicest-fitting T-shirts in the neighborhood. I never iron them, but I do take a little extra care. Here's how:

"Wash and rinse. Take shirt by shoulder seams and give a good shake to straighten. Now take by the hem and fold lengthwise in half, with the front on the outside. Hang by the hem with three clothes-pins. Then give a little tug downward by the shoulder seams and straighten the sleeves.

"When dry, take the hem in one hand, shoulder seams in the other and give the shirt a pull lengthwise. Then fold sleeves over toward the neck, fold hem up one third of the way, then over again. Now it's ready to stack in the drawer.

"After doing this a time or two, you'll find it's easy and really pays, for shirts never stretch wide or shrink up if done this way. They fit better and wear longer."

Tennis Shoes (see Sneakers, p. 365)

Tennis Shoes (see Sneakers, p. 365)

Tub Mat

From Nebraska: "When you launder towels in the washing machine, throw in your plastic bathtub mat, too."

Turtlenecks

Every time I take off a turtleneck sweater, I want to wring the manufacturer's neck because he isn't around either to wash my face before I take off the sweater—or dunk the makeup-soiled sweater afterwards!

I love the way turtlenecks look . . . and also because they keep the collars of my suits clean. But . . . I finally found the answer to laundering them.

If you turn them wrong side out before dumping them in your machine, the soil on the neck will come right out! If you don't, that soil will be on the inside when you scrub-a-dub and won't come clean . . .

Isn't that simple?

I think it should be against the law to sell a turtleneck without a zipper closing, don't you?

And women aren't the only ones who have trouble. Even men are complaining, and they don't even wear makeup.

Vinyl

If you're wondering whether a vinyl jacket can go in the washing machine, the answer is yes and no.

Use your own judgment. I had an inexpensive vinyl jacket embroidered with flowers that were rather dingy-looking, as was the lining.

Figuring I didn't have much to lose, I filled the washing machine with warm water and washed it along with a normal load of clothes. (You might want to use a gentle cycle, though I used a regular one.)

I put it in the dryer on a warm setting—along with the load of clothes—and the jacket turned out absolutely beautiful.

Wash, hanging up (also see Clothesline Post, p. 354 and Clothespin Bag, p. 354)

Here's a hint I find useful when hanging out wet laundry in cold weather:

Slip on rubber dishwashing gloves over a pair of cotton gloves.

Your hands will stay much warmer, honeybuns.

From Florida: "Rain or shine, I wash because I have several lines fixed up in my garage.

"I hang sheets first, then hang other clothes over them. They dry fast and it saves clothesline space. The next day, I take them all down, and put another load on the line."

From Idaho: "When hanging out wash on a windy day, I attach each piece to the next one on the line with a clothespin at the bottom.

"This keeps the clothes from wrapping around the line and makes taking them down lots easier."

From Nevada: "On a cold day, wash heavy items like towels and work clothes first because they need more hanging time to dry on the line."

From Idaho: "I have a washer and dryer, but like to hang clothes outside, if possible. I tied loops in my plastic clothesline every eighteen to twenty inches so I could dry wash-and-wear blouses, shells, pants, etc., on hangers.

"My clothesline looks a little bumpy, but the hangers never slip out of the loops and it's worth every knot I put in it."

From Vermont: "Where to hang up clothes after removing them from the dryer?

"My husband solved my dilemma. He purchased two inexpensive towel racks and attached them to the bottom of a high storage shelf located by the washing machine.

"Now I've got room for all the clothes plus the hangers, and I can even hang my long robes without having them drag."

From Rhode Island: "I dry my clothes with solar energy in good weather. I went out in the yard to collect them one beautiful day and wished I had some place to put the folded clothes as I took them off the line.

"So, I placed a folded lounge chair across the wheelbarrow and pushed it along beside the line as I took down the clothes. When finished, I rolled it up to the edge of the patio and carried the folded clothes into the house.

"I can't tell you that this is a timesaver, though, because when I went back out to take the lounge chair off the wheelbarrow to put it away, it fell open and I couldn't resist falling into it."

From Alaska: "As I take a sheet out of the washing machine, I fold the top hem to the bottom hem, holding them together with clothespins.

"This has saved me fumbling around when hanging up the wash.

"As I take a sheet out of the clothes basket, it is already folded and has clothespins in place ready to hang."

From Oregon: "I keep a rubber band around the shower arm.

"Now when I hang a drip-dry garment over the tub, I loop the hanger into the rubber band and the hanger doesn't slide off the arm and into the tub."

Wash, soaking

From Minnesota: "Instead of soaking clothes in the bathroom sink, I place them in a large plastic bag, adding water and soap and putting a rubber band tightly around the top.

"This way anyone wishing to use the sink may remove the whole bag and then replace it afterwards.

"Many times I wash the clothes by kneading the bag, and don't even get my hands wet!"

Wash, sorting (also see Colored Clothes, p. 355)

If you're starting out on your own, moving into your own apartment and feeling free as a bird, just maybe you don't know how to sort clothes for washing.

In the long run, you are much better off if you take the time to sort clothes carefully.

Put all whites and lights, such as bedding in pastel prints or stripes with white background, underwear, towels, etc., in one washload. White permanent press and man-made fabrics have a tendency to pick up the least little bit of color that's left in the water so it's best to wash them separately.

Check any new clothes you buy for colorfastness and read the care labels carefully.

Delicate fabrics, such as knits, sheers, etc., should be washed separately and require gentle agitation.

Never wash anything that gives off lots of lint with anything dark. Jeans, corduroys, and black or dark colors all attract lint like crazy.

Mix your load. By that I mean put a couple of sheets in with smaller items, such as pillow cases, underwear, T-shirts. The clothes

must have room to move around in order to get clean.

Always launder heavily soiled clothes together because if you mix them with slightly soiled garments the latter will come out of the wash dingy.

Close zippers and hooks to prevent their snagging other articles. Remove pins, ornaments and belts.

Whatever you do, check pockets and remove tissues or any papers (especially money!) from pockets because wet paper is hard to remove from fabric—and it could run if there's color printing on it!

If you follow these rules, your laundry should turn out real pretty.

From Virginia: "To make the sorting and putting away of clean laundry easier, I bought six plastic vegetable bins, one for each member of the family.

"As I fold the clean wash, I put it in the proper bin. Then it's up to the children to see that the clothes are put away in their bureau drawers.

"It gives them a chance to learn to be responsible and it makes sorting a clean wash easier for me."

From Iowa: "I keep three pillowcases in my hamper. I put white clothes in a white one, dark clothes in a colored one, and towels in a print one. It saves sorting time when I'm doing laundry."

Wash, whitening (cotton only)

To get dingy clothing whiter than white, try this never-fail trick:

For cotton, pour one gallon of hot water into a plastic wastebasket (enamel or stainless steel containers are acceptable but not—repeat, not—aluminum) and add one-half cup of automatic dishwashing compound and one-fourth cup of bleach, stirring well.

Let clothes soak for thirty minutes, then wash as usual. Use one half cup of white vinegar in the rinse water. The garments come out snowy white every time.

I have put stained pillowslips that were really yellow and badly soiled in this formula and they come out white as white can be!

Do not stir the mixture while the clothes are soaking. And do not re-use the mixture once it has become discolored. Pour it out and make a fresh batch.

Hope this brightens your day as well as your wash.

Washing Machine, cleaning

Maybe you didn't think of it but even a washing machine needs cleaning. Here's how:

Buy one gallon of distilled vinegar and fill your washing machine with hot water. Pour in the gallon of vinegar.

Let the washing machine run the full cycle—but without a wash in it!

This will clean the built-up residue left by washing powders and minerals in hard water areas.

Do this about every six months or at least once a year.

You'll be pleasantly surprised at how shiny your washing machine is.

Washing Machine, use as ice chest (see Ice, storing, p. 211)

Wool Knits (also see Hand Wash, p. 361)

From Maryland: "When hand-washing wool knits, I always let them drip in the dish drainer for an hour or so before rolling in a towel.

"It's an ideal place to get rid of a lot of the excess water."

PART II: SPOT CHECK

INTRODUCTION

I'm sure not going to get involved in the William Shakespeare-Sir Francis Bacon controversy involving who wrote what.

No, sirreee! That's not my department.

Still, know what I've always wondered? If maybe that brainy old

Bard of Avon got chicken soup on his doublet (or was it his triplet?) while writing *Macbeth?*

What better source of inspiration for those immortal words, "Out, out, damned spot!"

Wish I'd been around to bail out the bard . . . because a greasy chicken soup spot can be removed, though I doubt they knew this in Willie's day. In fact, most spots will do a disappearing act if you know how to treat 'em.

So . . . what I want you to do right now is pull up a chair and concentrate real hard. I've got lots to say about the do's and don'ts of treating spots and stains. And, believe me, every last bit of it is important! So read every word before you try to remove a spot!

Hot Water's a No-No!

First off, I want to throw some cold water on the idea that hot water plus detergent will take out everything except the zippers.

Forget it, hear?

Generally speaking, hot water's the worst thing you can apply to a spot. Hot water sets stains. So—and this is important—unless you're following specific instructions for removing a particular type of stain, NO HOT WATER!

And no ironing either, not unless you want the heat of the iron to press in that stain forever and maybe four or five days longer than that.

Pronto Does It!

Now for the next thing:

When should you remove a stain? Instantly's not a second too soon. Don't let a stain settle in or it just could settle in to stay!

Blot spills up pronto—and treat them before they dry. That's the best ticket of all. Do this, and sure as sunrise, you're tipping the odds in your favor.

If the fabric is not washable, whiz yourself off to the drycleaner. Be sure you give him chapter and verse, telling him what caused that spot and what, if anything, you applied to try and remove it. Once he has all the facts, he'll know what to do. And if there's more than one spot, be sure you point them all out to him—some drycleaners put stickers on the spots.

If you're taking a whack at spot-removal yourself, be sure to consult my Spot Check Chart (page 377). But first, read up on spot-removing techniques and formulas.

Work on the Wrong Side

Turn the garment inside out and work on the underside of the stain. There's a good reason why I'm telling you to do this:

If you work on the right side, know what you're doing? Forcing that old stain clear down through the fabric, that's what.

Work on a Clean Surface

A good place to work is on an ironing board. Put a thick piece of old toweling under the garment. Each time you take a swipe at that spot, move the toweling so you're always working on a clean surface. Remember, you're taking out that spot—not putting it back in!

Test Before You Try

Now, and this is really important, don't just get out the magic spot-removal formula and lavish it on. Leapin' lizzards, more dresses and suits have been ruined this way than oaks have acorns.

I know you'll be anxious and in a rush but hold your horses. The first thing to do is to test the formula on an inconspicuous spot—the underside of the hem, collar or belt, the inside of a pocket, or on an unexposed seam.

You don't want to go full-speed ahead only to discover the magic formula takes out the spot and maybe the fabric's color too, now do you? So, test before you try.

A Word About Fabrics

Praise be for those "care" labels that are on clothes these days. They spell out lots of the do's and don't do's and clue you to things like "never use chlorine bleach," etc. Even so, there are some things they may not tell you about . . .

Silk

Know what I've learned? Drycleaners are at their wit's end because customers are bringing them silk blouses and dresses that are beyond help. Scary, isn't it, when you know how much pure silk costs.

What are folks doing wrong? They're trying to spot-clean silk themselves, and that's a mistake. Once silk is wet and you start rubbing it, you can chafe and break off the surface fibers. Kaput! Ruined!

What's more, lots of silks are treated with water-soluble sizing that will leave a ring if you try to remove a spot yourself.

What's the best bet? Leave spot-removal to the experts. Take a silk garment to your drycleaner.

Arnel and Dynel

Avoid using acetone on these fabrics because acetone can dissolve them.

Wool

Avoid chlorine bleaches as they can cause permanent chemical damage to wool.

FOR WASHABLE FABRICS

When fabrics are washable, most but not all common stains can be removed.

Here is some useful information about some of the products used for spot removal:

Chlorine Bleach: Bleach shouldn't be used full-strength. A mixture of one part bleach to four parts water is about right.

Detergent Paste: This is made by mixing dishwashing detergent granules with enough water to make a paste.

Hydrogen Peroxide: The three percent solution purchased at drug stores can be used straight out of the bottle.

Vinegar: White vinegar should be diluted: one part vinegar to four parts water. White vinegar is suggested because cider or wine vinegar might spot light fabrics.

Important: Test all spot-removal products on an inconspicuous area before using. If they do not harm fabric, follow spot-removal technique suggested and then launder the garment.

SPOT CHECK CHART

Adhesive Tape: Get out a nice dull butter knife and scrape away all that gummy, gooky stuff. Do it carefully to avoid damaging the fabric. Then place the stained area on a pad of soft clean cloth, stain side down, and dampen a pad of cotton with grease solvent. Sponge the back of the stain with solvent. Repeat, using only a small amount of solvent each time. Work from the outside edge of the stain to its center, sponging irregularly around the edge so there will be no definite line when the fabric dries. Keep changing the absorbent pad so the spot is not resting on a soiled area.

Antiperspirant: Go over the spot with liquid detergent and (exception to the general rule) wash in the hottest water safe for the fabric. If the stain is heavy, place the garment face down on paper towels and sponge the stain with drycleaning solvent. Rub with liquid detergent, rinse and then launder in *very hot* water.

Beverages, fruit juices, cocktails: Do not use soap. Remove spot with detergent, vinegar or hydrogen peroxide bleach.

Blood: Soak in enzyme pre-soak product or dampen and sprinkle with unflavored meat tenderizer. Some detergents also have enzymes, but don't feature them—the same is true of some oxygen bleaches with pre-soak. Enzymes are great for removing all protein-type stains such as bloodstains or egg stains. Some enzyme pre-soak products are also whiteners.

Butter: See **Greasy Stains**

Candle Wax: Candlelight's romantic—but candle wax spots sure aren't. Use a dull knife to scrape off as much wax as possible. Then place the stain between white paper towels and press over it with a warm iron. Replace towels as they show wax. Go over the back of any remaining stain with a drycleaning solvent.

Carbon Paper: Work detergent into the stain, then rinse with cold water. If it's still there, put a few drops of ammonia on the stain and repeat detergent application. Rinse well.

Chewing Gum: Get out the ice cube tray and hold a cube over the gum to harden it. Now scrape it off with a dull knife. Go over the back of the stain with a drycleaning solvent.

Chocolate: How can something as yum-yum as chocolate leave such nasty stains? But it sure does. To remove 'em, use an enzyme soak, detergent, ammonia or hydrogen peroxide.

Coffee: Soak the spot in an enzyme pre-soak product or in oxygen bleach (if safe for the fabric). Then, and here's another exception to the don't-use-hot-water rule, wash in the hottest water that's safe for the fabric.

Cosmetics: Dampen the stain, then rub in a cake of soap, liquid detergent or detergent paste. Rinse off.

Crayons: See **Candle Wax.**

Cream: Soak in warm water with an enzyme pre-soak product

Deodorant: See **Antiperspirant.**

Fabric Softener: If you don't dilute fabric softener, it sure can stain things. But not to worry. Dampen stains and then rub-a-dub a bar of soap over them. Keep rinsing and repeating.

Fruit: Remove before stain dries with cool water. If stain is dry, soak in cool water, then work in a detergent and rinse. If safe for the fabric, use chlorine bleach when you launder.

Grass: An enzyme pre-soak product should do a job on a grass stain. Bleach will too, if it's safe for the product. After you treat the stain, launder the garment, and hang it out on the line. Sunshine will do the rest.

Greasy Stains: Don't you just hate it when greasy stuff gets on clothes? Here's what to do: Place the stain face down on paper towels and go over the back with dry cleaning solvent, working from center to edges, and always using a clean white cloth. Then dampen the stain with water and go over it with a bar of soap or liquid detergent.

Ice Cream: See Cream.

Ink: Hair spray takes out some ball-point pen ink stains. Also, you can use dry cleaning solvents, alcohol, or, if safe for the fabric, ammonia or bleach. Don't use milk. It could deposit another stain that's got to be removed!

Ketchup: See Fruit.

Lipstick: This is a tough one but, easy does it, and that stain should vanish. Work on the back of the fabric with dry cleaning solvent. You'll have to keep applying it, and keep changing the paper towels under the spot, too. Finally, dampen the stain and rub a bar of soap over it.

Mildew: Treat spots while fresh by washing thoroughly. Dry in sun. If stain remains, treat with a chlorine or sodium perborate bleach or hydrogen peroxide.

Milk: See Cream.

Mud: Let it dry, then brush well and soak in cool water. If stain still shows, rub a detergent into it, then rinse. Use chlorine bleach in the wash water if it's safe for the fabric.

Mustard: The best place for mustard is on a frankfurter. If you get it anywhere else, try using peroxide or vinegar to get it out. NEVER use ammonia.

Nail Polish: Nail polish remover's the obvious thing—but careful, please. DO NOT use remover on acetate or Arnel fabrics. Instead, send to a drycleaner. On other fabrics, sponge the remover over the back of the fabric. Just keep applying it until the stain fades away.

Oil (salad, cooking or vegetable): See **Greasy Stains.**

Paint (oil-base): Use the paint thinner recommended on the paint can, or turpentine. Rinse, then rub with detergent paste.

Paint (water-base): While that paint spot is still wet, rinse in warm water, then launder. If you let the paint stain dry, wave bye-bye to whatever's stained. You can't get dried water-base paint out—not even if you dynamite.

Pencil Marks: Usually a soft eraser (be sure it's clean) will erase pencil marks. If not, follow instructions for **Carbon Paper.**

Perspiration: Perspiration stains really ruin clothes, taking the color out of them. But, before you give up, friends, try this: Apply white vinegar (one part vinegar to four parts water), then rinse.

Rust: Lemon juice usually works wonders on rust stains, especially if, after washing the item, you hang it out and let the sun bleach it.

Scorch: Had the greatest success removing a scorch mark from my dad's suit with good old hydrogen peroxide. It took three or four applications but it sure worked. Now dad thinks I'm a genius—but fathers are like that, bless their ever-lovin' hearts. You also can soak a scorch in an enzyme pre-soak product, oxygen bleach or, if it's safe for the fabric, chlorine bleach. When you launder use hot water.

Tar: Follow directions given for **Greasy Stains.** If this doesn't work sponge with turpentine.

Tea: See **Coffee.**

Typewriter Ribbon: See **Carbon Paper.**

Urine: An enzyme pre-soak product's your best bet. And be sure to use chlorine bleach in the wash water, providing it's safe for the fabric.

Varnish: See **Paint, oil-base.**

Wax: See **Candle Wax.**

Wine: An enzyme pre-soak product or oxygen bleach should do it. And use really hot water. After laundering, if the stain still persists —why, launder again. This time, toss in some chlorine bleach if it's safe for the fabric.

PART III: THIS IS THE WAY WE IRON—AND DON'T IRON—OUR CLOTHES

INTRODUCTION

Like night follows day, so ironing follows washing. Even in this permanent-press era, there is always something that needs a little touch-up.

Well, if that's all that's needed—a collar, hem, cuff—why set up the ironing board? Why go to that trouble?

Instead, place a thick quadruple-folded towel on the kitchen counter and touch-up iron away.

Maybe you can avoid ironing altogether by hanging slightly wrinkled clothing in the bathroom while you run a hot tub. It will steam most wrinkles away.

Don't you sometimes wish there was a magic formula to remove the wrinkles that are—or inevitably will be—on one's face? —Hugs, Heloise

Curtains

From Arkansas: "This morning I hung permanent-press curtains in my kitchen. Not until they were up did I notice that the ruffles were wrinkled. I dreaded the thought of taking them down to iron as hanging curtains is not my favorite household chore. I got out an empty spray bottle, filled it full of warm water and sprayed the ruffles. Then I took my hand and smoothed out the wrinkles.

"When the curtains dried they looked just as if I had ironed them."

Dampening Clothes

If you ever have a batch of ironing to sprinkle, try my lazy person's shortcut method.

I slightly wet two bath towels and put everything to be sprinkled back in the dryer, running it on hot (this causes steam) for about five minutes or so. Remove quickly and wrap in a plastic garment bag from the dry cleaners.

If I don't get around to ironing that day I stash the bag in the refrigerator.

If I don't iron it within a day or so, I stuff it in my freezer! When I do get around to ironing, I remove the clothes from the freezer and let 'em stand for a bit. Sure is easy ironing.

From Minnesota: "A plastic nursing bottle is perfect for sprinkling clothes if you use a hot needle to make lots of extra holes in the nipple.

"You can either sprinkle the water or squeeze the bottle to produce more of a spray."

Double-Knit Fabrics (see Shine, p. 386)

Iron, cleaning

Sooner or later, it's going to happen. You're going to get starch on the bottom of your iron. How can you remove it from a plain iron —not the kind that has a nonstick finish?

Most people run the iron over a piece of waxed paper; others put salt on a brown paper bag and run the iron over that.

The old-fashioned way, which I really like, was to wrap a piece of leftover white candle in a scrap of worn-out bed sheet or pillowcase and then iron over it.

But an old native Hawaiian woman told me to break off a flat piece of cedar tree, leave it on the end of the ironing board and run the iron over it.

Golly whoopers! Does it do the trick! Just try it—takes all the goop off! Provided you have a cedar tree handy, that is.

Remember, now, I am talking about a plain iron and not one with a nonstick coating.

But the cedar does take all the starch off ('specially spray and heavy dip types), and does it ever smell mmmm-good!

What'cha got to lose? Your tree probably needs trimming anyway.

There are many products on the market that clean steam irons. If you prefer to use a home method, you might try mine.

Instead of water, pour the same amount of white vinegar into the iron and let it steam for about five minutes.

Then disconnect the iron and let it sit awhile. Empty the vinegar and rinse the iron thoroughly by pouring water in and out.

Be sure to wipe the bottom of the iron before using it, as some of the sediment may come through the little holes in the plate. I always run the iron over a damp washcloth before using it.

If your iron is too clogged, take it to a repairman. But before you get your dander up and throw away those hard-earned pennies, try my method first.

Iron, cord

From New Mexico: "I put a big safety pin on the square end of my ironing board and run the iron's cord through it. It works wonders! No more tangles."

Iron, steam (also see Iron, cleaning, p. 382)

From Kentucky: "I have a long spout watering can for house plants.

"It makes a good pitcher for pouring water in my steam iron also. I can direct the water right into the small opening without spills!"

Ironing (also see listings for specific garments, such as Shirts, Curtains, etc.)

From Iowa: "Sixteen years ago I found a method that makes ironing a snap—well, almost! Don't buy an ironing basket!

"It's too much of a temptation to let it fill up before starting on the ironing, and then it becomes a real chore.

"With no convenient place to stash unironed clothes, ironing is easier to get done immediately so you can forget it."

From New York: "Thought I'd share a hint that makes ironing a bit easier—and safer, especially for young homemakers like me.

"Before I start ironing, I pile up the clothing, putting the permanent-press fabrics on top and the cottons and woolens on the bottom.

"Then I set the indicator on the iron on low and start ironing. As I get lower in the stack, I change the heat indicator as needed.

"I know it seems logical to iron the things that need more heat first, but my way eliminates guessing whether the iron has cooled enough for those silky synthetics—the kind that melt before your very eyes when a too-hot iron touches them.

"Just remember to iron clothes from low setting to high."

Ironing, hanging up

From New Mexico: "I needed a place to hang clothes when ironing, so I put up a tension rod in the doorway between the kitchen and dining room. It is not in the way and is always handy."

Anybody ever do a time-and-motion study on ironing? If so, this lady from Louisiana deserves a prize:

"When I am ironing I like to save as many steps as I can so I hang my hangers on the leg of my ironing board.

"When I finish ironing a piece, I can reach down and get one without moving my feet."

Some clothes need a lot less ironing if they are put on hangers when they come off the line or out of the dryer.

If you have no place to hang them, hang them in a closet until ironing day.

Ironing Area

From New Hampshire: "Our garage is connected through a door to our kitchen. It is an ideal arrangement for me.

"I have made a special ironing niche for myself in the garage.

"First, I put a piece of old carpet on the floor, and then put up my ironing board. I place my hanger rack alongside of it, my never-empty clothes basket beside it.

"Now, when I want to, I just go and iron. It's easy and, best of all, I got rid of all the ironing paraphernalia in my kitchen."

Ironing Board, cover

Whenever I put a new cover on my ironing board I tear off two sheets of heavy-duty aluminum foil and put them between the padding and the cover.

Foil reflects heat, so my ironing goes nearly twice as fast, especially when ironing sprinkled clothing or using the steam iron.

Another ironing board cover trick: sometimes nylon does not come out wrinkle-free when ironed on those silver-type ironing board covers. Never found anything better to do the trick than old

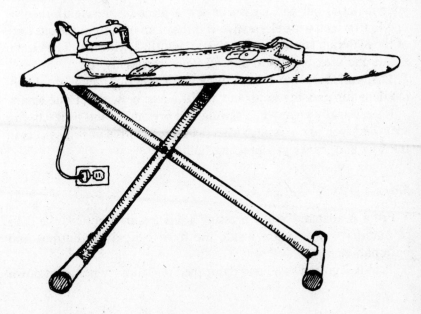

worn-out sheets like grandma used to cover her board with.

So if you are having trouble with ironing, do give these two ideas a whirl. I know you won't be sorry. I just couldn't iron any other way.

Shine (also see Seams, p. 515)

Double-knit fabrics are absolutely the greatest discovery since the light bulb, but they tend to get shiny when you press them and, once they get a shine, it's virtually impossible to remove.

The best thing to do to avoid shining the garment in the first place is to make a "sock" for your steam iron and use it to top-press all double knits.

A piece of wool knit is the best material for this sock. Dig around in your closet for an outdated garment or check at rummage sales for something made of wool knit that you can use. Also, check at remnant counters for scraps of wool knit. Other fabrics can be used, but wool won't transfer a shine to the garment you're ironing. If you use cotton, use a double thickness to make the sock.

To make the sock, trace around your steam iron on a piece of paper. Add one inch to this measurement and, using this pattern, cut your material out and zigzag or sew a piece of one-eighth-inch or one-fourth-inch wide elastic five-eighths of an inch from the cut edge of the material, stretching the elastic slightly as you sew. The elastic allows the sock to slip on and off your iron easily.

That's all there is to it, but I think you'll find this sock is absolutely fabulous for pressing knits and you'll never be without one again.

It's especially great when sewing and pressing seams as it lets you see where you are pressing, whereas a presscloth sometimes gets in the way and leaves you pressing "blind."

Shirts

From Alabama: "While pressing a white shirt I noticed the balls of lint that were caught inside the front behind the buttons and buttonholes.

"I took a cotton swab and dampened one end. By poking it down behind the button or buttonhole and pushing it, the lint came out—most of it stuck to the swab."

From New Hampshire: "The right way to iron shirt collars is to do the underside first, starting at the right point and working to the center. Then begin at the left point and work to the center. Next repeat the point-to-center ironing technique on the top side of the collar."

A man from Washington, D.C., whose job takes him traveling came up with this winner: "A shirt collar that is slightly wrinkled can be 'ironed' over a clean, hot, electric light bulb.
"This can come in very handy when traveling."

From Wisconsin: "I found a good use for the plastic-coated wires that come with sandwich bags. When I press my husband's French cuffs, I put one of these wires in each cuff after folding it up.
"It keeps the cuffs nice and flat until my husband wears the shirts."

From Oregon; "I put talcum powder on my husband's white shirt collars before and after ironing. It prevents the material from absorbing oil and grime during wear."

From New Mexico: "When ironing Western shirts with lots of those gripper snaps, put a bath towel on your ironing board and iron the shirts on the wrong side. The metal part will sink into the towel and you can easily iron over it."

Skirts, pleated

From North Carolina: "Next time you press a pleated skirt, try placing a sheet of coarse sandpaper under the pleats to hold them in place.
"This will save pinning the pleats together. Result: a nice, neat job."

Starch

Make your own spray starch. Make a pint of starch, and while it is hot add a half-inch square of paraffin and allow it to melt.

Store the starch in the refrigerator. Each time you iron, put the desired amount of starch in a window cleaner spray bottle. Add very hot water and there you go.

If the sprayer clogs between use, just spray hot water through it until it loosens.

From Illinois: "When using spray starch, most people spread the garment out on a flat surface and spray away.

"I've found that if I open up pillow cases, dresses, shirt sleeves, etc., and spray inside the garments it works better.

"It eliminates a build-up of starch on the ironing board and on the right side of whatever I'm ironing."

From Ohio: "I use cooked starch on my husband's uniforms. Sometimes it comes out pretty lumpy, but I solved this by using the quick method of cooling gelatin: I put ice cubes in the starch, stirring constantly until it melts.

"Not only do the cubes cool the starch in a hurry without putting in too much water but, to my surprise, they seem to keep the starch from getting lumpy."

Sweaters

After washing a woolen sweater, put it on a large bath towel to dry after blocking. Then take your trusty old rolling pin and roll and smooth it over the sweater a few times. It's easy as pie, pals.

No more wrinkles and the sweater will have a nicely pressed look when it's dry.

Tablecloths

To keep tablecloths from dragging on the floor while being ironed, pin a terry towel to the underside of your ironing board cover so it forms a sack under the ironing board. Put the cloth in the sack, pulling it out as you go. A plastic trash bag may also be used.

Wrinkles

Did you ever wear a permanent-press dress for a couple of hours only to have the back wrinkle from sitting?

Take a damp washcloth or sponge (use warm water) and moisten the wrinkled area.

Then hang the dress on a hanger and allow it to dry in an open area.

In most cases, the wrinkles will vanish and the dress will be ready to wear again without having to get out that iron.

Your Living Room

INTRODUCTION

Do you get the decorating dithers and the flimflam flutters when you're faced with a decision about buying something new for your living room?

Scary, isn't it, especially with everything costing so much. You're darned if you do, and darned if you don't.

If you're not 100 percent sure, if you think just maybe you're making a mistake and are hedging around about what you want and what you need, sit down, pour yourself a cup of coffee, and give the matter more thought. Then wait a bit . . . and even a little bit more.

Know what happens when you really put your mind to solving

something like a decorating problem? Why you zero in on all the possibilities, sort 'em out and, honest Abe, come up with an absolutely perfect solution. I don't know, but it's happened to me and to you too, I'll bet.

To give a f'rinstance:

A friend of mine has a cozy little summer cottage with a great big sun room that has fourteen windows. She had a shade on every single one, so you can imagine what a job it was to pull 'em all down when she wanted to shut out the sun so it wouldn't fade the furniture.

Exhausting—up and down, all day long!

"Well," she thought, "I've got to get curtains" and she rushed out to buy them. Halfway there, she changed her mind 'cause curtains would cut down on light in the afternoon and give that bright room the dismal drabs.

Then she thought about new decorator shades. Nope.

She considered Venetian blinds. Too dressy.

She brooded and thought and shopped and looked and talked about her windows for a whole year.

Then, know what happened? She visited a neighbor who had done his sun porch windows with bamboo shades—not one for every single window but a couple of big ones that cover windows that are grouped together—one to cover two windows at one end of the porch and ditto at the other end; two biggies to cover two sets of three windows along the side of the porch.

Well, you'd think my friend had discovered America—that's how pleased she was with the idea and the bamboo blinds she bought for her own sun porch. They're the perfect solution!

If she's said it once, she's said it a zillion times: "Thank my lucky stars, I didn't buy curtains or shades or Venetian blinds. Thank goodness I waited!"

So you see, folks, it's smart to curb impulse buying. Because if you give yourself time to sort out a problem, you're going to find not just any old solution but the absolutely right one.

It's just amazing how decorating problems can get you down. And sometimes the answer to them is simple as Simon.

Like, for example, putting up mirrored tiles to make a small room look barn-size . . . using a mural wallpaper to give vista to a room with no view . . . finding you can afford new furniture if you buy at auctions, garage sales or thrift shops.

And don't turn up your nose at that last suggestion, honeybuns, because it's a beaut.

Honest, there are so many nifty ways to save that shrinking old dollar.

A friend of mine is a "discount freak." So help me, Hannah, she never buys anything for top dollar. "Wouldn't enjoy it if I did," she says.

Instead, she keeps a sharp eye out for factory stores (they sell retail for just a notch above wholesale), for warehouse sales, and for the big whoppers at retail stores when you can pick up floor sample furniture for a song. And, believe you me, she can sing "tra la" about every last thing in her living room from carpet to sofa, right down to the last ashtray.

You know what's another good idea when you're decorating? It's to adapt, adopt or just plain copy what those high-priced professional decorators have done! You can get yourself some A-1 advice for free by reading decorating magazines and visiting model rooms in department stores.

Just don't give a quick one-two look. Take your time and study those nifty room settings. Find out what makes 'em tick.

That picture arrangement looks good, right? Well, why? Is it because the frames all match or because the flower prints all have the same color scheme, or what?

Analyze, friends, and find out the whys and wherefores and what you might be able to do with the same idea.

Or think about that dream living room in the ad. It isn't just super-expensive furniture that makes that room so dreamy, it's a lot of little decorator touches you could copy for peanuts, things like hanging plants and lots of greenery, an attractive window dressing, a clever use of color or wallpaper and so on.

Well, I guess you've got the idea. Use your noodle, learn to be a savvy shopper, stoop to a little copycatting and, wow, you can have a dream room even on a shoestring budget.

I've made my point. Mull it over as you thumb through some great living room tips that might solve problems for you. Have another cup of coffee first and, as you give it a stir, think of me, your friend —Heloise.

Ash Trays

What's such a big deal about buying an ash tray? Shouldn't be—but it is.

Don't just flip for the color or pattern. Make sure it's deep enough, too. The best ash trays have notched sides that hold a cigarette snugly while it's lit.

Bolsters

From Utah: "What do you do with the bolsters when a day bed is used as a bed?

"We anchored the bolster to the wall. It wasn't very difficult.

"We used a gold towel ring, fastening it to the wall with a molly screw secured in a wall stud. Then we took a chain, looped it through the towel ring and attached the ends of the chain to each end of the bolster. When we need to use the bed, we just pull it away from the wall and the bolster stays out."

Card Table

I recently received a brand new deck of very expensive plastic playing cards. The instructions with the cards said, "Do not use cards on plastic table tops."

Well, wouldn't you know that the only card table I own has a plastic cover. It never fails, does it?

I was bemoaning the fact to my neighbor over our second cup of coffee the other morning. She said her card table top was so disreputable, she was ashamed to use it.

Well, we put our two heads together and came up with a wing-ding of an idea. We discussed the fact that most gaming tables are covered with green felt, so why not ours?

Friends, it was as easy as falling off a log. We looked for green felt the width of a card table plus two inches. Since it comes in widths twice as wide as a card table, all we had to do was cut it in half and there was enough to cover both of our tables.

Covering the tables was a simple matter too. We just removed the little screws that held the tops in place, stapled on the felt and replaced the screws. That's all there was to it.

We now have practically new tables—well, they look new, anyway. The cost was mini and the effort the same.

Check your old card table and see if it needs a new top. My neighbor and I certainly do recommend it. It's cheap, quick and easy.

Coasters

From Illinois: "I got tired of cold drinks sticking to coasters causing the coasters to drop every time a glass got picked up, so I started thinking about a solution."

"Light dawned! We had some short-nap floor carpet scraps so we used them. After cutting circles, we glued them in deep coasters.

"Works fabulously!"

Coffee Table (also see Piano Bench, p. 399)

All brides do a lot of planning . . . but here's a tip from one who says she didn't plan far enough ahead.

From Missouri: "When we were buying furniture, I flipped for a square modern coffee table. Now that I'm the mother of a toddler, I sure wish my choice had been round or oval. Those sharp corners are a menace. I am so afraid my moppet will fall and hurt an eye that I've taped foam rubber bumpers to each corner."

Fireplace

Once in awhile we all run across something that will crack us up —send us out into orbit.

Well, if a friend didn't lead me to the greatest idea that I ever heard of.

It's a new way to save m-o-n-e-y! That's the stuff that used to buy us something . . . right?

So many of us have fireplaces, but now that wood logs are the price of gold inlays, we often hesitate to throw more dollars (that's a synonym for logs) on the fire.

So . . . what could take the place of logs and save those $$$?

The very newspaper you read every day, that's what!

And let me tell you how. Involves ecology, too.

A gentleman out in the mountains where I have a little old cabin uses a fireplace for heat.

Dadgum-a-mile if I didn't go into a trance when he told me how he gets his logs for nothing, folks.

After he reads his newspaper, he rolls it up tightly. Then he takes a metal can with the bottom and top cut out (think about a tuna fish or sliced pineapple can), and jams the paper through the can! This makes a metal band around the middle of the newspaper.

He has all his friends saving him newspaper "logs." When he picks them up each week, he leaves them outside near his garage so they'll get rained on.

That is the secret of it all. During dry spells when he is watering the yard he sprinkles 'em.

Now let's go back to the can.

After the papers are dried thoroughly, he puts can, paper and all

in his fireplace. They make wonderful logs and last nearly as long as oak! And you don't have to part with your gold inlays to amass this kind of log pile.

Isn't that terrific?

As each fire goes out, he takes his fireplace tongs and just lifts out the cans.

The crux of it all is that the woman of the house gets rid of her cans and those newspapers at the same time. Saves on those expensive plastic garbage bags, too. Look at the space those newspapers and cans take up.

I did learn after testing this gem that if you sprinkle a little laundry detergent mixed with some water on the papers you get a "back" log that will last for hours.

So get your fireplace-less friends to save you cans and newspapers. It'll sure save the dollars it costs to burn wood logs.

From Wisconsin: "In summer, I fill our fireplace with candle light.

"I take all the used candles of various sizes, and assorted colors and use bottles of various heights as holders. I arrange these in the fireplace. The taller ones are put in the back. Colors don't matter at all.

"After I light them, I replace the screen and how pretty it looks!"

Furniture, bargains

I once met a magician who'd furnished his entire living room with empty wooden boxes . . . it was magic of sorts.

He stacked them to make a floor-to-ceiling bookcase; cushioned them to create chairs; rested a door on top of two to make a coffee table.

Painted, papered and spruced up, they really looked great. And the price sure was right. You can't do better than "for free," now can you?

From New York: "Tuesday's the day when our sanitation department picks up big stuff—like furniture folks are throwing out. People put it out at the curb early in the A.M.

"I've found some great things (a card table, record cabinet and two lamps) just browsing about."

Hey, that's an idea . . . does your town have a similar system? If so, it's got possibilities because one person's trash may be another's treasure—Heloise

From Delaware: "I've bought almost all my furniture through the want ads in our local newspaper. They're the greatest for bargain buys because lots of times if families are relocating they sell things for a song. I bought a like-new sofa for about 25 percent of its value and a carpet for less than half price."

Furniture, marble (see Marble, cleaning, p. 398)

Furniture, polishing (see Furniture, polishing, p. 168)

Furniture, scratches (see Woodwork, scratched, p. 185)

Furniture, upholstered (also see Upholstery, p. 181 and Upholstery, velvet, p. 400)

From New Jersey: "Indoor cats needn't be de-clawed to save your upholstered furniture. Just clip their nails on a regular basis . . . and provide a scratching place for them.

I've never had a cat that would use a scratching post. My last two opted for a fabric-covered hatbox. I keep it in the living room so the sofa won't tempt them. And I also toss an old sheet over the sofa . . . just in case."

Furniture, water rings (see Furniture, water rings, p. 169)

Lamps, end table (also see Light Bulbs, p. 171)

Have you shopped for end table lamps lately? Sure beats me what designers have in mind. Some of those lamps are so short and squatty they hardly throw any light at all.

And light's what you need to avoid eyestrain when reading.

Make sure you get a lamp that's tall enough and has a shade wide enough to throw plenty of light on the subject.

From Mississippi: "I needed to get a long lamp cord off the floor next to an end table. Not liking the messy look a rubber band made, I notched the cover of one of those plastic egg containers pantyhose come in, rolled up the excess wire, stuffed it in carefully—so as not to pinch the wire—and capped the egg.

"With the plug outside the notch, it plugged in just at the wall.

"Very neat!"

Logs (see Fireplace, p. 394)

Marble, cleaning

Marble-topped furniture should be treated with the same care you would give any other fine finish.

Since marble is a somewhat porous substance, food and beverage stains that mar the finish of fine wood may also mar polished marble. Moisture rings may result from sweating glasses. Beverages containing acid fruit juices, such as wine, may etch the finish, so be sure to use coasters under glasses—and blot up spills immediately. Wash stains with water and a soft cloth.

If the stain cannot be removed with water, you'll have to apply a poultice made of white blotting paper (paper napkins, towels, or cleansing tissues) soaked in one of the following solutions, depending on the stain. Once in place, cover the poultice with plastic or place an upended glass over it to prevent evaporation of the moisture.

For organic stains caused by beverages, flowers, color dyes, use a poultice of hydrogen peroxide (20 volume) or full-strength household ammonia.

For oil stains caused by butter, milk, hand lotions, crayons, etc., apply a poultice of amyl acetate or acetone.

Rust stains caused by flowerpots, cans, nails or any metal that rusts call for a poultice soaked in a commercial rust remover.

A poultice may take from one to forty-eight hours to work, depending upon the stain.

On occasion, even though the stain has been removed, etch marks that resemble dull scuff marks will remain. Acid causes this, but repolishing the marble can remove them.

To do this, wet the surface with clear water and sprinkle on a polishing powder of tin oxide, available from hardware stores or marble dealers.

Rub the powder into the marble with a damp cloth and continue buffing until the etch marks disappear and the surface shines. For further protection, use a non-yellowing wax.

Hopefully this will solve your problem, although there is a limit to what can be achieved with home remedies. If marble has been severely abused or badly discolored, don't hesitate to ask a professional marble dealer for help.

In the meantime, sit down and have a cup of coffee while you mark this hint for now or sometime in the future when you find yourself face to face with this problem.

Odors

From North Dakota: "To remove cigarette odors after a party I burn scented candles. It really seems to help."

This is a goody—but if you don't have candles on hand, pour a cup of vinegar into a bowl and let it sit awhile to absorb the odors.
—Heloise

Piano Bench

From Indiana: "I cut four inches off the legs of an old piano bench, then refinished it and tiled the top.

"Makes a cute coffee table, and the top lifts for magazine storage, too!"

Sofa, sectional

From Michigan: "I have a three-piece sectional sofa on hardwood floors. The sectional wouldn't stay together when anyone sat down on it.

"My husband suggested cutting a piece of an old inner tube and slipping it over the back legs next to the wall to skid-proof it. Works like magic."

Television

From Connecticut: "Does your TV picture seem dull? Check the screen.

"Our TV was beside the fireplace and sooty. Boy, what a mess!

"Sure was a brighter picture when I dusted the screen."

My set happens to be seven years old but I never knew until this week that it had a "re-set" button just like my garbage disposal!

All the TV repairman did was push that little button and everything started working again.

I also have been known to call him 'cause the set wasn't working —only to discover the thing wasn't even plugged in!

True, those dollars would not buy much hamburger today, but they would help on the purchase of a chicken leg or two.

Well, that unnecessary visit from the repairman wasn't a total loss because here's a letter I had him write to you all. God bless him:

"When your TV goes blank and there is no sound or picture, you might save yourself a service charge by pushing that little red button on the back of your set (commonly called a circuit breaker). It is located next to the cheater cord. Just push it once and see if the set comes on.

"Sometimes the circuit breaker may be tripped by a sudden surge of current in the house. Again, push it and see if it functions properly.

"The main thing is, if you punch the little red button twice and it still trips, you know you need a professional repairman.

"The circuit breaker takes the place of a fuse and it never goes out. You can use it over and over again.

"These little buttons are not on all TV sets, but they are on most late models, both color as well as black and white."

Upholstery, velvet (also see Furniture, upholstered, p. 397)

A big puffy ball of nylon net (see Nylon Net, p. 217) is the ideal brush for furniture upholstered with velvet.

It's perfect for cut velvet because it gets into all the crevices; it will clean and smooth antique velvet; it will clean, but won't distort, crushed velvet.

Wall Hangings

Pictures sure aren't all you can hang on walls. There are lots of other things that look decorative, too.

Know what I did in a little living area? Hung a grouping of hats.

Know why? I needed a place to store them. Also needed something to dress up an empty wall.

Everyone just loves my mad hatter look. It's fun. And it's different.

I've also used a Chinese wedding obi as a wall hanging. Just smashing.

And I've hung all sorts of things—ribbons, keys, masks, posters, signs, framed slogans, cartoons, fans, even an abacus.

10

Your Sewing Room

INTRODUCTION

Looks like a lot of folks are into home sewing because it's an industry that's growing by leaps, bounds and giant steps.

Walk into a fabric store and you'll see what I mean—standing room only. And they're lined up two and three deep 'round those pattern books too because it sure costs lots less to make clothes yourself than it does to buy 'em.

So if you don't know how to sew, hop on the bandwagon, honey-chile, and learn a little. Everyone should have some stitchery skills.

Even if you don't want to make your own clothes, it's handy to be able to mend something so you don't have to go out and replace it . . . or pay a tailor to do a little old easy job like taking up a hem or stitching in a seam.

This isn't even mentioning the things you can make for home, sweet home, if you can run a sewing machine—curtains, draperies, bedspreads, and all at a fraction of what you'd pay if you bought them readymade.

And another thing: When you sew, you have a much wider selection of fabrics and styles.

Convinced that Heloise has made a point? Then take an afternoon, evening or weekend sewing course to fill an idle hour profitably because sewing sure helps to balance that battered old budget.

Or get a neighbor to teach you. Make it a swap—you do something for her, like babysit the kids or supermarket shop, in return for a lesson or two in sewing basics.

A friend of mine whose sewing savvy is nil—she barely knows how to thread a needle—made herself the greatest pinch pleated draperies

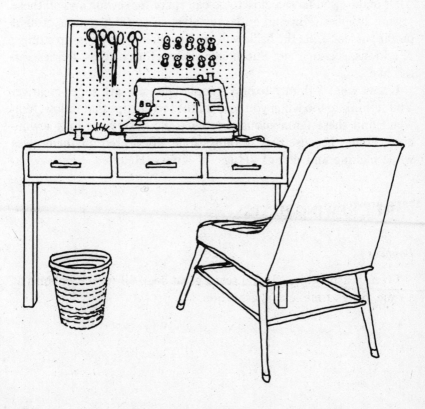

via ingenuity and the diagrams in a sewing book.

The ingenious part was using patterned sheets (bought on sale, natch) instead of yard goods. The sheets were hemmed, so all she had to do was put in pinch pleats—the diagram in the book showed her how. She doesn't know how to use a sewing machine and did it all by hand. Fantabulous!

Just shows what you can do if you try.

One complaint about sewing that keeps cropping up: "I love to sew but it's so much trouble setting up the machine . . ."

Thunderation! You're not going to let a flimflam excuse like that stand in the way of progress are you? I sure hope not.

If setting up really bugs you, make room for a sewing center in your home or apartment. You don't need 40 acres—just a corner will do for your sewing table, machine, etc. So you can leave a project in progress spread out and ready to work on, hide it all behind a decorative fold-up screen—but leave the machine open, so you can throw the start switch the instant you've got a moment.

Or maybe you have a closet you can spare for sewing and all those sewing supplies. Have an outlet installed so you'll have lots of light on the subject. Line the back wall with pegboard for hang-up storage of notions, scissors, etc. Put in side shelves for patterns, fabrics and the like.

Know what I think? I think people who sew are super-creative. You'll think so too when you read all the terrific tips that follow. You won't find these fantabulous shortcuts and easy ways in a sewing book, either, because they're things folks discovered for themselves while making and doing.—Hugs 'n' Kisses, Heloise

PART I: SEWING HINTS

Bobbins

From Washington: "If you sew a great deal, fill several bobbins at a time. Saves time and aggravation."

Buttonholes

From Vermont: "When making buttonholes by hand, mark the line on the material first.

"Then, with clear nail polish, brush along the mark. Let dry. Cut with a razor blade, being very careful to place the material on a magazine so's not to mar anything.

"You now can make a perfect buttonhole—no loose threads or raveling."

From Ohio: "When ready to bind buttonholes on hand knit cardigan sweaters, first mark your buttonholes on the grosgrain ribbon backing, then take small pieces of iron-on tape in the same color, cut to size slightly larger than the buttonhole and iron them to the ribbon over the buttonhole area, then cut the buttonhole through the ribbon and tape.

"Attach the ribbon to the sweater, matching buttonholes with the 'tape' side of the ribbon next to the wrong side of the sweater so it won't show.

"Bind buttonhole, sewing through tape and ribbon.

"You'll find the buttonhole retains its shape, doesn't pucker and is much easier to sew. Also, this technique keeps the ribbon from raveling around the 'cut' area.

"The sweater looks beautifully finished and can be either cleaned or washed without fear of frayed buttonholes."

Buttons (also see Buttons, p. 514)

Hey, hey! It's a lucky day for everyone who's had a problem with buttons that have metal shanks. You sew them on and they fall right off because the shank cuts through the thread.

So praise be for a simple but super solution from a North Carolinian who is a friend indeed:

"Forget thread when it comes to anchoring a button with a metal shank. Instead take a wire twistem, remove the plastic covering, and push one end of the wire through the shank and material, then back through the material again. Twist the wire ends together, then twirl the wire around to make it neat.

"The button's safe and secure."

Corduroy

Here's a whizbang way to get the stitch marks out of corduroy if you have to rip a seam or hem:

Take a stiff brush (I use an old toothbrush) and brush, brush, real hard along the stitch line. I brush both up and down and crosswise, too.

Then turn the corduroy over and press it on the wrong side with a steam iron.

Immediately turn it back over and use that old brush again. I'll bet you a cup of coffee that the marks, which were caused by the needle, won't show. Mine don't.

Cutting Board, table

Here's a doozy of an idea from a California husband who's truly a helpmate:

"My wife loves to sew but hates to set up for it, so I turned the den into a sewing center for her.

"There was just one problem: a table for her cutting board. The den seemed too small for one until I had a brainstorm.

"With hinges, I attached a 4 × 6-foot sheet of plywood to the wall. When folded down, this 'table' is supported on one side by a 1 × 4-foot railing screwed to the wall and on the other by a detachable leg.

"When not in use, the table, with leg removed (it screws out), folds up flat against the wall anchored there by two toggle bolts.

"On its now-exposed underside, I pasted a wall mural, framing it with one-eighth-inch paneling.

"It looks great and really does the job for her."

From Utah: "I don't have a regular cutting board for sewing, but use the dining table with the pad turned (leatherette side down, nappy side up). The nap holds even the slipperiest material in place while cutting."

Darning Cotton (see Thread, p. 416 and Socks, p. 511)

Darts

From California: "Instead of hassling with carbon paper, tracing wheel or marking chalk, let pins and scissors mark darts when you're sewing.

"To mark the darts, clip within the seam allowance where the pattern indicates sewing lines for the darts.

"Then push a pin through marking the point of the dart. Flip over and, on the other side, push another pin through the point of the dart on that side.

"Pull the layers of material apart and secure the pins.

"Match the markings and sew from the clip to the pin. Perfect every time.

"This not only saves time and wear and tear on patterns, but eliminates the need to wash marking lines out of the garment before wearing it."

Fabrics (see Linen, Rayon, Corduroy, Knits, Robe)

Facing

From Pennsylvania: "I use two-inch gauze bandage as facing for dresses and skirts.

"I like it better than bias tape and it's cheaper."

Fasteners

From Illinois: "Instead of sewing a snap fastener at the neck of your dress, stitch a narrow tab of material to one side of the opening. Sew the snap to the underside of this tab and to the dress under the tab.

"It makes a neat closing and is easier to deal with than the hook and thread loop you find on many ready-made dresses."

Hems (also see Lingerie, p. 513, Pajamas, p. 514
and Pants, p. 514)

Friends, what I'm here for is to try to help in any way I can, and I know taking up hems can be a real problem at times. But think of it this way: if you learn to do it yourself, you can save dollars on alteration. And hems needn't be a problem, really . . .

First, never just fold a hem over and hem it because there's no way it'll lie flat and look right. What you have to do is rip the hem all the way out before you turn it up. (You can save the thread for re-hemming, if you like.)

Next, press out the crease with a dampened press cloth—until the line disappears.

Try the garment on, then determine the length, and have someone pin it for a few inches.

At this point, decide if you have to cut off some material. If a hem is too deep, it won't hang properly.

A good rule of thumb: the depth of the hem should be about 2½ inches for a dress; 1½ to 2 inches for pants.

Sheerer fabrics can have deeper hems and still hang beautifully.

Finish the raw edge of the hem with seam tape if desired (depending on the material), or turn under the edge. On some fabrics—knits, for example—you don't have to do either as they don't ravel and you have less bulk. May not look as pretty from the inside, but no one is going to look that close!

Now, turn the garment inside out.

Cut a thin strip of cardboard and mark the depth of the hem on it. Work on your ironing board. Fold the hem over to that mark and carefully press the bottom edge of the hem with a warm iron, holding the hem in place as you work. Do this all the way around the garment, making a continuous line.

The hem is now creased and ready to be pinned in place. You'll find it is easier to pin if you first set the crease of the hem with your iron. Place the pins every few inches, keeping the fabric straight.

(At this point, it's a good idea to try the garment on again.)

After the hem is pinned all the way around, whip-stitch in place (using matching thread) with tiny stitches. Catch only a few threads of the material, so the stitches won't show on the right side. And don't pull the thread tight, or the material will pucker.

Once you have finished hemming the garment, press the underside first. Then top press, using a dampened press cloth. And I can't stress that enough: *use a press cloth!*

If you get a shine on some fabrics, you're just stuck with it for the life of the garment. Not anything you or I or anyone else can do is gonna take it out.

Here's a simple little sewing hint, but I have found it to be almost like having a third hand.

I use the presser foot on my sewing machine to hold the material taut when I'm hand-sewing a hem. It makes the work go faster and easier.

Ever wish you were an octopus? It sure would be handy while sewing . . .

But never mind, a clever seamstress in Illinois has a great suggestion for making hem-pinning a one-person operation:

"I use a floor lamp with a small flared shade. (You must use a shade that is small because it is important that the circumference of the lampshade not be greater than your waistline. If the shade is too large, the waistline of the dress or skirt won't fit around the shade.

"Pull the garment over the shade and pin the waistline to the shade exactly at the point where its circumference and your waist have the same measurement.

"Set the lamp on a table so you can stand up when measuring and pinning the hem.

"Decide on the length you want, and start measuring and pinning.

"I guarantee your hem will hang evenly."

From New Jersey: "Instead of pins use clip-type clothespins to hold a hem in place while you sew it."

Ever let down a hem only to discover the old hem line had left its imprint? Here's what to do:

Sponge undiluted white vinegar on the line. After the fabric has been saturated with the vinegar use a dry presscloth over the line. Press with a hot iron.

The mark or crease line will disappear like magic.

Hooks and Eyes

From Kansas: "When sewing on hooks and eyes or snaps, tape them to the garment with transparent tape first. Then they'll be easier to sew and won't slip, causing frustrating moments and evil thoughts.

"When the hook or eye is secured, the tape can be pulled off."

From Nebraska: "When you buy a card of those dandy hooks and eyes, don't tear off the little plastic case covering them. If you do, the sets you don't use will scatter and get lost.

"Instead, cut a slit in back of the card. After removing a hook and eye stick a piece of gummed tape over the opening.

"Your card will be good to the very last hook."

Interfacing

Did you know that nylon net (see Nylon Net, p. 217) makes a great interfacing? If one thickness is not stiff enough, double it until it meets your requirements.

I have used net interfacing for years and it holds up well.

Knits

From Nevada: "Have you tried to stitch lightweight acetate knit material only to have your machine skip along missing eight stitches out of twelve?

"To avoid this, I save old pillowcases (I save everything) and tear one-fourth-inch wide strips from them. I lay a strip where I want to sew and stitch down the middle of it.

"The percale is soft and not bulky, isn't noticeable and keeps the machine from playing hopscotch."

Lace (see Tablecloths, p. 420)

Linen

From Omaha: "While making a dress of linen-rayon which ravels, the thought occurred to me that soft nylon net (see Nylon Net, p. 217) would make good seam binding.

"It worked wonderfully! So soft and easy to sew over and the seams had absolutely no bulk."

Lining, repairing

If the lining of a jacket or coat rips, here's the easy way to repair it:

If the hem is tacked in place, rip the stitches out. With the hem free, you can reach up underneath the lining and stitch the rip on the wrong side so your mend won't show on the right.

Magnifying Glass

From Rhode Island: "I keep a small magnifying glass on my sewing machine to help me when threading the needle. Also keep one in my sewing basket for the same purpose."

Needle Threader

From Ohio: "I made a dandy needle threader.

"I took a thin strip of plastic—the kind that comes on cigarette packages—and put both ends through the eye of the needle as though I were using double thread. This left a loop in the plastic strip.

"Then I put thread through the loop and pulled both ends of the plastic strip through the needle's eye. The thread came through with them.

"Why don't I use a threader? Because the plastic strip is easier to see."

Needles (also see Pincushion, p. 413)

If people don't think up the darndest things! I didn't believe this tip would work but tested it and, so help me, José, it does:

From Missouri: "I am always misplacing needles which I like to keep threaded in case a quick repair job is needed, so I put the filter-tip of a cigarette—it fits exactly—in the center of a spool of thread, threaded a needle and used the filter as a pin cushion.

"I've done this with every spool in my sewing box. No more lost needles . . . and no more frustration."

Patterns

From New Mexico: "The large cardboard tubes from big rolls of gift wrapping paper are ideal for storing cut-out patterns after they're pressed and used.

"Roll the smaller pieces of the pattern on the tube, wrap the larger pieces around them and anchor with a rubber band. On the end of the tube attach a label with the pattern name, number and style. Then stack your rolled patterns on a shelf. You won't have to re-iron the pieces each time you sew."

From Georgia: "Just hit on a marvelous solution to the problem of storing patterns.

"Cut off the top of a gallon-size milk carton. Cover with adhesive-backed paper and—presto!—a pattern file.

"The container is just the right size for the envelopes the patterns come in.

"No more rummaging around in a drawer looking for the pattern you need."

From Kentucky: "Ever try taping a dress pattern to the fabric instead of pinning it?

"Here's all you do:

"After you have the pattern taped, take scissors and cut right through the tape along the edge of the material.

"When you're done, what a joy not to be bothered with removing pins.

"The remaining bits of tape are on the scraps you usually discard. If not, they can be pulled off easily."

From Hawaii: "When I couldn't find my tracing wheel to mark pattern lines, I tried using a dinner fork.

"I put the tracing carbon down as usual, then pressed down with the tines of the fork. It worked fine."

Pincushion

From Alabama: "A candle makes a great pincushion, one with a bonus:

"When pins are waxed, they slip through material easily."

From Kansas: "Ever blunt a machine needle only to find it's your last?

"Reach for an emery board and, using the fine side, pull the needle across it several times at an angle to sharpen that point."

From Iowa: "When sewing by hand, leave a short length of thread in the needle before popping it into the pincushion.

"The needle will be easier to find and it won't slide completely into the stuffing."

Scraps

What do you do with the leftover bits and pieces when you've finished sewing? Put 'em in a scrap bag because you never know when you might need a scrap to make a mend.

But you can use scraps for lots more than mending.

"I make fabric jewelry for my children," says a clever mother in Colorado. "My daughter loves the rings, bracelets and necklaces I stitch. I've even made my son a headband for an Indian headdress."

Lots of people make patchwork quilts with scraps. You also can make patchwork bedspreads, curtains, aprons, housecoats, skirts, etc., etc., etc.

One last thought: a friend of mine made the niftiest patchwork-look skirt. Know with what? With her husband's old ties!

Sewing Box

From Massachusetts: "My sewing table looked like one awful mess until I fell heir to a three-shelf fishing tackle box with pop-up trays.

"My thread and scissors all go in the bottom tray, my other notions go in the other two. When I want to sew, I lift up the tiers and all is handy.

"The nice thing, too, is that it can be closed and stored out of the way when not in use."

Sewing Center (also see Cutting Board, p. 406)

Planning to set up a sewing center? You might borrow an idea or two from a seamstress in North Dakota:

"One of my favorite pieces of equipment in my sewing room is a secretarial chair. It gives marvelous back support while I work. An added bonus: I can scoot around on the wheels to reach things.

"In addition to a chest of drawers to hold fabric, etc., I have a nut and bolt chest (found in any hardware store).

"Its drawers are about 2×5 inches and have a place for labels on the front. My drawers are full of buttons, snaps, hooks, bobbins, machine attachments, etc.

"I also have a pressing ham, sleeve board and iron. These all contribute to the beautifully finished look of a garment."

Sewing Machine

Do you get mad at your portable sewing machine every time you sew because it jumps and slides all over the place?

Set the machine on a small piece of carpet. Sure solves the problem.

From Texas: "A small paintbrush is handy for cleaning dust and loose threads out of your sewing machine."

For years I've fought a sewing machine drawer full of half used cards of seam binding and bias tape. It was a rat's nest of loose ends and tangled, mangled colors. Now I've hit on a solution.

When opening a package of tape, I slip the point of my scissors under one of the ends of the cellophane wrapper and slit it across carefully.

Then I slide the card of tape out, slipping the remaining unused tape on the card back into the cellophane wrapper for storage.

At long last that drawer is neat.

I "file" the cards of tape, so I can leaf through them as if they were folders in a file drawer.

By the way, it's easier to remove the paper label before sliding the card back in. Since you've used some of the tape, the card won't be too bulky for the return trip into the cellophane wrapper.

From West Virginia: "What a timesaver the presser foot on my sewing machine is.

"When I have to take out stitching, I catch the material under the presser foot and nip away with my seam ripper. It saves holding heavy drapes, etc., by hand and makes the job go lickety-split!"

From Illinois: "I had trouble threading the sewing machine until one day, when I had the needle out of the machine and threaded it before putting it back.

"It was so simple, I wonder now why I didn't think of it sooner.

"Now I take out the needle, thread it and replace it."

And here are two more needle points from a sharp-thinking seamstress in New Jersey:

"To make sewing machine needle-threading easy, hold a piece of white paper close to, but on the opposite side of, the needle's eye to bring the eye into focus. Or use a needle threader. If all else fails, get your eyeglass prescription changed."

From Mississippi: "To keep soft fabric such as rayon, nylon and polished cotton from sliding around as you sew, place a pillow case on your sewing machine table, so the material rests on it."

Snags

From Texas: "To take care of snags in double-knit fabric use a thin wire needle threader. Insert it through the fabric from the wrong side. Thread the snag through it, then pull to the other side.

"This is easier than using a needle and doesn't leave a hole in the fabric."

Thread

Let's hear a hoot and a holler and a "Honey, you're great" for the the stitchery expert in Colorado who solved a problem that's bugged me for years:

"To keep double thread from tangling, don't knot the ends together. Knot each end separately."

From Washington, D.C.: "Thread which is going to be re-used can be wound on strips of plastic cut from coffee can lids.

"Cut one-fourth-inch slits into the sides of the strips. They act as stoppers to hold the ends of the thread."

Betcha didn't notice what's done a disappearing act . . . darning cotton, that's what. It's almost impossible to find. But please don't panic because a resourceful homemaker in Oregon has one answer:

"I've found a good substitute—embroidery floss. It comes in a wide range of colors and you can control the thickness by the number of strands used.

"It's also great for hand-sewn button holes. Use four strands and the buttonhole will be strong, smooth and look professional even if you're shaky about tackling such a job."

Here's a bit of make-do magic from Mississippi:

"If I don't have the exact color thread on hand for mending, I can almost always make do by using two strands of thread which blend to the needed shade.

"For example, for ecru, thread your needle with light brown and white thread. For medium blue, use dark blue and light blue."

From Ohio: "When mending a dress or skirt of loosely woven fabric, I pull some threads from the inside hem or side seam in the skirt.

"What better match could you have for weaving or darning?"

From Louisiana: "We've used empty wooden thread spools as drawer pulls and cabinet knobs, made legs out of them for small cabinets and boxes.

"They even come in handy in the toy box. We've made toy abacuses out of them for the children and have used them as handles for a jump rope."

From Illinois: "We save empty thread spools (all sizes) and use them in decorating.

"We painted some of the spools and strung them with beads to make a really attractive and unusual room divider."

Zippers (also see Pockets, p. 514 and Slipcovers, p. 419)

From Indiana: "If a zipper gets off the track, take a razor blade and slit through the metal bottom of the zipper. Slip each side of the tab back onto the zipper track.

"Pull the zipper up, then sew the slit up, stitching across the teeth at the bottom."

PART II: SEWING FOR YOUR HOME

People think of the cleverest things, like these ideas for making curtains, drapes and other odds and ends for home, sweet home.

Ball Fringe (see Curtains, below)

Curtains

From Connecticut: "Recently I made curtains for my large kitchen windows from, guess what? Polyester double knit!

"I used nylon lace for the trim. My family went wild over them."
And boy, I bet they wash easy, with no ironing.—Heloise

From Ohio: "When trimming curtains with ball fringe, use the zipper foot on your machine and you'll have no trouble with the fringe catching between the feeder teeth."

Curtains, lace (see Tablecloths, p. 419)

Draperies

From Utah: "Why make buttonholes in the cotton liners of glass-fiber drapes? I hemmed the top and the bottom of each lining, then marked the place on the lining where the drapery hook should go.

"Instead of making buttonholes, I used an eyelet tool and punched a metal eyelet where the back of each metal pleat hook went.

"Then I put the drapes on the front of the hook, and the lining at each eyelet on the back of the hook . . . and hung as usual.

"So simple!"

Pillowcases

From Kentucky: "When pillowcases with embroidered hems wear out, the hem usually is still in good shape.

"I snip it off and 'hem' it to a plain pillowcase."

From Tennessee: "Instead of buying matched pillowcases when I buy sheets, I order an extra double sheet and—for a big saving, make five pillowcases with it—two from the top of the sheet which has the fancy border; two from the bottom of the sheet; one from the center."

Pillows

From North Dakota: "Wonder how many ladies use shredded foam to stuff pillows, toys, etc., and find the stuff sticks to their hands and arms?

"I've found a remedy: wash your hands and arms in fabric softener. Don't dry on a towel, but rub them until dry. Works real slick, no stuff clinging to hands and arms."

From Minnesota: "My friends who knit save their snips and snails and puppy dog tails of yarn for me so I can make confetti pillows!

"When I have enough for pillow stuffing I make a case of fine black or white nylon net (see Nylon Net p. 217) or tulle.

"I then snip the yarn filling into half-inch pieces, put them in the pillowcase and sew it up.

"The various yarn colors show through the net and look like confetti. Really pretty. Try it."

Slipcovers

From South Dakota: "When I was making slipcovers for my couch, I realized I didn't have another long zipper to put in the last cushion cover.

"It was too late to run to the store and I was expecting company the next day, so I had to finish the job.

"I used two short zippers, the top of one facing the top of the other. Together they made one long one."

Tablecloths

From Pennsylvania: "Here's how I repaired a lace tablecloth that had a slit about one inch long—like a knife cut.

"I took wax paper, laid it under the tablecloth where the cut was and got my clear nail polish and a straight pin or two.

"I loosely pinned the tablecloth to the wax paper so the cut edges of the slit were together. Then I applied just a little clear nail polish across the threads.

"After the polish dried, I couldn't tell there was a tear or slit in the cloth.

"You also could use this trick on sheer or lace curtains."

PART III: NEEDLEWORK

I just couldn't end this chapter without tossing in a couple of hints for you crafty needleworkers who make such beautiful things. Sure wish I had that kind of talent. But maybe it's better I don't— somebody's got to be an appreciative audience . . . and that's me, your friend, Heloise.

Crochet

From New Hampshire: "If you crochet a great deal, your finger gets sore because the thread cuts it. It needs protection.

"Crochet a 'finger' for that one finger the thread goes around."

From Alaska: "When you lay crocheting work down for a while, put a snap-type clothespin on the hook, thread and piece of work.

"This keeps everything together right where you stopped and keeps your work from unraveling."

From Delaware: "To keep threads from getting tangled or knotted when you crochet, try this:

"Run the crochet thread through a plastic soda straw. It sure keeps the thread free of tangles and knots."

From Illinois: "When I help my wife tie quilts with yarn, I have to thread the darning needle many times.

"To make the job easier and quicker, I use a small thin wire, make a loop and pass it through the eye of the needle.

"Then I thread the yarn through the wire loop and pull it back through the eye of the needle. Works very easy—no licking the yarn when trying to thread the needle."

Embroidery

From Alaska: "Of course everyone knows about using wax on thread to keep it from knotting, but I bet lots of people never thought of lightly waxing embroidery floss. It's especially great to keep French knots from knotting the wrong way."

Three cheers for this helpful husband in Nebraska:

"When my wife needed another embroidery hoop in a hurry I came to her rescue.

"I took the plastic lid from a large, round margarine container and cut out the center leaving the rim only. Then I cut off the bottom of the container. Then I placed the embroidery over the top of the margarine tub, snapped on the lid and, zingo, hoops.

"This is a great idea to use with children who are just starting to embroider."

Knitting

From Utah: "If you rub wooden knitting needles over a soap-filled scouring pad, they'll handle your yarn with lots more ease."

From Montana: "When you're ready to sew a knitted garment together use the plastic 'picks' that come with brush hair rollers. They not only hold the pieces together firmly but leave no holes."

From Idaho: "While knitting a sweater, I had only one stitch-holder (and needed two), so I shifted the stitches to a plastic straw.
"It served the purpose nicely."

Quilting

This hint is from a group of Minnesota experts who practice this old-fashioned needlework at weekly quilting parties:
"Use a white sheet as lining for a quilt and you'll find the quilt will be smooth and lump-free after washing."

Rug Hooking

From Louisiana: "The other day I was looking for a canvas to latch-hook a small rug for a gift for my parents.
"I came across a large nylon net onion bag. I cut out the size I wanted, taped the edges and presto! I had a new canvas."

The Great Outdoors

1

Outside Your Home

INTRODUCTION

Hi, home owners, the hints that follow are for you lucky folks who pay a mortgage instead of rent. It sure is worth the sacrifices you may have made because you not only have an indoors to enjoy but an outdoors, too.

In my book, one of the nicest things about a house is the yard, patio, porch, or deck that gives you living room under the sun and stars.

I sure like to lounge on the little deck behind my house and watch the seasons go by and the foliage change.

Okay, I know it's not all sunshine—especially not when the weatherman's blasting out blizzard warnings that keep your snow shovel on the ready.

Or when the paint's peeling and you know for sure you're going up in the world—up on a ladder, that is!

Or when the driveway's icy and you wish Hercules would lend a hand with those heavy garbage cans.

Yessiree, a house is work—but isn't it worth it?

Balance the drawbacks against the pluses and then answer one question: can anything beat having your own spread, as we Texans say?

Big or small, modest or mansion, it's yours, all yours—or will be when you make that last mortgage payment. That's what counts.

As for the inevitable chores, there usually are two ways to do 'em —the hard way and Heloise's way. That's what the tips that follow are all about.—Hugs 'n' kisses, Heloise

Ash Trays

From Connecticut; "Cover a three-pound coffee can with adhesive-backed paper to match your decor and empty all cigarette butts in it after an outdoor party.

"Cover with the lid and let stand until the following morning. No worry of an outdoor fire."

Barbecue (also see Barbecuing, p. 453)

From Kentucky: "An unusable charcoal barbecue grill makes a beautiful planter. First, remove the hood and motor (if any). Drill several holes in the bottom of the fire-bowl and use a wire brush to thoroughly clean off any rust or flaked paint.

"Spray inside and out with a good paint to retard rust.

"When the paint is completely dry, put in a layer of stones for drainage and fill the container with a mixture of good soil and peat moss.

"I planted a geranium in the middle of mine, surrounded by petunias and then put pansies around the outside.

"You also could put potted plants on the bottom shelf.

"Since most grills have wheels, you can roll your barbecue 'garden' around to sunny or shady spots, depending on the flowers you use.

"Our grill was about ready for the dump, but I now have an inexpensive planter—as well as a very attractive one."

Bird Seed (see Birds, p. 439)

Doors (also see Sliding Glass Doors, p. 180)

An accountant in New Mexico offers this advice:

"I have always applied decals to sliding glass doors so friends wouldn't walk through them. Well, it seems it's a good idea to apply decals to sliding *screen* doors, too.

"One of my clients was rushing off in a terrible hurry. He opened the sliding glass door with its decals but the screen door was closed, too, and he hadn't expected it to be there. Whammo! He crashed smack into it.

"Luckily, he wasn't hurt, just startled, but this prompted me to rush right out and purchase large colorful decals for the screen too."

From New Hampshire: "My son kept bumping his toy trucks into the door frame and chipping the paint.

"After touching it up for the umpteenth time, I bought clear adhesive backed plastic and covered the section of the frame that was getting those low blows.

"The paint shows through the clear paper and, thanks to the adhesive, it's staying in good condition."

From California: "Our toddler has learned to open doors. I didn't want to put a hook on every door in the house so I placed a soft sock on the knob of each outside door, fastening it with a rubber band.

"The doors are easily opened by adults who can squeeze the handles and turn 'em, but the socks just slide around the knob in a toddler's grasp."

If you have outside doors underlined by cracks that let in a lot of cold air, here's what to do. It may be an old-timer, but it still works:

Roll up a newspaper lengthwise and put rubber bands around it. (Cut it the same length as the width of the door.) Jam it under the door to shut out drafts.

As the door is opened and closed, the newspaper can be rolled aside or pushed back in place with your foot.

You could even cover it with some pretty paper or material.

Driveways

If you have messy grease or oil spots on your driveway, pour cat-box filler over them.

You'll be amazed how that stuff soaks up grease like magic.

Another solution to this problem, according to an expert—and you're not going to believe this—is cement.

Sprinkle it dry on a concrete driveway and let it sit for a few days.

Then sweep it off with a broom and you'll sweep away grease spots because it will absorb them.

If the first application doesn't do it, try one more time.

Recently, I discovered a quick, easy way to sand the driveways and sidewalks when they're coated with ice.

If you have a grass seed or fertilizer spreader, pour the sand in its hopper. Set it for the smallest hole opening and then just "push" your troubles away.

This method eliminates some of those painful backaches.

Drop Cloths (see Painting, p. 431)

Fences

"Don't fence me in," says a homeowner in Maryland, "because I'll probably have to paint it." In that eventuality, here's his hint:

"Use a paint roller to paint picket fences. It speeds up the work and covers every spot."

From New Mexico: "The paint flows more smoothly on picket fences if it is thinned a bit."

From a handy guy in Virginia, here's a trick I bet Tom Sawyer would have loved: "Paint won't waste or splash if you use a sponge to paint a wire fence.

"A sponge gets into those little creases of wire. It makes the work neater and faster. Don't forget to wear rubber gloves when you're sponging away."

Frisbees

From Illinois: "Don't throw away Frisbees. They make wonderful saucers to place under hanging plants so the water won't drip."

Garbage Cans

From Idaho: "Dogs kept poking about in our garbage cans until I sprang into action:

"I took two springs (like book straps or screen-door springs) and fastened one end of each spring to each can handle and the other end of each to the lid handle.

"We haven't had any problems since."

Is your galvanized garbage can a thing of beauty?
It could be . . .
Paint it the color of your house or paint a design on it or don't paint it but, instead, hide it behind a decorative wood screen.

Here's a good hint from an Iowa husband:
"Ever try to drag a trash can out in the ice when it's too heavy to lift? Even Atlas would give up. Not me.

"I put the can on one of the children's snow discs (round metal sleds) and slide it down the driveway."

From Oregon: "I bought three small self-locking plastic garbage cans. I put chow for my outside cats in one along with a scoop, and put it outside where I feed the cats. When I ring their dinner bell, they come running and I feed them right there. No carrying the food through the house anymore.

"I store birdseed (again with its own scoop) in another can.

"The third can, placed near the barbecue pit, keeps the charcoal dry, handy, and ready to use."

Gas Lights

From New York: "An easy way to clean the glass in our outdoor gas light is with spray-on oven cleaner. I leave it on for awhile and then wash it off.

"No scratching the glass that way, and it does the almost impossible job of getting off built-up grime, slush, snow and rain spots.

"Oven cleaner's good for extra grimy windows, too. But wear gloves to protect your hands."

Ladder

A dandy handyman in Vermont has this suggestion: "A wooden ladder that's used outdoors should be preserved against the elements.

"Instead of paint, use clear varnish to protect it. Then, rot or deterioration on any part of the ladder can be easily spotted and corrected."

Painting (also see Screens, p. 432)

What goes up can't come down until the paint is dry, so here's a tip for painting stairways:

Start at one side of each step and paint two-thirds of the way across.

Walk on the unpainted one-third until the other side is completely dry.

Then you can paint the unpainted side and, while you're at it, go two-thirds of the way across. This gives the center part of each step (which gets the most wear) a second coat of protection.

Years ago I discovered an easy way to paint window frames in a hurry without getting paint on the glass.

Cut newspaper into two-inch strips. Dip the strips into a bucket of clear water. Pull the strips between two fingers to wipe off excess water.

Put the straight edge of each strip on the glass next to the frame you're going to paint. That way the glass will be protected from paint smears.

The paper will come off easily when it dries but it'll stay in place while you're painting.

Masking tape can be used, too—but why buy it? Also, I want to warn you to leave the paper (or tape) on for only a short time. They should be removed after each pane is completed or else they're sometimes a stinker to get off.

From Utah: "When we painted the outside of our house we didn't have enough drop cloths to cover the flowers.

"I took extra large plastic trash bags and pulled them over each rose bush. When we were finished painting, I had the bags to re-use in my trash can."

Partying

From Florida: "When weather threatened a patio party, I decided to move everything into our attached two-car garage.

"I made a full length gold nylon net drapery (see Nylon Net, p. 217) for the garage door. To keep it from blowing, I zigzagged a continuous strip of drapery weights along the bottom.

"Gathering the net as I went, and using a stapler, I fastened the net to two (eight-foot) strips of soft wood and then nailed them to the door frame.

"After the party, I took the strips down, folded the net around each and stored my draperies away for another rain date."

Sandbox

From Florida: "Have you ever thought of putting the children's sandbox on wheels?

"Drill one large hole in each of the four feet so that metal dowel rods can be run through the holes. These rods should extend enough on each side so that small rubber tires (discarded children's wagon tires are ideal) may be attached.

"Put two thick nuts between each tire and the sandbox to keep the tires from rubbing against the box. Then drop pins through holes in the ends of the rods to keep the tires from working off.

"Now attach a plastic rope to one end and even the 'little ones' will be able to push and pull a hundred pounds of sand all over the yard."

Screens

From a pizza maker in Pennsylvania, here's another use for a tool of his trade:

"A pizza cutter with teeth (not a blade-type edge) does a great job of replacing the rubber gasket or molding around aluminum screens after new screening has been installed.

"Also, the corners of some storm doors come loose, but my trusty pizza wheel puts the rubber back without removing the window or damaging the screen wire."

You can buy screen patches but you also can make them, as this homemaker in Michigan does:

"To patch a screen, cut a piece of screening a little larger than the hole. Ravel the edges of the patch all around. Now bend the wires all the same way. Put the patch up to the hole in the screen and press the ends of the wires through the screen.

"Next bend all the wires back away from the hole, which cinches the patch and makes a neat mending job."

I have to confess I never can get screen patches hooked in or hooked on as this Michigan magician can.

My trick: I take the screen off the window and sew the patch on with invisible thread!—Heloise

A clever husband in Nebraska found this easy way to paint screens: "I run a piece of cord through the hooks on the top of each screen and then tie both sides of the cord to the clothesline. This way I can paint both sides of the screen on the same day."

From Florida: "My husband came up with a wonderful fix-it hint.

"We had a small hole in our screen.

"He cut a small piece of patch from some screening we had on hand and applied the patch with plastic glue."

Snow, Shoveling

From Minnesota: "When my fingers got wet and cold while shoveling snow, I thought of the thin plastic gloves I use when coloring my hair (they come in the package with the coloring). The next time I had to shovel snow, I put the gloves on under my wool ones. What a difference!"

From Massachusetts: "We use a rubber-tipped floor squeegee to remove a light coat of snow from our porch and stairs.

"It doesn't damage the wood as a shovel might and it's faster than a broom."

Stairways (see Painting, p. 431)

Swimming Pool (also see Wading Pool, p. 436)

Maybe I shouldn't ask but are you playing dirty pool? Is the backyard swimming pool full of gravel, soil, etc.?

Betcha it is if you've a mob of kids jumping out and diving back in again.

Try a trick that works for my neighbor. She uses a wading pool as a "stepping stone" to her pool.

Result: kids dunk their feet in the wading pool (leaving the residue there) before they dive into the swimming pool.

And, believe me, a wading pool is lots cinchier to clean. Just turn it over and dump it out!

Tool Box (also see Tool Shed, below)

From Vermont: "A sturdy ice chest (metal variety) makes a wonderful store-all for hammers, nails, and other tools that seem to clutter up the garage or workshop.

"The chest is not only a good place to store things, but serves as a sturdy stepstool to reach those impossible high shelves."

From Virginia: "My aunt bought a trash can with a lid and put it outdoors behind the house to store small garden tools . . . even garden shoes and gloves.

"When it rains, the lid protects everything from getting wet and rusty . . . and the can saves her countless trips up and down the basement stairs."

Tool Shed (also see Tools, p. 449)

It's true confession time . . . a homemaker in Nebraska is telling all!

"Wait 'til you hear what I did! I cleaned out the tool shed.

"We all have a place where we accumulate do-it-yourself supplies. This is the place where none of us can find anything—the hammer, the right size nail, etc.—when we want it.

"I took everything out of the tool shed, even the lawn mower—which I had to step over each time I wanted to get a hammer. I swept and wept.

"I put the big things back first—the extra camping equipment, etc. Then I went through gallons of paint. It was a disgrace how many of those cans were one third empty and all dried up because the tops weren't tight. If you have just a little leftover paint, put it in a jar, cap the lid tight and turn upside down. Add a label telling the brand name, color and what it was used for (house trim, screens, deck furniture, etc.).

"I found six cans of putty. Why does anyone need six? Five must have got lost in the clutter and hence I bought the sixth. Shame on me.

"The more I threw away, the more disgusted I got.

"As for all those little tin cans of odd screws, I sorted them out by size and filed like with like, kissing the rusty ones good-bye.

"The same with nails. I gave the rusty ones the old heave-ho.

"I got me one big jar and put in all the different-sized nails I thought I'd ever need and capped the lid tight.

"My heart broke when I got to paintbrushes suffering rigor mortis. I tried two different kinds of remover on them but soften they wouldn't. They had been stored in water but the water evaporated. Don't ever do this to a paintbrush.

"When I got to the tools, I found stuff that had not been used for years: an old pump, a no-good drill, a rusty pipe-cutter! Some I earmarked for trash, some for the swap shop. I only kept things I expected to use.

"What remains is all I really need. I even have a place to hang all my fishing rods and room to drive the lawn mower into a corner!

"Once you start a job like this, don't stop until it's finished. That's the secret of good cleaning. The more junk you find, the madder you get and the better cleaning job you do."

Wading Pool (also see Swimming Pool, p. 434)

From Maine: "Last year when I was ready to store a small, inflatable, plastic wading pool at the end of the season, I squeezed all the air out, closed up the valves and washed it in my washing machine. I added two bath towels and a little bleach and pulled it out before the spin, then hung it out. I rinsed it off with the hose while it was on the line and let it dry."

Windows (see Painting, p. 431 and Gas Lights, p. 430; also see Window Listings, p. 183)

Gardening—Outdoors and In

INTRODUCTION

No wonder Mary, Mary was so contrary. Bet she had trouble getting her garden to grow . . . just like your friend Heloise.

I've had lots of fun puttering around with plants and seedlings in the ready-made greenhouse I put up . . . even though my green thumb sometimes acts as if it were brown.

When it does, I just ignore it and putter some more. If anything's worth effort, it sure is a garden.

Nowadays, gardens grow indoors and out. Great land of Oz but plants are popular. And I know why:

A touch of nature is good for the soul, in fact it's the greatest.

If you're a city slicker, something green and growing takes the curse off all that concrete and cement. It makes you realize what life's all about.

Somebody asked if I talk to my plants. Well, doesn't everyone? I'm so pleased when they're doing well, I give 'em a verbal hug 'n' a kiss.

Don't let my Swedish ivy or philodendron know, but the two avocados I raised from pits are my absolute favorites. If anything happened to them, why, I'd wear my head at half mast for a year. Just couldn't stand it.

It's a real giggle to get a plant for free! Like my growing those avocados from pits. Know how to do it, dontcha?

Wash the seed and remove the pulp. Stick three toothpicks in the pit a little above midway, then rest the toothpicks on the rim of a jelly jar or glass, round bottom end of the pit down, and fill 'er up with water.

That water will evaporate, so you've got to keep adding and watching. The bottom half of that pit should be in water at all times. Put the glass in a warm spot—but not in direct sun.

When you've just about given up hope—it sometimes takes six weeks or longer—the pit will crack and, POP!, it will start to sprout.

Hallelujah!

But now comes the hard part. When the sprout gets six to seven inches high, you've got to cut it back to three inches. It's the hardest thing to do. Feel like I'd like to be blindfolded when I pick up those scissors . . . but it's the only way to make an avocado grow up strong. Cut it on a slant so that more of the surface is exposed to air. Some cut their avocado while it's rooting. I plant it first. The time to plant is when the roots are plenty thick and the stem leafs out.

Choose a 10½-inch terra cotta pot and put in lots of rich humus-type soil. But don't bury the pit—leave it half exposed. Plop the pot down someplace where it won't get too much direct sun.

Say a kind word every time you pass it, keep the soil moist and, before you can say, "George Washington chopped down a cherry tree—for shame on him!"—you'll have yourself a leafy plant. And pinch, pinch, pinch—the more you do, the fuller the plant.

And avocado pits aren't the only for-frees in the plant department, bless your thrifty heart, they're not!

Why, you can get a ferny beauty from planting a carrot top, a leafy vine from a sweet potato (one with lots of eyes) and a tropical treat from the top of a pineapple!

Not to mention the plants that'll grow from cuttings. Get friends to save you sprigs of Swedish ivy, philodendron, and the like, then stick 'em in water—but don't plant in soil until they have a few roots.

Don't be impatient, hear? Ma Nature takes her time, so you take yours!

Enjoy your garden, whether it's inside or out and, right this minute, stop what you're doing and say a loving word to your favorite plant from—your friend, Heloise.

Ants

From New Mexico: "Pour household ammonia down the center of an ant hill and you can start humming the funeral march. Also make a circle around the hill and fill it with ammonia.

"The amount you use is determined by the size of the hill but use plenty, from a cup to about a pint.

"If there is just a small bed or hill in the sidewalk cracks, a cup should do the job. Be sure you pour the ammonia in the center to kill underground residents. I take a stick and poke a hole in the center, then pour the ammonia in. This way I'm sure to get to the bottom of things."

Birds

From someone in Georgia who has lots of fine-feathered friends:
"To make a bird feeder, take a plastic milk jug and cut out a square large enough for the birds to get in close to the bottom.

"Keep the cap on the jug. To put bird food in the feeder just take off the cap and pour in the food.

"Tie the milk jug to a tree by running a piece of strong string through its handle."

From Rhode Island: "I keep a bird bath full all year long. To make it easier on me, both to fill it and watch them, the bath is close to the house and within easy reach.

"Somehow or other my coffee tastes so much better when I can just sit and watch our fine-feathered friends. They are so busy. My greatest delight is to see them bathe in the water, then get out and shake themselves off!"

From New Hampshire: "If your bird feeder's mounted on a post and squirrels get into it, skirt the lower part of the feeder (on all sides) with plexiglass. When the squirrels climb up the post, they'll be boxed in and have no place to go but down again."

Or circle the tree trunk with a wide metal band and you'll find they can't climb over it.—Heloise

Bulbs

From Massachusetts: "I know the foliage of bulb plants should not be cut off until it has died if you want to produce a better bulb for the coming year. But I hate the way it looks.

"My husband had a good idea. He cut off both ends of a wire coat hanger, about six to eight inches. These pieces make a very strong V-shaped metal piece to hold down these stems and leaves.

"He twists the foilage and folds it under, then pins it down with these coat hanger pieces. Only one is necessary for each plant and they really stay in the ground.

"This makes a neat bundle that can be easily trimmed off when the foliage dies. The wires can be removed and saved for next year. The planting of annuals near these bulbs completely hides the foliage until it is ready to be cut."

Compost

Save "fresh" garbage and use it to build a compost heap and you'll have free fertilizer. What goes into compost: Uncooked vegetables and fruit, peelings and cores, also egg shells, coffee grounds and tea leaves!

Fertilizer

From Hawaii: "I've always had trouble getting an even coverage of fertilizer with a drop spreader until I figured out a simple way to let me know where I'd been.

"I took a plastic bread wrapper and filled it about one-third full of lime, then I punched a few holes in the bottom.

"I hung the bag on the back right hand corner of the spreader using an 'S' hook made from heavy wire.

"The bag hung just a few inches from the ground and as I pushed the spreader, it bumped against the wheel, causing it to drop a thin line of lime on the grass, allowing me to see where I'd been."

Flower Arrangements (also see Planters, p. 445 and Plants, p. 446)

From Oregon: "To make miniature arrangements of garden flowers for each place setting, I use empty glass spice jars. The shaker tops are handy, too, because the slim stems slip right through the sprinkle holes and the flowers stay where I want them."

Flowers, picking

Words of wisdom from a green-thumbed gal in West Virginia: "When picking flowers, don't take any more leaves than necessary if you want your bushes to keep producing new blooms.

"After picking, cut the stems at an angle and scrape the lower part of the stem at several spots until green underbark shows. This will help the water to enter the stems.

"Condition the flowers by putting them first in room-temperature water for an hour, then in deep cold water in a dark place for a couple of hours or overnight.

"Cut flowers will last much longer if handled this way."

Gardening Gloves

From Nebraska: "Oven mitts make great gardening gloves for sticky jobs like pruning."

Grass Clippings

From Oklahoma: "When filling a plastic trash bag with grass clippings, you sure could use an extra pair of hands. To make the job easier, remove the bottom from an old twenty-gallon metal garbage can and turn it upside down. Put the plastic bag inside with its top cuffed around the edge of the can. It may need to be tied to keep it from slipping.

"When the bag is filled with the grass clippings, tie it shut, turn the can on its side and push the bag out."

Herbs

From South Carolina: "To pulverize herbs dried from my own garden, I rub them through a sieve."

Hose

Sure makes me feel good to know I'm not the only person in the world who's forgetful. This gardener in Iowa has her spells, too.

"I forgot to turn off the garden soakers and lawn sprinklers a few times last year and the water ran all night.

"A friend suggested that I hang an old, cheap bracelet on the outside faucet to remind me.

"Now, when I want to water the garden or the grass I slip the bracelet on my arm to remind me to turn off the water.

"When I turn it off, the bracelet goes back on the faucet, ready to give me a reminding nudge the next time."

From Michigan: "I have found the ideal way to store my garden hose.

"I took an old auto tire, put it on the garage floor, started with one end of the hose and wound it into the space where the tube normally goes.

"I just kept winding the hose 'round and 'round until it was all in the tire.

"My hose was only fifty feet long and the tire took care of all of it."

From Ohio: "Have you ever wondered where the end of the garden hose is when it's coiled or lying in the grass?

"Paint twelve inches at the nozzle end of the hose red and you'll know which end is which."

Kneeler Pads

From Missouri: "I use plastic foam meat trays as kneeler pads when working in my garden.

"They not only provide cushioning for my knees but warmth, too, because they seem to act almost like heating pads. This is very comfortable when one is working in the garden on a cool, damp day."

Leaves

From New Hampshire: "I have extra-sticky holly shrubs along my front walk. Each year in the fall, leaves from the trees accumulated on top of these bushes and worked their way down into the shrubs. I dug the leaves out with a gardening fork four times last year.

"This year I bought ten yards of 72-inch wide grass-green nylon net (see Nylon Net, p. 217) and put it over my shrubs.

"Most of the falling leaves blew right off the top of the netting, but those that stayed did no harm because when I removed the net, I removed the leaves with it."

From Kansas: "Guess what I do to hold my plastic leaf bag open?

"I shake it open, then clip one side to our chain-link fence with two clip clothespins.

"Makes it so much easier to fill, as I only need one hand to hold it open."

From Mississippi: "My modest rock garden was full of leaves and I dreaded having to clean it on hands and knees.

"Then I hit upon the idea of using a vacuum to blow the leaves out of the garden. It worked."

Mulch

From Washington: "Save newspapers to use as mulch for your garden.

"Either spread the papers out flat in several thicknesses, or tear them into small strips and put them around the plants.

"Thoroughly water them and they won't blow away."

Planters (also see Barbecue, p. 426, Flower Arrangements, p. 441 and Plants, p. 445)

From Florida: "I saved two plastic ice chests that had sprung leaks and couldn't be used anymore.

"What I did was 'dress up' my patio with them.

"I filled the chests with potting soil, planted geraniums in one and petunias in the other, and placed them on the patio.

"Quite an added attraction in our backyard."

From Wyoming: "If you like large house plants, but don't like the price you have to pay for those large planters, try using an inexpensive, galvanized mop bucket as a flowerpot.

"Spray-paint it (wipe with vinegar first or the paint won't stick) or glue on decals, add fringe or create a free-hand design with string or decorative scraps.

"Don't remove the handle because it makes it easier to move the plants."

From Alaska: "A plastic paint pail (often on sale for under a quarter) makes a great planter. Cover the outside with aluminum foil."

From Louisiana: "Want to grow a tree in your apartment? Plant it in a trash can cut down to the height you want. First punch holes in the bottom of the can for drainage.

"Use a round oil drip pan under it to catch excess water. You can buy one in a store that carries auto accessories.

"Before spray-painting the trash can and drip pan, rinse them off with vinegar; otherwise the paint won't stick to the galvanized surface."

From New Jersey: "Instead of stones or broken bits of clay pot, I use several layers of nylon net (see Nylon Net, p. 217) in the bottom of flower pots and planters."

I'm crazy about beautiful house plants that make a room look fresh and garden-like.

Clay pots are the most conducive to their health and further growth. I leave these pots natural in most rooms.

But in the living room, I wrap yarn (color-coordinated with the room) around the pot from the bottom up, securing it with a small amount of white household glue and leaving no spaces as I wrap.

This gives a unique textured effect. (Rug yarn is best.)

Put that about-to-be discarded lazy Susan under a large planter. Makes for easy turning.

Plants

From Texas: "When planting new cactus plants and/or repotting old ones . . . use a pair of ice or bacon tongs to keep from being jabbed."

From Delaware: "I hang small plants on a six-hook mug tree.

"It is very decorative and keeps all my new plants together. I am an African violet lover and am always rooting new leaves so the mug tree is constantly in use."

Plants, tying up

From Idaho: "Use a double-knit material instead of cotton to tie up plants. There is more 'give' to it and it doesn't harm the plant in any way."

Plants, watering

From New York: "We have crammed our enclosed balcony with plants. And, as a result, we have learned to cut down on our watering chores via a double-decker method.

"Pitcher by pitcher, we carry the water to our hanging baskets, but kill two birds with one stone since we have strategically placed other sturdy potted plants below them. The water dripping from above (like rainfall) takes care of the lower ones."

From Pennsylvania: "Watering hanging plants poses quite a problem. You have to contend with that drip, drip, drip . . . or lift the planter down and leave it for several hours after watering.

"I slip old shower caps over the bottoms of my hanging planters before I water them. Several hours later I carefully remove the caps and all that accumulation of dirt and drips."

From Florida: "My ingenious husband solved my problem of watering a rabbit hair fern in a hanging basket.

"He removed the top half of a one-quart plastic bleach bottle and with a heated finishing nail, punched holes, not only in the bottom but in the sides of the bottle. Then he affixed a wire to the top so that it could be hung on the same hook as the fern.

"When it's hung, he fills it with water that's distributed slowly and evenly.

"No more run-off water while watering. Therefore, the plant gets every drop it needs, and the watering container is hidden by the foliage."

I have been testing different kinds of philodendron—the velvet-leafed and the slick-leafed—and I've decided that the slick leaf is twice as easy to grow.

I have also learned that these plants must never be over-watered!

Never, never, over-water a philodendron. It's best to wait until the soil gets bone dry. A good way to test it is to put your finger on the soil. If it's the least bit moist, don't water. Once this soil is bone dry, flood it and forget it for at least a week.

Watering time varies in different homes because of humidity, air-conditioning, heating system, etc. But, when you see leaves starting to turn yellow, the most probable cause is too much aqua pura.

From a new mom in Minnesota: "An empty plastic bath powder can makes an excellent sprinkler for plants.

"Pry off the top with a dull knife, fill the can with water, snap the top back on and sprinkle away!"

From Florida: "When you turn on your lawn sprinkler, tote your favorite house plants outdoors and set them on the lawn under the sprinkler. This is especially good for most varieties of ferns. The sprinkled mist seems just the thing for them."

From Idaho: "If you have a 'brown' thumb in growing indoor plants, try this easy method:

"Once or twice a week stick your index finger up to the second knuckle in the pot's soil—if your finger is damp, don't water, if it's dry, do!"

Seeds

From Idaho: "When gathering pods from your garden for seeds, pull a nylon stocking over them and hang them to dry.

"When dry, shake, and the seeds will fall to the toe of the stocking. Cut off the foot, knot and store."

Save pull-top frozen orange juice cans for when you start seedlings. Open the cans on the *bottom* with a can opener.

Can you guess why? Because later on, after you've filled the empty cans with soil, planted seeds and are ready to transplant, you can pull off the top of the can (which is now the bottom) without disturbing the roots.

From New Jersey: "To start tomatoes, etc., put a few seeds in with houseplants and nurse them along the usual way."

A dear woman told me about soaking flower seeds for a couple of nights in ordinary tap water before planting them and in three days they came up.

I decided to try it myself and, believe me, she knew what she was saying!

I used six different kinds of flower seeds, soaked half of them for two nights, I planted the soaked ones in one place, the dry ones in another. Sure enough, the soaked ones were up and at 'em in three days.

From Wyoming: "When starting plants for my garden, I place the seeds on plastic meat trays between two pieces of paper toweling, which I keep moist at all times, covering it with wax paper to seal the moisture in. Within a few days, seeds begin to sprout.

"Then, I put soil in egg cartons and in each egg cup I place one sprout. I put the carton on the windowsill and water the seedlings each day, giving them plant food every two weeks until the danger of frost is over and they can grow in the garden."

Soil, mixing

From Utah: "Plastic bags come in handy when I'm gardening.

"I use a plastic bag when I want to mix a small portion of soil and fertilizer to put in flower pots. I add soil and fertilizer, secure the bag and shake away . . . couldn't be better mixed."

Tomatoes

Did you know you can pick tomatoes green, and if you wrap each one in newspaper they'll ripen slowly and beautifully! I use at least three thicknesses.

Be sure to store them in a cool place, but not in your refrigerator. After all, you want them to ripen slowly so that the juices and the taste will be there.

Wrapping the tomatoes in newspaper absorbs moisture if any of them happen to spoil, so the spoil won't spread like a disease from one to the other.

You know the story about one bad apple.

From Virginia: "I plant cherry tomato plants between maybells, zinnias and black-eyed Susans. Adds more greenery to the garden."

Tools (also see Toolshed, p. 434)

Paint the handles of tools like garden hoes and rakes a bright lemon yellow and they'll be easier to find if lost in heavy foliage or grass.

From Maryland: "Repair gardening tools before you put them away at the end of the season.

"If you want to paint the handles, there's a very easy way to do it. Just hang each tool upside down with string, rope or wire from a tree or clothesline.

"Makes the job much easier and they dry evenly and quickly."

Vegetables, rinsing

When rinsing the dirt off vegetables pulled fresh from the earth, use a large pot to catch the soiled water. Return it to the garden where it will be valuable. After all, you spent a long time preparing that soil—why wash it down the drain where it might just clog the pipes?

Vines

Oh, boy, folks, have I ever discovered something!

I have a vine that has been climbing a fence for eight years now.

That little critter wraps itself around and around and I don't like this at all.

The vine gives out what I call "sticky milk" wherever I cut it. And it's an icky mess when you get this goop on your hands or clothing.

Now I've learned the secret:

I got clippers and cut the main artery, the biggest stem leading to all those tentacles that took it wherever I didn't want it to go! Or grow!

I didn't even bother to remove them.

I just had patience and in a few weeks all the sticky juice dried up and I pulled up one dead vine.

No fuss, no mess, no bother and, best of all, no sticky milk substance.

Isn't that wonderful?

And to think that every few months I had been cursing that little devil and all his brothers.

Vines that grow where you don't want them to are an abomination.

I had one vine I planted in the ground so that it would climb up the chimney of my fireplace and impress all my neighbors.

Baloney!

I thought it was gorgeous until I found it was also growing down the top of the fireplace and into the house.

The same thing with vines and wooden eaves. They rot the wood, and until you pay that repair bill you haven't seen anything.

So, folks, heed my word. Save your money and most of all your energy by nipping a vine in the bud or, better yet, in the main artery.

Weeds

Wherever did they get the name "dandelion" for a weed? It's like a lion all right, but it's certainly not dandy.

I've fought them, tried choking and pinching them, even used weed killers, but they just wouldn't budge.

One of my neighbors explained to me that the little fuzzy ball on top was blowing off in the wind and spreading the seeds.

She had a candle in her hand. She lit it and held the flame under the little furry top and, heavens to old Betsy, if that little devil didn't burn and go right up in smoke.

I was so mad at myself that I hadn't thought of this. It's the simple things that most of us can't see.

From California: "You know the punch-type can opener that used to be so widely available for opening canned beverages? It's almost obsolete now, but if you have one don't throw it away. I've found another use for it. It is just the thing for getting out weeds that have grown up in crevices in the concrete.

"Now, if I only had a genie to attach it firmly to an old broom handle for me, I'd have it made."

Camping Out

INTRODUCTION

Hey, all you stay-at-homes, up and off your lounge chairs! It's great outdoors—try it, you'll like it!

Even city slickers are getting into the act and backpacking off to "rough it" on weekends.

The great thing about camping is that it needn't bust your bank-roll.

Sure, it's nice to have a fully equipped camper—but all you really need is a backpack and your own two feet—they'll take you where you want to go.

And getting there on shanks' mare is part of the fun.

A cream puff I know took off for a "Wilderness" camp-out last winter—smack drat in the middle of a blizzard. Gave her poor ol' mom a turn, it did.

Mom fretted away the hours 'cause, she said, "That girl turns blue just lookin' at the snow through a picture window!"

So what happened? Miss Cream Puff returned, eyes sparkling, cheeks glowing, and pooh-poohed mom's fears.

"Worry 'bout me?" she said in astonishment. "Why, I had the time of my life! I've signed up for next week's rock-climbing expedition. And then there's a canoe trip . . ."

Wouldja believe a tenderfoot could toughen up that fast?

Just take my word, it happens. And it could happen to you, if you'd give outdoor life a whirl and a twirl.

Start nice an' easy like . . . maybe with a long day's journey that takes you there and brings you back.

Then work up to an overnighter—and all the fun of settling into a sleeping bag and snoring away under the stars. There's nothing at all quite like it—just out of this world!

Honest, the letters I get about outdoor life . . . why, they're not really letters, they're more like poems.

And the hints that come with 'em . . . they're just the greatest. But, read on, and see for yourself.

Know something? It does the soul good to get back to Ma Nature. She's really a doll.

So, when you load up that trusty old backpack or start stashing supplies in your camper, know what to do? Put in an extra supply of laughs, smiles and campfire yarns from—your friend, Heloise.

Ant Catchers

From Montana: "When you go camping take along several small empty tuna or pineapple cans. They make great ant catchers! Fill them about three quarters full of water and place your table legs in each can."

Bathing

From Wyoming: "Thought other campers would like to know our solution for bathing when there are no bath facilities where we camp.

"We bought a small plastic pool at the local toy store and, oh, what a find!

"It makes a perfect tub and can be stored in a very small space."

Barbecuing

You no longer have to really rough it when cooking out. Now we have electric and gas grills, but then some of us still have that regular old pit and still have to follow a few safety rules!

Never use gasoline or kerosene to start your fire!

Read and follow the directions for using charcoal starter fluid.

Be sure to allow the fluid to soak into the charcoal before you light it. This will reduce the chances of a flash flame.

After your coals have ignited, never add more starter.

Keep the fluid out of the hands of children and keep children away from the barbecue area.

Never use charcoal grills or hibachis indoors. Besides the hazard of something catching on fire, the burning charcoal will use up oxygen and produce dangerous carbon monoxide.

Finally, never wear loose-fitting clothes when you're the outdoor chef. They could go up in a blaze.

If these rules are followed, it will be the meat on the barbecue pit that is cooked, and not you.

P.S. Don't eat too much!

Beds

From Georgia: "Here's a hint for those who own a camper that has a bed over the cab.

"These beds are so hard to make up so I just take two sleeping bags (the kind that open out flat) and zip them together to form one full size.

"Unzip the outside edge, climb in and zip up. The next morning the last one out zips it up and plumps up the pillows for a nice neat bed."

From Missouri: "This hint is for campers who have trouble making a bed that juts out over the cab in a camper.

"Spread your sheets and blanket out on your own bed at home just as you would if making the bed. Then fold each end over twice.

"When you are ready to make your camper bed, just unfold.

"This is doing it the easy way."

Clothes Rack

From New Mexico: "The last time we camped, I took our fold-away ironing caddy. It makes a dandy clothes rack.

"If you combine an ironing caddy and a closet type garment bag, you have a portable closet.

"Socks, underwear, etc., can be laid in the bottom of the garment bag."

Cooking (also see Stove, p. 458)

Since most camp stoves have only two burners, I take my double boiler with me when I go camping.

You can boil potatoes, rice or spaghetti in the bottom part while you heat canned vegetables in the top.

This leaves the second burner free for meat, spaghetti sauce or whatever.

From Colorado: "If you tear off the labels, food can be heated right in the cans.

"Remove the lids, place foil over the top and heat canned stews, chili, etc., as is. If you add a bit of onion, garlic powder, oregano, etc., canned food tastes a bit more like homemade."

From Minnesota: "You don't want to cook the first day of a camping trip, so why not make up a batch of stew or chili, freeze it and take it with you?

"Sure is a good feeling to have a meal ready—except for heating —when you arrive at your camp site."

From Nebraska: "I've found that serving soup for breakfast on a chilly morning hits the spot!"

From North Dakota: "I cook macaroni or spaghetti on the campfire in a coffee pot that has holes in the spout.

"Then you can pop on the lid, drain the macaroni or spaghetti and add the remaining ingredients. No colander needed."

Dressing room

From Illinois: "While camping we discovered a wonderful use for a hula hoop.

"You can easily hang a heavy shower curtain on one of these hoops, and string it to a tree for extra dressing room.

"Just snap metal shower curtain hooks through the curtain grommets and onto the hoop. Easy as one, two, three, and it gives you all the privacy you need."

Raise the flag and ring the bell for one of the cleverest ideas I've heard in a long while!—Heloise

First Aid (also see First Aid, p. 290)

Just a little reminder!

When camping, always carry a first-aid kit.

Among other musts it should hold antiseptic, bandages, aspirin and a pair of blunt-nose scissors.

Something you might never think of taking, vinegar, sure relieves itching caused by insect bites. It can also be used as smelling salts, if necessary; and it's great for sunburn—just pat it on.

Common household soda is another good item to have in your kit. Mixed with water, it makes an excellent pain reliever for wasp or bee stings. It also reduces the swelling.

Fishing

A good fisherman I definitely am not.

It kills me to sit all day and watch as everyone else brings 'em in, while the little devils just steal my bait.

Some fishermen tell the darndest stories. And they all compare bait. Well, have I got a new tall tale for them.

I found a dead grasshopper, put it on the hook and caught me a dilly.

You seldom find a hopper when you're fishing and wishing. And never at a lake, so I started looking around at home in the yard. And had success.

The trick is to catch them, so I keep bug spray on the porch. Now when I see one of the little darlings, I blast.

Then, know what I do? I pop it in a pill bottle and pack it in my fishing box.

Try it. But don't tell your fishing friends.

Nobody knows this but you and me and let's keep this a secret between one foxy fisherman and another.

From Minnesota: "A magnet is a must for your tackle box. Use it to attract fish hooks so you always know where they are."

Food Supplies

From Wisconsin: "How many times I have packed and repacked the ice chest for a camping trip, trying to find room for that big carton of eggs!

"It finally dawned on me to cut up two plastic foam egg cartons. I cut one in half, the other in thirds so I have mini egg boxes I can tuck in most anywhere and no problem if they get wet.

"I slip a rubber band around them so they'll stay closed."

Ice

From Virginia: "To make cubes for the ice chest for a camping trip, I fill zippered plastic bags three-fourths full of water and freeze them.

"The big bonus: There isn't any messy water in the bottom of the ice chest.

"We don't even waste the water when the ice finally melts but use it in the puppy's bowl. Once it even came in handy to add to the radiator when the car overheated."

From New York: "I'm a graduate university student and my work often takes me into the field on weekends for overnight trips.

"Funds are extremely limited, and the groceries involved often strain the budget. The matter of an extra dollar or so for ice cubes was a problem until I found the solution:

"Cut the end off empty soda pop cans, fill the cans with water and freeze. Three or four of these 'giant cubes' will keep the contents of a small foam cooler safe for eating for forty-eight hours.

"Six or eight of them may be frozen together into a plastic bag, forming a block, which will last three days or more in the camper refrigerator.

"The ice is always ready when it is needed, it costs nothing and the money saved may be applied to a special goody we otherwise could not have afforded."

Lantern

From Nebraska: "Did you know that if you hang your lantern on a foil-wrapped tree limb it not only will protect the tree but also reflect the light?"

Mattresses

From Iowa: "For our camping trip, I purchased long pieces of upholstery foam, the size of each child's sleeping bag.

"These foam pieces are useful because they never need to be inflated like an air mattress and the sleeping bags never slip off them at night.

"They keep the bags off the damp ground and are easy to store, rolled up or flat on the floor of the station wagon."

Meals

From Indiana: "An empty soda pop carton is perfect to carry a jar of mustard, powdered coffee creamer, jar of jelly, etc., on a camping trip.

"It also can be used for cans."

Nylons

From Nebraska: "I think the handiest item in our camping kit is a bag of old nylons.

"In an emergency these old nylon stockings, tied together, make a good rope.

"Also, they make good bags for the children to put their collections in."

Packing

From Indiana: "When two of my children were packing for a lengthy backpack trip, I suggested they put small articles in those mesh bags one gets with onions, grapefruit and so on.

"Some of the bags were long enough to knot at the end, others were tied with a twist tie.

"Because mesh bags are see-through it was easy for them to find an article immediately. Bonus: the mesh bags lasted far longer than plastic bags would have, besides providing 'air conditioning.' "

Raft, rubber (see Swimming, p. 459)

Rope (see Nylons, above)

Stove (also see Cooking, p. 454)

From Minnesota: "By covering food and slipping it underneath a campstove, you create a warming oven. If the stove is too low, put bricks under each end and raise it enough to do the trick.

"This way everyone's food is warm at the same time."

From Idaho: "A square of thin sheet iron doubles as a stove when you cook out. Just suspend it across large stones and build a fire underneath."

Swimming

Why blow yourself inside out trying to inflate a rubber raft? Here's an easier way:

From New Jersey: "My raft is the kind that has a small tube on top of a larger one. I set my hair dryer on cool, and hold its hose over the larger tube to inflate it."

Ohh, don't you know daddies are just gonna love this hint. —Heloise

Tablecloth

From Indiana: "I sew twelve-inch ties to the four corners of old bedspreads so we can take them on camping trips.

"We use them for tablecloths and tie the corners to the table legs so they won't blow in the wind."

Tent, folding

From Wisconsin: "Every camping season, the one job my husband dislikes most is folding the tent. This means cleaning off the wet soil and brushing off the damp leaves from the bottom.

"To eliminate one of his peeves. I bought a 9 × 12-foot painter's drop cloth, the same size as the tent.

"We place this thin plastic film on the ground before setting up the tent. It keeps the bottom of the tent dry and clean."

Tent Flap

From Washington: "Instead of zipping the flap on your tent (in our case, the add-a-room on our tent trailer) each time you enter or leave, buy a couple of yards of nylon net, (see Nylon Net, p. 217)

"Fold the width in half and hem top, bottom and one side. My friend put stones inside before hemming the bottom. When hung on the door, their weight swings the net back into place when you enter or leave.

"We snapped clothespins on the bottom of ours and also used clothespins on the top to hold it over the door opening.

"With five children, there is so much wear and tear on the zippers (plus time lost zipping), that we found this idea helpful."

Toiletries

From Kansas: "Here's a space-saving hint:
"Those little prescription pill bottles are handy for many things.
"They are just the right size to divide deodorant, toothpowder, cream, lotion, etc., for individual use.
"Saves taking along the big family-size containers."

Towels

From Illinois: "To cut down on soiled towels when camping, we tie a roll of paper towels to a tree.

"They are real handy and disposable. No laundry or lost towels either."

Of course, you add a plastic bag to dispose of them.—Heloise

Wagon

From Texas: "On a mountain camping vacation, we managed to squeeze in a small wagon for our eighteen-month-old girl.

"On hikes, monument tours or such, a rope on the handle made it easy to pull her along.

"In camp, she entertained herself collecting rocks and sticks or putting her dolls in the wagon.

"We also used the wagon to carry our five-gallon water container to and from the pump.

"We met many folks carrying (should we say lugging?) children, who said, 'I sure wish I'd thought of that.'"

Water

From Nevada: "We had a fifteen-gallon oil drum (with lid) steam cleaned to hold water at the edge of our campfire.

"It supplies all the water we need for dishes, bathing and washing out socks or underwear.

"A few minutes after the fire is lighted, the water is warm enough for clean up before supper. The evening bonfire keeps the water warm enough for 5 A.M. wash-up.

"The water in this drum is not used for cooking or drinking."

Here's a hot idea from a family in South Carolina that loves going camping:

"I have a good idea for those who would love to have hot water when needed on a camping trip.

"If you have a thirty-cup coffee pot, take it camping. Fill it with water and plug in to the electricity."

Only when you know there is an outlet, natch.—Heloise

You and Your Car

INTRODUCTION

Where cars are concerned, I guess the main thing we think about these days is gas.

Everyone knows you can save on gas by keeping that speedometer at a steady 55 mph. But would you believe that bad driving habits waste fuel like crazy?

Now hold onto your hats for this one but . . .

Depending on the driving errors you make, you can waste up to 44 percent of the fuel in your tank.

Doesn't that knock you out?

And you don't have to take my word for it . . . that's what the

AAA discovered in driving tests. wow!

What might you be doing that you shouldn't be doing if you want to make every last drop of gas give you full value? Things like . . .

Starting up too rapidly.

Stopping short on a dime.

Changing lanes constantly. (That weaving in and out doesn't get you anyplace, but it sure does eat up gas.)

Driving too fast. (Keep a check on the fuel gauge to see what you use at 55 mph and what you use if you break the law of the land and speed. You're in for a surprise.)

Hitting the brakes. (You should prepare for stops—easing up when you know a stop sign or traffic light's coming. But if you're speeding, why you might have to slam on those brakes like crazy. And that's wasteful!)

Some of the things you can do to conserve gas don't have the first thing to do with the actual driving. F'rinstance;

Keep the windows closed, so air flow doesn't make your engine work overtime.

Use the car's ventilation system—instead of air conditioning—when it's warm but not hot.

Keep your trunk empty (except for SOS supplies), because a heavy car requires more gas to move it along.

Keep your engine clean.

We all have to do a big re-think on when, where and why we drive. Lots of times, we could walk on short errands (and that's a bonus for the waistline!).

The gas shortage isn't going to go away—and the price of gas isn't going to decrease (you betcha, it's not). That means the name of the game is Conservation. Maybe a good way to be a winner in that game is to check out your owner's manual to find out what tune-ups a car needs to run at peak efficiency.

Drive safe and slow—but not too slow (not under 25 mph) because that wastes gas too.—Hugs, Heloise

Aerial

Know the red or green plastic tubes used to protect golf clubs? Slip one over the car aerial so you can locate it easily in a parking lot.

Bicycle

Not everyone gets places in a car—some go by bike. And since bikes are stored in the garage, I decided to plunk these useful tips down right here:

To store a bicycle so it won't rust over the winter, here's what to do:

Before you put that bike away, be sure to clean it thoroughly with warm, soapy water to remove all the dirt you have accumulated all summer long. Then rinse and dry it real well.

Wipe all the metal parts with a cloth that has been soaked in machine oil. This will prevent rusting and dirt accumulation.

So that your bike won't be resting on its tires for several months, tie a rope around the seat and handlebar stem and suspend it from a hook on the garage ceiling or wall.

When that good ol' summertime comes around again take your bike down, sponge it with sudsy water to remove oil and dust; rinse and dry very thoroughly.

Check and re-inflate tires to recommended pressure. Now you're all set to hit the bike trails. Be very careful and have fun.

Car (see specific car listings)

Car, emergencies

Here are some emergency measures for unlucky motorists who run out of gas or break down on the road:

Get the car off the road and onto the shoulder.

Raise the hood and trunk of the car and/or attach a white handkerchief to the left door handle to signal distress.

Set up emergency blinker lights or flares. Sure hope you carry them in your trunk. (It's important!)

Car, oil-check

If you patronize a pump-it-yourself gas station, don't forget to keep a check on your oil supply.

Make a note on your calendar to give you a mental nudge to check that oil.

Car, starting

From Minnesota: "The temperature is down below freezing, .you're bundled up to go to work and your car won't start. Pandemonium!

"It's happened to me—but not any more. Now I take an ounce of prevention.

"Before I go to bed on a cold night, I plug in an extension cord with a light on the end and place the lit bulb between the engine and battery and close the hood.

"Leaving the bulb on overnight seems to keep things from freezing up—and my car starts easily in the A.M. no matter how cold it is."

Car, washing (also see Floor Mats, p. 466, Grill, p. 467 and Windshield, cleaning, p. 469)

Before going through the car wash, dip nylon net (see Nylon Net, p. 217) in water and take a swipe at icky spots—bugs, droppings, whatever. Then run the car through.

Beautimus! (How d'ya like that for a word?)

And a couple of other things:

Stash a bottle of white vinegar in the trunk. And a lint-free rag too.

Wet the rag, then pour your vinegar on it and wipe those windows. Watch that goop disappear—works like magic!

From Idaho: "Guess what takes tar off a car?

"Laundry pre-wash spray. Squirt it on and the tar drips off!"

Nylon net (see Nylon Net, p. 217) works wonders on those stubborn spots.—Heloise

Clip Board

From Missouri: "A 9 × 14-inch cookie sheet makes a great clip-board.

"We use one for car trips—holds maps, papers and even coloring books.

"Oh, yes, the 'clip' part of the board is a snap clothespin."

Floor Mat

That old washing machine sure can work magic . . . It washes just about anything:

From Missouri: "Put the floor mats in the washing machine with a few old towels and let it clean the mats while you clean the car!"

Foot Rest

From New York: "I'm uncomfortable sitting in a car because I have short legs, so my husband made me a foot rest.

"He covered a two-inch thick board with scrap carpet and put it on the floorboard on the passenger side.

"I now have something to press my feet against and also a support, if he stops suddenly."

Gas, conservation (also see Introduction, p. 462)

Know what the experts estimate? Automobile trips—to shop, see friends, visit the doctor or dance teacher, or attend an athletic event —average five and a half miles one way per family. If you planned ahead and combined errands and appointments and thus took one less trip each week, you could save fuel . . . and money.

Glove Compartment

I always used to lock the glove compartment and don't know why I did. Nothing in it but maps and junk!

Some one ripped it out. They got nothing for their trouble but I got a repair bill.

So learn from my error.

Keep your glove compartment unlocked. It not only might save you filing an insurance claim but paying an increase in your policy rates.—Heloise

Grill

From Florida: "Driving south in summer? Tie nylon net (see Nylon Net, p. 217) across the grill of your car to make a 'bug catcher.'

"If any bugs get through this first line of defense, put some baking powder on a damp sponge and rub-a-dub-dub them away."

Handbag

Does your handbag slide off the seat when you drive? Do you drive with windows shut because you're afraid someone might grab your purse at a stop?

Here's the easy solution to both problems from a woman driver in Mississippi: "Slip the straps of your bag through your seat belt!"

Keys

From Alabama: "If I don't want to forget a package when visiting, I leave my car keys on top of it.

"Even if I walk out the door without the package . . . I don't get very far without the keys!"

From Ohio: "Did you ever lock your car, then discover the keys were still in the ignition? I avoid this problem by carrying a duplicate ignition key in my handbag."

Men can carry an extra key in their wallets—Heloise

I sure can identify with this Georgia gal because she's just like your friend Heloise. She drives off and then starts wondering if she left a stove burner on. But she's got the problem licked:

"To remind myself to shut burners off, I leave my car keys on a hook over the stove. Then I'm sure to check the burners before I step on the gas."

Litter Bag

To make a litter bag for your car, use an empty tissue box, an empty washed-out milk carton, or the plastic bags that sometimes appear on your doorknob at home filled with sample products. They already have a hole for hanging on your car's window handle. A clothespin bag lined with plastic works, too.

Luggage

From Maine: To eliminate bulky suitcases on a car trip, I leave the clothes on hangers and slip them inside a large plastic trash bag so I can lay them flat in the trunk or on the back seat.

"Pleasing plus: when you travel with plastic 'luggage', as I do, there's no need to unpack.

P.S.: On the return trip, the bags are used for soiled clothing."

Steering Wheel

From Florida: "In summer I cover my steering wheel with a towel so that the scorching summer sun won't make the wheel too hot to touch when the car is parked. Towels also keep plastic upholstery from becoming hot seats."

Telephone Book

From California: "I keep last year's city telephone directory in the trunk of the car. It's a handy thing to have.

"If I forget an address or want to look one up, it's ready for reference."

Thermos Bottle (see Vacuum Bottle, below)

Trunk

From Maryland: "I put a heavy corrugated carton in the trunk to organize overloaded grocery bags, keep loose library books and records from sliding around and stash bakery boxes in, topside up, so the frosting won't get squashed."

Vacuum Bottle

From New Mexico: "A long, heavy sock makes a good case for a vacuum bottle.

Windshield, cleaning

From Vermont: "When my windshield has ice on it, I grab a big handful of nylon net scraps (see Nylon Net, p. 217), twist a pipe cleaner around them and make a scraper that works like a charm."

Windshield Wiper

From South Carolina: "Often when windshield wiper blades don't do a good cleaning job, all they need is a scrubbing to get rid of the dirt that's slowing them down or causing them to smudge up."

SECTION FOUR

Strictly Personal

I

Looking Good

INTRODUCTION

Lord love a duck, but don't I get hopping mad when I see how much things cost, especially cosmetics and groomers.

You know and I know that what we're paying for is not just that lipstick or after-shave, but the fancy packaging, not to mention the advertising that lures us to buy.

I'll betcha the actual production cost of the product accounts for just a smidgen of what you pay for it.

But good news, chickadees, there is something you can do about this problem . . . at least some of the time. You can use your noodle, that's what.

F'rinstance . . . did you ever stop to think how many beauty helpers you can find right on your pantry shelves, in your fridge or medicine chest?

No, your friend Heloise hasn't flipped her wig. I really mean it.

Take olive oil . . . it's just about the best darned lubricant there is for dry skin. And ditto for safflower, cod liver and mineral oils. Coat your face, even your body, with these and your skin will be smooth as silk, maybe even satin.

You guys use them too, hear, because not even Robert Redford would look good with weatherbeaten skin, and weatherbeaten's what skin gets if it's overexposed to sun, cold or wind.

You can use oil to condition hair, too. Warm it up, massage it in, then wrap your head in a towel and sit under the dryer for a spell. The greatest for dry hair . . . and at a fraction of the cost of going to a salon.

Then there's witch hazel. I'll bet a fortune cookie you guys never thought of slapping it on for aftershave.

"Bracing"—as they say in the commercials. And a great astringent for oily skin, too.

You can do super stuff with eggs—and not just make omelets. To make hair shine, whip two yolks and mush 'em into freshly shampooed, towel-dried hair. Let the glop sit a spell, then rinse it off. Fantabulous!

Didn't think I was going to let you waste those egg whites, did you? Would Heloise do that? Use them "as is," or get out your mixer and whip them up frothy, and spread them on your clean face for the most terrific skin-tightening mask ever. Just avoid the under-eye area because that skin is sensitive, so you should never, ever apply a mask to it.

Do you like oatmeal? I love it . . . and not just for eating. Mix a handful with water to make a paste, then apply to skin. Let it dry then rub-a-dub scrub it off. The best skin-refining treatment I know. And for pennies—that's the best part.

And don't throw out used tea bags. Pop them in a plastic bag and store 'em in the fridge. One A.M. if you look in the mirror and scare yourself silly 'cause your eyes are all puffy, remember the tea bags. Dampen them with cold water and place them over your eyes. In about ten minutes those puffs will look like defla-tion's set in.

Tea—the camomile kind—makes the greatest rinse for hair that needs highlights. It will give you so many you'll have to wear sun-glasses or squint when you look in that mirror.

I'll bet you throw away cucumber peels. For shame, if you do. On a hot day, press those peels over your hot, perspiring face and it's instant cool, the greatest feeling!

Who says you have to be Cleopatra—or Mark Antony—to enjoy a milk bath? No sirree. Just be you and toss a cup of pow-dered milk in the tub, then run the water, for the smoothest beauty bath ever.

Next time you eat an avocado, cut it in half and save the skin. Rest your elbows in the skin cups and they'll be real smoothies.

If skin's dry, rub a clean avocado pit over it because it's chock full of lubricating oil.

You can't beat these last two for budgetwise tips! Why, these treatments are free because you would have thrown the skin and the pit out, right?

Honest to Betsy, chickadees, if I know something for true.it's this:

Now that you've gotten those rusty wheels turning, you're gonna sit down and think a spell and start remembering all those home-made treatments your grandmother and mother told you about. Know something? They'll work for you just like they worked for them, and that's the greatest.

When it comes to beauty-grooming tips, don't go away. You've just had a sampler 'cause there's more to come and, even if you're a super smartie, you don't know everything.

I know this for sure because people keep finding the greatest ways to do things. There's nothing makes a body an expert faster than tackling a job and learning by trial and error. That's how some of the greatest inventions and ideas in the world got thunk up in the first place—Hugs, Heloise

PART I: GROOMING HINTS

Antiperspirant (also see Bottles, deoderant, p. 493)

From South Dakota: "If you ever have used a highly concentrated roll-on antiperspirant you may have noticed that crystals form on the screw-on lid making it very difficult to open.

"If you will put a little moisturizing lotion on the bottle where the lid screws on, it will impede the formation of these crystals and your bottle will open easily at all times."

If you store the bottle upside down, the antiperspirant will always roll on—Heloise

Out of deodorant? Not to worry. Dust underarms with baking soda and relax 'cause you'll enjoy social security until you can buy your favorite roll-on, cream or spray. This is also a good one for people who are allergic to commercial products.

Bath

So many times after a hard day's work neck and shoulder muscles hurt . . .

Well, here is the greatest way I've found to relax at the end of a day:

Fill that bathtub up with hot water, then get the *thickest* bath towel you can find and dump it in the water.

Now, hop in and sling that towel around your neck and shoulders! Wow! Keep dipping and dunking it in that glorious hot water. It's the greatest. And keep letting out water and adding more hot!

Another thing: let the hot water run a second, hold the bath towel under it and throw it back around your shoulders again. It's a wee bit hotter that way.

For free relaxation, what do you have to lose?

That little old hot bath towel really relaxes muscles! You can even hold each end of it and rub-a-dub-dub, pulling it this way and that, back and forth across your shoulders.

It's free! It's free! It's free!

Bath Oil

Pour about a teaspoon of plain baby oil in your bath water for an inexpensive bath oil. It will remain in one spot and you will think it won't work, but it sure does!

But sometimes I just don't have time for a bath, and want to combine the benefits of my shower with the softness provided by the baby oil bath. So, after I shower and rinse, I take an old washcloth and hold it under the hot spray. Then I shake drops of that baby oil on the hot, wet washcloth and go over my body. I then step back under the warm shower for a mite.

When I get out, my body "beads." When I towel-dry, no oil shows whatsoever, but my skin feels absolutely lush. You know that stuff-you-like-to-touch feeling?

I keep one special cloth for this purpose only. Never use the same cloth for soaping as this removes the oil.

Blemishes, concealing (also see Foundation, p. 481)

Know the "goop" you buy in a tube to cover up blemishes on your face called "cover-something?" And it does?

Well, my cousin taught me that instead of putting the makeup directly on your face, it's better to smear some on your finger and then wipe it or, better yet, pat, pat, pat it over the blemishes.

Works like a charm, luvs. Doesn't look as if you were doctoring your face with "smear 'em" makeup. So natural looking . . .

Breath Sweetener (see Garlic, too much, p. 134)

Brush

From Idaho: "I usually use a quart jar of hot water with ammonia added to clean my hair brush, but once, when I was out of ammonia, I decided to try a baking soda and hot water solution. It worked like magic."

Brush, makeup

Makeup artists use brushes to apply shadow and powdered blusher. Allows 'em to control the application and get it in the right places. For bargain prices, buy small artists' paintbrushes—they work like a charm and are cheap-o.

Comb (see Brush, p. 477)

Compact

If the powder in your compact gets hard, take a piece of fine sandpaper or an emery board and gently rub it across the powder.

If you store your powder puff upside down in your compact the powder won't cake. It's the oil and makeup from your skin that cause this problem.

Contact Lenses

From Illinois: "When my daughter dropped her contact lens down the bathroom drain, I took a long-handled screwdriver, wrapped some absorbent cotton around it and stuck it as far down the drain as it would go.

"The lens stuck to the cotton and up it came."

From Kansas: "When I clean my lenses, I use one of those small spice or herb jars with the perforated plastic lids.

"This allows me to wash my lenses, drain the water, rinse in the same manner, and not take the chance of losing a lens in the sink."

Curlers (see Rollers, p. 487)

Dentifrice

Did you know you can dip your toothbrush into baking soda and go over your pearly whites with it just as you would with toothpaste? Moisten the brush slightly. For flavor, store cloves in the "soda toothpaste" canister.

Baking soda works for dentures, too. Brush it on dentures, then soak 'em in a glass of water with two teaspoons baking soda.

Dentures

From Missouri: "If you wear dentures and feel that they need a quick clean-up, use a small piece of nylon net (see Nylon Net, p. 217). I always carry some in my purse for this purpose."

From Alabama: "Here's an eating hint for denture-wearers: when eating, cut each bite-size piece of meat through each tine of the fork.
"This will cut the bite into four easily chewed pieces even though it still looks like one piece."

Emery Boards

From Arizona: "Don't throw away emery boards if the middle is still useful.
"Take scissors and cut right down the middle and you'll have two more good sides on the board for filing your nails.
"Also, this will sharpen your scissors at the same time."

Eyeglasses (also see Eyeglass Case, p. 492)

Guess what? A drop of vinegar on a tissue is the most spectacular thing yet to clean glass lenses. But don't use on plastic!

From Wisconsin: "Hair spray was making white spots on my dark plastic eyeglass frames.
"I washed them thoroughly with warm water and soap and dried them. Then coated the frames with a thin film of good old petroleum jelly and polished. (Don't get it on the lens.)
"They shine like new."

From New York: "Hair dye ruined three eyeglass frames and then . . . a stroke of genius.
"Now I wrap the ear pieces of my glasses with aluminum foil when my hair is being colored and the dye doesn't get on them."

From Virginia: "Our son was always taking off his glasses to wash his face and misplacing them or knocking them off the counter. So my husband attached an old eyeglass case to the wall in the bathroom near the wash basin.

"This keeps the glasses safe and sound and they are always easily found."

Eyelash Curler

From Nebraska: "Spread a very thin coat of petroleum jelly on your eyelash curler before using it!

"Not only does this prevent sticking and pulling, it also cuts down on eyelash brittleness and breakage—besides adding a gorgeous gloss to your eyelashes!

"A quick swipe with a tissue after each use of the curler keeps it clean as a whistle."

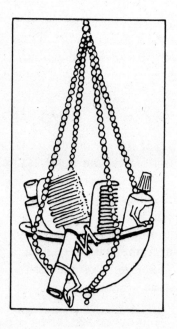

Eye Makeup (also see Eyes, dark circles, below)

You know what I like best for removing eye makeup? Petroleum jelly or baby oil! Either gives the dry, delicate under-eye area a lubricating treatment even as it softens eye makeup so it can be floated away with a tissue.

Oh, so cheap!

Eyes, dark circles

From Tennessee: "Many women have that age-old problem of dark circles under their eyes.

"My suggestion is to cover them with the thickened makeup that accumulates on the rim of the makeup bottle. You'll find it's just the right consistency to cover up."

Feet

Here's a funny from a honey in Iowa: "When your feet hurt, all you have to do is take off your shoes. So when your head hurts, will it help if you take off your hat?"

From Wisconsin: "You can take a shower and relax tired feet at the same time if you put the stopper in the drain. Then you can soak your feet for as long as you shower."

Fingernails (see Manicure, p. 485)

Foundation (also see Blemishes, concealing, 477)

I'm gonna teach you something that a friend taught me. It's about putting on foundation cream makeup. Many contain a moisturizer nowadays, but sometimes they are hard to smear on.

The secret?

Water!

Yep. Just plain old water from the tap. Before applying the cream, hold your hand under the cold water faucet, then wipe your face all over with the wet hand.

Then dip into the jar and dab on the cream. Take your hand and spread away. It will sorta melt all over the skin. It's scrumptious. Really!

Before I learned this technique, I really rubbed to spread that foundation. Eventually rubbing and pulling causes wrinkles, gals. You can only stretch skin so many times before it forms a wrinkle. Think that one over . . .

So wet your face first and, when you feel a slight pull on your skin, slightly dampen your hand again. You will be amazed at the difference it makes when foundation dries.

It takes only a few minutes and I have noticed that it puts a new, glossy fresh look on my skin because, since I've been doing this, I have quit wearing powder altogether.

You don't have a thing to lose, so try it.

Apply makeup base with a sponge and you'll get even coverage.

Hair *(see specific hair listings)*

Hair, summer care

In the swim season, the sun's hot. Boy, what it can do to your hair!

To prevent excessive damage, try to avoid over-exposure to the sun . . . at least wear a hat or a scarf.

The chlorinated water in swimming pools is hard on your hair, too. It tends to dry it out and make it very brittle.

Salt water is another cause of dried-out hair. Just remember to shampoo or rinse hair immediately after a swim, whether in a pool or in salt water. Alternate, using shampoo one day, lathering up with conditioner the next, and always rinsing thoroughly. This is a trick a hair care expert taught me.

Fortunately, only your hair shaft is damaged when exposed to too much sun and salt water. The roots are not affected.

Try to make it a habit when you leave home to pick up your sun hat just as you do your sunglasses.

Hairbrush (see Brush, p. 477)

Hair Coloring

If you use a color rinse on gray hair but like a light streak at the temples, here's what to do:

Wind up one or more strands at the front—the ones you want light —and wrap them in aluminum foil. Then apply the color, as per directions.

When hair has processed, unwrap the foil-covered strands, and you'll have a light streak or two.

To keep hair dye from staining your skin, smooth petroleum jelly on your forehead and around the sides of your face.

Hair Curling (also see Rollers, p. 487 and Home Permanents, p. 484)

Would you like the ends of your long hair to have just a little curl?

When you go to sleep at night, put your hair on top of your head in a bun. Just bend over and brush all the hair forward, catch it with your hand, then straighten up and twist the hair into a bun.

The trick is to dampen the bottom three inches and then wind this tightly around the core of the bun (like a big pincurl).

When you brush your hair out, it will turn under just a little at the ends.

From Oregon: "If you have a short tight, curly Afro, use fabric softener sheets to roll hair on.

"One sheet will make at least four spongy end papers.

"These sheets also make the curlers a little easier to sleep on overnight as they cushion the scalp."

Hair Drying

From Missouri: "I have very long hair. After washing it, it takes a while to dry, so I take a large towel and drape it over my shoulders so it hangs down my back.

"Then I comb my hair and let it dry without getting my back and clothes wet."

Hair Spray

So help me, Hannah, hair spray's not just for hair. Listen to this:

From Idaho: "I tracked down a big fly that had gotten in the house and I bombed it with water-soluble hair spray. It really does the trick and there is no unpleasant insect spray odor in the house.

"This hint is helpful for anyone who is allergic to insect spray.

"If you happen to spray the wall, the spray dries clear and is water soluble."

From Nevada: "When I was buying a gift for a friend, I told the clerk I wouldn't purchase it unless she could remove the price, which had been written with purple marker.

"That sweet gal grabbed a can of hair spray, squirted away and wiped it off with a facial tissue."

Hands

From Ohio: "When my hands become rough, I use baby powder to soften them.

"I rub the powder on my hands as you would hand lotion and in a few minutes they feel smooth. It sure works wonders!"

From Wisconsin: "To remove stains from around the cuticles and from the little crevices on your fingers and elbows, try cuticle remover!

"Put a dab on a little piece of cotton and rub and massage away. Then rinse. No soap is required."

Home Permanents

From Indiana: "I cut my own hair and give myself home permanents.

"To keep the waving solutions from burning my forehead—the excess sometimes runs down—I cream my face before starting the wave.

"I leave the cream on as long as the solution might drip, then wipe off the cream and wash my face well."

From Montana: "I just gave myself another home permanent and discovered that if you roll the curl just above your forehead forward instead of back like the rest, it won't form a ridge.

"Another thing. I washed my hair, waited a few days, then wet it and followed the perm directions.

"No frizzies."

Lipstick (also see Lipstick, p. 492)

From New Hampshire: "If the cover to your lipstick gets loose, cut a narrow strip of adhesive tape and put it around the bottom of the tube.

"The cover will then fit over the tube snug and won't keep falling off in the bottom of your purse."

Manicure (also see Emery Boards, p. 479)

Fingernails are composed of horny layers of dead cells held together by the substance called keratin. Nails tend to split and peel when this is destroyed by detergents or from the constant pounding involved with typing. Illness or drugs often can affect the nails, too.

Fingernails should be filed as uniformly in shape as possible. They should be kept oval or round for some jobs, such as typing. Otherwise, they should be tapered but never to a sharp point.

Don't neglect nails and cuticles for weeks at a time and suddenly go to work on them with a vengeance.

Keep nails smooth at all times with an emery board.

Apply glycerine, cuticle remover or lotion, massaging it around the cuticle gently, gradually pushing the cuticle back. Gently does it.

If cuticles are tight and cling to the base of the nails, soak in warm vinegar and water (half-and-half) for five minutes. Then apply glycerine and rub with a blunt orangewood stick.

If you have hangnails, trim them carefully.

Remember the cuticle around the nail is holding the nail in place. When the cuticle is cut away or broken, the skin around the nails rolls back and causes hangnails. Never cut cuticles unless absolutely necessary.

Rinse nails with warm water, and scrub gently with a small brush, then rub them dry.

Before applying polish, dip a small piece of cotton in vinegar (yep, plain old household vinegar) and wipe each fingernail. This not only will leave your nails absolutely clean but also will make them more pliable . . . and the polish will adhere to nails longer.

If you can't apply colored polish neatly, it is far better to use clear polish.

The correct procedure for applying polish is: one clearbase coat, two coats of polish, a top coat.

Gals, there's no reason why we can't have good looking nails. The dime stores are loaded with inexpensive tools.

I'm disgusted with fingernail polish—the kind with the white stuff in the bottom that you have to shake and shake and shake to mix. You could shake your hand off.

I've finally learned to store the bottle on it's side instead of standing it up when I put it away.

This way, the white goop is on the side of the bottle and you can mix it quicker by using the brush.

How could I have missed something so simple all these years?

From Ohio: "If you grease the treads of nail polish bottle caps with petroleum jelly, the caps won't stick to the bottle."

Mustache

Although a mustache is one thing I haven't had to cope with, I suppose it can be a problem for guys and here's a tip from a mustache-wearer in Arizona:

"I've noticed that my mustache sometimes gets messy looking. Besides an occasional trimming, I have found that an extra toothbrush makes an excellent dusting brush.

"After I munch something I give my mustache a dust off so it never looks crummy."

Nail Polish (see Manicure, p. 485)

Perfume

When you have a very expensive perfume you want to get the most out of it, so . . .

Put a few drops on a small ball of cotton and apply it behind your ears and on your wrists. Then tuck the cotton ball in your bra and the scent will last all evening.

In fact, the scent stays in the cotton for weeks so when you get home tuck the cotton in your lingerie drawer and you will have sweet-smelling undies.

Permanent Wave (see Home Permanents, p. 484)

Razor

Have you ever cleaned your safety razor? I don't mean just running it under hot water, but scrubbing it with a toothbrush. I never had. I always swished it around in the hot water and set it on the side of the tub.

So now I know better.

Once in a while I open it up and scrub all that gunk out with an old toothbrush.

The other little pointer I finally learned is to set the razor on its side, not with the blade edge down.

Rollers (also see Hair Curling, p. 483)

From Vermont: "So I won't lose the plastic picks for brush rollers, I stick them in a plastic kitchen scrubber."

From Delaware: "Because my hair's super curly, I made giant-size curlers from empty six-ounce and twelve-ounce orange juice cans. I removed both ends of the cans, then covered them with corduroy. I use giant bobby pins to hold them in place."

From California: "Here's a new use for a clothespin bag! I use one to store hair rollers.

"To make it do extra service, I attached a small pocket for the pins that hold the rollers in place.

"You can sew on more pockets to hold a comb and brush, etc.

"The really nice part of this idea is that the bag can be hung on the arm of a chair when you're setting your hair, and then hung in the closet out of the way until the next time you use it."

From Florida: "When I wash plastic rollers, I place them in a mesh fruit bag.

"The curlers can be swished around in soapy water and then held under running water to rinse.

"I hang them up to dry in the same little bag."

I've got a handy trick for girls who set their hair on jumbo rollers. Sometimes they don't stay in too well, so . . .

Take a half slip that has an elastic band around the top, put it over your head around the rollers. Then tie a long piece of yarn around the open end of the slip to keep it shut.

Now you've got something to hold those pesky rollers in place through a restless night.

From Maine: "To dampen each section of hair when you are setting it on rollers, cut a three-inch piece from a fine-grained sponge, dampen it and use it to moisten each strand."

Shampoo (also see Bottles, shampoo, p. 491)

It can be a problem when you're in the shower ready to wash your hair, and discover you have forgotten to loosen the top of the shampoo bottle.

When I buy shampoo I pronto put it in an empty squirt bottle—the kind dishwashing detergents come in—then I label it.

These bottles are plastic and have a top that opens with a little pull, closes with a push.

So convenient—and free.

Do you wear you hair in a short tapered cut? After a shampoo, nothing makes this kind of style dry quite as neatly as does a band of nylon net (see Nylon Net, p. 217) wrapped around it while it's still wet.

Make every drop of shampoo count: To use those last drops in the bottle, add a little water, shake the bottle, then use it. Works for conditioner, too!

Shaving Cream

Want in on a little secret that I snitched from men who shave with shaving cream?

I use it in the shower to shave my legs, and I usually buy whatever is on sale or the cheapest brand.

Well, last time I picked up a can of menthol, it smelled so good that I just foamed some on my face. Wow!

Let me tell you, it felt so good that I was tingly all over.

When I rinsed it off, my skin felt glowing. I figured I had hit on a good idea.

So, now, whenever I get into the shower or tub, I pat some all over my face and leave it on while I bathe. When I'm done my face feels like I've just had an expensive facial.

Give it a try . . . I really think you'll feel like smiling all day.

Here's a handy-dandy for new fathers: if you run out of shaving cream don't panic. Just reach for a bottle of baby lotion (not oil) and slather it on. It sure serves the purpose in a pinch.

Shower Cap

From Maryland: "This is for those who complain that shower caps are made only for women with misshapen heads.

"Go ahead and buy the usual huge cap. Put it on, and adjust a big pleat from ear to ear across the head, tapering from the deepest part at the crown.

"Remove the cap and fasten the pleat with strips of clear adhesive tape for a custom fit."

Toothpaste, (see Dentifrice, p. 478)

PART II: SECOND TIME AROUND: GROOMING RECYCLE

INTRODUCTION

There are lots of little money-saving tricks you can use to get the last cent of value from cosmetics and grooming aids. And I don't mean just the tips that follow because mainly they suggest ways to use the containers cosmetics are packaged in.

Nope . . . your friend Heloise is cooking on another burner.

What I'm thinking about right now are the smidgens . . . the little bits that are left in containers and bottles. Mainly when something gets down to a smidgen you toss it out. Right?

You shouldn't. Here's why:

It can be used.

When your lipstick's worn down so far you can't apply it, here's what to do: use it as blusher. Dab some in the palm of your hand, then add a drop of hand lotion or moisturizer (makes the lipstick easier to apply). Blend the two, then dot on cheeks.

This is one of those Jim-dandies that saves a day when you've run out of blusher and are worrying that you'll have to face the world looking anemic. Remember this goody, and you won't!

And what about the foundation that's caked in that bottle? Add a few drops of water or moisturizer shake well, and you've got enough left for a few more applications.

When nail polish gets thick (and that's what happens if you forget to screw the cap on real tight), don't throw it out. Instead, add a few drops of nail polish remover, give a shake. It should be thin enough to use.

Never throw out those pretty dusting powder boxes and the fluffy puffs that come with them.

Instead, buy a shaker container of baby powder or talcum (much cheaper, too) and pour it into the dusting powder box. How's that for a money-saving idea?

As for perfume or cologne you're weary of . . . why let it take up shelf space? Add a drop or two to the rinse water when you wash your lingerie. Mmmm, nice!

What I like to do with empty perfume bottles is tuck 'em in with lingerie. Sure scents slips and nighties in a heavenly way.

So you see, if you put on your thinking cap you can find lots of ways to save pennies here and there—and if you save enough they sure add up.—Hugs 'n' kisses, Heloise

Bottles, deodorant (also see Antiperspirant, p. 476)

From Oregon: "An empty roll-on deodorant bottle makes a remarkably efficient dispenser for glue.

"Pry off the plastic ball top. After washing and drying, fill the bottle with glue and replace the ball. Keep the cap screwed on tightly after each use to be sure the glue does not dry out and render the rolling ball inoperative. Store upside down if you can.

"A roll-on spreads just enough glue to do a perfect job—and we all know how glue travels!"

Empty roll-on bottles also are great for tanning lotion and cologne. Just love to roll-on an application, don't you?—Heloise

Bottles, hand lotion

From a clever penny-pincher in Pennsylvania:

"After carefully washing two empty glass hand lotion bottles (the kind with the pump dispensers), I covered the outsides with découpage, then gave them a coat of shellac.

"Salad oil went in one bottle, vinegar in the other.

"With a squirt or two from each my salad is seasoned."

Bottles, shampoo (also see Shampoo, p. 488)

From a rootin' tootin' ten-year-old in Nevada:

"The squeeze bottles my sister's shampoo comes in make great water guns."

Brush, shaving

From Utah: "When a shaving brush gets too old to use, it makes a wonderful shoe polish applicator."

And gals, listen to Heloise, it also makes a soft complexion brush, so if you can get your mitts on one, why, get ready to lather up for lovelier skin.

Brush, mascara

Never throw out a mascara brush. After cleaning, it's the handiest for brushing eyebrows or cleaning typewriter keys, jewelry, etc.

Containers, deodorant

From Montana: "The handiest little containers can be made from push-up deodorant stick holders.

"I keep bobby pins in one, cotton tips in another, etc. The bottoms can be pushed up or down, making it easy to pick out contents.

"I use nail polish remover to take off the printing on them and tape appropriate labels around each."

Eyeglass Case

From Illinois: "Open-end thick cloth type eyeglass cases make wonderful pot holders.

"Just slip an old one over a pot handle. It sure saves having those messy pot holders hanging around the stove."

Lipstick

From Oregon: "Melt the lipstick left in a worn-down tube and use for coloring decorative candles."

Lipstick Case

From Ohio: "Empty lipstick cases (clean 'em carefully first) make great needle holders."

Your Wardrobe

PART I: WARDROBE HINTS

INTRODUCTION

Who'd think that getting dressed could be such a challenge? But sometimes it is, if you know what I mean.

Ever have one of those days when you had trouble zipping into, gartering up or tugging on? (You know what I'm talking about—dresses, girdles and shoulder bags.)

And you guys, what about ties? Aren't there days when they make you drat-ratted mad 'cause they won't tie right?

When this happens, I'll bet you get so wild you'd like to pull that tie tighter than tight. Better not! You could cut off your breath and, believe me, breathing's a handy thing to be able to do.

Or how about boots? When you've just got seconds to spare or you'll miss the A.M. train, what happens? Nothing!

You tug and tug and tug some more and can't get the dratted things on.

I sometimes think clothes are out to get us. And I haven't even gotten around to the "Lost-But-Not-Found Department."

There you are, all dressed up but not ready to go because you can't find the matching belt, your collar stays or one of your earrings. It's enough to drive a body clear up Mt. Everest, not to mention right through the ceiling.

Well, stop fretting, sugarplums, because there are folks out there who say "Pooh" to such problems. Know why? They've licked 'em, that's why.

Okay, atomic scientists and space-age engineers aren't going to think this is earth-shaking news . . . but I do!

Wow! I really get chills-and-shivers excited when someone comes up with a solution to something that riles me up and ruins my day. It may be a little thing—but little things count, right?

So a round of applause—and, because you can't strain the quality of "merci," another one, too—for the guys and gals who solved the aggravation-makers I've mentioned here and others I didn't get 'round to. All their fantabulous ideas follow.

But one last thing before I forget it: you'll find lots more tips about clothes in the laundry and sewing chapters, because we not only wear 'em, we wash and iron 'em, mend 'em and sew 'em, too.

Kisses, luvs, and extra hugs to you genuine geniuses who contributed to this chapter.—Heloise

Belt

Ever have a bathrobe, coat, suit or dress get unwearable because the matching belt slipped out of the loops and got lost?

Wow! Who can afford that these days?

Don't wait until it happens. Right now get a needle and thread and tack that belt to the loops or, better yet, sew it with a few invisible stitches to the center back of the dress, coat, robe or suit.

Then you won't have to worry about losing it if you wear it open instead of tied.

Boots

From Arkansas: "Here's a hint to make unlined rubber boots slip on easily. Just spray the insides lightly with spray-on furniture polish.

"The boots slip on like magic—unless they are too small.

"Don't do this if the overshoes are lined as the polish might make the lining oily."

From Vermont: "If you have trouble zipping up high boots, hook the top of a wire clothes hanger into the eye of the zipper, pull and the zipper will glide right up."

Bra (also see Bra, p. 512)

Don't you hate the look of a white bra showing through a sheer blouse? I do. Know how to make a bra invisible? Wear a flesh-colored one under sheers.

Bridal Gown

Brides, sentimental lovies that they are, always want to know how to store a wedding gown.

Checked with the Guild of Professional Drycleaners and this is what they had to say:

The first thing to do is have your wedding dress and veil professionally cleaned.

Get a storage box with a tight-fitting lid, one large enough to hold your dress and veil without squashing them.

Now, lay your dress on the bed, spread out the skirt and lay blue tissue paper over one side of the skirt. Fold the skirt over several times, placing tissue between each fold. After this is accomplished, fold the bodice down over the skirt.

Wrap the veil the same, placing tissue paper between each fold.

Take a large, dark plastic bag (such as is used for leaves), and put both dress and veil inside and fold over the open end several times; seal well with masking tape; place in the large storage box.

This should keep your dress and veil in perfect condition because the bag and box seal out the light, air, moisture and dust that discolor and ruin such treasures.

Make sure to store in a dry place. High humidity can cause mildew, which can leave a ruinous stain.

I'm sure when you have that little girl and she grows up, she will be tickled pink that you went to all this trouble to preserve these things, so dear and beautiful, just so she could wear them on her wedding day!

Collar, stays

Here's an idea to save both your temper and hubby's when he loses his shirt collar stays. Even worse—if he loses just one! He need not be late for work or an important engagement. Just quickly make a new stay or two from any emery board you happen to have around.

The "grip" of the board's sandy surface keeps the stay in place.

If he loses your make-do's, who cares!

Earrings (also see Earrings, p. 508)

Doggone and heck a mile!

How many times have you lost one clip-on earring?

It's like losing one glove—might just as well lose them both.

Well, I have lost so many earrings that I've been in a dither. I've tried every hint that has come in. Hints like when you use the phone (this is always where we lose them, right?), hold the earring in your hand.

After losing many, I've finally learned that if you clip the earring you took off on the same ear that the other one is on, you can't lose it.

Just take my word for it, gals, this idea works. Eventually someone is going to ask, "Are you crazy?" And when you ask why, they'll tell you you have two earrings on one ear . . .

From Rhode Island: "Have you ever thought of using pierced earrings for sweater studs?

"I don't have pierced ears, but I buy these earrings just for this purpose. They really add to the appearance of an otherwise plain sweater."

Garters

From New York: "If you find it difficult to connect back garters and hose, try fastening garters before pulling up your girdle all the way.

"It's easier!"

Girdle

From Utah: "If you've ever struggled with a girdle on a hot, sticky morning you'll love this cool idea:

"Put your girdle in the refrigerator when you go to bed.

"It's a real cool way to start the day."

Gowns

If you are wearing a long dress on a rainy or sloshy day, cut two holes in an extra large garbage bag, and step inside it. Pull it up to your waist and secure with a belt.

You'll have no problem with dirty splash marks on your gown. And the bag is large enough not to wrinkle the dress.

A friend of mine who was a bridesmaid for a wedding held during a blizzard solved this problem another way.

She tied a skip rope around the waist of her gown, then looped her long dress over it, blouson style.

Handbag, over-the-shoulder

From Virginia: "Here's how I solved the problem of keeping the chain handle of my over-the-shoulder purse from slipping off my shoulder.

"I took a heavy hook from an old fur coat and attached it right under my coat collar at the shoulder seam. Then I hooked a chain link of the shoulder strap to the hook and that was the answer."

Handbag, plastic

You and I know that we save plastic handbags from year to year. Aren't they a mess when you take them out months later?

They're out of shape and look absolutely awful.

Now an idea hit me which I tried on one of my plastic bags:

I took my hair dryer, turned it on hot, put the hose inside the bag and let it blow away on hot for a few minutes.

This made the plastic so warm and pliable that the "wrinkles" fell out. As soon as the bag was soft, I stuffed it with a bath towel folded to fit the shape of the purse. It looked like new again a few hours later.

Those of you who do not have hair dryers can open a window, lay your handbag on a towel and let it sit in the sun until one side gets hot.

When it softens, stuff it with a folded bath towel and turn it over and repeat on the other side. This may take a day or two, depending on how the sun shines in your window, but it works.

Hosiery (also see Hosiery, p. 509 and Static Electricity, p. 504)

From Illinois: "If you spray the heels or toes of nude nylons with hair spray, you can get a lot more mileage out of them!

"Hairspray also helps keep a run from running more."

And so does fingernail polish.—Heloise

From Montana: "Aren't you dismayed at the way your big toenail cuts through nude-toe pantyhose? I've licked the problem:

"I cut off a one-inch piece of half-inch wide transparent first-aid tape for each big toe. I place the tape a quarter-inch down from the toenail edge and smooth it over the nail, across the nail edge and down the back of my toe.

"It stays put through several showers, is virtually invisible and works so well I haven't had a breakthrough for the longest time!

"When I shared this idea with my husband, he said he'd try it, too, as his big toenails go through his socks."

Here's a helpful hint on how to store stockings:

When you take them off, knot them loosely so they will be in a matching pair.

If they haven't a run, make the knot at the ankles. If they are loaded with snags, tie them in the middle.

Wash and dry them knotted, and never unknot them until you are ready to put them on again.

At a glance, you can see which good pair or which snagged or runny pair (for wear under slacks) you want.

This simple method helps identify stockings at a glance when you are in a hurry.

If pantyhose have a run in one leg only, cut off that leg. Then, when a matching pair gets a run in one leg, snip it off too. Wear the two pairs of one-legged pantyhose, one over the other, for a money-saving bonus—a new pair!

About holes in the toes of stockings and socks:

Instead of pulling hose on tight over your feet, pull the toes of the hose out a little to give your toes room after your shoes are on. It helps keep big toes from pushing through hose.

From Indiana: "I recently started wearing support stockings.
"Putting them on was a chore until I started dusting my feet with cornstarch, especially the bottoms and the heels."

Jewelry (also see Earrings, p. 496 and Ring, p. 502)

From Wyoming: "When attaching charms to a charm bracelet I place a drop of glue on the small ring opening to prevent loss.
"Saves money on soldering and works like a charm."

From Colorado: "If you drop a tiny screw or a small stone from a piece of jewelry in the house, fasten a scrap of organdy or nylon stocking securely over the end of your vacuum hose with a heavy rubber band.
"Run the vacuum over the suspected area, checking the hose cover frequently, and you will soon find the lost object intact."

Keys

From Kentucky: "Who hasn't been frustrated trying to find keys in the bottom of her purse?
"Finally (in pure desperation), I used a large safety pin to secure a shower curtain ring to the inside of my purse, near the opening.
"Now I reach in and unsnap my keys with one hand.
"Works great when my arms are full of packages!"

From New Hampshire: "Have you ever gotten to the door of your house and had to dig into your handbag for your house keys?
"Well, when I'm going home by bus, car, or whatever, I take my keys out of my purse while still sitting.
"This saves me so much trouble especially if I have a baby in my arms or am loaded down with packages."

Lint Removal

You can buy a special brush in the notions department that picks up lint and cat or dog hairs. Know what also works? Cellophane or masking tape!

Wrap it around your hand, sticky side out, then press over lint or hair. Instant pickup!

Necklaces

From Georgia: "A good way to store long, dangling chain necklaces is to hang them from a square of cork attached to the wall.

"Not only does this keep them untangled, but it also makes a nice display and they are easy to see when you are choosing your jewelry for the day."

From Wisconsin: "If a pendant falls off a chain, thread a needle and tie the thread onto the end length of the chain, then gently pull the threaded needle and chain through the pendant's loop. It's quick and easy."

Nylons (see Hosiery, p. 499)

Pants

From Nebraska: "When you enter a public rest room, if you are wearing a pants suit, reach down and turn each cuff up, pulling it to the knee.

"This will prevent soiling your slacks on the floor."

Be ready for emergencies and always pin a safety pin on the inside of slacks in case a button comes off or the zipper breaks.

From New Hampshire: "I have beautiful shag rugs but discovered when wearing pant suits that the pant legs worked like a magnet in attracting lint from these rugs.

"By the time I was dressed and ready to go out, the pants were always in a terrible mess. I finally got the idea of turning up the pants legs halfway to the knees and then, as I got out the door, turning them down again. No more lint problems and it certainly takes less time than trying to get de-linted or de-fuzzed."

Pantyhose (see Hosiery, p. 499)

Price Tags

No more broken fingernails pulling stubborn pins out of price tags if you try this tip from a keen teen in Connecticut.

"Slip the teeth of a small comb around the head of the pin and it can be removed easily."

Raincoat

For an emergency raincoat use one of those large plastic trash bags.

Slit a hole for your head in the bottom of the bag, make a slit on each side for your arms, and slip it over your head.

This is the best rain slicker in the world and can be used more than once, too.

Ring

From Texas: "If you have an allergic reaction to a favorite ring, apply a thin coat of clear fingernail polish around the inside of the band."

Shoehorn

A mother in Iowa says a tablespoon makes a great substitute shoehorn.

A policeman in Wisconsin has another idea: "The end of a belt not only serves as a good shoehorn, but is extra handy if I have a backache because it is long enough to reach my shoes without my having to bend over."

Shoes, polishing

A natty naval officer in Virginia came up with this sparkler:

"For a quick and easy way to polish shoes so they look like you've had a professional do it, borrow your wife's floor polisher.

"Turn the waxer on its side on a chair, apply your shoe wax to your shoes and, when dry, flip on the waxer switch and polish to a high shine."

A savvy bachelor in New York had this shiny idea:

"When my leather shoes need a quick cleaning and polishing, I use spray-on furniture polish.

"Rub it in good with your fingers and wipe off excess with a towel. It is also good for white shoes before wearing them. Helps to keep black marks off, makes them nice and soft, too."

From Nebraska: "Rub a clean pencil eraser over scuff marks on patent leather shoes and they'll vanish pronto."

Ever notice that wax polishes don't cover the scuffs and that most liquid polishes don't leave a nice shine? What to do:

Apply the liquid first, let it dry, then apply the wax polish and buff. You'll find the worst looking shoes will take on a nice-as-new finish.

Shoes, squeaky

A smarty Idaho bachelor says his shoes no longer announce his arrival because he's discovered how to de-squeak them:

"I have a shoe that squeaks. I put two thumbtacks on the bottom of the shoe under the arch on each side of the metal arch support.

"Lo and behold, if it didn't stop that squeak!"

Shoes, tight

To stretch tight shoes, put identical small jelly or jam jars in each and let 'em sit a bit 'til the shoe stretches into a more comfy fit.

Slacks (see Pants, p. 501)

Slip, substitute (also see Static Electricity, below)

From New York: "I wear a pajama bottom under a long gown instead of a half slip.

"It gives me leg room and is so comfortable."

Sneakers (also see Sneakers, p. 365)

A thrifty mother in Maryland discovered a way to salvage sneakers:

"When rubber separated around the canvas, I used to throw them out, but no more.

"I find that if I thread a needle with fishing line, then double it and tie a knot, I can sew along the canvas and some of the rubber and get the sole to hold for many more weeks of playing."

From Oregon: "When you buy a new pair of sneakers, put a piece of adhesive tape inside the shoe where your little toe rubs the side. It will prevent the shoe from wearing out so soon!"

Stockings (see Hosiery, p. 499)

Static Electricity

Whoops! Doesn't it drive you daffy when your dress or slip swishes up, showing more leg than you'd like to reveal? Or when your slip sticks to your nylons when you walk?

Static electricity's the culprit. There's a spray you can use to avoid this, but I know another trick:

Add one tablespoon of white vinegar to the final rinse water and you'll defuse that static electricity and solve the problem.

Ties

If you men have trouble tying your ties, try this:

Wrap the tie around your thigh and tie it facing you. Then loosen it, slip it off your leg and pull it over your head and around your neck.

This trick makes for a perfect knot every time . . . and no more getting all twisted up trying to tie a tie looking in the mirror.

Travel, packing

From New Hampshire: "My husband travels a great deal.

"I hit on the idea of making packets, putting a coordinated shirt, tie, socks and handkerchief for each day he's away in a plastic bag.

"After wearing each outfit, he puts the soiled clothes back in the empty bag, thereby separating the dirty clothes from the clean ones in his suitcase."

From Michigan: "Pierced earrings are tiny and easily lost in a large suitcase.

"When traveling I pack them on a card punched with holes.

"The card slides down in the pocket of my bag and is easy to handle. My earrings are in view and I can make a quick selection."

From Michigan: "When I go on vacation, I use a hair roller to wrap my chains around, securing them with a bobby pin.

"No frustrations of knots or tangles."

Umbrella

From Kansas: "To repair the broken rib of an umbrella, cut a one-eighth-inch length of wire from a coat hanger. Use it as a splint on the broken rib, securing it with masking tape."

Veil

From Arkansas: "To keep a face veil from crushing, fill it with tissue paper, then place it in a plastic bag, blow up the bag, put a rubber band around it and that's that.

"Your veil will stay in shape. The bag may be hung up or put in a box."

Wedding Dress (see Bridal Gown, p. 508)

Wig

From West Virginia: "Here is a tip for you women who wear wigs:

"By the end of the day, without fail, you fight the Battle of the Wispy Neck Hair.

"No matter what you do, those wisps won't stay up. Here's how I waged war on wisps:

"I bought two small hair combs. After putting my wig on, I slip them up under the back, catching all those little neck hairs and holding them securely underneath my wig.

"The combs keep the wisps up—and the wig snugly down."

It's time to share an idea with you about what to do with a wiglet or wig when traveling.

At bedtime, stuff the wig with toilet paper, then perch it on a soft drink bottle. It makes a perfect wig stand. Or try this: Slip a roll of toilet paper over the bottle's neck, then slip your wig on it.

The paper roll is soft enough so that you can use wig pins to anchor the wig and do additional setting or combing if necessary.

The wig is easily rotated on top of the bottle for combing and spraying.

Wig Form

"Know what to do to make wig forms stay securely on any table, vanity, bureau, etc.?

"Glue a record (an old 33 does fine) to the base of the form. This will support the form and will keep it from tilting."

PART II: SECOND TIME AROUND: WARDROBE RECYCLE

INTRODUCTION

Put on your thinking caps, honeypots, and let's play a guessing game.

The subject is: wardrobe.

The question is: what do you own—and might just be throwing out 'cause it's old, worn or you're just plumb sick of it—that could be recycled into the following?

A tack pin for a bulletin board that really looks nifty . . .

A clothespin bag that's nigh on the sturdiest . . .

A shoe polisher that really shines 'em up . . .

A camisole that's as lacy as you like 'em . . .

A wet mop that does the dandiest job on those kitchen floors . . .

A scarecrow to keep those birds from eating your berries . . .

Give up? Well, I'm not going to make it easy for you, no sirree. You'll find all the answers follow—but you're gonna have to search for 'em.

Know why? They're alphabetically listed not by what they turned out to be, but by what they were originally.

I did not do this to be tricky, friends, but so that, for example, if you were tossing odd socks into the trash, you'd be able to look up socks and—like magic—find something useful to do with them.

Sure, I know that homes and apartments are smaller than they used to be and that you can't save everything. But, for budget-balancing's sake, save things that are useful. Why go out and pay big bucks for an item when you've got the makings for it right on hand . . . and maybe even headed for the trash can.

Doesn't make sense, does it?

And sense is what we've all got to make these days to save cents that add up to dollars.

Think nifty and thrifty!

If you don't want to splurge on another cup of coffee, have a "free" cocktail on me. Throw some ice cubes and a splash of lemon juice into a glass. Pour the water you cooked spinach in over those rocks, season to taste with salt and pepper, then down the hatch.

Honest, this isn't only delicious, it's also packed with all those good-for-you vitamins.—Hugs, Heloise

Bridal Gown

From Kansas: "Know what my clever daughter did with her bridal gown?

"First, she cut it apart and made a baptismal dress for her little girl.

"A few years later, she made a first communion dress for that same child with the remaining fabric."

From Idaho: "I chose a simple bridal gown so I could dye it and wear it as an evening gown later. It's deep green—and looks sensational."

Dresses

From South Dakota: "I've made pillowcases from old cotton dresses—and pot holders, patchwork and doll's clothes, too."

Earrings (also see Earrings, p. 496)

From Ohio: "What do you do with one leftover post-type pierced earring when you've lost the other one?

"Don't throw it away. Your bulletin board can use it as a push pin."

From South Carolina: "When I lose an earring, I save its mate in a trimming box I keep with gift wrap supplies. An earring can supply sparkle plenty when clipped to a bow."

Handbag

From New Hampshire: "Scraps from old leather and plastic purses make patches for elbows on jackets or knees on jeans."

Hat

From Washington, D.C.: "Don't throw out a felt hat. It can be cut to fit the bottoms of lamps, bookends, ceramics, etc., so they won't scratch furniture tops. Apply with glue."

Hosiery (also see Hosiery, p. 499)

From New Jersey: "The cut-off feet of nylon hose make wonderful mothball bags to thumbtack in your closet or wardrobe.

"Hang them near the top of the closet, as this way the fumes go downward and leave a protective odor."

Jeans

From Florida: "If you cut cut the legs off jeans to make shorts, use the scrap jean fabric to make a clothespin bag! Sure is good and sturdy."

Jewelry (see Earrings, p. 496)

Nightgown

From Maryland: "A long nightgown that wears out at the neck and shoulders can be rejuvenated.

"Cut off above the waist, under the arms. Make a casing and insert elastic.

"Now you have a strapless summer nightie."

Pants (also see Pants, p. 514)

From Nebraska: "I recycle my old pants suits into pull-on pants for my toddler. Here's how:

"Fold the pants pattern down the front to show you where the crease should go. Then, when laying out the pattern, line up the crease on the pattern with the stitched-on crease on the pants you're recycling.

"I've made several pairs of toddlers pants with the stitched-in crease already done for me. Just don't be careless as I was once, when I cut the back part of the toddler's pants from the front of my old slacks.

"You can also can make toddlers' jumpsuits from old slacks.

"Zippers can be salvaged, too. So can the elastic waistband."

From Delaware: "I cut a square out of the top of a pair of old slacks and inserted a waist area piece from an old pair of pantyhose to make maternity pants.

"It worked! Now I'm going to make several more pairs."

Pantyhose Containers

Here's a Letter of Laughter from Missouri: "I stash small change in an empty egg-shaped pantyhose container. Makes sense, doesn't it? 'Cause this is my nest egg!"

Shirt

Wear one of your husband's old shirts as a cover-up over your own clothes when feeding the baby or doing messy chores.

It is easy to take off when the doorbell rings

Bonus: the shirt can be tossed in the machine and, if drip-dry, needs no ironing.

From Idaho: "Make a "Big Papa" clothes hamper from a man's flannel shirt. Button up the front to where you want the opening, then sew the bottom and the cuffs shut.

"Hang it behind the bedroom door for a personal clothes hamper."

Need a new slipcover for a pillow? Make one with a soft shirt he no longer wears.

From New York: "Use discarded white shirts to make linings for little girls' dresses.

"A shirt's buttons are the ideal size for children's clothes, too."

Shoe Polish (also see Shoes, polishing, p. 503)

A sixth-grader in Mississippi came up with this idea while polishing his brother's shoes:

"Do you know the liquid shoe polish bottles that have a sponge top you press down on to get the polish out?

"Well, when you use up all the polish in the bottle, remove the rubber top and wash sponge out real well, and the bottle can be filled with paint.

"Then, if you want to paint small objects that a big brush would mess up, you can use this little dispenser."

Slip (also see Slip, substitute, p. 504)

From Illinois: "Instead of buying camisoles for see-through blouses, I took some of my older slips, cut them off a little below the waist and pinked the bottom.

"I used the skirts of some of the longer satin slips to make pillowcases that I use to keep my hairstyle intact as I sleep."

From Louisiana: "I recycled all my too short half slips by turning them into camisoles.

"Here's how: turn the slip upside down so the lace around the bottom of the slip becomes the top of the camisole. Add straps.

"The waist elastic will still be around the waist, or slightly lower. The bottom of the camisole, being elasticized, will stay in place better."

Socks

From Montana: "If you can't find any darning cotton, cut off the top of an old sock and unravel it. Some socks unravel from the top, others from the bottom. Works like a charm and you have strong thread because socks unravel in two strands."

PART III: WARDROBE-MENDING AND MAKING-DO

Do you put things off . . . tackling that tiny rip in a seam, tightening a button that's looking loose? Well, my face is red, too. I know better and you do, but we all let things slide.

Know what I'm gonna do? Embroider this motto, frame it, and hang it over my closet door: "A Stitch in Time Saves Nine."

Bra

Those of you who wear bras with cloth straps could do what I did.

I bought insert lace (same on both edges) and stitched it to each strap using the biggest stitch on my machine. I bought peach for white straps so they'd be a little bit more flesh-colored as well as pretty and feminine if they decided to do a peek-a-boo.

Seems like there's nothing more unsightly than a bra strap showing when it shouldn't.

From South Carolina: "To be honest, I'm too lazy to sew on a patch when the wire of an underwire bra pokes through. Instead I patch it with a moleskin corn plaster. It's self-sticking and does the job.

"If you're in a fix, you can tape a cotton ball over the wire for short-term use. I've also used stick-on bandages in a pinch—or should I say a poke?"

Buttons (also see Buttons, p. 405)

Know how bottom buttons on coat dresses and some coats tend to pull, ripping the dress or coat? Here's how to avoid that:

Remove the bottom two buttons while the garment is still new. Carefully sew a patch on the garment, not the facing, to reinforce the fabric so the button will not pull out and tear the garment when it's replaced.

The patch should be done with tiny stitches that are not visible on the right side of the garment.

Another way to skin this pesky cat:

Instead of a patch, use a small square of iron-on interfacing. A real boon for this sort of thing!

Jeans

From North Carolina: "Here's how I mend the knees of my son's jeans:

"I rip out one side-seam on the outer leg (most jeans have a straight seam, not flat-felled) and thus have an easy-to-reach, flat surface to sew the patch to. For reinforcement, sew a heavy-duty patch inside, a decorative one outside.

"Afterwards, I sew up the side-seam and the jeans look great."

Lingerie

From Utah: "So that the stitching wouldn't show when I shortened several nightgowns, I used lace hem finish—but on the right side of the fabric instead of the hem."

From Texas: "I tried to iron my favorite slip with an iron that was too hot and—sizzle!—burned a hole in it.

"My mom's suggestion saved the day . . .

"I appliquéd a lace heart over the burn."

Long Johns

From Idaho: "Now that a lot of people are wearing long johns again, here's a tip that makes them more comfortable.

"Sew a piece of one-inch wide soft elastic on the bottom of each leg, stirrup-style.

"It keeps them from bunching at the ankles and they look neater."

Maternity Clothes

From Massachusetts: "Finding the right shade of stretch panel for the tummy often is a problem if you're making maternity skirts or slacks. I've always dyed white stretch material to match . . . and hoped that it would. But here's a cheaper, easier method.

"Buy an inexpensive nylon sweater in a bargain store. Cut off the bottom eight or ten inches and open the side-seams.

"It already is hemmed on the bottom, so thread elastic through the hem and sew the panel in place.

"You can use the top half of the sweater for a dickie or shortie sweater under a suit jacket.

"You waste nothing, and it's inexpensive because one sweater will make two panels."

Pajamas

From Maryland: "When my daughter's pajama pants got too short, I cut the legs from a pretty pair of socks and zigzag stitched them to the bottom of the pajamas."

Baby, it may be cold outside but it'll be snug-as-a-bug inside, if you follow a warming trend set by a seamstress in Nebraska:

"Use a blanket to make really warm pajamas for the kids. You can get two pairs from a double blanket. Use the binding to make ruffled cuffs."

Pants (also see Pants, p. 509)

From Iowa: "Instead of hemming my son's pants when I shorten them, I use four snaps in each leg so I can unsnap them when they go in the wash.

"This makes it a cinch to make the pants longer as he grows taller."

Pockets

From New Jersey: "Sew a double square of nylon net (see Nylon Net, p. 217) folded at the top, to make a pocket conveniently located on the underside of a pocketless coat, sweater, apron, etc.

"No one will know it's there."

From Florida: "I bought tiny zippers and sewed one on the top of the left outside pocket of each of my childrens' coats and jackets.

"Now they don't lose their lunch money or bus tokens!"

Got a hole in your pocket? You can mend it temporarily with adhesive-backed bandages. Press two on one side of the pocket, then turn the pocket inside out and bandage over the hole on the other side.

Zingo! Frustration's gone!—at least for awhile.

Seams (also see Shine, p. 386)

Here is one of my favorite "Inflation-fighter" tips from a Georgia gal who's hip to saving ways.

"Before wearing new clothes, machine-stitch stress seams and resew all buttons with strong thread."

Isn't this a dandy idea. I think so. Bet you do too.

But will you do it? You should . . . saves aggravation, rips, tears and lost buttons.

From Indiana: "Usually I sew the cut-out parts of a dress together and then finish the seams.

"But while working on fine material that raveled easily, I zig-zagged all around the pieces . . . and then sewed them together.

"It was far easier, faster, and looked better, too."

Shirts

From Montana: "When the cuffs on several of my husband's long-sleeved shirts frayed I turned them into short-sleeved ones.

I left the buttons attached to a small piece of shirt cuff in my sewing box so that when he loses a button I know which button goes on what shirt."

From Indiana: "To make a collar extender for a shirt, use a shirt button and a piece of strong thread.

"Start as when sewing on a button in the regular way, but leave an extension of about one-half inch thread between the button and shirt collar.

"When a tie is put on, the extension won't be noticed."

Skirts, enlarging waist (See Slacks, enlarging waist, below)

Slacks, enlarging waist (also see Maternity Clothes, p. 513)

Hope you don't need this expandable idea . . . but if you do, you'll bless the "sew" clever woman in Nevada who thought it up:

"Need to make slacks wider? Cut off a cotton glove finger, sew a button on it and then attach the cut end of the finger over the spot where the old button was."

Sweaters

If you use grosgrain ribbon to make the facing for a cardigan sweater, be sure to shrink the ribbon first or you could wind up with a puckered front.

Even ready-made cardigans have this problem. It's a wonder manufacturers don't think to do something about it.

To shrink the ribbon, put it in hot water and let it soak for a few minutes, roll in a towel to remove excess moisture, then press with a fairly warm iron."

Sweaters, darning

From South Dakota: "I've finally learned how to darn knitted sweaters, suits, and so on.

"Stretch a piece of nylon net (see Nylon Net, p. 217) over an embroidery hoop. Put the knitted garment on top, place the top of the hoop in position, then do your darning.

"You will find that the nylon net reinforces your stitches so they will not gather together."

Naturally, trimming the excess!—Heloise

help from

To the homemaker, no matter what gender, age or marital status. We all need help at one time or another.

And to my dear mother, who in 1959 started "Hints from Heloise" and the idea of sharing hints with each other. She taught me at an early age to care about you, the ones that have helped make Heloise a household word.

A special thanks to my daddy, I couldn't have done this without him.

General Introduction

Hello, this is your friend Heloise. Since you're reading this book, I figure you could use some help!

Actually, we *all* need help. No matter how efficient and organized we are, the moment sometimes arrives when nothing is more important than knowing how to get ball-point ink out of a shirt, or how to remove a plastic bread bag that's gotten stuck to your toaster. What then?

Since my first book, *Hints From Heloise,* was published, I've found out from thousands of people in every corner of the country that sometimes the littlest things going wrong make for the most frustrating problems. I started making a list of them. The list grew. Boy, do we have problems!

Well, now *Help! from Heloise* is here, with solutions to those problems that seem to pop up most. Whether you need an ounce of prevention or—sometimes it happens!—a pound of cure, *Help!* is at hand.

How to Use This Book

If you turn back to page 7 and look at the Table of Contents, you'll see what's in this book. There are three parts—one each for inside, outside, and all around your house—and twelve chapters.

I almost called this book "P.S. from Heloise"—*P* for the Problems we plan to avoid, *S* for the Solutions we sometimes have to have ... in a hurry! Well, fact is, each chapter in this book contains dozens of *P*'s and *S*'s—solved problems, questions with their answers—all organized under alphabetical headings so you can find 'em fast. And I often find that one good idea leads to another, so I've put in lots of cross-references to help you on to greater things.

In addition to these *P*'s and *S*'s, every chapter is stuffed full of additional tips that may help you from having some problems in the first place. Wouldn't you rather pour a cup of water into the broiler pan *before* broiling hamburger patties than spend time scrubbing and scrubbing the pan *afterwards?*

At the back of this book is an Index to everything—Problems, Solutions and all the hints. It's the best way to find what you're looking for—and to find related things you didn't realize you needed to know, too.

Heloise's House

Before you start turning to find the "helps" you need, you may be wondering about something people ask me all the time: Where does Heloise find these hints in the first place? The answer, of course, is that most of them are found by *you,* and shared with me when you write in, and shared *by* me with everyone who reads this book.

I also have a "test house," my home in Texas, where my staff and I combine and carefully test the best suggestions America has to offer —and we even invent quite a few of our own!

The Heloise Philosophy

You know, lifestyles are changing, and family units have changed from the "perfect" family with mother, father, 2.5 children and one pet with a two-car garage, to almost anything-goes. Men are now getting custody of the children. Women are working full time and spending more time away from home.

I feel that today the term "homemaker" means anyone who has to do some laundry, wash his or her own hair, take the garbage out, or even fix that first cup of coffee in the morning. (In my family, we were taught that if you were old enough to walk then you were old enough to help out around the house. It may be only carrying the napkin from the dinner table to the kitchen, but it's a start.) *Every* homemaker who helps around the house can use *Help! from Heloise.*

So the hints and solutions in this book are for everyone, and they're for everyday problems. Some of the hints you may know already, but if you're like me, some of them you'll absolutely flip out about. How smart we all are when we all put our heads (and our hints) together!

I'm constantly learning from the readers of my newspaper column and from people who read my books, who send in their best ideas to me to share with others. Often the most obvious-sounding solution is the one everyone has been searching for. That's what the entire Heloise philosophy is—Caring and Sharing.

My best wishes to you, may all your problems be very small and easily cured. If not, remember I am here to help whenever I can with those big ones too. If I can't, I can listen to you and let you know that there are millions of others with the same or worse problems, and I love each and every one of you!

—Hugs, Heloise

PART ONE:

Inside the House

INTRODUCTION

A house, a home or an apartment—no matter where you live, the inside is your domain.

The trend in housing seems to be more and more towards the compact, the easy-to-care-for. More people are moving into condos, into smaller houses with little tiny yards (we call them garden homes here in Texas). The whole world seems to be going for "smaller is better," even in our cars.

The first section of the book is just what the title says, "Inside the House"—the things that go on inside, the things you must care for and the things that you do for yourself.

I have broken this down into five major areas of the home.

The first and foremost is the kitchen. We all know how important the kitchen is to any family. You can live without a dining room or a living room, but it sure is hard to live without a kitchen.

Your kitchen may be very large with all the gadgets in the world, or it may be just a sink, coffee pot and a hot plate. No matter, it's still the place that is the heart of the home.

I don't care what you do, how large your living room is, or your den or the area you entertain in, it seems everyone always ends up in the kitchen. Right? When I lived in my tiny apartment I would carefully plan things so that no one had to go into the kitchen to get anything. Food was already out, drinks and ice and glasses were on the patio, etc. There was no reason for even me to go in there.

You guessed it. Out of twenty people that came over one night, fifteen of them ended up in that tiny kitchen, shoulder to shoulder. So I gave up. If that's where everyone is going to end up anyway, let's make the best of it.

In my home now, the kitchen is large, and we even have a center island that is three feet by four feet and forty inches high. I put chips, dips and cheese out and make my kitchen a real entertainment area. Everyone likes it and so do I.

The next chapter is about probably the second most important room in the house. The bath. Unless you live in the backwoods, or have a roughing-it type of retreat, you have indoor plumbing and at least one bathroom, if not several.

That old bath sure does get a work out, doesn't it! If there are children or teenagers in your family, I bet you never thought anyone could spend so much time in there.

If you are lucky enough to have your own bath that you don't have to share with anyone, I would say that is really a luxury. If you are like most people, you have to share the bath area with someone. This section will give you good advice on coping with the problems that arise.

Laundry problems have got to be some of the most-asked questions that I get in my column. We are all stuck with doing a little laundry now and then, even if it's only hand washing those special garments in the bathroom sink, or trying to sort socks. Yuck. Sometimes I wish all socks came in only one color. Even though some might say it would be certainly boring, it sure would make laundry day a heck of a lot easier!

The problems and solutions in this laundry section are the ones I get asked, over and over and over. Simple, tried and true, but the hints will make your laundry day a bit brighter and lighter.

Inflation has become a way of life. With the cost of clothing going up like everything else, more and more readers are sewing and repairing, rather than discarding and buying new. Sewing and mending and taking better care of clothes is very important. I think you will see from this chapter that if you will take a few minutes to do it correctly, then it will save you time and money in the long run.

If you aren't a seamstress, you still may have to sew on a button, or at least pin it on for the time being. There are a lot of short cuts and easy ways to do these things, and I hope you will remember them when you need the help.

Last but not least in this section is my favorite chapter: Miscellaneous. If I could put everything under this heading, wouldn't you have a time finding what you want!

Miscellaneous covers things like carpets, closets, furniture care, and some real good information on storage.

Welcome to my world—and may this section on "Inside the House" help when you need it!

—Hugs, Heloise

Your Kitchen

Let's pour a cup of coffee and talk a few minutes about a very special place.

A kitchen is just a room in the house until folks move in, and then it becomes the heart of the home. People lend the warmth and glow that make your kitchen that very special place.

On a cold rainy day, there's no better gathering place than the kitchen table for coffee with a friend. When the kids come home from school tired and hungry, you know the first place they go. And, of course, the kitchen's a very special place when the kids are all in bed and you and hubby can share a cup of hot chocolate and the news of the day.

Your kitchen tells others a lot about you. It says, "I like bright colors and I'm a gregarious type," or "I like cool, refreshing greens," or "I like a quiet cozy nook," or "I prefer uncluttered, modern,

529

functional things," or "I'm a soul who loves the beauty of yesterday." And, though we are all different in our likes and dislikes, we
all want our kitchens to be a happy place for ourselves and our
families.

We all know how much activity is connected with this heart of the
home, and it seems as if all the chores that begin there never get done.
I can remember mother saying so many times, "Just top clean and
do what you have to do and then when you really feel like it, do the
heavy cleaning."

Well, one thing about the kitchen that bugs me is cluttered counters. I don't know about you, but if my kitchen is presentable I feel
like a million dollars and my day goes much smoother. Have you
noticed that the mood YOU are in is the mood that the whole
household gets into? T'ain't fair but it's true.

The rest of the house somehow doesn't seem insurmountable after
I've gotten the kitchen done. I always clean the counters and table
off first; that way, if unexpected company drops in at least you have
a place to sit down for coffee. However, you need to do what suits
YOU best. Don't do something a certain way because it works for
your neighbor, unless it works for you.

Success in running a kitchen efficiently does require a little planning and a little organization. I love a little saying that someone
passed on to me—PLAN YOUR WORK and WORK YOUR
PLAN!

There are three things that really have helped me manage in my
own kitchen, and that's (1) having a telephone with a l-o-n-g cord
so I can keep on working while I talk (sometimes I just sit down and
scoot along the floor washing cabinets); (2) writing a menu and
shopping list out and posting the menu for the week on the fridge
so I know at a glance what to thaw and what to cook; and (3) writing
my most-used and favorite recipes on cards and taping them to the
inside of my cabinet near the place where I store my staples and do
my mixing.

We are all in this kitchen thing together! All of us have to clean
ovens and refrigerators. All of us have to mop spills. All of us have
to get the cabinets "back between the fence posts." So I have com-
piled this special chapter. We'll lend each other a helping hand and
get our kitchens shipshape. We'll go from Rags to Dishes!

ACCESSORIES

Bulletin Board

Problem   *I don't have space for a kitchen bulletin board.*
Solution   Purchase some "chalkboard paint" and chalk
                 paint the inside of a cupboard and you'll have an
                 instant message center!

*   *   *

Tape lists of birthdays and anniversaries to your bulletin board and
they will be less likely to slip your mind.

*   *   *

An "inspirational board" will turn a gloomy day into a sunny one
and turn a frown into a smile. Clip poems, sayings, cartoons, pictures
of loved ones, whatever gives you a lift, to this special bulletin board
that you can go to when needed. Try it, it really works!

Canisters

Silver cleaner will make your aluminum canister sets shine like
new!

*   *   *

P   *The aluminum canisters I have leave black marks
         on my cabinet.*

S   Glue pieces of moleskin or little pieces of felt on
         the bottom.

*   *   *

If you break fingernails trying to get canister lids off, glue some knobs
on the lids.

*   *   *

P   *I use apothecary jars for canisters. I detest filling
         them because it is so difficult.*

S   Try this: Cut a small hole (about the size of a
         nickel) in the corner of a plastic bag. Put the bag
         in the canister and pull the top of the bag around
         the neck of the jar; now you can dump "whatever"
         in the bag and it will flow through the hole into
         your apothecary jar.

*   *   *

P   *I have a gorgeous set of ceramic canisters but the
         lids won't fit tightly.*

S   Go ahead and use them, but put your ingredients

in plastic bags, twist them closed with a twistie, and place them in your canisters.

* * *

To clean ceramic canisters, use a mild ammonia-and-water solution or a commercial window spray.

* * *

The jars that freeze-dried coffee comes in are super as canisters for those folks who live alone and don't want or need regular-size canisters.

* * *

Use small jars to store quantities of one or two cups of flour, sugar or coffee to use in a pinch.

* * *

P   *What can I do with an old canister set?*
S   Put the canisters in your bath to store hair rollers, cotton balls, cotton swabs, makeup, etc., or put them in a child's room to store crayons, puzzle pieces and small toys. In your kitchen you could remove the lids and use the canisters to store long spoons, spatulas, etc.

* * *

P   *I have some new canisters of dark wood. I'm afraid that water and spills on the cabinet will mar them.*
S   Why not glue some garden hose washers underneath them to raise them slightly out of the path of spills?

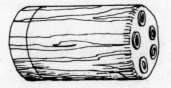

Curtains

P	*How can I restore body to limp dacron curtains?*
S	Soak them in a solution of 1 cup Epsom salts and 1 gallon of lukewarm water; rinse by hand.

*   *   *

P	*My curtains snag when I slip them on the rod.*
S	Put a piece of transparent tape over the end of the rod, or slip a small plastic bag over the rod and secure it with a rubber band before putting your curtains on the rod.

*   *   *

An old pair of cafe curtains with rings, stitched face to face and turned inside out, makes a great laundry or storage bag. Thread a piece of rope or cord through the rings.

*   *   *

P	*The curtain over my kitchen sink constantly looks bad because of water spots.*
S	Some folks with this problem have switched to terry cloth curtains over the sink. When dirty or spotted, just toss them in the washer and dryer and rehang. Shutters that can be opened while your sink is in use are a solution, but unfortunatley will cost you something.

*   *   *

To cover an unsightly kitchen shelving area, place a tension-type curtain rod to hang a curtain over the opening. Match your kitchen colors.

Place Mats

P	*How do I get the grooves clean on my patterned place mats?*
S	Use an old toothbrush and scrub them with detergent.

P   *I love the look of place mats on my wood table, but I worry that they aren't enough protection from spills.*

S   Cut a pad the size and shape of your place mat out of an old quilted mattress cover or those flannel-backed moisture pads that can be found in the baby department of your store. Put this pad under your place mat. This extra pad will surely solve the spill problem, but I would check to see how much protection they offered before placing anything really hot on them.

*   *   *

P   *How can I keep my plastic place mats from sticking to my table?*

S   Glue felt strips on the back, or line them with nylon net.

*   *   *

P   *I get so tired of hunting through drawers for place mats; I think I would use them more if they were handier.*

S   A multi-skirt hanger will hold mats in your pantry. You can even store them under the sofa cushions (at least they'll stay flat!) If you do have to put them in a drawer, be sure it is one that is close to the table and easy to get to.

*   *   *

Fingertip towels make washable, practical place mats for small children.

Potholders and Oven Mitts

Crocheting pot holders? Use rug yarn for durability.

*   *   *

A child's toy rolling pin makes a darling holder for pot holders. Screw two cuphooks in the pin and attach it to the wall; or, take a wooden spoon (paint if desired) and screw two cuphooks in it and attach to wall.

*   *   *

Pot holders can be made out of worn-out silicone ironing board covers, old mattress pads and stretched-out thick socks, just to name a few materials.

*   *   *

P   *What can I do with worn-out oven mitts?*
S   When the oven mitt loses its protection, give it to hubby to wash the car with.

Scrubbers

The nylon net bags that onions and potatoes come packaged in make fantastic scrubbers. Just fold the bag into a square and stitch along the edges. Slip a washcloth or a sponge inside one of the bags and it makes a super dishrag scrubber.

*   *   *

You'll wonder how you ever did without these wonderful scrubbers. Stuff a sponge into the knee area of an old, clean, nylon stocking. Cut and tie knots in the ends. Keep one in the kitchen, one in the bath, and one in the car for those trips to the car wash.

*   *   *

P   *I have seen nylon net scrub brushes made by using a plastic bleach bottle. Can you tell me how it's done?*

S   Take 72-inch-wide nylon net and cut it into six strips three inches wide. Then, lay one strip on top of the other until all six are in a pile. Now, gather them all together through the middle. Next, cut out the handle from your empty bleach jug; be sure and leave about one-half inch or so of the bottle along with it. Now, use a hole puncher and punch holes about every one-half inch along the plastic edge.

Get a strong string and stitch the net to the plastic by going through the center line of the net, then through the holes of the plastic, and finish by separating each row of net so it will be "bushy" and stand out.

Spice Racks (Also see Spices, p. 587)

P   *I just got married and received several spice racks. Any suggestions for making use of the duplicates?*

S   Lucky you! Some of us scrounge around at garage sales and such trying to pick up the old ones because they're so handy! Put one in your bath or bedroom to store makeup in or fingernail polish and remover. You can store straight pins, needles, and other small sewing items. Hubby probably would love to have one to store his nails, thumbtacks, screws, etc., there.

*   *   *

P   *I would love to have a spice rack but I'm really on a tight budget. Any ideas for a homemade one?*

S   You bet your boots I've got some ideas! A 2-pound

cardboard cheese box covered with shelf paper or adhesive-backed paper will hold six cans of spices.

*   *   *

If you don't have a spice rack, a lazy Susan is great for holding your spices in a cabinet.

*   *   *

Alphabetize your spices in their storage space to save time locating them.

Towels (Also see Towels for the bath area, p. 634)

Plan on doing a lot of cooking or baking? Pin a washcloth or small towel to the belt of your clothing or apron, and you'll have a handy cloth to wipe your hands on.

*   *   *

A really handy item in your kitchen is a "refrigerator" towel. This type of towel buttons together and can be hung over the door handle of your refrigerator.

*   *   *

P   *How can I keep a kitchen towel from falling off the towel rack?*

S   You can sew gripper snaps on the towel, or you can pin the ends together with a safety pin or clothespin. If you have a paper towel holder, sew two towels together (all ends), slip the towel over the dowel, replace the dowel and you have a "rolling" towel.

APPLIANCES, LARGE

This section was written to help you with problems encountered cleaning appliances as well as to give a few hints for making your appliances do "double duty"!

Be sure to make a file folder or an expandable envelope to store all your instruction books, warranties and sales tickets. Keep all of this information together in one file; it sure beats digging through a dozen drawers and tearing the house apart.

Before you call a repairman or take an appliance to a serviceman, be sure to check to see if it is plugged in or if you have blown fuses or tripped circuit breakers.

*   *   *

P   *I'm a bride-to-be and I'd like some suggestions in choosing appliances.*

S   Best wishes for a long and happy life! I'd be happy to give you a few hints . . . first of all, ask yourself, how often will I use it? Where will I store it? How will I clean it, and also, how heavy is it to move? If you don't know what features to look for or what prices are reasonable, pick up a copy of a major store's catalog and look through it. You can get an idea of what the basic features and capabilities are, as well as what "like-to-have" (I call them "gingerbread") features are available. You can also get a pretty good idea of what price you'll have to pay.

*   *   *

When you move, leave the instruction books and warranties to those appliances that will be left in your home for the new owner.

Dishwasher
(Also see Cleaning dishes and glassware, p. 571)

Judging from the letters I get, some of you are having problems with your dishwashers. That's a shame because your dishwasher was built to be a boon to you. Once you master a few "basics" you'll realize the full benefit your machine was designed to give you.

Number one, the water needs to be hot enough to do the job. If your dishes aren't getting clean, or film and water spots are left, this is probably the reason. Some machines have built-in "boosters" that heat the water to the correct temperature once the water is in the machine. If yours doesn't have boosters, you can check the temperature by letting the water run out of your faucet until it's as hot as it's going to get. Fill a tall glass with the hot water and drop a tablespoon of your dishwasher detergent in there. If the detergent mostly dissolves before it reaches the bottom of the glass, the water temperature is hot enough. If not, you may need to turn up your water heater a bit. The temperature should be around 120°F. A word of caution: Small children are easily scalded and some have even died from scald burns due to water that was between 140°F and 160°F.

If you're sure your hot water heater is at the right setting, it may be that you're trying to run the dishwasher right after baths or while doing laundry, and there's simply not enough hot water available. Try rescheduling your dishwashing time to make sure you have really hot water on hand.

Another problem can be the dishwasher detergent itself. You should pick up that box *at the store* and give it a good shake. Don't put it in your basket if it doesn't sound loose and powdery. Old, lumpy detergent just won't get the job done.

Where do you store that box of detergent once you get it home? I used to store it under the kitchen sink until I found out that it's far too warm and moist under there. Find a cool, dry shelf and keep the box spout closed tightly.

If you'll check that filter in the bottom of your dishwasher regularly and keep it free and clean, your dishes will come out cleaner. Face it, if there's guck and pieces of food in that filter, it's just going to recirculate over your clean dishes until you get that filter clean.

Slivers of broken glass, spoons that have fallen to the bottom (I have even found matchsticks) that get under the waterflow arm or in the filter can mess up the whole works!

Another tip is to load dishes properly. If you block the spray of water from reaching all the dishes, you simply can't expect sparkling dishes.

I have found that some brands of detergent unfortunately do not work as well as others. Try changing brands and see if that helps get your dishes cleaner. Also, if you are not filling the detergent cup to the manufacturer's suggested level, especially if you have hard water, that could mean the difference between so-so clean and *really* clean and sparkling dishes.

Folks who prerinse dishes before putting them in the dishwasher (lucky me, mine come out clean without prerinsing!) have problems with other members of the family not knowing whather or not the dishes in the machine are ready to use or ready to wash. Some readers have made little signs saying "Wash me" or "I'm washed" which they attach to their machines with little magnets.

If etching is a problem, try not to overload your dishwasher and do use the right amount of detergent. Etching is caused by a combination of things; mainly it's because the water is too hard or too soft and because the dishes are not thoroughly rinsed. This causes a silica film to build up on the glassware. To be on the safe side, always hand wash fine crystal. Also, be sure and see if your fine china is specified dishwasher-safe. Gold-plated flatware should *never* be placed in a dishwasher.

* * *

Remove the entire flatware basket to unload flatware—saves steps!

* * *

If you want to wash small items in your dishwasher, tie two pint-size plastic baskets (like the ones you get from the grocery store with strawberries) together with twisties.

* * *

P   *I have trouble with small forks and such falling to the bottom of the dishwasher.*

S   Place a plastic scrubber in one of the sections of the silverware basket and stick those small items through it.

* * *

Put nylon net in the silverware basket to prevent small flatware from falling to the bottom of the dishwasher.

* * *

P   *The inside of my dishwasher is discolored.*

S   This is probably due to hard-water lime deposits. With an empty dishwasher, set one cup of bleach in the bottom rack and run through a wash cycle (do not run dry cycle). Then, run one cup of vinegar through an entire cycle. NOTE: Do not try to "short-cut" it and run both the vinegar and bleach through at the same time. Bleach should not be mixed with other substances due to poisonous gases that can form. Read the labels!

*   *   *

If you normally wash small loads, why not wash seldom-used dishwasher-safe glassware each time you run a load? You won't have such a chore to do when you need it.

*   *   *

If you only run a load through your dishwasher every two days or so, place a glass of water on the bottom rack and put the flatware in it to soak until "wash time." You won't have any hardened, stuck-on food on your flatware.

*   *   *

If you want to sweeten the smell in your dishwasher, add a half a box of baking soda and run the machine through a rinse cycle.

*   *   *

Do not place gold-decorated china, hand-painted dishes, hollow-handled silverware, wooden ware or heavy glass such as lead crystal in your dishwasher.
(Also see Cleaning Dishes, p. 571)

*   *   *

P   *The racks on my dishwasher won't slide freely.*

S   Take a soap pad and vinegar and scour the metal part the rollers glide on.

*   *   *

P   *How can I keep the water from splashing all over? I have the portable dishwasher that drains in the sink.*

S   You can cut the bottom and top off of a bleach bottle, and the handle, and then place the discharge hose through the handle slot. Or, you can let the water drain into an empty shortening can; the water will fill to the top and then overflow into the sink drain without splashing.

*   *   *

If your dishwasher goes out, remember you can use the racks for draining dry (your dishes will still be out of sight, too!).

DISHWASHER—OUT OF ORDER?
Check the following before calling repairman:

1. Is it plugged in?

2. Is there a fuse blown or a breaker tripped?

3. Is it clean under the filter-strainer? No food, spoons, or gook under there?

4. Is the detergent flowing freely in the box? Shake the box—if it's lumpy the soap won't clean good.

5. Is the water hot enough? Check your hot water heater temperature.

6. Is there something lodged in the solenoid that won't allow the washer to fill or drain?

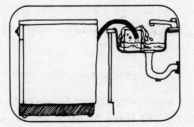

Freezer
(Also see Refrigerator, p. 549)

Full freezers are more economical to operate than empty ones. You can even stock your freezer with rolls of paper towels, macaroni, crackers, cookies, and so on to fill up those empty spaces.

*　　*　　*

P   *Do you know of a simple way to inventory freezer contents?*

S   I think I have two really good ways to do this. The first is to make a list and place it in a zippered plastic bag that you've taped upside down on your freezer door. You can mark off items used and add new items. Keep a pencil handy by your list.

     Another way that will be well worth the time and effort is a peg board. Make a peg board about two feet square and space nails two to three inches apart and in rows about four inches apart. Write above each nail the items you freeze such as corn, peas, beans, pork, chicken, etc. Hang a tag under each item—one tag for each package you have in your freezer. When you use an item take a tag down; when you put an item in your freezer add a tag.

*　　*　　*

You don't have to have tape to mark plastic freezer containers. A black crayon or marking pen works super.

*　　*　　*

Color-code your meats and you won't have to open or dig through your freezer: For example, red for beef, yellow for chicken, blue for pork, etc.

*　　*　　*

P   *I need some suggestions to make defrosting easy.*

S   Hon, I don't think there is any way to make defrosting "easy," but there are a few tricks to make it less hard!

First of all, as a safety measure, unplug your refrigerator from the wall. Place a thick layer of newspapers or several old towels on the floor in front of the refrigerator. Remove all the food from the refrigerator (you can pack it in an ice chest if you want to take your time). Keep a pail or a garbage can handy if your sink's not handy to throw the big chunks of ice in.

Never chip away those ice chunks with an ice pick or any other sharp object that might puncture a line or the compartment lining.

A hand-held hair dryer works super for melting the ice and speeding things up. (Caution: remember that electrical appliances are dangerous if they come in contact with water.) A pan of real hot water set in the freezer compartment helps, too. If your hands get cold, try putting on some rubber gloves.

After you're done with the job, place a couple of layers of waxed paper on the freezer shelf before putting your food back in. Next defrosting time, the ice will just glide off the paper. A light coat of vegetable oil spray around the bottom and walls should also help.

*   *   *

Use oven mittens when rearranging or defrosting your freezer to keep from getting "cold" burns on your hands.

*   *   *

P   *After I defrost my freezer, the packages stick to the shelves.*

S   If you'll wait just a bit and let the freezer freeze slightly before you put the packages back in, they won't stick.

*   *   *

P   *When I defrost my chest-type freezer, I have a problem getting the water out when the ice melts*

S   Take several thick towels or old bath mats and lay them on the bottom of the freezer and then all you'll have to do is pick them up and wring them out.

* * *

P   *I have a chest-type freezer and cannot keep stacks of food from falling over.*

S   Take heavy grocery bags and label them. For instance, put vegetables in one, meats in another. It will help to keep your frozen food separated and the bags will help support the stacks.

* * *

P   *The ice in my freezer compartment has an "off" taste.*

S   This is probably because food in your freezer or refrigerator compartment is not sealed airtight. Be sure and put onions, as well as other strong foods, in foil, plastic wrap or a tightly-sealed jar.

* * *

P   *How can I tell if the power was off to my freezer while I was away on vacation?*

S   Put a few ice cubes in a plastic bag and set the bag in your freezer. When you return, if the cubes are still shaped the way you left them, no problem. If the cubes are misshapen or melted a little, that would indicate a power loss or malfunction occurred while you were away.
        (See also *Refrigerator—Out of Order,* p. 553)

* * *

"If you're going away on vacation or an extended trip, store your valuable papers such as insurance policies, wills, birth certificates, etc., in the freezer or refrigerator (be sure you put them in a moisture-proof plastic bag).

In case of fire, usually the refrigerator or freezer isn't totally destroyed, and you may save the headaches and time involved in replacing those papers.

Oven
(Also see Stove, p. 553)

P   *What is the best way to clean my oven?*

S   My favorite way is to wipe the inside of my oven with plain old ammonia before I go to bed at night. Then the next morning it simply wipes clean as a whistle! Or, you can use a commercial oven cleaner the same way (the oven cleaner works better if your oven is slightly warm).

You can wash all your removable oven parts in your dishwasher. If you don't have a dishwasher, soak those parts in your sink or bathtub with dishwasher detergent (put something down to prevent scratches if you use this method).

*   *   *

P   *I simply cannot get the glass on my oven door clean.*

S   If you've tried cleaning the grime off with vinegar, ammonia or a window cleaner and that hasn't worked, your problem is probably guck in between the panes. In this case, if you can, unscrew the window panel on your oven door to get to those "inside parts" of the window.

*   *   *

P   *The numbers on my oven dial are so worn I can't see them*

S   Take a yellow crayon and rub it all over the numbers on the dial. Then gently wipe off the excess crayon. You should have easy-to-read numbers once again. Paint with clear nail polish.

*   *   *

Never line your oven completely with foil—heat simply cannot circulate properly if you do.

*   *   *

Your oven rack makes a great rack to put over the fire for a weiner roast. Take it along next time you go camping!

*   *   *

Always use dishes or cookware with lids in the oven to prevent boil-overs and spills. Aluminum foil can be used for covers. Never fill a dish to capacity.

*   *   *

P   *I was told to choose shallow casserole dishes for my microwave. How come?*

S   A shallow casserole exposes more food surface to microwave energy. That's why it's preferable to a deep dish.

*   *   *

P   *Why do I need straight-sided dishes for microwaving casseroles?*

S   It's because food in casseroles with sloping sides can overcook around the edges. Straight-sided casseroles will cook your food more evenly.

*   *   *

Did you know you can cook "heaps" of bacon at one time in a microwave? Just layer bacon on paper towels in a baking dish. Rotate the dish after half the cooking time.

*   *   *

When you barbecue, cook an extra amount, freeze and reheat in your microwave later. Same yummy taste!

Refrigerator
(Also see Freezer, p. 544)

Your vegetable bins make super extra bowls for mixing salads for large groups.

* * *

Never immerse cold vegetable bins made of glass in warm or hot water. It may crack them. Let them warm up to room temperature before you wash them.

* * *

P *The vegetable bins are always sticking.*

S Clean thoroughly, wipe dry, and apply a light coating of vegetable oil spray.

* * *

Do not block air circulation by lining your refrigerator shelves with aluminum foil or by using mats. Your refrigerator will not cool properly without proper air circulation.

* * *

P *How can I clean under my refrigerator—it seems impossible!*

S Take heart! Wrap some nylon net or old rags around a yardstick to wipe underneath.

* * *

Be sure to vacuum thoroughly underneath your refrigerator at least once a month. Dust on the condenser coils can spell a big repair bill. Also, a vacuum simply won't reach up behind your refrigerator, so it needs to be blown out at least once a year. If you don't have the apparatus to blow it out, call a serviceman to come do this for you.

It may cost, but it's a small price compared to the price of a new refrigerator.

*   *   *

P   *I can't keep fingerprints off my refrigerator door*

S   Try waxing your refrigerator with a kitchen cleaner-wax product made especially for that kind of finish. That should help. But I think your best bet would be to keep a little towel hanging on the door handle. Maybe everybody would grab the handle and the towel at the same time and eliminate prints in the first place. If not, at least you could give it a swipe "in passing" and keep those fingerprints from getting out of hand (no pun intended!).

*   *   *

If you dislike cleaning the dust off the top of your refrigerator, cover it with plastic wrap and just pull it off and toss it away when it becomes dusty (no one will notice the plastic wrap on top). The plastic wrap will adhere better if you just slightly moisten the top of the refrigerator before you put the plastic down.

*   *   *

P   *I have rust streaks on the inside walls of my refrigerator.*

S   Make a little paste of baking soda and water and apply. Most stains will vanish.

*   *   *

P   *I've got ugly brown stains on the glass portion of my refrigerator.*

S   Use full strength hydrogen peroxide to remove them.

*   *   *

P   *The finish on my refrigerator has yellowed.*

S   There are commercial car rubbing compounds

that will lighten the finish on your refrigerator. You may have to make more than one application, but the results are well worth the time and effort!

* * *

When moving, or disconnecting your refrigerator, be sure to read your instructions for disconnecting the ice maker (if you're fortunate enough to own one!). Water lines may need to be cut off.

* * *

P   *The walls on my refrigerator always have moisture on them.*

S   You need to check the gaskets and the catch to make sure your door is sealing tightly. An easy way to do this is to use a dollar bill or a piece of paper. If it can be inserted between the door of the refrigerator and the refrigerator itself, it means you need to have the gaskets or possibly the catch replaced or fixed (sometimes a good cleaning alone will solve the gasket or catch problem).

* * *

P   *I can't get rid of an odor in my refrigerator.*

S   If you're sure the source is not a food or spill,

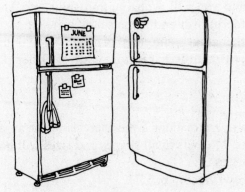

remove everything from your refrigerator and clean it thoroughly. Be sure to clean every crack and crevice, including cleaning under the gasket.

Some models have a drain tube and you should check the tube and the pan it drains into. Also clean the area underneath the vegetable bins. A cleaning solution of warm soapy water followed by a water and vinegar rinse should eliminate the odor.

If you set a saucer or cup of baking soda or a cup of vinegar in your refrigerator, you will keep it sweet smelling.

*   *   *

Never, never, never store an old refrigerator outdoors or in a place where a small child could climb inside. Always remove the door of any junked refrigerator or place the refrigerator with the door flush against a wall when stored. In some cities there are safety organizations which will come pick up discarded refrigerators and dispose of them.

*   *   *

P   *The door won't stay shut.*
S   More than likely, the gasket around the inside of the door needs cleaning. Gently pull the gasket up and you will probably find spills, etc. Use an old toothbrush and some soapy water to clean under the gasket and this problem should disappear. (Also see Refrigerator—Out of Order p. 553)

*   *   *

Make your refrigerator door a message center or an art gallery for your little ones. Magnets in all shapes and sizes will hold your notes or artwork in view.
(See also *Bulletin Board,* p. 531)

REFRIGERATOR—OUT OF ORDER
Before calling a serviceman, check the following:
1. Is the refrigerator plugged in?

2. Is there a fuse blown or a breaker tripped?

3. Does it need defrosting?

4. Vacuum underneath it and around the back.

5. Check the gaskets to make sure they close tightly.

* * *

If your refrigerator goes out, pack your food in an ice chest. For frozen foods, dry ice can be purchased. A fairly small amount of dry ice will keep frozen foods frozen for several days, and there is no mess to clean up such as with ice melting.

If you "ice down" your foods in an extra bathtub or washer not in use, the water will simply drain out and you'll have no mess.

Stove (Also see Oven, p. 547)

If you're one of those people who automatically go YUCK at the mere mention of the word "stove," join the club! I guess that's the biggest, never-ending job we've got—keeping that critter clean!

However burdensome stove care is, it sure beats cooking Abe Lincoln-style, in a fireplace, or hauling in wood like great-grandma did for the old wood burner! Keep that in mind, and take good care of that feast-fixing family friend.

Whoever said "An ounce of prevention is worth a pound of cure" must have been talking about stovetops and ovens! I'd like to share with you some of the things I've learned (mostly the hard way) about caring for stoves.

Keep some baking soda handy in case of grease fires (a fire extinguisher in the kitchen is your best bet). Be sure to keep the baking soda on the refrigerator or near at hand—never on the back of the stove because you may have to reach across the fire to get to it. Remember, throw a lid on the skillet to smother out the fire; in an oven fire, leave the door closed.

Store matches in your kitchen in a can with a lid. Also, you can toss used matches in an empty soft drink can to prevent wastebasket fires. (Also see Candles, Caution p. 700)

* * *

P *How can I get and keep my burner bibs clean?*
S Vinegar and baking soda are a few of the household items you can try. Remember that oven cleaners, ammonia or soap pads may pit or scratch chrome burner bibs (and most *are* made of chrome). Once you get them clean, line them with foil to keep them clean.

Also, a nifty trick is to cover burners not in use (especially when you're frying) with a pie tin or plate while using other burners. Spills, boil-overs and splashes will be kept to a minimum on burner bibs if you practice this.

* * *

P *The flames don't burn evenly on my gas stove.*
S Remove your grates and look at your burners. Clean them well with a toothbrush and make sure they're grease-free. Then take a toothpick and poke it in each little hole. More than likely, the stove has some clogged up holes.

* * *

P *My stovetop burners are really grimy.*
S Soak them in a little water and dishwasher detergent for an hour or so and scrub well. Then wash them in the dishwasher.

* * *

P *Why does the burner on my gas range emit soot?*
S This is a sure sign your burner needs adjusting. The utility company in our area usually does this as a free service for customers. Why not check with your local utility company on this?

Some stoves have a drip tray. Pull or remove your stove knobs and lo and behold! There's a little tray that slides out. These trays get covered with glob and gluk—and did you know that cockroaches feast on that mess? So, keep 'em clean!

* * *

If you'll use a paper towel or napkin to wipe off the grease before you tackle your stove, you'll find it makes an easier and faster job of cleaning it when you take your cloth and soap or whatever to clean it.

* * *

Covering the electric buttons on your stove with plastic wrap to keep grease from getting in them will save you a heap on a service call later on!

* * *

If you have the type of stove where you can turn off the pilot light on your gas burners, you can save quite a few pennies by turning it off and using matches each time to light your stove. Also, in the summer your kitchen will stay much cooler without that pilot light on.

* * *

P   *I have a tiny space between my stove and cabinet that catches spills.*

S   Put strips of transparent plastic tape along this space. You can also buy an aluminum strip to cover the gap.

* * *

If you're lucky enough to have a timer on your stove, use it to remind yourself when to take clothes out of the washer, when to leave for appointments, take medicine, make a phone call, etc.

* * *

P   *My new wallpaper behind my stove is getting grease spots on it.*

S   Clean that wallpaper thoroughly and then cover it
with *clear* adhesive-backed paper and it will stay
fresh as a daisy for years to come!

* * *

A neat (and best of all, free) splatter guard can be made by tying or
fastening three foil TV dinner trays together and placing them
around your skillet while frying.

* * *

The grates of your stove can be placed on a cabinet and are super
for cooling pies and cakes. You won't have to hunt for the old cake
rack.

* * *

P   *My vented hood filter is grungy.*
S   If "grungy" means covered with grease, I gotcha!
Just place the whole filter into the dishwasher and
will you be amazed. If you don't have a dishwasher, soak and rinse it in the bathtub or sink in
dishwasher detergent and water.

* * *

Use red nail polish to mark the "off" position on your stove knobs.
This will conserve energy and money from stoves being left on accidentally.

* * *

P   *Keeping my aluminum stovetop clean is difficult.*
S   If hot sudsy water won't do the job, try a paste of
cream of tartar and water, or a commercial aluminum cleaner. Aluminum is easily discolored and
pitted, so be very careful "concocting" home
remedies.

* * *

P   *My ceramic stovetop is discolored.*
S   Vinegar to the rescue, again! Just wipe some white

vinegar on, let it sit a minute, and wipe clean. Voila!

* * *

P   *My chrome doesn't shine.*
S   Use vinegar or window cleaner to make your chrome sparkle! I promise once it dries you can't smell a thing.

* * *

P   *My coppertone stove looks dingy.*
S   You probably have a soap film or buildup of some type. Put a little vinegar on a cloth and rub. Or, add one-half cup cornstarch to a gallon of warm water and wipe with this mixture.

* * *

P   *The enamel finish on my stove is chipped.*
S   Porcelain repair kits are now on the market. Colors can be mixed to get just the right shade.

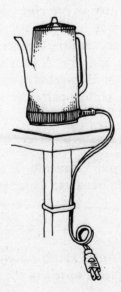

APPLIANCES, SMALL
(Also see Utensils, p. 603 and Appliances for the bath, p. 610)

If you know you're going to be on the phone for a long period of time, gather your small appliances near the phone and polish while you talk!

*　　*　　*

If you plan to use an electric appliance on a dining table, place strong rubber bands on the table legs and thread the cord through. If someone trips on the cord, the cord will come loose from the wall, but the appliance will be more likely to stay on the table.

*　　*　　*

Why not make pockets in your appliance covers to store cords in? Color-code plugs with squares of plastic tape (blue for toaster, red for mixer, etc.) or paint *T* for toaster, *P* for percolator, etc., on the plug with fingernail polish.

Blender (Also see Mixer, p. 561)

P　　*Is there an easy way to clean my blender?*
S　　The easiest way is to add a little soap and water, put the top on, turn the blender on and let it clean itself. Rinse and dry. A baby's bottle brush will reach those hard-to-get-at spots. Of course, never immerse the bottom part of your blender in water.

*　　*　　*

Don't let liquids stand in your blender for long periods of time. Three or four hours won't hurt it, but avoid longer periods of time (it's hard on the gaskets).

*　　*　　*

P　　*My blender leaves marks on my cabinet.*
S　　Glue little pieces of felt to the feet of it.

P   *I use my blender for orange juice, and rings of orange pulp are difficult to remove.*

S   Put a little water and some cracked ice in your blender, pop the top on and zap for a few seconds.

*   *   *

P   *I used a fork to push food down to the blender blades and I ruined my blender. Please warn others of this.*

S   Use a plastic straw to push food down near the blades instead of a metal utensil and you won't have a torn-up blender.

Can Opener, electric, (Also see Can Opener, p. 604)

P   *How can I clean my electric can opener?*

S   First of all, unplug it before you begin to clean it. Use hot, soapy water and an old toothbrush to get under the teeth of the blade; follow with a hot water rinse. Never immerse an electric can opener in water. You can also use a pipe cleaner to clean under the blades.

   After cleaning, lubricate your can opener using a cotton-tipped swab and cooking oil.

*   *   *

When your electric can opener doesn't open like it used to, replace the cutting wheel instead of the entire unit.

Coffee Pot/Maker/Percolator

P   *When I run out of coffee filters, is there a substitute?*

S   In a pinch, make your own filters out of heavy-quality white paper napkins.

*   *   *

P   *My percolator is still good but the glass knob do-esn't fit tightly.*

S   Wrap a strip or two of aluminum foil around the knob until it fits snugly. By the way, you can get a replacement top for under a dollar at appliance repair shops.

*   *   *

P   *The spout on my percolator needs cleaning—I think it's causing a bitter taste in the coffee.*

S   Yep, that will do it. Grab a piece of nylon net and push it through the spout with a stick or pipe-cleaner.

*   *   *

P   *I have a new automatic drip coffeemaker but my percolator is still good. What can I do with the percolator?*

S   You can boil eggs in it, boil weiners or small ears of corn, or keep it full of hot water to make instant tea, coffee or hot chocolate.

*   *   *

P   *My coffeepot has stains inside it.*

S   Put a couple of tablespoons of automatic dish-washing detergent in it (make sure it's *not* alumi-num) and let it perk for a few minutes. Rinse well.

Crock Pot, see Slow Cooker, p. 570)

Disposal

If you don't have a disposal and you don't want vegetable scraps in your trash, liquefy them in your blender and use the liquid for fertilizer around your trees and shrubs. Or, flush the liquid scraps down your commode.

*   *   *

P   *Sometimes my disposal doesn't work.*
S   Many disposals have a restart button that will need to be pushed. It is usually red.

Knives, electric

Use an electric knife to slice angel food cake—works super!

*   *   *

To avoid accidents, disconnect electric knives immediately after use.

Mixer (Also see Blender, p. 558)

P   *When I'm mixing, the batter always comes up the beaters to the base of my mixer and makes a mess.*
S   Spray the beaters with a vegetable nonstick spray before you start mixing.

*   *   *

P   *My mixer bowl slides*
S   Place a damp cloth or towel under it.

*   *   *

P   *My mixer causes splatters all over everything*
S   Use a large brown bag, cut the bottom out and place the bag over the bowl and the mixer. The splatter will go only on the bag. Or, if you place the bowl in your sink, you will only have the sink to rinse out when you're finished.

*   *   *

If you use one certain bowl for mixing, store your beaters and spatula in that bowl—no more hunting.

Skillet, electric

You can use your electric skillet to cook corn-on-the-cob, or you can heat rolls in it by placing the rolls on a cake rack in your covered skillet.

*   *   *

Make little foil "bowls" to place different types of leftovers in and heat them in your electric skillet.

*   *   *

P   *What can you do with an old electric skillet that doesn't work anymore?*

S   How about removing the legs from it and using it as a skillet on top of your stove? Or, if it's beyond that (like mine was), it can make a nifty feeding bowl for your pet.

*   *   *

P   *How can I get black carbon off the bottom of my electric skillet?*

S   Dampen the bottom of your skillet, sprinkle automatic dishwashing detergent on it, and then place several damp paper towels over this. Let it sit for a while. Repeat if necessary.

*   *   *

To fry in a practically grease-free way, prop up one leg of your electric skillet slightly. The grease will then drain down to one side.

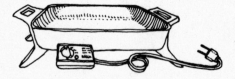

Slow Cooker

Keep apple cider hot for a large group, heat it in your slow cooker and then reduce the setting to keep the cider warm.

*   *   *

Use your slow cooker to keep candy coatings warm (especially good for dipping cherries).

*   *   *

P   *Help! How do I get dried-on food and goop out of my slow cooker?*

S   Fill the slow cooker with water and dishwashing liquid and let it "cook" for one-half hour or so. It'll be easy as pie to wash then.

*   *   *

You can cook hot dogs in your slower cooker, too. Cook the weiners for twenty to thirty minutes and then set the buns on top of the weiners for the last ten minutes. Be sure the buns are placed on top of the weiners or they will get wet if they fall in the juices at the bottom of the slow cooker.

*   *   *

If you have to apply hot packs to an injury, keep the hot pack solution hot in your slow cooker.

*   *   *

If you're serving food to a large group, borrow four or five slow cookers and put the meat in one, vegetables in another, potatoes in one, rolls in another and so on. The food can be kept at serving temperature while you wash your pots and pans or attend to last-minute details.

*   *   *

If you need a large strainer, use the basket from your large party-size percolator.

Toaster

You can make a toaster cover and two pot holders to match from one valance if you are buying new kitchen curtains and want to put those old ones to good use.

*　　*　　*

P   *My toaster finish has lost its lustre.*
S   Polish it with a little ammonia and water, or white vinegar using a soft cloth.

*　　*　　*

P   *Is there a way to heat English muffins in a toaster?*
S   Stick a toothpick through the top of the muffin and let the toothpick lie across the opening of the toaster. This will allow most of the muffin to drop into the toaster yet remain suspended by the toothpick.

*　　*　　*

P   *How do I get stuck toast out of a toaster?*
S   Use a wooden spatula. Be sure to unplug your toaster before digging with the spatula.

*　　*　　*

Did you know that most toasters have a hinged tray on the bottom that catches crumbs? Be sure to keep the crumbs out of your toaster (remember, they attract bugs).

Waffle Iron

P   *My waffles always seem to stick on my waffle iron.*
S   Never leave a waffle iron wet; always clean and dry it thoroughly; then, temper your iron. Waffle irons need to be tempered after each use.
　　Clean the iron and then brush the iron with

salad oil. Or, temper the iron by rubbing both sides of a piece of bread with *unsalted* fat, let the bread brown. This will grease the squares.

CABINETS
(Also see Medicine Cabinet, p. 614)

Until someone invents a kitchen cabinet impervious to kids and hubby, I guess we'll have to keep on cleaning kitchen cabinets!

I clean mine whenever they start bothering me (from the looks of them now they haven't bothered me in a long time!)—sometimes it's late at night, sometimes it's when I need to work off a little steam, or sometimes it's on a cold, rainy day.

Sometimes it's just like Christmas, stumbling across things I'd forgotten I'd had! Not being "tall," I can tell you "persactly" what's on the lower two or three shelves. But if Robert Redford were hiding on my top shelf, I'd never find him!

The best way to organize your cabinets is to think YOU! If you're tempted to place your items in the order you saw in the latest home decorating magazine, it probably won't work. Put some newspapers all over your floor and then empty everything onto your floor. If you've got pots and pans and lids in three different places, why not toss them all in an old dishpan or a cardboard box and set them in a handy lower cabinet near your stove.

If you're reaching over that pan you use only to bake fruitcake in during the holidays, move it and others like it to a box and store them on a shelf in your utility room or garage or some other nook. It's better to go fetch them once or twice a year and wash them up than to fret and fume every time you have to move them to get to an item you use daily.

Also, why not keep only the size pans you use every day and store those extra pans and odd-size pans? You only have four burners, so why keep gobs of pans around? You probably use the same ones over and over.

If you have a worn-out chest of drawers or can pick one up cheap at a garage sale, they are super for storing cookie cutters, small utensils, cake decorating kits, etc. A friend of mine with a large accumulation of plastic food-storage containers keeps the lids to them in a drawer. She gave up trying to keep the lids with the bowls (her four kids kept them scattered in every drawer), so she places all of them in a chest drawer and they're easily found. You can set the chest on a back porch or in the garage or utility room if you don't like the looks of it in your kitchen.

If you don't like stooping or it's hard on your back, who says cleaning supplies have to go under the sink? Put them on a shelf you can easily reach and store seldom-used items under your sink. If you have little ones around it's a lot safer to store cleaning supplies up higher anyway. There's some good hints in this chapter on how to secure cabinets from young children, so we'll talk about that in a minute.

I hope that this little section will guide you in organizing your cabinets. Well-organized cabinets will save you time, and make preparing and serving meals a lot easier. It will do wonders for your disposition, too!

Decorating

P   *I covered my old cabinets with adhesive-backed paper but there are bubbles in it.*

S   Just prick the bubble with a pin or needle and press it down. The pin hole won't show.

Doors and Drawers
(Also see Drawers, p. 722) and Childproofing, p. 847)

P   *How can I keep my baby out of the kitchen cabinets?*

S   Try hooking a dog collar through the handles over knobs, or rubber bands or shower curtain rings (three hooked together) through the handles.

*   *   *

P *My cabinet doors have magnetic catches that are really hard to open.*

S Try putting a little piece of transparent tape over the magnetic catches.

* * *

P *The catch on my metal cabinet is broken and an always-open cabinet door is bugging me.*

S An easy way to solve this is to take a little magnet and glue it where it catches.

* * *

Need a little table for a visiting child? Pull out a lower cupboard drawer, lay a cookie sheet on it and close the drawer until the cookie sheet fits snug.

* * *

If you're blessed with drawer space, tuck those spice cans away in a small drawer—oh, so handy!

* * *

P *I want my toddler close at hand to keep an eye on him, but his banging pots and pans when I'm in the kitchen is driving me "buggy."*

S If space will allow, clean out one lower shelf of your kitchen cabinets and put only his toys there. Tell him that this is HIS shelf, but all the rest are YOURS.

He'll be happier and so will you.

* * *

Remember, don't store poisons or cleaning supplies where a baby or child can get to them. If you do have your cleaning supplies under your sink, keep a bicycle lock handy and when children visit, put it between the handles of your sink cabinet.

Interiors

P   *I have a hard time seeing to the back of my lower cabinets.*

S   Its probably because they are dark. If you paint the inside of the cabinets with a coat of bright, white paint, it will really make a difference. Painting just the inside back wall may work. Lining the sides with tin foil to reflect some light also helps.

*   *   *

P   *My pots leave marks on my shelving paper.*

S   Just stick a paper plate under each pan when you store it. (You can use the same plate over and over.)

*   *   *

Write your most-used cookie recipes, cornbread recipe, etc., on 3 × 5-inch cards and tape them to the inside of your cabinet near your flour and sugar. You won't have to drag out your cookbook as often.

*   *   *

P   *My cleaning supplies are always a mess.*

S   You can tote your furniture polish, window spray, all your cleaning supplies from room to room in a sturdy plastic tub and then just slide the whole thing under your sink. This is what I do, but I don't have children around who can get into that place.

*   *   *

Line your shelves with aluminum foil or wax paper. It will protect your shelves and they will be easier to clean next time. Just wad the lining up and throw away.

*   *   *

If your family is always asking where something is, you can save wear and tear on the old vocal cords by placing a little fruit sticker or magnet on each shelf. Just holler back, "It's behind the banana!" or whatever.

* * *

Store a few spoons, some plastic cereal bowls and plastic juice glasses in your lower cabinets, and even small children can set a breakfast table and prepare cereal.

Metal Cabinets

P   *My metal cabinets look simply awful.*

S   Well, of course, sanding them down and repainting them is the best way. But if that sounds like too much work or if you're pinching pennies (and who isn't these days), try covering them with adhesive-backed paper. You get a variety of colors and designs.

* * *

P   *I'm replacing my metal cabinets with new wood ones. Any suggestions for using the metal cabinets elsewhere?*

S   Would be great to have extra storage for tools in the garage, or how about storing books or magazines in them up in the attic?

Wood Cabinets

P   *How can I get grease spots off my wood cabinets?*

S   Wet a cloth with a little water and vinegar and wipe over the spots. Dry with a clean cloth or paper towel.

* * *

P   *How can I polish my wood cabinets?*

S   One reader suggested using *neutral* shoe polish paste. She said it made her cabinets look as good as new. I would do just a little test spot in an inconspicuous place before I tried any kind of polish or wax on my wood cabinets.

DISHES AND GLASSWARE

A flat rubber sink stopper placed under a bowl will keep the bowl from slipping. This is especially helpful for a handicapped person.

*   *   *

Buy white dishes to fill in broken dish sets.

*   *   *

An old warped hi-fi record covered with plastic wrap makes a cute cake plate for a teen-age party.

*   *   *

Taking a dish to a covered luncheon or picnic? Make sure you get it back by writing your name and address on a piece of transparent tape with a permanent ink marking pen. Stick the tape to the bottom of the dish; even if it's washed, your name will still be readable.

*   *   *

Tired of your dishes? Why not swap sets with a neighbor or friend for a few weeks?

*   *   *

Chips and Scratches

P   *Is there any way to salvage fine china that has nicks and chips?*

S   Try gently sanding down the nicks and chips. The fine, wet-looking sandpaper with a cloth backing seems to work best. You can take it to a professional.

*   *   *

P   *My ironstone dishes have gray scratch marks.*

S   These marks are caused from scratches due to improper storage. To remove the gray marks, rub the dishes with a baking soda and water paste and wipe clean. Store your dishes with circles of felt or paper or paper plates between items. If you can, store the cups on hooks to prevent scratching.

Cleaning
(Also see Dishwasher, p. 539)

P   *How can I remove stains from my plastic dishes?*

S   Rub a paste of baking soda and water over the stains. Or, use a very diluted bleach and water solution.
(Caution: too strong a bleach solution may take the glaze off.)

*   *   *

P   *I would use my lovely "special dishes" more often if they weren't dusty and didn't require washing for each occasion.*

S   If you have storage space in your cabinets, wash your set of dishes and then cover all the glassware with small plastic sandwich bags. Use larger plastic bags to dustproof the serving pieces.

Or, some folks that don't wash a whole load of dishes in their dishwashers take a few of their "special dishes" and add to the load—that way, you avoid washing the whole set at one time when that "occasion" arises.

*   *   *

Gold-banded or gold-decorated china and glassware should never be washed in an automatic dishwasher.

*   *   *

A thought: Although it certainly is convenient to use disposable dishes when taking food to families of deceased persons, it actually may be better for the families if we used our special china dishes. The bereaved person needs to get out of the house, visit friends, and not totally withdraw. Cleaning and returning the dishes will help the grieved person stay in touch.

*   *   *

Be sure to rotate your dishes. Put the just-washed plates on the bottom of the stack and use the ones off the top of the stack. All of your plates will then stay fresh and dust-free.

*   *   *

P   *I have some beautiful glasses that are stained and discolored.*

S   Drop a tablet sold for cleaning dentures in your glasses with water. Should do the trick!

FLOORS

On the subject of floor care, a dear gentleman named Bobbs said it all: "When I see a spot on my light color vinyl, it may be only a shadow, so I just eye it for a moment. If it doesn't go away then I clean it up. If it wiggles I step on it!"

I hope there are no more Cinderellas tied down to scrubbing and waxing floors day after day. I think this section will "free" you from the drudgery part and give you time to go to "the ball" or the grocery store or the post office or other exciting places!

Cleaning and Maintaining

P   *I mop my floor, yet it never looks really shiny.*

S   You probably have a film left on the floor. Mix one-half cup vinegar with about a gallon of lukewarm or cool water and go over the floor after you've mopped. Be sure your mop is clean.

*   *   *

P   *We are moving into a beautiful new home and we want to keep the floors looking like new.*

S   I'll be glad to give you a little advice! This is what my mom taught me to do. (1) Dust the floors daily either with a dust mop or a vacuum cleaner so that tracked-in dirt or grit is not ground into the floors. This applies mainly to the traffic areas—it is not necessary to dust under the couch, bed, etc., *every* day. (2) Wipe up any spills immediately. (3) Take time to read the cleaning instructions and recommendations of the manufacturer for your type of floor or carpeting. (4) Always test an unfamiliar product by spot cleaning or treating in an inconspicuous place.

*   *   *

Set your table legs in coasters or rubber casters to keep them from making indentations on your kitchen floor. Moleskin sheets or plasters you buy at the drugstore work well, too.

*   *   *

P   *My child got crayon marks on my terrazzo floor.*

S   Would you believe a plain old eraser will get them up? An eraser also will sometimes help remove heel marks.

*   *   *

Having trouble dusting your floors in the nooks and crannies? Put on an old pair of wool socks and put those little footsies to work!

Take the socks off and shake them into a trash bag when they've accumulated the dust and then go back to it! You get some exercise, too.

*   *   *

P   *How can I pick up small pieces of shattered glass without cutting myself?*

S   Pick up the pieces with a dampened cotton ball, or heavy paper towel.

*   *   *

P   *How do I get black heel marks off my vinyl floor?*

S   First, try a damp cloth and baking soda, or rub a little nongel toothpaste on the mark.

*   *   *

P   *How can I get up a gooey spill?*

S   Pour salt on most gooey spills and let dry. Then sweep it up and throw the mess away.

*   *   *

P   *How do I get the white water spots off my asphalt tile?*

S   Rub a little liquid vegetable oil on the spot *only*. It may take more than one application, but it will do the job.

*   *   *

P   *I can't get rid of a squeak in my hardwood floor.*

S   Take a thin bar of soap and rub it down in the crack or "squeak area" as much as you can. Wipe off the excess soap. Or , melt some paraffin in an old pan you can throw out (better still, use an empty coffee can) and add a small amount of light brown shoe polish to match your floors. Gently work the mixture into the crack or squeak.

*   *   *

P   *I have some horrible scratches on my hardwood floor.*

S   Rub walnut or pecan meat into the scratch. You may have to repeat this several times. This really does help.

*   *   *

To keep your favorite rocker from scratching or marring hardwood floors, glue a piece of weather stripping or strips of felt on the bottom of the rocker.

*   *   *

To avoid splashing wax or cleaner on table legs, set each leg in an aluminum square and then fold the square up around the table leg.

*   *   *

P   *My entrance way is a mess in winter. I'm afraid the salt and water tracked in will ruin my floor.*

S   It sure will, luv. Why not put a plastic drop cloth down as a liner, and then a piece of indoor-outdoor carpet right in front of the door?

*   *   *

Out of floor wax? Add one-half cup cornstarch to a gallon of luke-warm water and mop. It will make your floor shine better than the same amount of wax will.

*   *   *

Remember, the more you buff paste-waxed floors, the fewer folks you will have slipping down.

*   *   *

Use nylon net to scrub with when removing wax buildup.

*   *   *

To prevent gumminess and streaks, buff the entire floor before and after applying wax.

*   *   *

If your washer or dryer is in your kitchen area, don't try to wax your floor while they are in operation. The heat they put out can make your floor gummy and it will not dry properly.

Floor Covering

Bored with a dingy, drab kitchen floor? Buy some adhesive-backed paper with a large flower print. Cut out the flowers and stick them around the floor.

*   *   *

P   *How can I remove vinyl tiles?*
S   Some of my readers have suggested putting foil over the tile and ironing over the tile (wool setting) for a few seconds. Then repeat the ironing after a bit and lift the tile off with a spatula or pancake turner.

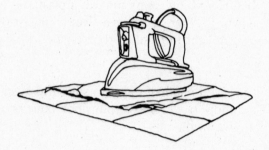

If you want to make a throw rug warm and cozy, place newspapers underneath.

*　　*　　*

To keep throw rugs from slipping, glue or stitch those foam fabric-softener sheets to the backing, or put a thick foam-rubber pad under the rug.

*　　*　　*

Avoid discoloring your new kitchen floor—do not use scatter rugs with rubber backings on the new no-wax flooring. The rubber backing will cause discoloration over a period of time.

FOOD PREPARATION
(Also see Cooking Out, p. 788)

I just love to open up a magazine and view those luscious foods pictured there. (Honestly, I sometimes think those calories jump right off the page and land in *me!*) It's a joy to create dishes that please our family and friends.

But, as we all know very well, casseroles, salads, soups, whatever, just don't happen! And that's what this section is about—ways to make food preparation easier, more enjoyable, more efficient, and perhaps a little more economical.

*　　*　　*

Planning a buffet? Write the names of the dishes you're going to serve and put them where you plan to arrange the dishes on the serving table. You won't be as likely to forget any salad or refrigerated dish when you are ready to serve.

*　　*　　*

When mixing messy things, if you put your bowls in the sink, all the spills go down the drain. No messy countertop cleanup.

*　　*　　*

Want to save a few pennies on the paper towel bill? Place some newspapers under a couple of paper towels to absorb grease and drain food on.

*   *   *

P   *I love to experiment with new recipes, but keeping the pages of my cookbook clean and open is a pain.*

S   One way to solve that would be to slide a rubber band across the pages, or take a glass pie plate and place it upside down on your cookbook. An added bonus is that the curved bottom of the pie plate actually magnifies the print!

*   *   *

A handy and cheap way to have a recipe card holder is simply put the card in the tines of a fork and then put the fork handle in a glass!

*   *   *

P   *Is there any way to salvage scorched food?*

S   Yes, but you have to act fast. Immediately take the pan to the sink and set it in cool water. Do not scrape the pan. Carefully transfer the food that is not scorched into another pan. The scorched food will stick; the good food will not.

Need to transport a pot of soup or casserole? Place the pan or dish in a large zippered plastic bag and seal. If spills occur, the bag catches them.

*   *   *

Training a young cook? Hold the spoon backwards when stirring to avoid burns; the splatters will be away from the youngster.

Bacon

P   *What can I do to keep bacon from sticking together*
         in the package?
S   Roll your bacon package in a tube shape and put
         a rubber band around it before you refrigerate it.

Bananas, freezing

Got some overripe bananas? Mash them up and put them in a plastic bag. Freeze. Use them later for making banana bread.

Breads, Buns, and Rolls

Have trouble getting bread to rise in cold weather? If you have a gas oven with a pilot light, just pop in the bread and let it rise. Or, turn the oven to 200°F, let it heat, then turn it off and put the bread in to rise.

*   *   *

Ever try putting aluminum foil under the napkin in your roll basket to keep them hotter longer? Or, a preheated ceramic tile really does the job.

*   *   *

P   *Does anybody know what to do with leftover hot*
         dog buns after a cookout? They're usually so dry
         and hard!
S   Just slice 'em into sticks. Butter them, sprinkle a

little garlic powder and Parmesan cheese, and then toast them in your oven. They are dandy crumbled over salads. Another favorite of mine is "instant pizza." Spread tomato paste over the bun, put a slice of your favorite "pizza-type" cheese on top, some pepperoni (salami is good, too), other toppings you like, and then bake until the cheese melts. Yummy!

Brown Sugar

P   *How can I soften hardened brown sugar?*

S   Place the brown sugar in a jar or plastic bag. Put a damp paper towel across the top of the sugar. Redampen the paper towel if necessary; the softening process may take several days. To keep brown sugar soft, always store it in a plastic bag. Or, put a piece of apple with the sugar in the box.

Butter

To soften butter in a hurry, measure it and then take your potato peeler and shred it.

Cabbage Odor

P   *I love cabbage but don't like the smell it leaves in my house.*

S   How about adding a little vanilla or cinnamon to a pan of water and let it steam while you're cooking cabbage—it will mask the cabbage smell.

Cakes

Dislike getting those fingers greasy when greasing a cake pan or casserole? Slip your fingers into a plastic sandwich bag and grease away.

P   *How can I keep cakes from rising up in the middle?*

S   Wrap a strip of wet toweling such as terry cloth around the outside of the cake pan. Reducing the oven temperature also helps. In addition, grease the bottom of the pan only (don't grease the sides); this seems to help.

*   *   *

P   *My chocolate cakes always look tacky because they have the white flour on them that I used to dust the pans with.*

S   If you dust the pans with cocoa instead of flour, you can eliminate that little problem forever!

*   *   *

P   *My mix cakes sometimes seem a little dry and crumbly.*

S   Just add two tablespoons of cooking oil to your mix. It makes your cake more moist and gives it a better texture.

*   *   *

P   *What can I do when the frosting is too thin?*

S   Add a little powdered sugar until you have the desired consistency.

*   *   *

Want picture-perfect cake slices? Freeze your cakes first and then slice.

*   *   *

Sprinkle some powdered sugar onto your cake plate and your cake won't stick.

Canned Food

Here's a tip from my college days when living in a dorm with no kitchen. Fill the bathroom sink with the hottest water possible. Place a can of soup, spaghetti or whatever in the sink and shake the can occasionally. Add more hot water every now and then, and you'll have a heated meal.

Citrus Peels

Lemon or orange peels are easier to grate when frozen.

Cookies

P   *How can cookies be kept soft in a cookie jar?*
S   Put a slice or two of bread in the cookie jar.

*   *   *

Leftover icing? Spread the icing between two cookies for a delicious treat.

Corn Silk

P   *How do I get corn silk off of corn on the cob?*
S   Get that old faithful kitchen toothbrush and brush
        downward on the cob.

Dough
(Also see Rolling Pin, p. 607)

P   *Dough sticks to my rolling pin.*

S   Try placing the rolling pin and the pastry cloth in a plastic bag and keeping it in your freezer until used. An old, clean knee sock makes a good cloth to prevent dough sticking.

Eggs

P   *Is there anything at all I can do if I run one egg short right in the middle of making something?*

S   There's nothing more frustrating, right? Well, just grab one teaspoon of that old standby cornstarch *or* one teaspoon vinegar and substitute it for the missing egg. This will squeak you by just fine for *one* missing egg, but of course it won't work for any more. Also, you'll need to increase the liquid in the recipe by three or four tablespoons.

*   *   *

P   *My egg whites never seem to stay stiff and sometimes never even get stiff—what am I doing wrong?*

S   Your utensils and bowl must be grease-free; absolutely no egg yolk allowed; let your eggs warm to room temperature before you beat them. While beating them, add one teaspoon of cream of tartar to each seven or eight egg whites.

Fish

P   *How can I tell if a fish is fresh?*

S   The eyes have it! The eyes should be bright and clear. A fresh fish will have red or pink gills, and its scales will be shiny. Don't buy a fish that has sunken or cloudy eyes.

Food Coloring

P   *I accidentally added too much food coloring to a batter. Could I have fixed it?*

S   If you haven't stirred it in, next time grab some paper towels and soak up the excess coloring with the towels.

Gelatin

P   *I love to take molded gelatin salads to luncheon but I can't keep them looking as firm and pretty as they are when I take them out of the refrigerator.*

S   This is a problem especially when the weather is a wee bit warm. However, if you'll add a mere teaspoon of white vinegar to your recipe, this will help your gelatins keep firm.

Gravy

P   *What can one do when the gravy turns out too thin?*

S   Reheat the gravy. Dissolve a little cornstarch in water and add to the gravy and stir.

Hamburger shaping

I have several gadgets in my kitchen for shaping perfectly round hamburger patties. But I get in a hurry and just grab this old standby which works just as super! Just take a full No. 2½ can out of your pantry, clean the bottom, press down on the patty and then trim.

Meatloaf

Need to hurry up that meatloaf for supper? Bake five or six small ones instead of one large loaf.

Meringue

P   *How can I make a really fluffy meringue?*

S   Add one-fourth teaspoon of white vinegar to three egg whites. The vinegar really does make a difference!

Milk

P   *My child doesn't like to drink milk.*

S   Add a little food coloring or vanilla flavoring to it. It will look and taste better.

Onions

P   *How do I keep onions from making me cry when I'm cutting them?*

S   The best thing I've found is to keep those onions refrigerated until you need one. The colder the onion is, the less you'll cry. Other readers have said it helps if you keep your mouth closed tightly, or peel them under cold, running water,

Parmesan, serving

Baffled as to how to serve Parmesan cheese? A covered bonbon dish is an excellent choice.

Pie

Want to bake pies up ahead of time for a holiday and don't have enough pie pans? Mix up your pie fillings, line your pie pans with foil, add filling and freeze. When frozen, remove pie-shaped fillings and leave in freezer. This way, you don't tie up your pie pans in your freezer, and you can finish baking your fruit pies when you have the time.

*　　*　　*

P   *How do bakers get that lovely sheen on their pie crusts?*

S   Vinegar! Yep, then take that pie crust out of the oven just a few minutes before it's ready, brush the top with a little white vinegar (or cider), and then plop it back in the oven.

Potatoes

P   *How can I keep the skins of my baked potatoes from cracking?*

S   The secret to this is to rub butter or shortening over the potatoes before you bake them.

Salt

P   *How can I keep salt flowing freely in the shaker?*

S   Add a cracker or a few grains of rice to the shaker. Also, remember to keep the salt in a warm, dry place.

*   *   *

P   *How can I keep sugar and salt from getting caked?*

S   If you'll put a glass or mixing bowl over the shaker or bowl, you won't have caked sugar or salt.

*   *   *

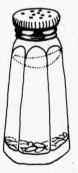

Attach a 2½-inch strip of cellophane tape to make a tab on salt or cereal boxes with the metal spout. Grab the tab to open—no wear and tear on the fingernails.

* * *

P   *How can I keep salt and pepper from spilling when I try to fill my shakers that have the filler holes on the bottoms?*

S   Put masking tape over the holes before filling, or put some grains of rice in first and then fill.

* * *

P   *The holes on my salt shaker are too large.*

S   Make a bit of paste with flour and water. Put some in a couple of holes, and when it dries the paste works like cement.

* * *

P   *What can I do if I run out of salt?*

S   Cut off the top of the cardboard salt container. Under the little metal "funnel" is usually enough salt remaining to get you by.

* * *

P   *What's the solution to too-salty food?*

S   If the dish can take it, add a pinch of sugar.

Spices
(Also see Spice Racks, p. 537)

P   *My herbs and spices don't keep very long, but friends of mine have spices that remain fresh for long periods of time. How come?*

S   The culprit is probably heat. Are you storing your spices next to your stove? Herbs and spices should be stored in a cool, dry place.

* * *

If you live alone and like to experiment with different spices, why not buy a spice you'd like to have and give half to a friend and vice versa! Then both of you wouldn't be out the expense or accumulate seldom-used spices.

*   *   *

You'll find it convenient to keep chili powder in a glass shaker jar.

*   *   *

Mix up cinnamon and sugar for cinnamon toast and keep it in a salt shaker.

*   *   *

P   *I goofed and got a dish too spicy; what should I have done to save it?*

S   If you can, make up another batch unseasoned and combine the two. In some instances you can add another can of cooked pinto beans, tomato juice or canned tomatoes. Sometimes adding catsup or a few drops of vinegar helps.

Strawberries

Don't wash strawberries before refrigerating—they will become mushy. Store them in a colander or plastic woven basket so the air can circulate.

Syrup

To make syrup or honey easier to pour out of a measuring cup, rinse the cup with hot water before pouring the syrup or honey in to be measured.

Tea

P   *How can cloudy tea be cleared up?*

S   Refrigeration will cause tea to turn cloudy. Leave it at room temperature until you are ready to serve it. You can clear up cloudy tea by adding a little boiling water.

Vegetables

P   *Is there a way to keep colors of vegetables from fading out while cooking?*

S   For greener cabbage and redder beets, etc., just add a little vinegar to the water while they are cooking. Did you know this will cut down on cooking odors, too?

Waffles

P   *I always have too much leftover waffle batter.*

S   Just go ahead and cook the waffles up and freeze them until later. To heat, just drop them in the toaster.

*   *   *

P   *My favorite waffle recipe is 2 cups biscuit mix, 1*
   egg, ½ cup oil, and 1½ cup club soda. Since this
   batter will be "bubbly," it will not store well.

S   You should cook it all at once.

SUBSTITUTIONS

BAKING POWDER:	2 tablespoons cream of tartar,
	1 tablespoon baking soda, and
	1 tablespoon cornstarch
BROWN SUGAR:	½ cup granulated sugar, ½ cup molasses, plus ¼ teaspoon baking soda
BUTTER:	⅞ cup vegetable shortening or lard
BUTTERMILK:	1 tablespoon vinegar or lemon juice plus enough fresh milk to make one cup
CAKE FLOUR:	All-purpose flour. For one cup measure, level off and remove 2 tablespoons
CORN SYRUP:	1 cup sugar and ¼ cup water
EGG: (ONE ONLY)	1 teaspoon cornstarch per egg or
	1 teaspoon vinegar per egg. Also, increase the liquid in the recipe by 3 or 4 tablespoons.
FLOUR:	For 1 tablespoon: 1 tablespoon cornstarch OR 1 teaspoon rice starch OR 1 tablespoon arrowroot
FROSTING:	Top with marshmallows a minute or so before removing pans from oven.
HONEY:	For 1 cup, use 1¼ cup sugar plus

	¼ cup water (do not use this substitution in delicately balanced recipes).
MILK:	½ cup evaporated milk and ½ cup water to make 1 cup milk. Or, use
	1/3 cup instant nonfat milk plus
	1 cup water (less 1 tablespoon water).
POWDERED SUGAR:	1 cup granulated sugar and 1 tablespoon cornstarch. Put in blender.
RED FOOD COLORING:	Red-colored sugar (like that used for Christmas baking) or unsweetened powdered soft drink mix
SHORTENING:	Peanut butter for pie crusts
SOUR CREAM:	1 cup evaporated milk plus 1 tablespoon vinegar, OR 1 cup cottage cheese blended with 1 tablespoon of milk and 1 teaspoon lemon juice.
	Also, try 1 cup plain yogurt with 1 tablespoon vinegar added.
SUGAR:	Light or dark brown sugar may be used tit for tat. However, there will be a light molasses flavor.
TOMATO JUICE:	½ cup tomato sauce plus ½ cup water
TOMATO SAUCE:	8-ounce can whole tomatoes zapped in the blender
UNSWEETENED CHOCOLATE:	3 tablespoons unsweetened cocoa plus
	1 tablespoon shortening or butter

WHIPPED CREAM: Slice a banana or two (to taste) in
                      the WHITE of an egg and just beat
                      until stiff.

No rolling pin? Place dough in a plastic bag and use a large unopened straight-sided beverage bottle as a rolling pin.

FOOD STORAGE

Nonrefrigerated Food

To help cut down on pantry clutter, store rice, beans, raisins, etc., in plastic containers.

*   *   *

P   *Please tell me how to get rid of weevils?*
S   First, take everything out of your cabinets and
        destroy every box or bag that is visibly infested
        with weevils. Check everything including flour,
        meal, cereals, dried fruits, spices, dry pet food,
        pasta products, dry beans and peas.
            To destroy unhatched eggs, place cartons in
        which weevils are not visible in the freezer for four
        days at zero degree temperature or in a 150°F to
        160°F oven for thirty minutes.
            Next, scrub the shelves with hot, sudsy water
        using a stiff bristled brush. Then spray the shelves,
        crevices and cabinet doors with insecticide and
        leave them closed for three to four hours.
            After doing all of the above, put everything into
        sealable glass jars before returning food to the
        shelves.
            Also, buy small quantities of staples and get into
        the habit of freezing them before using. Open each
        package when you bring it home from the store
        and immediately return any infested item (along
        with a sales receipt).

Refrigerated Food
(Also see Refrigerator, p. 549)

P   *I store foods in bowls with lids but the odors still seem to permeate my refrigerator, and the food does not stay fresh as long as it should.*

S   A lot of the popular glassware bowls are not sealed tightly by their lids. Place a piece of plastic wrap over the bowl before you place the lid on.

*   *   *

To store canned pet food that has been opened, so your fridge won't smell, place the can inside a coffee can with a plastic lid and keep in your refrigerator.

*   *   *

P   *I can't seem to keep vegetables fresh very long in my refrigerator.*

S   If you line the bottom of your vegetable bin with newspapers covered with paper towels or napkins, you'll find that your lettuce and other veggies and fruits will stay fresher much longer.

*   *   *

Start a "distress bin"—when vegetables look pretty sad, toss them in that special bin to remind you to use them up right away or to prepare soup.

*   *   *

P   *How do I prevent ice crystals in ice cream once I've opened it?*

S   Cover the unused portion with plastic wrap before you put the lid back on and put it in the freezer.

*   *   *

Check your favorite grocery store and find out which days they receive produce deliveries and which days they put out fresh meat. It does make a difference which day you shop!

POTS AND PANS

The Food and Drug Administration states that cookware made of aluminum is perfectly safe. The grayish substance sometimes seen on this type of cookware is harmless. Cast-iron pots and pans have been used for generations of homemakers—and the iron absorbed into foods while cooking is actually beneficial. If a cast-iron pot is not kept seasoned, some foods may turn dark and look unappealing, but this will not affect you.

It is safe to use pans with nonstick coatings after the coating have been worn or partially chipped off. The FDA reports that this coating is not dangerous to use under these conditions.

The only precaution I would give would be about using pans or pots galvanized with zinc. Certain foods which are acidic (such as tomatoes) should not be cooked in them, since zinc salts can be formed and can be toxic.

*   *   *

I can't say this too often—always turn handles toward the rear or side of the stove where a child can't reach up and grab them. Even if you don't have children, it's a good safety habit.

*   *   *

An old dish drainer makes a great storage container for pan lids.

Aluminum

P   *My aluminum pans are discolored.*
S   Boil either two tablespoons vinegar or two table-

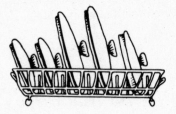

spoons cream of tartar in the pot for twenty minutes.

*   *   *

P
S

How do I shine aluminum cookware?
Cream of tartar works fairly well; however, I would suggest a commercial cleaner made especially for aluminum. DO NOT use any cleaner that contains ammonia—it will pit the aluminum.

Cast Iron

P
S

How should I care for my new cast-iron skillet?
How lucky you are! I have letters from friends who have been using the same skillet for as long as fifty years! Obviously, they have given theirs TLC (Tender Loving Care).

More than likely, your new skillet has been preseasoned and no further seasoning is necessary. Just wash thoroughly (never in the dishwasher), dry and always lightly grease before storing.

If you've acquired a skillet that's discolored or has rust spots, you need to reseason your skillet as follows: First, get all the rust off, using a scouring pad if necessary, then wash and dry. Next, coat the inside of the pan heavily with unsalted grease (preferably suet). Coat the lid also. Place the skillet in the oven for about two hours at the lowest possible temperature. After an hour or so, wipe more grease on the sides of the pan again. After two hours, wash in good soapy suds—your skillet is now ready for use.

After each use, wash in warm, soapy water (don't use scouring powders). Wipe thoroughly, dry and then coat the inside of the pan with oil or shortening or nonstick vegetable spray.

Think DRY when you're thinking of caring for

cast-iron cookware. Wipe dry thoroughly with a cloth or paper towel. Crumple up a paper towel or newspaper and put it in the skillet to absorb moisture. Or, place your skillet back on the stove and heat it until all the moisture is gone and then store it in your cabinet. Be sure and store it in a dry place after use. If you have an oven pilot light, your oven will make an ideal storage place.

Cleaning

P   *Food always sticks to my pots and pans and makes it hard to wash them.*

S   Some folks make up hot, sudsy dishwater and wash them as soon as the food is put in bowls. Others fill a pan with water and stick the lid back on it as soon as the pan is emptied. The whole secret to the matter is not to let the food dry out and become crusted on the pan. Let it soak until you find time to wash it.

*   *   *

P   *How should a burned pot be cleaned?*

S   Dampen the pot and sprinkle baking soda on the burn. Add a little vinegar and let it stand for twenty minutes. Then wash as usual.

*   *   *

Got a pan that needs scrubbing and no scrubber handy? Grab a plastic glass and turn it upside down. Loosen the "goo" with the rim of the glass.

*   *   *

P   *My skillet has baked-on grease.*

S   Use a piece of nylon net and a little baking soda and water paste. Spray-on oven cleaner can be used. Of course, wash thoroughly.

Copper

P   *How do I shine copper cookware?*

S   Make a paste of lemon juice, salt and flour, and rub it on. Or, there are very good commercial copper cleaning compounds on the market.

Nonstick Coating

P   *My skillet is nonstick coated and it keeps getting scratched.*

S   First of all, do not use metal utensils in a skillet with this kind of coating. Secondly, always put a paper towel inside it when you store it so that other pans or articles will not scratch the inside. Also, nylon net makes a perfect scrubber and will not harm the coating.

*   *   *

P   *I love a particular skillet of mine but the coating is shot. Any way I can salvage it?*

S   Sure is! Have hubby or someone with an electric drill with a wire brush attachment grind all the coating off. You'll still have a usable skillet.

Stainless Steel

P   *How do I shine stainless steel cookware?*

S   Oven cleaner works well to clean baked-on grease, and will help put a shine back on. Ammonia and water can be safely used on stainless steel to clean and shine.

*   *   *

If you have baked-on grease on stainless steel pots and pans, wet a cloth with ammonia and place the cloth and your pot in a plastic bag. Tie the plastic bag tightly and let it sit. This method will even clean around the handles. Caution: do not use this procedure on aluminum pans.

*   *   *

P   *I have water rings on my stainless steel pots. How can I get them off?*

S   Saturate a cotton ball with alcohol and rub.

Teflon, see Nonstick Coating, **p. 597.**

SINKS
(Also see Sinks in the bathroom, p. 622)

Kitchen sinks. Boy, oh, boy, they sure do take a lot of abuse sometimes, don't they? From washing the baby, to giving the pet ferret a bath, doing hand laundry and then all the "kitcheny" things like soaking pots and pans and scrubbing the broiler.

Not many of us have ever read an instruction book on the care or wear and tear of a sink, but there really are a few do's and don'ts.

Don't ever, and I mean ever, put hot grease down your sink drain. I know, I know, you always do and have never had any trouble. Well, you are really a lucky one.

My husband is a plumbing contractor and I was told in no uncertain terms, "NO!" When I asked sweetly, "Why not?" I got this explanation. Think, my dear. Where does all that stuff that you suffer the poor little kitchen sink to force down go? The plumbing in your house sometimes looks like a snake.

If you put grease in, even while running hot water, somewhere down the line it will probably congeal and stick to the sides of your pipes. Do this several times, along with the rest of the garbage you put down there and you are asking for trouble.

Before washing out the frying pan, just wipe it out with a paper towel and then proceed to wash and rinse. Don't take chances. Also, to be on the safe side, no coffee grounds or long celery strings should ever grace your drain.

Do run hot water and a little liquid soap once in awhile and a handful of ice with cold water to clean the blades of your disposal.

Don't (again from the professional in my family) use abrasive cleaners on your sinks. Even some of the supposedly mildly abrasive and liquid-type cleaners are still going to take the finish off your sink. You keep using those and you are really going to be in a lot of trouble later on.

Once that glaze is gone, your sink will look like the Fourth Army marched through there and no one bothered to clean their boots.

Do use a spray-on foamy cleaner. You can use baking soda and even sprinkle dishwasher detergent on it and scrub-a-dub without scratching the finish.

The same goes for your bathroom sink and the tub. No abrasive cleaners . . . I know we were all raised to sprinkle that compound and scrub away. If you continue to do this, you will scrub away your nice finish and then be stuck with a tub that no one wants to even sit in. And, honey child, it sure isn't cheap to replace a sink or tub . . . believe me, I know!

Cleaning

P   *How can I get rid of black marks on my sink from pots and pans?*

S   They can be bleached out, or use nylon net and baking soda. After you get rid of the marks, prevent them from recurring by putting a plastic place mat in your sink before washing pots and pans.

*   *   *

P   *I like the results of bleach, but I can't stand the smell.*

S   After you've rinsed the bleach out of your sink, swish a little fabric softener around in the sink and then down the drain.

*   *   *

P   *We moved into an old apartment and the sink looks horrible—rust stains.*

S   Try making a paste of salt and lemon juice or a full-strength solution of hydrogen peroxide. There are some excellent liquid rust stain removers sold comercially that are easy to use.

*   *   *

P   *How do I get stains off sink mats?*

S   Put your mats in your sink or your bathtub, spray them with a presoak compound and let them soak clean. Or, try sprinkling a little automatic dishwashing detergent and water on them and letting the mats soak clean. I don't recommend using bleach because bleach is too harsh on the mats and can cause color fading.

Drains and Stoppers
(Also see Drains in the bath area, p. 651)

P   *I have a single sink and the water starts standing because of my dishpan covering the drain.*

S   Set your dishpan on a cake rack and this will allow the water to drain. Be sure and protect the sink from being scratched.

*   *   *

If you drop a small item down the drain, it can be retrieved by bubble gum (chewed, of course!) stuck onto a piece of wire (or a clothes hanger).

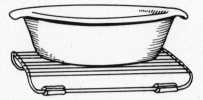

P   *I keep losing things because the holes in the drain are too large.*

S   Put a piece of nylon net across it or stuff a piece in the drain. Or, cut the top off of a scouring powder can, twist a piece of wire through two of the holes and insert this in your drain. It fits perfectly in most drains..

*   *   *

P   *My kitchen sink "clogs" frequently, and I need to learn how to unclog it myself.*

S   One way is to pour one cup baking soda and one cup vinegar into the drain. When it foams up, add one pint of boiling water.

Another method is to add about a cup of laundry detergent, followed by a half gallon of boiling water, and then flush with hot tap water.

*   *   *

As a preventive measure in the future, try adding a little vinegar to your dishpan or dishwasher to break up the grease and help keep grease clogs out of your sink.

*   *   *

If your plunger isn't handy try covering the drain with the palm of your hand and making an up-and-down "plunging" motion with your hand.

If that old plug has about had it, slip it into a plastic bag and then insert it in the drain. You'll get a little more life out of it.

* * *

If you can't get the drain stopper out by pulling, remember you can work some stoppers loose by a twisting motion.

Sink and Counter Area

A piece of peg board cut to fit one side of your sink will give you extra counter space when needed. If you cut a hole in the peg board above the opening for your disposal, you can rake the scraps right into the disposal.

* * *

Get some carpet padding and a piece of carpet and place it in front of your kitchen sink. When you're standing in front of that sink washing dishes, that carpet feels almost as good as kicking your shoes off!

* * *

If you face a blank wall while at your sink, try putting a big mirror on that wall. You can set a pretty flower arrangement where it will be reflected in the mirror, and I guarantee your sink nook will be much cheerier!

* * *

P   *I set a hot pan on my laminated countertop, and now I have a very ugly burn spot on it.*

S   One thing you can do is to stick one of those bathtub appliqués over the damaged area and then scatter some more here and there to give the effect of "planned" decor.

* * *

No sink top? Cover a board with adhesive-backed paper or paint or stain it; lay the board across the wash basin when needed.

Stainless Steel Sink

P   *I'm a little nervous about caring for my new stain-*
        less steel sink.

S   Just remember that abrasive cleansers are a no-no.
        Baking soda, and silver polish are especially good
        to use for cleaning stainless steel sinks because the
        main problem with stainless steel seems to be
        water spots. Vinegar is super for removing water
        spots.

        To shine stainless steel, rub a little mineral oil
        over it and buff with a dry cloth.

        Stainless steel will stay looking good if you wipe
        the sink dry after each use. Keep a towel handy
        and get in the habit of drying your sink, and I
        guarantee you'll be proud of your stainless steel
        sink.

UTENSILS
(Also see Appliances, small, p. 558)

I used to be one of those poor souls who could never find a big
stirring spoon or spatula or turning fork—until one day I lumped
'em altogether in an empty coffee can and covered the can with
adhesive-backed paper.

You could hang your utensils by your stove on cup hooks or bend
the "branches" on old coffee mug trees to hang them on. Also, you
can buy a peg board about two feet by three feet, cover it with
adhesive-backed paper if you like, and arrange cup hooks to hold
your cooking utensils.

                        *   *   *

P   *My cooking utensils get tangled together in the*
        drawer and slip around out of place.

S   If you will thumbtack a kitchen towel to the bot-
        tom of the drawer and store your utensils upside
        down, they will not slide around.

Can Opener
(Also see Can Opener, electric, p. 559)

Protect your nails. Hang a small pair of pliers on the inside of your cupboard door to lift off cocoa lids, baking powder lids, and so on.

*   *   *

P   *How can I prevent "beet red juice" or sticky fruit juice from splattering all over when I open a can?*

S   Gently make a small opening with a beverage can opener in the can and pour off an inch of juice and then open as usual.

*   *   *

Put a napkin on the palm of your hand and under the bottom of the can to prevent spills on the floor when using a wall can opener.

*   *   *

P   *I get frustrated because I have to dig through the drawer to find my can opener.*

S   Several solutions to this nuisance—tie a ribbon or yarn on the opener to spot it easily or attach it to a magnetic hook on your refrigerator.

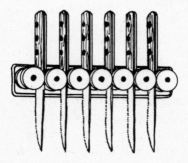

Knives

P How can I store sharp knives?

S Fill a coffee can or plastic container about three-fourths full with uncooked rice and store the knives blade down in the can.

* * *

Make it a habit to place all sharp knives on the drainboard to be washed by hand instead of slipping them into the dishwater.

* * *

P *How can I make an inexpensive rack for holding my knives?*

S One neat way is to glue thread spools together on a board as closely as possible. The blades will drop between the spools but the handles won't.

* * *

P *I have a beautiful set of knives with handles made of ebonite (looks like hard plastic). They have become whitish and dull with hard water deposit.*

S Get a soap-filled pad or fine steel wool. Do NOT wet them. Scour with the grain of the handle, rubbing vigorously. This will remove soap film. Then pour vegetable oil on a tissue and rub hard on the handles.

* * *

Scrape a serrated steak knife across cheese spread on crackers or cream cheese sandwiches to make a pretty shell design.

Knives, electric
  (See p. 561)

Measuring

P   *I always have to fumble around in the morning looking for the coffee measure.*

S   Slip a heavy rubber band around the can or jar and stick the measuring spoon under it.

*   *   *

Before using containers as substitute measuring cups, be sure they are a "true" measure; for instance, a quart mayonnaise jar sometimes holds more than four cups liquid.

*   *   *

Did you know that the cap off certain small bottles of vanilla measures one teaspoon, and off some larger bottles measures one tablespoon?

*   *   *

If you save yogurt cups, they measure exactly eight ounces and they are throwaways, no cups to clean up!

*   *   *

Cut a measuring chart out of an old cookbook and tape it to the inside of your cubpard near your staples. Sure comes in handy!

*   *   *

P   *I have a hard time reading the numbers on my measuring cup.*

S   Make those marks stand out by going over them with waterproof felt-tipped markers or red nail polish. Also, remember to hold the glass cup up and look across to the other side to read the numbers.

*   *   *

Fasten hooks on the underside of a cupboard to hang measuring cups. Pick up an extra set of measuring cups at a garage sale and store them in your canisters.

Buy a couple of inexpensive sets of measuring spoons and keep them in your flour and sugar canisters. A set stored in your mixing bowl is handy.

*   *   *

P   *My measuring spoons get separated or all tangled in the drawer.*

S   One solution is to hang or tie them together on a key chain.

Rolling Pin
(Also see Dough, p. 583)

Heaven help a duck! Did you know that you can fill a hollow, plastic rolling pin with a beverage, freeze it, and then you have a nice cold drink to carry along? Hubby could even tote one along in his golf bag!

*   *   *

P   *I was told not to wash my rolling pin.*

S   Some folks never wash them, just shake them off and place in a plastic bag to store. I wash mine by hand with warm sudsy water and dry thoroughly. Of course, we're talking about the wooden kind. No problem caring for the hollow, plastic kind.

Spatula

Use a putty knife (buy one at any hardware store) to remove pieces of fudge, brownie squares, etc. You'll wonder how you ever got along without one!

Spoons

P   *We at the office have tried everything to keep the sugar and creamer spoons clean and dry at the coffee area. Nothing seems to work!*

S   Spell out "cream," "sugar," and "stir" with plastic tape in raised letters. Use red tape or a bright color. Stick the tape words on the handles of the spoons.

* * *

P | *What can I use my seldom-used grapefruit spoons for?*
S | They really do come in handy when you want to core tomatoes and apples.

* * *

P | *Do wooden spoons need to be seasoned?*
S | Sure do! Scrub your spoons clean and place them in hot water for a minute or so. Towel dry. Let 'em dry thoroughly (several hours). Then heat some cooking oil to medium hot and dip the spoons in the hot oil. Let them cool and then wipe dry. Seasoning keeps the spoons from absorbing cooking odors.

Stainless Steel Flatware

P | *How can I get my stainless flatware to shine?*
S | Soak the flatware in hot water and a little ammonia; rinse and dry. Soaking in vinegar and water does a super job, too.

Strainer

Instead of a conventional metal strainer, purchase a fish net strainer (the kind you use with an aquarium). It stores flat, is rustproof.

* * *

If you don't have a strainer, clip nylon net around a bowl with clothespins.

* * *

A tea strainer works well as a flour shaker or sifter.

2

Your Bath

Problems in the bath area seem to be more centered on things like storage, taking care of the tub and shower, making bathroom accessories like shower curtains, carpets and rugs last longer, and most difficult, keeping it in order.

The bathroom doesn't have to be a mess and always in need of cleaning. Everyone and anyone who uses it should be responsible for keeping it neat and clean.

When I got married, one of the things that David and I agreed on was separate bathrooms. We were lucky enough to be building our house, so we could do this, and let me tell you it has saved many a fight. I can't complain about shoes or socks on the floor, he can't complain about fighting his way through hanging pantyhose or the sink filled with hand washing.

If you do share a bathroom, there are things you can do to make

609

it easier for all concerned. This is where good old common courtesy comes in. No one likes to find hair all over the sink, or the top always off the toothpaste . . . so think about those who have to follow you. Pretend you are a guest at someone's home—and always pick up after yourself!

There are some good hints on how to recycle, repair and make last longer all those little items in the bath that add up to money. Hints on how to save a shower curtain, help save a bath mat, and even how to use the hundreds of soap slivers you end up with will help you save many dollars.

At the end of the chapter is a really nifty substitutions list that just might save a shopping trip sometime when you are out of just one thing. In fact, you can use some of these substitutions all the time, and again those saved pennies will start to pile up.

APPLIANCES
(Also see Appliances, small for the kitchen, p. 558)

Curlers and Curling Iron

Problem	*My electric curlers create so much heat when I use them in the bath.*
Solution	Cover them with a hand towel before and after using, to help reduce the heat. Be sure there is no chance of fire.

*   *   *

P	*The cord to my electric curlers drives me crazy.*
S	Save a toilet paper cardboard roll, fold the cord up

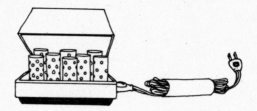

and stuff it inside so you have just enough slack to plug it in.

* * *

P   *My electric curlers don't work anymore. Any suggestions on what I can do?*

S   Heat your curlers in boiling water. Then use as usual.

* * *

Need to press a hair ribbon in a hurry? Why not grab that curling iron!

Electric Toothbrush
(Also see Toothbrush, p. 620)

An electric toothbrush with a spare brush can be used to clean rings and to clean around faucets.

Hair Dryer

Use your hair dryer to dry water spots on clothing.

* * *

Some hair dryers will fit nicely into the tumbler hole in toothbrush holders. A convenient stand!

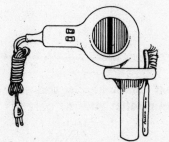

BATH AREA

Bathtub, cleaning
(Also see Shower Stall and Shower Head, p. 616)

Supervising a child at bathtime? Why not clean the bath while you have to be in there anyway?

*   *   *

P   *How do I get a yellow ring off my procelain enamel tub?*
S   Even though it is not a rust stain, liquid rust remover will probably get it off.

*   *   *

P   *How do I get a rust stain off my bathtub?*
S   First, try lemon and salt, then, if that doesn't work, use a liquid rust remover, rinse and dry. Never leave the rust remover on very long. Also, DO NOT use liquid rust remover on a fiber glass tub.

*   *   *

An old nylon stocking is perfect to scour your tub with. When finished, just toss in the trash.

*   *   *

If bending over or kneeling is too hard on your back, buy a child's mop or extra toilet bowl brush or long-handled car wash brush to scrub your tub with.

*   *   *

P   *My knees hurt when I kneel to clean out the bath-tub.*
S   Use your garden kneeler pad or keep two sponges to kneel on that you use only for this purpose.

*   *   *

P   *What is good for removing stains from fiber glass tubs?*

S   A paste made of baking soda and water left on the stain overnight will usually remove the stain. Use a damp cloth and scrub. Never use anything abrasive.

Bathtub Mat

P   *I hate a soggy bathtub mat.*

S   Most nonslip mats will stick on the tile wall by themselves and dry. Or, cut off the top of a bleach bottle, poke some drain holes in it, roll the mat up, place it in the container and stand it in the corner of your tub to drain.

Decor

The bath area is ideal for some plants that need steam and moisture—and they add to the decor as well.

*   *   *

P   *What will remove decals from tubs?*

S   A prewash spray works well if you let it sit a while. Then, gently try to pull up the edges. Applying extreme heat, as from a hair dryer, will help loosen the glue.

*   *   *

P   *I removed some decals from my porcelain enamel tub, but there are stains remaining.*

S   Scrub the stain with automatic dishwashing compound and hot water.

*   *   *

If your bathtub really looks shot—no more glaze or lustre, but is otherwise still in good condition—why not consider having it professionally resurfaced or reglazed? Let me tell you, chickadees, it's sure cheaper than a new tub!

Drains
(Also see Drains and Stoppers, p. 629)

P   *I can't clean under the drains in my tub or sink.*

S   Take a steel crochet hook to pull out hair, etc., from a drain where you can't remove the strainer.

*   *   *

P   *The drain is sluggish.*

S   Is there some hair or gook under the strainer? Clean it out. (Some strainers pull up, some twist up.) Also, pour one cup baking soda down the drain. Wait a minute or so and then pour one cup of vinegar down the drain; follow with one-half gallon of *boiling* water.

*   *   *

Drains smell? Pour baking soda and hot water down the drains once a month.

Medicine Cabinet
(Also see Cabinets in the Kitchen, p. 565)

P   *I use several different shades of lipstick and they really mess up my medicine cabinet when they fall over.*

S   Use the plastic top from any spray can to hold two or three lipsticks.

*   *   *

P   *I always knock over at least four bottles trying to get something in the back of the bathroom cabinet.*

S   Put your bottles, small boxes, etc., on a lazy Susan

and all you have to do is twirl it around to get the bottle that you want.

Mirrors

Got a bunch of girls hogging the mirror? Why not hang a full-length mirror horizontally in the bathroom!

*　　*　　*

P　　　　*I hate foggy mirrors.*
S　　　　Use your hair dryer to defog them; hang a towel over the mirror before beginning your shower; or keep a small windshield wiper blade handy to wipe the glass.

*　　*　　*

Can't see the back of your head when blow-drying your hair? Mount a mirror on the wall behind you in addition to the mirror in front of you!

*　　*　　*

Use your soap slivers to leave messages on your bathroom mirror. That's one way to get it clean!

*　　*　　*

P   *What can I use in place of mirror cleaner that I'm buying at the store?*

S   Ammonia and water works well. Newspapers are super to wipe with—won't cost you a penny, either.

Shower Stall and Shower Head
(Also see Bathtub, Cleaning, p. 612)

To mend holes in a shower curtain, repair them with strapping tape (not masking tape).

*   *   *

Place extra shower curtain hooks on the inside of the curtain between folds. Use the hooks to hang small things and hose on to dry. When the curtain is pulled, the drying garments don't show.

*   *   *

P   *I hate a yucky, damp washcloth sitting in the corner of the bathtub.*

S   Use the corner tag on the washcloth and hang it on a shower curtain hook. If your shower hooks are closed, open one or two just for this purpose.

*   *   *

P   *My shower curtain "hovers" around me.*

S   Wet it on the side next to the tub, plaster it to the tub and it will stay put. Or, attach magnets or

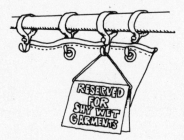

fishing weights to the hem to make it hang straight down.

*   *   *

P   *I have mildew on my plastic shower curtain; how can I get it off?*

S   Machine launder the curtain in one-half cup bleach and your usual laundry detergent. Throw in a couple of light-colored towels at the same time for "rubbing" action. If you stretch your shower curtain open the full length of the tub to dry each time, you will be less apt to have a mildew problem. Also, you can cut the mildewed bottom off a curtain and still have a usable curtain.

*   *   *

P   *I like to wash my shower curtain but how do I keep the plastic from wrinkling so?*

S   Always remove the curtain from your washer after the rinse; never spin one dry. To get the wrinkles out, put the curtain in the dryer on very low heat for just a couple of minutes and then rehang immediately.

*   *   *

Tired of an old shower curtain but can't afford a new fancy one? Buy some nylon net, fold several thicknesses, punch holes for the rings using your old curtain as a guide, and you'll have a pretty new curtain for a fraction of the cost! Use a plain plastic shower curtain as a liner.

*   *   *

Save old shower curtains for painting or remodeling. Cut in squares to protect carpeting in bad weather, or save for a mattress protector for visiting children. Throw an old curtain over the spare tire to keep suitcases from being scuffed in the trunk of your car.

*   *   *

P   *We live in an older apartment and it is impossible to lower the curtain rod. Consequently, all shower curtains are too short.*

S   Instead of one set of rings use three sets forming a chain effect at the top; or, replace the curtain with plastic draperies that are available in longer lengths.

*   *   *

P   *My shower curtain won't slide on the rod.*

S   Rub a bar of soap or baby oil on the rod.

*   *   *

Some shower curtains can be tinted. Also, felt-tipped permanent ink pens can be used to color white or light areas of the outside of a shower curtain for a color scheme change.

*   *   *

Tarnished rods or unsightly shelving poles can be covered with plastic slip-on covers.

*   *   *

P   *I have a dark-colored curtain that always has water spots and soap film.*

S   In between washings, try spraying the inside of it with prewash spray, let it sit awhile and rinse.

*   *   *

P   *How do I get black off an aluminum shower frame?*

S   An automobile rubbing compound works well.

*   *   *

P   *I can't unclog lime deposit buildup in the shower head.*

S   Unscrew the head and soak it in vinegar; then, use an old toothbrush to scrub it clean. You may have to use a toothpick to poke through the holes.

For a slippery shower with no mat, place a terry-type hand towel on the shower floor.

* * *

P *How can I get a straight flow from my shower spray?*

S If it won't adjust to straight, secure a plastic sandwich bag tightly over the head and cut one corner off. Be sure water flow is low-medium.

* * *

P *The shower track needs cleaning—how can I do it?*

S Use full-strength hydrogen peroxide, saturate cotton balls and pull them along the track with a tweezer.

* * *

A tiered wire or plastic basket hung in the corner of the shower will provide storage for quite a few bath items and drains well.

* * *

P *The wall side of our tub is wallpaper and is not protected from the spray of the shower.*

S Using a tension rod, hang a clear plastic liner over the wallpaper. When the shower is not being used, open the curtain to display the wallpaper.

BRUSHES

Hairbrushes

P   *Any quick way to clean my hair brushes?*

S   A little hot water and a dab of hair shampoo works great, rinse well.

               Putting hair brushes in that old standby of ammonia and water in a glass jar does wonders.

               For plastic-type hair brushes, you can put them in a sock, tie a knot in the ankle part and drop in your washing machine along with a load of laundry.

Toothbrush
(Also see Electric Toothbrush, p. 611)

Why not keep sets of toothbrushes for everyone in each bath in your home? This might make things less hectic at busy rush times.

*   *   *

Buy a few extra toothbrushes on sale and keep them on hand for guests.

CARPETING, CLEANING AND MAINTAINING
(Also see Carpet, p. 703)

P   *How can spots on the carpet around the toilet bowl be removed?*

S   More than likely, those spots are bleached out and can't be removed. However, take a crayon the color of your carpet and color over the spot. Then put your iron on low setting, place wax paper over the spot and apply heat until the crayon is melted.

Be sure that cleanser from the toilet bowl brush is not dripping and causing the spotting.

*   *   *

P   *I washed my bath carpet and it shrunk.*

S   You can salvage the rug by sewing fringe around the edges, wide enough to make it the original size.

*   *   *

Two or three old bath towels sewn together make a nice bath mat that is easily washed.

*   *   *

P   *I bought a fur-type rug and it looks matted and tangled.*

S   Brush that "critter" with an old stiff hair brush. A little fabric softener in the rinse cycle will help with those things.

*   *   *

P   *The edges of my bath carpet ravel.*

S   Spray the underside edges with hairspray or apply clear glue to the edges.

* * *

P   *The throw rugs on my tile bath floor slide.*

S   Sewing some used foam fabric-softener sheets on the backing will help keep it in place.

* * *

P   *The small rug that fits around the base of the toilet will not stay in place.*

S   Sew elastic loops on the rug and hook the elastic loops over the bolts at the base of the toilet.

SINKS
(Also see Sinks in the Kitchen, p. 598)

SINKS AND BATHTUBS—NO ABRASIVE CLEANERS, PLEASE. This is the same story as enamel kitchen sinks . . . use spray-on foamy-type cleansers or liquids. Once you scratch and mar the finish, you will be cleaning and cleaning and never get the surface clean and shiny.

* * *

P   *Why can't toilet bowl cleaners be used on tubs and basins?*

S   Because that's talking apples and oranges! Toilet bowls are usually vitreous china; tubs and basins are cast iron or steel with bonded porcelain finish. Don't take a chance on ruining the finish on your fixtures. Carefully follow instructions on all cleaning products. Remember, cleansers are carefully formulated for different finishes.

* * *

P   *How can I repair porcelain chips on my sinks?*

S   Buy a porcelain repair kit; the oil paint can be tinted to match your porcelain to a "T."

*   *   *

Attach your old "scrubber" toothbrush to your cleanser can with a rubber band and have it always handy.

STORAGE
(Also see Storage Space for odds and ends, p. 721)

Only one bathroom and several people who want to keep their things in the drawers? Use sturdy shoe boxes. They can be put under the sink or wherever. Just slide them out, use what you need and put the whole thing back.

*   *   *

P   *I don't have enough shelf space in my bathroom to store all the cans of hairspray, etc.*

S   Hang a see-through shoe bag on the back of the door or even on the wall behind the door. Everything slips right in. You can see what you need; if

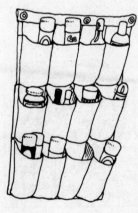

there are a lot of people in the family they can each
have a row of pockets.

*   *   *

Do you sometimes put your rings on the bathroom or sink counter
and then walk off and leave them and worry about them? Then you
should use one of your seldom-used little dainty bowls, or a small
pretty ash tray to hold all your pieces of jewelry when you need to
take them off for washing dishes, doing laundry, painting, etc.

*   *   *

P   *My makeup brushes are always rolling around in*
       the drawer.
S   I use a pretty little vase or an extra wine glass to
       hold them, right out on the counter.

*   *   *

Avoid spilling or breaking bottles of shampoo by transferring your
shampoo to clean, empty, plastic detergent bottles. Label them properly, of course.

*   *   *

P   *Where can I keep that extra roll of toilet tissue so*
       I don't have to crawl under the bathroom basin?
S   Use a boutique tissue box, cut the bottom out and
       slip in one roll of tissue. This can sit on the back

of the commode or in any convenient place and looks attractive.

*   *   *

P   *Our bath does not have a toothbrush holder.*

S   How about a glass "frog" that's used for flower arrangements, or put up cup hooks for your brushes that have holes in the handles.

*   *   *

P   *I don't have enough shelf space in my bathroom.*

S   Small wicker baskets look cute hung on the bathroom wall, and sure do hide clutter. Each member of the family can have his or her own.

*   *   *

A wooden case for soda pop bottles mounted diagonally on the wall is a handy nook to store small personal items. Paint it, of course, to match your bathroom colors.

TILES

P   *How can I get grout clean between my ceramic tile?*

S   Make a paste of bleach and scouring powder (luv, remember that bleach and ammonia DO NOT mix, so check the powder to make sure it contains no ammonia) and scrub with an old toothbrush or fine-grade dry steel wool pad on dry ceramic tile. Then rinse well.

Dingy grout can also be painted with latex paint.

*   *   *

P   *My ceramic tile shower walls are covered with scum.*

S   Make a paste of bleach and scouring cleaner (use a cleanser that has NO ammonia), then scour with nylon net and rinse well. You can use a prewash spray, let sit and wipe clean. (No fiber glass, please.)

After you have the wall clean, if you'll simply get in the habit of wiping down the wall with a towel after each bath, the walls will stay scum-free. Also, switching from regular soap to a detergent soap will help immensely!

TOILET BOWLS AND TANKS

Brushes

P   *Where can I dry the toilet bowl brush?*

S   Place the brush under the commode seat hanging over the bowl and let it air dry.

*   *   *

To protect the finish on your bowl, don't use a worn toilet brush. The metal can scratch or destroy the finish.

*   *   *

Don't have a brush holder? How about an old flower pot or an empty bleach bottle with the top cut off.

*   *   *

To keep the brush holder from getting rust, line the holder with a plastic bag.

Cleaning

P   *How is a ring around the toilet bowl removed?*

S   Pour two to three cups of household bleach OR vinegar (don't mix—use only one product at a time) in the bowl and let it sit overnight. Liquid rust remover will sometimes remove the ring.
    It may be that the clean water tank on the toilet may be the cause of the ring. Be sure that the tank is kept sediment-free to insure that clean water is going into the bowl. Liquid rust remover may also be used to clean the tank.

*   *   *

To prevent rust on the screws on the toilet seat, paint the screws with clear fingernail polish.

*   *   *

P   *I hate to clean the top of the water cabinet in the back of the commode. It gets covered with dust and powder so quickly.*

S   Cover the top with a hand towel or cut an old

place mat in half and use that. Just flip it over
when needed and wash it once in awhile.

Water Flow
(Also see Water Conservation, p. 635)

Find out where the main water valve cutoff is for your home *before*
an emergency situation arises.

* * *

P   *How can I stop a toilet from overflowing?*
S   First, open the tank lid and pull up on the rod or
arm that goes to the float. This will stop the flow
of water. Keep a piece of wire handy to hang over
the side to suspend this arm in the "Up" position.
Then determine what the stoppage is and clear the
bowl with a plumber's helper. Also, there is a valve
on the base of the toilet that will shut the water
off.

* * *

P   *How can I displace water in the toilet tank to conserve water?*
S   Put an open glass jar (like a medium-size mayonnaise jar) upright in the tank.

* * *

P   *The toilet doesn't seem to have as much water flow
as it used to.*
S   Check under the rim. It could be that the holes are
clogged with lime deposit and water simply can't
surge through. You can carefully poke into the
holes with a paper clip. Use a hand mirror so you
won't have to stand on your head!

* * *

Unsightly or missing knobs over the bolts at the base of the toilet? Some rounded deodorant bottle caps will fit.

*   *   *

P   *I want to clean stains out of the bowl. How do I lower the water level?*

S   Use a quick up-and-down motion with a brush or mop, or better yet, from as high as possible pour a bucket of water quickly into the commode. The water level should lower and stay that way since you are not flushing the toilet thereby letting more water out of the tank.

*   *   *

P   *What do I do when the toilet won't flush?*

S   Remove the top from the water tank. Check the floating "ball" that operates the valve that fills the tank with water. Check the wires and arms which hold the float. Bent coat hangers and paper clips can be used as temporary spare parts in a pinch.

    The usual cause of not flushing is that the lift wire has come loose from the flush ball or the trip arm. The flush ball is the stopper that regulates the flow of water into and out of the bowl.

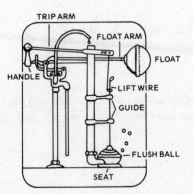

TOILETRIES
(Also see Wise Shopping, p. 635)

Bothered with perspiration on your wrist from your watch? Rub
your skin with a roll-on antiperspirant and let dry before putting on
your watch.

*   *   *

P   *What can I use if I run out of deodorant?*
S   Plain old baking soda is a terrific underarm de-
    odorant. Just pat on with an extra powder puff.

*   *   *

Out of eyebrow pencil? Use a soft lead pencil in a pinch, but only
on brows. *Don't* get near your eyes.

*   *   *

P   *I don't have an eyebrow brush.*
S   Those old toothbrushes come in handy for making
    beautiful eyes. I use a stiff one to separate my
    eyelashes (it's ten years old and still going strong).

*   *   *

Brown eyeshadow can be used to contour; if it is a little dark, mix
with powder.

*   *   *

Lipstick mixed with a dab of hand lotion, will work great as rouge.

*   *   *

Don't leave your perfumes and colognes out in the direct sunlight
. . . sunlight will cause them to evaporate and maybe even change
the fragrance.

*   *   *

P   *I love the bath powder that goes along with the perfume I buy, but both cost so much.*

S   Mix a box of the "expensive stuff" half and half with plain baby powder or baking soda, or spray a little of the good perfume on some baby powder, close tightly and let dry. It will do the trick.

*   *   *

P   *I love dusting powder, but besides dusting me, the floor sure gets a workout.*

S   Stand in the tub and you can just rinse away whatever misses your body.

*   *   *

Old bathpowder puffs are great to throw in your lingerie drawer to add a little extra fresh, beautiful fragrance.

*   *   *

P   *What can I use to scrub my face with?*

S   Oatmeal is the old standby. Also, a little salt with a drop of oil is very abrasive and can be used, but be careful not to overdo it.

*   *   *

P   *My little ones have such a hard time with the big bars of soap, so they don't wash their hands as well as they should.*

S   Cut the larger bars in small hand sizes so your little ones feel that they were made "especially" for them. They will be more likely to use the soap since "it's mine." Also, save the little soap slivers just for them. They don't have any excuses when they have their "own" soap!

*   *   *

P   *What's the difference between a soap bar and a detergent bar?*

S   Soaps are made by the action of alkali or fat and

fatty acids; detergents are synthesized chemically
from materials derived from petroleum.

*   *   *

Don't throw away the wrappers from bars of soap . . . slip them in
between your linens or, if you have a guest room that isn't used often,
place these wrappers on the pillow until the day your guests arrive.
When your company pulls back their sheets, they will smell a lively
fragrance rather than mustiness.

*   *   *

P   *I hate fighting with the last few squirts of shampoo*
       in the bottom of the little plastic tube.

S   Hang the tube from the bottom end with a clip-
       type clothespin that has that little hanger on it.
       Hook it on your shower curtain rod. All the sham-
       poo will be right at the top end the next time you
       use it.

*   *   *

To keep hair from "souring" between shampoos, rinse the hair with a mixture of one-fourth cup apple cider vinegar and three-fourth cup water after your shampoo.

*   *   *

P   *What can I use as a hair conditioner?*

S   Mayonnaise—works wonders! Rub it in, let it sit, and then wash. Or, beat one whole egg and rub it into your hair. Let it sit for five or so minutes and rinse out well . . . added protein.

*   *   *

P   *We go through a box of tissues a day when a member of the family is sick—and the tissue costs so much.*

S   Use a boutique tissue box, cut the bottom out and after taking the cardboard roll out of the toilet tissue, put the roll inside. You have easy pop-up tissues, very cheap, and they can be carried about if you travel from room to room.

*   *   *

P   *Toothpaste costs so much—what can I use instead?*

S   The recipe is 1-½ cup salt, 1 pound baking soda, and ⅛ ounce bottle of oil of wintergreen (or your favorite flavor). Simply blend well.

*   *   *

Want to get the last of the toothpaste out of a tube? Put the cap on tightly, place it on the floor, and step on it. Or, put a pencil at the end and roll up the tube all the way to the opening. . . . You will be surprised how much more paste comes out.

*   *   *

Disinfect toothbrushes and holders with alcohol when colds are going around.

*   *   *

Did you know that toothpaste will get marking pen ink off skin, get rid of onion and garlic odor on skin, and also take skid marks off of some vinyl floors?

*   *   *

Don't forget to brush your tongue once in a while to help have a fresh breath.

*   *   *

P   *My safety razor needs a thorough cleaning.*
S   Put a denture cleanser tablet in a pint container with water; put your razor in there and let it soak clean. Scrub with an old toothbrush and your razor will look like new.

*   *   *

Hot water bottle sprung a leak? A temporary solution is a piece of adhesive tape over the leak; apply a tire inner-tube patch to mend it permanently.

TOWELS

Remember, towels are used to dry off clean bodies and hands, so save yourself time and money by not washing them after each use.

*   *   *

P   *We never have enough towel racks to hang towels on when company comes.*
S   Give each a coat hanger marked with their name or color-coded and then you can hang several of these on one towel rack.

*   *   *

Want a pretty way to set out guest hand towels? Roll them up and put them in a pretty wicker basket or flower pot set out on the counter.

*   *   *

Pretty, heavy-duty paper towels folded and placed in napkins rings make nice guest towels.

* * *

If you find that the washcloths on your matched towel sets wear out faster than the towels, purchase two washcloths per set.

* * *

P   *How can I get my family to use a towel more than once?*

S   Assign each person a certain color, or a different pattern and assign each person a towel rack or hook.

* * *

For guests, use colored plastic tape to mark their towels.

WATER CONSERVATION
(Also see Waterflow for the toilet, p. 628)

P   *Which uses the most water—a bath or a shower?*

S   A shower takes five to fifteen gallons per minute; a full tub bath, thirty to fifty gallons to fill the tub. A shower lasting five or six minutes would use more water. The moral is: take a short shower and a half tub bath.

WISE SHOPPING
(Also see Toiletries, p. 630)

It seems like every time you go to the store, the prices are never the same. They are a few pennies higher than the last time. The price increase of things may slow down a bit, but you can be pretty sure that they aren't going to go back down.

What really got to me one day was looking at the price on a can of tuna and being shocked that it was the same as two weeks before! Now, that's unusual!

We all know that you should shop sales, use coupons and comparative-shop. Sometimes I don't have the time or want to waste the gas to go to three different stores to get their specials. You need to ask yourself if it's worth saving a nickel on a roll of toilet tissue when you have to drive ten miles to another store.

I think the best way to save money is to buy in bulk. If you have the space to store paper products and things that will keep six months to a year—and you can afford it—by all means buy a lot.

I wait until things like paper towels, napkins, toilet paper and tissues are on sale; then I buy twenty or thirty packs of toilet paper and ten boxes of tissues. Yes, I might look silly rolling up to the checkout counter with a basket full of nothing but toilet paper, but I guarantee that we have never run out. You know that the next time you go into the store it's going to cost more, so why not?

Buying in quantity like this may not be practical for you if you don't have a place to put it. Have you ever thought of stuffing toilet paper, paper towels, etc., under a bed? No one will see it, it's not going to go bad, and so what if it gets a little dusty—it's all wrapped up anyway! Think about it.

SUBSTITUTIONS

AIR FRESHENER:	Strike matches
BOWL CLEANER:	Full-strength bleach OR
	vinegar (not together)
COLD CREAM:	All-vegetable shortening
CREME RINSE:	Fabric softener diluted with water (use with caution)
DENTAL FLOSS:	Coarse thread

DEODORANT:	Baking soda
FACIAL MASK:	Shaving cream
GLASS CLEANER:	Alcohol, ammonia or vinegar
PUMICE STONE:	Nylon net
SHAMPOO:	Mild liquid dishwashing detergent diluted with water
SHAVING CREAM:	Baby oil
TALCUM POWDER:	Cornstarch, or cornstarch and baby powder
TOOTHPASTE:	Baking soda plus salt and flavoring

The Laundry

Wash day blues! As far as I'm concerned, it should be wash day whites!

Laundry problems seem to be the questions most often asked. It seems that the same problems bug most everyone. "How do I get ball-point ink out?" "How can I get my things white?" or "What about smelly tennis shoes?" The answers are in this chapter!

After living in an apartment all my life and having to use the apartment washing machines or drag everything to the laundromat, it is a real luxury to have a washer and dryer at home.

Laundry day for me was always a pain. I don't know why, but pulling all those wet clothes out of the washer and then lugging them across the laundry room into the dryer was just really hateful. The worst part of doing laundry was the folding and putting away. I hated it—and I lived alone and had only *my* laundry to do.

WELL, I am now married and live in a house with my own washer and dryer and it is hog heaven. I do my laundry and David does his own—that way there are no complaints about lint on the socks or "You lost my favorite T-shirt" or "Why is this white shirt gray?" I still hate folding and putting everything away, but the satisfaction of seeing the bottom of the laundry basket makes it bearable.

My personal philosophy on getting the dreaded deed done is to do it a little at a time, or as needed. For some people I know that's not practical, but if you have the facility in your own home or close by it's worth it. It's like cleaning an oven to me—if you do it a little at a time then it isn't hard to clean, but if you wait and wait and let the gunk build up, boy, oh, boy, do you have a chore ahead of you!

There is a very useful spot and stain listing in this chapter with some really good information. You will probably get tired of hearing me say, "Use prewash spray" or "Grab the box of dishwasher detergent" (I don't own any stock in any company—have never gotten a free box or can) but the stuff is great! I tried to give you home remedies, things that you have on hand, that you can use since few of us keep cleaning solvents or things like that around.

If the answer to your problem isn't here, let me know and I will be sure to include it in the next book or print it in the column.

Good luck! Because sometimes that's what it takes to get the laundry done, have everything match up, not fade, and be lint free. AMEN!

COLORFASTNESS

If the tag on clothes, linens, etc., says "colorfast," that means the colors are set and should not run. If it doesn't say anything about it, you have to be careful when laundering.

Always read the care instructions on the labels of all garments you plan to buy. If it says "dry-clean only," think if you want to spend the time and money to always get it dry-cleaned. Be sure you are prepared for it to run, if the label doesn't say colorfast.

*　　*　　*

Problem   *I bought a new T-shirt and the color ran.*

Solution   It's painful (and expensive) to learn from experience, isn't it? Next time soak your new shirt in cold water and white vinegar before washing. The vinegar and cold water "set" the color.

*   *   *

P   *How do I test for colorfastness?*

S   Soak a small portion of the garment for two minutes in a light suds at the temperature you will be using for regular washing. Look for traces of dye. If the dye does bleed, wash that item alone.

*   *   *

A very simple way to test for colorfastness when you get a garment home is to wring out a wet washcloth or rag and rub over an inside seam. If color comes off you can bet it's gonna bleed when you wash it.

*   *   *

P   *My new colored towels are almost too pretty to use —how can I keep them looking new?*

S   Always wash them in warm water with detergent and tumble dry them. You should wash dark colors separately. Because the dyes in vibrant colors may be sensitive to bleach, I do not suggest bleaching colored towels.

DETERGENTS, FABRIC SOFTENERS AND BLEACH

Always check the unit price when buying laundry detergent and the likes—bigger is not always cheaper. It pays to check.

*   *   *

A metal grapefruit spoon is great to open detergent boxes with—sure beats breaking a fingernail.

*   *   *

Never, never, never use liquid dishwashing detergent in your clothes washing machine—you will end up with enough bubbles to float you to the moon!

* * *

P   *I am tired of lugging a measuring cup to and from the laundromat. Plus I have lost several.*

S   The plastic type 8-ounce yogurt or sour cream cartons are perfect. Measure and mark if you use less than eight ounces. If it gets left behind, big deal, and it sure is lightweight!

* * *

P   *I use the very concentrated liquid detergent, and I feel I'm wasting so much that is left in the cup.*

S   If you will use a soft plastic cup, you can throw it in the wash and get every last drop used . . . no money wasted here.

* * *

P   *I hate measuring detergent. It is such a chore to look at the measuring cup and figure out how much half a cup is.*

S   Use the plastic tops from cans, or even sturdy frozen juice cardboard cans; measure one-half cup

or whatever you want and cut off the juice can
. . . most large tops are one-half cup.

*　　*　　*

P   *I ran out of laundry detergent at midnight and
really didn't want to go to the store.*
S   In a real pinch, I have used one-fourth cup powdered dishwasher detergent BUT only on clothes
that can stand a little bleach. This is for an emergency situation—don't use it all the time.

*　　*　　*

P   *I ran out of fabric softener in the middle of doing
my laundry.*
S   You can use the creme rinse that you rinse your
hair with. Mix one or two capfuls to a quart of
water and pour in the machine on the rinse
cycle.

*　　*　　*

P   *What can I do if I forget to put liquid fabric softener in the wash at the right time?*
S   Put just a dash of the liquid fabric softener on a
washcloth and toss it in your dryer; you have your
own homemade fabric softener sheet!

*　　*　　*

P   *My towels don't absorb moisture as they used to.*
S   It may be that you're using fabric softener too
frequently on your towels. Stop using fabric softener for a few washes and that should help. Then
use maybe every other time.

*　　*　　*

Out of household bleach . . . hydrogen peroxide can be used on many
things to remove stains. Always first test a spot that doesn't
show.

DRYING

Indoor Drying

P   *I do hand laundry in my tiny apartment. Where can I hang all the things I have to dry. I have no balcony.*

S   If you have a lot of things to hang up to dry, put them on coat hangers, and you can hang a lot of hangers over your bathtub shower rod. You can put several bras and slips on just one hanger. If you worry about dripping, use your old plastic shower curtain to drape over the floor.

*   *   *

Putting up extra towel racks is worth the cost of having the space to hang dry items.

*   *   *

P   *I hang my clothes in the basement to dry and it takes forever.*

S   Turn on a fan to circulate the air and they will dry much quicker.

*   *   *

P   *I always run out of pants hangers and hate to go buy some. The pants legs crease when hung on a regular wire hanger.*

S   Use two hangers at a time and place a magazine over the bottom, then cover with plastic bags over them and staple or tape 'em together. (I like this way.) If you have time, you can tie old pantyhose around them.

*   *   *

P   *I have several garments that say "dry flat" and I really don't have any place to do that.*

S   If you can, spread them out on some plastic or
        paper on the hood or trunk of a full-size car, in the
        garage, natch. When the bathtub is not in use, it
        makes a marvey place to lay things out to dry. It's
        out of the way, and you can shut the curtain and
        not even have to see the laundry.

*   *   *

For extra strength in wire hangers, put two together and tape them
at the neck; they will hold most heavy garments.

*   *   *

If you have dresses that have little spaghetti straps or a large neckline
and always fall off the hangers while drying, just fold them over the
hanger at the waistline—no wrinkles and they won't fall off.

Machine Drying

P   *When I dry my laundry at the laundromat, I hate
        having to run three different dryers (which cost
        money) just because I have things which need dif-
        ferent temperature settings.*

S   Put all your things in one dryer and stop it after
        a few minutes to take out those quick-drying
        things. Then a few minutes later, pull out the
        things that are dry and finally leave the heavy-duty
        things in the longest.

*   *   *

P   *My clothes come out really wrinkled even after
        going through the dryer.*

S   You might be overloading your washer and dryer.
        Things need room to move around. If you pack the
        washer tight, natch they are going to twist and
        wrinkle. Also, the dryer should never be stuffed—
        or else, Wrinkle City!

*   *   *

If you remove permanent press fabrics immediately from the dryer, give them a shake, and place them on hangers, they will usually remain wrinkle-free. Sometimes just a light touch-up with a warm iron is all that's needed.

*   *   *

P   *I hate having to use my hand to clean the lint filter on my dryer.*

S   Don't throw the fabric softener sheets away when you are finished with them; just grab a used one and wipe that lint away.

*   *   *

Never place "rubberized" items such as girdles, bras, etc. in a dryer on high heat. If you do, they will ruin. Always use low heat or air-dry setting to dry them.

Outdoor Drying
(Also see Blankets, p. 661 and Drying Carpet, p. 705)

P   *Can I dry blankets outside?*

S   Yes, if you avoid drying them on very windy days or in bright, direct sunlight. High wind may stretch a wet blanket and bright sun could fade some colors. If possible, hang them lengthwise over two or more lines to keep the blanket's shape and to speed drying time.

*   *   *

P   *I live in an apartment and do a lot of hand washing to save money, but I've run out of places to hang things to dry.*

S   If you have a balcony or area that gets sunlight and is secluded from public view, garden chairs turned upside down make super little clotheslines.

*   *   *

Short of line space? You can place lightweight things over some of the clothes or sheets that have already been hung.

*   *   *

P   *My hands get cold when I hang my laundry in chilly weather.*

S   Fill a hot water bottle with hot water and put it in your laundry basket; every time you pick up something to hang, hold the bottle for a second to warm up those hands. Or, you can wear rubber gloves.

*   *   *

Wash towels and work clothes first because it takes longer for them to dry on the line.

*   *   *

P   *I have so much laundry to hang on the lines that there is never enough space to hang it, and I have to do it in shifts.*

S   Honey child, you are going to love this one and it is so simple you are going to say, "Why didn't I think of that?" Hang the clothes crosswise on the lines, from one line to the other, instead of length-

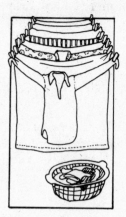

wise. You can hang a lot of laundry on just two
lines.

Ironing
(Also see Post-washing, p. 664)

Sprinkled some ironing and can't get to it? Put it in a plastic bag
in the refrigerator and it will keep for several days. Or, stuff it in your
freezer. But don't forget!

*   *   *

P   *I have a tiny apartment and really hate putting up
the ironing board for just one shirt.*

S   Can I help you? I can iron on the floor better than
most people using an ironing board! Just put a
thick towel down, sit yourself on the floor and iron
away.

A more conventional way is to put a few magazines or newspapers on the kitchen counter, cover
with a towel, and use your counter for a hurry-up
ironing board.

The dadgum easiest and quickest way is to
throw a towel over the corner of the bed, and you
even have a curved edge for the shoulder seams.

*   *   *

P   *I have to iron long tablecloths for a church banquet—how can I keep them from dragging on the
floor?*

S   First of all, if you can iron them at the banquet hall
and put them directly on the table, they will not
wrinkle. Also, put a card table by your ironing
board to drape the tablecloth over—it won't drag
on the floor.

*   *   *

P   *I hate ironing handkerchiefs and little things like that.*

S   Place the light things on top of each other, iron, turn over and iron again. You get double-duty!

*   *   *

P   *It seems that my ironing is more wrinkled when I pull it out of the basket than when I put it in.*

S   For those things that you have to iron, don't throw them in the basket and pile things on top of them. Hang them loosely on hangers or lay them out flat somewhere. The less wrinkles to contend with, the better.

*   *   *

P   *I hate walking back and forth to each closet to hang up the clothes when I am ironing.*

S   Put one of the metal hooks that slips over the front of the door and gives you a place to hang clothes on the back on the closest door to you. Do all your ironing at once, then grab the clothes that go to each room and make only one trip.

*   *   *

P   *My iron has a buildup of starch.*

S   If it is a light buildup, you can scrub the cool iron with some nylon net, or an old toothbrush and a

little baking soda. If you have a nonstick coating on the iron, never use anything abrasive. If the buildup is rather heavy and has been on there a long time, most home remedies don't work well.

* * *

Buy a tube of iron cleaner (you can find it in fabric stores); it is as easy as pie to use and you will have a slick-bottomed iron in nothing flat. It costs only about a dollar and lasts well over a year.

* * *

P   *My steam iron is clogged.*
S   Pour white vinegar into the iron and let it steam for about five minutes. Then unplug the iron and let it cool for awhile. Empty the vinegar out and rinse the iron thoroughly by pouring water in and out.

HAMPERS
(Also see Sorting, p. 664)

P   *I am always forgetting to wash something that I didn't put in the hamper, like a bathrobe or blanket.*

S   As soon as you think about it, write yourself a note and throw it in the hamper. When you see it, you will know right where to go and nothing will escape getting washed.

*   *   *

P   *So many times things to be cleaned are not that soiled, and I hate crunching them up and putting them in the hamper.*

S   Hang the item wrong side out in your laundry or closet. Then on laundry day you know at a glance what needs to be washed, and they are hardly wrinkled.

*   *   *

P   *Getting the heavy, overstuffed laundry basket from the bathroom to the laundry room is almost impossible.*

S   Loop a dog leash or something sturdy through a handle and drag the beast. Much easier than lifting and carrying.

*   *   *

P   *My clothes hamper smells mildewy sometimes.*

S   Be sure that there is no dampness in there. Always air-dry things before throwing them in the hamper. This is a great place to throw those small soap slivers. They will keep things smelling fresh in most cases.

I am not a miracle worker—if you run a gym, nothing is going to keep that hamper from stinking —short of putting all gym clothes in a plastic bag (and I am not going to be responsible for what happens when you open it up!).

*   *   *

P   *My laundry hamper smells worse than my son's tennis shoes.*

S   That's pretty bad, but one sure way is to do the laundry as often as is needed. But if you can't get those things out in a hurry, sprinkling a handful of baking soda in the hamper every now and then will sure help. It won't hurt your clothes at all; just shake it to the bottom of the hamper when you pull the things out to wash.

*   *   *

P   *My family just won't clean their pockets before putting things in the hamper.*

S   Finder's keepers is the rule—if its money it's yours, if it's a frog they can have it back! Place a large clean coffee can or catchall in the spot where the laundry is done. If they don't sort through the pockets, then it's all yours.

       You can place a can or note in each hamper as a reminder.

HAND WASHING
(Also see Detergents, p. 640)

Soaking items in the bathroom? Place them in a clean plastic bucket or trash basket with water and soap and put it in the tub or shower.

If anyone needs to take a bath, they can simply remove the container and replace it afterwards.

*   *   *

P   *I hate hand washing lingerie.*
S   Wash it in your machine using a gentle or delicate cycle. Or, using mild detergent and cool water, place the articles in the bathtub and rub-a-dub-dub using a plumber's helper with a rubber suction (clean, of course!). Drain the water, refill and rinse. Do not put nylon lingerie or delicate fabrics in a dryer.

*   *   *

P   *I hate hand washing my underwire bras.*
S   I put mine in a pillow slip, or laundry bag, close the end and run them through the washing machine on gentle cycle. It's better to air-dry but depending on the fabric content it might go in the dryer. Always check the label.

*   *   *

When hand washing small items in the sink, you can use a tiny plastic glass, like a juice glass, as a plunger. Just "squash" the glass up and down and make your own washing machine cycle.

*   *   *

P   *Can I hand wash a silk blouse?*
S   Yes, I do mine using a mild liquid detergent and cool water (a gentle, swishing action)—no twisting or wringing—rolling it in a towel first, then hanging it up to dry, out of direct sunlight. Remember though, if you try to remove a spot yourself on silk, it will circle. So, leave spot removal on silks to professionals. Iron on the wrong side with a pressing cloth—be sure to use low setting.

*   *   *

P   *How do I launder sweaters?*

S   Wool or part wool sweaters can be washed by hand in a mild detergent. Dissolve soap or detergent in lukewarm water, and squeeze suds through the sweater. Rinse gently and thoroughly. Gently squeeze (don't wring) out as much water as possible. Roll the sweater up in a thick towel and squeeze gently to remove excess moisture. Lay the sweater out flat to dry (be sure and shape it).

*   *   *

P   *I have some dingy clothes which need whitening.*

S   This has got to be the greatest! Especially for kids' white socks and baby clothes. Pour one gallon of hot water into a *plastic* container. Add one-half cup of automatic dishwashing compound and one-fourth cup of bleach. Stir well. If clothes can't stand hot water, let it cool first. Let the clothes soak for thirty minutes, then wash as usual. Use one-half cup vinegar in the rinse water.

JEANS AND SNEAKERS
(Also see Patching, p. 686)

P   *My kids' jeans have "white spots" on them.*

S   If the white spots are caused from bleach or faded, or if the white spots are threads of the material showing through, this tip will work. Pick a crayon the color closest to the jeans and gently rub it across the faded area. When you've reached the wanted shade, put a piece of waxed paper over the area and press with a warm iron. The heat will set the color to keep it from washing out for awhile. The color will eventually wash out, but just repeat the application.

*   *   *

P   *I have a lovely jeans outfit that's only a few months old, and the vest and blazer are so much darker than the pants.*

S   You should always wash matching pieces, or multi-piece outfits together. If there is any fading or color change, they will all change at the same time. You could wash the two darker pieces a few times and see if they fade to match the pants.

*   *   *

P   *I hate stiff new jeans.*
S   I use a plastic laundry tub (you could use a clean plastic trash can) and cold water, plus a cup or so of fabric softener, add my jeans and let them soak overnight.

Just pop them in the washer the next day; using the fabric softener, water and wash as usual. Sometimes it still takes a few washings to get them comfy—but this helps wonderfully for that first wearing.

*   *   *

P   *I want to keep my new jeans dark blue as long as possible.*
S   Before you put your jeans in the wash, turn them inside out. Also, dry and iron them (if you do) inside out. Washing your jeans in cool water helps. If you are line drying, it helps to hang the jeans in a shady spot to prevent fading.

*   *   *

P   *I hate washing shoe laces—I always lose them.*
S   Untie them from the tennies and either sprinkle with detergent and scrub with a toothbrush or tie the laces through a shirt button hole and run them through the wash.

*   *   *

After washing your tennis shoes, use a spray-type soil repellent to give them a good going-over on the outside. It will help keep dirt from grinding in and they are much easier to get clean the next time.

LABEL DEFINITIONS

P   *Sometimes I find the cleaning instructions on the labels in clothing confusing.*

S   I didn't realize one could come across so many different labels. Natch, these labels are put in clothes by the manufacturer for a purpose so it pays to "read and heed." Hope the following list will help you understand those labels a little bit better!

BLOCK TO DRY: Shape the garment to its correct size and shape while drying.

COLD WASH—COLD RINSE: Use cold water from faucet or cold temperature setting on the washing machine.

COOL IRON: Iron item at lowest setting.

DAMP WIPE: Just wipe with a damp cloth or sponge with a little mild detergent. Surface clean only; do not soak or get item wet.

DELICATE CYCLE—GENTLE
 CYCLE: Can be washed in the machine that has this setting; if not, wash by hand.

DO NOT IRON: Do not iron or press using heat.

DRY-CLEAN ONLY:	The article can be dry-cleaned professionally or you can clean it in a self-service dry-cleaning machine.
DRY FLAT:	Lay garment on flat surface to dry.
DURABLE PRESS CYCLE— PERMANENT PRESS CYCLE:	Use appropriate machine setting. Or, use warm wash, cold rinse and short spin cycle.
HAND WASH:	Launder by hand only with mild liquid detergent in lukewarm or cool water. Item may usually be dry-cleaned.
HAND WASH ONLY:	Launder by hand only in mild liquid detergent in lukewarm or cool water. No machine washing or dry cleaning.
HAND WASH SEPARATELY:	Hand wash alone or with same colors.
HOME LAUNDER ONLY:	Do not use commercial laundry (temperatures are too hot).
HOT IRON:	Iron at hot setting.
IRON DAMP:	Dampen the article before ironing.
LINE DRY:	Hang damp and allow to dry.
MACHINE WASH:	You can wash and dry the article by your usual washing method.
NO BLEACH:	No kind, no how!
NO DRY-CLEAN:	Do not dry-clean. Follow label instructions for cleaning.
NO SPIN:	Remove garment before final machine spin cycle.

NO WRING—NO TWIST: Line dry, drip dry or flat dry. Wringing or twisting of garment may cause wrinkles or loss of shape of garment.

PROFESSIONALLY DRY-CLEAN
ONLY: Do not use a self-service machine. Have garment cleaned only by professional cleaners.

STEAM IRON: Iron or press with steam.

TUMBLE DRY: Can be tumbled in dryer at recommended heat on label.

TUMBLE DRY, REMOVE
PROMPTLY: Can be tumble dried in a dryer at recommended heat but if your machine doesn't have a cool-down cycle, remove the article at once when tumbling stops.

WARM WASH—WARM RINSE: Use warm water from faucet or warm machine setting.

MACHINE WASH SEPARATE: Machine wash alone or with same colors only.

MACHINE WASHING
(Also see Pretreatment, p. 666–668)

Machine Washing Procedures

If your washer or dryer doesn't work, these hints may save you an expensive service call. For either one, check to be sure it is plugged in and if a fuse is blown or a circuit breaker tripped. For the separate appliances, check the following:

WASHING MACHINE

1. Are the water faucets turned on?

2. Is there a kink in the hose?

3. Is the selector button pushed in all the way?

4. Is the load of clothes balanced? Some washers turn off automatically if the load of clothes becomes "lop-sided." Rearrange the clothes and push the button to start the machine again.

5. Is the lid closing tightly? There's a button under the lid that cuts the machine off when the lid is raised.

DRYER

1. If gas, is the striker working properly or is the pilot light on?

2. Does the lint trap or filter need cleaning?

3. Is the exhaust vent blocked?

4. Is the door closing tightly?

*   *   *

Even your washing machine needs cleaning now and then. Fill the machine with hot water and pour one quart of vinegar in. Run the machine through the entire cycle. There can be a residue left by detergents and minerals in hard water areas, but the vinegar wash will clean it.

*   *   *

P   *I think I have hard water.*

S   Here's an easy way to see if you have hard water problems: Add one-fourth teaspoon powdered laundry detergent to one pint of warm water. Shake. If there are no suds or if the suds don't stay "sudsy," the water is probably hard. Increase the amount of detergent you use and give clothes an extra rinse, using a little vinegar.

*   *   *

P   *Long-sleeve shirts always tangle in the washer, and it's like pulling eye teeth to get them undone sometimes.*

S   Simply button the sleeves to the front of the shirt-(button one or two buttons of the shirt) and no more problem.

*   *   *

P   *Help! I was doing the laundry and the machine looked like Mt. St. Helens with all the suds.*

S   You can sprinkle them with salt, and then rinse well; it won't hurt the fabric. Running a bar of soap through detergent suds will kill those little devils instantly . . . this is good to know when washing dishes.

*   *   *

P   *With everyone in our house doing their own laundry, keeping up with washing instructions can be a problem.*

S   Post the general laundry instructions in a place where all can read easily at a glance what temperature, how much detergent, etc.

*   *   *

P   *Is it necessary to rinse clothes in hot water?*

S   No! The disinfecting and cleansing of the detergent has already taken place. You're merely rinsing out water from clean clothes, and cold water works just as well as hot. Plus, we all need to conserve energy any way we can!

*   *   *

Add about a cup of white vinegar to your rinse water. The vinegar dissolves all the "gook" and soap film residues and gets your wash cleaner. Don't worry about hurting your clothes—one cup of vinegar is too mild to harm fabrics.

*   *   *

Give your clothes an extra spin in the washer after they have gone through the usual cycles. You will be amazed at the extra water left in garments. They will dry faster in the dryer, and line dry quicker, too.

Blankets
(Also see Outdoor Drying, p. 645)

P   *My blankets don't come out soft and fluffy after they're washed.*

S   Rinse them in two cups of white vinegar to a washer full of water. The vinegar will help restore their softness and fluffiness, and they'll smell fresh, too!

*   *   *

P   *My blankets need cleaning but it costs so much to take them all to the cleaners—dare I try to wash them myself?*

S   No problem, if you follow a few basics. Check the label on your blanket to see if it is washable. Then fill your washer with detergent and water. Make sure the detergent is *completely dissolved* in the water before adding the blanket. Put the blanket evenly around in the water and let it soak fifteen to twenty minutes. Then start the washer and let the blanket agitate on gentle for about three minutes.

       Rinse them in two cups of white vinegar to a washer full of water. The vinegar will help restore their softness and fluffiness, and they'll smell fresh, too!

Delicates
(See Hand Washing, p. 651)

Delicate fabrics such as knits, sheers, etc., should be washed separately and require gentle agitation or hand washing.

Diapers

Never use ammonia to disinfect diapers. Your baby will wind up with an A-1 case of diaper rash if you do. Wring the diapers out and wash them in your washer using hot water and detergent. Rinse thoroughly (two rinses are preferable for diapers), adding one-half cup vinegar in the final rinse.

Items, heavy

P   *My rubber-backed bath mat peels and comes off in the washer—a mess.*

S   Wash and dry it in a pillow case; if a pillow case is too small, make one out of an old sheet.

Small Items

P   *I always lose my baby's tiny socks when I put them in the washing machine.*

S   Those lovely little socks can be troublesome, but if you will simply safety pin them to a towel or large piece of clothing they will never be lost again.

Laundromat

If you have to do your laundry in a laundromat or in your apartment laundry room, you know how frustrating it is when you want to do your laundry and you don't have the "correct change, please!" Always keep a cookie jar (even if it's only a mayo jar) with extra quarters, dimes and nickels . . . you will then be assured of always having the correct change for the laundry. If you need mad money, it's there—at least enough for a pizza!

*   *   *

If you take your wash to a laundromat or you can't hear the timer on your washing machine or dryer, carry a little egg timer with you

. . . it sure saves on leaving your things in too long, which can cause unnecessary wrinkles in permanent press things.

* * *

If you use a laundromat, it's worth the time at home to sort your laundry into the loads that you will have to do. If you get there and there are only two machines available and you have three loads, it is a simple matter to at least get two done without much hassle.

Lint

P   *My clothes end up with lint all over them.*
S   Turn the garments inside out before washing. If you do your wash at a laundromat, wipe the inside of the machine out first with wet paper towels before using.

Pretreatment
(Also see Stains and Spots, p. 665)

Part of the reason that pretreats and presoak cleaners work so well is that you put them directly on the offending spot. Keep a squeeze bottle (clearly marked) that you have filled with liquid dishwashing detergent handy . . . give those nasty spots a quick squirt, a little rub, and toss in the machine—you might be surprised!

* * *

P   *I always forget which clothes need extra treatment when it is laundry time.*
S   As soon as you take an item off and you know that it needs to be spot-treated or whatever, pin the spot with a safety pin or put a clothespin on it to draw your attention to it on laundry day.

Post-washing
(Also see Ironing, p. 647)

P   *After wearing a dress only once, sometimes it is still*
         clean enough for me to wear it again, but I hate to
         hang it in my closet with the newly laundered
         clothes.

S   If you will hang a garment up immediately after
         taking it off, your body heat will make most wrin-
         kles fall right out. Let the item air well before
         putting it in your closet and it will be ready for
         your next wearing without a fuss.

Silk
(see p. 652)

Sweaters
(see p. 653)

SORTING
(Also see Hampers, p. 649)

P   *Sorting clothes—there are so many people in my*
         family that just putting the clothes away after
         washing is a major chore.

S   Sort them all in one place and divide them so that
         each person has their own pile. Then let them put
         their own things away.

*   *   *

P   *Finding the right size sheet to match the pillow*
         cases is a really hunt-and-seek chore in my house.

S   If you have different size beds, mark the size of
         each sheet on one edge with a permanent marker
         . . . twin, king, etc. Then you can see which sheet

it is without having to pull out and unfold.

If you will make a package when folding the laundry, you won't ever have to search for the lost sheet again. One top, one bottom, and the pillow cases (all the same size and pattern) all folded together. Pull the whole kit and kaboodle out and no more looking for the lost pillow case.

*   *   *

P   *Turning socks right side out drives me up the wall —my boys just won't listen.*

S   Wash them the way they throw them in the hamper; if it doesn't bother them to wear them inside out, it shouldn't bother you. Look at it this way— they will be right side out every other wash time!

*   *   *

P   *Matching up socks is the world's worse chore when laundry day comes.*

S   Tie them together loosely at the tops, or pin them together: or, buy all one color and never have to worry again!

*   *   *

P   *I can never tell which socks are my son's and which are my husband's—they both wear the same size now.*

S   Code them: Use blue thread for one and red for the other. Whip a few stitches in the top of each sock.

STAINS AND SPOTS

It seems the whole world is one big spot. I don't know if we are just a messy lot, or it's a fact of nature that very few things remain stain-free for a lifetime.

This section on stain removal should help you through the irritating times at home when you get a "spot" on something and want to know how to get it out.

A lot of the solutions to these problems are simple things you have around your house because I have tried to make it as easy for you as possible.

The first and foremost rule to stain removal is to get to it ASAP (as soon as possible), if not quicker. The general rule is: Flush with cold water then proceed to do your magic.

Always consider what the stain is, how long it has been there and what kind of material you are working on.

I wouldn't touch velvet or silk with a magic wand. When in doubt, *don't.* If you have something that is very expensive or very special, it is worth the money to take it to a professional cleaner. They know what they are doing. Always tell them what the stain is, and don't be embarrassed to tell them if you have done anything to it to try to get the stain out. If you aren't honest, when they put their cleaning chemical on it, there might be a reaction that you won't like.

For home care, the simplest is the best. Following all instructions both on the garment and on the bottle of whatever you are using is very important. If one thing doesn't work, be sure to rinse well before going on to the next or you might end up with a hole in the fabric.

When removing a spot, work from the back of the material first; you don't want to push that stain in even more. Always blot from the outside of the stain in; otherwise, you will end up with a larger spot than you began with.

Prewash sprays are great, but remember, most of them need to be rinsed in warm water to work well. Also, just spraying on and tossing into the machine sometimes isn't enough. A little elbow grease, or wrist action, is required first to work at the spot.

Read instructions and information *before* starting to spot treat something instead of afterwards when you have already ruined your favorite shirt or blouse.

*   *   *

P   *My clothes are gray.*
S   Check your water supply. If it's cloudy or has
         sediment in it, naturally your clothes are going to
         look that way, too. Maybe the water is too hard

and you need to use an extra amount of detergent and also a fabric softener. You might be overloading your washer; clothes need to agitate freely.

* * *

P

S

Ring around the collar—I hate it and I know it's not my fault. I only do the wash!

You are right, honey child. Ring around the collar is not the fault of the person doing the wash, but the person who wears the shirt. I am not saying that the person who wears the shirt doesn't bathe, it's just a basic fact of nature that no matter how well you scrub the back of your neck there are oil glands back there that really do get a workout.

If you will have the wearer of the shirt take a piece of white facial tissue or a white washcloth, put some rubbing alcohol on it and rub over the back of his neck, he will see the result and know it's not your fault.

There are several things that you can do to prevent this. Be sure the neck is clean by rubbing it with alcohol before putting on the shirt. If it is really bad, one can put an antiperspirant on the back of the neck providing there are no allergies . . . it really helps.

If shirts do have ring around the collar, you can rub chalk into the "ring" to absorb the oil prior to laundering his shirts. Also, you can use prewash spray on it. Another good way to get rid of it is to rub in some hair shampoo before your usual washing. This is where that old extra toothbrush comes in handy, too. Just give a little scrub-a-dub-dub and no more yuck!

* * *

For spit-up stains on baby clothes, make a paste of unseasoned meat tenderizer and water, rub it on the stain, and wash as usual, rinsing in vinegar and water.

*   *   *

P   *I have tried several things but can't get a stain out —what can I try now?*

S   Some folks have good luck with the hot sun and lemon treatment; it depends on the stain but it's worth a try. Wet the stain with lemon juice and spread the garment out flat so the sun's rays will get to it full strength. Leave the garment out all day.

*   *   *

P   *What are some common stain removers?*
S   A list of common stain removers are:

1. *Chlorine Bleach:* Don't use bleach full strength. One part bleach to four parts water is about right. Always read the bottle instructions.

2. *Detergent Paste:* Mix enough detergent granules with water to make a paste. Test materials for light bleaching.

3. *Hydrogen Peroxide:* The three percent solution can be used straight out of the bottle (you can buy this at a drugstore).

4. *Vinegar:* Use only white vinegar (cider or wine vinegar might spot light fabrics). One part white vinegar to four parts water.

HELOISE'S GUIDE FOR STAIN REMOVAL

ALCOHOL: Rinse hurriedly in a cold water and vinegar solution. If the alcohol is spilled on the carpet, sponge up the alcohol spot quickly with a water and vinegar solution and then dry with paper towels. If the color has "bled," the damage can't be undone.

ANTIPERSPIRANT: Blot the spot with a paper towel moistened with a solution of vinegar or baking soda. Soaking may be required. Wash in the hottest water safe for fabric.

BALL-POINT INK: Hair spray works well on most inks. Spray and blot the stain with a clean cloth.

Fingernail polish remover (if safe for fabric) and prewash sprays will work on some ink stains.

BEVERAGES, FRUIT
JUICES, COCKTAILS: Do not use soap. Remove spot with liquid detergent or hydrogen peroxide bleach.

BLOOD: Flush with cold water first and use a liquid detergent next. Dampen and sprinkle unflavored meat tenderizer and let sit. Hydrogen peroxide is another very good home remedy if fabric can take light bleaching. Just pour on and let bubble away, then rinse out in cold water.

CANDLE WAX: Flick off as much of the hard wax as possible with your fingernail or a plastic credit card. Place paper towels on either side of the material where the wax stain is and iron on a low to medium setting, depending on the fabric. If any stain remains, go over it with liquid detergent and water, and then rinse or wash as usual.

CANDY: Rub a little detergent on the stain with cold water and rinse; for stubborn red stains, soak the item in strong laundry detergent and a little bleach (if material will take it), or treat with prewash spray.

CATSUP:

Blot up as much as possible. Rinse or soak in cold water. Spray with prewash product. Liquid detergent works sometimes.

CHEWING GUM:

Place an ice cube on the gum to harden it. Then scrape it off with a spoon. Go over the back of the stain with a prewash spray and wash as usual. You can also put the garment in the freezer to harden the gum and then scrape it off.

CHOCOLATE:

Always use cold water. Use a prewash spray, ammonia, or sometimes hydrogen peroxide. Work into fabric and let set. Rinse out in cold water.

COFFEE:

First rinse in cold water, then bleach if safe for the fabric, or use nonchlorine bleach (powdered). This is an exception to the "don't use hot water" rule: After spot treating wash in the hottest water safe for the fabric.

COSMETICS:

Grab that bar of soap and wet the stain a little and rub-a-dub-dub! If the stain remains, use straight liquid detergent, work into the spot and launder as usual.

CRAYON:

See "Candle Wax." Use same method.

FRUIT:

The sooner you get to the fruit stain the better. Flood the stain with cold water and then treat with a prewash spray. If the stain has dried, soak it in cool water. Then work some detergent in the stain and rinse. Use a color-safe bleach when laundering.

GRASS:

If material is bleach-safe, use bleach according to bottle directions. If not, use hydrogen peroxide to soak in, then launder as usual.

GREASE: Treat with commercial degreaser product. Or place the stain face down on paper towels and go over the back with dry cleaning solvent, working from the outside in. Always use a clean white cloth. Then, dampen the stain with water and go over it with a bar of soap or liquid detergent. Hair shampoo will break down some types of grease.

LIPSTICK: Treat with prewash spray and rub the spot with a clean paper towel. Keep applying the spray and keep changing the paper towel. Finally, dampen the stain and rub a bar of soap over it. Wash as usual.

MILDEW: Lemon juice and salt, or white vinegar and salt will kill the mildew. Place in sun. Wash as usual. Always wash separately—you don't want to spread that stuff.

MILK: Soak in warm water using an enzyme presoak product.

MUSTARD: Use peroxide or white vinegar to get it out. Don't use ammonia. Wash as usual.

TEA: See "Coffee."

URINE: (carpet) Absorb as much of the liquid as possible with paper towels. Then go over the area from the outside in with a solution of white vinegar and water. Keep blotting with paper towels until no wetness comes through. If a stain remains, a mild solution of liquid detergent and water should do the trick, being sure to rinse well. You can sprinkle with baking soda or salt to absorb any extra moisture, and it helps deodorize.

If you use salt, be sure and empty the vacuum after picking up.

URINE: (clothing)

Soak the stain in an enzyme presoak product with a little bleach. Wash as usual. Sponging with diluted white vinegar or perborate bleach may help restore the original color. NOTE: Do NOT use ammonia on diapers.

WINE:

I have great luck with pouring club soda on the stain, then rinsing in cool water. If the material is bleach-safe, go to it (natch, according to bottle instructions). Dishwasher detergent does wonders on stubborn stains like wine. Make a paste with a little water and scrub with an old toothbrush. Wash in the hottest water possible for the material after first spot treating.

4

Sewing

Sew! If you think this chapter is going to tell you how to make a suit or whip up some new slip covers for your sofa, I hate to disappoint you, but that's not the kind of information most of you ask Heloise. What this chapter will help you with are some of the problems that we fimble-(no, not nimble-) fingered people face.

I, for one, can fix almost any garment with a few safety pins, some glue or tape, and a lot of luck. I won't guarantee that my kind of mending will last forever, or is really the "proper" way, but it will hold me through most any day, and then some.

The problems you face and feel frustrated about are the problems that we all encounter one time or another. So, don't feel alone when the bobbin runs out and you have just sewn the straightest seam in your life, or the button you sewed on yesterday falls off right in the middle of lunch.

I hope you never know sheer panic such as I did at a dinner party in a very fancy restaurant with a pretty new dress on, when the nylon thread from the hem caught on something and unraveled all the way to the restroom.

That's when what I like to call my "Heloise ingenuity" comes to the rescue. Well, it was either come up with some way to fix it, or start a new style for the messy, raveled look. Tape to the rescue! I popped over to the front desk, explained my plight and the desk clerk gave me an entire roll of tape (bless his sweet soul). It worked beautifully.

I know some people who hem all their blue jeans with silver duct tape. They swear that it holds through washing after washing, and nary a stitch sewn. All power to you if that's what you can live with. Remember, it's you that has to live with it. If tape and safety pins don't bother you, then by all means do your best. The most important consideration is how it looks on the outside . . . if safety pins show through, then I suggest you look at yourself the way others will see you.

If you can't mend a garment back to its original look, and it just can't be worn, don't give up. We all need lounging-around clothes or grubbies to wear while washing the car and potting plants.

Do you know that industrial shops like plumbers, mechanics, etc., pay for a box of rags (at last check it was seventeen dollars here in San Antonio) . . . you just might have a gold mine in your sewing hamper. Put all your scraps, unmendables, etc., to good use. Give them to the grease monkey in your family, or use them to wipe up spills or really greasy messes, and then have no guilt about throwing them away.

Get out that needle and thread and save a shirt today . . . it may turn out to be your favorite. I am still wearing my father's military shirts that are over fifteen years old and my very favorites.

BUTTONS

Cut buttons for doll clothes out of a plastic lid using a paper punch, then poke holes for the thread with a hot needle (only adults should handle a hot needle).

Problem   *Keeping those teensy little buttons in place when making garments for a wee one is so hard.*

Solution   Roll a small piece of regular tape in a circle, sticky side out. Stick the tape onto the back of the button, then position the button on the fabric. It will stay in place while you stitch; then cut away the tape using small, curved cuticle scissors.

*   *   *

P   *I hate having to use several strands of thread when sewing on buttons that get a lot of wear and tear.*

S   Nylon fishing line, or dental floss, is very strong and will hold through most any rough treatment.

*   *   *

Having trouble sewing on a coat or suit button? Slip a round toothpick or tines of a fork between the button and the fabric. Sew the button on over the toothpick or tine. Remove the toothpick (or tine) and wrap the remaining thread around the thread holding the button, forming a post. This creates some "play" in the button and it won't pop off.

*   *   *

To keep matching buttons together, stick them to a strip of cellophane tape. Cover with a second strip of tape. Snip off buttons as needed.

P   *Buttons, buttons, buttons—they're all over my sewing basket.*

S   Use those nifty twisties from bread or plastic bags. Slip them on and you can even color-code.

* * *

A real quick way to keep buttons together is to slip them on a large safety pin and pin it closed.

MACHINE SEWING

Bobbins

P   *I don't have enough bobbins.*

S   In a jam, transfer the thread left on one bobbin onto a three inch piece of plastic straw. Now you have an empty bobbin to use. The straw will fit back on the spindle of my machine to use as the top thread. Why don't you try it on yours?

* * *

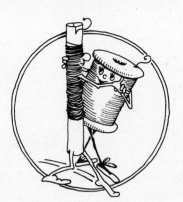

P   *I always run out of bobbin thread right in the middle of a project. It drives me batty.*

S   Fill two or three empty bobbins with the various colors you need . . . no more frustration. Bonus: you can use the thread for hand stitching. A few extra bobbins are worth the investment.

*   *   *

P   *I have the hardest time remembering how to wind my bobbin and put on the zipper foot on my machine. I know it's silly, but . . .*

S   Always keep the instruction booklet nearby. If you have a permanent sewing area, place those pages in easy sight, or tape them to the back of the machine.

You can also tape the threading diagram right on the machine.

Height Adjustment

P   *I'm a shortie and I cannot find a table low enough for my portable sewing machine.*

S   Try using a typing table (used ones can be found very reasonably priced).

To keep down vibration, put a sheet of one-inch foam rubber under the machine. The height of the table, even for a "shortie," should be perfect.

*   *   *

Your sewing machine table makes a wonderful extra display, or serving table when not in use. Just cover with a pretty tablecloth or printed sheet.

Needles

P   *Changing needles in my sewing machine is a major chore. I seem to be all thumbs.*

S   Slip a needle threader into the eye of the sewing machine needle. You can hold the needle steady while inserting it into the correct position, yet your fingers will be back out of the way.

Oiling

P   *I am always having to have my machine cleaned and oiled.*

S   A sewing machine is like any other electric appliance that moves; you should keep it as dust-free as possible. Always cover it when not in use; it will save you money in the long run.

*   *   *

P   *I oil my machine but I got oil on the fabric as soon as I started sewing.*

S   Stitch through a blotter (or paper towels) to catch any excess oil, or stitch through a layer or two of scrap fabric first.

Pedals

P   *The foot control of my sewing machine "wanders" and I'm forever chasing it.*

S   Glue a piece of foam rubber or self-gripping tape on the bottom of the control. It will stay put.

*   *   *

P   *The foot pedal on my machine gets unbelievably dusty and dirty, even though I consider myself a good housekeeper. I know this will cause damage eventually.*

S   Cover the pedal with a plastic bag and place a twistie around it to close it. It will keep it clean and dust-free, and this is important, considering replacement costs. You can use it as long as it doesn't slip around. If it does, place it on a piece of foam rubber.

*   *   *

P	*I have always used a sewing machine with a knee pedal. My new one has a foot pedal, but I prefer my old knee one.*
S	Place the foot pedal at the correct height and tape it to the leg or pedestal, etc., of your sewing machine with masking tape.

Seams

Save yourself time from getting up to go iron each seam one at a time. Sew all small pieces at once, then iron them all at the same time.

Static

P	*I'll be sewing along and suddenly my machine starts acting cantankerously.*
S	Some of the fabrics we sew on today cause a buildup on the needle and machine that you are unable to see. Also, hair spray, grease in the air, etc., cause buildup. Clean the needle, the bottom of the pressure foot, and also the tension discs often with plain old rubbing alcohol and a cotton ball, or cotton swab.

Supplies, machine
(Also see Machine sewing, p. 676)

P	*My sewing machine has no drawers for holding sewing paraphernalia and other drawer space is already at a premium in our house.*
S	Make a small (or as large as desired) shoebag-type holder and hang it over or near your sewing machine. It will keep all those little odds and ends

such as a tape measure, seam ripper, scissors, etc.,
together in one place.

* * *

Hang a calendar towel on the wall behind your sewing machine so
you can see it at a glance.

Besides making an attractive wall hanging, you will have something to pin your guide sheet to when sewing, without damaging the
walls.

* * *

Put a double band of stretch or knit fabric around the neck of the
sewing machine to put the pins in as you sew. They are right there
and always handy.

* * *

P   *How can I mend a loosely knit sweater or fabric
without the pressure foot catching in the loops?*

S   Use the reverse stitch and sew backwards. The
rounded edges on the back of the pressure foot will
glide over the loose weave with nary a snag.

* * *

P   *How can I tell when the tension on my machine
needs adjusting?*

S   Put a dark spool of thread on the top spindle,
white thread on the bobbin; then, stitch on a neutral color material. If the top tension is too loose
or tight, it will easily show up. The same with the
bobbin. Adjust until you have a perfect stitch.

* * *

P   *I am a novice seamstress with a new sewing machine and keep forgetting how to thread it properly.*

S   Cut the thread off at the spool when you want to
rethread with another color, etc., but leave it in all
the stations. Put on the spool with your new color.

        Tie the new color onto the old one with a double

knot and *gently* pull it through all the tension stations, and if the knot is not too large, through the eye of the needle.

You'll be ready to continue sewing in a jiffy.

* * *

P   *I can't thread elastic through a casing easily.*

S   Stitch down the seams that will be inside the casing (before making it, of course); then afterwards, the elastic should glide right through.

* * *

P   *How can I topstitch when my machine has only one spindle to hold the spool of thread? One thickness of thread doesn't seem to do the job.*

S   Try using a piece of heavy plastic drinking straw as a post extender. The more narrow paper straw would probably work best since the holes in a spool of thread sometimes aren't very large.

* * *

P   *I sew a lot and find it difficult to thread my sewing machine needle because the polyester threads fray so badly.*

S   Tape a small piece of soap to the top of your sewing machine. (If you are afraid it might harm the finish, fold a piece of foil or a piece of plastic and place it under the soap).

When ready to thread the needle, dampen the thread and roll it on the soap with your finger.

This seems to seal and stiffen the thread so it will go through the needle easier.

* * *

When threading your sewing machine, put the pressure foot in the down position onto the pressure plate.

This will give your fingers more room to get at that ornery small needle hole with the thread.

If you cannot see well enough to thread your sewing machine needle while it's in the machine, remove it, thread it, then reinsert it in its proper groove.

PATTERNS AND CUTTING

Taking care of a pattern is really worth the effort. If you find a pattern that you like and one that fits, etc., you can use it over and over.

Finding the perfect pattern, or one that you really like may take some time. The hardest part is that you really have to be honest with yourself. When the pattern says thirty-six inches around the hips, if you are thirty-nine or forty, honey child, that isn't gonna cut it. I know we all like to fit into a size smaller, but when you get home, no one knows but you . . . so by all means, be realistic.

If you can't seem to get all those pieces back into that tiny paper envelope, there really is a simple solution. Place the smaller pieces all on top of the larger ones, press lightly with a warm iron and fold to fit.

If you have a lot of patterns to store, roll them up, place each one in a brown paper lunch bag, and cut off the picture and all the outside information (amount of material, accessories needed, etc.) and tape them to the outside. It's all there and easy to locate. You can even make little notes to yourself such as, "like this pattern," or "was easy to sew," or "only needs one zipper."

Take care of those patterns and they will take care of you . . .

*   *   *

P   *Sewing saves so much money, but, oh! how I hate to cut out the garment when I'm really in the mood to just start sewing.*

S   Besides having to cut out the garment, many times you can't find matching thread or may have even misplaced the pattern.

You can solve all these problems by cutting out two or three items at once, then placing each one in a separate box, along with needed sewing notions and instructions.

Then, on the day you are in the mood to sew, you won't take a chance of getting "out of the mood" as everything will be at your fingertips.

*　　*　　*

P　　*How can I cut fabric in a perfectly straight line?*

S　　As you know, the sales people who work in fabric stores use a grooved table to measure and cut. You can do the same thing by pulling an extendable table apart slightly and using the center opening to guide your cutting. Keep fabric taut as you cut.

*　　*　　*

Before cutting a pattern out, be sure to measure yourself (or whomever you are sewing for) and the pattern to be sure you have the same measurements. . . . sometimes a size twelve can be a ten or even a fourteen. . . .

*　　*　　*

P　　*I don't have a cutting table, and I'm unable to get down on the floor to cut fabric.*

S　　Use the dining room (or any long) table extended as far as possible. If you have a protective pad, turn it slick-side down, to protect the table from pins. If you find the dining room table too low, ask for help and set the table on four cans of equal height. Canned goods out of your pantry work fine.

*　　*　　*

P　　*How can I lengthen a pattern without having to cut the piece apart?*

S　　Merely pin down the length of the pattern to the "adjusting line," be it the waist-, hip- or hemline. Place a pin directly across the cutting line at this point so when you come to it you will naturally stop. At this point, unpin your pattern, and slide it down, adding the extra length needed. Repin and continue cutting.

P   *When I use tape for my pattern it always tears the pattern or leaves gunk on the material.*

S   Pink hair tape is perfect and is especially good for materials like leather and Ultrasuede that really shouldn't be pinned.

*   *   *

P   *What can I use if I don't have a tracing wheel?*
S   A pizza cutter works just like a tracing wheel.

Hand Sewing and Mending

Place a small pillow in your lap when doing hand sewing. You won't have to lean over so far to see what you are doing.

It gives you a smooth, soft surface on which to work and is a wonderful backsaver. Especially nice when embroidering.

*   *   *

P   *My eyesight is poor and I can't sew well on dark fabric when doing hand sewing.*

S   Use a white thread, along with a dark one through the needle. The white thread will enable you to see where you have stitched. When you're finished, remove the white thread.

*   *   *

P   *The hem came out of my dress and there was no way to repair it at the moment.*

S   Tape the hem carefully with clean adhesive-backed tape, or even double-sided sticky tape.

*   *   *

P   *When I let a hem down, the crease mark shows.*
S   Dampen the crease with white vinegar. Place a press cloth over the material, then press with a moderately hot iron.

*   *   *

P   *I discovered a hole in my pants pocket at work and didn't have a needle and thread to sew the tear.*

S   Either pull the pocket out, or work from the inside and wrap a rubberband tightly around the hole. It will keep you from losing your belongings until you have time to mend it properly.

*   *   *

Going to the doctor's and have to wait, or have a long-winded friend? This is the time to do that mending. Just take one or two small pieces at a time. My, how the work flies!

Learning to Sew

P   *I want my little girl to learn to sew, but I'm not sure of a good way to begin to teach her.*

S   To start her off, cut up scraps of material you have left and let her make a patchwork quilt for her doll's bed.

She will learn how to put the colors and pieces together and how to sew them.

What's more, she will have the special pleasure of using something which she has made all by herself.

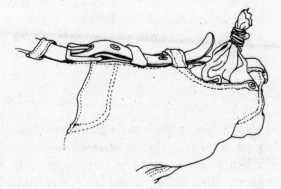

Marking

Use a leftover sliver of soap for marking seams, hems, etc. The mark will disappear after a hot iron hits it. Better than tailor's chalk.

*   *   *

P   *I use a lead pencil to mark darts, etc., but I have a terrible time getting it off.*

S   Don't use a pencil. Use a sliver of soap instead. It will wash right out.

*   *   *

P   *Tracing darts always tear the patterns after a few uses. Now what?*

S   When the pattern is new, make holes in the pattern where the darts should be and stick on little round paper reinforcements like those you use on notebook paper. Each time you mark your pattern, use a piece of chalk through the reinforced holes.

Organizing

P   *I am really messy when I sew and I hate to clean up after myself.*

S   Tape a large grocery or shopping bag to your sewing machine or cutting table and toss those tiny fabric scraps and bits of thread in it. Once you get into the habit, I promise your sewing area will be a mess no more.

Patching

P   *My sons get holes in their jeans even before I can wash them twice (or so it seems).*

S   When patching holes in jeans, especially in the knees, since you are doing it anyway, put a patch on the inside as well as the out. Double protection.

Prevention is the answer, though. Start out by putting patching on the inside. No one will see them and it will save you a lot of work later.

*   *   *

P   *Those iron-on patches don't seem to stay put very long. The edges curl.*

S   If that is the case, it's worth the extra time to just run a line of stitching around the edges.

*   *   *

P   *I hate sewing on patches! And I have three boys in scouting!*

S   First, use a fabric glue to hold the patch in place. Just a dab—then when it dries, stitch the patch on in jig time! No slipping or sliding.

Professional Touches

P   *I get so tired of the same old look. Seems as if you can spot my homemade clothes a mile away.*

S   Check mail order catalogs and fashion magazines to keep up with the latest looks and colors. You'll get lots of ideas from them. Sometimes adding an extra pocket here, a little trim there, will jazz up your clothes.

SCISSORS

A quick way to "oil" your scissors is to carefully rub them in between your fingers and thumb. There is usually enough natural oil to lubricate the blades without a lot of drip or fear of too much oil on your scissors.

Be sure to give your scissors a good cleaning and oiling every once in a while, as they will get a slight buildup of threads and grime from the material you cut. (Always wipe well and cut some scraps first before using to be sure no oil is left).

* * *

P　*My sewing scissors are always missing, and it's not me that moves them from my sewing area.*

S　Little hands do seem to spirit them away, don't they? Tie your scissors to your machine, or sewing table, with a long piece of yarn (if you want it to look pretty), or twine, etc. They won't go very far.

* * *

P　*I hate running back and forth to snip little threads when I am pressing things. And sometimes I don't get around to doing it later.*

S　Attach an extra pair of small scissors to the end of your ironing board with enough slack so you can use them. (Caution: if you have little ones around, be sure they don't think this is a play toy).

* * *

P　*Any way to quickly sharpen my scissors?*

S　For everyday scissors, cutting sandpaper or a steel wool pad helps sharpen them enough. If you have special sewing scissors that you paid a few bucks for, take them to a professional.

* * *

P　*I always stab myself reaching into my sewing basket to locate my scissors.*

S　Stick the pointed end of your scissors into a piece of cork, and no more worries.

SEWING POINTERS AND SUPPLIES
(Also see Organizing Your Sewing Box, p. 185)

Basting

P   *I could cry when the gathering is nearly perfect— and nearly finished—then the basting stitch breaks.*

S   Never trust just one row of basting stitch. Take the extra time to stitch three gathering rows about three-eighths inch apart, leaving long strands on each end to work with. If one thread breaks, you will still have two to hold on to. Always pull the bobbin threads from each end, working toward the center.

Bedspreads

P   *I want to make a ruffled bedspread for my little girl's bed, but panic at the thought of keeping all those gathers intact until I can stitch them in place.*

S   "Steal" a spool of monofilament fishing line from your husband's tackle box. Lay the fishing line (don't cut it off the spool) on the ruffle just above the seam line. Zigzag *over* the line, but don't catch the fishing line in the stitching. Continue all around the ruffle.

When finished, the line will slide easily through the material. If you knot the line first, you can gather it up some as you go, if you like. Stitch the ruffle onto the spread, being careful not to catch the fishing line. Pull it through and re-wind.

Belts

P   *I can't make belt loops that look neat.*

S   The easiest way I've found is to use about six strands of sewing thread, six inches long. Slide the strands under the pressure foot and use a zigzag stitch catching all six strands. Neatest and quickest belt loop you ever saw!

*   *   *

P   *Turning belts, straps and suspenders of new garments is such a struggle.*

S   After sewing your belt inside out, attach a safety pin of appropriate size to the closed end of the belt and just push it through (large end first) to turn it right side out. The pin glides easily through the material and you can feel where it is as you work it along. No chance of losing it.

Collars

P   *I can't get collar points to look tailor-made*

S   After trimming the collar seam close to the points, turn the collar right side out. Thread a needle and tie a rather large knot in the end. Insert the needle through the stitches at the collar point and pull it through. Cut the thread off close to the fabric and you have a "professional" pointed collar.

Equipment

P   *I'm told using the proper tools helps to give home sewing a more professional look, but after pricing hams, sleeve rolls, etc., my budget says, "wait awhile."*

S   No need to . . . make your own! A roll of toilet tissue covered with foil, then with terry cloth or any fabric which will withstand the heat of an iron, makes an excellent pressing ham. Or, use an old wig form as a pressing ham, covering it per above. Great!

A half-used roll of paper towels, covered as suggested above, can be used as a sleeve roll, and a small pressing board to fit inside a pants leg, or whatever, can be made from an empty cardboard tube that fabric stores use to roll bolts of material.

Pick one up the next time you're buying fabric. (Or just go in and ask for one. Most stores just throw them away.) Pad it somewhat, then cover it with any desired fabric. This board can even be used as a seam board for pressing straight seams. Just stand it on its side.

This equipment is so handy and lightweight, you can keep it right at your sewing machine.

And, you surely can't beat the price!

*　　*　　*

Use a magnet to pick up spilled pins and needles off the floor.

*　　*　　*

P　　*My seam ripper is always missing.*

S　　Glue a small magnet to your sewing machine head. The metal part of the seam ripper will quickly adhere and hang on. Just remember to always put it there after each use.

Fabrics, difficult

P　　*Single knit T-shirt material always curls on the edges.*

S　　Lightly spray starch the cut edges and let dry. You will give it just enough stiffness to make it easier to work with.

*　　*　　*

Sewing velvet and need to press some pieces? Place them right side down on top of a heavy terry or turkish towel, and press gently.

*   *   *

P   *I sew a lot of heavy fabric and the needle sticks.*

S   Lightly rub a bar of soap across the seam line and it will help the needle go in easily.

*   *   *

P   *When I sew the new sheer fabrics, the seams always pucker.*

S   Try using strips of tissue paper under each seam as you stitch. It will help keep the fabric in place, thus causing less pulling and tugging, and it tears right off.

Fasteners (hooks, etc.)

P   *I can't match up snaps when sewing them on a garment.*

S   Sew the small part of the snap on first. Rub a piece of chalk over the little point, then carefully place the top piece of fabric over the snap in the proper position and rub the back with your finger. The chalk will mark the spot for the top part of the snap.

*   *   *

P   *The eye part of my hook & eye came off and I couldn't get to a sewing box.*

S   A small safety pin on the wrong side of the fabric works as an eye in a pinch.

Fitting

P   *I would love to sew for my grandchildren but I don't live close to them so fitting is a problem.*

S   Ask their mother to draw the outline of the child on a piece of butcher paper, or something similar. Include waist measurement, height, arm length, etc., on the drawing. Fitting will then be a cinch. They will enjoy doing it, too. What a wonderful record of growth later on.

Leftover Fabrics

Cutting off a pair of jeans? Save the legs to make a "ditty" bag for a catchall for the kids, or a clothespin bag.

Organizing Your Sewing Box
(Also see Sewing Pointers and Supplies, p. 689)

P   *My sewing box looks as if a tornado hit it . . . always*

S   A small metal or plastic tool box is good. Also, the small plastic boxes with lots of little drawers in it can store many different items, and you can see what is in each drawer.

*   *   *

P   *I always stick myself on loose needles in my sewing box.*

S   Drop them in a clear plastic pill bottle and snap on the top. Tape an adhesive bandage on the out-

side and just slide your threaded needle through the padded part of the bandage after using, like a little pin cushion. Wrap the extra thread around the bottle.

*   *   *

P   *Spools of thread in my sewing box become un-wound and the ends get so tangled I have to cut them to get the spools apart.*

S   Once you get them apart, tape the ends of the thread to the spool with a smidgen of clear adhesive tape. The thread won't come unwound, and it's a simple matter to remove the tape when the thread is to be used. Save the tape and reuse it later on the same spool.

This is a good rainy day project for the kids. They love it!

Another idea which works well is to put the spools of thread of like colors in a clear plastic bag. Close the bag with a twistie, then place them in a drawer of your box. The colors can be easily seen for quick selection and the tangling problem is solved.

*   *   *

An empty adhesive tape spool makes a handy holder for a tape measure.

*   *   *

P   *My knitting needles get scattered to the four winds.*

S   Save an aluminum foil box to store those needles in.

Retrieving Needles

Before discarding a pin cushion, cut the covering with your scissors.

Hold it over a pan or pie plate, etc., and carefully check the sawdust inside for pins and needles. Amazing, sometimes, how many are buried inside.

* * *

Put a pin cushion in the guest bedroom, along with several needles threaded in different colors of thread. Stick a few safety pins of assorted sizes in the pin cushion, also.

Your guests can sew on a button, etc., without asking you for assistance and will appreciate your thoughtfulness, even if the items are not needed.

Rickrack

P   *For the life of me I can't sew narrow rickrack in a straight line.*

S   First tape it in place with transparent tape. Stitch right through the tape, then the tape is easily pulled off afterwards.

Sleeves

P   *Putting in sleeves frustrates me!*

S   One of the simplest ways I know to put in a sleeve is to stitch it in before sewing up the side seams. It's easier to ease in the fullness and then the entire side seam can be sewn in at one time.

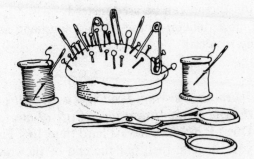

Zippers

P   *When I put a zipper in a garment, it puckers after laundering.*

S   This is due to the zipper shrinking. Zippers, as well as seam tape, hem tape, lace, etc.,—even the fabric, if it is washable—should be preshrunk before sewing into a garment. Nonwashable fabric, such as woolens, should be professionally blocked.

*   *   *

P   *My zipper always sticks and I have a heck of a time getting it up.*

S   Use a lead pencil. The graphite in the lead helps, but don't use too much and get it on your garment.

THREAD HANDLING AND STORING

P   *I can never find the color of thread I want without digging through the maze of thread stored in a drawer.*

S   Drive headless nails at an angle into a peg board, or the right size board for you. Hang the board over your sewing machine and you will be able to select the color needed quickly and easily, without having to hunt and seek.

*   *   *

As I never seem to have the right color thread when I need it, I find that clear nylon thread can be used instead.

It's a little more difficult to use when doing hand sewing, but it will match any material.

*   *   *

P   *When hand sewing, I can't get a nice little knot in the end of the thread for the life of me.*

S   Don't fret, 'cuz I have a hard time, too. First, wet your fingers, then put the end of the thread between your forefinger and thumb, then wrap the thread around your forefinger once, and kinda roll the thread to the end of your fingers so that it catches on itself, and slowly pull to form a knot. Got that? If all else fails, sew a few stitches and tie a knot then.

* * *

P   *My thread always curls up when I am hand sewing.*

S   Starting at the needle end, run your fingers all the way down the thread to the knot to untwist it and you can also slowly draw the thread between a warm iron and the ironing board to untwist it.

* * *

P   *The thread always frays and I never can get it through the eye of the needle easily.*

S   A squirt of spray starch or hair spray to the rescue! Press it between your fingers, let dry and it will go right through.

* * *

When using polyester thread for sewing by hand, it's prone to snarl and twist in a most aggravating way.

To overcome this, get into the habit of giving your needle a counterclockwise quarter turn each time you pull the thread through the material.

* * *

P   *Static electricity causes polyester thread to knot so badly it makes hand sewing difficult.*

S   Rub a fabric softener sheet or a candle over the entire length of thread in your needle. You'll have no more tangles.

* * *

P   *You wouldn't believe how tangled embroidery thread becomes when I work with it!*

S   Use one of those sponge hair rollers. Just wrap the thread around the curler, then close the fastener.

*   *   *

To hold a lot of spools of thread, use a plastic foam wig stand.

Insert sturdy toothpicks about one inch apart—all over the "head"—then put a spool on each one. A matching bobbin can also be placed on the toothpick.

Looks very colorful placed in your sewing room with the different shades of each color grouped together. Easy to grab the one you want.

SUBSTITUTIONS

A dollar bill is one eighth of an inch more than six inches. Knowing this can be handy if there is nothing else to measure with.

*   *   *

An old, clean lipstick case makes a super portable sewing kit. It holds needles and safety pins. Great to tuck in your purse or travel kit.

*   *   *

P *I don't sew often and hate to buy a pin cushion.*
S Use a big sponge. An old cloth-type powder puff
   works well and smells nice, too.

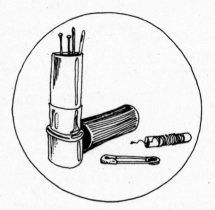

5

Odds and Ends

Sometimes it's hard to put things in the right place, so this is the answer to all of those "where does this go?" questions.

This chapter will help you with problems from carpets and candles to closets. You'll find answers to insect troubles, furniture and painting questions and storage dilemmas.

Carpet care is something I'm constantly asked about—particularly the removing of spots and stains. I want to stress that if you have a major problem with your carpet, by all means call a professional. It's worth the money to have the problem taken care of by an expert if you aren't sure what to do. Beyond that, home carpet care has a few basic rules. You should vacuum often, clean up spots and stains as soon as possible and give your rugs a complete cleaning at least every eighteen months.

If an entire carpet doesn't need cleaning, you can have just the traffic pattern cleaned at much less cost.

Other sections in this chapter will give you some good tips on caring for candles and what to do if you have a problem with candle wax. Closets are a world of their own, and the problems with them are very easy to solve.

So if you have a problem that you can't find the solution to anywhere else, look through these odds and ends.

CANDLES

Candles are so romantic, aren't they! I just love to eat dinner by candlelight, and they make such a nice touch when decorating.

One of my favorite hints about candles is an idea that is super. If you have a fireplace, you know how dull they look in the summertime when you are not using them. Candles to the rescue. Fill your empty fireplace with a few candles, light them at night, and you can enjoy a warm glow all summer.

*   *   *

Never go off and leave candles burning. Even if they are in votive holders they can be a hazard.

*   *   *

Problem *I have so many bits and pieces of candles left over —I hate to throw them away.*

Solution Use a coffee can and carefully melt all of your little scraps together, add a wick, and you can make your own "leftover" candle.

*   *   *

P *My candelabra holds ten candles, and they always sell them by the dozen.*

S Always buy the same color, or wait until you have ten different colors and have a rainbow of colors.

*   *   *

Putting a candle in front of a mirror will reflect the light more.

P   *Lighting candles is a chore—I always burn my fingers*

S   Use a piece of spaghetti to light your candles. It's very long and you can get down into the holders when the candle has burned down.

*   *   *

P   *I always scorch my hand when lighting candles on a birthday cake.*

S   Remember to start from the inside first, or work from the top of the cake down. Use a long fireplace match.

*   *   *

Always burn your candles a few seconds, blow out and then trim the wicks before your dinner party. Then they will all burn evenly and light easily.

*   *   *

P   *My candles just don't burn very long and they drip, drip, drip.*

S   If you will keep your candles in the freezer, they will burn longer and hardly drip at all. Don't ask me why, but it sure works at my house!

*   *   *

P   *My 12-inch candle broke right before my company arrived.*

S   Hold it under hot running water to soften the wax, then press together with your fingers.

*   *   *

P   *My candles never stand upright.*

S   You can wrap tape around the bottom to get a snug fit, or put some clay in the holder and press the candle down.

*   *   *

P   *How can I remove candle wax from my candle holder?*

S   If the holder can stand hot water, just soak it in the sink and most of the wax will rub right off. Never scrape at the wax if your holder scratches easily.

*   *   *

Make your own candle holder. Use a drinking glass or jelly jar, fill it with salt or sand and put your candle down in this. Safe and also attractive!

*   *   *

P   *I hate blowing candles out—I usually get wax everywhere.*

S   Why not cup your hand behind the flame while you blow? This keeps the wax from splattering.

*   *   *

P   *I use candles for decoration—how can I clean them to keep them looking fresh?*

S   Use a soft cloth dampened with rubbing alcohol.

CARPET
(Also see Carpet, cleaning and maintaining, p. 620) and Scraps, p. 707

When you put carpeting in your home, there are a few questions you have to ask yourself before you start looking:

1. How much do I want to spend?

2. How much traffic wear and tear will the carpeting have to stand?

3. Do I want this to last twenty years, or just a few years?

4. How much time will I have to spend taking care of it?

When you answer these questions you will then have a good idea of what to buy.

If you have children and your carpet is going to get a lot of wear and tear, people running in and out all day long, then you need something that will hold up well. If it's for an area that doesn't get much traffic, you can buy something that isn't as sturdy.

Be honest with yourself about how long you want to keep it. I don't know about you, but after five or so years, I am ready for a change. If you pay twenty dollars a yard, you are not going to want to pull it out in just a few years. I personally would rather buy less expensive carpet and replace it more often than live for twenty years with expensive carpet that I'm tired of.

The padding underneath will make cheap carpets feel like the good stuff. Put more money into thick padding, and when you walk on it, it will feel like the thick carpet.

If you are going to vacuum every day (which you should) then you can put down short, cut pile. But if you know that you aren't going to pull out the vacuum except on Saturday, then don't get a carpet that will show dirt, foot marks, and all the things that end up on the floor.

Cleaning
(Also see Stain removal, urine, p. 671 and Carpeting for the bath area, p 620)

P   *I have deep shag carpeting and find it difficult to care for.*

S   Pick up litter and crumbs before they have a chance to settle deep into the rug. There are special rakes to keep the pile upright. Be careful when using rug shampoo machines. Rotating brushes tangle and untwist individual yarns.

*   *   *

Put a plastic bag under furniture legs after shampooing to prevent rust marks on the carpet.

*   *   *

P   *I want to shampoo my carpet but it will be impossible not to walk on it until dry.*

S   It won't hurt to walk on it if you put down brown paper bags over the traffic area.

*   *   *

P   *Dirt and animal hair seem to cling to my carpet near the baseboards and is difficult to vacuum.*

S   Dampen a sponge and wipe the carpet, or buy an extra toilet bowl brush just for brushing up next to the baseboards.

*   *   *

P   *Candle wax dripped on my new carpet.*
S   Scrape off as much of the wax as you can with a dull knife. Cover the remaining wax with paper towels or napkins. With your iron on synthetic setting, place the iron over the napkins. As soon as the napkin shows wax, replace the napkins and "iron" again. Repeat until all the wax is removed.

P   *Is vacuuming really all that important?*
S   You bet your carpet! The more often you vacuum, the longer your carpet will last.

You should do it every day lightly to remove dirt, etc., and then *really* good once a week. If you don't, the longer the dirt and debris sits on the carpet, the deeper it gets ground in and the harder to remove.

Don't just run over it quickly, either. When you are vacuuming for real, go over the area slowly and crisscross to be sure you give the vacuum a chance to really get all the dirt up.

Drying
(Also see Drying clothes, p. 643)

P   *Any way to dry a damp spot quickly?*
S   After you have blotted up as much moisture as possible with paper towels, you can use your hand-held hair dryer to dry the area.

*   *   *

P   *Our carpeting got soaked when the window was left open and it rained.*
S   If it is a large area, and it really soaked through, you should call a professional to come out and extract the water. If the carpet is just surface-wet, you can dry it out yourself; but if it got down into the padding, you must pull up the carpet and let that dry out. If you don't, Mildew City.

Indentations

P   *I moved some furniture and now I have identations in the carpet that I can't get rid of?*
S   Moisture from a steam iron and brushing the nap of the carpet will get your carpet to straighten up.

Of course, you don't want to place the steam iron directly on the carpet—just hold it above to let the steam get on the carpet, and then brush the carpet with your hand or an old hairbrush.

*　　*　　*

P　　*I can't get rid of deep pile indentations in my deep shag carpet.*

S　　Take a hairpin to pry up the matted areas. Put the hairpin through the loop and pull gently.

Petproofing
(Also see Stain Removal, urine, p. 671–672 and Insect Problems, p. 209)

P　　*How can I get rid of fleas in my carpet?*

S　　Since fleas that result from developing larvae can live several weeks without food, you have to be sure you get to the source of the problem—namely, the eggs.

Carpets, rugs, upholstered furniture and the pet's bed have to be thoroughly vacuumed. Then apply an insecticide. Be sure the product doesn't stain before you spray or sprinkle your carpets and upholstered furniture. You must reapply in a few days.

*　　*　　*

P　　*How can I get pet urine stains out of my carpet?*

S　　The only way to avoid a color change or dye loss in your carpet is to act quickly. The first thing to do is grab some paper napkins or paper towels and blot up as much of the urine as possible. Throw down a handful at a time. Keep removing the paper towels and adding more until you see no more moisture. By stepping on the paper covering the wet area, your weight will help the absorption of the urine into the paper.

Next, take one teaspoon of nonalkaline detergent (such as used for laundering fine washables) and mix it with one-half pint of lukewarm water. Blot, don't rub or brush, this mixture into the stain. Work from the outside edge to the center of the stain. Put a little solution on the stain and blot, then rinse with tap water.

A mixture of one-third cup white vinegar and two-thirds cup lukewarm water will help deodorize. Repeat the blotting process. Remember, keep blotting until there is no more moisture on the towel or napkin. After getting up all you can, sprinkle salt or baking soda on the spot to help absorb whatever moisture is left and to deodorize. Finally, put down a half-inch layer of paper towels or napkins and weight them down with a heavy book and allow about six hours for it to dry.

Repairing

P   *Cigarette burns in carpet!!!*
S   Trim the burned yarns off with scissors. Get some "fuzz" from around the baseboards or clip a few yarns here and there in inconspicuous places. Place some household glue into the hole and glue the yarns in the hole. Place paper towels over, weight down with books and leave for twenty-four hours.

*   *   *

For a surface scorch from a cigarette on your carpet, rub a silver dollar or a fifty-cent piece on the scorch. The burned part should flick right off.

Scraps

There are a whole slew of things you can do with carpet scraps and what a way to save money! You can pick a handful up at your carpet dealer for very little. Watch for sales for carpet remnants, too—it's an ideal way to really get your money's worth. Below are just a few ideas for you.

1. To soundproof and deaden noise in some rooms, install carpet scraps on the ceiling, and walls, if you can.

2. Cut down on noise in the kitchen area or where there is no carpeting on the floor. Glue carpet scraps on bottoms of tables and chairs to absorb noise.

3. Great to put under sewing machines and typewriters to keep them from scooting around and to absorb noise.

4. Wonderful for lining windowsills, etc., where you put your plants to sun. No drips or rust spots.

* * *

P   *I was told not to use leftover carpet scraps as throw rugs in the heavily traveled areas.*

S   Yep, that's true. Feel the back of a piece of carpet and you'll notice it is somewhat abrasive. Anything abrasive on top of your new carpet will cause premature wear. If you want to use the leftover pieces, glue some sheeting on the backing first.

Static Electricity

P   *I am plagued by static electricity from our carpet.*
S   Sometimes putting a little moisture in the room
        such as filling a vase with water or using a vapo-
        rizer will solve the problem.
            Or, spray a little antistatic spray on the soles of
        your shoes (never directly on the carpet).

CLOSETS

Do you hate to clean out a closet? Do you have a hard time finding
what you want in your closet? Do you dread opening the door for
fear of what's there?

This section will help you arrange, rearrange, clean, and fix your
closet!

Before going any further, I want to give you Heloise's never-fail
method for getting a closet in tip-top shape.

You have to be dedicated and ready to really clean your closet out.
Not just going through to see what you don't want, but attacking full
force.

Start at one end and work your way through each piece of clothing. If there is the slightest question, take it out and throw it on the
bed. Ask yourself honestly: "Have I worn it in a year?" "Does it still
fit?" And this is real honesty!—"Is there really any hope?"

Now that you have a pile of clothes and shoes on the bed, go
through them again. If you put something back, remember it the next
time you clean out. If it turns up twice, it should be a candidate for
the out box.

It will make it easier to "get rid of" if you know that whatever you
don't keep is going to a charity, or church, etc.

Doors

P   *I have noisy sliding closet doors.*
S   Buy some rubber buttons (the kind made to go
        underneath toilet seats or on each side of a shower
        door). Tap them into the door jamb at each side

of your door frames to prevent the doors from banging.

* * *

Make sure closet doors can be opened from the INSIDE to prevent small children from becoming panicky or perhaps suffocating. Also see p. 339

* * *

Be sure to keep closet doors shut most of the time, especially on walk-ins. It's like heating or cooling an extra room.

Linen Closet

When putting your fresh linens away, always rotate them. Put the newly washed towels and sheets on the bottom and then always work from the top. You should rotate clothes, too. Be sure and inform your family of the system.

Don't be like the man who read the hint and started taking his shirts off the bottom of the stack without saying anything to his wife. She was putting the fresh ones on the bottom of the stack, not saying anything to him. He couldn't understand why it seemed like he was always wearing the same two or three shirts.

* * *

If you have closet space, or an extra shelf in your bedroom, put the sheets you use on that bed in there. Saves you a few steps going back and forth.

* * *

Linen cabinet too cramped? Fold your towels in half and then roll them—they will take up less space.

* * *

P   *I love satin sheets—my husband hates them.*
S   Use the satin bottom with a cotton top that matches the pattern, or a cotton bottom and satin top.

Mix and match sheets for something a little different. A brown solid with a brown and white stripe.

Odor

P   *My closets are always damp.*
S   A temporary solution would be to use your vacuum cleaner to put in warm, dry air, or a room dehumidifier would help. (Leave a small light on.)

*   *   *

P   *My closets are musty.*
S   Be sure they are well ventilated. Open closet doors a few hours each day or night and let them air out. Never put dirty clothes back in the closet.

*   *   *

P   *Frankly, my closets just smell.*
S   Be sure you follow the above advice. To keep a "sweet smelling" closet, I sprinkle baking soda on the floor and in shoes; I make my own deodorizer by using a small jar—punch holes in the lid and drop in a few cotton balls with oil of wintergreen (or your favorite fragrance.).

*   *   *

P   *When I store my clothes away in a bag, even though they are clean they still smell musty when I take them out.*
S   Slip a used fabric softener sheet or the wrapper from your bar of soap in the bag.

Organizing

P   *I can never find anything in my closet.*
S   Arrange your closet by putting all blouses together, pants, skirts, etc. Then hang them by color

within each category. If you want to, you can mark the section to make it easier. Group all shoes together by color, too. If you want a blue blouse and a pair of pants, you know just where to find them.

*   *   *

P   *I have to share a closet with a roommate.*
S   Divide the closet evenly and either put up a marker in the middle, or, to add a little decoration, paint each half a different color.

*   *   *

Make your closet do double-duty. To make more space in a crowded closet, put two poles on one side. Hang skirts and blouses on the higher one and shirts and trousers on the lower one.

*   *   *

P   *My kids can't reach the clothes rod in their closets.*
S   Attach a piece of wire or strong cord to each end of the pole, forming a loop in the part hanging down. Run a second rod through the loops.

Bookcases can easily be made by removing sliding closet doors and adding shelves if you are converting an unused bedroom into a den.

* * *

If you have clothes that hang in the closet and don't get worn much, it is a good idea to vacuum them once in a while to get rid of dust, etc. If you can, always store them in light plastic cleaner bags to keep the dust off. Don't ever put real leather or leather-type garments in plastic; they must breathe to stay healthy. Same goes for furs.

Poles

P   *My hangers won't slide on the wooden poles in the closet.*

S   Rub furniture polish on the poles or place shower curtain rod plastic covers over them.

FURNITURE

Arranging
(Also see Floors, p. 588)

Need to balance a piece of furniture? Use a garden hose washer instead of a piece of paper—works better and won't show.

* * *

P   *I'm having a hard time deciding how to arrange my furniture—and it's hard work moving it around.*

S   Make a scale drawing of your room. Cut out pieces of paper for your furniture to scale, and move the furniture around on the paper until you decide how you like it best. No backache for you!

* * *

P   *How can I move heavy furniture without scratching the floor?*

S   Put flattened-out milk cartons, magazines or pot holders under the legs, and just slide.

*   *   *

P   *Our sectional sofa is always sliding.*
S   Cut small pieces of foam rubber or sponges to fit under the legs of the furniture.

Dusting and Polishing

A baby's brush or a thin paint brush are super for dusting ornately carved furniture or bric-a-brac shelves.

*   *   *

P   *Furniture polish costs so much—surely you have a goodie!*
S   How's this! Mix one-third cup each of boiled linseed oil, turpentine and vinegar. Don't try to boil your own linseed oil—you can buy it at a paint or hardware store. Mix the ingredients together and shake well before using. Pour on a soft cloth to apply and wipe completely dry with another clean, soft cloth.

*   *   *

P   *I love lemon oil polish but I always seem to get blobs on my rag—and that means too much oil on my furniture.*

S   Fill an empty window cleaner bottle with lemon oil. Spray the polish on the dust rag—no more blobs!

Repairing

P   *My child stuck some adhesive-backed pictures on my furniture.*

S   Rub vegetable oil or mayonnaise on the stuck paper, leave it awhile, and it should come right off without damaging the furniture.

*   *   *

P   *I'm just sick—I now have a cigarette burn on my table.*

S   Dip a cotton swab in clear fingernail polish *remover* and rub over the burn very carefully. If the burn remains, scrape the burn gently with a dull knife until the discoloration is removed. Fill the depression that is left with clear fingernail *polish*. Apply a thin layer, let it dry, apply another layer, let it dry, and so on until the hole is filled up. Then cover with regular furniture polish.

*   *   *

P   *I want to repair some holes in unpainted wood furniture with patch plaster but can't match the light brown shade of the wood.*

S   Mix instant coffee into a little plaster until you get the right shade.

*   *   *

P   *I have some leather-topped furniture and someone spilled alcohol on it.*

S   Alcohol will bleach the leather white, so get some saddle soap and clean the entire top of the table. After it is thoroughly dry, apply a scuff-type liquid polish to the area (use a color that matches as closely as possible) and don't use too much polish. Test a spot. If it stains the leather too dark, pour the polish on a clean cloth and very lightly coat the entire top of the table to even the color.

*   *   *

P   *I'm just at a loss what to do—I have a scratch on my new dining room table.*

S   Rub the scratch with the meat of a pecan or walnut. Or, take a crayon of the same color of the table (or an eyebrow pencil) and fill in the scratch. But try the pecan meat trick—it really works super!

*   *   *

P   *How can I remove a water stain from my furniture?*

S   If it is a fresh water ring, blot and buff with a soft cloth. Use mayonnaise and cigarette ashes mixed together. Rub it in well; let it stand for a while.

Upholstery

P   *I have dark-colored upholstered furniture that collects lint.*

S   Since constantly vacuuming it isn't much fun, use an old clean nylon stocking or pantyhose to wipe it down. It will pick up the lint.

*   *   *

P   *I need new furniture throws but they are so expensive.*

S   Shop around for a sale on bedspreads. A spread can be used instead of a throw and is usually a lot cheaper (good choice of colors, too!).

Recovering your living room furniture in a luxurious fabric that won't stand the wear and tear of your darling grandkids—why not save the old washable slipcovers. Everyone will be more at ease when they come to visit.

INSECT PROBLEMS
(Also see Petproofing carpet, p. 706)

P   *How can I keep ants off a picnic table?*

S   Fill tin cans with water and set each table leg in a can. On permanent concrete tables, saturate strips of cloth with insect repellent and wrap around each table leg.

*   *   *

P   *Flying insects in my bedroom at night drive me crazy.*

S   Sheer frustration, right? Try this. Keep lights off in your room, but open the door to the bath or another room and turn on the lights there. The bug will fly towards the light in that room and you can close the door and shut the bug out of your room.

*   *   *

To preserve an insect in a jar for a child's observation for a few hours, cover the jar with a nylon stocking held secure by a rubber band. Water can be dripped through the nylon without drowning the creature.

*   *   *

P   *I'm allergic to insect spray.*

S   When there's a stinging critter you'd like to get rid of, use hair spray or spray starch to zap 'em in their tracks. Some deodorant sprays will also do the trick.

P   *How can roach infestation be prevented?*

S   First of all, roaches come inside primarily for food and water. Remove those two sources and half the battle is won. (Don't forget the pet feeding dish.)

The second thing to do—and this positively has to be done well and done often—is to destroy any and all eggs. Roach eggs, or sacs, are brownish in color, about the size of a grain of rice, or larger. Any dark place is a haven for roaches. Thoroughly vacuum areas such as the motor under the refrigerator, under all furniture (turn chairs upside down and look under the seats), pipes under the sink, under the dishwasher, under stove burners, behind the water closet at the back of the toilet, under the washing machine, back of the piano, folds and headings of draperies, behind bookcases, behind dressers, etc. After the eggs have been vacuumed up, get rid of the bag and apply a good roach spray.

*   *   *

P   *Any home remedy for roaches? It costs so much for a professional.*

S   Yep. Here's a favorite that does work, although not as fast as a commercial spray. Place a mixture of boric acid and sugar in cupboards and other places where roaches are. CAUTION: This mixture is poisonous, so be sure children and pets cannot get to it. Also, remember if there's any food, water or garbage left out, the roaches won't be as likely to feed on this poison.

PAINTING

After opening a new can of paint, using a hammer and a large nail, punch five or six holes in the lid retaining groove. Of course, be careful not to slop paint around. When you dip the brush in the paint and then wipe it against the side of the can rim, the paint fills the groove as it always does. But with the holes, it runs right back into the can.

* * *

Write the date, brand and color of paint used under the light switch for a handy reference.

* * *

A skateboard makes a nifty scoot-along seat when painting baseboards.

Paint Splatters

Flattened-out corrugated boxes are good to cover floors with when painting.

* * *

Glue a large plastic-coated paper plate to the bottom of open paint cans to avoid splatters and spills.

* * *

Ever caught in the midst of painting and have to drop everything? Put the roller or brush in a plastic bag; make sure the bag is airtight. Your brush or roller will remain moist for a while.

Keep a small bottle of paint handy for touch-ups (a nail polish bottle and brush is terrific for this).

* * *

P   *How can I keep paint from running down my arm?*
S   Slit a paper plate in the middle and push the brush handle through it.

* * *

Baby oil will remove most paint spots from skin.

* * *

When painting baseboards, use a window blind slat or piece of cardboard to put along the floor edge—no paint on the floor or carpet.

* * *

Painting a bathroom? Wet some newspapers and place over the bottom and sides of the tub—they'll cling, and no paint drips on the tub.

* * *

Wrap hardware in foil before painting. This means metal parts like door knobs, hinges, pulls, etc.

Steps

Paint the lowest step white for safety.

* * *

P   *How can I keep everyone off the steps long enough for me to repaint?*
S   Why not paint every other step, let them dry, and then paint the remaining ones.

STORAGE SPACE
(Also see Storage in the bath area, p. 623)

The secret to solving storage problems is to utilize every nook and cranny to the best advantage. Boxes can be stored under beds, and small items such as children's toys can be combined into an old canister set. Think DOUBLE-DUTY! Used lozenge boxes can be used to store hair pins. Cancelled checks can be stored in the cardboard boxes cheese comes in; packets of salad dressing mixes, soft drink mixes, or even baby's socks can be stored in boutique facial tissue boxes.

It's a lot of trouble, face it, to make a place for everything and keep everything in its place. But once you organize your storage space to the fullest advantage, it's downhill and shady the rest of the way!

*   *   *

Blankets

P   *I have no room at all for storing blankets.*

S   Lay them out flat between your mattress and bedsprings.

Cedar Chests

P   *I need to mothproof some clothing but I don't have a cedar chest.*

S   Line a drawer with heavy-duty foil; wrap the contents securely in heavy-duty foil and then scatter moth crystals or balls throughout the drawer.

*   *   *

P   *The cedar aroma has disappeared from my cedar chest.*

S   Using fine sandpaper, rub *with* the grain lightly to restore the scent. Vacuum to remove the dust. If this doesn't restore the cedar scent, purchase some oil of cedar and wipe the *inside lid* of the chest only. Lay a strip of plastic or foil on top of clothes so the oil will not get on clothes.

*   *   *

Remember, a cedar chest can be dangerous to a small child. Keep it locked or better yet, remove the lock so a small child cannot be trapped inside.

Drawers
(Also see Doors and Drawers, p. 566)

P   *I need more drawer space for my baby's things.*

S   Use see-through closet bags with shelves (the kind made for shoes or sweaters) to store baby's blankets, sheets, sweaters, etc.

Garage
(Also see Garage and auto care, p. 756–760)

P   *We have room in our garage to store lots of boxes, but it's hard to locate the box we need without rummaging through everything.*

S   Use a clipboard and make a note of everything you put in a box. Label the filled box "A," "B," "C," etc. Keep the master list in the house and you can locate the desired item pronto!

Out-of-Season Storage

P   *I have no place to store seldom-worn or out-of-season clothes.*

S   Pack them away in large flat boxes and store them under your bed. Or, use heavy-duty plastic trash can liner bags (make sure they're closed tightly) or store things in empty suitcases.

* * *

Store seasonal items such as heaters or fans in plastic garbage bags. They'll be dust-free and ready to go when you need 'em (they'll last longer, too).

PART TWO:

Outside the House

Introduction

So much more goes on in our lives besides doing the laundry and cleaning the kitchen. Thank heavens!

This second part of the book, "Outside the House," is about those things that come up around our home—and away from it.

Chapter six, "Things that Grow," is about plants, flowers and gardens. Whether you live in a house or in an apartment, you probably have at least one growing green thing (and no, I don't count mildew in the shower!). There are all kinds of technical books around about the do's and don'ts and the how-to's of plant care, so this chapter follows the Heloise school of thought. That means let's do it the easiest and quickest way.

The problems in Chapter six are the simple ones that you and I face every day. A lot of the solutions are homey-type things that a plant "expert" may never have heard of. But I know these things work for me and have worked for my readers for over twenty years. I think you'll find them helpful when it comes to taking care of those delightful companions that don't talk back and don't ask questions!

"Auto Care" (Chapter seven) is another of the very important things we sometimes need help with. We have become such an auto-mobile society and depend so much on our cars that it's a must to keep our cars in tip-top running shape. With the cost of cars today, buying a new one can be almost as big an investment as the down payment on a home used to be.

In the auto care chapter, I'll tell you the little things that you can do for yourself, from how to help your car smell good to how to solve potentially serious problems with some very, very simple solutions.

If you're like me, the very mechanical things are better left to a professional but the easy things like washing, waxing, and making spiffy, you can do all by yourself. To start with a dirty, depressed-looking car, to wash it, clean the inside, polish all the chrome and then be able to stand back and view the finished product feels great!

Car care doesn't have to be difficult. If you start out with the right attitude, you will make things very *easy* for yourself later on. As with cleaning a kitchen, if you do things a little at a time, as they're needed, it's not hard to have a clean car.

"On the Move"—Chapter nine—could be an entire book just about moving and traveling.

Moving can be traumatic when we have established roots and friendships and have invested a good part of our life in one place. But there's a plus side. Moving can be a new start; we get to see new things. As much as I disliked leaving my friends, I always was excited about meeting new ones at the other end. And you know, the friends I "left behind" are still my friends. Distance needn't destroy a friendship.

I learned from many, many moves as a military brat, and a lot of traveling for business that the key to making things easy—or shall we say as painless as possible—is to PLAN. Preparation is essential. Don't wait until the last minute to find out that the movers are only movers and not packers, or that they won't take your grandmother's rocking chair because it's an antique. Call, ask questions, write things down.

Moving and traveling sometimes go hand in hand. For the traveler who leaves home with a suitcase and a plane ticket, the most important rule is still to PLAN. I never go anywhere without writing out my itinerary and checking all reservations ahead of time.

Learning the art of packing is not so hard if you decide first what you are going to take. Lay it all out on the bed, stand back and ask yourself whether you really need all of those clothes. Probably not. Then, pack your suitcase. After it is packed and closed, pick it up and heft it for a moment. How heavy is it? You are probably the one who is going to have to carry it. Can you leave anything else at home?

Traveling, camping, gardening and even moving should be enjoyable experiences. I hope you don't get into problems, but if you do, the chapters in Part Two will help you out!

—Hugs, Heloise

Things that Grow

Things that grow! Let's see: children grow, pets grow, the cost of things keeps growing, and we all grow older, don't we?

Some of the really nice things that grow are green, smell nice and really look pretty. Namely, plants, flowers and that nifty garden of yours.

Flowers bring so much joy, are so simple to arrange and can make a sad or rainy day perk up. Flowers can bring sunshine when there is none, can say, "I'm sorry," "I love you," or "I miss you."

I love flowers because it's the way I say, "Thank you for being so nice." Don't you feel special when you receive some flowers? I know I do.

Next best thing to fresh flowers are indoors plants that make a dreary apartment come alive, or a dull office look a little more comfortable. When you put pretty green plants in an area, it helps make it more comfortable and homey. Remember, too, that you

don't have to go and buy expensive plants. Part of the fun is getting
a little bitty thing for eighty-nine cents and watching it grow into a
big beautiful addition to your house, apartment or room.

FLOWER ARRANGING
(Also see Indoor Plants, p. 745)

Need some greenery for an arrangement in a hurry and none to be
had? Carrot tops are a good substitute. Or, go into your yard and
snip a few branches of leaves from your shrubs.

* * *

Problem	*When I make an arrangement, the side I work from looks great, but the back looks terrible—and I want it to look pretty from all sides.*
Solution	Work in front of a mirror, and you can see what you are doing all the way around.

* * *

P	*I crush the flowers laying them on the sink while making an arrangement.*
S	Use your dish drainer and place it over a sink full of water. The flower stems can stay in water and the blossoms will be held apart.

* * *

P	*I have trouble keeping flowers arranged in a large, wide-mouth flower vase.*
S	Cut a circle of plastic foam to fit into the top of the vase and punch holes for the stems to go through. Or, you could crisscross transparent tape across the top of the vase and just stick the stems through the open squares made by the strips of tape.

* * *

No florist frog? Children's dough compound or a piece of plastic
foam works well.

* * *

Stems too small to fit firmly in the holes of the frog? Cut green drinking straws in short lengths. Insert the stems in the straws and the straws into the frog.

* * *

P   *I like to make arrangements with roses but the blooms never open all at once.*

S   Go ahead and cut your roses in the bud stage. They won't open if you keep them in the refrigerator. Leave the buds in the fridge until you have enough for an arrangement. They should all open at about the same time when you take them out.

* * *

P   *I always end up scarred when I try to arrange roses with thorny stems.*

S   It will help if you will wear gloves, but also using a clothespin or kitchen tongs will keep you away from the thorns.

Dyeing

P   *I know shasta daisies can be dyed, but I don't know how to do it.*

S   Cut the stems at an angle. Mix one-half cup water with one small bottle of food coloring. Stand the

stems in the coloring for several hours to dye the flowers. The solution can be reused. This also works on other flowers.

Maintaining Freshness

P   *Fresh flowers are so lovely, but sometimes so sad when the entire group seems to die at the same time.*

S   Silk flowers are really nice and you don't have to water them. They don't die on you, but they don't smell pretty and you do need to dust them.

Well, you can have your fresh flowers and silk, too. I saw the loveliest arrangement that was part silk flowers and part fresh ones, and it was really difficult to tell which was which.

After asking around, I found out that this was a continual bouquet. They pull out the fresh flowers when they look bad and add new ones when needed. To keep the live flowers watered, they wrapped the stems in a wet tissue and put 'em in a plastic bag held in place by a rubber band and then placed them in the container. You could buy some orchid tubs to put them in. Isn't that a nifty idea!

*   *   *

When you have fresh flowers or a loose arrangement, you should cut the stem off a little each day, and when you do trim them, be sure that you cut at an angle so there is more stem exposed to drink up as much fresh water as possible.

*   *   *

P   *A beautiful arrangement of flowers was delivered and they died the next day.*

S   You should check the water in arrangements immediately. The florist can't send them out with water in them, so the first thing to do is give those beauts a drink of water.

*   *   *

If you receive flowers or a potted plant as a gift and they die the next day or are really in bad shape (natch, you have watered them and not abused them), call the florist who delivered them and tell him. Nine times out of ten he will be more than happy to replace them.

Sometimes there are conditions beyond the florist's control that have caused the flowers to expire before their time, and if this is the case don't hesitate to let him know. If you don't tell him, he will have no way of knowing that something was wrong.

*   *   *

P   *I got some fresh cut flowers that really looked rather droopy . . . Should I have sent them back?*

S   Flowers need a little TLC (Tender Loving Care), too. Remember, they go from the florist cool storage, to the truck or car, and then into your home —and every one of these places has a different temperature. Pop them in the fridge for an hour or so and see if they perk up.

*   *   *

P   *Any way I can salvage a cut arrangement? Some of the flowers look good though a few have had it.*

S   Pick out the flowers that have fallen by the wayside and add some greenery or new flowers—go to your garden and snip a little. They will look lots better!

*   *   *

P   *The stems of most flowers are always too short to arrange in my favorite tall vase.*

S   Put some pretty marbles or colored pebbles in the vase to the point where the stems reach; not only will it help hold the flowers, it is really very attractive.

*   *   *

P   *Does it hurt to leave flowers out all night?*

S   You really should put them someplace cool for the nighttime, even if it means moving them to the floor. Be sure to watch out for pets because some flowers are poisonous.

*   *   *

The ideal temperature for flowers is between 40°F and 50°F. Always place your flowers someplace that is cool. You can put them in the fridge at night to make them last. Remember, florists keep flowers refrigerated, and usually at a temperature somewhere around 40°F. So, pop them in the fridge.

*   *   *

P   *I had a flower arrangement for a dinner party and the stems drooped, making the arrangement look terrible.*

S   If the stems are small enough, insert them in plastic straws. Also, a great way to extend stems.

*   *   *

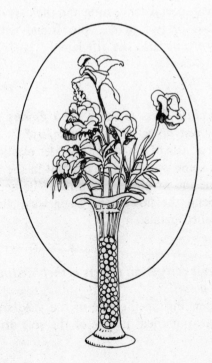

P   *Does it hurt flowers to clean the stems off?*

S   Not in the least; one of my sources even uses a
vegetable brush to lightly brush the stems to clean
them. This helps keep the water clean, too.

*   *   *

P   *My fresh cut flowers don't stay fresh.*

S   Cut flowers last longer if all leaves are removed
from the stem part that is under water.

*   *   *

When you get flowers, snip one-fourth inch off the bottom of the
stem while holding the stem under water; the stem seems to absorb
water faster that way.

Money-savers

P   *I like to take flowers to friends in the hospital but
I can't afford arrangements.*

S   Buy a special coffee mug and then arrange a single
flower or two in it. Your friend will enjoy the
flower and also the gift later.

Transporting

P   *My child loves to carry fresh flowers to school—
how can he get them there safely?*

S   Cut a little of the top off a 2-liter plastic bottle and
put some water in it. Then put in the flowers and
some foil or plastic wrap over the neck.

   Send the flowers on their way, and have no
crushed petals.

*   *   *

P   *I never can get cut flowers to their destination without a spill.*

S   Depending on the size of the vase and arrangement, put them in one of the soft drink cartons

made for 32-ounce bottles, or set them in a cardboard box or grocery paper sack weighted down with an old catalog or magazines.

Water Tips

P   *Do I have to change the water every day in my flower arrangement?*

S   You really should change the water as often as possible, and every day is best.

*   *   *

Don't put fresh flowers on top of the TV to display them. The heat will make the water evaporate very quickly and your flowers will not last long at all.

*   *   *

P   *My mother always told me to add a teaspoon of sugar to the water when I put cut flowers in a vase.*

S   It's an old wives' tale, but who knows! It surely can't hurt. I sometimes add a little soft drink in the

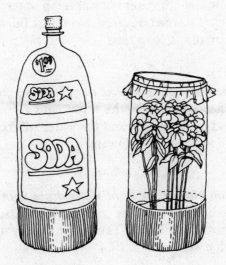

hopes that it's like a shot of glucose . . . seems to help.

*   *   *

P   *I would like to use a clear vase that I have but the water looks yukky.*

S   To keep the water from clouding up, add one tablespoon of bleach to one quart of water. Change often.

*   *   *

P   *I want to change the water in my flower arrangement but it is so large that I just hate taking the whole bunch out of the vase.*

S   Use a turkey baster to remove the old water and add the new without ever disturbing the arrangement.

*   *   *

P   *I add fresh water to my flowers and they still look pretty sad.*

S   When you add or change the water for flowers, use warm water and they will draw it in much faster. Now, not hot water but warm tap water will do the trick. I learned this from my florist Ed, and he has been at it a long time.

*   *   *

P   *The water always looks terrible in my flower vase.*
S   When you change the water, add a few drops of food coloring to it and the water will be as pretty to look at as the flowers!

*   *   *

P   *I am plagued by hard water deposits in vases.*
S   Take heart! Let the vase soak in a solution of vinegar and water. Then wipe clean with a bit of nylon net.

P   *Quite frankly, my flower arrangement stinks.*

S   The stench from the flower stems is the culprit.
Add a few drops of bleach in the water next time.

GARDENING

Gardens! How wonderful if you are lucky enough to have a yard or an area where you can grow big beautiful plants.

Gardening to me really means starting with earth and an idea. If it's flowers and plants, beautiful. Or, even better yet, a vegetable garden! How wonderful to plant those seeds, tend your garden through the weeks or months, and then, like raising a child, see and enjoy the finished product.

With more and more of us trying to save money, one sure-fire way is to have a vegetable garden. In this section on gardens, I have given you some tips that should make it a little easier on you to get that job done.

* * *

An old garbage can with the bottom rotted out is an excellent container to start a compost pile in. Just toss in fruit peels, vegetable scraps and the like, and pop on the lid. When the compost is ready to put on your garden, just pull off the can and start spreading.

Personal Protection

P   *I can't work around the shrubs in my garden without getting stuck with thorns and branches.*

S   Cut the arms off an old heavy sweatshirt and slip them on when you're working around thorns.

* * *

Save soap slivers and drop them into an old nylon stocking. Tie the stocking around an outside faucet for a quick cleanup when you are through gardening.

* * *

P   *My roses "attack" me when I'm trying to cut them or work on my bushes.*

S   Wear long oven mitts and it makes the task less painful.

*   *   *

P   *My fingernails are a mess after gardening.*

S   Run your fingernails along a bar of soap before you start digging in the dirt and they'll be easier to scrub clean.

*   *   *

P   *I absolutely kill my hands carrying dirt and rocks to my garden in my pail.*

S   Use a piece of old garden hose or a small rubber tire and slip the piece around the wire handle. When you carry the bucket it won't cut into your hand.

*   *   *

Pin a hand towel onto your waistband to wipe the sweat off your forehead and out of your eyes while working in the garden on hot days.

*   *   *

P   *How can I beat the heat while working in my garden?*

S   Wet a large handkerchief, wring it out and put it on your head, then put on a wide-brimmed straw hat. Let the handkerchief hang back on your neck almost touching your shoulder. You may look like a sheik, but you stay cool!

*   *   *

P   *My knees kill me when I'm gardening.*

S   If you're a gal, wear an old nylon stocking and stuff the knee area with a sponge. Or, stuff an old hot water bottle with stockings to kneel on.

Pestproofing

Some folks plant marigolds in their vegetable gardens to repel insects.

* * *

P   *Rabbits seem to love my garden and I can't keep them out.*

S   I've heard that planting garlic amidst your vegetables will make them feel "unwelcome" and they'll leave!

Planters

No room for a garden? A wheelbarrow makes a wonderful moveable bed, and hanging baskets can grow certain types of vegetables.

Row Markers

P   *My row markers get blown over or torn up.*

S   Use plastic spoons (write with a waterproof marker)—they're sturdy and last. Better still, make a diagram of your garden and keep it in a notebook. Last month's calendar can be used and the squares are already marked off.

Stakes

P   *My gladiolas grow tall and then fall over.*

S   Straighten a coat hanger and make a loop at one end. Stick the straight end into the ground and let the flower come up through the loop; it will support the flower. If your flower is already kinda tall, don't close the loop until you stick the coat hanger in the ground next to the flower.

GRASS

P *I was trying to sow grass seed in my yard and could not tell if I had covered it evenly.*

S If you mix your grass seed with a little kitchen flour, you can see where you have sown the seed.

*   *   *

P *Mowing my sloped lawn is getting the best of me.*

S Get you some old golf shoes. The spikes will give you traction and they certainly won't hurt the grass. Always mow crosswise and not up and down.

*   *   *

Got a lot of grass to trim along a sidewalk? Sit on a skateboard and roll yourself along.

Grass in Cracks

P *What will kill grass in sidewalk cracks?*

S Plain old table salt will do it. Just pour a generous amount anywhere you don't want grass. (It will kill most other plants, too.)

*   *   *

An old linoleum knife is good for getting out weeds and grasses in borders, cracks and hard-to-get-at places. The hooked blade works great.

Seeds
(planting, starting, watering)

Put your seeds in some soil and water in the cups of a plastic foam egg carton. Place plastic over it and you have a neat little "hot house" to help them sprout.

P   *Any way to get seeds to sprout fast?*
S   Place seeds on a plastic-coated paper plate be-
        tween two wet paper towels and cover with plastic
        wrap. Keep them damp and warm.

*   *   *

For small seedlings use 3-ounce paper bathroom cups with drain
holes punched in the sides and bottom. You can plant cup and all
outside in the garden without having to disturb the roots.

*   *   *

P   *It may sound dumb but I can't remember when to
        plant my seeds.*
S   With all folks have to remember these days, don't
        feel bad! Tape your seed packs to your calendar on
        the appropriate planting dates.

*   *   *

Retain the seed packets and staple or glue them to an index file card
or place in a notebook. Comes in handy next planting time—you can
note whether you liked that variety, how well it did, etc.

*   *   *

P   *I have a horrible time getting tiny seeds sown prop-
        erly.*
S   Punch holes in the soil with an old ballpoint pen
        or chopstick. Then, use a salt or pepper shaker (a
        Parmesan cheese can works well, too) to shake
        small seeds into the holes.

*   *   *

Seeds planted in mid-summer should be planted deeper so they are
protected from the hot sun while they germinate.

*   *   *

P   *Birds won't leave my seeds alone.*
S   Spread nylon net over the soil. Some folks say
        placing artificial snakes along the garden rows
        frightens away birds.

P *I practically kill seedlings trying to water them.*

S Use a sprinkler bottle or an eyedropper. You are using too high a water pressure on the little things.

HOSES AND WATERING

P *I lose my temper every time I hook up the hose because the faucet is right over my flower bed and the hose smashes my plants.*

S Twist a coat hanger into an M-shape and stick it in the flower bed. Then, let the hose lie in the M-groove . . . instead of resting on the plants.

* * *

P *My hose turns into a fighting snake when I try to roll it up.*

S Get an old tire and wind the hose around and around inside the tire. It'll stay put.

* * *

P *How can I repair a leak in a water hose?*

S Pour some melted paraffin on the leak and let it harden. Then, wrap tape around the leak.

P   *I don't have time to water my garden by hand.*
S   Get an old water hose and poke holes all along it.
               Just lay the hose alongside the row and you'll have
               a nice "soaker."

INDOOR PLANTS

Haven't we all gone plant crazy!

It used to be that the only place you saw real live growing plants was at your grandmother's or the flower shop. Now they are everywhere, from your favorite restaurant to the dentist's office. Why, I even saw a few in my neighborhood gas station!

Plants are growing, living things, and I am of the belief that plants can feel and tell good vibes from bad ones. (You may think I am crazy, but there are a lot of people who think like I do.)

Do you think that plants are like animals, that they can tell a good person from bad? I mean, why is it some people have green luscious plants no matter what they do or don't do to them. Then, there are the poor souls who read every book, who pinch, trim, feed, water, repot and pray. Nothing grows, not even weeds. Does that mean that they have bad vibes?

I must have changed, or at least changed my attitude towards plants, because I used to kill everything, and I mean everything. I even killed a cactus once. Do you know how hard that is . . . those buggers live in the desert all alone for years and survive, and I would bring them into my house and bingo . . . el-dead-o!

Now, boy, oh, boy! Do I have a green thumb, maybe not deep green, but green enough. My best luck is with avocados. You say those are very hard to grow? Not so, at least not for me.

As I said just a minute ago, I think what has changed is my attitude. That must be the key. Plants are like horses. If they know you are afraid of them, or afraid of taking care of them, they will prove you right.

I once threatened a plant that was kinda looking frumpy that if it didn't perk up I was going to put it down the garbage disposal.

Do you know that little devil came back to life and sprouted a bunch in the next few weeks. Maybe it was my imagination, but I swear they know.

The key to having healthy plants is to decide exactly how much time and effort you can put into taking care of them. If you know that all you are going to do is water them once a week and maybe feed them once a year, then for heaven's sake, get good, hardy plants which will survive, even if neglected. I like corn plants—they will take all kinds of abuse and still reward you by growing. They are nice to have around, aren't they!

*   *   *

An old swing set will hold lots of hanging baskets.

*   *   *

An old aquarium is a good place to plant an herb garden.

Drainage

P   *The drain holes are so large that when I water my plants I am losing soil each time.*

S   Tear off a small piece of steel wool pad or use some nylon net and stuff it up in those holes; the water will drain but no soil will escape.

*   *   *

P   *I need something to use for a lightweight drainage layer in the bottom of hanging planters.*

S   Use the plastic foam leftover from meat trays (cut up in small pieces) and packing boxes.

Fertilizers

P   *How can I use egg shells to fertilize my plants?*

S   Put your egg shells in a pan or some container with a lid, add water to cover and let sit a day or so. Water your plants with this and they will be strong and pretty.

P	*Any home-style fertilizers?*
S	I have always put my leftover tea and coffee (no cream or sugar, please) diluted with tap water on my plants every now and then and they look super. No, my plants don't stay awake at night from too much caffeine!

Freeze-proofing

P	*During the winter my plants that sit in the window for sun sometimes "catch cold" at night.*
S	Place a piece of large cardboard between the glass and your plants at night to protect them from the cold coming through the window. Remove during the day.

Leaf cleaning

Leaves of plants should be dusted every now and then. A great way to clean plants with big leaves is to pull those mismatched socks over your hands and wipe away—you get both sides with one swipe.

*   *   *

P	*How can I dry my plastic flowers after hand washing them?*
S	Put them in a pillow slip and hang them on your clothesline or from the shower head nozzle. (If hung in the sun, the pillow slip will keep them from fading.)

Pestproofing

P	*One of my plants got infected and the others around it caught the bugs.*
S	When any plant gets attacked by bugs, always move it away from the other plants. Putting a clear plastic cleaner bag over the plant will help keep the little critters from spreading.

You don't have to go out and buy all kinds of insecticides for many of the bugs and insects on your house plants. You can simply use a mild solution of liquid detergent and water and wipe the leaves and affected area. Then wipe with clear water.

Potting

P   *Do I have to start my avocado in a glass of water?*

S   No, you can pop the seed right into the soil and keep it well watered. I sometimes start mine out by putting it in a pot with another plant and wait until it gets its first good growth before transferring it to its own pot with soil.

*   *   *

P   *I do all of my potting on the balcony and don't have room for large bags of soil, rocks, etc. Any space-saving ideas?*

S   You can use old sponges, broken pieces of pottery or even nylon net to cover the holes in pots instead of rocks. When I plant, I put everything in a flat cardboard box (the kind that a case of soft drinks comes in) and work from there. Soil in one corner, gravel or rocks in the others, and hardly any mess to clean up.

*   *   *

P   *Do I have to repot my plants completely?*

S   No, scrape away the top inch or two and work around the roots with a small spoon. Apply new potting soil the same depth as that removed. This is, however, a short-term solution.

*   *   *

P   *I love to start new plants from old ones but flower pots cost so much.*

S   Have I got a goodie for you. The 2-liter plastic bottles that soft drinks come in are a boon to the home gardener. You can make almost any depth container that you want by cutting off the top of the bottle with a serrated knife. Then using a heated metal ice pick (careful here), punch holes in the bottom for drainage.

I absolutely love these for my avocados. You can plant them near the top of the bottle and watch the roots grow.

* * *

P   *I hate transplanting my tiny plants—it always disturbs the roots when I have to pull the plant out of the starter pot.*

S   Start your plants in paper cups and you can just cut the cup away from the root system. Using juice cans with both ends cut out (and set on a tray) makes it easy to gently push all the dirt and roots through without hurting the roots or plant.

Shaping and Staking

P   *My ivy plant hangs down into the kitchen sink— yet I don't want to cut it off.*

S   Use a U-shaped hairpin to anchor the trailing vines back into the dirt.

* * *

Hang onto any kind of broken plastic-type recorder tape. They can be used to tie and stake all kinds of plants. The tape stretches and doesn't damage tender stems.

Watering and Misting

P   *When I water my hanging plants, the water drips all over the place.*

S   Instead of pouring on lots of water, place a handful of ice cubes on top of the soil. They will slowly melt and nary a drop to drip.

If you need to pour on water and are afraid of drips on the carpet, put your old plastic shower

curtain or a few plastic cleaner bags on the floor
to catch the drips.

* * *

Want to give all your house plants a nice rainy day—bring them all
into the shower or tub, turn the shower on low and it's raining inside!
After turning off the water, close the door and let them soak up the
moisture while they drain.

* * *

P   *How often should potted plants be watered?*
S   A good way to tell is to thump the pot or con-
       tainer. If it sounds hollow, chances are the soil is
       dry and needs water. If it thuds, then there is some
       moisture in the soil.

* * *

P   *I want to take a trip, but there is no one to water*
       my plants while I am gone.
S   Never fear. You can water your plants well, and
       then tie clear plastic cleaner bags around the
       plants and make a mini-terrarium. You won't even
       have to move your hanging plants. Be sure they
       are not in direct sunlight, and when you come
       home, gently open the bag and let the plant adjust
       before ripping it off and exposing it to a sudden
       change in air.

       If you have a lot of plants, you can do about the
       same thing in the bathtub or kitchen sink. Put
       something like an old towel down so you won't
       scratch the tub, place all your plants in there and
       water heavily, cover with plastic, and off you go.
       If you want, you can run about an inch of water
       in the tub for extra moisture (be sure the stopper
       is in). My plants survived two weeks like this.

* * *

An easy way to slowly water outdoor and indoor plants is to use a
2-liter plastic bottle and poke a small hole in the side near the

bottom. Fill it with water and set this right down in your plant, or just on top of the soil where it won't mash the plant. Drip, drip, drip . . . great for when you go away from home for awhile.

* * *

P   *What if I have small plants I want to water slowly?*

S   Grab a paper cup and punch a small hole in the side near the bottom. Push it down about one-half inch into the soil and fill it with water.

* * *

P   *I need a watering can with a spout, but they cost too much.*

S   Save a plastic bottle that dishwashing liquid came in, or a large shampoo bottle with a little spout that opens and closes. Be sure and rinse it well. You can direct the stream of water and even control the flow. Didn't cost you a penny!

* * *

P   *I know I should mist my plants, but I don't want to spend the money for a mister.*

S   Use your plastic bottle that window cleaner comes in, after washing and rinsing it well. Some of them even have an adjustable spray nozzle.

TOOLS

During the months the garden tools are in frequent use, you will find it handy to keep a bucket filled with sand mixed with any type of oil so that the tools can be dipped in for a quick cleaning and oiling. Be sure to wipe off any oil before using them.

Cleaning

P   *I have a time getting the "goo" off my pruners.*

S   Spray your pruning shears with a vegetable oil

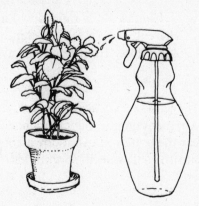

spray *before* use and the goo will slide right off for
easy cleanup.

* * *

P   *I lose small tools in the grass or else I step on rakes
and stuff.*

S   For safety's sake, paint the handles of those tools
a real bright color or wrap bright colored plastic
tape around the handles. Added bonus: you will
always know your tools on sight.

Money-savers

Don't know what to do with a worn-out lawn mower? Convert it to
a gardening carryall, or use it to haul garbage cans on.

* * *

P   *I don't have much of a garden and hate to spend
a lot of money on tools.*

S   A crow bar or some jacks from the car will work
as a digger. I use a pencil to break up the soil in
my potted plants when they need to be aerated. A
beverage can opener that has a point makes a
dandy weeder.

Auto Care

The life and well-being of your auto is strictly up to you. Plants, pets and children seem to have a way of taking care of themselves when they have to, but your car will just sit there and die if you let it. This chapter deals with little problems that we all have, from smelly cars to losing the key and getting locked out. There are some very good preventive tips that I hope you'll keep in mind.

We are all concerned about how to save money and nowadays anything to do with a car is going to cost you money. Most of us are keeping cars longer, which means that you must maintain one as best you can for it to serve you well.

If you are a single woman and don't know anything about car care, take the time to learn as much as you can. No matter how simple, every little bit helps. Take an auto class for women; they really teach you a lot. Even if you don't do it yourself, you will know what they are talking about when you go to have your car worked on.

A very important thing to remember when it comes to your car
. . . if there is something wrong or you suspect that there is something
wrong, don't hesitate to take it to be checked out. The longer you
wait, the worse it will probably get. It's not going to go away and
will most likely end up costing you more.

Always keep good records. Keep a maintenance book either in the
car or someplace in the house that you can get to easily. Record
everything from dates of oil changes, tire rotations, to tune-ups.
Keep your receipts, too!

I suggest that you leave the major problems like repairing your
transmission to the professional. May all your problems be small.

DOORS, KEYS AND LOCKS

Doors, sticking and squeaking

Problem	*The doors on my car do not close easily.*
Solution	Roll your car window down a little, and then close the door. It's the tight-fitting doors and windows designed to keep water out that also traps air inside the car.

*   *   *

P	*Squeaky doors bug me. I squirted some oil on the hinges and had to keep wiping off the drips. They still squeak.*
S	Maybe the oil you used was too thick and didn't get far enough into the hinges where the squeak was. Trying using a light oil in an aerosol can. It should penetrate the hinges and be less messy.

Keys and Key Rings

P	*I'm afraid I'll lock my keys in my car—what should I do if this happens?*

S   The best advice is to carry an extra key in your
        purse or wallet. There are little metal boxes with
        magnets that will attach someplace where you can
        hide a key.

                        *   *   *

P   *I hate leaving my entire key ring when they park
        my car for me at the garage.*
S   Use two key rings and put just the ignition key on
        one and give them that. I carry a safety pin on my
        key ring and take off only the ignition key and slip
        it on the safety pin.

                        *   *   *

P   *I carry a lot of keys and I need to change them
        often, but all the key rings are hard for me to open.*
S   Use a metal-type shower curtain hook that opens
        like a safety pin. You can easily slip as many keys
        as you want off or on. An added bonus: you can
        hook it to your belt loop.

                        *   *   *

If you stop at a friend's house and don't want to forget something,
leave your car keys with the item. You won't get very far without
your keys!

                        *   *   *

If you have a lot of different keys in your family you should always
clearly mark or code them. Don't put your name and address on your
set of house keys, put your neighbor's or your business phone. If they
are lost, you don't want the finder to know which house they open
up, do you?

                        *   *   *

P   *My car lock sticks sometimes.*
S   Don't ever oil the lock—it really will mess it up.
        Instead, rub your key with a soft lead pencil really
        well. When you insert the key in the lock you will

"treat" the sticky lock with graphite from the pencil lead. You can buy a small tube of graphite at the auto parts store.

*   *   *

P   *My door lock freezes in winter.*

S   There's not much you can do about the freezing weather, but you can heat your key with a match or cigarette lighter before putting the key in the lock. The hot key will melt the ice. Caution: the key will be very hot—handle with care.

GARAGE
(Also see Garage as storage space, p. 722)

P   *There is enough junk (valuable, I am sure) on the floor of my garage to outfit an entire family—I can't even get my car in.*

S   Hang as much as you can on the garage walls and even the ceiling. Things that you don't use often should be the highest up. Get that stuff off the floor and your garage will look a whole lot bigger. Be sure the things are hung securely so they won't fall on your car.

In and Out

P   *Driving into and out of my garage is terrible— the space is so narrow (I have scraped the car twice).*

S   Attach some pieces of rubber or foam rubber to the sides of the garage where you are most likely to "get" a fender or side. It sure saves the paint.

*   *   *

P   *I either bump the front of the car or else I can't close the door when I put the car in the garage.*

S   Park the car just perfect and then suspend a ping-pong ball on a string down from the ceiling where it touches right in front of your windshield. You now have a perfect "liner-upper."

*   *   *

P   *The new drivers in my family can't judge distance very well and keep "nudging" the wall with the front bumper.*

S   Hang an old tire right where the bumper would hit, and no problems—just like parking a boat.

Floor Protection
(Also see Mats for the car, p. 758)

Save old floor mats to put on your garage floor to catch oil drips; even leftover strips of carpet help. Or, place an old cookie sheet or large flat pan filled with sand or wood shavings on the garage floor. It will catch the oil drips from your car and protect your floor. It looks neat and the sand or shavings can easily be replaced when they get saturated with oil.

*   *   *

P   *I have terrible black oil spots on the floor of my garage, and I have tried everything to clean them up.*

S   If you can't clean it, cover it. Clean up as much as you can and then paint a large black strip and tell everyone it's your personal parking place!

*   *   *

If you have to walk across the lawn to get to the garage, put an old throw rug on the garage floor in front of each car door. Helps keep the tracking down from sandy or wet shoes.

INTERIORS

Write the date your inspection sticker is due and your license renewal date on a strip of adhesive tape and stick it by your speedometer. No fines for you! They are not tax deductible!

*   *   *

A small thing, but it will sure save wear and tear and steps for a gas attendant: write your license number on a strip of adhesive tape and put it on your gas credit card, or use punch tape.

Mats
(Also see Floor Protection for the garage, p. 757)

P   *In rainy weather water gets tracked in on the floor mats and just sits there, with no place to go.*

S   Carry a large kitchen sponge under the seat. Throw it down to sop up the water.

*   *   *

P   *Floor mats—I absolutely hate washing them.*

S   If you wash the car at the car wash the high power spray will clean them in a jiffy. When washing your car at home, just use an old toilet bowl brush, or your work broom to sweep away the dirt.

Odors

P   *Quite bluntly, my car has a bad odor.*

S   After cleaning it thoroughly, put baking soda in the ashtray. Also, tucking a bar of fragrant soap in the car will freshen it.

Organizers

Don't smoke? Convert the car ash tray to a candy or gum dish or a loose change tray. I taped a fabric softener sheet in mine so the change would not rattle around.

P   *My car needs a "hump" to fit a car caddie on.*

S   Some just don't have them—buy a small TV lap tray; glue two plastic foam beverage cups to the tray. The tray sits on the floor of the car and the cups stick up. Set your canned drinks in the plastic foam cups. Glue on another cup to hold pen, paper and change.

* * *

P   *I have a car pocket which hooks over the back of the front seat—the side seams have split open.*

S   To repair and reinforce it, put about four thicknesses of nylon net strips between the split pieces and sew them together.

* * *

P   *I get rattled trying to keep track of tickets, directions, pen, paper, etc.*

S   Stretch two large rubber bands around the driver's visor, slip the items you need under them.

* * *

P   *I hate fumbling through a glove compartment—and everything falls out.*

S   Group things in plastic bags and close the bags with twisties. Maps, pens, glasses, etc. You can then see what you need without emptying the whole compartment.

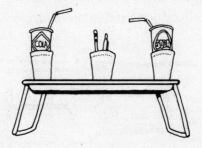

Upholstery

P   *My grandchildren's shoes make polish marks on my car's upholstery.*

S   Keep a clean pair of socks around to slip on *over* their shoes in the car. No fuss about getting little ones' shoes back on.

MAINTENANCE
(Also see Camper and Trailer Safety, p. 787)

Air Conditioner

P   *The air conditioning won't work.*

S   Check the fuses. The fuses are usually under the car dash on the left side. The markings "A.C." mean air conditioner, of course. It's a good idea to keep some spare fuses in your glove compartment. Some sizes of fuses are used for two or more accessories. If the fuses don't solve the problem, see your serviceman.

Antenna

To keep your antenna moving up and down more easily, rub it with a piece of wax paper every now and then.

Batteries

Need to clean a car battery in a hurry? Pour a bottle of cola on it and brush the battery posts and cable connectors. Then flush it off with clean water.

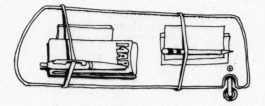

P   *How can I tell if I have battery trouble?*

S   If the starter works normally there is usually no battery problem. If the starter is sluggish, turn on lights and as you watch one light (dash, dome, etc.) try the starter for a second or two; if the light goes very dim the battery is probably weak. Further check requires equipment.

Belts, engine

The belts that are turned by the crankshaft pulley of your engine operate your generator (or alternator), power steering, air conditioner, radiator fan, etc., are necessary for your car to operate properly. Some older cars have one belt; some have two and three. Have the belts checked by a mechanic every now and then, especially when you have your car greased and the oil changed. Most service stations routinely check them at that time. Have them tightened or replaced if needed. It's no fun to be on the road or in traffic and have a belt break.

Convertible Top

P   *I have a sportscar with a leaky canvas top.*

S   Try mending it with dental floss or nylon fishing line. It's probably going to take two people to "push and pull" the needle through the top. You might try sturdy iron-on patches used on blue jeans if you can get the right color.

Dents

P   *I got a dent in my car the other day at the supermarket. Can I fix it myself?*

S   Try securing a rubber suction-type "plumber's helper" over the dent and pull. Sometimes the dent will pop out. This will not work on all dents, but it's sure worth a try.

Fluid and Oil Changing

P   *I can't ever find the funnel when I fill up the "fluids" on my car.*

S   A plastic detergent bottle works well. Cut off the bottom, stick the neck in the filler hole and pour away!

*   *   *

P   *I change my own oil—what can I use to dispose of old oil?*

S   Plastic beverage containers or plastic milk jars are good to catch the old oil in. Some service stations are accepting old oil for reprocessing; find one nearby and donate your used oil for recycling.

*   *   *

P   *I can't remember when I need to change the oil, rotate the tires, replace the air filter, etc.*

S   Install a blackboard on a wall of your garage. When you drive your car, you can glance at the board to jog your memory.

*   *   *

There may be times when you don't use a whole quart of oil. Save the leftover. The plastic lid from a one-pound can of coffee fits perfectly over the opened oil can.

Guarantees

Keep your repair bills handy. Your guarantee may still be good —no use paying for the same job twice.

Radiator

P   *I want to make sure my radiator is in good condition—how can I check it?*

S   Look for water under the car for a large leak. Check the water level frequently for small leakage and look for wet spots around the radiator, hoses and water pump.

Tires

Tires should be inspected every now and then, and each time you have the oil changed. The car is put up on a lift to change the oil and the tires can easily be checked all around. Look for nails, glass, cuts, blisters, cracks in the sidewalls and how the tires are wearing. Uneven wear usually means that you need the wheels aligned and balanced or rotated. These jobs cost much less than new tires!

*   *   *

Soft Top (See Convertible Top, p. 761)

Water Hose

P   *Can I repair a water hose temporarily?*
S   Drain the water out first and let it cool. Wipe the outside of the hose dry, and wrap two or three layers of duct tape tightly around the leak. Refill the water and drive slowly to the nearest repair place.

Windshield Wipers
(See Windows and Windshields, p. 754)

ON THE ROAD

Breakdown at Night
(Also see Trunk Supplies, p. 767)

P   *For safety's sake is there something I can do to make my car seen at night should I become stranded?*

S   Put a large X of reflector tape across the inside of your trunk lid and inside the hood. Lift the trunk and hood, and your car can be more readily seen from a distance.

*   *   *

No flares? Flatten clean dry milk cartons and store them in the car trunk. When needed, pull them open and add a little dirt or gravel to the carton to keep it from tipping over. Ignite the milk cartons and they will burn for a few minutes.

Following Another Car

P   *I always lose someone in a strange town when I have to follow them in my car.*

S   Attach a colored cloth or scarf on the lead car, making it easy to spot. If they have a radio antenna that sticks up, tie it to the top of that.

Gas Cap

Lost a gas cap at a self-serve? Why not use clear tape and stick an address label sticker to the gas cap—write your phone number on it, too. You'll get a call from the station.

Hatchback

Got a hatchback? When you go to the drive-in, park the car with the rear facing the screen, fold down the back seat and you've got a neat place to lean back and enjoy the movie. A cooler of drinks, some snacks, and the fresh air—good summer fun!

Lights

P   *Help! I always forget to turn the car lights off.*

S   Put a clothespin on your ignition key as a reminder, or if you have a pull-out light switch hang a tissue on the switch.

Out of Gas

P   *I got stuck on the road with no funnel to use for pouring gas in the car.*

S   In a real pinch you can use rolled-up newspaper, foil, or even the road map out of your car. These make a very good makeshift funnel. Be sure to dispose of any gas-soaked material safely.

Parking

P   *I really have trouble remembering where I've parked at these huge shopping malls.*

S   Look at the huge letters of the store nearest you. Make a mental note of which letter your row is closest to.

Seat Belts

P   *Disappearing seat belt buckles drive me up the wall.*

S   Cut a slit in plastic coffee can lids just big enough to slip the buckle part through—the lids will keep them from sliding between the seats. Smaller plastic lids may do the trick and not get in your way.

*   *   *

P   *My shoulder harness seat belt is so tight it is really uncomfortable and pins me back in the seat—so I don't use it.*

S   Put a spring-type clothespin on the belt in *front* of where it goes through the guide on top of the seat back or the top of the car. Make it comfort-

able, but not real loose—just so you won't be tied down.

When you come to a quick stop, the belt will hold you. The pin will not interfere with the belt reel from catching and stopping you from going forward abruptly. It just stops the belt from going back into the reel and being tight across your shoulder.

Seat and shoulder belts should be worn at ALL times to prevent deaths and injuries.

Shoes for Driving

P   *I always mark up my new shoes when I am driving.*

S   Carry an extra pair to change into when you get into the car. That black from the pedal is hard to get off.

Starting

P   *What should I do when my car won't start?*

S   Make sure the key is on and inserted all the way in. Some cars won't start unless they are in park or neutral gear. If the car won't crank at all, check out the battery by hitting the horn or turning on the lights. If the horn won't honk or the lights won't come on, it's probably the battery.

If you suspect battery problems, check the battery cables where they connect to the battery to make sure they're tight.

If the battery is strong enough for the starter to "turn over" the engine and it won't start, check to see if you have gas.

Get qualified help if none of the above solves the problem.

Stuck Wheels

P   *What can I do if I get my car stuck in mud?*
S   Find something you can use to get traction—dry
            sand, boards, newspapers—anything handy that
            causes traction. Don't spin your rear wheels—
            you'll just dig in deeper.

Theft

Thieves can make a stolen car almost untraceable. Cut one of your
old plastic credit cards so it can't be used and drop it down a side
window. Water won't hurt the plastic. Very few thieves will take time
to dismantle a car door. If it's found, your card will be positive
identification that the car is yours.

Trunk Supplies

Got an old flannel-backed tablecloth? Use it to wrap tools you
want to keep in the trunk of your car. It keeps them from sliding
around on sharp turns.

*   *   *

Always keep an old blanket in the trunk of your car. You can use
it if you get stranded in the cold, for sun protection from the heat,
or to keep your clothes clean if you have to crawl under your car.

*   *   *

A spur-of-the-moment picnic is great fun. If you have a supply of
paper plates, cups, paper towels, a can and bottle opener stored in
an empty ice chest in your car, all you have to do is stop and buy
sandwich fixings, drinks and ice—not too great a cash outlay.

*   *   *

You should always keep a few emergency-type supplies in your car
trunk. I don't mean a whole auto supply store-just some simple
things that may save you a lot of trouble:

1. A small roll of yellow reflector tape. If a headlight goes out, put some on the bulb and at least it will pick up light from oncoming cars and they will know you are not on a motorcycle.

2. Flares or milk cartons (See *Breakdown at Night,* p. 763)

3. A few thick rubber bands . . . great for holding a flashlight to your wrist if you have to change a tire alone at night.

4. Baking soda for small electrical fires. Never put water on an electrical fire.

5. Always have spare fuses handy . . . sometimes you can't get to a station to replace one that burned out or they may not have the right size.

6. Be sure your car has the proper jack and tools needed to change a tire; there are certain things you just can't substitute.

Oh, yes—become familiar with the instructions on how to change a tire or at least know where they are so you can show them to some kind soul who is willing to change it for you. Three cheers for kind souls!!!

Waiting Line

P   *I get so frustrated and edgy waiting in lines at the bank, the gas station, etc.*

S   Make yourself a kit or box to keep in the front seat for times like these. You can make out a grocery list, write a letter, do your nails, read a book, munch on something, clip coupons—anything to pass the time and let you relax a bit. Caution: be sure your car is in neutral and your brake is engaged so that you do not roll into the car ahead of you.

Weather, hot

P   *The steering wheel becomes so hot in the summer —ouch!*

S   Keep an old pair of gloves in the glove compartment to drive with until it cools down. Or, lay something over it before getting out of the car.

*   *   *

P   *Glare and reflection are a problem to me in the summer when I drive.*

S   Place a piece of dark felt on the dashboard to help cut the sun's rays.

*   *   *

P   *I don't want to wear long sleeves in the summer, but I don't like "driver's arm" sunburn on long trips.*

S   Make a loose-fitting sleeve out of remnants and carry the sleeve in your glove compartment. Before starting out, slip the sleeve over your arm and pin it to the shoulder of your garment.

*   *   *

That straw cushion you use in the summer will also insulate you against a cold plastic seat in the winter!

Weather, cold
(Also see Doors, Sticking and Squeaking, p. 754–755 and Windows and Windshields, p. 772)

When starting up in cold weather, pump that old accelerator a couple of times first. It gets the intake system charged with fuel.

WASHING YOUR CAR

Bumpers

P   *How do I get rust off my car bumper?*

S   Wad up a piece of aluminum foil and rub the spot briskly. This will not fill up the pits, but it will make for a nicer appearance.

P   *Old bumper stickers—how can I get them off?*

S   Spray the sticker with prewash spray, let it sit for a few minutes, and then, using a little elbow grease, rub it with stiff brush or a piece of nylon net.

Decals
(see p. 772)

Cleaning Supplies

P   *Mechanic's hand cleaner is expensive to buy and my family goes through it like it's free.*

S   There are a few things you have right in your kitchen that will do the job. Did you know that sugar or salt work well as an abrasive cleaner when mixed with a little liquid detergent, vegetable oil or cooking lard?

　　　Your family may look at you funny at first, but just mix some up and let them give it a try. Put some lard, and sugar or salt in an old coffee can and leave it by the outside sink or faucet.

*　　*　　*

An old diaper pail is good to store all your cleaning supplies and rags in when going to the car wash. (Also see Scrubbers, p. 763)

*　　*　　*

Socks that have lost their mate make super wash rags, or use them to apply wax and buff the car.

*　　*　　*

If you have kids and soda pop in the car, you're gonna need a couple of disposable diapers under the seat to wipe up spills—they absorb like super!

*　　*　　*

P   *I'm short and I can't reach the top of my pickup to wash it.*

S   Grab that old kitchen string mop—dip it in some soapy water and wipe away!

*   *   *

P   *Yuck! My hands get so dirty when I do the simplest chore on my car. I'm a lady and really enjoy doing these things but oh, the condition of my hands.*

S   Rub a thin layer of petroleum jelly on your hands before starting, and the grease and grime won't get embedded in your skin.

Grills

P   *Ick! Bugs on my car's grill are so hard to get off.*

S   Using baking soda and a damp sponge, or baking soda paste and a piece of nylon, scrub them away.

*   *   *

P   *I hate cleaning my car's grill.*

S   Use an old vegetable brush or even a toilet bowl brush to scrub the gunk off.

Headlights

Speaking of headlights . . . if they are dirty and covered with bugs, the maximum amount of light is not going to shine through. So don't forget to clean the lights when the rest of the car gets a bath.

Undercarriage

P   *My car is caked on the bottom with goop—how can I possibly get under there and get it off?*

S   Put your lawn sprinkler under the car and turn the water on full blast. No sense breaking your back! This will get lots of it off, but the buildup of grease

and oil will have to be cleaned off by a professional.

Wheels

P   ***Spoke wheels are a pain to clean.***
S   Not if you use foamy-type bathtub cleaner and a
     toilet bowl brush.

Windows
(See Windows and Windshields, below.)

Woodgrain

P   ***The woodgrain on our station wagon has lost its
     sheen and looks kind of tacky.***
S   Rub in some good neutral shoe wax and buff.

WINDOWS AND WINDSHIELDS

Going on a long trip? Keep the windshield clean by using premoistened towelettes. The greasy film comes off easily.

*   *   *

When you replace your windshield wiper blades, save an old one—
put it under the seat for a quick swipe inside of the windows when
they fog up. Did you know it's not how much you use your wiper
blades that determines if they should be changed, but how long they
have been on your car? It's exposure to the air, sun and all the bad
things that are floating around that cause them to deteriorate. So
check them often because when you want them to work well on a
dark rainy night, that's not the time to find out you need new ones.

Decals

P   ***I have a decal on my window that just won't come
     off.***

S   Spray it with prewash spray and tape a wet sponge over it . . . let it sit awhile and usually this will help dissolve the paper and glue. Don't ever scrape at it with a sharp knife, etc. Some windows and windshields are covered with a plastic film and you might scratch it and the glass.

Fogging Up

If your windshield and windows fog up or collect a lot of moisture while you are driving, don't use your hand—all you do is smear that stuff around and the oil from your hand will cause a real mess. Stuff an old oven mitt under the seat, slip it on and wipe away . . . it absorbs a lot of moisture.

*   *   *

P   *My windows fog up.*
S   Turn on the air conditioning system. The other choice is to open a window.

Icing Over

P   *In icy weather I have to go to a parked car with iced-over windshields and windows.*
S   If you think there will be ice on your car when you return to your parked car, here's a way to try to prevent it. Spread a piece of plastic over the windshield and secure it with small magnets on the metal windshield molding. Closing the doors on the sides of the plastic will hold it that way.

         Also, you need to see out the front side windows so hang a plastic trash bag out each window and roll them up to hold the bags in place. If the wind is blowing, a few paper clips or bobby pins stuck in between the window and the rubber molding on the door will hold the bag down.

It's a lot easier than scraping thick ice off when you are in a hurry to get to work or go home.

* * *

P   *What can I do when the windshield and windows ice over?*

S   If you don't have a plastic or hard rubber scraper, a plastic credit card makes an emergency ice scraper. Do *not* use metal to scrape a windshield 'cause it will scratch it. Start your car up and turn on your defroster while you are scraping.

Wax

P   *A film of hot wax from the car wash is on the windshield of my car.*

S   Wet a cloth with vinegar and wipe the windshield and windows clean.

Camping and RV's

The call to the wild, getting back to nature, or getting away from it all. The different kinds of "camping" are about as varied as the different flavors of ice cream.

I have a little Hill Country lakeside cabin that I call my retreat and to me that's roughing it. I do have an almost complete kitchen (that means no microwave) and indoor plumbing and even a bathtub to soak in. Some people will say that's just going to another house, and maybe it is to you, but to me it's "getting away from it all."

Whatever makes you happy is what's important. If you really like to rough it and carry everything into the wilderness on your back, GREAT! Maybe you like to go by trailer, or pop-up camper, and set up with a few conveniences. You might be like me—just going to another location with fresh air, a fireplace and the smell of the woods is enough.

Many of the problems are all the same whichever way you do it. They usually center around food, cooking and keeping track of things. When you go away, remember that this is supposed to be an enjoyable time for you and the family. The secret to having a good time is to make it as easy as possible. That means: If you can't eat it, wear it or sleep in it, don't drag it with you. The more you take, the more you have to keep up with and pack up.

If you go for a day or a week, please remember what you are there for. To enjoy Mother Nature, relax, and have a good time. If you spend all your time cooking or cleaning up, it's a drag. Take a few minutes to plan and figure out how you can make everything as easy as possible and thereby avoid all the "boring" stuff.

Last but not least, if you can bring a little nature home with you, like a pine cone or sea shell or a pretty leaf, you can look at them and enjoy your good memories for a long time.

ADVANCE PREPARATION
(Also see Advance Planning for moving, p. 801 and Loading the Car, p. 815)

When you know you're going camping quite a few weeks in advance, why not write or call the Chamber of Commerce in the area for anything of special interest to see.

You might be surprised what's available just down the road, or just a few miles away.

*   *   *

Problem   *I always forget something we really need.*

Solution   Some day when you're not rushed, sit down and "think through" an entire camping trip. Write down everything you need to cook with, menus for a week or so and all the food and seasonings to cook them with, what clothes each member of your family needs, all the toiletries needed, etc. Include flashlights, extension cords, light bulbs, perhaps a radio or fan, a rope with clothespins, coat hangers, matches in a waterproof container, and so on. Make lists and put them in a safe place.

When camping time comes, you can pack knowing you haven't forgotten anything.

*   *   *

Don't throw the plastic liquid detergent bottle away when you are finished. Take it on your next outing. Fill it with water when you get there and you have a handy dispenser for soapy water for quick cleanups.

*   *   *

Start a "camping box." Fill a box with one-of-a-kind dishes, pots, pans or broken sets of dishes that you have gotten at garage sales. After a while, you'll have a complete camping set that you can keep stored separately, ready to go on a moment's notice.

*   *   *

Save all the old tennis shoes to use for "river shoes." Even old, torn, shot tennies your kids have outgrown could be passed on down to other "camping" families' kids.

*   *   *

P   *Toothpaste, soap, deodorant, shampoo costs so much in the individual sizes needed for camping.*

S   Save that little dab still left in each tube or container before it's completely gone and stash it away. The old budget won't be hit so hard come vacation time. You'll have enough grooming aids to give to everyone.

*   *   *

P   *If I can survive the first meal on a camping trip, I've got it made.*

S   Don't let it get you down. When you're tired from the trip and the kids are starving, don't try to hunt for ingredients and cook. Take that first meal already prepared from home (fried chicken or sandwiches or such). Eat and then set up camp. Sure saves wear and tear on the nerves.

*   *   *

P   *Buying food to take on a camping trip wrecks my budget because of all the extras involved.*

S   Those "extras" are expensive but really add to everyone's enjoyment, don't they! To keep the old budget more in line, buy a dab of this or a can of that each payday, or whenever, two or three months before your vacation. Put them someplace where you won't be tempted to use 'em.

One more word of advice . . . take along enough food for the entire stay if no major food store is nearby. Having to purchase food in tourist areas will wreck the budget even more.

*   *   *

If you know there's an electrical hookup at the campsite, take along your electric skillet. Fantastic!

AT THE SITE

Camping Etiquette

FOOD FOR THOUGHT: We go camping to get away from the day-to-day routine of life—right? I realize we all have our likes and dislikes, but if you're camped right next to several other adventurous

families, be considerate of their feelings. After all, they came to get away from it all, too.

If you have radios or TV's, keep them low. Everyone may not have your taste in music. You "country kickers" may be camped next to the "Boston Pops"!

Lights? Turn them out at a reasonable time, so those "early birds" can get enough sleep.

*   *   *

P   *I love to go camping but I'm bashful meeting other campers.*

S   Bumper stickers telling what campgrounds you've been to would be a good conversation starter. Also, the old standby "May I borrow a cup of . . . ?" or "How can we get there from here?" are icebreakers.

Cleaning Cookware

P   *Camping is fun, but cleaning the camp stove afterwards almost spoils it all.*

S   Camping was meant to be fun, not drudgery. So line every possible square inch of that stove with aluminum foil before using.

When it's time to pack up, cleanup will be a breeze.

*   *   *

P   *I have to use my good cookware and it gets blackened on the bottoms.*

S   Line the pans with foil on the *outside* and just toss the foil into the trash when finished. Or, coat the bottom and sides of each pan with dishwashing detergent; the soot will wipe off the pans with a wet cloth.

Dressing and Bathing Area
(Also see Keeping Dry, p. 781)

P   *We need extra dressing-area space as our tent is*
        rather small and our family is rather large.

S   Pack a large umbrella and an old (but good)
        shower curtain. Hang the umbrella by the handle
        (upside down) on a tree limb and hook the shower
        curtain onto the tip of each metal rib of the um-
        brella. It's practically custom-made for this pur-
        pose.

        You'll have a dressing area which is completely
        private and so easy to take down again when you
        get ready to move on.

        A word of caution: Take the whole thing down
        if it looks like rain. This is a fair-weather tip only.

                    *   *   *

Hate to wait in line for family members to finish with their morning
shower in the *one* shower stall? Have each one wear only a beach
robe to the shower house and dress upon returning to camp.

Saves time and keeps from getting clothes wet on the shower floor.

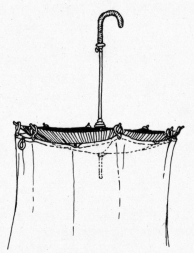

P	*How does a person keep his sanity trying to wash his hands or take a shower when there's no place to lay the soap except in the dirt or shower floor?*
S	Try this! Save those last little pieces and slivers of soap from home (or use a new bar). Put the soap in a nylon stocking and tie shut. Tie the stocking around the faucet or the shower head. Or, tie it to a tree branch near the water bucket or faucet.

Keeping Dry
(Also see Sleeping Bags, p. 786)

P	*Our clothes always get damp when we are camping.*
S	If you'll store them in plastic zippered pillow protectors, they will keep clean and dry.

*   *   *

P	*I never manage to keep my clothes dry when I go to the campground shower—there's never any place to stash them while showering.*
S	I could have kicked myself when I came across the solution to this one. I was the person who tried to

hang a towel, washcloth and a complete change of
clothes on one tiny nail—unsuccessfully each time
I tried it. All you have to do is carry along a plastic
shopping bag with all your things in it and hang
the bag on that one tiny nail!

*   *   *

P   *All our clothes wind up on the floor of the tent—*
        usually damp and dirty.
S   Fasten a screw-type hook in the main pole of the
        tent. Hang a garment bag or a plastic shoe bag
        with shelves on the hook. The clothes won't fall to
        the ground and the see-through plastic will elimi-
        nate the "tossing around" to get to them.

*   *   *

P   *At our last picnic we had a sudden shower and all*
        our supplies got wet.
S   If you'll buy a small plastic trash can with a tight-
        fitting lid, you can store all your paper goods in it
        with no need to worry about sudden showers.

*   *   *

P   *The bottom of my tent gets wet.*
S   Plastic drop cloths that painters use are pretty
        cheap. Throw one on the ground before setting up
        your tent.

Labeling Tent

P   *It is really hard for the little ones (and adults) to*
        find our tent in the camping area, they all look
        alike after awhile.
S   Attach a small flag or colored handkerchief or
        something distinguishable to the highest point of
        the tent or to a car antenna or trailer top. Most
        anyone will be able to spot their home base if it's
        marked with a brightly colored flag.

Signals
(See signals for children, p. 782)

Storage

P   *Since we won't damage trees by driving nails into them, not having a place to hang numerous items is very inconvenient.*

S   Punch several holes in a man's leather belt. Buckle it around the tree trunk, then insert pegboard hooks in the holes. You'll have space to hold several pieces of camping equipment, or whatever.

*   *   *

P   *There's no cabinet space in my trailer's little bath —toothpaste and such rattles around—it drives me crazy!*

S   Mount spice racks inside the bathroom door or on the bath wall to stick personal items in.

*   *   *

P   *My mom bought me a plastic tote bag to carry my swimsuit and towel to the pool. I lost it (and the one before it, too)*

S   Sounds to me like you've got a mom who's not too happy about that! Save those plastic rings that hold six-pack cans of drinks together. Remove the entire plastic as one piece. When you've got a bunch of them, get some string and just start tying them together in the shape of a tote bag. Two of the plastic holders will make the bottom. Cut a handle from another. If you lose this one, at least it was free!

*   *   *

P   *My spray deodorant, etc., as well as my underclothes are so cold early mornings. Brrrrr!*

S   Before you crawl into your sleeping bag at night, place the deodorant and underclothes at the foot or bottom of your sleeping bag. Next morning both are nice and warm—well worth any inconvenience from sleeping with a can of deodorant!

*   *   *

P   *The kids can't find the shampoo, etc., since it is never put back twice in the same place after someone uses it.*

S   Take along a plastic shoebag to keep all these personal items in place. And label each pocket as to contents. A shoebag is also a dandy place to keep first-aid necessities handy, too. You can hang it from any convenient spot.

*   *   *

A neat carrier for knives, forks and spoons on camping trips or picnics is a lunch kit—either metal or plastic. The flat, square type works best.

Just set it out on the table come mealtime and let everyone help themselves.

*   *   *

Large coffee cans or fruit juice cans are great to store utensils in.

*   *   *

Place your opened milk cartons and cans of juice in plastic bags and twist-tie shut, just in case of spills in your ice chest.

*   *   *

P   *I can't seem to keep track of my roll of paper towels. It keeps coming unwound or rolling off the picnic table.*

S   Just put a rope or twine through the cardboard tube in the center of the roll of towels and tie it fast to a tree. Real handy and no lost towels. (No laundry to do later, either.)

Sunburn Protection

P   *I love outdoor camping activities, but the sun doesn't like me. My skin sunburns severely, even though I use a sunscreen lotion.*

S   The amount of sunscreen protectives in a lotion vary, so learn to read labels. If your skin is extremely sensitive to the sun, choose one with a high "SPF" (sun protection factor).

For example, one with an SPF of 8 means you can stay in the sun eight times longer than you could with no protection.

It would also provide maximum protection against the sun while permitting limited tanning. Lesser numbers would provide less protection and allow for more gradual tanning, so know your skin type.

Also, choose a sunscreen with a "water resistant" label. These claims can only be put on products that meet government testing, requiring that the sunscreen maintain the initial SPF during a forty-minute period of water immersion.

This means it won't wash off in the water and you won't have to reapply your sunscreen every time you go for a dip—at least for forty minutes!

BEDDING

Mosquito Protection

P   *We sleep in our station wagon but we have to keep the windows rolled up because of mosquitoes and that makes it miserably hot.*

S   Get some long, small-holed nylon net pieces wider than the car door and hang them over the inside of your doors. Then close the doors and roll the windows down. If the net blows, place magnets on the window frames to hold the net in place.

*   *   *

P   *How can I keep mosquitoes and insects away from my baby at night?*

S   Put nylon net over the baby's crib or playpen.

Sleeping Bags
(Also see Baby Bed for camping, p. 797)

To keep sleeping bags from slipping off the mattress at night or to make the ground "softer" carry inch-thick pieces of foam along that match the length and width of the sleeping bags.

These take up very little space when rolled tightly.

*   *   *

P   *The damp ground gets my sleeping bag clammy.*

S   Before putting your sleeping bag down, put an old plastic shower curtain on the ground, then spread a lot of newspapers for extra insulation.

*   *   *

P   *My sleeping bag never smells really fresh when I pull it out to use.*

S   You can air it out in the sunshine. Better yet, sprinkling some baking soda inside, or putting in a few fabric softener sheets before storing it will help keep it sweet smelling.

Sleeping in Car

P   *We sleep in our station wagon but have no curtains for privacy.*

S   Pack a can of the window cleaner that leaves an opaque film after applying. Rub this on the windows at night; just wipe it off in the morning.

Not only will you have privacy during the night but you will also have the cleanest windows in the camp!

CAMPER AND TRAILER SAFETY
(Also see Maintenance for the auto, p. 760)

Word of Caution: If you are pulling a trailer with a car, never, never let anyone ride inside the trailer . . . you never know when something might happen and sudden stops can be dangerous.

*   *   *

If you're traveling in a pickup camper and there's children riding in the back, it's a good safety idea to replace thin camper glass with safety plastic.

CLOTHING

Clean Clothes

P   *My kids always look like "river rats" on the trip home.*

S   Pack a clean set of clothes (minimum a shirt) and tennis shoes (at least a clean pair of shoelaces if you don't have other tennies). Don't let the kids know you've got them until time to go home. They'll look spic and span if you make any restaurant stops or visits to friends on the way home.

*   *   *

This is a wonderful hint! When I was small and we were traveling and camping, my shirt got so dirty that my mother turned it around so the dirty part was in back—you know how important first impressions are! So at least when someone saw me from the front I looked OK.

The real kicker was—when the front (really the back) got awful, she turned my shirt inside out and I looked all clean (on the outside) for a day or so more. This may be funny, and it was, but it sure kept me looking half decent for a while.

Laundry
(Also see Chapter 3, The Laundry, p. 638)

P   *I like camping but I don't like the smell of the clothes to be laundered after the trip.*

S   Put two or three fabric softener sheets in with the soiled clothes. They will smell much fresher.

*   *   *

P   *Doing laundry while camping out is for the birds.*

S   Save your old clothes, the ones that you won't wear any longer or ones that are not in the best of condition. Wear them while camping; when soiled, add them to the fire or just throw away. I agree—who wants to wash clothes? You are supposed to be getting away from it all!

*   *   *

Use a clean garbage can or diaper pail with a tight-fitting lid. Place your dirty clothes in it along with soap and water and put the can in the trunk of your car. When you get to your next campsite, all you'll have to do is rinse them out and hang them up to dry. Viola! The jostling of the car acts like a washing machine.

COOKING OUT
(Also see Food Preparation, p. 577)

Camping Menu

When making up your camping menu, put a number by each meal and the corresponding number on top of the cans for that particular meal.

Tape the menu somewhere in the cooking area at the campsite;

then sometime when the kids want to prepare the meal or you just want to be lazy for a change, just tell them to match the numbers and fix the meal.

You'll get to enjoy your vacation, too, by doing this little bit of extra planning ahead of time.

Charcoal

To quickly start a charcoal fire in the barbecue grill, get a large (46-ounce) juice can and cut out both ends. Punch three or four rows of large holes around one end of the can.

Place the can upright in the bottom of the grill with the holes of the can at the bottom. Stuff a sheet of crumpled newspaper in the can, then fill with the desired amount of charcoal, leaving two or three inches of space at the top. Light the paper through the holes in the can with a match.

The holes in the can let the fire draw and the charcoal will begin to burn very quickly. After it takes on the familiar gray look, remove the can with tongs or a thick mitt. Replace the grate and you're ready to bring on the goodies to grill.

*   *   *

P   *We love to grill but charcoal bags are so bulky and spills can mess up the car (not to mention your hands when you're picking it up).*

S   Store charcoal in egg cartons or put it in plastic bags and close with a twistie.

Condiments
(See Food Storage, p. 792)

Keep all those packets of salt, pepper and catsup you get from fast-food places to use on your picnics. They are free, sealed and disposable.

*   *   *

Use the cups in a muffin tin to hold pickles, onions, relish, mustard, etc., on the picnic table. After a meal, just cover the whole tin with plastic wrap or foil and it's ready to use next time.

*   *   *

P   *I dislike dragging condiments from the camp "pantry" to the camp table.*

S   Put jelly, coffee cream, mustard, etc. in an empty plastic soda pop carton. Makes a nifty tote, or just leave the carton on the table.

Covers, Food

P   *I cover the food left on the table to keep flies off but the kids come along to look and uncover everything.*

S   If you'll just toss a large doubled piece of small holed nylon net over the food and weight the net down, they can find what they want and reach under the net. Or, use clear plastic wrap that kids can see through without uncovering the dish.

Eggs

P   *I'm a city boy who doesn't like cold eggs and bacon on a camp-out.*

S   No one does! Put your bacon and eggs in a plastic foam cup and they'll stay warm for quite awhile.

* * *

P   *Help! How can I travel without breaking eggs and spoiling them?*

S   Why not break the eggs into a bowl before you leave and then pour the eggs into a hollow plastic rolling pin and keep it cold? Pour the eggs out as you need them.

Hot Dog/Marshmallow Roast

P   *The kids always complain their hands get too hot when they roast weiners or marshmallows.*

S   Get some aluminum pie tins or heavy-duty paper plates and run the roasting stick through the middle and down near where they hold it. This will reflect the heat and keep those little hands cool. They will have roasted weiners, not fingers.

* * *

Take along sticks or wire coat hangers for roasting marshmallows or weiners. Invariably, if you get to the campsite at night the kids want to do the roasting first thing, and sticks are sometimes nowhere to be found, or hard to find in the dark.

Ice

If ice cubes melt too quickly in your gallon jug of lemonade or whatever, freeze ice in margarine tubs or whipped topping containers, etc.

The larger size of cubes will last longer and won't dilute your drink so readily.

*   *   *

P *A friend told me to pack my food in dry ice—will dry ice harm my food?*

S Heavens no! Dry ice is carbon dioxide in a solid form. However, it will freeze anything it comes in contact with. It's terrific for keeping food frozen or extremely cold. Don't put vegetables and such in contact with it. Don't handle dry ice barehanded. A few chunks tossed in with your "wet ice" will keep it from melting so quickly. You can find out where dry ice is sold in your ad pages in the phone book.

*   *   *

P *How can I keep my salad fresh until we get to the campsite?*

S Put your salad in the top part of a double boiler and fill the bottom with ice. If you have a set of bowls that fit one inside each other, you can use the largest one to hold ice and then place the smaller one inside it with the salad in it.

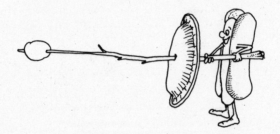

Water

P   *It seems I spend all my time boiling water for this and that when camping.*

S   If you have electricity, take the biggest electric coffee pot or urn you can find and keep it "churning" all the time. You'll have plenty of hot water when you need it.

*   *   *

P   *I like to back pack but I can't figure out how to get really cold water in a canteen.*

S   Fill the canteen one-third full of water the night before and place it in your freezer (leave the cap off the canteen). Next morning, fill it the rest of the way up with water and put the cap on. Juice can also be done this way.

*   *   *

Freeze water in clean milk cartons for ice. When the ice thaws you'll have nice cool drinking water. While it's thawing it will keep other perishables cool.

EQUIPMENT

Canvas

Don't spoil a camping trip by having a leaky canvas roof. Check out your pop-up camper *before* you leave. It's a good idea to store those campers under a shed to prolong the roof's life.

Clothespins

Always carry a large supply of clothespins; they come in so handy for everything—from clipping your napkins together so they don't blow away, to clipping open a road map to the right spot. And natch, the old standby to use in hanging wet clothes!

Cups

Never have enough cups for a large thermos bottle? Hang a few extra cups on the thermos with a shower curtain ring.

*   *   *

P   *The cost of paper cups for a camping trip for our bunch looks like the national debt.*

S   And invariably you run out, right? Why not get a different color or design plastic glass for each member of the family (plus a few extra) and have each one use the same glass all day long.

Flashlights

Keep your flashlight in a plastic bag twisted shut. A sudden shower won't do it a bit of good nor will dropping it in the river or lake.

Glassware, transporting

P   *I am always worried about the glass jars and things breaking.*

S   When you pack your camping or trailer things, use all those old socks that hang around. Cut off the foot part and slip the rest around each glass thing. This cushions the jars and will keep them from banging together.

Utensils

P   *I can't afford two sets of utensils, and when we go roughing it I end up "missing" a few things here and there.*

S   Take the time to clearly mark all your items, down to knives, stirring spoons, pots and pans. You can either tape an address sticker with your phone number using clear, see-through tops. Or, mark them with your name or initial using bright red nail polish. When something ends up in another campsite, it's a dead giveaway that it belongs to the "Joneses."

I have a Chinese-style knife that was made for my mother in China in 1948 that is perfect for slicing vegetables, etc. I put my name and phone number on it per above instructions, and took it to a chili cookoff. Naturally, it disappeared from our spot and I was sick—do you know I got a phone call a few days later and it was returned—it's worth the effort.

* * *

P   *I hate washing forks and knives when camping— I am supposed to be on vacation.*

S   Save all the little plastic utensils you get from drive-ins, etc., and take them along. After one use, you can toss them in the garbage if you don't feel like washing—that's what paper plates and plastic forks are for, dear!

* * *

P   *I dislike having to wash my dishes and silverware before every meal, yet I want to insure that they are clean.*

S   Just place the dishes and eating utensils in a plastic bag and close it with a twistie. You can remove those needed for each meal, reclose the bag and nary a pesky fly or crawly bug will have a chance to cause you all that extra work.

* * *

If you don't have a water faucet at the campsite, use a plastic gallon milk jug or bleach bottle (wash it thoroughly) and poke a small hole in the bottom. Plug the hole with a golf tee or small cork. Be sure to tie these to the jug or you may lose the stopper and your water.

Fill the jug with water and tie it around a low-hanging tree limb. Put a bar of soap in a nylon stocking and tie it to the tree.

Now, to wash your hands, just remove the stopper and grab the bar of soap. Really works great!

FUN ACTIVITIES
(See Playtime for children, p. 813)

Take along bottles of bubbles—the dime store variety. While spending time around the campfire, blow bubbles into the smoke. It's fun to watch them rise with the hot air and float around.

At night, let the kids follow them with the flashlight and watch the pretty colors they make. (Should go without saying, but NEVER let the kids get close to a campfire, of course.)

*   *   *

Smaller children can get bored camping after a day or two, so take along a small riding toy or tricycle.

They'll have a grand time riding around the campsite and will be entertained if they are too small to swim unsupervised.

*   *   *

Waterlogged and wanting do so something a little less strenuous, yet keep those kiddos (and some adults) entertained?

Try a game of pitching washers. All it takes is six or eight large washers about 2½ inches in diameter (available at hardware stores) and two holes dug in the dirt. The holes should be slightly larger than the washers and a couple of inches deep.

The game is played the same as horseshoes, so put the holes about twelve to twenty feet apart (depending on the age and size of the players). Every washer that lands in the hole is a point. Two players compete against each other, using three or four washers each.

Lots of fun and the washers take up next to "nil" storage space, are easily available, and ever so easy to carry with you.

*   *   *

When the family is sunburned and tired of swimming and hiking, take a little side trip and see what the country has to offer.

PACKING
(Also see Packing for moving, p. 303 and Loading the Car,- p. 815)

Plastic bags are space savers. If you eliminate large bulky boxes and cartons, you'll have a lot more room. Remember, many boxes of food are not completely full. Put meal-size servings of instant mashed potatoes (you can even put in powdered milk and salt and add the water and butter later), noodles, macaroni, biscuit mix and so on in plastic bags and close them securely. They tuck under things and in corners nicely.

* * *

Carry soap in a margarine tub to keep it dry.

* * *

Duffle bags or pillow cases "stuff" in the car trunk and under cots much better than suitcases.

SUBSTITUTIONS

Baby Bed

Take along your baby's playpen. It can serve as a bed or a supervised play area, and you can put a sheet over the top for shade. It is a safe way to take your baby along with you to the swimming hole to watch while you swim.

Colander

A plastic woven box that strawberries come in makes a camping colander that doesn't take up much space and can be discarded before returning home.

Grill

P *There is no room in our subcompact car to carry along a grill for barbecuing.*

S Stuff four 3-pound coffee cans and your oven rack

into the car. When you want to barbecue, fill the cans with water or sand, place the oven rack over them, and you're ready to go! You could even carry charcoal briquets in the cans and use them for cooking. More space saved.

Napkin Holder

An empty coffee can makes a good napkin holder.

Table

Need a "table"? Place a board between two tree forks—makes a good dishwashing center or storage table. Tie the board securely so it doesn't "tump" over.

Tablecloth

P   *Our tablecloth always blows and flaps in the wind.*
S   Use an old fitted bedsheet and just slip it over the corners of the table. If you already have a pretty tablecloth that you want to use, get some double-sided sticky tape and tape that bugger down.

Tent Maintenance

P   *Our last tent tore at the top center pole. I don't want this to happen to our new one as replacement is too expensive.*
S   Invert a tin or plastic funnel over the center pole before inserting it in the hole to raise the tent; it will reinforce the ring at the top of the tent and help to prevent its ripping out.

Towels

P   *Towels and washcloths take a beating when camping. Worse yet, many times they get lost.*

S Save all your old, frayed towels, etc.,—those you have to replace from time to time. Just put them aside and on the next camping trip drag them out and take them along instead of your good ones. You won't cringe if you see one down in the dirt or feel too badly if one disappears.

On the Move

When it comes to problems about traveling and packing and moving to a new location, I know how it feels, and I can sure help you solve them. The first place to start is getting ready to leave. If you are just going on a short trip it doesn't take too much planning to get organized. If you are making a major move, then settle in and read this chapter and get ready to get it done. The questions in this part are the ones that I receive time and time again, the ones everyone has troubles with.

I like moving. It is the only way to really clean out closets and sort through all that stuff in the "catchall" drawer and honestly—now I mean honestly—get the garage or attic "gone through."

I have always told you, "Clean when you are in the mood," but this is an exception. You are being forced to get it done. Do plan ahead and do a little bit at a time. Do one closet, one drawer or one shelf at a time. When the "big day" comes, most of it should be ready to pack. The other section in this chapter deals with traveling, both business and pleasure. Getting between here and there really can be a nice experience. I've had to learn how to make it both efficient and enjoyable since I travel a lot for business, doing spots on TV shows, going on book tours, and giving speeches. I have learned, sometimes the hard way, the ins and outs, the shortcuts and the ways to make it easy.

There are times that I am traveling so much that I am on a plane and in a different city every day. I never check luggage; I always carry it with me and so far have never missed a plane.

I promise you, your transit time doesn't have to be difficult . . . all you have to do is take it a step at a time. Don't be afraid to ask questions: "Is this plane going to San Antonio?" and "Is this the right way to the airport?" You will save a bundle of time and mistakes.

If you are traveling by car, current maps are important. Have someone, somewhere, that you can call in case you get lost.

Planning is very important; if you plan well, there will be no major problems. Above all, remember there is only so much you can control. If a plane or train or bus is late, or your luggage is lost, you had nothing to do with it. Do the best you can, but don't let it ruin your vacation or spoil the fun for others.

ADVANCE PLANNING
(Also see Advance Preparation for camping, p. 776)

Problem	*We are moving cross-country and will be driving two cars. We need a way to communicate with my husband who will be in the lead car. We don't have CB radios.*
Solution	Buy little colored plastic flags, letting different colors represent messages (i.e., BLUE, stop for gas, YELLOW, let's eat). Let the kids be the flag wavers.

Moving Day Meals

P   *Anything I can do to help my neighbors when they are moving?*

S   One of the nicest things you can do is fix a farewell meal for them on moving day. Nothing is worse than spending all day packing and then having to clean up to go out and eat. Put everything on disposable plates and they can enjoy their last meal in their home without having to wash a dish—what a thoughtful person you are!

Newspapers

P   *I always feel like a lost sheep in a new town.*

S   Subscribe to the newspaper in that town for a few weeks *before* you move. Things won't seem so strange to you when you arrive and you'll be familiar with the stores from their ads.

Phone Directories

Take a phone directory along with you when you leave a city. Frequently, you'll need the addresses of doctors, banks, schools, etc., in your old hometown.

Prescriptions

If you use prescription drugs, have them refilled before you leave (your doctor will probably need to send records to your new hometown doctor). Carry along your medications, extra eyeglasses, and important papers with you on the trip. You'll feel better knowing they're in your possession.

LUGGAGE

Choosing luggage

P   *I dread traveling by plane because it is so difficult for me to manage a heavy suitcase.*

S   Two smaller suitcases are easier to manage than
         one large one. If your luggage should decide to
         take another plane than the one you're on, at least
         you stand a chance of getting one suitcase on your
         flight!

Extra Luggage

P   *We never have enough room for everything in our
         luggage on the return trip.*
S   Plan ahead and pack an extra bag in your suitcase.
         The cloth type that folds up is ideal; it won't take
         up much room and when you discover you have
         overstuffed your suitcase, you'll have instant extra
         luggage at no extra cost.

Labeling

P   *I always have a terrible time distinguishing my
         luggage from all the others that look like mine.*
S   Mark yours with something different—a red yarn,
         pompom or a big green bow.

*   *   *

P   *My luggage tag came off and it took forever to find
         and identify my luggage.*
S   Always tape identification on the inside, just in
         case.

Lost Luggage

P   *My bag got lost for days on my last airplane flight.*
S   Watch when you check in and be sure they put the
         correct destination on your luggage.

*   *   *

P   *It never fails that my luggage gets lost or arrives a
         day late.*

S   Prevention is the key. Never put anything in your
           suitcase that you must have—medicine, money,
           traveler's checks, house keys, etc. Take a very light
           carry-on bag that will fit under the seat. Fill it with
           makeup, shaving gear, toothbrush and paste, any
           medicine that you must take, and an extra shirt
           and change of underwear—just in case. Enough to
           see you through until the "misrouted" suitcase
           arrives.

Luggage, substitutions

P   *We're making extended visits to our children but
           we don't like living out of a suitcase, and they have
           no extra drawer space.*
S   You could purchase a lightweight fiberboard chest
           of drawers and pack your things in that instead of
           a suitcase. Lay the chest in the back seat or trunk.
           Clothes can be carried in the car on hangers. Use
           the chest at your children's homes.

MOTELS AND HOTELS

P   *Our motel room is a mess only a few minutes after
           we get there and looks like a whirlwind hit it.*
S   If you are only staying for a night or two, there is
           no need to unpack everything. Pull out only what
           you need and then try and put it back when you
           are finished with that article. When it's time to go,
           packing is a snap!

Carrying ID

When you're traveling, always have your "staying address" on
your person. Your driver's license showing your address back home
is not going to help the police locate a relative staying back at the
hotel if something should happen to you.

Be sure your child has some kind of identification on his or her person when traveling.

Correspondence

P   *I like to send postcards to my friends but it's hard to get around to addressing them while on my trips.*

S   Type or write friends' addresses on those adhesive address label sheets before you leave on your trip. When you want to send a card, peel a label off and stick it on the card and mail away. You could have your friends give you a few of their address labels. This would be easier on you!

Fire Exits

Always check where the fire exit is in your hotel or motel . . . . make a mental note how many doors down and which way. If the halls are filled with smoke it's hard to read the exit sign.

Ironing
(See Ironing, p. 647)

P   *How can I do touch-up ironing in a hotel room with no board?*

S   Take along a travel iron and a pillow case. Buy a
         newspaper at the hotel, put it in the pillow case,
         and you have a small "ironing board" to do touch-
         ups on.

*   *   *

P   *Any way to unwrinkle clothes?*
S   Hang them in the shower away from the stream of
         water (close the bathroom door) and steam them
         a few minutes with real hot water.

Laundry

P   *I hate putting my soiled clothes in with my clean
         ones when traveling.*
S   Pillow cases or zippered laundry bags are great.
         The cases tuck nicely in corners and don't take up
         much space.

*   *   *

P   *Dragging along a bottle of detergent to do a small
         amount of hand laundry takes so much room.*
S   Use a little squirt of your hair shampoo.

*   *   *

P   *I wash clothes in the motel sink—but they never
         seem to dry.*
S   Before hanging them up, roll them in a towel and
         squeeze as much moisture out as possible; then use
         your hair dryer to blow them dry if you are in a
         hurry.

*   *   *

When traveling, to solve the problem of never having enough hooks
to hang things on in the motel bathroom, take along a few of those
plastic clothespins with the hook at the top.

These can be hung over towel bars, shower rods and cabinet knobs.

Lost and Found

Take a matchbook from each motel or hotel that you visit. If you should leave something behind, you will have the name and address of the motel handy.

Night-lights

Dark motels or strange bedrooms can upset small children. When you travel, carry a night-light along. Even *you* can make your way to the bathrooms more readily.

* * *

Carry along a lightbulb with sufficient wattage in case you want to read and the light in the motel room is not bright enough.

Soap

P   *Tiny bars of soap in hotels and motels are such a nuisance to use when showering.*

S   Take along a regular-size bar of soap to use in the motel and drop the motel bars into your handbag to use at service station stops.

* * *

Tuck away the small bars of soap and a cloth in a plastic bag for roadside restroom stops.

Towels

P   *My husband and I get our towels mixed up in hotels.*

S   Follow one easy-to-remember rule in traveling . . . let your husband's things always be on the right and yours on the left. This goes for towels, drinking glasses, clothes in the closet, clothes in the drawers, and even as nearly as possible, when

packing the suitcases. This will be his big chance
to *always be right!*

PACKING
(Also see Packing, p. 811)

Bed Linens

P   *When moving it's really a pain to locate bed linens
         in a hurry to get the bed made for the little ones.*

S   Leave an old fitted sheet on the mattress . . . slip
         the top sheet and pillowslips and maybe a light
         blanket inside it. It's all there ready for you when
         you want to put them to bed.

Cleaning Supplies

Put all your cleaning supplies in a wastebasket along with the mop
and broom, and make sure it's the *last* thing on the moving van
(remember, last things in, first things out).

Clothes

P   *I have to pack some clothes for moving and I don't
         want them to get a musty smell.*

S   Place bars of soap in with your clothes (of course,
         be sure that the clothes are clean before packing
         them).

Dishes and Glassware

P   *Washing dishes and glasses that have been wrapped
         in newspapers is a lot of trouble and sure takes a
         lot of time.*

S   Watch for a sale on paper towels and stock up.
         When you are packing to move, wrap all your

"kitchen" things in the paper towels and you
won't have to wash a thing when you start unpack-
ing . . . bonus, you will have a lot of paper towels
for all those dirty hands at your new home!

* * *

Bath and kitchen towels are good to pack dishes and crystal in when
preparing to move.

Drawers

P   *It takes me forever to arrange kitchen drawers
when I move in.*

S   Dump the contents of each drawer into a plastic
bag (you've probably got them arranged like you
want them) *before* you move. Then, at your new
house just place the bags in a drawer and unpack
at leisure. You'll pretty much know exactly where
stuff is and just about where it was at the old
house.

Essentials

P   *Last move we made, we arrived dead tired and had
to unpack boxes before we could do anything.*

S   Take a box along with you in the car that has
essentials like toilet paper, towels, soap, washcloths, can opener, tableware, coffee pot, etc.
When you get there you can open a can of something and feed a hungry child. You will probably
be too tired to eat out!

Hardware

P   *Every time we move, buying nuts and bolts and
picture hangers costs a fortune.*

S   As soon as you take a picture down or remove a
           curtain rod, put the hangers, etc., in a little plastic
           bag and tape the bag directly to the picture or rod.
           They will be right there when it's time to rehang.
           Don't forget where you packed the hammer!

Labeling

P   *Even though I color-coded my packing boxes, I
           can't find what I want easily without having to go
           through twenty kitchen boxes.*
S   When you are packing, number each box K-1 or
           B-2 and so on, and keep a list of approximately
           what goes in it. When you want the blankets for
           your son's room, you know which room and which
           color-coded box it's in. Look at your list and you
           can find the number.

                    *   *   *

P   *Any way to make the move any easier—I wound up
           with forty boxes marked "miscellaneous."*

S   Yes, there sure is, for you and the mover. When
       you start moving, assign each room a color. Yel-
       low for the kitchen, blue for the first bedroom,
       green for the living room, etc. When you pack a
       box or carton, put a strip of that color tape on
       the box to indicate which room it goes in. Col-
       ored felt-tip markers can also be used. You
       should put a strip of the colored tape or a col-
       ored piece of paper over the door jambs in the
       new house to direct the mover. When the mover
       unloads the cartons he'll know which room to
       place the boxes in.

                    *   *   *

P   *I don't want my refrigerator to smell after being*
       closed up for so long during our move.
S   Be sure it is clean, clean, clean, and put some
       charcoal in some panty hose and then tie them in
       the door; also put some in the freezer. Stuffing the
       whole thing with newspaper helps absorb odors
       also.
       (Also see Refrigerator, p. 546)

On Arrival

P   *We are moving and I have to go house-hunting in*
       a strange city; how will I remember what's what
       and where's where?
S   First thing, buy yourself a map of that city and a
       little notebook. For every house you look at, trace
       the route to the house on your map and circle the
       location. Make a few notes about the house in your
       notebook (address, color, size, price, distance from
       schools, churches, shopping, etc.). You'll be able
       to easily decide which houses you want to go back
       and look at again.

                    *   *   *

When moving into a new neighborhood, it is very important to teach your children their new phone number and address. You think you get confused—think how a small child feels! If they can't remember this information, it is a good idea to have them wear an ID bracelet (homemade is fine). Or, you can even have them wear a little name tag showing their name and address. This will turn out to be an icebreaker in meeting other kids in your area.

TRIPTAKING

Children
(Also see Identification, Child, p. 814)

P   *We love to travel with our child, but the car does get pretty cluttered.*

S   Hang a shoe bag over the back seat to hold small toys, crayons, bottles, etc.

*   *   *

In the summertime, the first things kids want to do when they get to the motel is swim, so tuck their swimwear in a little bag and have it handy. You won't have to unpack or unload all those suitcases right away.

*   *   *

P   *How can I make a sleeping or play area in my car for my small child.*

S   Place the suitcases on the floor of the car of the back seat. Then lay a baby mattress across them to make the "floor" level with the seat. By spreading a quilt or two across them you have a good area for the baby to sleep or play in during stops. Remember, a baby, too, should be protected by a restraining device.

*   *   *

A metal cake pan with a sliding lid is a good lap desk for traveling children. Crayons, color books, etc., will store inside the pan, and the lid makes a good writing surface.

*   *   *

Older children might enjoy taking along a notebook and making a journal of the trip. The journal can be used for a souvenir or for a school report.

*   *   *

P   *We need a way to help keep our two older children occupied.*

S   Give each of them a large map of the United States and a colored pencil. They can watch for license plates from the various states and as they spy one, mark it on the corresponding state on the map.

        Not only will they have fun spotting the different plates, but it will help them to learn the location of each state.

*   *   *

Stop and buy sandwich makings and drinks, then find a nice roadside park. While you are eating your snack you can walk around and rest your back and legs. It's great to let the kids "let off steam."

*   *   *

P   *We love to stop for picnics, but sometimes we can't find a table.*

S   Put a folding TV tray in your trunk . . . just set it up and you have a place to put all your lunch goodies on.

*   *   *

P   *I give my kids a drink when traveling, but then minutes later they are asking for another.*

S   If you will give them a cup of crushed ice instead of water, it will occupy them longer and still quench their thirst (real or imagined!). Keep a small foam chest full of crushed ice and a few cups inside the car.

*   *   *

Put ice cubes in a plastic bag closed tightly with a rubber band. Punch a hole in a corner to drink from. Less spills and mess than a cup of water and it keeps youngsters happy for awhile.

*   *   *

P   *Our young children get so restless sitting in the restaurant waiting for our orders after they've sat in the car for so long on our trip*

S   Have one parent go in and order for everyone, letting the children have the freedom to move around outside (under supervision, of course). You won't have fussy children squirming or arguing about what to order.

*   *   *

P   *I would like to provide my preschooler with some type of identification as I worry about her straying from the campsite.*

S   Make the child a wrist band out of twill tape. Use indelible, waterproof ink and write her full name and the number of your lot and campsite on it. Fit it on her wrist securely and stress to her that she must keep it on at all times.

P   *I'm always turning around to supervise the kids in the back seat while driving.*

S   That could be very dangerous. Clip a mirror on the dashboard or put one on the driver's sun visor.

*   *   *

P   *My kids could make a mud puddle in the Sahara Desert with just one teaspoon of water—they get so dirty when we travel.*

S   Resign yourself and just carry along a detergent bottle filled with a little soap and water and take a washcloth and towel. Easy to wash off little dirty faces and hands just before you arrive.

*   *   *

P   *My child always spills his drink in the car.*

S   Use one of those training cups with the lid and spout—even an older child enjoys drinking from them.

*   *   *

P   *My family loves to stop at the beach when traveling but I dislike sand tracked in the car by the kids.*

S   Dampen washcloths and put them in plastic bags fastened with a twistie. As the kiddos get in the car, have them wipe their feet off and put the sandy cloth back into the bag.

Loading the Car

Take along an electric coffee pot or hot pot to heat water in. Use instant coffee, and you have "room service" right in your room. When your feet hit the floor, you can have that morning cup of coffee right there to enjoy while you dress for breakfast. Oh, so nice, and cheap!

*   *   *

Take pillows with several cases on them to make things more comfortable in the car. As one case becomes soiled, slip it off and the pillow will be ready to use with a fresh one already on. The dirty case can be used to hold dirty laundry.

*   *   *

P   *I don't have any garment bags but I need some-thing to protect my suits in my car.*

S   Button up the clothing inside an old raincoat or use several plastic cleaners' bags.

*   *   *

P   *I want to carry some dresses on a rod in the back seat of my car, but they hang down too far and drag.*

S   Put cardboard tubes on the hangers and then lay your dresses across the hangers just as you do pants. They won't wrinkle or drag on the car floor.

Map Reading

P   *I can't drive and read the map at the same time. I need some navigating help.*

S   If you are traveling alone, write out your travel route in advance. Pin the route to the seat of your car or tape it on the dash. No one can safely drive and read a map at the same time.

Medicine

P   *Traveling with large bottles of all my vitamins takes up room.*

S   Count out the number of days you will be gone and take only what is needed in small suitable bottles or plastic bags.

Money

Before leaving on a trip, accumulate some change and put it in a small purse. Have it handy for telephones, pay toilets, and drink machines along the way.

Packing Suitcase
(Also see Loading the Car, p. 815, Packing, p. 808, and Personal Items, packing, p. 818)

Clothes

P   *My clothes always arrive wrinkled.*
S   Roll your clothes or pack with plastic bags—put the heavier things in the bottom of the suitcase.

*   *   *

A space saver when you are packing is to roll all belts, ties and even small things like slips, and put them inside your shoes. Don't let any space go to waste.

*   *   *

Always prepare an itemized list of articles in your suitcases. In case they are lost, the carrier will ask for such a list and it will save you time and hassle. Keep the list in your purse or pocket.

*   *   *

P   *I hate pulling everything out of my suitcase just to get one thing that always seems to be on the bottom.*
S   A really nifty way to pack it is to put everything in large, clear plastic bags. Shirts in one, pants in another, shoes, toilet articles, etc. Then all you have to do is slip just one bag out, and the rest stays neat.

*   *   *

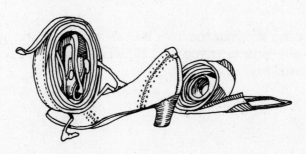

P   *I either take along too many clothes or not enough.*

S   You need to make out a "clothes menu" before you go. Plan each day's activities and what you will wear. Mix and match—all the same color scheme—and your accessories and outfits will "go further."

*   *   *

P   *I'm always forgetting my slip or black shoes, etc.*

S   Write out a master list. Start thinking from shoes up—shoes, stockings, slip, dress, jewelry, etc.— and use this list to pack from.

*   *   *

P   *Every time I go through the security check they practically have to dump out my handbag or purse.*

S   Plan for it, dear. Put all the things in your purse in several small plastic bags and they can just lift the bags out instead of digging around. Sometimes it's embarrassing, isn't it!

Personal Items

A handful of safety pins and a few threaded needles stuck to the inside of your suitcase will come in handy when a button pops off or a hem comes undone.

*   *   *

Travel often? Save time and space by buying sample-size toiletries and leaving them in your suitcase.

*   *   *

For traveling, slip your toothbrush inside a clean plastic hair roller or small pill bottle after you have cut an opening in the top. Slip it into a plastic bag.

*   *   *

P   *I hate packing a wet toothbrush.*
S   Blow it dry with your hair dryer.

*   *   *

P   *I love the convenience of towelettes when I travel, but they cost too much.*
S   Moisten cotton pads with a mixture of rubbing alcohol and water (half water and half alcohol). Put them in a small jar with a tight-fitting lid. These are cooling, soothing, and you can throw away the jar prior to returning home.

*   *   *

Those premoistened towelettes are not just for baby—use them to remove makeup, wash your hands, or just revive tired feet!

*   *   *

You can carry a wet paper towel in a plastic pill bottle—handy to use for changing the baby, then just toss in the trash.

PART THREE:

All Around
the House

INTRODUCTION

The third part of this book is about the people and pets in your life.

Putting together Chapter ten, "Babies and Children," was a simple matter of putting good information into logical order. Can you apply logic to children, though? That's one question I'm not going to even attempt to answer! But the information is all here for you—to help with those little wonders when they stump you! When you are frustrated and at wit's end, just remember that children (no matter what age) don't necessarily do things *to* parents, they do them just 'cuz they're kids.

There are no required courses on how to raise children; parents don't have to go to school or get a license somewhere. Parents just do their best, make the best judgment they can at the time, and hope. So if you have a problem with your kids, I hope the answers are here to help in your day-to-day battle to stay one step ahead of the children (sometimes one step behind, and that's called "picking up after").

Chapter eleven, "In Sickness and in Health," is for those among our family and friends who don't have it so easy. Sometimes, when someone we love is handicapped, even though it may be only temporary, it is difficult to deal with. What do you do when you have to have an ice pack in a hurry and you have none in the freezer ready and waiting? How do you help someone who has a broken leg and can't get up the stairs or carry out the garbage? This chapter of the book will help you solve these problems and many more.

To be handicapped doesn't mean to be totally dependent on others. There are a lot of hints in Chapter eleven to help those who are less able to do things for themselves.

The elderly—or Senior Citizens, if you will—are able to do a lot for themselves, and it helps them maintain a positive outlook to know that they can. We have some nifty hints for them as well.

If you own pets, you know that they are just like members of the family. I have a household full of them, so Chapter twelve, "Pets," has been a joy to put together. I used to say that I own a dog, but she really owns me—and that doesn't bother me in the least! Tequila is a little 3-pound chihuahua that has been my roommate and companion for over six years. She is twelve years old now and so she is quite an old lady but still in good health and perky as ever.

When I got married, I told my husband, David, that along with me came Tequila. That agreement was all right with him, because *he* had a macaw (large parrot) of whom *I* wasn't overly fond. So our family of animals now includes Rocky who has finally come to like me a bit . . . not a bite, just a bit.

To those, add little Fussy, a cockatiel who sings in the early morning and sometimes flies into the glass window when he is out of the cage. The only way I can keep him from doing this is to make sure the drapes are closed.

The last of our pet family, but most surely not least, is Fred the Ferret. You are probably asking yourself "Did she mean another parrot?" No, a ferret is a small animal, similar to a mink or weasel, and a real delight to watch. How, you ask, did Heloise end up with a ferret as a pet? Well, it's a long story but the ending is, I saw one in a pet store and the rest is history. Fred is a little unusual in that he is an albino, which has caused some problems. When we put him in his cage, we put newspaper down just like you do for hamsters, but the newsprint started turning his white coat of fur black. This was a problem for Heloise. Solution: I used shredded brown paper bags instead, and give old Fred a bath every few days.

How do you bathe a ferret? Just like you do a baby in the kitchen sink! The fun part is using the hair dryer to dry him.

So off we go—All Around the House.

—Hugs, Heloise

10

Babies and Children

Children make the world go round and round, don't they? Sometimes you're tempted to ask yourself if they really are worth it—
usually when they've just tracked mud in on your clean floor—but
then a little one comes up with a posy and a hug for no special reason.

This chapter gives you the benefit of experience of mothers who
have been through it all, from handling the 2:00 A.M. feeding to
entertaining a bored preschooler on a rainy day.

Parenting calls on inner resources and strength and most of all,
love. We all need to remember that no one is going to be a perfect
mother or father, and that to do your best is all anyone, or any child,
can ask. You may look back on the times when you didn't know to
put ice on a bump or let a little one suck on a popsicle instead of
holding an ice pack to his lip . . . but remember, love can more than
make up for the mistakes you think you've made along the way. If

826

children know you love them, some of the mechanics of mothering don't seem so important.

Give your children lots of hugs, and maybe they won't know that the toast was burnt and you scraped it off. I won't tell.

BABIES

Announcements

Problem	*Being nonsmokers, we would like a suggestion for something to pass out besides cigars when our new baby arrives.*
Solution	Why not have ball-points printed with "It's a girl" or "It's a boy."

Baby Book

P	*Keeping my baby's book up-to-date is a real problem.*
S	If the book is handy, it will be easier. Keep it on a bedside table and enter things each night. Or, keep note pads around to jot things down, then transfer them to the book later. Use a kitchen calendar to make quick notes.

Bathing

P	*My baby gets so bored when I bathe her in the sink.*
S	Cut out some pretty pictures and put them on the cabinet where she can see them. Or, hang a pretty mobile above so she can look up and see something besides blank wall space.

* * *

P	*Drying my baby seems so difficult with his squirming around.*

S   Use a big beach towel and completely wrap baby
         up. He will be easy to hold and no problem with
         missed wet spots.

*   *   *

Cold lotion doesn't feel too good on baby's skin. Put the plastic bottle
(with the cap on tightly) in the baby's tub (or other sink) during the
bath so it can warm. Warm the shampoo this way, also.

*   *   *

P   *Baby powder is very expensive for me. Can I substi-*
         tute?
S   Mix the powder with a box of cornstarch or baking
         soda to make it go further. Both are wonderful and
         safe to use.

*   *   *

If you bathe baby in the kitchen sink, place a hand towel or small
piece of foam rubber in the bottom and baby won't slip. Makes a soft
cushion, too.

*   *   *

P   *My baby is so slippery when I bathe her—I am*
         really afraid sometimes she will slip.
S   If you will leave a T-shirt on when bathing the tiny
         one, you can hold on easily. No slippery skin.

*   *   *

P   *My baby slips in his plastic bathtub.*
S   Lay a towel in the bottom of the tub; I think
         nonskid appliqués would be too rough and
         scratchy.

*   *   *

P   *Every time I bathe my baby, she spits up.*
S   Some wee ones don't like to be jostled—are you
         bathing her right after a feeding? Why not bathe
         your baby before you feed her and see if that helps?

P   *My baby is too large for his infant tub and really*
      too small for the family tub.

S   Use a plastic laundry basket that is the woven
      type. You can put this in the tub and baby in it.
      The water flows in and out and he stays in one
      place. Never, never leave a child alone in water—
      no matter how shallow the water is.

Beds and Cribs
(Also see Baby Bed for Camping, p. 797)

Beds

A towel rack attached to the outside end of baby's crib is so handy
to hold blankets, towels, and such. Just be sure that your baby can't
pull them into the crib.

*   *   *

For a very tiny baby, you can keep all the things that you need close
at hand, like powder, pins, wipes, etc., at the end of the crib. Just
hook a bicycle basket at one end of the crib to hold all the essentials.
Of course, when baby starts pulling himself up, move the basket to
another spot.

*   *   *

Beach towels make good summer blankets for baby. Easy to wash
and dry.

P   *Our baby's room is drafty. How can I keep the draft off the baby at night?*

S   Take the mattress out of the crib and slip a blanket under the springs. Pull up the sides of the blanket and secure the sides to the crib railings. Replace the mattress.

*   *   *

P   *Putting my baby back in a cold bed after an early morning feeding always wakes her up.*

S   Keep a plugged-in heating pad with a towel wrapped around it next to the baby's bed; as soon as she is lifted from the bed, put the heating pad in. When you return her bed is nice and warm.

*   *   *

P   *When the weather gets cool, the plastic liner that I use on the baby's crib makes the bed so cold.*

S   Place a large beach towel between the liner and the sheet.

*   *   *

P   *My baby kicks the covers off.*

S   Fasten men's suspenders to each side of the cover and secure loosely under the mattress. Or, using shower curtain rings, attach the blanket to the side rails. You can sew blanket "pillowcases" to slip the baby into.

*   *   *

Placing baby's crib at a diagonal from the corner of the room makes it easy to change the sheets, etc. You can get to your baby from both sides of the bed and there's no chance of little fingers touching the wall.

*   *   *

P   *My little "darling" drives me up a wall shaking his bed and watching it walk across the room.*

S   It's amazing how those little ones can figure out things at such an early age. If you want to outsmart him, put sponges underneath each leg of the crib . . . that creepy, crawly crib won't crawl.

*   *   *

P   *I hate to put my baby back in a damp bed—even though I have changed the sheets.*
S   Use your hand-held hair dryer to quickly dry out those damp spots and warm the bed.

*   *   *

P   *The little ones in the neighborhood always seem to ring my doorbell during my baby's nap time.*
S   Post a picture of a sleeping baby on the door. Even the smallest tyke can tell that it's not the right time to ring the bell.

*   *   *

P   *I have to wash so many sheets for such a tiny baby.*
S   Use only one sheet on the crib. Tuck the sheet in the top as usual, then fold it halfway back up the bed. It's kinda like "short-sheeting," but a tiny baby never gets down to the bottom anyway.

*   *   *

Ever had to completely change a wet crib at three o'clock in the morning? Next time you make the bed, make it up "twice," with rubber pad, sheet, rubber pad, sheet, etc. When the bed gets wet, remove the top sheet and rubber pad. The dry bedding underneath is ready to use.

Bottles

P   *How do I get that chalky deposit out of my baby's bottles?*
S   Boil the bottles in water with one or two cups of

vinegar added, for ten minutes or so. To prevent
this chalky deposit, add a little vinegar to the
water each time you sterilize the bottles.

*   *   *

P   *The plastic bottles my baby uses have developed an
        odor.*
S   Boil the bottles for a few minutes in baking soda
        and water.

*   *   *

P   *No matter how well I clean baby bottle nipples, they
        get so clogged.*
S   Use a toothpick to gently push through the hole.

*   *   *

P   *Every time I wash bottles, caps and nipples in my
        dishwasher, they scatter.*
S   Put them in a nylon net bag with a drawstring
        closure.

*   *   *

P   *My baby can't hold a bottle because it's slippery.*
S   Make a tube out of a small sock and slip the bottle
        inside.

*   *   *

P   *Even though my baby can hold her playthings, her
        bottle seems to be impossible.*
S   Place one of the colored plastic rings around the
        bottle. It will attract her attention, and since she
        is used to holding it, she will want to hold the
        bottle.

*   *   *

P   *The baby bottles in the fridge are always falling
        over and are really bothersome.*

S Use a cardboard carton that soft drinks come in. The compartments will hold six bottles, and they won't fall over every time you reach in the fridge.

* * *

P *When my friends and I visit, getting baby bottles mixed up is a disaster.*

S Put a different colored rubber band or a small piece of tape on the bottles to color-code them.

* * *

P *How can I keep plastic disposable bottles from leaking when traveling?*

S Put a piece of plastic wrap over the bottle opening before putting on the nipple and cap.

 Remember, water temperature and bottle temperature should always be checked, using the crook of your elbow. Your hands are less sensitive to heat.

* * *

P *I just dread dragging myself to the kitchen to warm the bottle for the 2:00 A.M. feeding.*

S Before going to bed, heat the bottle to the right temperature, while at the same time filling a wide vacuum bottle with hot water to warm it. When the baby bottle is ready, pour out the hot water, pop in the bottle, and close the lid. Keep this by baby's crib and you won't have to take an extra step.

* * *

Heat baby's bottle in a coffee can. It's deeper and more narrow, and the bottle will heat faster. Remember, the can will be hot so don't touch.

* * *

P   *I want to go out but I worry about how to keep baby's bottle warm.*

S   After you warm the bottle to the right temp, put it in a clean, round, potato chip can, put the lid on and wrap in a towel. When it's time to eat, the bottle is still warm.

*   *   *

P   *I hate to have to spend the money for a bottle warmer.*

S   If you have a slow cooker, this works just great. Keep it turned on low. The water isn't hot enough to boil, but warm enough to get the milk to the right temperature in no time.

*   *   *

P   *Weaning my baby from her bottle is almost impossible.*

S   When it is time to start getting her away from the bottle, take the lid off and let the little one start drinking from her old favorite bottle, then move onto a cup.

*   *   *

P   *My little one just refuses to drink from a cup and won't touch anything that isn't in his bottle.*

S   This just might do the trick . . . fill the bottle with something that doesn't taste as good as whatever you put in his cup . . . for example, put very diluted juice in his bottle, and the good stuff in the cup. When there is a "taste test"—guess which one will be picked!

Bathtime

P   *My toddler loves to play with plastic toys in the bathtub, but oh, the mess afterwards.*

S   Keep a nylon net bag handy to put those drippy
       toys in after the fun's over. Just hang it over the
       faucet handle to drip dry.

       To delight the small fry, cut animals such as
       frogs, turtles and fish out of colorful construction
       paper. Coat them with paraffin, let dry, and they
       will float on the water.

       Fun at bathtime!

Colds

P   *My young baby doesn't sleep well when she has a
       cold.*

S   Try propping up the head of the bed with books
       or pillows under the mattress; if your baby is very
       young, use the infant seat to keep baby's head
       elevated. The baby will breathe easier in an ele-
       vated position and will be able to sleep more com-
       fortably.

Diapers

There are always days when everything gets off schedule or seems
to go wrong! Be prepared by having a supply of disposable diapers
(even though you don't ordinarily use them) and ready-to-use formula on hand, prescribed by your pediatrician, of course.

*   *   *

To keep those diaper pins gliding easily through the diaper, just stick
the pin in a bar of soap before using.

*   *   *

P   *I hate to throw away a new disposable diaper which
       can't be used because the tab's pulled off.*

S   Don't! Keep an adhesive bandage or some adhe-
       sive tape handy and make a new tab.

*   *   *

P	*Occasionally I have to dry diapers indoors, but I don't really have the room to dry as many as my baby needs.*
S	Hang two coat hangers on your shower curtain rod. Pin one corner of a diaper to one hanger, and the other corner to the other hanger. Fill up the hangers (they're parallel), and it's just like two short clotheslines, side by side.

When those two "clotheslines" are full, start with another two hangers. You can really hang a bunch this way.

*   *   *

Ever been caught with sopping wet plastic pants for baby and no dry ones to be had? Wash them out, then dry them in a hurry, using your electric hair dryer.

*   *   *

You like soft things next to your skin and so does your baby. Add a fabric softener to your last rinse or use a softener in the dryer for your diapers. Besides being soft and feeling good, the diapers will be easier to pin.

*   *   *

P	*Sometimes while visiting, I can't find a place to lay a soiled diaper when changing a baby.*
S	A fancy bedspread or carpet just isn't the spot, right! Well, get one of those plastic "flying saucer"

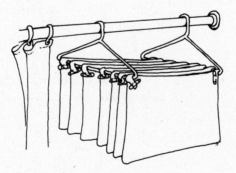

shaped toys with the curled edge and stick it in your diaper bag.

It's a perfect place to plop the diaper down temporarily and the plastic toy is light and easily washed.

*   *   *

Take along some empty coffee cans with plastic lids to put soiled diapers in when away from home.

*   *   *

P   *I ran out of premoistened towelettes.*
S   Keep a supply of diaper liners handy to use as wipes. Have a vacuum bottle of warm water nearby to wet the liners.

*   *   *

P   *I wish I didn't have to put a cold diaper on my baby at night.*
S   Slip a few diapers (perhaps a gown, too) under your electric blanket or heating pad. Diapers will be nice and warm for baby's change.

Feeding

P   *My little one loves fresh bananas, but those little fingers just can't hold them.*
S   Slippery banana slices can be a hassle. Roll them in graham cracker crumbs and they'll have something to hold onto.

*   *   *

P   *It never fails that when I'm feeding my "little darling" she dumps the entire bowl of food on her head. Help!*
S   Before feeding her put a plastic shower cap on her head. Make it a game and she won't know it's for her own good—and your sanity.

P *I need a bib for myself when I feed my little one! It seems like more food ends up on me than in his mouth.*

S Mom should have a bib, too. Slip on a large man's old shirt, or anything that covers most of you.

*   *   *

P *My youngest (eighteen months) insists on feeding herself, and oh, what a mess at the table.*

S Give the lady her own space, as the saying goes . . . put her in a regular chair and be sure she is secure. Then belly up a TV tray and it should be just about her height.

*   *   *

P *Handling a bowl, spoon and baby too, is sometimes a chore.*

S Use a tea or coffee cup that has a handle so you can hold onto it securely. And even if little hands hit it, you don't have to worry about it being dropped to the floor.

*   *   *

Small plastic spoons, like the kind that come with ice cream or ice tea are perfect for feeding a baby. They are tiny for their mouths and the plastic isn't as hard on their gums as metal is.

An iced tea spoon is much easier to feed baby with than a regular teaspoon. The bowl is smaller and fits those little mouths.

* * *

Baby learning to feed himself or herself? Spread strained meat from a jar of baby food on a cracker. They can hold a cracker easier than a spoon.

* * *

P *I can't get my baby to swallow his liquid vitamins once I get them into his mouth.*

S From the smell of them, who'd want to! But, when baby won't swallow, just gently blow in his face. It really works.

* * *

P *There is no closet in my baby's room.*

S Suspend a hula hoop toy from the ceiling and hang the clothes hangers on it.

* * *

P *I can't afford curtains for my baby's room, but want something "baby-looking."*

S Buy summer receiving blankets (much cheaper than curtains) and hem an edge to slip a rod through.

* * *

A sturdy card table covered with a mattress pad makes a nifty dressing table for baby.

* * *

Got a huge baby gift to wrap? Why not buy a disposable plastic or paper tablecloth? It usually doesn't cost as much as a couple of packages of wrapping paper and it surely will be easier to manage! Cute, too!

High Chairs

P   *When visiting friends who don't have a high chair*
         or booster seat, my small one's chin rests on a table
         when we eat.

S   The phone book to the rescue (if you live in a large
         town). I can remember some of my best meals,
         sitting on top of large (fat) books with a small
         pillow as a cushion. There are some grandparents
         who have a special phone book. It's last year's
         edition, covered with adhesive-backed paper . . .
         not much extra money spent for a chair booster.

                          *   *   *

If you don't have the time to take the high chair to the car wash for
a good cleaning, put it in the shower. Let the shower run a while,
and all the built-up grime should go down the drain, with a little
help.

                          *   *   *

P   *My baby's high chair gets pretty gunked up with*
         spills.

S   Make it easy on yourself to clean! Just stick it
         outside in the rain or turn the lawn sprinkler on
         it.

                          *   *   *

P   *My baby slips down in his high chair.*

S   Safety pin a towel or tie a bib to the back of the
         seat of the chair. No slipping, and the towel will
         catch spills, too.
             You can also put strips of adhesive tape or foam
         rubber on the seat of the chair for "grip."

                          *   *   *

P   *My young son has a way of tipping over his high*
         chair.

S   If you attach a large screen door hook to the back of the chair and when he is in the chair, hook it to the wall, you'll never fear about the tot falling over. You could even put a hook on each of the back legs for safety.

*   *   *

P   *My little girl is big enough to sit in the high chair, but she wobbles from side to side.*

S   Make some bumper pads for her. You can roll up hand towels or even a bath size towel. Then just place them on the sides of the high chair and your "precious" can bob and weave but she won't wobble out.

Injuries

P   *I can't keep the little hands of my baby protected when injured.*

S   Clean and bandage the area, then cover it with a baby stretch sock.

Nailtrimming

P   *My baby really protests having his nails cut.*

S   Use blunt pointed scissors to cut his nails while he is sleeping.

Pacifier

P   *My baby always manages to drop his pacifier and screams until I get it sterilized.*

S   Tie a pretty ribbon onto the pacifier and pin the ribbon to his clothing, or attach it to his high chair.

*   *   *

A fussy baby in a waiting room is not much fun for mom, baby or others. Stash a few little toys or items in a plastic bag that will amuse the baby. Also, a little sweet-coated dry cereal tucked in a sandwich bag is a lifesaver at times!

Playpen (See Baby Bed for Camping, p. 797)

P   *I "inherited" a mesh playpen which is in good condition except for looking horribly dirty and dingy.*

S   Put a solution of bleach and water in a spray bottle and spray the mesh liberally, scrub and then rinse *well.* Afterwards, if there is a remaining bleach smell, spray a little liquid fabric softener on the mesh. If the playpen is completely washable, the high pressure hose at the car wash would be great!

* * *

P   *My toddler aggravates his older brother who's trying to build with blocks.*

S   Try putting the older brother in the playpen out of the reach of the exploring but well-meaning brother!

Quick Meals

Got a "starving baby" who can't wait for anyone to dress for breakfast when you're on a trip? Mix dry powdered milk (if okay with your doctor) with dry cereal. Just add hot faucet water at the motel. Jars of fruit can be added for a yummy taste. Feed baby, dress at leisure, and everybody's happy!

Security Blanket

P   *I have a toddler who won't part with his blanket— that thing is dragged around through the dirt— yuck!*

S   Cut the blanket in half. Then, after awhile, cut the blanket in quarters. He can't drag the small part through the dirt—at least, not very easily—and an added bonus is that part of his beloved treasure can be in the wash. You'll always have a clean part to give to the child.

Stroller

P   *I love to go shopping, but my little one is not old enough to sit up in a stroller.*

S   Put the baby in a plastic infant seat and then place the seat in the stroller. Of course, make sure the baby is well secured.

Teething

P   *How can I make my teething baby feel better?*

S   Fill a sterilized nipple with water and then freeze it. Place it on a baby bottle and give to your baby. For an older baby, chewing on a piece of frozen weiner is sheer delight!

Traveling

Baby fussy in the car? Pin or tape some bright pictures above the car seat to amuse the child.

*   *   *

Take along your baby's car seat on a long train or bus trip. They get tired of being held and mom's arms need a rest, too.

*   *   *

An inflatable child's swimming pool makes an excellent temporary travel bed for a wee one.

Walker

P   *My baby's walker makes marks on my walls.*

S   For bumpers, split a few short lengths of old
        garden hose and place on the edges of the walk-
        er.

CHILDREN

Beds, Bedding and Bedtime

P   *My three-year-old likes to sleep on a top bunk at his
        cousin's house—I worry that he might slip through
        the rail.*

S   Take a full size bed sheet, fold it in half widthwise.
        Hang the sheet over the rail and tuck both ends
        under the mattress.

*   *   *

Ever think that when your youngster lies on the bottom bunk he or
she has nothing to look at—tack some "interesting" fabric or pictures on the underside of the top bunk to brighten up the spot.

*   *   *

A neat way to place bunk beds is to slide the lower bed under the
upper one at a right angle (put both footboards on one bed and both

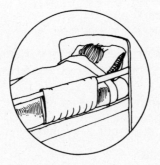

headboards upside down on the other). This doesn't take up as much room as twin beds.

* * *

P   *My daughter wants a canopy bed, which is out of the question right now.*

S   An inexpensive "canopy" of nylon net may satisfy her until her dream comes true! Find an old umbrella and take the cloth cover off so you only have the skeleton left. Fold the ribs down on one side so you have only half an umbrella. Using the cover folded in half for a pattern, cut three layers of nylon net. Make two-inch net ruffles to go along the edge and along each rib.

Now, tack the net cover on the half umbrella skeleton. Then add your ruffles around the edges and along the ribs. If you like, add a few silk or plastic flowers here and there.

* * *

P   *My daughter is weary of her old headboard—any suggestions for an inexpensive change?*

S   Take the headboard down and hang woven straw mats or straw decorations above the bed, or tack a fake fur rug over the headboard for a new look.

* * *

P   *My little one stays black and blue hitting her legs on the corner of the bed.*

S   Tie sponges on the bed frame legs. They won't show under the spread.

* * *

P   *My son refuses to make his bed in the morning.*

S   Strip off all the sheets, blankets, pillow cases, and spread—fold them and put them under the pillow. Remaking a bed from scratch is not much fun—

two or three times of this should make him willing
to make his bed as he should.

*　　*　　*

P   *My "little" boy is no longer little—any way I can*
     "stretch" his twin bed to fit him?

S   Buy some foam rubber as firm as you can find. Cut
     it the width of the bed and the depth of the box
     springs and mattress combined; make the foam
     about six inches long to extend the bed. Cover the
     foam with material. Put this on the edge between
     the headboard and the mattress, and the bed is six
     inches longer. (You might need a bed slat to sup-
     port the foam insert.) This works only when the
     bed frame is open at the foot.

*　　*　　*

P   *My little boy sometimes wets the bed—and over-*
     night visits make him (and me) edgy.

S   Carry along an old waterproof shower curtain to
     slip under the sheet. The mattress will be pro-
     tected.

*　　*　　*

P   *My little girl drives me "crazy" at night asking for*
     a drink every ten minutes.

S   Keep a plastic bottle of water or juice by the bed-
     side and a small plastic glass. It will save you steps
     and she can have her drink anytime.

*　　*　　*

Daddy travel a lot? Have him read some bedtime stories onto a tape
recorder. Makes "missing him" a little easier on the kids. (Mom likes
to hear his voice, too . . . kinda like a long-distance phone call.)

Car Pools

P   *I drive a car pool with preschoolers and I fear I*
     may smash one of their fingers in the door.

S   Before you close the door, make a game of it—like "Everybody, hands on your head."

*   *   *

P   *My little girl is joining a car pool—she is afraid she won't remember the right car.*

S   Buy different colored toy cars to match cars in your car pool and write or tape the last three numbers in the license of that car on the toy. Each day pack the right color car in her lunch or in her school bag. Then she'll know what color car to look for in the afternoon and will be sure it's the right car by the last three numbers.

Chicken Pox

Use your hair dryer to give relief to chicken pox itching. Put it on warm if the child feels chilly or on cool if the child feels hot. *Only you* should use the hair dryer—don't give it to the child.

Childproofing
(Also see Doors and Drawers in cabinets, p. 566)

P   *My toddler locked herself in the bathroom and both of us were upset, to say the least.*

S   If you will put a thick towel over the top of the door, your child can't completely close it.

*   *   *

P   *My child is always pulling drawers out and may get hurt.*

S   Stick a sock in the side for a wedge—very little ones can't pull the drawer out.

*   *   *

Do you have a curious little tyke in your household who loves to dial numbers on the phone?

Place a large rubber band over the receiver buttons to hold them down. If "Junior" decides to make a long-distance call, he can dial away but the numbers won't connect.

Clothes/Dressing

When making or buying clothing for two or more children of the same sex, don't buy things exactly alike, no matter how cute you think it is at the time.

By the time the youngest child has gone through the oldest child's hand-me-downs, not only is the child sick of looking at the same shirt, but you are, too.

If you want to dress them alike, buy different colors of the same design. At least you'll have some variety.

*   *   *

P   *My child needs help putting on her coat.*

S   You can teach her easily this way. Lay her coat on the floor with the lining facing up. Have the child

stand by the collar, bend down and slip her arms into the sleeves, then toss the coat over her head.

* * *

P   *My toddler is so fussy when I'm dressing her.*

S   Try dressing your child in front of a full-length mirror. The mirror fascinates a child and will distract her.

* * *

P   *My little girl's hair is too thin to hold a barrette.*

S   Glue a rubber band on the inside of the barrette; it will grip well and keep it in place.

* * *

P   *Every time I cut my children's hair, they complain of hair in their eyes even though I use a cloth and am careful.*

S   Put one of those "sun visor" shades on them when you cut their hair. Much easier.

* * *

P   *I have the hardest time remembering the length of laces needed for my kids' shoes.*

S   If you can remember the number of holes in his or her shoes, and multiply six by that number (one side only), then you've got it made.

For instance, if there are five holes on one side of the shoe, multiply five times six, which means you need to buy 30-inch laces.

* * *

A prewash spray and a little elbow grease will remove most scuff marks from children's vinyl shoes.

* * *

P   *My son is forever scuffing up his good shoes.*

S   Cover up those scuffs and scratches with a felt-tip
pen that matches the shoes. They come in a variety
of colors.

Give it a second coat of liquid furniture polish
or shoe wax to bring out the shine.

*   *   *

P   *My little girl has several pairs of lace-trimmed
socks which go with special outfits, but I always
have to frantically hunt for the matching pair.*

S   Next time, after laundering the dress and socks,
pin them together. No more searching for the
socks at the last minute.

*   *   *

P   *I have the hardest time keeping up with my children's socks, and when they do end up in the wash,
there's always a "lone" stranger with no mate.*

S   When buying socks for the kiddos, buy all the
same color, or preferably solid white. That way, if
you do happen to lose one, you'll still be able to
have a pair.

*   *   *

Socks worn out but still good in parts? Try this!

Use the stretchy tops to protect knees and elbows a little more when skating. Use the good tops as wrist and leg bands on pajamas and jacket cuffs.

A small child's worn-out knee-hi socks, when the tops are stitched together after cutting a U-shape for the crotch on each sock, make cute little pantyhose for a doll.

How about a nifty sleeping bag for a fashion doll?

What kid couldn't use a marble bag! Make a casing and add a draw string. Cut the foot off, gather the cut end and tie in a little "top knot." Roll the edge up and you have a cute "toboggan cap" for a favorite doll.

*   *   *

P   *My little boy can't manage the zipper pull on his coat.*

S   Put a notebook ring or metal shower curtain hook on the zipper pull. He can slip his fingers in and pull.

Emergencies

Keep an easy-to-read list of emergency phone numbers by the phone and teach your children how and when to use them. If the child is too young to read but can pick out numbers, place pictures of a policeman, fire truck, etc., with the appropriate telephone numbers in large writing next to each picture.

Organizing Room, Closet and Supplies
(Also see Organizing closets, p. 709)

P   *My son has decided to organize his room—he wants a storage area for his sports equipment but I can't afford one right now.*

S   Hope you were sitting down when he decided to "neatenize"! Shocks like that are hard on mom's system, right? Anyway, find a bar stool and turn it upside down. Stuff baseball bats, bow and arrow, golf club, football, etc., in that center area, and hang baseball gloves and caps on the legs.

* * *

Like a nice neat closet with everything in its place? Try making some separator disks like you see in clothing stores to separate the sizes of garments. Make them out of plastic lids.

Label each, such as slacks, skirts, blouses, dresses. The kids will know right where things go, and mom can see at a glance what's needed to round out a wardrobe.

* * *

When small children are unable to reach the closet rod to hang their clothes, a good learning device would be suction cuphooks attached to the inside of the closet door.

As the child grows the hooks can be moved up, but in the meantime the child can learn to hang up his or her clothes and feel a little more independent, not to mention the help mom gets.

* * *

P   *My little boy collects tiny little cars and other "treasures"—I need a place to display and store them.*

S   Save large 46-ounce juice cans. Cut one end out, being sure there are no sharp or jagged edges. Paint and then glue them together (arrange them on their sides). The cans make round cubbyholes which can be hung on your child's wall or placed on a shelf.

* * *

A plastic laundry basket makes an excellent toy box. No hard corners to bump heads on, and it fits easily on the closet floor out of sight.

* * *

Toys all over the room? Grab an old pillowcase and have a "police call" with the kiddies.

P	*My daughter is "too big" to play with dolls but she can't quite bear to put them away yet.*
S	She can have her cake and eat it, too! Hang her dolls and stuffed animals from the ceiling. It's really cute for a young girl's room.

* * *

P	*School mornings are so hectic that the children are continually leaving the house without all their school things.*
S	Have each child put a cardboard box in his room in a handy place. The night before, put all homework, books, gym clothes, lunch (if possible) and school money into the box.
	Next morning it's a simple task to grab everything up as they go out the door. Kinda like an "in and out" basket in an office.

* * *

Want a unique cover for that school textbook? Cover it with an old road map (and protect it with clear self-sticking plastic if you want).

Interesting to say the least! Especially if it's your own area. Wouldn't a city map with your neighborhood on the center front be neat! You could pinpoint all your friends' streets.

Playtime
(Also see Fun Activities in Camping, p. 796)

P	*Our apartment is a little difficult to find—how can I make it easier for my child's guests?*
S	Tie or tape some balloons to your front door to make it easy to spot.

* * *

Want to have a "ball" at your next party? Fill a balloon almost full with water with a few drops of food coloring added. Put in the freezer and when frozen, split the balloon off with a knife. You will have a colorful ice ball to keep the punch chilled.

*   *   *

Smaller children love door prizes. They all like to go home with something (it needn't be expensive).

*   *   *

P   *My child wants party favors for her party—any suggestions for an inexpensive favor?*

S   Save empty rolls from bathroom tissue and fill them with pieces of candy. Wrap the rolls in gift paper and tie both ends of the wrapped roll with ribbon.

　　Make a fabric place mat and have each guest sign his or her name in pencil. Later, liquid embroidery the place mat and your child has a souvenir of the party.

*   *   *

A good icebreaker for an older child's party is to ask each guest to bring a baby picture. Post them and have each child write down who he or she thinks each picture is.

*   *   *

P   *My little girl wants to play musical chairs at her birthday party—almost impossible in our tiny apartment.*

S   Instead of chairs, use cardboard squares for the children to stand on—musical "squares"!

*   *   *

P   *Pin the tail on the donkey is a popular party game but I think pins are too dangerous.*

S   Make your own version of the game. Draw a large bunny and use cotton balls (stick tape on them) to play "Pin the Tail." Safe and just as much fun!

*   *   *

P   *My little boy loves to play ball but he gets frustrated because he can't catch well yet.*

S   Make him a "basket scoop" out of a half-gallon bleach bottle to catch the ball with. These games are very popular now.

*   *   *

Even a small child can be of service to the community! They can copy regular bingo cards on larger pieces of cardboard with large print to donate to nursing homes for older people to use. Bottle caps could be spray painted for markers.

*   *   *

Want to delight your youngster? Poke a peppermint or other flavored hard stick candy right through the center of an orange. The child will have a "candy straw" to suck up the juice of the orange.

*   *   *

Save those detergent bottles! Partially fill them with sand or water to weight the bottoms down. An old rubber ball, a driveway, kids—and instant bowling alley!

*   *   *

P   *I need a recipe for some play clay that I can make at home for my kids.*

S   Put 2 cups of salt and 2/3 cup of water in a pan and heat slowly until near boiling. Mix 1 cup of

cornstarch and ½ cup water and add to the salt and water mixture. Stir until thickened, cool and store the dough in a plastic bag in your refrigerator.

Another recipe you may use is to mix 4 cups flour and 1½ cups salt. Slowly add 2 cups water. Mix well. You will have to knead the dough for about ten minutes, then store the dough in airtight containers and place in the refrigerator.

Food coloring may be added to both these recipes.

*   *   *

A plain cardboard box makes a nifty desk for your child. The bottom of the box will be the desk top. Cut off the flaps. Draw and cut out a semicircle on the bottom of the long sides of the box. Your child's legs slip through this cutout and presto, instant desk!

*   *   *

P   *My child loves to fingerpaint but I'm afraid of ruined clothing.*

S   Let her wear one of dad's old, worn-out shirts. Put it on your child with the buttons in the back. Instant painter's smock.

*   *   *

P   *My kids love games but the game boards really get frazzled.*

S   Cover the boards with clear shellac before you give them to the kids—the coating will sure make those games last longer.

*   *   *

P   *My kids are always "hounding" me to take them to play miniature golf—it's too expensive to go as much as they would like.*

S   If there's an area in your backyard or a vacant lot nearby, they can design their own golf course and place a few tin cans in the ground for the holes. I think they'd have just as much fun!

*   *   *

Having a hard time choosing a gift for a young person? How about a "party pack"? Older children love to give parties but the family pocketbook feels the pinch. Give a supply of paper goods, some balloons for decorations, etc.

*   *   *

Remember, a child with braces on his teeth often can't enjoy the refreshments you serve at your child's parties. Make sure you have something softer for them to eat—usually hard candies, apples and such are a no-no for brace wearers.

*   *   *

P   *Serving birthday cake to a group of kids can really be a hassle.*

S   Use flat-bottomed ice cream cone cups and fill them half full with cake batter. Bake in a muffin tin at 350° for twenty minutes, or until done. When cool, ice them and they are easy to serve.

*   *   *

P   *My children feel they're a little old for coloring books, but they need a quiet activity on a rainy day. Help!*

S   Have them cut words or sentences out of newspapers or magazines and then glue them on stationery or notebook paper. They can have "typed" letters or messages to send to their friends!

*   *   *

A game for a rainy day is a coin toss. Get an egg carton and let the children take turns tossing coins in the egg cups. They could even practice their math by adding up the total number of coins that landed in the cups, and the number of pennies, nickels and dimes in the total amount.

Hours of fun can be had on rainy days playing pickup sticks using long spaghetti!

*   *   *

Make a "family" of dolls for your youngster. Save clean dishwashing detergent bottles and draw faces and hair with marking pens.

*   *   *

Wonder what to do with old Christmas or other greeting cards? Save them for "sicktime." They can be cut up to make little jigsaw puzzles (stash the pieces in a plastic sandwich bag), or they can be assembled to make an autograph book or scrapbook. Also, it's fun for a child just to cut out the picture.

*   *   *

When you leave children with a babysitter and prefer that they only watch certain programs, mark the programs on the TV schedule and inform the babysitter which programs the children are allowed to watch.

*   *   *

P   *Being from a large family with one TV, we get into arguments about which program to watch.*

S   Be democratic. Vote on the programs and the majority wins. Or take turns. You watch your favorite, then let the others choose theirs.

        Better yet, turn off the set and read a book once a week!

Signals
(Also see Identification, child, p. 814)

P   *We go camping a lot and I once lost my child for a little while.*

S   Tie a whistle around your child's neck—if he or she gets lost, you can follow the shrill sound.

P	*I have several small children and I'm afraid one will slip out of the house without my knowing it.*
S	Put a hook on the screen door above their reach, or attach a bell to both the front and back doors so you will know when anyone opens the doors.

*   *   *

To save a few steps while caring for a sick child, give the child a bell to ring if he or she really needs something.

Snack Money

P	*My kids always lose their snack money at the swimming pool.*
S	Sew a small pocket on an old towel and fasten it completely shut with a safety pin.

Spills

P	*My little girl always knocks over her drink.*
S	If you are using plastics, try switching to a heavier weighted glass or a small mug.

Toys

P	*My kids love to get new toys (as all kids do), but they soon tire of them and the toys are doomed to a life of neglect.*
S	"Absence makes the heart grow fonder," they say —and it's true with toys, too. When the child tires of certain toys, pack them away for a few weeks or months. When you drag them back out, they'll seem like new toys all over again. Then you can pack up the present group for a later reunion!

*   *   *

P   *My child "collects" stuffed animals, and some of them are really getting grimy from so much love and attention.*

S   If they are stuffed with straw or some substance where they can't be washed, try sprinkling cornmeal or cornstarch on them and letting it set awhile to absorb the oil and dirt. Brush it out.

I've found, though, that if you will cut a small opening in the bottom of the toy and remove all the old stuffing, more than likely you can hand wash it in a cold water wash. Remove any trim, such as felt eyes, etc., that might be damaged if wet.

Dry it in the dryer, or use a hair dryer. Once dry, restuff it with a washable filler such as foam or cut-up panty hose. Stitch the opening closed, and you have a clean fluffy, ever-so-cuddly toy!

*   *   *

P   *My toddler is allergic to stuffed toys but she refuses to part with her favorite animal.*

S   Remove the stuffing and replace it with nylon net

or old panty hose. You can then wash the stuffed
toy as often as needed.

*   *   *

If a wagon is on your list for that son or daughter, drill a couple of
small holes in the bottom to allow water to drain out.
Helps keep the wagon from rusting out.

In Sickness and in Health

This chapter deals with those of us who can't peel an apple because of arthritis, or can't bend over and clean out the bathtub because of back trouble. The term *handicapped* doesn't only apply to those who are permanently disabled. It can mean anything from not being able to carry a cup of coffee because you are on crutches, to having a hard time hearing the phone because you are slightly deaf.

I had a fractured leg and was in a cast and on crutches for two months, and then had to walk with a cane for another two months. I was not supposed to put any weight on the broken leg for the first two months so I couldn't even put my foot down.

I learned the hard way that many things that we take for granted can be so difficult and frustrating. My biggest problem was getting my meals and especially my morning coffee into the living room so I could park on the couch for the morning.

Such a simple task—but when you can't carry anything because you have to use crutches, and can't even put your foot down, the smallest task becomes a real irritant. At first I had a relay system. I placed little TV tray tables every few feet, and then putting the cup of coffee on one, I would hobble-hobble to the next one, place the cup down, and so on until I reached the couch.

The thought of doing that more than once a day was enough to make me stop drinking coffee, or at least have only one cup. Then the light dawned. I filled my vacuum bottle up with coffee and cream, etc., put the lid on tight, and just rolled it across the floor with my good foot. I even put a cup hook on my crutches so I could hang and carry my empty coffee cup. I had three cups of coffee without ever having to get up. Do you know I still do this (although I don't roll it on the floor!) when I am sick in bed. It's great for soup, juice and even fresh ice water without ever having to put your feet on the floor.

What I am calling "home aid" is a "first-aid" section Heloise-style! I'm not going to tell you how to deliver a baby, or put a broken arm in a cast. I am going to give you information for common problems.

The problems and solutions that you find in this chapter are simple, easy things that you can do. If there is ever any doubt or questions in your mind, call a doctor. Your health and your family's health is too important to take a chance on.

I want to leave you with my favorite "home-aid" remedy for a headache. My mother used to brush my hair and then give me a neck massage . . . don't ask me why but it worked. I think it was the TLC that really did the trick!

ADVANCE PLANNING FOR EMERGENCIES
(Also see Sunburn Protection, p. 785)

Caution: Any first-aid hint given in this chapter is NOT intended to be all inclusive in all emergency situations nor are these complete first-aid directions. You should have an up-to-date first-aid handbook and first-aid kit. However, the problems discussed here are everyday household situations that may not require professional medical attention. If in doubt, see a doctor.

Babysitter, information for
(Also see Identifying Locations, p. 865)

Problem   *I have just started babysitting. What information do I need to ask the parents for in case of an emergency?*

Solution   First, find out how to reach the parents or nearest relative in an emergency, and the street address and apartment number of the home in which you're babysitting in case of fire. The police and firemen have to know where you are before they can come help you. Second, if the parents cannot be easily reached, they should leave you a notarized medical release form authorizing you to get treatment for the child. Third, you should know the baby's doctor's name and phone number and any other emergency phone numbers you might need.

Escape Route

You and your family should have a prearranged escape route and meeting place in case of fire. Make sure any guest in your home is aware of the fire plan. Also, give your guests a flashlight—you may be able to find your way around your home in the dark but maybe a guest can't—especially in a traumatic situation.

First-Aid Kit

You may never need it, but you should always have a first-aid kit handy . . . even if it is a lunch box, old makeup case or overnight bag filled with a few supplies. This should be labeled clearly and put in a specific place so everyone knows exactly where to go if needed. You can buy a complete first-aid kit, which I think is well worth the money. If you want to make your own, the things I have listed are the bare minimum that you should have to take care of the very minor cuts and scrapes at home:

1. Adhesive bandages of all sizes and shapes. They sell a multi-type package at the drugstore.

2. Adhesive tape to hold dressing in place.

3. An elastic-type roll to hold bandages or compresses in place or to wrap an ankle.

4. Sterile gauze that is sealed in packages.

5. Scissors that stay in the first-aid kit.

6. Soap and cotton balls. If you run out of antiseptic spray, you can gently wash a cut, etc., with a bar of soap and it will disinfect it.

7. A thermometer for taking temperature . . . this is very important if you have to report to a doctor.

8. Tweezers are a must for removing splinters.

Flashlight

Keep a flashlight near your bed for emergencies.

Identification, child

Teach a little one his or her last name, street address and phone number by making it rhyme.

Identifying Locations
(Also see Babysitter, information for, p. 864)

If you have an emergency, firemen and policemen need to be able to find you quickly. Make sure you can describe your house and its location clearly. At night, turn on the porch lights as well as the headlights and flashing lights on cars that may be parked in your driveway or at the curb.

*   *   *

Always be sure your house numbers can be seen clearly from the street. Paint them on the curb with fluorescent paint so they can be spotted at night.

*   *   *

If you live in an apartment complex or building, leave the front door open, or throw a towel over the balcony to identify your apartment. If possible, have someone waiting outside to direct the emergency help.

Phone Lists

Be prepared for emergencies. Write phone numbers you'd need in an emergency and tape the list next to or on your phone.

Ready Coins

It's good to write phone numbers needed in emergencies on a card and tape some coins on the back of it for pay phones—keep this card in your wallet.

AT-HOME TREATMENT

Bone Fractures

P   *What are signs of a bone fracture?*
S   Swelling, discloration, or painful to the touch are signs. It's important not to wait long to get X-rays and medical attention. Improperly healed fractures can cause problems down the road. So, better be safe than sorry—when in doubt, seek medical attention.

Cuts and Burns

P   *I don't understand the difference between first, second and third degree burns.*

S   First degree means redness with mild swelling, limited to the outer layer of the skin. Second degree means a deep-red oozing tissue with blisters, extending to the inner layer of the skin. Third degree means a loss of all skin, including glands and hairs; the skin may be charred, coagulated, or white and lifeless. With third degree burn or extensive second degree burn, or with the very young or elderly, a physician should be consulted immediately.

*   *   *

P   *A minor burn is so painful.*

S   Hold the area under cold running water, or immerse it in a pan of cold water. Hold an ice cube over the spot, or keep some clean damp sponges in plastic bags in the freezer for these minor burns around the home. Cold will help relieve the pain and also keeps swelling down. Never, never put grease or butter on a burn.

*   *   *

P   *How should I treat minor cuts?*

S   Check to make sure no glass, etc., is in the wound. Flush out the wound with hydrogen peroxide if available. Wash the surrounding area and the wound with soap and water. If you can't stop the bleeding, press directly on the cut with a sterilized cloth or gauze. Remember, any redness or swelling is a sign of infection—see your doctor if this occurs.

Hot Soaks and Packs

P   *Whenever my little toddler injures a finger it's next to impossible to get him to soak it in a pan of water.*

S   Fill the pan with the proper soaking solution, then put in some of his favorite small plastic toys or some interesting and safe kitchen gadgets for him to play with.

    The soaking time will pass a lot faster for both of you.

*　　*　　*

P   *I have to apply hot packs frequently.*
S   Keep the solution hot in your slow cooker.

Liquids

P   *When my children are sick with colds and fever, I have a hard time getting them to drink the required liquid.*

S   Keep frozen popsicles made of fruit juices handy during the cold and flu season. When they don't feel like drinking from a glass, the cold popsicle is usually too tempting to resist.

    Keep popsicles handy for bumped and bruised lips, too.

    Make several different flavors so they'll have a choice.

Medication, Giving and Taking

    Remember, medication should be kept in a place away from little hands. Although we call the cabinet in the bathroom a "medicine cabinet," if you have children in the house, it is a good idea to keep all aspirin and other medicines in a place that only adults can reach.

P   *I have a hard time remembering to take my "daily dose."*

S   Get in a routine—if you take your medicine in the morning, put it by your toothbrush or in the kitchen next to your coffee cup.

*   *   *

P   *I have to take quite a few pills each day and I always worry about forgetting to take one.*

S   Take out the number of pills you need to take that day and place a ball of cotton back in the medicine bottle. Lay the number of pills on top of the cotton in each bottle and replace the caps. Each medicine stays in its original container and you can tell at a glance whether you took a pill.

*   *   *

P   *I can never remember when my children are supposed to take their medicine.*

S   Put a small piece of adhesive or masking tape over the hour on the clock when it's time for the medicine. When you give the child the dose, take the tape piece off and place it over the next time.

*   *   *

Help that wee one's hurt go away. When putting a disinfectant such as Mercurochrome on an injured knee or elbow, paint a "happy face" over the injury. Bring a smile through those tears.

*   *   *

P   *My little ones drive me crazy asking "when do I have to take my medicine next?"*

S   If you have an old clock that doesn't work, set the time at the hour they are supposed to take their medicine next. Then they can "see" the hour. If you want to, you can use a working clock and set the alarm for the "correct time, please."

*   *   *

P   *I'm an adult but I still have a hard time getting down unpleasant medicine.*

S   Suck on an ice cube for a couple of minutes before taking the medicine—it will numb the taste buds.

*   *   *

P   *Whenever I give liquid medication to a bed patient using a spoon, I usually end up spilling it on the person or the bed.*

S   Measure the medication into a clean, plastic pill bottle and mark the correct level with a piece of tape. Then the patient can easily drink the liquid without spills.

*   *   *

P   *I think more liquid medicine ends up on my little one's chin than in her mouth.*

S   Hold a small paper cup under her chin. Whatever dribbles into the cup can be mixed with a little water, and she can drink the rest down. Sometimes, when giving liquid medicine, every drop is important, so don't waste any.

*   *   *

P   *Childproof caps drive me up a wall. I can't get them open—and I don't even have children in the house.*

S   You can ask your pharmacist not to use childproof bottle caps when you know there is no danger of children getting ahold of the bottle. Remember, take your time opening any bottle. Read all instructions, it really is easy to do!

*   *   *

Do not tell children medicine tastes good or is "candy." Accidental poisonings can result. Explain what the medicine is and why it has to be taken by the child. Be honest about the taste. Give the child a little juice or cracker before and after they down the medicine.

Stings and Bites and Rashes

Did you know that white vinegar will help stop the itching in insect bites or stings? Also, baking soda and water paste is good.

*   *   *

P   *How do I remove a stinger?*

S   If there is a stinger, get it out using tweezers. Don't
         squeeze the stinger out. Then wash the sting area
         with soap and water. Apply cold pack (ice cubes
         will do) to the area.

                    *   *   *

P   *I was told not to pull a tick off my skin—what is
         the right way to remove one?*

S   Don't pull the tick off because the head might not
         come out of the skin. Cover the tick thoroughly
         with petroleum jelly. Leave on for about thirty
         minutes. If the tick does not fall off after thirty
         minutes, grasp it firmly near its head with tweezers
         and slowly remove it. Make sure the whole tick,
         including its head, is removed. Wash the bite area
         with soap and water. Destroy it, being careful not
         to touch it.

Poison Ivy/Oak

P   *What should I do if I meet up with poison ivy or
         oak?*

S   As soon as possible after exposure, wash your skin
         thoroughly with warm water and soap and then
         pat on calamine lotion.

Sunburn Protection
(See p. 785)

CASTS AND CRUTCHES

Never, never stick anything down a cast. Pencils and coat hangers
are a no-no. Your skin is very sensitive and can easily become in-
fected.

                    *   *   *

P   *I have a cast on my arm and I can't get a blouse over it.*

S   Go to a thrift store and buy some men's shirts with deep armholes. Have someone hem the sleeves at a length you like, and square off the shirttails. These new "blouses" will do until you get the cast off.

*   *   *

P   *My ugly white arm cast just doesn't go with anything I wear.*

S   Get a supply of different colored tube socks. Cut off the foot part, slide one on, then color-coordinate your cast with whatever you are wearing!

*   *   *

P   *I have a cast on my leg and it itches like crazy. What can I do?*

S   Blowing air or baby powder down inside the cast with a hair dryer will usually give relief.

*   *   *

P   *My toes get so cold, and I can't put a shoe or sock on because of my cast.*

S   Make mini-socks. Use some old or mismatched socks and cut off just the toe part, or at least as much that will cover your toes. You can use a little piece of tape to hold it on.

*   *   *

P   *The cast on my leg gets so heavy.*
S   Always prop up your leg as much as possible to help the circulation. If you are on crutches, you can turn the crutch upside down and rest your foot on the hand grip.

*   *   *

P   *My cast just looks awful–it's so dirty*
S   Grab the bottle of white shoe polish and clean your act up! You can dab here and there or do the whole thing.

*   *   *

P   *I am so afraid my son's cast is going to get wet when he's out playing.*
S   Cover it with plastic wrap, or a plastic cleaning bag. Be sure and tape it well; this will also help keep it clean. Be sure and remove the wrap when he comes in, so the skin can breathe.

*   *   *

P   *My friends signed my cast but now the ink is all smeared.*
S   As soon as they sign their name, let it dry and then cover with clear nail polish so it won't smear.

*   *   *

P   *I have been on crutches only a few days and my hands are killing me.*
S   If you will pad the hand grip it will make it much more comfortable. You can use sponges or foam rubber. I placed a pretty piece of scrap material over the sponge, and it looked nicer, plus it didn't crumble up.

P   *The rubber that covers the top of the crutches (where it goes under your arm) is all dried out and falling apart.*

S   First, replace it with a new one, or make your own, then always cover it. A real easy way is to use the little footlet socks that women wear for tennis.

*   *   *

P   *I can't even stand up long enough to wash a few dishes or put on my makeup—my crutches get in the way.*

S   If you can lean, you have it made. I used two old barstools, one in the kitchen and one in the bath. Just lean against them, or even sit on them and you can do a multitude of things. I even spent an afternoon potting and repotting my plants, after setting everything up on a table and sitting on my stool.

*   *   *

P   *I can't carry anything.*

S   Attach a cup hook (like you use in your kitchen cabinets) on the outside of each crutch and bend the hook part a little. You can hang an empty coffee cup on it or an old purse for carrying various small items. Also, you can wear an apron with pockets.

*   *   *

P   *While walking on crutches, I got aching muscles from trying to hold up my foot that was in the cast.*

S   A heavy leather belt attached to the handbar of the crutch would make a little "hammock" to hold your foot and cast when you sit down.

*   *   *

Through with your crutches? Instead of stashing them away, why not leave them at your doctor's for a patient who can't afford crutches?

Know you're going to have surgery and be on crutches for a while? Practice with them before the surgery. It will make all the difference in the world!

HELPS FOR THE ELDERLY

Arthritis

P   *I have arthritis and it's difficult for me to hold a pen.*

S   Push that pen through a small rubber ball. Or, wrap masking tape around and around until it's large enough for you to hold.

*   *   *

P   *I have arthritis and can't hold a toothbrush.*

S   Take a wooden spool or dowel; have someone drill a hole large enough to insert the handle. Then glue the handle of the toothbrush in it. The large spool or dowel is easier to grasp.

*   *   *

P   *I can't hold newspaper pages in place.*

S   Staple the sections where they are folded so that they open like a book. Or, tear the paper in half to make it easier to manage.

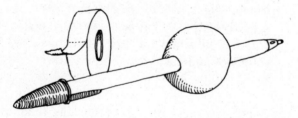

Bathing

P   *How can I help a weak or feeble person bathe?*

S   Set a lawn chair in the tub and turn the shower on. A person too weak to stand under the shower or pull himself out of the tub can sit in the chair and bathe. If you think the chair might slip, put a towel under it. Also, a towel will prevent marks in the tub. A hand-held shower is super.

     *   *   *

P   *I have been ill, and the full force of the shower is too much for me.*

S   Attach a hand spray to the tub faucet. They are easy to regulate and you can get the water just where you want it.

     *   *   *

If you have to bathe and can't get a foot or leg wet, sit on a stool, and keep the foot or leg outside the tub.

Bathroom Safety

P   *I want to make my bathroom safer for my elderly parents—any suggestions?*

S   Attach grab bars close to the tub, shower, sink and toilet to prevent falls. Use nonbreakable soap dishes and drinking glasses. Be sure medications are clearly marked (relabel them if necessary in large enough print to be easily read). Of course, put nonskid adhesive strips or decals in the tub and shower floor. Wall-to-wall carpeting provides better footing. A night-light is a must. Ideally, a telephone in the bath to summon help in an emergency would be nice.

     *   *   *

P   *I have difficulty getting out of the new, lower style tubs.*

S   Turn over onto your hands and knees and push yourself up. And take it slowly!

Bed, getting out of

P   *I can't get out of bed in the morning—no joke!*

S   Tie a piece of rope at the bottom to the bedpost, tying knots at intervals to have a good grip, or on the side of the mattress frame. Grab the rope and pull yourself up! Pin the rope to the sheet or blanket at night so it's handy come morning.

Car, riding in

P   *How can I help my disabled friend into the car?*

S   Spread a couple of plastic trash bags on the front seat. Help her to back up to the seat, sit down on the bags and slide back as far as possible. Then lift her feet and swing them around "frontward." It's also easy to get a person out of the car using the plastic bags to "slide" on.

*   *   *

P   *I have trouble lifting my legs to get in and out of a car.*

S   Why not wear slacks? You can use the legs of the slacks to grasp and pull your legs up and around.

Cooking

P   *I'm afraid to cook on my daughter's electric range —the buttons are confusing and I can't see very well.*

S   Have your daughter mark the medium heat and off buttons with a fluorescent sticker or fingernail polish so you can see them.

P   *I am disabled and can't peel vegetables with just one hand.*

S   Have someone drive a long nail through the center of a board. Just stick the potato or whatever over the nail and peel away.

*   *   *

Old curtain rods make good "hookers" to reach canned goods too far back on shelves.

Dentures

P   *I dropped my dentures brushing them—how can I avoid breaking them?*

S   Fill up the sink bowl with water before brushing them, so in case you do drop them, the water will cushion the blow—no more breaking for you!

*   *   *

P   *My dentures never smell really fresh.*

S   Soak them in a small amount of mouthwash and water.

Dressing

You can make a handy hook to help handicapped people pull up trousers, socks, etc., with a wire coat hanger.

Pull the pants hanger part to form a long handle, with the "hook" part at one end. Pinch the wires close together and wrap them with colorful plastic tape.

Put the tape on the loop end of the hook to prevent snagging clothing or scratching the skin. You'll find it to be a real handy tool for a lot of things.

* * *

P   *I can't bend over to put on pantyhose or stockings.*
S   Get a pair of scissor-type kitchen tongs. Cover the end of the tongs with a "snagless" material such as velvet. Use the tongs to pull up the hose.

Eating

P   *I have to wear a bib when eating, but I can't keep a napkin in place bib-style.*
S   When you have to use a napkin bib-style, use a chain-type eyeglass holder and clip it on the napkin.

* * *

Use heavy dishes such as pie plates or even new, clean ash trays for a disabled person to eat on. Also, rubber mats (sink protectors) make super table mats that won't skid.

* * *

P   *I have a hard time seating myself at the table.*
S   Place a sturdy turntable (like you use in a kitchen cupboard) on the chair and then put a round pillow on top of that. Sit down sideways on the chair, and then turn to face the table.

Eyesight, poor

P   *I can't see regular print but I love to read—why don't stores sell books in large print?*

S   You may not find too many large print books for sale, but check at your local library. They do have large print books, if you'll just ask for them.

*   *   *

Left your glasses and can't read a menu? Put a hole in a matchbook cover or a piece of paper and look through this.

*   *   *

When writing to someone with poor eyesight, use black ink on white paper. If you'll write large and distinctly, and leave more space between words and lines, the person can usually read the letter without having to ask a neighbor or friend.

Gifts

P   *I need some gift ideas for elderly persons.*

S   If they're still keeping house, a gift of meat for the freezer is appreciated (the cost of meats really cuts

into a fixed budget). If you decide on clothing, consider warmth and ease of closing. Buttons are hard to manage for arthritics. A zipper closing in back is also hard to manage. Flowers, candy or a favorite food (check if permitted on diet) are welcome. A goldfish bowl would be enjoyed by a confined person (with fish, of course!).

Hearing, hard of

P   *We love grandpa but this is driving us bananas! He is hard of hearing and when we all watch TV together he blasts everybody else out of the room.*

S   You can now buy a portable radio that has a TV band on it; it picks up the sound of the TV programs in your area. Since it has an ear jack on it, give it to grandpa to turn up as much as he likes, and the rest of you can listen to the TV set at normal volume.

*   *   *

P   *I can't hear the phone ring.*

S   Set it in a metal pan. Also, most phones have volume dials on the bottom of them. Be sure to check that it's turned up. If you still can't hear it, your phone company can install bells or other devices that will amplify the sound (for a fee, of course).

Phone Calls

P   *I'm elderly and I love to get phone calls, but I can't move very fast and I miss a lot of calls.*

S   Tell those friends and family to let the phone ring twice, then hang up and call back about two minutes later. That will give you time to get to your phone and perhaps settle down in a chair.

Strokes

P   *How can I communicate with my dad who's had a stroke and can't speak or write.*

S   Give him a large mail order catalog and a cookbook. He can point to the item or food he wants.

Wheelchair

In a wheelchair? Use a pair of kitchen tongs to pick up dropped articles.

SICKROOM

When you are caring for someone at home, there are some very nice things you can do to make their rest more comfortable. If you are in bed for only a day, or a week, it's no fun. So let's make it as easy on the sick one as we can.

Bed

P   *When I'm in bed, the covers are so heavy on my feet I feel like I am tied in.*

S   Get a large cardboard box and cut out two opposite sides. Turn this over and place it at the foot of the bed between the bed and the heavy covers. Slip your feet in the box opening and the covers won't mash on your feet.

*   *   *

P   *The pillow slips get soiled from perspiration so quickly; I hate to change the entire bed.*

S   Put several pillow slips on the pillow at one time. You can remove one and have a fresh one right there without having to disturb your patient very much.

P   *When my little one is sick, he wants all the pillows in the house to hug and prop him up.*

S   Roll up some soft towels and put inside a pillow case. This is a great way to use your old, clean panty hose. Stuff them in a pillow case that closes, or fold over the end of your regular one and safety pin it shut.

*   *   *

P   *When I am sick in bed my feet freeze even though I put on socks.*

S   Remember the old days when they would warm a brick, wrap it in a towel and put it in the bed to warm your feet? Use a heating pad and keep it at the foot of your bed for toasty toes. No heating pad? A hot water bottle wrapped in a towel stays warm and cozy for quite some time.

Feeding

The sense of smell usually gets dulled when a body's under the weather. A good way to help stimulate the appetite or create some interest in mealtime is to cook up something "smelly" and let the odor drift to the sickroom. My mother always fried onions or bacon, and even if I wasn't very hungry I sure was ready to nibble when the

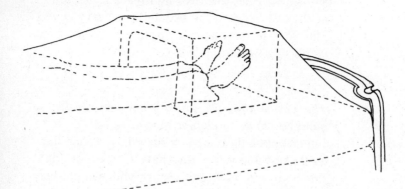

food came. Some folks can't resist salivating at the first smell of a chocolate cake or homemade cookies! It's worth the effort.

* * *

When someone's sick, eating usually isn't much fun. Make mealtime as attractive as possible. For grownups, pull out the special china or pretty teacups. Most sick ones can't eat too much at one time, so use little salad or dessert plates to put food on. Colorful napkins will help make things look a little brighter.

* * *

P   *It never fails—whatever I fix for my husband when he is sick and stuck in bed, it is never what he wants to eat.*

S   Give him a choice. Before fixing anything, make out a daily menu and let him mark what he wants to eat . . . works great on children and husbands.

* * *

P   *It is so hard to manage a glass to drink from while lying in bed.*

S   Use a small coffee mug or anything with a handle so there is something to hold onto. Also, whenever you give someone in bed a liquid, fill the cup only one-third to one-half full and it will be easier to drink.

* * *

P   *Carrying and serving soup to someone in bed is like an accident looking for a place to happen.*

S   How true! My mother always served any liquid in a gravy boat, and only filled it halfway. It is much easier to refill the "special bowl" than to worry about spilling it. The gravy boat even has a built-in spoon rest and doesn't slide off the saucer.

* * *

If utensils are hard to handle, use iced tea spoons, or even baby spoons . . . much easier for sick and weak hands to hold.

*   *   *

Many times a tray is too large for a little one. Use a deep bread pan and place a glass and small bowl inside.

*   *   *

P   *No matter what I do, something on the tray spills when I am serving a meal to a sick person in bed.*

S   Place a damp hand or kitchen towel on the tray first, then put dishes on it; things won't slide around. Even if something does spill, no problem.

Hot Water Bottle

P   *I don't have a hot water bottle.*

S   You can make a substitute hot water bottle by using a heavy-duty rubber glove. Fill it with water. Close it tightly with a strong rubber band and wrap it in a towel. A plastic bottle with a tight-fitting lid can also be used in bed.

*   *   *

P   *After being in bed awhile, I don't have the energy to take a tub bath or shower.*

S   Have someone put a few washcloths in hot water (maybe add a drop of light cologne), wring them out well and roll 'em up tight. You can wash face, hands, neck, etc., and feel refreshed and clean without much effort.

*   *   *

P   *My kids sometimes can't make it to the bathroom when they get sick.*

S   If you have someone in bed who might vomit, keep an empty trash can or heavy paper bag lined with a plastic bag next to the bed, just in case.

P   *I just can't get out of bed to shampoo my hair.*

S   Rub and pat some cornstarch or baby powder in your hair. Let it sit a little to absorb the oil; then brush, brush, brush. A little rubbing alcohol on a cotton ball dabbed around the hair line will remove most oiliness also.

*   *   *

P   *Sometimes it is just too exhausting to get out of bed, but I sure want to brush my teeth.*

S   Give them the old navy dry brush. Put toothpaste on the brush, no water, and brush away. Then, take a sip of water and squish around in your mouth, then empty into a bowl or glass. A quick way for "fresh breath" is a dash of mouthwash in a glass of water, gargle and empty.

Time-savers

P   *I feel like a marathon runner, going back and forth to the sickroom for a glass of this, a sip of that.*

S   Keep a filled ice bucket by the bedside. Also have fresh water, juice, and maybe a thermos with hot water and a teacup, etc. A few clean glasses and some napkins. If you have an extra thermos, fill it with soup and they can sip, sip, sip whenever you want.

*   *   *

For anyone who is in bed and doesn't have "full-time" nursing, be it family or friend, here are a few hints for you. I try to remember these things whenever I am sick and when my husband is sick in bed, too. Sometimes it is disturbing to a sick person to be asked all the time, "Want anything?"

Here are some other suggestions if you are stuck in bed for a few days and recuperating. Along with fresh water, ice bucket, etc., I keep a few cans of little nibbles, a slow cooker to heat something if I want to, crackers, cookies, whatever I might feel like eating, by my bedside. If you don't have much room on your night table, bring in an extra table, a card table; even a sturdy wood-bottomed chair covered with a towel works as a storage place.

Most sick people don't know what they want and eating can be difficult so "finger" food is perfect. A basket of fruit, mainly easy things to eat like grapes, bananas, plums, etc., along with a knife and a roll of paper towels, makes it easy to grab a bite anytime.

It may take me a few minutes to get set up, but once I have everything I might want, I don't have to leave the bedroom.

A phone by the bed is essential; especially if you are alone you need to get to the phone easily to call for help when necessary. It also helps pass the time talking to friends. The old standbys of books, magazines and things you haven't read are good. If you feel up to it, this is the time to write a few notes or take a mental inventory of your household goods.

*   *   *

When you are very sick, resting, relaxing and gaining strength are vital.

Want to know Heloise's remedy for a healthy, happy family? My prescription for feeling good—A HUG A DAY KEEPS YOU THAT WAY!!!! Now remember, it's just as important to give as it is to receive. When times get bad, and no one is around to give me a hug, I pick up my dog and hug her; when she wags her tail, I feel just as good knowing I have made *her* happy!

Pets

The wonderful world of pets! If you have any kind of animal in your household, you know that pets are a "whole other world."

I am an animal lover—and to prove the point I have four pets: two birds, one ferret, and one dog. If that doesn't make me pretty qualified to answer your questions and solve your problems about animals, I don't know what does! (Next to being a vet.)

This chapter is not a complete handbook on pets by any means. The problems that you read here are ones that millions of people have encountered over many, many years. Yes, some are very simple. But if it's the first time you have puppies or kittens in your house, you sure want to know the easiest way to take care of them.

Caring for a pet is kinda like taking care of a small child. They can't really tell you what they want or how they feel in words, but you can usually figure out what's wrong or what they need in a general sense.

The old saying about a dog being "man's best friend" sure hits close to home. Dogs and cats and birds can be man or woman's best friend. I used to think that birds didn't cuddle or show affection. Well, some of them do. The love and affection that grows between any animal and its owner is something very special. So take care of your little friend!

The following hints are about the animals that most of you have and write to me about. If I left something out about your pet boa constrictor, I am sorry but I can't cover every kind of pet so I've tried to stick with the more common varieties. Please don't be offended!

Remember, love your pets, treat them right, and they will be loyal to you and return your affection.

BIRDS

Birds! I have two so I could fill the next pages with my own problems and solutions. But rather than bore you, I have narrowed it down to the questions I get the most.

When I say, "I know what you mean!"—boy, do I!

Cage

Problem *Cleaning the perch is the absolute pits.*
Solution Take it outside and hose it down; then use an old sturdy brush to scrub. A suede brush is perfect.

*   *   *

P *The bird cage just doesn't seem to hold all that birdseed when my little bird starts eating and making a mess.*
S If you will use a large strip of nylon net, long enough to go around the cage and about twelve to eighteen inches wide, you can wrap it around the cage, from the bottom up, and nary a seed will leave its premises.

Feeding

P   *When I try to put water in my bird cage, the bird pecks at me.*

S   Use a kitchen baster to squirt the water in the dish.

*   *   *

P   *I fill the feed dish full, but the bird only eats half and I have to throw the rest out.*

S   You can take the little dish outside and blow into it and all the hulls will go out. I only fill mine half full to start with. I may have to watch to see he has food but I think it's much easier.

*   *   *

P   *How can I retrieve my bird when he gets out of the cage, without both of us ending up upset.*

S   I know what you mean! My cockatiel is named Fussy, and you can guess why. He thinks that we are trying to murder him when it's time to go back in the cage. The best way we have found is to throw a lightweight towel or piece of cloth over him, then gently pick him up and into the cage.

Feeding Outdoor Birds

To feed the birds in winter, save your fat and suet scraps and put them in mesh bags like the ones onions come in. Hang this outside and watch them flock!

*   *   *

P   *I love to feed the birds outdoors, but birdfood costs so much.*

S   Save your bread crumbs, pizza crust, etc., in a large plastic bowl. Empty the bottom of your toaster, too, and the birds will love all the goodies.

*   *   *

P   *Any good things I can give to the birds to help them build their nest.*

S   This is the ultimate in recycling. Save all your little strings, dryer lint, etc., and put them outside for the birds. They love it, and that's what I call "back to nature."

*   *   *

P   *I can never tell when my hummingbird feeder is out of water.*

S   Add red food coloring to the water and you can tell at a glance when water is needed. Humming-

birds are attracted to the red color so you can paint stripes on the feeder with red nail polish and it will attract them, too.

CATS

If you have some friends taking care of your cat, here are some rules and regulations (standard for all animals) to follow:

First and foremost, leave the name and number of your vet just in case anything happens. Take your cat's or dog's bed and familiar things along. It helps to have a piece of your clothing for him to curl up in; your smell is on it and the animal feels a little better.

Naturally, you want to leave as much food as the animal will need for the length of time you are gone.

If you can, call a few days later to be sure there are no problems. It sure doesn't hurt to tell the adoptive parents any peculiar habits your friend has . . .

I babysat a cat and the first night he disappeared. I was frantic thinking he got out somehow and was sick. Then he finally showed up, inside a cabinet. When his owner returned, she said, "Oh, I forgot to tell you he can open doors and drawers and likes to hide." Sure would have saved me some heavy worrying!

Caring For

P   *I'm expecting a little one, and I don't want our cat in the baby's room—yet I hate to keep the door closed all the time because I will need to hear the baby.*

S   Take your regular door down and put up a screen door temporarily. You could even paint it to match your baby's room!

* * *

P   *My cat's foot was injured and the vet told me to soak its foot for a few minutes several times a day. I never did figure out an easy way to do this.*

S   Put the medicine and water in a small plastic bag. Put the cat's foot in it and tape it shut. Hold your pet while the foot is soaking.

* * *

P   *How can I make a homemade identification collar for my cat.*

S   Get a piece of elastic (it should fit loosely) and write your name and phone number on it with indelible pen.

* * *

P   *I can't afford cat box deodorant.*

S   Shred or tear up newspapers and mix with baking soda. You are recycling the papers and they are easily discarded.

* * *

P   *The plastic liners I buy for the litter box are too thin.*

S   Buy poly trash bags at the store—they're sturdier; the kind you use in the kitchen.

* * *

Unused disposable diapers make great cat box liners.

* * *

Cut several litter box liners at once.

* * *

P   *I want to make some inexpensive toys for my cat.*

S   Make a ball of nylon net and attach a small bell, or fill a plastic pill bottle with rice and glue on the lid.

* * *

P   *My cat needs a dry place to sleep outside.*

S   Turn an old foam ice chest upside down and place it on top of the lid. Cut a hole in one end for an entrance and add some scrap material to make it cozy. You can place the "house" on the porch or some other place. The foam is insulating and provides a dry, cozy cubbyhole.

*   *   *

Want a nifty house for your kitty? Build a home out of plywood scraps and *carpet* the roof. Kitty will use the carpet (hopefully) for a scratching post.

Catproofing
(Also see Stain Removal, Urine, p. 671)

P   *I vacuum but I can't seem to get up all the cat hairs.*

S   Before vacuuming, dampen a broom and sweep over the area with it.

*   *   *

P   *Cat hairs are everywhere and just don't come off the chairs when I vacuum.*

S   Use a damp sponge to wipe them off.

P   *My cat eats my houseplants.*
S   Put a pot of grass near your cat's feeding dish.
            Hopefully, the cat will ignore your plants.

                        *   *   *

P   *My cat jumps up on tables.*
S   Spray a little bit of water in its face when it jumps
            up (it won't hurt your cat). It won't take long to
            break the habit.

                        *   *   *

P   *My cat claws the upholstery.*
S   All cats need to "claw." If you nail a scrap of
            carpet on a board or box, perhaps the cat will claw
            that instead. It needs *something*. Rub catnip on
            the scratching post and it should help your cat
            know where to scratch.

Feeding

According to my vet, it's OK to give cat food to a dog; but a cat
can't survive on dog food. There are some extra things in cat food
that they must have. So don't give your kitty dog food. It's not all
the same.

                        *   *   *

P   *I can't keep ants out of my cat's feeding dish.*
S   Set the feeding dish in a larger dish which has a
            little water in it.

                        *   *   *

An empty cottage cheese container makes a good feeding dish for
cats. Cover any remaining food with the lid.

                        *   *   *

P   *I need a feeding "trough" for my kittens.*
S   Those flying-saucer-shaped toys make super ones!

Grooming

If your cat or small dog splashes around when you bathe them in the sink, try this. Cut a head hole and arm holes out of the bottom of a large plastic trash bag. Slip your head and arms through the holes and you have a waterproof smock. You will stay dry but will still have to mop up the floor!

* * *

P   *My little cat sheds so much.*

S   Did you know you can vacuum your pet? Some animals just love it. You should start out a little at a time so they don't get scared by the noise.

Travel

Driving with a cat and want cool water for it without a mess? Put some ice cubes in a margarine tub with snap-on lid; as they melt, they will provide water along the way. Add cubes as needed.

DOGS

If you care for a dog, you not only take care of him, but you also love and care about him. I have a darling little 3-pound dog, Tequila, that is part of my family. So when it comes to caring for dogs, I CARE!

* * *

Before your dog gets lost, write a complete description of him and also tuck a photograph away with the shots record.

You think you can remember each marking, but sometimes it's difficult—especially when you are upset over the pet's being lost.

Caring For

Don't ever leave a dog in the car in hot weather. In 85°F weather outside it can become 102°F inside a car in ten minutes with the windows rolled up. Even with the windows opened a little, the temperature can reach 120° in thirty minutes. You may come back to a dead pet.

* * *

P   *I take my dog with me to the store but I have to tie him outside and several times the leash has come undone.*

S   Attach a small leather collar that will buckle to the hand strap—it's easy to attach to a pole or post.

* * *

P   *Our new puppies keep wandering away from "mama" and crying.*

S   Line a child's wading pool with old carpet or newspapers. "Mom" can come and go but the puppies can't.

* * *

P   *On rainy days, my dog tracks mud through the house something terrible.*

S   With kids going in and out, so does Rover, right? You can't be there to wipe the dog's feet every time, so just throw down some old rags or towels where the dog crosses to come in. Most of the muddy footprints will come off on the towels instead of on your floors.

*   *   *

P   *How can I get dog urine stains out of my carpet?*

S   See Chapter five—the section on stain removal, p. 163 and p. 198. I've gone into quite a bit of detail there about petproofing.

*   *   *

P   *Our new puppies whine all night long.*

S   An old ticking clock will sometimes do the trick. Just wrap in a towel and put it in their bed. Sometimes a heating pad or hot water bottle wrapped in a towel helps. Remember, they are used to cuddling up to something warm!

Feeding

P   *Sometimes when my dog is "feeling blue" she just won't eat her dog food.*

S   Animals aren't the only ones . . . you like a change of taste, too. My little chihuahua will always give in to butter and sugar mixed together and rice with a little beef broth poured over. Check with your vet to be sure this is OK for your dog's diet.

*   *   *

P   *My little dog has lost all her teeth! She is so fond of table scraps.*

S   I know what you mean. My sweet dog lost all of her teeth, too. Dog food was a complete turn-off.

My vet said anything I could feed her—as long as it was a balanced diet—was OK. So into the blender went beans, meat, veggies, etc.—and she lapped it up.

*   *   *

P   *My dog doesn't like dog food and we don't have enough scraps to feed him.*

S   Add leftover gravy to the dry food, or some beef broth made with bouillon cubes—anything to give the dry food a "homemade" flavor.

*   *   *

P   *I can't get dog food out of the can without a mess.*

S   Open both ends of the can and then push the food through with the lid. It'll come out clean as a whistle.

*   *   *

P   *My little dog cannot eat a can of dog food in one day—it is so smelly in the fridge.*

S   Not if you store the can inside a coffee can that has a plastic lid.

*   *   *

P   *My dog food always dries out before I can use up the whole plastic bag.*

S   Empty it into a jar large enough to hold one bag, add a little vegetable oil and put the lid on tight. It will stay moist and fresh.

*   *   *

Remember, dry dog food stored in just the bag or an open container will attract varmints and bugs, not to mention drying out.

*   *   *

P   *I get tired of dog dishes sliding all over my kitchen floor when I feed my dog.*

S   Place the dishes on a piece of foam rubber.

*   *   *

P   *My bowser keeps turning over his water dish. Since there is no one home during the day, I worry about him.*

S   Dogs have to have plenty of fresh water to stay healthy, don't they! Try driving a stake or stick in the ground. Use an angel food cake pan and place the center hole over the stake.

*   *   *

P   *I can't get my dog to swallow a pill.*

S   Wrap the pill in a ball of cheese, hamburger or peanut butter. Gulp and it's gone!

*   *   *

P   *My dog still won't swallow a pill easily.*

S   Coat the pill in butter—have your dog's neck up —as if he is looking up at the ceiling. Put the pill in his mouth as far back as you can; hold his mouth shut and rub his neck. He has to swallow! Of course, my dog weighs only three pounds so this is easy to do!

Grooming

P	*I like to bathe my small dog in the tub, but there's so much hair that gets in the drain.*
S	Put a piece of steel wool pad over the drain and it will catch the hair. Toss it away after the bath.

* * *

P	*My dog got in some oil, and a soapy bath simply didn't do the job.*
S	Next time, rub cornmeal all in the hair first to absorb the oil. Then bathe the dog.

* * *

Take your dog in the shower with you, that is, if it is small. It's easy to soap and rinse it without a big wet mess.

* * *

P	*How can I get dog hair out of my dog's wire brush?*
S	Take a toothpick and "weave" in and out to remove the hair.

* * *

P	*My little dog just shakes and shivers after her bath.*
S	Use your hair dryer on the lowest setting and dry her in a jiffy. Don't get too close—hold the dryer a good distance away.

* * *

Use an old sock to make your little dog a sweater. Cut off the foot part, and make two holes for the front legs.

FISH

There is an Oriental saying that looking at water is calming. I have heard that watching fish in an aquarium is also very relaxing, not to mention interesting. If you have a family member stuck in bed for some time, a gift of a little fishbowl would certainly help. A new interest, something to watch (that doesn't have dials and commercials) and maybe even a little companionship.

Aquarium

P   *The power went off and I lost some expensive fish because the tank wasn't aerating.*

S   To make a temporary aerator, punch a small hole in the bottom of a No. 3 coffee can. Fill it with water from the fish tank. Set the can on the corner edge of the tank where drops of water will slowly drip back into the tank. When the can empties, refill it and continue the procedure.

*   *   *

P   *My aquarium has a yucky crust built.*

S   After emptying, scrub the aquarium with nylon net and vinegar; rinse extremely well before putting your fish back.

*   *   *

P   *The bubbleless filter siphon sucks up small fish in my aquarium.*

S   Cover the siphon hole with nylon net secured by a rubber band or string. Be sure the tube is not constricted.

*   *   *

A lighted aquarium will soothe your child and he will have something to watch while he falls asleep. It provides just enough light to keep him from being fearful.

* * *

P   *The plastic plants I placed in my aquarium refused to stay upright.*

S   Take a circle of nylon net, place three or four marbles on it, and gather. Put the stems in the gathered net and fasten the net around the stems securely with a needle and thread. Place the weighted bag in the gravel.

Fishbowl

P   *My little girl is too young for a fishbowl and our cat won't leave a goldfish alone.*

S   You can make her happy by giving her a little goldfish bowl on which you've glued some fish decals on the outside back. Add a little fern, some colored gravel, etc., and your little girl has her very own fishbowl!

* * *

Brandy snifters make darling goldfish bowls.

* * *

If you have an aquarium that sits against a wall, tape a pretty scene on the back glass; it will look lovely!

HAMSTERS

P   *I have had to replace several hamster cages because of rust spots.*

S   Place a square of tile in the cage to protect the floor.

P   *Is there an easy way to retrieve an "escaped" hamster?*

S   Take a box with a lid; make a hole in the lid big enough for the "escapee" and lay a paper towel over the hole and put some food on the towel. When the hamster becomes hungry, he will go to the food and drop down in the box below. Cushion the bottom of the box with crumpled newspaper.

*   *   *

P   *My kids' hamster loves to play in its treadmill—but the thing squeaks and is annoying.*

S   Oil the treadmill using vegetable oil applied with a cotton swab.

*   *   *

P   *When I clean my gerbil's cage, I can't keep up with him while he is out.*

S   If you put him in the bathtub, he will stay there until you are ready to replace him in the cage. He can't climb the slippery sides of the tub.